# THE POCKET
# A–Z
# OF THE
# KNIGHTS
# TEMPLAR

A Guide to their History and Legacy

GORDON NAPIER

This book is a revised, condensed edition of *A–Z of the Knights Templar*, ISBN 978-1-86227-386-3, by the same author.

First published 2014
by Spellmount, an imprint of The History Press
The Mill, Brimscombe Port
Stroud, Gloucestershire, GL5 2QG
www.thehistorypress.co.uk

British Library Cataloguing in Publication Data.
A catalogue record for this book is available from the British Library.

ISBN 978 0 7524 9867 6

Typesetting and origination by The History Press
Printed in Great Britain

# THE POCKET
## A–Z
### OF THE
# KNIGHTS
# TEMPLAR

# Introduction

# The Knights Templar

In Jerusalem, in the wake of the First Crusade and its bloody triumph, there was born a religious brotherhood of a kind never seen before. In about AD 1118 this embryonic Order, comprising a handful of men, established itself on the site of the ancient Hebrew Temple. They became known as the *Poor Knights of Christ and the Temple of Solomon*, the *Knights Templar*, or simply the *Templars*.[1] Setting themselves apart from other knights and nobles, the Templars took religious vows before the Patriarch of Jerusalem. They renounced worldly comforts and committed themselves to a harsh, monastic way of life. It was to be monasticism with a difference, however, for they were to retain their arms and armour and become warrior monks. This union of monasticism and militarism was a new concept within Catholic Christianity, and some observers were troubled by the contradiction. Others were concerned lest the Templars neglect the internal battle against spiritual forces of darkness while they engaged in physical warfare against those deemed infidels and enemies of Christ.

The Templars lived communally, devoted themselves to prayer, and embraced poverty, chastity and obedience. In addition they pledged their swords to the defence of pilgrims, guarding them from the bandits and marauders and guiding and sheltering them along the arduous way to the sacred places. The early Templars received enthusiastic support from Abbot Bernard of Clairvaux, the charismatic and visionary leader of the Cistercian Order, who was later to be canonised. St Bernard's endorsement resulted in the Templars' incorporation into the heart of the ecclesiastical establishment. They received their formal Rule, as well as general recognition by the clergy, at the Council of Troyes in 1129. A great noble, Count Hugh of Champagne, meanwhile, gave the Order an aristocratic seal of approval by joining it himself. He swore allegiance to their founding Grand Master, Hugues de Payens, who had embarked for the East as the count's own vassal. Before long, Church edicts were issued, giving the Templars such extensive powers and privileges that in theory they answered only to the Pope.

The Holy Land had been recovered for Christianity from the Muslim powers. While enduring much suffering and spilling much blood, the Crusaders had effectively created a Christian confederation there, comprised of the four states of Edessa, Antioch, Tripoli and Jerusalem. The fledgling Kingdom of Jerusalem became pre-eminent, but was surrounded by enemies and remained in peril. The scene of Christ's Crucifixion and Resurrection was held sacred by all of Christendom. Once Jerusalem was won, the struggle was to retain it. It soon became clear that the Order of the Temple could serve an additional function contributing to the defence and expansion of the kingdom's frontiers. The Templars' potential was appreciated in the principality of Antioch, to the north, where they received some of their earliest castles. Catholics with sufficient means made generous donations of land and capital to the Order. They believed that by making such endowments they aided the Holy Land's physical defence, and also helped to assure spiritual salvation for themselves and their families. Pious nobles proved ready to join the Order as knights, while commoners joined as sergeants or serving brothers. Soon the Templars evolved into a formidable army, spearheaded by knights in white mantles emblazoned with red crosses. An Armenian chronicler wrote of them as Christ-like paladins, who appeared 'as if sent by Heaven' to defend the Christians from Turkish marauders. The Templars' martial activities in the Holy Land were facilitated by an expanding support network in France, England and other kingdoms, where soon the Order became a familiar presence in society.

After 1144, when Edessa fell to the resurgent Muslims, the Second Crusade was proclaimed. In the course of this campaign the Templars came of age as a fighting force. They contributed leadership and financial assistance to the expedition of Louis VII of France as it crossed Anatolia, saving the King's contingent from certain annihilation. At around this time the Order also began to commit knights to battle against Muslims in the Iberian Peninsula, the reconquest of which was coming to be portrayed as a second front in a virtually ongoing Crusade. The Templars and their counterparts, the black-clad Knights Hospitaller, continued to bolster secular armies fighting on the frontiers of Christendom. They fought in Spain against the Almohads and in Eastern Europe against the Mongols, as well as against the Turks, Arabs and Mameluks in the Levant. Their foe was often equally zealous and invariably possessed a significant numerical advantage. On a number of occasions the Templars fought to the brink of their own extinction.

The Templars' most famous defeat was at Hattin, against the Sultan Saladin, the nemesis of the Kingdom of Jerusalem. Poor and divided leadership – not least, perhaps, the failings of the Order's own Grand Master Gerard de Ridefort – propelled the Christians towards this disaster in midsummer of 1187. Saladin captured their leader King Guy and (what was worse) the True Cross. The Christians had carried the sacred relic into the battle, as they had into many through the years. After the battle, the Sultan executed his Templar and Hospitaller captives. So many other Christian knights had been killed or taken prisoner at Hattin that there were few left to defend the towns, castles and cities, which capitulated to Saladin's might over the ensuing months. Eventually came the turn of Jerusalem, and soon the Muslims again controlled the Holy City.

Europe had not yet lost its Crusading enthusiasm, however. The Third Crusade, led by King Richard the Lionheart of England, restored the coastal cities of the Holy Land to Christian rule. Meanwhile, new knights came to replace the fallen brethren of the Military Orders, who were considered martyrs. The Orders played an active role in the fight back, especially at the Battle of Arsuf, where Saladin's army was scattered. The Christians might have followed up this victory by retaking Jerusalem, but realised that they had insufficient men to hold on to it afterwards. Having reached a stalemate, the conflict was suspended and a truce was made.

The Templars avoided participation in the infamous Fourth Crusade, which veered off course and pillaged Christian Byzantium. Likewise they kept out of the Albigensian Crusade, which ravaged the Languedoc in the name of eradicating heresy. They were, though, active in the ill-fated Fifth Crusade in Egypt, and in the Sixth, when the Holy Roman Emperor Frederick II secured – through diplomacy – the restoration of Jerusalem to the Christians. In the second quarter of the thirteenth century an internecine power struggle between the Pope and the Emperor led to political Crusades being preached within Europe against Frederick II himself; Frederick being viewed as a threat to the Papal States, which his domains encircled. The Templars as a rule disdained to fight against other Christians, even on the Pope's behalf. In 1244 in the East, meanwhile, allies of the Sultan of Egypt, the Khoresmians, took Jerusalem by storm, and subjected it to rapine and pillage. Soon afterwards the Christians suffered another heavy defeat, at the Battle of La Forbie, where almost all the Templars were killed or captured. Though the Order would again resurge, it was perhaps the beginning of the end.

The Seventh Crusade – that of the saintly King Louis IX of France – came next. Louis invaded Egypt with Templars as his vanguard, but was not fated to achieve great success. The Templar contingent, after initial triumphs, was decimated when it accompanied Louis's bellicose brother in a fateful charge into the town of Mansourah. The knights were trapped and massacred. The victorious Mameluks, a caste of slaves-turned-warlords, soon seized power. Lauded by a Muslim chronicler as *Islam's Templars*, these Mameluks subsequently burst out of Egypt into Syria and Palestine and, after defeating the Mongols, turned against the Christians. In unrelenting campaigns, they whittled away the territory of the Frankish settlers. Europe, meanwhile, had turned in against itself. Successive Popes were distracted by their wars in Italy and Sicily. They offered indulgences to those prepared to take up the sword for the *Guelf* cause against the *Ghibellines*. Papal wars against Frederick's successors absorbed money and manpower, much to the detriment of the Latin East and to the dismay of Templars. The condition of the vestigial Kingdom of Jerusalem continued to deteriorate as the thirteenth century wore on. In 1291, when no Crusaders came to reinforce them, the Templars there perished defending the last corner of the last major Christian stronghold, the city of Acre. They fought on almost until the walls of their fortress tumbled around them. Yet even after this final failure of the Eastern Crusades, the Templars survived as a powerful organisation throughout Europe, at least until the fateful events of 1307.

The Templars still possessed their widespread and lucrative estates, and since coming into being had also branched out into banking and other commercial enterprises. Yet having been founded for the defence of the Holy Land, with the fall of Acre they had lost their principal *raison d'être*. Even as they continued making valiant attempts to regain a foothold on the Syrian shore, they were more vulnerable than they imagined to being attacked from the rear. They had become, perhaps, both an uncomfortable reminder to Europe of its failure in the long-neglected East, and a handy scapegoat for this failure.

King Philip IV of France (called Philip the Fair) suddenly accused them of betraying the Christian cause. He claimed that they were guilty of secretly repudiating the faith and of performing nocturnal rites both blasphemous and depraved. Royal agents seized every Templar in France following dawn raids carried out on Friday 13 October. The Templars were soon delivered into the hands of the Inquisition – an institution founded to stamp out religious heresy, but by this time subservient to the Capetian state. At the same time Philip sequestered the Templars' property.

Pope Clement V was originally outraged by the King's action, and tried to halt the heresy trials. By then, however, many Templars had confessed under torture. The Pope, under sustained pressure from Philip, had little choice but to go along with the destruction of the Order. Clement sealed the Templars' fate by calling for them to be arrested in every land where they were established, and to be held and put on trial in the name of the Church. Thus commenced perhaps the largest trial in world history. In France many Templars, who had retracted their initial confessions, were burnt, protesting their innocence and their loyalty to Christianity.

Their international brethren, meanwhile, from Ireland to Cyprus, were seized and brought before Episcopal tribunals, and though not all could be convicted, the Order's name was widely tainted with suspicion.

In 1312, Clement V convened the Council of Vienne, where the Templars' fate was to be decided. The Pope, having imposed silence on the unhappy congregation, issued *vox in excelso*, a solemn proclamation that abolished the Order of the Temple for all time. Two years later, in Paris, the last Grand Master was called to publicly repeat the confession that had been forced from him some years before, and to hear his sentence. Jacques de Molay used the occasion instead to retract his confession and to insist that the Order of the Temple was wholly innocent. He declared himself ready to die in atonement for the moment of weakness in which he had confessed to lies through fear and torture. Geoffroi de Charney, a fellow Templar dignitary, supported him in this stand. Before the day was through the furious King had ordered both men to be burned alive. It was the end of the Knights Templar. Both King Philip and Pope Clement were dead within the year, and soon after that the King's line died out amid strife and betrayal. In the imagination of many, however, the Templars lived on.

## Author's Note

Words in the text in **bold print** are those names and topics that have individual entries. Saints are listed by first names (e.g. **George, St**), unless in a place name (e.g. **Sainte Eulalie de Cernon**). Contrary to recent convention, I have tended to give names and dates as they would have been familiar to those involved in the subject of this book; hence, for example, *Jacques de Molay* instead of the Anglicised *James of Molay*, and the traditional AD.

# Select Chronology of Templar History

| Event | Year |
|---|---|
| **First Crusade** invades **Holy Land** | 1098–9 |
| **Baldwin II** comes to throne | 1118 |
| **Foundation of the Order** | *c.* 1118 |
| **Field of Blood** | 1119 |
| Council of Nablus | 1120 |
| **Council of Troyes** | 1128–9 |
| Templars gain castles near **Antioch** | 1136–7 |
| *Omne Datum Optimum* | 1239 |
| **Second Crusade** | 1148–9 |
| Crusaders capture **Ascalon** | 1153 |
| **Amalric I**'s campaigns in **Egypt** | 1163–9 |
| Templar ambush of **Assassin** envoys | 1173 |
| **Saladin** comes to power | 1174 |
| Battle of **Montguisard** | 1177 |
| Fall of **Jacob's Ford** | 1179 |
| Battles of **Cresson** and **Hattin** | 1187 |
| Saladin takes **Jerusalem** | 1187 |
| **Third Crusade** | 1188–92 |
| **Fourth Crusade** sacks **Byzantium** | 1204 |
| **Albigensian Crusade** begins | 1209 |
| **Fifth Crusade** | 1221 |
| **Sixth Crusade** (that of **Frederick II**) | 1228–9 |
| Foundation of the **Inquisition** | 1231 |
| **Richard of Cornwall**'s Crusade | 1240 |
| Battle of **Liegnitz** | 1241 |
| Strife between **Military Orders** in **Acre** | 1241 |
| **Khoresmians** take Jerusalem | 1244 |
| Battle of **La Forbie** | 1244 |
| **Seventh Crusade** | 1247–54 |
| **Ain Jalut** (**Mongols** v. **Mameluks**) | 1260 |
| Mameluks invade Holy Land | 1261 |
| **Edward I**'s Crusade | 1271–2 |
| Fall of **Acre** | 1291 |
| **Arrest** of the Templars | 1307 |
| **Trials** of Templars | 1308–10 |
| **Council of Vienne** | 1311–12 |
| **Burning** of **Jacques de Molay** | 1314 |

# The Templar A–Z

## A

### Abbasids

The Abbasid dynasty reigned as Caliphs in **Baghdad**. The Abbasids were the spiritual leaders of the Sunni **Muslim** world, recognised throughout the Middle East as the successors of Mohammed. The **Crusaders** understood the Caliph to be the **Pope** of the **Saracens**; however, by this time Abbasid power had waned. In 1055 the Caliph had been reduced to little more than a symbolic figurehead, with a **Seljuk** Sultan holding the real power.[2] Even so, the Caliphs retained an aura of semi-divinity. The **Mongols** deposed the thirty-seventh and last Abbasid Caliph, al-Mustasim, in 1258, after the sack of Baghdad. The Caliph died along with 80,000 of his people, who were slaughtered by the Mongol hordes.[3] **Hulagu** supposedly had al-Mustasim trampled to death beneath horses' hooves, having rolled him in rugs so that none of his sacred blood would splash on the ground.

### Abbey of Notre Dame de Mont Sion

The Abbey of Notre Dame de Mont Sion was the home of a small religious Order operating in the **Holy Land** during the era of the **Crusades**. The community served the abbey on Mount **Zion** in **Jerusalem** and also had a monastery on Mount Carmel, which later became the seat of the **Carmelites**. The monks of the Abbey of Sion, according to **Jacques de Vitry**, were **Augustinians**, linked to the **Canons of the Holy Sepulchre** – the same religious Order as that which had custody of the **Dome of the Rock** on **Temple Mount**, and that supported the foundation of the Knights Templar. The Abbey of Mount Zion itself probably predated the Crusades and originally had an Eastern Orthodox monastic community. It is thought that after the success of the **First Crusade** the **Latin** brethren arrived, possibly being the same mysterious Italian monks who had founded the Abbey of **Orval** and then suddenly departed from it. There is some suggestion that these monks could also have had links to **Peter the Hermit** and **Godfroi de Bouillon**.³ When the Crusaders lost the Holy Land, the monks of the Abbey of Zion evacuated to Sicily and were apparently absorbed by the Jesuit Order in 1617.

## Abraham (unknown ancient date)

The Biblical Patriarch Abraham was the mythic ancestor of the **Jews**, via his son Isaac, and the **Arabs**, via Ishmael. He travelled from Ur in Mesopotamia to settle in Hebron. His God became the God of the three monotheistic religions. The scene of Abraham's abortive sacrifice of Isaac, Mount Moriah, came to be identified with Temple Mount in Jerusalem, where the Templars would be based.

## Abraxas

The Abraxas (or Abrasax) is an enigmatic figure, depicted as a warrior with a cockerel's head and with snakes for legs. The creature holds a round shield and a flail whip, supposedly representing wisdom and strength. **Gnostic** sects apparently used small stones, carved with images of the Abraxas, as magical charms, in the first centuries AD. ('Abraxas' may be the root of the magic word 'Abracadabra!') Abraxas images were used by the Basilidean sect of **Alexandria**, whom the early fathers of the **Catholic** Church condemned as **heretics**. Abraxas is said to have represented the supreme deity, from whom emanated the angels, one of which, as the Gnostics thought, was the flawed Jehovah who created the material world. Obviously to medieval Catholics all this would have constituted grave heresy, and the chimera-like image would have appeared outlandish and demonic. The issue of whether there was a secret group within the Templars, which diverged from Catholic Orthodoxy, is still an open question. An intriguing indication that this might be the case is a version of their **seal** bearing the image of the Abraxas. Around it is the legend *Templi Secretum*. Whether the Templars knew the true meaning of the Abraxas, or merely used it as a heraldic device, is hard to assess.

## Accusations against the Order

The Knights Templar in **France** were **arrested** on **Friday 13** October 1307, three weeks after King **Philip the Fair** had issued secret instructions for this, saying it was necessary because the Templars were guilty of terrible, supremely abominable crimes. According to the accusations, though the Templars were outwardly a respectable Christian brotherhood, secretly they were blasphemers and **heretics**. The accusations were subsequently made public. The definitive list was drawn up only in August 1308 and was probably the work of the King's minister **Guillaume de Nogaret**. It contained many items; mostly covering practices allegedly taking place during the Templars' **initiation ritual**. The list was well calculated to besmirch the Order's reputation and to rouse popular revulsion. The main charges were as follows:

That the Templars **denied** and renounced **Christ**, and made initiates spit at (or otherwise defile) the **Cross** during their secret reception ceremony. They taught that Christ was a false prophet and not God.

That the Templars did not perform or believe in the sacraments of the **Catholic** Church, and their **priests** failed to speak the proper words during the **mass**.

That the Templars were guilty of **idolatry** and unholy worship. They worshipped severed **heads** (some had three faces, some one, some a **skull**. The idol had the power to bring them riches as well as to make the trees flower and the land germinate). A black **cat** also manifested.

That the Templars wore **chords** around their middles, which had touched these idols.

That at their receptions initiates were made to give or receive obscene **kisses** by the presiding **Master**, and afterwards encouraged to engage in **sodomy**.

That the Templars were sworn to **secrecy**. Those who refused to go along with these things were killed or imprisoned. The rest were forbidden to **confess** to anyone except to a brother of the Order.

That the Templars held that the **Grand Master** and other lay brothers could **absolve** sins.

That the Order was greedy and corrupt and sought to enrich itself by any means, legal or otherwise.[4]

The Templars in France were cruelly **tortured** by the **Inquisition** and by royal agents. Confessions (to some or all of the above charges) were secured from many of them by these means. The accusations were apparently first made by a former Templar called **Esquin de Floyran**. Little if any material evidence could be produced pointing to Templar guilt, and none of the spies apparently sent into the Order by King Philip seem to have been called to testify.

## Acre
Acre is an ancient Mediterranean port long seen as the gateway to the **Holy Land**, if not part of the Holy Land itself. The **Crusaders**, under

King **Baldwin I**, captured the city in 1104. After the Battle of **Hattin** in 1187, Acre was one of the many Christian cities that fell to **Saladin**. The beleaguered **Guy de Lusignan**, having been captured at **Hattin** and subsequently released, was turned away from **Tyre** by **Conrad of Montferrat**, and so took his meagre forces to besiege Acre, establishing a fortified camp on the beachhead. This was in turn surrounded by Saladin's army, but held firm, and became the nucleus of the Christian fight-back that became known as the **Third Crusade**. Many died of disease and injury, but supplies and reinforcements continued to arrive from Europe. The English and French Crusaders under **Richard the Lionheart** and **Philip II Augustus** eventually joined the Christian camp, and recovered the city in 1191, having successfully kept Saladin's relief force from the besieged **Muslim** garrison.

The Siege had been long and bloody (it was compared to the mythic siege of Troy). The **Grand Master** of the Templars, **Gerard de Ridefort**, had died in the course of the fighting, and Queen **Sibylla of Jerusalem** and her two young daughters died during an epidemic in the Crusader camp. After the Crusaders' victory, the Muslim prisoners were executed on Richard's orders.[5] With Acre secure, Richard was able to march south and to defeat Saladin again at **Arsuf**. Acre, meanwhile, became the effective capital of the vestigial **Kingdom of Jerusalem**. It lacked the spiritual draw of **Jerusalem** itself but was more important strategically, and it became the political and economic hub of the Christian territory, also playing host to Muslim merchants, for the Holy Wars did not long put a stop to commerce.

To the north of Acre was the suburb of Montmausars, created to accommodate the Christian refugees from the Muslim conquests who swelled Acre's population during the thirteenth century. The whole city was surrounded by formidable fortifications. The 'Accursed Tower' was part of these defences, on the inner of two walls. The name dated to the costly siege of Acre during the **Third Crusade**. The outer wall had towers named after their sponsors, including the Towers of the Patriarch, the Legate, King Henry II, the English, the Countess of Blois, the **Hospitallers** and the Templars.[6]

The Templars had their compound in a fortress by the sea in the southwestern corner of the promontory on which the city stood. According to the **Templar of Tyre**, the towers of the Templars' base at Acre were topped by four gilded lions, which were 'a noble sight to look upon'. A grand palace for the **Grand Master** also lay within the enclosure (perhaps indicative of the onset of a degree of decadence). The Hospitallers and **Teutonic Knights** also had their headquarters in the city.

The Bishop of Acre, **Jacques de Vitry**, newly arrived from **France**, found the city full of vice and corruption. Acre was also often the scene of acrimony among various Christian factions. There would be strife between supporters of the **French**, **German** and **Cypriot** claimants to the throne, and the Palestinian

Frankish barons, as well as between the Italian merchant communes. The **Military Orders** became embroiled in some of these internecine quarrels, symptomatic of the Christian state falling apart before its final destruction. Despite being without stable government and being torn by factionalism, the city survived until the siege commenced by the **Mameluks** in 1291. Even today it contains Crusader remnants, including parts of the Hospitaller Citadel and a Templar **tunnel**. The Templar fortress by the sea at Acre was the last part of the city to fall under the Mameluk onslaught. Its ruins are now under the water.

The Siege of Acre of April to May 1291 was effectively the Christians' last stand in the East. The Mameluk sultan **Al-Ashraf Khalil**, the son of **Qalawun**, brought a mighty army out of **Egypt** and the defenders of Acre, largely abandoned by the West, perished on the walls.[7] The Grand Master of the Templars, **Guillaume de Beaujeu**, led a daring sortie out and he and his brethren subsequently fought off sustained assaults on the fortifications. The city's moat filled with dead bodies as the Muslims pressed the offensive. When the Accursed Tower fell, Guillaume rushed to lead the counter-attack, where he was mortally wounded. At last the Mameluks gained entry to Acre. As desperate street fighting raged, many of the citizens streamed out of the doomed city by sea. The **Patriarch**, Nicholas of Hanape, took so many refugees onto his boat that it capsized and he was drowned, while the unscrupulous Templar captain, **Roger de Flor**, founded a career in piracy by extorting vast sums from any who would flee on his own ship. Other Templars fought on, under **Peter de Sevrey** their **Marshal**. They guarded the citizens who could not escape in their citadel by the sea, once the Muslims cut off the harbour. On 18 May 1291, they made such a determined resistance that al-Ashraf offered terms, and the Templars agreed to surrender in return for the safe passage away of the refugees among them. On 25 May, a Mameluk Emir with 100 warriors was dispatched to oversee the surrender, and raised his banner over the citadel. His men at once began to molest the women and children, provoking the Templars to kill the Mameluks and tear down their banner, hoisting again their own flag, the **Beauseant**.

That night De Sevrey ordered **Theobald Gaudin** to take the Templars' **treasure** to **Sidon** by boat, and most of the civilians were also evacuated by sea, though others volunteered to stay to help in the fight. The next morning de Sevrey and his staff left the citadel under a flag of truce, having been invited to renewed negotiations. When they reached Al-Ashraf's camp they were seized and beheaded. The remaining Templars fought on against the final Mameluk assault for three more days, until the undermined walls collapsed around them and the Mameluks poured in to finish them off. The Mameluks then systematically demolished much of Acre. Those citizens who survived the massacre but who failed to escape were taken as **slaves**. The fall of the capital so demoralised the remaining Latin Christians that soon afterwards

**Sidon**, **Tortosa** and **Pilgrim's Castle** were evacuated for **Cyprus**. After this time Acre went into steep decline, and it is today little more than a backwater.

## Adam de Wallaincourt (died *c.* 1310)

Adam de Wallaincourt was a Templar referred to in a document produced by the Templars during the **Paris trials**, defending the Order from the **accusations** made against it. The document claimed that this brother Adam de Wallaincourt had wished to find a harsher religious Order and had entered the **Carthusians**, for a while. However, he had found it unbearable and had returned to the Order of the Temple, subjecting himself to humiliating **penances** in order to be accepted back. (His penances had included fasts, eating on the ground, being flogged by the priest and crawling naked before the altar during masses.) The brothers defending the Order called for this man to be brought to testify in its defence, as it was unlikely that someone would have suffered all that to return to an Order guilty of all that the Templars were charged with.[8]

## Ad Extripanda

*Ad Extripanda* was the title of a **Papal Bull** issued by Pope **Innocent IV** in 1252. It granted the **Inquisition** the authority to use **torture** against suspected **heretics**, in order to extract **confessions**. The edict also gave the secular authorities the right to seize a portion of the property of the condemned heretic. This was in accordance with ancient Roman law, a harsh and authoritarian system that was making a return to the statute books. *AD Extripanda* also officially sanctioned the practice of passing convicted heretics 'to the secular arm' for execution by **burning** alive at the stake. The custom of burning to death unrepentant or relapsed heretics was already in place.

## Ad Providam

*Ad Providam* was the title of a **Papal Bull** issued by **Clement V** on 2 May 1312. This was towards the end of the **Council of Vienne**. It granted most of the property of the Order of the Temple (which had been abolished and outlawed in the bull *Vox in Excelso*) to the Order of the Hospital, so that the **Hospitallers** could use it for the purposes for which it had originally been granted to the Templars. It also transferred all the Templars' former privileges. The various kings, who had hoped to retain the confiscated land, were compelled to go along with the decree, for the most part. Exempted were the Templar lands in **Iberia**. There the land would go to other, smaller **Military Orders**; some were newly founded ones that rose from the ashes of the Temple.

It was a coup for the **Catholic** Church that it managed to retain the Templar lands for the Hospitallers and not see them dissipated by the kings and distributed to their favourite courtiers. The bull called the Hospitallers 'athletes of the lord' and praised them for bearing hardship, danger and heavy losses in the defence of the faith overseas. *AD Providam* states that the Templars were blemished and stained with depravity.[9] The transfer was confirmed in another bull entitled *Nupter in Concilio*. However, this bull of 16 May emphasised the exception of the properties in Iberia.[10] Other bulls from this time, meanwhile, reveal that owing to pressure from the bishops, the Hospitallers' new privileges were suspended.

## Agnes de Courtenay (1136–84)

Agnes de Courtenay, Countess of **Jaffa** and **Ascalon**, was an influential figure in **Jerusalem** in the mid- to late twelfth century. She was the daughter of Joscelin II de Courtenay, the Count of **Edessa**, the sister of **Joscelin III** and the wife of **Amalric I**, although the marriage was annulled for political reasons on his succession to the throne, after which she married first Hugh of **Ibelin** and then Reynald Grenier, the 'ugly, intellectual' lord of **Sidon**.[11] Her children by Amalric were King **Baldwin IV** and Queen **Sibylla**. Agnes was the power behind Baldwin IV's throne. Her decisions had a critical bearing on the fate of the **Kingdom of Jerusalem** in several respects. She secured the appointment of **Heraclius** as **Patriarch**. She also encouraged Sibylla to marry **Guy de Lusignan**, and along with **Gerard de Ridefort**, leader of the Templars, engineered Sibylla and Guy's accession to the throne. **William of Tyre** called Agnes a 'grasping woman, detestable to God'.[12]

## Agnus Dei

*Agnus Dei* is Latin for 'Lamb of God'. It is a symbol of the martyred **Christ**, and Christian sacrifice. The lamb has a halo and holds a banner bearing a **cross**. Sometimes in Christian iconography, the lamb was also depicted bleeding, with its blood flowing into a chalice resembling the **Holy Grail**. The *Agnus Dei* is also associated with St **John the Baptist**, who proclaimed Jesus to be the Lamb of God, which takes away the sins of the world (John 1:29). The Templars and the **Hospitallers** both used the symbol, in carvings around their buildings and on their official **seals**. Some believe that as well as its conventional interpretation as a symbol of Christ, the *Agnus Dei* was chosen because of the word's relation to the Latin *Agnito* meaning 'knowledge'. In London, carvings of the lamb can be seen on St John's Gate, which is all that remains of the Hospitallers' Grand Commandery in Clerkenwell. It can also be seen around the Inns of Court, off the Strand, where the law society of the **Middle Temple** inherited the lamb device from the Templars, along with the premises, which had formerly been the Templars' British headquarters.

## Ain Jalut

The Battle of Ain Jalut, fought in Palestine on 3 September 1260, was a **Mameluk** victory over the **Mongols**. The Mongols under **Hulagu** had conquered Persia and Mesopotamia, massacred the population of **Baghdad**, and received the submission of **Damascus, Aleppo, Antioch** and Armenian Cilicia. In 1259, Hulagu had returned to Mongolia with most of his horsemen, in order to advance his interests following the death of the great Khan, his brother Mongke. He had left an army in the Middle East under General Kitbuqa. The Mongols remained an imminent threat, therefore. Kitbuqa's ambassador arrived in Cairo, and delivered the usual ultimatum. He demanded the Mameluk regime offer total submission to the Mongol Empire or await its fate. The Mameluks responded by sending back the envoy's head.

Led by the Sultan **Kurtuz** and by the general **Baybars**, the Mameluk army marched out, crossing the Christians' territory of southern Palestine. The leaders of the vestigial **Kingdom of Jerusalem** were unsure whether to involve themselves directly, and (as it is usually claimed) declined Kurtuz's offer of an alliance, although they agreed not to impede the Mameluk army's progress.[13] One chronicle says the Christians did become actively involved. According to the annals of St Rudbert of Salzburg, the Sultan 'of Babylon' joined to himself Templars, **Hospitallers, Teutonic Knights**, 'and all the Church overseas', and did battle with the Tartars (Mongols), and God granted that he defeated them.[14]

The Egyptian-led force intercepted the Asiatic horde at Ain Jalut (the pools of Goliath) in Galilee, though Baybars kept the bulk of his troops hidden behind ridges. He organised a classic Mameluk feigned withdraw (also a favoured Mongol tactic) and then unleashed the hidden reserves. For once the Mongols were on the receiving end of slaughter, and soon Kitbuqa himself was captured and beheaded. The Mongol threat to the Franks of Syria/Palestine was over, replaced by the threat of the ascendant Mameluks. Baybars killed Kurtuz and became Sultan himself. Having driven off the Mongols, he was poised to begin the destruction of the Christian states, beginning with **Antioch**.

## *Al-Adil* (1145–1218)

Abu-Bakr Malik al-Adil was an **Ayyubid** Sultan. The Crusaders knew him as Saphadin. He was a younger brother of **Saladin** and had negotiated on his brother's behalf with **Richard the Lionheart**, thus being instrumental in the treaty that brought the **Third Crusade** to a conclusion. Previously a proposal had been on the table that would have seen al-Adil ruling the Kingdom, married to Richard's sister Joan.[15] The lady's objections to marrying a non-Christian and al-Adil's disinclination to convert put a stop to that idea, and it is unlikely the Muslims ever took the proposal seriously. Al-Adil eventually succeeded as Sultan in Syria. He also ruled in **Egypt** and favoured a policy of peaceful relations with the **Franks** in the East. He also established trade links between Egypt and the **Maritime Republics**, especially **Venice**. Meanwhile the pragmatic **Grand Masters** of the Temple, **Gilbert Erail** and **Philip de Plessies**, signed and preserved treaties with al-Adil, which preserved the peace in the years before 1217, when the **Fifth Crusade** invaded Egypt. Al-Adil, in declining health, failed to prevent the **Crusaders** from investing **Damietta**.

## *Alamut*

Alamut was a remote fortress in northern Persia (Iran), an eyrie in the mountains south of the Caspian Sea. Its name meant *the eagle's perch*. It was long regarded as impregnable. It became synonymous with the Shi'ite **Muslim** sect the Nizari Ismailis, better known as the **Assassins** or Hashishin. In 1090 the sect had infiltrated the garrison, and from then until 1256 it served as their stronghold. They held numerous other castles in the area besides, as well as in Syria. The Assassins in Syria were subordinate to the leader in Alamut, and probably acted on his orders, or at least with his permission when moving against Templar lands or assassinating Crusader barons. Followers of the Assassin sheik (the first of which was **Hassan I Sabbah**) were 'brainwashed' into becoming ruthless murderers, usually targeting Sunni potentates. Their leader expected them to embark upon their bloody missions without expectations of returning alive. Then as now it is hard to account for such fanaticism, but the promise of paradise and **houris** was a strong motivation. Legend has it that there was a beautiful secret vale near Alamut, an earthly paradise where novice Assassins were taken to be entertained by beautiful young women trained in the arts of gratifying male desires. The young men, after a short stay in this garden, were drugged, and then revived elsewhere, and told that they had been in paradise. They would naturally be filled with a longing to return. However, they would be told that the only way they could do so was to show blind loyalty to the leader of the sect. They had to perform the murder he ordered and be captured and executed as a result, thus achieving **martyrdom**. Marco Polo, who passed Alamut while on his travels to the East, recorded the legend of this false paradise. By then, however, the castle was a ruin and the Assassins had been scattered by the **Mongols**.

## *Alanus Marcel* (died *c.* 1228)

Alanus Marcel (or Alan Martel) was a Templar Master or **Grand Preceptor** of **England**, presiding from around 1218. He is commemorated in a modern stained-glass window in **Temple Church, London**. He was the recipient of a letter from **Peter of Montaigue**, telling of how the **Fifth Crusade** had been trapped in **Egypt**, leading to the surrender of **Damietta**, and appealing for help.

## *Al Aqsa Mosque*

The Al Aqsa Mosque is an **Islamic** place of study and worship in **Jerusalem**. This large building occupies part of **Temple Mount**, adjacent to the **Dome of the Rock**. It comprises part of the sacred complex of buildings known to the **Muslims** as the Al-Haram al-Sharif. It was built in the years from AD 674, possibly on the site of a **Byzantine** Church. The mosque was a scene of slaughter in the wake of the capture of Jerusalem by the **First Crusade**. It seems that subsequently **King Baldwin I** began to convert the building into a royal palace. **Baldwin II** eventually assigned part of it to the nascent Order of the Temple. **Hugues de Payens** and his associates set themselves up there and subsequently used the building as their base. Later Templars probably added the building's great porch, with its central **Gothic** arch, which can still be seen, as well as extensive additions now lost. The building remained in Templar hands until the fall of Jerusalem to **Saladin**, who had it ritually cleansed and restored as a mosque. The Templars never returned to this their first home, even after **Frederick II** negotiated the return of Jerusalem to the Christians. Part of the Emperor's treaty with **al-Kamil** had stipulated that the mosques of Temple Mount were to remain in Muslim hands. The Crusaders sometimes referred to the Al Aqsa Mosque as the **Temple of Solomon**, while calling the Dome of the Rock the Temple of the Lord. (This does not necessarily mean that they believed the Mosque actually to be the original Temple built by King **Solomon**.)

## Al-Ashraf Khalil (died 1294)

Al-Ashraf Khalil was the **Mameluk** Sultan of **Egypt** who brought about the annihilation of the Crusader state by capturing the Christians' last major stronghold at **Acre** in 1291. He was the son of **Qalawun**, who had already much reduced the Crusader holdings and destroyed various cities. Qalawun mustered his armies for the final assault in 1290, but died before he could lead them against Acre, passing that distinction to al-Ashraf. Al Ashraf united the forces of Egypt and Syria. He imprisoned the envoys from Acre, including a Templar called Bartholomew Pizan, who attempted to negotiate, and proceeded to commence the siege, bringing over 100 siege towers, trebuchets and ballistas to bear. Though the defenders fought valiantly the cause was hopeless. Al Ashraf Khalil destroyed Acre and its Christian population, taking many into **slavery**, and completed his sweep by taking **Sidon**, **Tyre** and **Beirut**, before returning to Cairo. He later entered **Damascus** in triumph, preceded by 280 fettered prisoners.[16] Khalil favoured Circassian Mameluks over **Turkish** ones for promotion, and this led to his assassination by a disgruntled Turk.

## Albert I of Habsburg (1255–1308)

Albert of Habsburg held the titles King of **Germany**, King of the Romans and Duke of Austria. He was the son of Rudolf of Hapsburg, who set the family on the path to pre-eminence. His title King of Germany was contested by Adolf of Nassau-Wielberg, whom Albert defeated in battle in 1298. In 1303 **Boniface VIII** recognised Albert as future **Holy Roman Emperor**. **Clement V**, however, turned down Albert's appeal to be so crowned. Albert expressed doubts concerning the accusations against the Templars and like **James II of Aragon** was reluctant to move against them in his lands before being formally requested to do so by the **Pope**. Albert was murdered on 1 May 1308 by a disgruntled nephew, while en route to suppress a revolt in Swabia.

## Albigensian Crusade

The Albigensian Crusade was a military campaign called by Pope **Innocent III** in 1209 and dragging on for many decades. It was directed against the dualist **Cathar** sect in Occitan-speaking south-western **France**, and the nobility of Toulouse and the **Languedoc** who sheltered and defended the Cathars and refused to persecute them. Its pretext was the murder of the papal legate Pierre de Castelnau, and one of its leaders was another uncompromising churchman, **Arnaud Amaury**.[17] Innocent III promised the French-speaking northern knights who embarked on this war the same spiritual rewards as it did those who made their way to fight the Muslims in the **Holy Land**. Initially, Count **Raymond VI of Toulouse** had born the Church's condemnation and had been **excommunicated** for his reluctance to stamp out the heretics.

Raymond VI of Toulouse managed to deflect the initial wrath of the French host away from Toulouse and towards the territory of his nephew, Viscount Raymond Roger Trencavel. The Catholic armies stormed the Town of Béziers, pushing an ill-planned sortie back in through a gate unwisely left open. They slaughtered the population indiscriminately on St **Mary Magdalene**'s day, even massacring those sheltering in churches. They then moved on to **Carcassonne**. After a worthy defence, Viscount Trencavel was lured out of his city to negotiate. He was seized and died a prisoner while his people were dispossessed. **Simon de Montfort**, one of the leading Northerners, took over Carcassonne and continued the war, pursuing the Cathars and the southern nobles (for example the Count of Foix) who opposed him. Simon took Toulouse itself, and even defeated **Pedro II of Aragon** when Pedro intervened on the Occitan side. Later, De Montfort's skull was crushed by a rock hurled from a catapult operated by women on the walls of Toulouse. He had gone there to recapture the city, which had risen up against his harsh rule following the return from exile of Count Raymond VI and his son Raymond VII. This reversal inaugurated a few decades of Occitan resurgence. However, a Church-sponsored trade embargo impoverished the area, while renewed French campaigns, including the royal Crusade of 1226, brought more massacres and gradually brought Occitania into submission.

Captured Cathars were routinely **burned** in large numbers during the Albigensian Crusade. It may be that the **Military Orders** sheltered some fugitives, but on occasion they were also compelled to play host to De Montfort and his allies. De Montfort stayed with the Templars in Montpellier in early 1215 while on campaign, for example. The Templars endeavoured to preserve their neutrality, in the main, nonetheless, despite their avowed loyalty to the Pope. They were mindful that their true calling was in the **Holy Land**, and were loath to take up arms against their neighbours in the Languedoc.[18] The effect of the war was to pull the Occitan-speaking region into the orbit of **Capetian** France rather than **Aragon**. Catharism was brutally persecuted. From the 1230s onwards, the people of the ravaged region were subdued by the fearful and intrusive presence of the **Inquisition**. In a sense the attack on the Cathars was a prelude to the attack on the Templars. Out of the Albigensian Crusade was born the ruthless institution that would be the Templars' nemesis.

## Aleister Crowley (1875–1947)

Edward Alexander 'Aleister' Crowley was a prominent and notorious occultist. He tried to found a new pagan religion called 'Thelema' based on individual will. He adopted the maxim 'do what thou wilt', and was a member of such occult groups as the Hermetic Order of the Golden Dawn and the *Ordo Templi Orientis*. Courting controversy, he identified himself with the Beast, and sometimes used the name **Baphomet**, linking himself to the idol allegedly worshipped by the Templars. He was influenced by the ideas of **Eliphas Levi**.

## Aleppo

Aleppo was a great city in Syria that the **Byzantine Empire** lost to the **Arabs** in AD 637. It was a little to the south of the midway point between **Antioch** and **Edessa**, and was a threat to both the principality and the county. It became the seat of a **Seljuk Turkish** ruler. The **Franks** under **Baldwin II** unsuccessfully besieged it with **Muslim** allies in 1124. Aleppo became even more of a thorn in the Crusaders' side when it was united with Mosul in 1129 by **Zenghi**. In 1138, Aleppo's people fell victim to a terrible earthquake, which killed many. The city was later ruled by the **Ayyubid** dynasty, and then occupied by the **Mongols**. Aleppo is famous for its great medieval citadel, which still dominates the city.

## Alexander IV, Pope (1199–1261)

Reginaldo Conti was elected Pope in 1254, succeeding **Innocent IV**, and assumed office as Alexander IV. He tried to persuade the kings of **England** and Norway to embark on a campaign against his **Hohenstaufen** enemy **Manfred**, the son of **Frederick II**, offering Crusade indulgences in 1255. Armies of **Guelfs** and papal mercenaries attacked Lucera in Apulia, where **Manfred** was sheltering amid the largely **Muslim** population, but Manfred emerged the victor. Later Alexander himself lost control of **Rome** to **Ghibelline** sympathisers and fled to Viterbo where he ended his days.

## Alexandretta

Alexandretta (now Iskanderun in eastern Turkey) was a port in between Armenian Cilicia and the Crusader principality of **Antioch**. In the early 1150s it was taken from the Armenians by **Reynald de Chatillon**, on behalf of **Manuel I**. Reynald subsequently gave it to the Templars for their assistance in his campaign. Soon after Reynald and the Templars allied with the Armenians.[19]

## Alexandria

Alexandria is a port city at the mouth of the River Nile in **Egypt**. It was founded in antiquity by Alexander the Great. It was a centre of Greek culture, with an active **Jewish** community. The city also became important to early Christianity, and was a centre of **Gnostic** thought. It was conquered by the **Muslims** in AD 640, but remained the seat of a Christian **Patriarch**. During the period of the **Crusades** it was perhaps the most important port in the eastern Mediterranean. It traded with the **Levant, Byzantium** and the Italian **Maritime Republics**, which maintained mercantile outposts there. Their presence in this Muslim city scandalised pious minded Muslims as well as Christians, the latter being particularly alarmed by the Italians' readiness to trade in weapons and other war materials.[20]

Alexandria was several times raided by Crusaders and even briefly occupied by them. **Saladin** first fought the Crusaders in a battle near the city. Alexandria's famous Pharos Lighthouse, one of the Seven Wonders of the World, was still standing at this time, though its ancient library was long lost. Alexandria was also the original burial place of St Mark, until his body was stolen and smuggled out by merchants of **Venice**. Venice retained particularly strong links with Alexandria and rather than jeopardise these steered the **Fourth Crusade** away from this intended target.

## Alexius I Comnenus (1048–1118)

Alexius I Comnenus was the **Byzantine** Emperor at the time of the **First Crusade**. He seized the throne from Nikephorus III in 1081. It is he who appealed to Pope **Urban II** for western military assistance against the **Seljuk Turks**, but he got more than he bargained for. Alexius insisted upon receiving oaths of loyalty from the Crusade's leaders when they passed through **Constantinople**. These were not vows the Crusaders had much intention of keeping, for most of the great lords desired to fight on their own behalf and keep any spoils for themselves. Later, Alexius, believing them to be already vanquished, failed to aid the Crusaders at **Antioch**. This soured an already strained relationship between the Greeks and **Franks**.

## Alfonso I of Aragon (1073–1134)

Alfonso *el Batalador* (The Battler) was King of **Aragon**. Crowned in 1104, he was the son of King Sancho Ramirez, and succeeded his brother Pedro I. He welcomed the Templars into his kingdom in the 1130s, keen for them to play a part in the ongoing **Reconquista**. Alfonso was a tireless and successful warrior who had already regained much territory. He conquered Zaragoza, Tarazona, Tudela, Daroca and Calatayud between 1118 and 1120. Alfonso endowed the Templars and **Hospitallers**, and also tried to foster more localised Orders such as the Confraternity of Belchite, dedicated to supporting the Reconquista. The King was married unhappily to Urraca, the daughter of Alfonso VI of Castile. They produced no heirs, and the marriage was eventually annulled.

In 1131, while besieging Bayonne, Alfonso I made an extraordinary will. It bequeathed the Kingdom of Aragon to the **Canons of the Holy Sepulchre**, to the Hospitallers and to the Templars. The will explicitly left to these Orders all the lordships over all Alfonso's subjects including lords and bishops.[21] The three Orders were unable to claim this legacy in its entirety.

It might be added that in 1131 the Templars were a fledgling institution, hardly tested. This bequest was an extraordinary vote of confidence. Such an arrangement was unacceptable to the Aragonese barons. On Alfonso's death they chose as his successor his brother Ramiro, despite the fact that Ramiro was a monk. He was brought out of his monastery for long enough to be married and to sire a son and heir, and then allowed to return to his vocation.

## Alignment of Templar Churches

It has been noticed that many Templar **churches** are not aligned perfectly east–west, as most other Christian churches are. There is a strong tendency for them to be aligned to the north of east, by anything between ten and thirty-five degrees. One theory has it that this is intentional, and that the churches align with the position of the sunrise on the mornings of the feast days of the saints to which the churches were dedicated. This is termed 'patornal alignment'. A couple of churches seem to have aligned with the rising sun on 29 August, the feast day of **John the Baptist**. The famous **Temple Church, London,** and the ruined church at **Dover** apparently shared this alignment (16° north of east), while the Templar Chapel at **Ribston** was so aligned as to face the rising sun on 22 July, the feast of **Mary Magdalene** (pointing 33° to the north of east).

## Al-Kamil (died 1238)

Al-Kamil Mohammed al-Malik was the **Ayyubid** Sultan of **Egypt** during the time of the **Fifth Crusade** and the **Sixth Crusade**, that of **Frederick II**. He was the son of **al-Adil** and the nephew of **Saladin**. He commanded the force supporting **Damietta** against the Fifth Crusade's siege, but on his succession was obliged to withdraw to Cairo to impose his authority, enabling the Franks to encircle and capture the port. In 1219 and 1220, Al-Kamil attempted to negotiate with the invaders, but they snubbed his offers, either through mistrust or over-confidence. The Papal Legate **Pelagius of Albano** turned down the return of **Jerusalem** with rebuilt walls and the **True Cross** in exchange for Damietta, because Kamil refused to also cede **Kerak** and Montreal. In 1221 the flooding river arrested the southward march of the Christian army short of the town of **Mansourah**, which al-Kamil had fortified.[22] The stranded Crusaders were forced to surrender.

Later, the Emperor Frederick II arrived in the East as part of the **Sixth Crusade**. He had already established good relations with al-Kamil, via the envoy **Fakhr al-Din**, whom al-Kamil had sent to Sicily. The Sultan had intimated to Frederick that he would return Jerusalem to the **Franks** in exchange for the Emperor's assistance against his rivals, particularly al-Muazzam of **Damascus**, who had become Egypt's enemy. In the end the assistance was no longer required, as al-Muazzam had already died. However, Frederick II negotiated a new treaty with the Sultan, and managed to persuade al-Kamil to restore Jerusalem, **Bethlehem** and Nazareth to Christian hands, supposedly for a ten-year period. Al-Kamil lost face in the Islamic world by agreeing to this, despite the clause that Temple Mount would remain under **Muslim** control, and the clause preventing the Christians from refortifying the city. According to **Matthew Paris**, meanwhile, the Templars, envious of the Emperor, had written to al-Kamil intimating that he might like to ambush Frederick at the River Jordan. Al-Kamil had responded not by attacking Frederick but by alerting him to the Templars' treachery. This had cemented the Emperor's friendship with the Sultan and they subsequently exchanged many valuable gifts, among which was an elephant that al-Kamil sent to Frederick. Al-Kamil was no Jihadist, and showed himself willing to make peace with the Crusaders in order to concentrate on other matters. In his final days he had to contend with **Khoresmian** and **Seljuk** encroachment and with hostility from a nephew in Damascus.

## All Hallows by the Tower

All Hallows by the Tower is a church standing adjacent to the **Tower of London**. The original building was the scene of the trial of some of the English Templars, who fervently defended the Order's innocence. The undercroft of the church houses a stone altar table, said to have been brought by the Templars from **Pilgrims' Castle** prior to their suppression.

## Almoural

Almoural is a picturesque Templar **castle** in **Portugal** that survives in a good state of preservation. It is situated above the River Tagus, and was occupied by the Templars from 1175.

## Amadeus de Morestello (mid-thirteenth century)

Brother Amadeus de Morestello was the **Master of the Temple in England** at the time of **Henry III**. He received a Templar envoy dispatched from **Acre** in 1260 by the **Grand Master, Thomas Bérard**, to tell the western brethren and the royal courts of Europe of the arrival of the **Mongol** hordes in the Middle East, and of the great danger to the **Holy Land**, which was already being ravaged. This messenger, 'compelled by intolerable necessity', reached London in thirteen weeks, travelling from Dover to **London** in a single day. Unless aid arrived quickly, the Templars' appeal stated, then a ghastly annihilation would be visited upon the world.

## Amalric I, King of Jerusalem (1136–74)

Amalric I was the second son of **Fulk V, Count of Anjou**, and of Queen **Melisende**. He succeeded his brother **Baldwin III** as King of **Jerusalem** in 1163. Prior to that Amalric had been the Count of **Jaffa** and **Ascalon**. He was said to be tall and fairly handsome but grew fat as he aged and he never possessed the charisma of his brother. He was married to **Agnes of Courtenay**, the daughter of Joscelin II, Count of Edessa, but was forced to divorce her by the barons and prelates, on grounds of consanguinity. However, their children **Sibylla** and **Baldwin IV** were recognised as legitimate. Amalric cemented a **Byzantine** alliance by marrying Greek princess Maria Comnina, producing another daughter, **Isabella**.

Amalric launched three invasions of **Egypt** (in 1163, 1164, and 1168), being involved in shifting alliances with rival Viziers there, and initially having support from the Byzantine Emperor **Manuel I Comnenus**. The Vizier Sharwah, after finding himself deposed by his **Fatimid** master, made alternating appeals to **Nur ed-Din** of Syria and to Amalric for their assistance in reinstating him. In the latter campaigns Amalric came up against **Shirkuh**, the Kurdish General sent with an army by Nur ed-Din. General Shirkuh was the uncle of **Saladin**, and it was close to **Alexandria** that Saladin first met the Christians in battle. Arguably it was Amalric's invasion of Egypt that set Saladin on the road to power. In Amalric's absence, the **Holy Land** was vulnerable to attack from Nur Ed-Din. At one point the Sultan attacked the principality of **Antioch** and besieged the castle of **Harenc**. The Prince of Antioch, **Bohemond III**, rode to relieve the siege, but subsequently grew overconfident and against advice for greater caution attacked the Sultan's much larger army, lured by a feigned retreat. Bohemond and his forces were either slain or captured. Only seven of sixty-seven Templars escaped.

Amalric fell out with the Templars on several occasions. He hanged twelve of them in 1166, accusing them of surrendering a cave fortress in Transjordan too easily to Shirkuh.[23] The Templars, under **Bertrand de Blanquefort**, refused to accompany Amalric on the invasion of Egypt in autumn 1168, on the grounds that this violated a peace treaty. Perhaps they also feared that the expedition jeopardised the security of the Kingdom. The Templars' disobedience further angered the King. The Grand Master of the **Hospitallers, Gilbert d'Assailly**, supported Amalric and it was at this time that the Hospitaller Order completely militarised. Amalric and the Hospitallers attacked the Egyptian town of Bilbies and massacred its inhabitants. The expedition was ultimately unsuccessful, and Gilbert resigned in its aftermath.

Amalric's feud with the Templars came to a head in 1173. He was in negotiations with the Syrian **Assassins**, who had promised (no doubt falsely) to convert to Christianity and to enter into an alliance against Nur ed-Din on condition that Amalric release them from their tribute obligation to the Templars. The Templars probably knew that the Assassins were professional back-stabbers, both literally and metaphorically, and sought to prevent Amalric from an unwise alliance. Perhaps to pre-empt their treachery, a party of Templars ambushed and slew Abdullah, the representatives of **Sinan**, the **Old Man of the Mountains**, thus sabotaging the intended treaty. The King demanded that the Templars hand over those responsible for the ambush, especially its leader **Walter de Mesnil**. The Grand Master, **Odo de Saint-Armand** refused. Amalric descended upon **Sidon** (where the Templars were holding their General **Chapter**). He seized Walter and took him away to prison in **Tyre**. The King sent apologies to Sinan but had no chance to renew the talks concerning an alliance. He died in 1174. Such was his enmity for the Templars by then that he had been planning to call on the **Pope** to have the Order punished.[24]

## *Amaury de la Roche* (died *c.* 1271)
Amaury de la Roche was a Templar **Grand Preceptor** of **France** from about 1262, based at the **Paris Temple**. King **Louis IX** had asked the **Pope** that Amaury be assigned this position and the Grand Master **Thomas Bérard** had consented. Before this Amaury had served as Grand Preceptor of **Outremer**. In 1267 Amaury received letters from the Patriarch of Jerusalem, William of Agen, concerning the dire situation in the East as a result of **Mameluk** incursions, instructing him to relay this to the Pope, and requesting finance.[25]

## *Amaury de Lusignan of Cyprus* (died 1310)
Amaury (or Amalric) de Lusignan was the brother of King **Henry II of Cyprus**, and was the ruler of **Cyprus** in late 1307 when **Clement V**'s order for the **arrest** of the Knights Templar arrived (*Pastoralis Praeeminentiae*).

The instructions put Amaury in a difficult position because to some extent he owed his power to the Templars. They had assisted him in overthrowing his brother the previous year. Amaury also doubted the charges, but equally did not want to incur the anger of the **Pope** and of **Philip the Fair**.

The Templars on Cyprus initially resisted the agents sent to arrest them, but eventually submitted to being placed under guard on their own properties. Amaury, meanwhile, was murdered in his palace in mid-1310, by one Simon of Montolief. Soon afterwards the Templars' enemy Henry II was restored to the Cypriot throne. Conditions deteriorated for the Templars thereafter and many died in the dungeons of the fortress of **Kerynia**. Several of the witnesses at the Templar trial on Cyprus (just prior to Amaury's murder) were returned exiles, nobles who had been loyal to Henry II, and who opposed the Templar-backed overthrow.

## America

There has been speculation that the Templars (or members of a supposed secret society founded by surviving Templars in **Scotland**) may have travelled to America, perhaps some decades after their **suppression** in Europe. **Henry St Clair, 1st Earl of Orkney** is usually linked to this theory, as are certain carvings at **Rosslyn Chapel**. The Templars were great mariners, and in principle their ships would have been perfectly capable of crossing the Atlantic. Viking archaeology on Newfoundland provides evidence of the existence of the short-lived colony of Vinland. It is feasible that the Templars could have learned of the existence of the New World from Scandinavian sources, and sailed there after the suppression, possibly after a sojourn in **Scotland**. Speculative authors have seen this as a possible explanation for the disappearance of the fleet from **La Rochelle** on the eve of the arrests in 1307. There is, however, no evidence for Templar knowledge of the Americas. There is a rock carving in Westford, Massachusetts, supposedly resembling a Knight's effigy, and a round tower of uncertain origin in Newport, Rhode Island.[26] The so-called 'Westford Knight' is so indistinct as to be hardly there at all, however.[27] The Newport Tower, meanwhile, could possibly be seen as the remains of a Templar round church, but the conventional explanation seems more credible; that it is the base of a seventeenth-century windmill or signal beacon.

## Amio of Ais (died c. 1212)

Amio of Ais was a Templar who apparently fell from grace within the Order. He was recorded by 1179 as holding the exalted position of Grand Commander, or Lieutenant Master of the West. In the preamble to one document he described himself as 'Amio, by the Grace of God called **Master** of the Temple of **Jerusalem** and noble procurator in regions this side of the sea' (as opposed to **Outremer**). The document was addressed to all

Christians ready to bestow favours on the earthly Jerusalem, which would earn them a place of habitation in the heavenly one. It was a call to resolve disturbances and scandal in the Church in the name of the 'higher peace'.

By 1190, Amio was evidently in the **Holy Land** and was made **Seneschal**, but did not last long in this position, being replaced for unknown reasons by a Seneschal appointed by **Robert de Sable**. Under **Gilbert Erail**, Amio's career suffered even more, and he was apparently demoted to a simple Brother of the Order. He evidently left the Order, after twenty years of service, and returned to the secular world. His name appears in charters from the thirteenth century as a lay witness. He participated as a secular knight, alongside his former brethren, in a mission to relieve **Baghras** and was last heard of in 1211. He does not seem to have parted on bad terms with the Order, and all this belies the claim by chronicler **Michael the Syrian**, that anyone who committed to the Knights Templar and fell short was killed by the sword.

## Anagni, 'Outrage' of
Anagni is a town in central Italy. The Papal Palace at Anagni was the scene of the scandalous episode in 1303 when a party of French troops, led by **Guillaume de Nogaret**, minister of **Philip the Fair**, descended on the palace to arrest Pope **Boniface VIII** on trumped-up charges of **heresy** and sorcery. Their intention was to force Boniface to attend a Church council in **France** where he would be judged. **Scairra Colonna**, the leader of an Italian faction hostile to Boniface, was also involved, and at one point allegedly struck the **Pope**. The Pope was held under house arrest, but the loyalist people of Anagni rallied to free him. Even so the traumatic episode had taken a toll and Boniface died soon after. The outrage at Anagni remained a source of controversy, and it overshadowed subsequent events. De Nogaret was **excommunicated**. King Philip and his ministers pressurised **Clement V** to convene a posthumous trial of Boniface in tandem with the trial of the Templars, in order to rewrite history and portray an attack on the Church as a defence thereof. In 1311, Clement formally vindicated Philip's actions, praising his Christian zeal, and also pardoned Guillaume.

## André de Montbard (1103–56)
André de Montbard was a **Burgundian** of noble birth. He was one of the early members of the Knights Templar. He went on to become fifth **Grand Master** of the Order, presiding between 1153 and 1156. André was an uncle of **Bernard of Clairvaux**, Bernard apparently being the son of André's much older half-sister Aleth.[28] André's access to St Bernard and Bernard's influence within the **Catholic** Church helped ensure the official recognition of the Templars at the **Council of Troyes**. André apparently arrived in Europe some time before the other founding Templars, charged with gain-

ing support for the **Holy Land** and negotiating with **Fulk V, Count of Anjou** to come east to marry **Melisende**, the heiress to the Kingdom of **Jerusalem**. André returned to the Holy Land and served as **Seneschal** of the Order under **Everard des Barres**. André also served under **Bernard de Tremelay**. He participated in the capture of **Ascalon** from the Egyptians in 1153. He was elected Grand Master after de Tremelay perished there.

## *Andrew Michael Ramsay* (1686–1743)

'Chevalier' Andrew Michael Ramsay was a Scottish **Jacobite** and **Freemason**, living in exile in **Paris**. He was a well-known writer, and had been a tutor to the young Charles Edward Stuart (Bonnie Prince Charlie) in **Rome**. As a Freemason, Ramsay was apparently Chancellor of the French Grand Lodge. He gave a speech in 1736 known as Ramsay's Oration. The theme was the world being 'nothing but a huge republic', which could be unified by the philanthropic and fraternal spirit of Freemasonry. In this speech, he was the first to suggest that Freemasonry began in the **Holy Land** during the **Crusades**, among **knights** who gathered together from all parts of Christendom into one sole fraternity. After his speech 'Knights Templar' degrees began to appear in Masonic Lodges.

## *Andronicus Comnenus* (1118–85)

Andronicus Comnenus was a **Byzantine** prince and later Emperor. Several times he fell out of favour with his cousin the Emperor **Manuel I**. At times he was honoured, at other times he was a prisoner or a fugitive. He was governor of Cilicia for a while but went on the run from Manuel I with Philippa of **Antioch** (the second daughter of Raymond of Poitiers, whose sister was **Maria of Antioch**, Manuel's wife). Andronicus appeared in **Jerusalem** and ingratiated himself with King **Amalric I** (his fortune in embezzled Cilician taxes may have had something to do with this). Amalric made Andronicus lord of **Beirut**. Andronicus then eloped with **Theodora**, his own niece and the widow of **Baldwin III**. The lovers passed between **Muslim** courts, including that of **Nur ed-Din**, before setting themselves up in a castle in Anatolia.

When Andronicus was out raiding, his own castle was stormed by the Byzantine Governor of Trebizond, who took Theodora and her children to **Constantinople** as prisoners. Andronicus had to make grovelling apologies to the Emperor to ensure their return. He did not forgive the humiliation. Andronicus later stepped in to end the power struggle that broke out in Byzantium on the death of Manuel I.

In 1182 he brought an army to Constantinople and subsequently murdered Maria of Antioch, her young son Alexius II and various other members of Manuel I's family. Andronicus then assumed the Imperial throne himself, and minted coins showing himself being crowned by Christ.

He had officials who had been loyal to the old regime impaled on stakes. He also killed Renier of Montferrat, the brother of **Conrad** and **Boniface** and husband of Manuel's daughter Maria. Andronicus spared only Alexius II's young fiancée Agnes, a French princess, and took her for his own, though over fifty years her senior.

Andronicus launched a notorious attack on **Latin Christians** living in Constantinople, especially the **Venetian** merchant community. (Later, Doge Enrico Dandolo would lead the vengeful Venetians in the **Fourth Crusade** and desecrate Constantinople.) Andronicus also attacked the Byzantine aristocracy, hoping to remove potential rivals. Byzantine nobles thus supported an invasion by William of Sicily, which Andronicus just managed to defeat at Thessalonica. Meanwhile, Constantinople rose in support of the young prince **Isaac Angelus**, whom Andronicus had attempted to arrest. When Andronicus returned to the city he met a grisly death at the rebels' hands.[29]

## *Angevin Dynasty (Plantagenet)*

The Angevin Plantagenet dynasty began with the Counts of Anjou (**France**). After the advantageous marriage of **Geoffrey Plantagenet** (the son of **Fulk V Count of Anjou**) to the Empress **Matilda** (the daughter of **Henry I** of **England**), the dynasty became the ruling house of England also. **Henry II** and **Richard the Lionheart** ruled an Angevin Empire, as extensive on the Continent as the British Isles. The French lands were largely lost in the time of King **John**.

The Plantagenet arms consisted of a red shield with a gold lion. By the time of King John, three lions *passant guardant* featured. According to legend the Angevin dynasty descended from a demonic witch or siren named Melusine (sometimes depicted as a serpent or fish from the waist down, and sometimes with wings). She was supposed to take this form every Saturday because of a curse. One day, one Raymond of Poitou encountered her in a forest, and proposed marriage. She accepted on condition he never enter her chamber on a Saturday. He broke the arrangement one day and discovered her in her half-serpent form. The incident was forgiven and forgotten by both parties until one day he unthinkingly called her a serpent during an argument before the court. She took the form of a dragon, flew from the castle, and was never seen again. Demonic ancestry or not, the Plantagenets were famously hot tempered. It was said of Henry II's rebellious sons 'from the Devil they come and to the devil they will go'. The Templars received great favour under the Angevin kings. They were granted alms, lands, and trusted positions as royal councillors and treasurers. They were also mediators in negotiations with the King of France.

The county of Anjou itself was lost to the Kingdom of France in 1206. The title ended up in the possession of an unrelated **Capetian** Prince, **Charles of**

**Anjou**. 'Angevin' thereafter could also refer to the dynasty Charles founded, which ruled in Naples and Sicily from the 1260s.

## Anglo-Saxon Chronicle

There are several versions of the Anglo-Saxon Chronicle, which records the history of Britain in old English, up to and immediately after the Norman invasion. Historian monks at various monasteries produced different continuations. One version records the arrival of **Hugues de Payens** in **England**, after meeting with the **Henry I** in Normandy, and then passing north to **Scotland**, on a drive to recruit volunteers for the **Holy Land**. It records that the Templar received many gifts of gold and silver to aid the cause of **Jerusalem**, and that a great multitude followed him back. The Chronicle claims these multitudes felt duped when they arrived in the East because there was not a great battle with the **Saracens**. This probably referred to the abortive attack on **Damascus** planned by **Baldwin II of Jerusalem**.

## Antichrist

The Antichrist is a sinister figure constructed by apocalyptic Christians interpreting various passages in the Bible, including parts of the book of Ezekiel and **Revelation**. The name 'Antichrist' itself only appears in the first and second Epistles of John (**John the Evangelist**). Revelation does, however, speak of the 'Beast' and also seems to foretell the coming as a powerful ruler, who will be a great deceiver and enemy of **Christ**. Various individuals through history have been identified with this diabolical being, who is supposed to be an agent of the Devil, if not the Devil incarnate. Some Christians speculated that Mohammed could have been the Antichrist (**Islam** has its own Antichrist figure, the Dajjal); while others in the thirteenth century convinced themselves the Antichrist was the Emperor **Frederick II**. To slightly later Templars like **Richard Bonomel**, meanwhile, it must have seemed like the Antichrist was leading the **Mameluk** rampage.

The Templar brother **Henry d'Arcy**, at about the same time, commissioned or composed a work on the Antichrist, revealing that the Order took an interest in matters eschatological. Building on the obscure references in the Bible, d'Arcy's disquieting tract states that the Antichrist will be the opposite of Christ. 'Christ came humbly, and he [i.e. the Antichrist] will come arrogantly; Christ came to uplift the humble, and he will crush them; Christ came to justify sinners, but he will come to exalt felons.'[30] This Antichrist would destroy holy law while being called Almighty God. Henry d'Arcy anticipated the Antichrist would be of the Jewish tribe of Dan, because the Bible (Genesis 49:17) compared Dan to a serpent. He would be born 'in sin' but his mother would also be entered by the Devil at the moment of his conception. He would be a son of Hell, a vessel of venom, possessed by

Satan in the same way Christ was by the Holy Spirit. He would set up his throne in **Jerusalem**, perform miracles and bring nations under his terrible power. His reign would be presaged by the severing of nations from **Rome** (and the return of the prophets Enoch and Elijah), and characterised by a great persecution of Christians. Antichrist would eventually be destroyed 'by his own power' and the end of the world, amid flames, the resurrection of the dead and the last Judgement would soon follow. 'Be of great heart and undertake boldly to do good, and God will help you,' concluded d'Arcy.

Apocalyptic anxiety accompanied the turn of the fourteenth century and the failure of the **Crusades**. **Philip the Fair** and his minister **Guillaume de Nogaret** cast first Pope **Boniface VIII** and then the Templars as secret servants of Antichrist. Conversely, an anonymous song at the time of the **suppression** of the Templars cast Philip himself as Antichrist, accusing him of subverting the Church and plotting against **Christendom**.[31]

## Antioch

Antioch was an ancient city located on the border between Turkey and Syria. It was one of the centres of the **Roman** and **Byzantine** Empires, and the seat of a Christian **Patriarch**. Though conquered by **Muslims**, much of the city's population remained Christian. In AD 1098 Antioch was the scene of one the **First Crusade**'s most remarkable victories. The **Crusaders** besieged the city for nine months, during which starvation took its toll, within and without. Then word came that a Muslim relief force was on its way under Kerbogah of Mosul. The Christians' situation looked so hopeless that the Norman **Stephen of Blois** deserted with his men. He met **Alexius I Comnenus** with a Greek army coming to relieve the Crusaders, but told the Emperor to turn back, as in all likelihood the Crusaders were already dead. Stephen of Blois was mistaken. At the last minute, with inside help secured by **Bohemond of Taranto**, the Crusaders had taken the city. However, Kerbogah's army then appeared outside Antioch, and the weakened Franks seemed doomed after all. Their morale was lifted when the **Holy Spear** was unearthed in their midst following a hermit's vision, and the relic helped to inspire them on to fresh victory.[32] Antioch was to become the capital of one of the Latin states. The principality's Latin rulers were:

| Ruler | Reign |
|---|---|
| **Bohemond of Taranto** | 1098–1105 (with Tancred as regent 1101–3 and 1105–6) |
| **Tancred de Hauteville** | 1108–12 (Prince/regent for Bohemond II) |
| **Roger of Salerno** | 1113–19 (Prince/regent) |
| **Baldwin II of Jerusalem** | 1119–26 (Protector/regent) |
| Bohemond II | 1126–30 |

| | |
|---|---|
| **Fulk of Anjou/of Jerusalem** | 1130–36 (regent, disputed by Alice of Antioch) |
| **Raymond of Poitiers** | 1136–149 |
| **Constance** | 1149–63 (with **Reynald de Chatillon** 1153–61) |
| **Bohemond III** | 1163–1201 |
| Bohemond IV | 1201–16 |
| Raymond Roupen | 1216–19 |
| Bohemond IV (again) | 1219–33 |
| Bohemond V | 1233–52 |
| **Bohemond VI** | 1253–68 (ruled in Tripoli until 1275) |
| **Bohemond VII** (titular) | 1275–87[33] |

Up until the Battle of the **Field of Blood** in 1119, it seemed the principality might emerge as a power in its own right, independent of the **Kingdom of Jerusalem**. However, the aftermath saw the principality becoming a Jerusalemite protectorate. Subsequently the **Byzantine** Emperors, notably **John Comnenus** and **Manuel I**, sought to re-establish their authority in the region. The early Templars gained several castles in the principality of Antioch, mostly in the northern frontier region known as the Amanus March, which included **Baghras** and Roche Guillaume.

Bohemond VI of Antioch, hoping to safeguard his city, offered tribute to the **Mongols** in 1260, thus winning the particular hatred of the **Mameluks**. Antioch fell to the latter in 1268 whereupon the Sultan **Baybars** destroyed it almost completely. The population was either enslaved or massacred and the city never recovered. The Templars of Baghras withdrew, meanwhile, seeing that the principality was lost.

### *Antonio Sicci de Vercelli* (thirteenth–fourteenth century)

Antonio Sicci de Vercelli was an Italian notary who testified at the Papal Commission in **Paris** in 1311. He was not a Templar but had had worked for them for some forty years in the East. His testimony included a version of the story of the **Skull of Sidon**, and also the allegation that a Templar preceptor of **Sidon** had made himself a blood brother with the Sultan of **Egypt**.

### *Apocrypha*

The Apocrypha, or Apocryphal Gospels, are those scriptures that were not selected for inclusion in the official or canonical Bible. Some of these were subsequently suppressed or destroyed, being deemed either unreliable, irrelevant or dangerous. There were always some who thought the Book of **Revelation** should be considered apocryphal, even though it was essential to Christian teachings about the end of the world and the last judgement. Other books were included in the Bible that have subsequently been rejected (at least from modern English Bibles). These include the Books of **Maccabees**, Tobit and Judith, which were included in an apparently Templar Old Testament produced in **Acre** in the late thirteenth century. The Templars also seem to have known of a fourth-century 'Apocalypse of St Paul' describing St Paul making a visit from Heaven into Hell, and being moved by the plight of the damned. This seems to be the inspiration for one of the works composed by or for Brother **Henry d'Arcy** of Temple **Bruer**. There were other books that were forbidden by the Church. Many were known of but thought lost, until the discovery of the **Dead Sea Scrolls** and the **Nag Hammadi** library with its **Gnostic** Gospels. Curiously not all esoteric, apocryphal writings were viewed as **heretical**. For example some that emerged during the **Fifth Crusade**, and that seemed to contain predictions of Christian triumph, were seized upon by the Papal Legate **Pelagius of Albano** and used to encourage the Crusaders. These works in Arabic included the *Prophecy of Hanan*, son of Isaac, and *The Revelation of the Blessed Apostle Peter to his Disciple Clement.* [34]

## Arabs

The Arabs were a semi-nomadic, Semitic race native to the Arabian Peninsula and the Middle East. They traced their origins to the patriarch **Abraham** via Ishmael, son of Abraham's concubine Hagar (Genesis 16:1–16). Renowned warriors, they won a widespread empire and spread their language, culture and beliefs after the time of Mohammad and the rise of **Islam**. They developed a more sophisticated civilization following the conquest of Persia and **Egypt**. They conquered much of North Africa and southern Spain as well as much territory in the East. By the eleventh century in the Middle East, however, the Arabs themselves had fallen under the domination of the **Seljuk Turks**. These conquerors subsequently adopted aspects of Arab culture and religion.

## Aragon

Aragon is a region in north-east Spain. In medieval times it was a kingdom in its own right, also covering much of Catalonia. Its capital was Zaragoza, after the reconquest of that city by **Alfonso I** 'The Battler'. The Kings of Aragon were also Counts of Barcelona, and sometimes overlords of Navarre. The Templars became extensively established in Aragon, with their administrative centre in Barcelona, governing Templar houses north of the Pyrenees as well as in Spain. The Order played a part in the wars of the **Reconquista** against the **Moors**. The Templar castles of **Miravet** and **Monzóm** were among the strongest in the kingdom. **Alfonso I** was a great patron of the Order, and in his will, left the entire Kingdom to the **Hospitallers**, the Templars and the **Order of the Holy Sepulchre**. This will was disregarded however, though the Templars did gain control of a number of fortresses and various other revenues and privileges. The Templars were also granted lands in areas recently recovered from **Muslim** rule. Here they were often obliged to encourage the resident Muslims to remain on the land as well as to encourage new settlers to these regions. The Templars became influential courtiers in Aragon. The Master of Aragon had special responsibilities including being tutor to the royal princes as well as mediating between the King and the Church or the nobility.[35]

The wars against the Moors in Aragon sometimes took upon the characteristics of **Crusades**. Just as the reconquista was completed, ironically, Christian Aragon itself became the target of a Crusade preached by the papacy. This stemmed from the Aragonese monarchy's establishing a link to the **Hohenstaufen** Crown of Sicily, when Peter III of Aragon married Constance of Sicily, the daughter of **Manfred**. The Aragonese kings asserted a claim to Sicily and became the latest representatives of the **Ghibelline** cause against the papal/**Guelf** faction. Aragon repulsed a **Capetian** invasion, but later relinquished its claim to Sicily. King **James II** restored Aragon's good relationship with the papacy (and was seen as a potential leader of an expedition to the **Holy Land**), but his rule of Sicily was never officially recognised.

James II was sceptical about the **accusations** made against the Templars in 1307. However, he soon turned against the brethren, ordering them to surrender to royal custody.[36] The Templars declared their innocence, but were not ready to capitulate, withdrawing to their castles and preparing to withstand sieges by royal armies. James soon captured the castle of **Peníscola** and took the Grand Preceptor **Exemen de Lenda** into custody, but other Templars held out much longer, most notably **Ramon sa Guardia** in Miravet. At length the resistance faded and the Templars and their lands were taken into custody. The trials revealed nothing conclusive. The Templars were not systematically tortured and none of them apparently confessed. James II eventually won the right to deliver the Templars' properties to the new Order of **Montesa**, which resembled the Order of the Temple, but was dependent on the crown. Aragon remained a separate kingdom until 1479 when its King Ferdinand II married Queen Isabella of Castile, creating the unified Kingdom of Spain.

## Architecture

Crusader architecture in the Holy Land was usually in the late **Romanesque**/early **Gothic** style that they developed, which also showed traces of Byzantine and Arabic cultural influences. Greek and Syrian/Palestinian Christian artists were employed to decorate the walls of the churches with paintings and gilded mosaics. The Templars were great builders. Like the **Hospitallers**, they spent much of their revenue building formidable **castles** in the **Holy Land** and **Iberia**, or improving pre-existing ones. They also built **churches** and chapels, both in the East and in their **preceptories** across Europe. Early examples of their churches were often **round churches**, such as that at **Tomar**, and **Temple**

**Church, London**. The circular plan echoes the shape of the **Holy Sepulchre**. In silhouette, however, some of these churches more closely resembled the **Dome of the Rock**, with a squat, cylindrical central tower supported by columns and spacious arches. The Templars also built polygonal churches, such as the octagonal chapels at Laon, Segovia and **Metz**. Early Templar architecture took its aesthetic lead from the **Cistercians**, and rejected excessive ornamentation. A number of Templar churches and chapels do contain decorative elements, though, including carved **heads**, often adorning corbels. Some Templar buildings also retain original **wall paintings**.

To build their various structures, the Templars took on mason and carpenter brothers. In Jerusalem the Brethren were also associated with a sculptors' workshop near **Temple Mount**. The Templars built other buildings including domestic, industrial and agricultural structures, from dovecotes and barns to bridges, wharves, mills and city walls. Great examples of timber-framed Templar barns survive at **Cressing** in Essex.

## *Archives, Templar*

The Central Archives of the Knights Templar were never found at the time of the Order's **suppression**. Many documents would have been amassed over their two centuries active in the **Holy Land**. The documents would have been kept at **Jerusalem** and then at **Acre**. Like the **Hospitallers**, the Templars probably rescued their archives from Acre and brought them to **Cyprus**, assuming the documents escaped the cataclysm of 1291. What happened thereafter is a mystery. In 1307 it is possible the Templars either carried them away to some new hiding place or had them destroyed. They were never produced during the trials. Some documents of Templar origin found their way into the archives of the Knights Hospitaller, which moved from Cyprus, eventually to **Rhodes** and then to **Malta**. Another theory has it that the Templar archives were destroyed when Cyprus fell to the **Ottoman Turks** in 1571.[37]

## *Archives, Vatican Secret*

The Vatican Secret Archives are a vast collection of historical records and diplomatic documents kept at **Rome**, distinct from the Vatican Library.[38] Some of these papers and Papal promulgations at various times have been classified highly secret. They are said to cover thirty miles of shelves, and some date back to the seventh century. The earlier records and texts seem to have been lost. The archives contain some records relating to the Templars and their **heresy** trials. These have been examined over the centuries. Some documents were brought to **France** to be examined by **François Rayounard**, following **Napoleon Bonaparte**'s conquests in Italy. They were subsequently returned. More recently Dr Barbara Frale rediscovered the **Chinon Parchment** in the Vatican.

## Ark of the Covenant

The Ark of the Covenant was a sacred **Jewish** treasure and religious symbol in Old Testament times. It may be considered a **Holy Relic**. According to scripture it was constructed on the instructions of **Moses** (Exodus 25:10–28). It had the form a large chest of acacia wood, covered in gold, with winged, golden cherubim on its lid facing each other. It was carried on two poles, which slotted through rings attached to the chest. It was attributed with great sanctity and fearful powers. God himself was somehow supposed to reside within the Ark, and to communicate with Moses from between the wings of the cherubim. The Ark contained the tablets of the law, the Ten Commandments, which Moses received during the Exodus from **Egypt**. At first the Ark was housed in a portable shrine called the Tabernacle. Levite priests attended it, and even they had to tread carefully. (The high priest himself could only enter the Holy of Holies once a year.) The Ark's mystical power could be very destructive to God's enemies. It devoured in jets of fire the two sons of the High Priest Aaron who entered the tabernacle making offerings that were deemed undesirable (Leviticus 10:1–2) The fall of the walls of Jericho was attributed to the Ark, and it brought nothing but misfortune to the Philistines when they captured it (so much so that they sent it back). In the tenth century BC, or thereabouts, the Ark was installed in **Solomon's Temple** in **Jerusalem**. At some stage thereafter it was lost. Certain Jewish lore had it that the Prophet Jeremiah had the Ark hidden in a secret chamber under **Temple Mount** or elsewhere in Jerusalem, just before the Babylonian invasion. Some have speculated that the Templars and **Cistercians** learned of this myth – and that the Templars' secret purpose in Jerusalem was the recovery of the Ark.[39] Even if this were so there is nothing to suggest that they ever found it there. Meanwhile, an **Ethiopian** legend, the ***Kebra Nagast***, claims that the Ark was removed by **Menelik I**, a son born to **Solomon** and the Queen of **Sheba**, who took it to his mother's realm in Africa. The Christian Kingdom of Ethiopia still had ties to the **Holy Land** in Medieval times. Another theory has it that the Templars encountered the exiled Ethiopian prince **Lalibela** and even accompanied him back to Ethiopia on a quest for the Ark.[40]

Despite their association with the Temple of Solomon, the Templars do not often seem to have used the Ark of the Covenant as a symbol. It was also never mentioned at their **trials**. The Templars much revered the **Virgin Mary**, however, who was sometimes compared to the Ark, and mystically associated with it. Both she and it were thought of as vessels containing the essence of divinity, and **Christ** himself, in Christian thinking, embodied a new Covenant between God and Mankind.

## *Armand de Perigord* (1178–1244 or 1247)

Armand (or Hermann) de Perigord was the sixteenth **Grand Master** of the Knights Templar. He was elected in about 1232. There was tension among the Christian factions at this time of his election. The **Hospitallers** were supporting the imperial party (those loyal to **Frederick II** and his representative Ricardo Filangieri) and favouring an alliance with **Egypt**. The Templars, under Armand's predecessor **Pierre de Montaigu**, had sided with the Ibelin lords against the Imperial faction, supporting the claim of Alice, Queen of Cyprus to regency in the vestigial **Kingdom of Jerusalem**, and tended to favour an alliance with **Damascus**. The anti-Imperialist party gained ground, expelling Frederick's forces from **Cyprus** and restricting them to **Tyre** on the Levantine mainland. In 1237 the Templars lost 120 knights after a skirmish with forces from **Aleppo**, encroaching between **Atlit** and **Acre**. Armand trusted the Egyptians even less than the Syrians, accusing them of imprisoning Templar ambassadors in Cairo. In 1242, he abandoned a peace treaty with Egypt that had been arranged by **Richard of Cornwall**. He initiated a violent attack on **Hebron**, which had remained in Egyptian hands. The Templars then retook Nablus and acted with uncharacteristic brutality against the **Muslim** population there.

Armand also led the Templars into open conflict with the Hospitallers (under Pierre deVielle Bride) at **Acre**. The Hospitallers allied with the imperial agent Filangieri, in an attempt to re-impose Frederick II's authority in the city. The Templars joined the Ibelins to oppose this, and ended up besieging the Hospitallers in their compound. The Templars also turned against the **Teutonic Knights** and ejected the imperial party from Tyre. Armand de Perigord organised a coalition with Damascus, meeting al-Mansur Ibrahim, the Muslim Prince of Homs, at Acre to seal it. The prospect of a Damascene/Frankish alliance unnerved the Sultan of Egypt, who called on the services of the **Khoresmians**, a Turkic tribe from east of Persia who had been displaced westward from their homeland by the **Mongol** advance. The Egyptians engaged these Khoresmians as mercenaries, and the tribesmen descended on the relatively defenceless **Jerusalem**, where they massacred the Christian population and defiled the churches. The forces of Acre, under **Walter of Brienne**, and including Armand de Perigord and the Templars, joined with the Damascenes to confront the Khoresmians, who now joined forces with the Egyptians. They clashed at the battle of **La Forbie** in October 1244, where the Egyptians and Khoresmians triumphed. Armand de Perigord was among hundreds of prisoners taken to Egypt. It is possible he died then or that he lived three more years in captivity. In any event **Richard Des Bures** effectively replaced him as Grand Master.

## Armour

The armour worn by the Templar Knights was the standard protective gear
of knights of the period. It consisted of a chain mail *hauberk* (a long sleeved,
hooded tunic) and leg defenders, or *chausses*, made from hundreds of small
metal rings linked together and riveted. There were certain refinements over
the 200 years during which the Templars were in operation. The hood (coif)
became a separate piece for example, enabling freer movement.[41] In addition the Templars wore plate metal **helmets**. By the mid-thirteenth century
this was the fully enclosed great helm, with eye slits and ventilation holes.
Some additional pieces of plate armour were also being introduced by the
late thirteenth century. This chain mail was worn over a padded leather
jerkin called a *haubergeon* or *aketon*, quilted to keep its padding in place, and
adding protection. All of this cannot have been pleasant to wear in the heat
of the Middle East. Cloth mantling over the helmet may have helped stop
the knights' heads cooking inside their helmets. Above their body armour
the Templars wore a mantle of white. They sometimes also wore a white
cloak or **cappa** with a red **cross** on the shoulder. Templar **Sergeants** and
**Turkopole** mercenaries probably wore less heavy armour. The Sergeants did
not wear the white cloaks and probably had black or brown mantles.

## Arnaud Amaury (died 1225)

Arnaud Amaury was the **Cistercian** Abbott of Cîteaux and one of the leading figures of the Albigensian **Crusade**. He was present during the slaughter
of the people of Béziers. The Abbot reputedly told his troops, who had asked
how to distinguish **Cathars** from **Catholic** believers, 'Kill them all, God will
know his own.' After the town fell, many of the people fled to a church in
the upper town, which was dedicated to **Mary Magdalene**. The Crusaders
trapped them there and slaughtered them. (The chronicles say 7,000
people died, although this is reckoned unrealistic, as the church could only
have contained about 1,000.) In one morning the town was wiped out.
Altogether some 20,000 people, 'regardless of age and sex' as the Abbot
proudly informed Pope **Innocent III**, were killed. This terrible massacre was
the first of the 'Crusade', and occurred on 22 July, St Mary Magdalene's
day, 1209. The Abbot also probably instigated the betrayal of Viscount
Trencavel who was made prisoner though under a banner of truce, and the
burning of 100 or more Cathars captured the following year at Minerve.
He went on to become Archbishop of Narbonne. He also took a lead in
Crusades in Spain.[42]

## Arnold de Tarroja (c. 1110–1189)

Arnold de Tarroja was a Templar who became **Grand Master** in 1179. He
had previously served as master of Spain and Provence. During a truce

with **Saladin**, Arnold visited Europe along with Roger de Moulins, Grand Master of the Hospitallers and Heraclius, Patriarch of Jerusalem, seeking aid for the Holy Land. He fell ill in Verona and after his death was succeeded by **Gerard de Ridefort**.

## *Arnulf of Chocques* (died 1118)

Arnulf Malecorne of Chocques was a **Catholic** priest who accompanied the **First Crusade**. As the Duke of Normandy's Chaplain, he was sceptical about the **Holy Spear** discovered at **Antioch**. He was less sceptical about the **True Cross**, which he himself discovered for the Crusaders in **Jerusalem**, having (according to one version of events) imprisoned the Greek and Syrian ecclesiastics and threatened them with torture to make them reveal its location.[43] Arnulf became the unofficial **Patriarch** of Jerusalem immediately following the city's fall in 1099, ignoring the traditional rights of the Byzantine Church to fill that position.[44] He was soon replaced by **Dagobert of Pisa**, but eventually regained the title of Patriarch in 1112. He was unpopular with the Eastern Christians for forbidding anything but Roman **Catholic** services in the **Holy Sepulchre**, and with his fellow Franks for sanctioning the bigamous third marriage of **Baldwin I**. Arnulf, suspected of corruption, was deposed in 1115 but appealed to Pope Pascal II and was again reinstated providing he annul the King's marriage.

## *Arrests*

The Templars in **France** were arrested throughout the country in the early hours of **Friday 13** October 1307. Three weeks before, King **Philip the Fair** had dispatched secret instructions to his *baillis* and *sénéchaux*, telling of the inhuman crimes of the Templars and ordering that they be arrested and detained. It was a large-scale operation, efficiently and ruthlessly carried out. Contemporaries, such as the chronicler Jean de St Victor, were shocked by the King's sudden move. The Templars were mostly caught entirely by surprise by the dawn swoop, and some 15,000 members of the Order, from the **Grand Master** down to the humblest serving brother, were seized. They were arrested in the name of the **Inquisition**, and the process of interrogation and **torture** began almost at once. Meanwhile their lands and properties were taken into royal custody. The arrest warrants suggested that the king acted after prior consultation with the **Pope**. This was evidently not so, as two weeks later Pope **Clement V** expressed his indignation at this assault on an Order under the Church's protection.[45]

It seems a handful of Templars, including **Gerard de Villiers**, the Preceptor of France, had caught wind of the planned arrests and escaped by sea from **La Rochelle**. One Hugh de Châllons also reputedly escaped, possibly with de Villiers, along with the Order's **treasure**. **Hugues de Pairaud**, with a dozen or more companions, was arrested in Poitiers while awaiting an audience with the Pope. The Templars in other countries were not arrested until after the publication of *Pastoralis Praeeminentiae* on 22 November 1307, and the arrests beyond France were carried out with much less zeal and organization. In **Aragon** and **Cyprus**, frontier territory where younger Templars served in a more active capacity and where their Preceptories were more like fortresses, they made a show of resistance while protesting their innocence, but even there they had little spirit for a struggle against their own sovereigns and other Christians.

## *Arsuf*

Arsuf (or Arsur) was an ancient town and fortress near **Sidon**. It was taken by the **Crusaders** in 1101, but fell to **Saladin** in 1187. **Richard the Lionheart** recovered Arsuf for the Christians after the famous battle there in 1191. The Battle of Arsuf was, for the Christians, the high point of the **Third Crusade**, which dispelled the myth of Saladin's invincibility.[46] Richard marched the Crusader army south along the coast, after his previous victory of **Acre**, with the objective of taking **Jaffa**, before turning inland towards **Jerusalem**. The Templars rode in the Crusader vanguard, followed by the Bretons and Angevins, the Poitevins under **Guy de Lusignan**, and the Normans and English under Richard. The **Hospitallers** under Garnier de Nablus protected the rear along with archers and crossbowmen.[47] The heraldic banners of the nobles and multifarious other flags flew above the battle-hardened army on the move, while the English fleet kept pace out at sea and the baggage train trekked in between the fighting men and the shore. The soldiers were harried relentlessly on all sides by Saladin's mounted archers and dart-throwers for much of the way, but retained formation and kept moving. The Sultan's army included Bedouins and black Africans, as well as Arabs and Turks, and greatly outnumbered Richard's. On 7 September, outside Arsuf, Saladin intensified the harassment in an attempt to provoke the Crusaders into battle. The sweltering air hummed with arrows. At length, Richard ordered his force to halt and face the enemy, hoping to use his infantry formations as a protective screen in front of the waiting cavalry, and to withstand the assault until the right moment.

After fending off the bruising assault throughout the morning, the Hospitallers on the northern flank decided they had endured enough, and solicited Richard's order to charge, in vain. The Marshal of the Hospital, the knight Baldwin de Carron, took matters into his own hands, calling on **St George** and charging at the Turks. The Templars followed, then the other troops. King Richard regained the initiative, repulsed a Muslim counter-attack, and led another series of charges. He saw the action through to a great victory. The scattered Turks retreated into the wood of Arsuf and Saladin was forced to withdraw. Other nobles prominent in the battle included **Henry II, Count of Champagne**, and James of Avesnes, who was killed. The battle of Arsuf was a less spectacular victory for Richard than Hattin had been for Saladin, as the Muslim army was able to depart and escaped total destruction.

The town of Arsuf remained in Christian hands over the following decades, dominated by the **Ibelin** clan. In 1261 they sold it to the Hospitallers. **Baybars** and his **Mameluks** besieged Arsuf in 1265, after taking **Caesarea**. Two hundred and seventy Hospitallers led a valiant forty-day defence, during which ninety of the knights perished. In the end, the Mameluk mangonels mounted on siege towers breached the walls of the lower town. The citadel, crowded with refugees, held out for three more days before negotiating surrender in exchange for a promise of safe passage away. Baybars went back on his word. All the Christians were seized and taken into **slavery**.

## Art

The Templars were an active order. Unlike other monastic Orders they were not devoted to contemplation or scholarship. They tended to eschew elaborate ornament on their clothing and equipment, as well as on their buildings. However, many Templar chapels were beautifully decorated with carvings and wall paintings. In the East they may also have featured mosaics by artists influenced by **Byzantine** and Syrian styles. Certainly other Crusader churches did, notably the Church of the Nativity in **Bethlehem**.

Grotesque carved heads aside, the Templars do not seem to have favoured the overtly dark or horrific imagery that appears in some strands of **Catholic** art. In the few original Templar **wall paintings** that survive there is little sign of a 'doom' scene of the damned being tormented by **demons** amid the flames of Hell. The Templars instead favoured figures of saints (as at **Metz**), scenes of knights and castles (as at **Cressac** and **San Bevignate**) and abstract designs and **symbolism** (as at **Montsaunes**). The Templars in **Jerusalem** sponsored an important workshop near their headquarters, where sculptors produced works to adorn their chapels and other buildings.[48] Sculptors from the Templars' workshop carved royal tombs including that of the boy-king **Baldwin V**.

The **Hospitallers** were also artistic patrons, as fragments of murals in their castles at Margat and **Krak des Chevaliers** show. Unfortunately, relatively little Crusader art survived the destruction of the **Kingdom of Jerusalem**. The victorious **Saladin** purged **Temple Mount** of Templar accretions and the **Khoresmians** ravaged the **Holy Sepulchre**, while the royal tombs were destroyed in more recent times. Reused fragments of non-figurative Templar sculpture, including mouldings and capitals, survive in certain Muslim structures in Jerusalem. Other surviving jewels of Crusader art include the icons in the Monastery of St **Catherine** in Sinai.

## Arthur, King (fifth century?)

King Arthur was a mythical king of Britain, probably based on a **Celtic** warlord who fought the Saxon invaders who poured in after the departure of the Roman Legions. Stories of Arthur appear in early Welsh texts. By the medieval period Arthur had become a central character in a body of romances and legends collectively termed the Matter of Britain, wherein Arthur was the ideal (and yet flawed) king presiding over a chivalrous court of Knights of the Round Table at Camelot. Arthur's court is the backdrop to the **Holy Grail** Romances, such as the writings of Jean Bodel and **Chretien de Troyes**. Most of the Grail stories and *chansons de geste* concern the adventures of the knights who embark on the Quest (especially Perceval) more than they do Arthur himself.

## Arwad

Arwad (or Al-Ruad) is the small island off the coast of Syria. It lies two miles out to sea from the port of Tartous (or **Tortosa**, as the **Crusaders** knew it). The island contained the Biblical city of Arvad. This island was the scene of the Templars' final action in **Outremer**. A garrison clung on and in 1300 the Templars, now under **Jacques de Molay**, sent a few hundred reinforcements there from **Cyprus**. The **Mameluks** sent a fleet of sixteen galleys to besiege Arwad, starving the garrison into submission by 1303. The Templar commander **Hugues d'Empuries** negotiated safe conduct for the Christians away to the safety of Cyprus, but was betrayed. The Mameluks, predictably, reneged and killed or enslaved all their captives.

## Ascalon

Ascalon was an ancient port city in the **Holy Land**, between **Gaza** and **Jaffa**. The Crusaders defeated the **Fatimid** Egyptians at a battle near Ascalon in 1099, safeguarding the newly taken **Jerusalem** for the time being. Ascalon was important strategically as it controlled the route to the Sinai peninsula and **Egypt**. The strong fortress there remained a thorn in the Crusaders' side, being a base for **Muslim** raids into the south of the **Kingdom of Jerusalem**. King Fulk (**Fulk V, Count of Anjou**) built several castles facing Ascalon to counteract the threat, including one at Gaza that he gave to the Templars. The Crusaders did not conquer Ascalon itself until 1153 when it fell to **Baldwin III** and a force including many Templars and **Hospitallers**. The Templars were led by **Bernard de Tremelay**, who died leading a rash assault. **William of Tyre** accused the Templars of rushing in and trying to prevent their allies from securing a share of the glory or the spoils. The city later fell to **Saladin** in the aftermath of **Hattin**, whereupon the Sultan had much of it dismantled including its walls and its fine churches. What remained of it was captured by **Richard the Lionheart** and the army of the

**Third Crusade**. They laboured to rebuild its walls, only to have to demolish them again as a requirement of the peace treaty. Seventy years later the **Mameluks**, under **Baybars**, finally destroyed the city.

## Assassins

The Assassins, also known as the *Hasishiyun*, more properly called Nizari Ismailis or Batinites, were a heterodox **Islamic** sect, active in the twelfth and early thirteenth century, who inspired both fear and disgust. They were radical Shi'ites; bitter enemies of the Sunni caliphate and the **Seljuk** imperial establishment of Malik Shah. They used targeted killings to advance their political and religious cause. Their devotees believed that the reward for the murders they committed was a place in paradise. The Assassins' method was to infiltrate the household staff of their intended victim and earn his trust before stabbing him in the back with a dagger. They hoped to be executed soon after and thus to attain the delectable rewards of **martyrdom**. The Assassin sect was established in Persia, among disaffected Shi'ites who opposed the Sunni ruling class. Their effective founder was **Hassan I-Sabbah**, who infiltrated the castle of **Alamut** and converted sufficient numbers of its garrison to the Nizari philosophy that he was able to take control of it. Hassan became known as the 'Old Man of the Mountain'. A branch of the Assassins was also established in Syria, in mountains bordering the Crusader state. Their castles included Qadmus and Masyaf, and they were also a fearful presence in **Damascus**. In 1129, **Buri**, the successor of Tughtigin, had the vizier al-Mazdaghani beheaded for protecting the sect. There followed a massacre of those suspected of Assassin affiliations, carried out by Damascus's Sunni citizens, although the sect later had its revenge and killed Buri himself.[49]

The Assassins' relationship with the Crusaders alternated between convenient alliances and open hostility. **Jacques de Vitry** referred to them as the 'brotherhood of the knife', saying they believed that only blind obedience to the Old Man of the Mountains led to salvation. The Assassins spread their intimidating shadow over the Christians, too, and murdered several prominent Crusader barons. They notably killed **Raymond II of Tripoli** and **Conrad of Montferrat**, and they attempted to kill de Vitry himself, as well as Lord Edward (**Edward I** of England). It is possible the Assassins, for all their religious pretensions, were not above contract killing. Blind obedience was certainly a central tenet in the Assassins, and brainwashing of some sort must have been used to secure it. When **Henry II, Count of Champagne** visited an Assassin stronghold in the early thirteenth century, the Sheik proved his men's absolute loyalty by ordering a pair of them to jump to their deaths from the battlements, and by asking if the visitor would like to see a repeat demonstration.

The Assassins had some contact with the **Military Orders**, particularly the Templars. The sect's lands faced the Templar castles of **Tortosa**, La Colee and **Chastel Blanc**. At some point the Templars imposed a tribute obligation on the Assassins. In 1173, the Syrian Assassins, under Rashid ed-Din Sinan, sent overtures to King **Amalric I** offering an alliance in exchange for the abolition of this tribute, but this was broken up when the Templars ambushed the returning ambassador and slew his party.[50] King Amalric was furious and punished a Templar called **Walter de Mesnil**. Several questions arise from this, especially how come the Templars, if they had the power to impose a tribute duty on the Assassins, did not use that power to stop the sect's murderous activities within Christian territory? At any rate, later, when **Louis IX** arrived in Acre after the fiasco of the Seventh Crusade, he found himself confronted by a delegate of the sect. According to **John of Joinville**, the delegate boasted of the Assassin's ability to kill any ruler they chose, and that Louis too might find a dagger in his back if he did not pay them tribute and release them from their obligations to the Military Order. The King sent the Ismaili away, and recalled him in the presence of the Grand Masters of the Temple and the Hospital. This time the delegate was reluctant to repeat his demand. It is notable, though, that Louis saw fit to exchange gifts with the Old Man of the Mountain, and did nothing to provoke the sect against him.[51] The Assassins, however, had not long to survive as a regional power. The coming of the Mongols precipitated their destruction, and the sect faded into obscurity after 1256, when the Mongols destroyed Alamut.[52]

## *Augustine of Hippo, St* (354–430)

St Augustine was an early father of the Roman **Catholic** Church. Augustine's writings influenced monasticism and are the guidelines used by the various **Augustinian Orders**. They also strongly influenced the thinking of St **Bernard of Clairvaux**. Born in what is now Algeria, Augustine studied in Carthage and taught in **Rome**. He was influenced by the Manichaeans but rejected **Gnostic** Dualism and came to preach salvation by faith alone. He kept concubines and was somewhat licentious in his early life, and famously prayed 'give me chastity and continence, but not yet!' After a spiritual conversion, however, he joined the Catholic Christian clergy and became an advocate of celibacy. He became Bishop of Hippo in AD 391. Augustine advocated an anti-materialistic outlook, something evident in later **Cistercian** thinking. This world view implies that the flesh and the physical world were somehow the domain of Satan. Such an outlook would be reflected in the **Rule** of the Knights Templar. Augustine was also a strong proponent of the doctrine of Original Sin, in opposition to the followers of Pelagius, whom he denounced as **heretics**. Augustine advanced the theory of a morally just war, which would help to make the **Crusades** and the **Military Orders** become acceptable within a Christian framework.[53]

## Augustinian Order

There were several monastic fraternities following the precepts of St **Augustine of Hippo**. These, in the Middle Ages, included the **Canons of the Holy Sepulchre**. If the Templars were one and the same thing as the elusive Knights/Fraternity/**Order of the Holy Sepulchre**, the protégés of the Canons, then this may account for Augustinian sentiments in their **Rule**. However, the **Cistercian Order** also had Augustinian influences.

## Avignon

Avignon is a city in southern **France**. In medieval times it contained a Templar Preceptory. The city tried to assert its independence during the **Albigensian Crusade**, and in 1226 it withstood a siege by **Louis VIII**, falling eventually, though not before the squalid conditions suffered by the besiegers hastened Louis's death by fever. During the reign of **Clement V**, the city became the seat of the Holy See, although the move was never popular with the faithful.[54] **Rome** was undergoing a period of instability at this time and the **Popes** preferred to avoid it. Clement V settled permanently in Avignon in 1309, converting the **Dominican** Priory for his use. Succeeding Popes built a great Gothic fortress-palace in the city, the *Palais des Papes*. The Avignon Popes were all French, and to a greater or lesser extent dominated by the **Capetians**. After the death of Gregory XI in 1378, the year after he returned the Papacy to Rome, Avignon became the seat of a succession of Antipopes. The Schism lasted until 1417.

## Axum

Axum is a city in northern **Ethiopia**. It contains towering obelisks or stelæ that date back to the first century. Also there is a shrine dedicated to Our Lady of Mount Zion. There, a monk of the Ethiopian Orthodox Church guards what is locally believed to be the lost **Ark of the Covenant**. Tradition has it that the Ark has resided in Ethiopia since Biblical times, where it was brought by a claimed son of King **Solomon**, **Menelik I**. Axum itself was the centre of an ancient kingdom, which adopted Christianity in about AD 300. Though the shrine where the Ethiopian Ark is kept today was only built in the twentieth century, it stands amid the ruins of much older buildings.

## Ayme d'Oselier (died 1316)

Ayme d'Oselier was a **Marshal** of the Knights Templar, the last to hold that post. He remained in **Cyprus** when **Jacques de Molay** returned to

France. The Marshal tried to negotiate at first with Balian d'Ibelin and the officials of **Amaury de Lusignan**, the ruler of Cyprus, who came to take the Templars into custody. He was prepared to cede control of Templar estates but not to give up his arms of the order's **treasure**.[55] Ayme organised Templar resistance for a time, and meanwhile had most of the treasure hidden. Amaury de Lusignan threatened to have the Templars put to death unless they cooperated. Ayme d'Oselier met Amaury's representative at the castle of Nisso, and came to terms. With other Templar dignitaries, he went to Nicosia and delivered a declaration before the court, stating the Order's fidelity to the **Catholic** faith. As inventories began of the Templar houses in Nicosia, Ayme and his brethren withdrew to their fortress in Limassol, where they prepared to resist. They were besieged and in June 1308 obliged to surrender. The marshal was imprisoned in Khirokitia.

Ayme and the other Templars pleaded innocent when they ultimately came to trial between May and June 1310, and many witnesses defended them. However, when Amaury was murdered and their deposed enemy **Henry II of Cyprus** returned from Cilicia and regained the throne, the Templars luck began to run out. The Pope ordered new tribunals, this time accompanied by **Inquisition torture**. The brethren were probably subjected to harsh treatment, and many including the Marshal died in custody in the Castle of **Kerynia** in 1316. It is alleged that he had been involved in a second plot against Henry II in June 1311.

## Ayyubids

The Ayyubids were a Sunni **Muslim** dynasty of Sultans, reigning in either Syria or **Egypt** or both, and also in parts of Arabia. Of Kurdish extraction, they were the family of **Saladin**. The name derives from Saladin's father, Najm ad-Din Ayyub. In order to gain power for the dynasty, Saladin had overthrown the **Fatimid** Caliphs in Egypt and the heir of **Nur-ed-Din** in Syria. Power struggles within the dynasty were fairly frequent, but they were also capable of uniting against the Franks (as they did, for example, in order to resist the **Third** and **Fifth Crusades**). After Saladin, the Ayyubid Empire came to be dominated by his brother **al-Adil**, who in turn disinherited his nephews. Al-Adil was succeeded by his sons, **al-Kamil** in Egypt and al-Muazzam and al-Ashraf in Syria. Al-Kamil, the dominant brother, was succeeded by his son as-Silah **Ayyub**. The last Ayyubid ruler of Egypt was Ayyub's son **Turanshah**, who was murdered by the **Mameluks** at the time of the **Seventh Crusade**. The Ayyubid rulers in Syria, meanwhile, were first forced into submission by the **Mongols** and then swept aside by the Mameluks.

## *Ayyub, Sultan as-Silah* (died 1249)

Al-Malik as-Salih Najm al-Din Ayyub was an **Ayyubid** Sultan of **Egypt**. He was a son of **al-Kamil**. He overthrew an elder brother to become ruler of Egypt in 1240. He installed the **Mameluks** as his bodyguard and promoted them to positions of authority. He initiated a persecution of Coptic Christians, whom he suspected of collusion with the **Franks**. It was he who summoned the **Khorezmian** Turks to attack **Jerusalem**. He joined with these mercenaries and defeated the Franks and their **Damascene** allies decisively at the battle of **La Forbie**. Ayyub was ailing at the time when the **Seventh Crusade** invaded Egypt, but he managed to muster his forces at **Mansourah**. On the eve of the invasion, Louis and Ayyub exchanged menacing letters. Ayyub, responding to Louis's bluster, predicted that the Muslims would crush the arrogant invaders, but may not have been so confident as he tried to appear.[56] He was furious to hear that the Muslim garrison had abandoned **Damietta**, as soon as **Louis IX** and his army had landed. Ayyub had some of the deserters executed, but spared the commander **Fakhr al-Din**. When Ayyub died, Fakhr al-Din and Ayyub's widow, Shaijar al-Durr, initially concealed the fact, and issued proclamations in the late Sultan's name.

# B

## *Baculus*

The Baculus was the staff carried by the **Grand Master** of the Knights Templar and a symbol of his authority. This Staff of Office is sometimes given as 'Abacus' (possibly due to an error of translation made by Sir **Walter Scott** during his research for his novel *Ivanhoe*). The Baculus was probably made of gold and capped by a disk or octagon containing the *Croix Pattée*. The Baculus, with the addition of a stepped base, as in a **Calvary cross**, is a device often found on Templar **grave slabs**. According to the Templars' **Rule,** the **Master** was to hold a staff and rod so that he might both support the weak and strike down the vice of delinquents. The Baculus was also called the *Pedum Magistrale*.[57]

## *Baghdad*

Baghdad, the capital of modern Iraq (former Mesopotamia), lies on the Tigris river in the centre of the country. It was the seat from the mid-eighth century of the **Abbasid** Caliphs, the spiritual leaders of Sunni **Islam**. Baghdad had its golden age in the ninth century, when its population reached almost one million, making it comparable only with **Constantinople**. Baghdad declined somewhat under the **Seljuk Turks**, who made it the capital of their empire after AD 1055 and the seat of their Sultan. (The Caliph was retained as a religious figurehead.) A great blow to the city in its early phase came in AD 1258 when it was taken by the **Mongols**. Some 800,000 people were massacred, including the last Caliph. The city became part of a Mongol province. It was again sacked in 1401 by Timur-e Leng, another Mongol warlord. The city eventually became part of the **Ottoman** Empire.

## Baghras

The **castle** of Baghras was one of the first major fortresses given to the Templars. They renamed it Castle Gaston and greatly extended it. It lay in the north of the Crusader territory, in mountainous Amanus Marches, in the principality of **Antioch**. It guarded the strategic Belen Pass, on the road between **Aleppo** and Antioch and the ports of **Alexandretta** and Port Bonne. The castle was situated on a high, rocky crag, and from there the Templars could control the border with Armenian Cilicia (southern Anatolia). It was lost to **Saladin** in 1188, and subsequently occupied by Armenian King Leo. The Templars took it back in about 1216, in alliance with Bohemond IV of **Antioch**, though it seems the **Hospitallers** sided with the Armenians against the Templars at this time.[58] In the 1230s, the Templar garrison withstood a siege by the army of Aleppo.

When the **Mameluks** were marching on the northern principality, Brother Geraut de Saucet, Preceptor of Antioch, based in Baghras, knew that the castle had inadequate provisions to make much of a defence. He appealed to **Thomas Berard**, the **Grand Master**, for the love of God to send supplies and reinforcements. No reply was forthcoming and the garrison grew nervous about the prospect of encountering Baybars in their parlous state. One of them, Gins de Belin, turned traitor. He mounted his horse while the others were eating and rode to deliver the castle keys to the Sultan. Meanwhile the brethren decided that they could not defend the castle and so decided to destroy its contents before withdrawing to la Roche Guillaume, farther north. This, as it happened, was exactly what the Grand Master issued orders for them to do, but they went ahead with the evacuation before the orders arrived. Subsequently the garrison were charged at **Chapter** with abandoning the castle without permission. (If they had waited for the order to come they might have died waiting.) The Chapter at **Acre** decided that under the circumstances they should be allowed to remain within the Order. The ruins of Baghras may still be seen in what is now southern Turkey.

## Balantradoch

Balantradoch (or Ballentradoch), now known simply as Temple, was the Templars' first and most significant Preceptory in **Scotland**. It is situated in Midlothian, near the River Esk. The name Balantradoch derived from the Gaelic for 'stead of the warriors'. King **David I** of Scotland, following the visit of **Hugues de Payens**, granted the land to the Templars. Today little remains of this once extensive Preceptory besides a roofless chapel and an archway in an adjacent field, near the village of Temple. The old church is located about five miles from **Rosslyn Chapel**. The ruined church at Temple is oblong in plan with steep gabled ends with mullioned windows. There is a niche for a tomb effigy and a **piscina**. The graves surrounding indicate that the building continued to serve as the parish church for many centuries after the **suppression** of the Order, and it only fell into ruins in the nineteenth century when a new parish church was built to serve the village. Some of the graves seem to contain **Masonic** symbols. The square and compass are visible on one close to the church, others show the **skull and crossbones**.

## Balcanifer

The Balcanifer, or Gonfanier, was standard bearer of the Knights Templar. He carried their banner, which was called **Beauseant**, into battle.

## Baldock

Baldock New Town is a market town in Hertfordshire. The Templars founded it in the twelfth century, on land given by Gilbert de Clare in 1148. They encouraged settlement from around the region. The layout of the medieval town is still visible around the town centre, though there are no visible Templar remains. Not far from Baldock lies **Royston Cave**. There was a theory that the name Baldock was derived from *Baldach*, an old French word for **Baghdad**. It would have been strange, though, for Templars to name a foundation of theirs after the capital of their Saracen enemies.

## Baldwin I, King of Jerusalem/Baldwin of Boulogne/Baldwin of Edessa (died 1118)

Baldwin (Baudouin), Count of Boulogne was a leader of the **First Crusade** and the brother of **Godfroi de Bouillon**. Venturing off independently in 1098, he allied with the Armenians of **Edessa**, and soon took over as Count. He married the Armenian princess Arda, the daughter of Thoros I of Cilicia (his first wife Godvera de Toeni having died in Anatolia), and established the first **Latin** state, the county of Edessa. He resisted a siege by Kerbogha, and sent supplies to the beleaguered Crusaders at **Antioch**. At the end of 1099, he and **Bohemond** visited **Jerusalem**. The following year, on Godfroi's death, Baldwin succeeded as the city's ruler. Unlike Godfroi, Baldwin had no qualms about using the title of king. He granted Edessa to his cousin Baldwin of le Bourg, (who would succeed in turn as King **Baldwin II**).

Baldwin I felt the resentment of **Tancred** who blamed him for the deaths of some of his men during the First Crusade. Baldwin also encountered initial opposition from Daimbert of Pisa, the Latin **Patriarch** who had wanted to set up a theocracy in place of the developing secular monarchy.

The Patriarch refused to crown Baldwin in Jerusalem, and **Bethlehem** had to suffice. Others had opposed Baldwin's succession, seeing Godfroi's legitimate heir as Eustace of Boulogne, Baldwin's older brother, but Eustace, who had returned to France, did not press his claim. Once secure in power, Baldwin I fought campaigns year on year to expand and defend the fledgling **Kingdom of Jerusalem**. He captured **Arsuf** and **Caesarea** with **Genoese** assistance. In 1101 he defeated invading Egyptians at Ramlah but in 1102 was mauled by another Egyptian army there and had to flee, later to triumph at **Jaffa**. In 1104 he captured **Acre**, while **Beirut**, **Tripoli** and **Sidon** were added to the Kingdom in subsequent years, and invasions from **Damascus** and **Aleppo** were repulsed. Baldwin brought in Syrian Christians from east of the Jordan to help repopulate Jerusalem. He also, on several occasions, acted as a mediator between feuding Latin barons.

In 1108 Baldwin I put his wife in a convent (apparently on the pretext that she had been raped by pirates) and bigamously married Adelaide, the widow of the **Norman** King Roger of Sicily, who brought much needed funds in exchange for the promise that her son Roger II of Sicily would inherit Jerusalem. The new Patriarch **Arnulf** sanctioned the bigamous marriage but was later forced to annul it and Adelaide was sent home.[59] Baldwin had fallen ill, and this was blamed on the sinfulness of the marriage. When Baldwin recovered he led an expedition to **Egypt**, where he again fell ill, apparently after catching and eating some strange fish from the Nile. He died while being carried back, at Al-Arish in the Sinai.

## *Baldwin II, King of Jerusalem/Baldwin of Le Bourg/Baldwin II of Edessa* (1217–1131)

Baldwin (Baudouin) of le Bourg (or le Bourcq) was a son of Hugh, Count of Rethel and a cousin of **Godfroi de Bouillon** and of **Baldwin I**. He assumed the crown of **Jerusalem** on the latter's death in 1118, having hitherto been his replacement as Count of **Edessa**. Some would have preferred once again to offer the crown to Eustace of Boulogne, the brother of Godfroi, who was still alive in Europe, but the support of the Patriarch **Arnulf** and of Joscelin de Courtenay ensured that Baldwin II became king. Baldwin II was also related to many key families in north-eastern France and **Champagne**, including the houses of Montlhery and Le Puiset (as well as possibly being an relation of Pope Calixtus II).[60] In the first year of his reign, Baldwin II received **Hugues de Payens** and the other pioneers of the Knights Templar, who were also connected to this region and its network of noble families. The king endorsed and supported them as a new **Military Order**, granting them space in the **Al Aqsa Mosque**, which had hitherto served as a royal palace. The Templars were to be useful guardians of the holy places and the **pilgrim** roads. Their leaders seem to have become quite close to him, additionally, and gained positions of trust.

Baldwin later wrote to St **Bernard of Clairvaux**, requesting that he take up the cause of the Templars and help them to receive official recognition.

Immediately on becoming king, Baldwin II had to contend with **Muslim** invasions. He had to fend off the **Seljuks** from the east and the **Fatimids** from the south-west. The Christians suffered heavy losses against the former near **Antioch** in a battle that became known as the **Field of Blood**. However, he succeeded in relieving Antioch and salvaging the principality. In 1123, Baldwin II himself was captured by Balak of **Aleppo** while leading a patrol in the north. Balak held him prisoner for two years, during which the kingdom was governed by the constable, Eustace Garnier. The King later escaped with Armenian help and united the armies of the Crusader states to confront the Seljuks at the Battle of Azaz, in 1125, gaining a victory over an army from Aleppo. He failed, though, in an attempt to take Aleppo itself in the same year.

Baldwin II was married to the Armenian princess Morphia and they had four daughters. The eldest, **Melisende**, was married to **Fulk V, Count of Anjou** who arrived in the East in 1129, having received Baldwin's assurance that he would become his full heir. Fulk, as well as being very rich, had a reputation as a strong man and Baldwin II doubtless thought that he could unite the squabbling barons. As for Baldwin's other daughters, Hodierna married **Raymond II of Tripoli**, while Alice of Antioch married Bohemond II of **Antioch**, and Loveta/Joveta, who had served as a hostage during the king's captivity, became Abbess of Bethany. Also in 1129, Baldwin II mustered Crusader forces against **Damascus** (probably with the help of the early Templars) but the city under Buri withstood the siege and Baldwin was forced to withdraw. In his last year, Baldwin was obliged to march on Antioch to restore order after the death of Bohemond II and Alice's attempted coup. On his deathbed, having returned to Jerusalem, Baldwin revised the succession arrangements, leaving sovereignty jointly to Fulk, Melisende and the infant **Baldwin III**.

## *Baldwin III, King of Jerusalem* (1130–63)
Baldwin (Baudouin) III was the first son of King **Fulk** and Queen **Melisende**. He reigned as King of **Jerusalem** during the turbulent mid-twelfth century. During the **Second Crusade**, Baldwin went along with the questionable advice of the Emperor **Conrad III**, and led the Crusaders in an attack on **Damascus**, which had hitherto been a useful ally against **Aleppo** and Mosul. The attack was as ill fated as it was ill conceived. The Crusaders departed, leaving the **Kingdom of Jerusalem**, if anything, weakened.

Having come of age, Baldwin struggled to pry the reins of government from his mother's hands, and for a time a civil war threatened. The **Haute Cour** partitioned the Kingdom between Melisende and Baldwin, with the queen ruling the south. Baldwin, never happy with the arrangement, invaded Jerusalem to oust his mother. He probably had Templar support in this. Melisende, in accordance with the final settlement, had to be content with ruling Nablus. Even so this power struggle between mother and son was a scandal at a time when the realm was under constant peril from **Nur ed-Din**'s gathering forces. Subsequently, Baldwin III became a more effective and by the end a generally well regarded ruler. In 1153 he campaigned successfully in the south with Templar help, and captured **Ascalon** from the Egyptians. In 1158 Baldwin was married to **Theodora**, a young niece of **Manuel I Comnenus**, but they were still childless when Baldwin died four years later. The throne was passed to his brother **Amalric I**.

## *Baldwin IV, King of Jerusalem* (1161–85)

Baldwin (Baudouin) IV was the son of **Amalric I** and **Agnes de Courtenay**. He was raised in **Jerusalem**. His tutor and mentor was **William of Tyre**. One day when the prince was playing with other boys, William noticed that he was injured and yet felt no pain. William correctly diagnosed this as an early symptom of **leprosy**. This cruel disease would render Baldwin increasingly disfigured and disabled. It would eventually deprive the **Kingdom of Jerusalem** of one of its most valiant Kings.

In 1174 Baldwin came to the throne at the age of thirteen, with Miles of Plancy serving as regent. Miles, an unpopular character, was soon assassinated in the streets. He was replaced as regent by **Raymond III of Tripoli**. Three years later the young king, with **Reynald de Chatillon** and the Knights Templar, defeated **Saladin** and his invading army in the south-west at the battle of **Montguisard**. Baldwin fought bravely, wielding his sword with his left hand, his right having been rendered useless by his condition. The King went into action again in 1179 to repulse a raid by Saladin. Allied with Raymond III of Tripoli and with the Templars under **Odo de St Armand**, Baldwin initially defeated the raiders crossing the Latani river. The Christians then fell foul of Saladin's main force. Baldwin fell and was unable to remount by himself. Another knight carried him from the battle to safety, as his guards hacked their way through the enemy. Others were less lucky. **Grand Master** Odo of the Templars was captured. Soon afterwards, Saladin took and destroyed the newly built castle of **Jacobs Ford**, which the Sultan considered a threat to the security of **Damascus**.

King Baldwin IV's leprosy worsened, meanwhile, depriving him of his sight and his ability to walk. Still he proved an able ruler. When in 1183 Reynald de Chatillon was besieged by Saladin at **Kerak**, Baldwin mustered the army of Jerusalem, and went to lift the siege. The strain of the expedition took its toll though and the King died in 1185. Baldwin IV had made a will leaving the Kingdom to his nephew **Baldwin V**, whom he had crowned as co-ruler to ensure his succession. If anything should happen to the child, the succession was to be decided by the **Pope** and the Kings of Europe. Owing to the machinations of **Sibylla** and her supporters his will went ignored and her second husband **Guy de Lusignan** took the throne.

## *Baldwin V, King of Jerusalem* (1177–86)

Baldwin V was the child of **Sibylla** by her first husband William 'Long-sword' of Montferrat. Baldwin succeeded his uncle **Baldwin IV** in 1185 at the age of seven, having been nominal co-ruler since 1183. Again **Raymond III of Tripoli** acted as Regent. The Templars provided security at the coronation in the **Holy Sepulchre**. Afterwards the Order entertained the royal party at their headquarters. Seven months later the Templars escorted the boy-king's body back to the Holy Sepulchre for burial, from **Acre** where he had died. A succession crisis followed. The terms of Baldwin IV's will were disregarded. Sibylla emerged as Queen with her second husband **Guy de Lusignan** as co-ruler. They were supported by the Templars under **Gerard de Ridefort**, who had been central to the coup.

## *Baldwin IX of Flanders (Baldwin I of Constantinople)* (1172–1205)

Baldwin IX, Count of Flanders (IV of Hainalt) was a leader of the **Fourth Crusade**. He was a nephew of the Crusader **Philip of Alsace, Count of Flanders**. Baldwin married Marie, the daughter of **Henry I, Count of Champagne**, and left her as regent in Flanders when he embarked on Crusade in 1202, she being unable to accompany him due to pregnancy.[61] In 1204, after the sack of **Byzantium**, Baldwin's comrades elected him the first ruler of the **Latin** Empire of Constantinople, which was then being established. The Templars did not contribute significantly to this controversial adventure. However it seems Baldwin had in his staff a Templar called Brother **Barozzi**, who was sent to inform Pope **Innocent III** of the conquest. Meanwhile Marie sailed to **Acre** in 1204, unaware of the diversion of her husband's expedition. She died of plague before she could reach Constantinople. The following year, after the Battle of Adrianople in Thrace, Baldwin was captured by the Bulgarians and died soon after. According to one version of events, Baldwin met a grisly end. He had his hands and feet cut off and was thrown into a deep valley where he died after three days.

## *Baldwyn Encampment*

The Baldwyn Encampment appears to have been a **Masonic** Templar group active in **Bristol, England**, in the last half of the eighteenth century. A document of theirs, from 1780, evokes the name both of the Templars and the **Hospitallers**, implying that members of the encampment were confused about the separate identity of the two historical **Military Orders**.

## Balian of Ibelin (c. 1142–93)

Balian of **Ibelin** (or d'Ibelin), son of Barzan, was a prominent baron of the **Kingdom of Jerusalem**, famed as the leader of the defence of **Jerusalem** before its fall to the Sultan **Saladin** in 1187. Balian, a tall and skilful knight, held the lordship of Ibelin as a vassal of his elder brother Baldwin, the lord of **Ramlah**. Both brothers fought alongside **Baldwin IV** and the Templars at **Montguisard**. Subsequently Baldwin IV had his little nephew (**Baldwin V**) crowned as his co-king and heir, at the **Holy Sepulchre**. Balian had the honour of carrying the boy-king to the church on his shoulders. Unfortunately Baldwin V was not to live long. **Balian**, meanwhile, married Maria Comnena, the widow of **Amalric I**. The d'Ibelins supported **Raymond III of Tripoli** and his faction in opposition to **Guy de Lusignan**. However, with Templar help Guy manoeuvred into power. Balian and Raymond grudgingly paid homage, but Balian's brother Baldwin of Ibelin refused and was exiled to **Antioch**.

In 1187 Saladin besieged Tiberias. Though Balian and Raymond advised a more cautious strategy, Gerard de Rideford and Reynald de Chatillon persuaded King Guy to take the combined Christian army north to do battle. The result, at **Hattin**, was an unmitigated disaster for the Christians. Balian of Ibelin and Raymond III fled from the battle once the inevitability of ruin became apparent.[62]

Balian escaped to Tyre. Subsequently, he sought Saladin's permission to ride to retrieve his family from Jerusalem. Saladin allowed him to cross his lines in exchange for Balian's solemn promise that he would not remain there to defend the city. When Balian arrived in Jerusalem, though, Queen **Sibylla**, the people and the **Patriarch Heraclius** begged him to stay to lead the defence. Jerusalem had very few soldiers left, including, apparently, only two Templars, and the city was packed with frightened refugees. Heraclius argued that an oath to an infidel was not binding, and persuaded Balian to stay. One of Balian's first moves was to create new knights from among the common people. He prepared the city for the inevitable onslaught, which arrived in September. The assault was vicious, a bombardment from trebuchets and ballistas, and a constant storm of arrows, rocks and Greek fire that kept the city's physicians hard pressed to treat all the wounded. Balian led a stubborn resistance, holding out for more than two weeks against unrelenting assault. In the end the Patriarch persuaded Balian to negotiate with Saladin, rather than see the survivors annihilated.

When they spoke, Saladin announced to Balian his intention to slaughter the Frankish population of Jerusalem, in revenge for the massacre of Muslims by the **First Crusade**. Balian said that if so then he would have his Muslim prisoners killed and the **Dome of the Rock** demolished: and that he and his men would kill their own families before coming out to fight to the death. Before Saladin triumphed his army would be decimated.[63] Bluff or not, it caused Saladin to relent, and to negotiate terms whereby the Franks could leave Jerusalem in safety in exchange for a ransom. Balian surrendered Jerusalem on 2/3 October 1187. Saladin took the city and many **slaves**, though as a gesture of grace he allowed some to go free regardless of their ability to pay the ransom. Balian and his family went to Tripoli.

## Balsall, Temple

Temple Balsall was a rural **Preceptory** in Warwickshire. During the **suppression**, the last Templars from there were held for a time in a grim dungeon at **Warwick Castle**. The Balsall estate was eventually passed to the **Hospitallers**. The surviving church, dedicated to St **Mary**, is an elegant building made of a pinkish stone, and is surrounded by trees, fields, streams and meadows. The Hospitallers completed the building in the 1330s in the Decorated Gothic style. The east end has an Edwardian stained-glass window featuring a Knight Templar. The west wall has a rose window. There are many carvings around the church including dogs and other creatures on the buttresses, and **heads** under the eaves reminiscent of those at **Temple Church, London**.

## Baltic Crusades

The Baltic Crusades were a series of campaigns fought throughout the thirteenth century and beyond, with the aim of conquering and converting the pagan tribes of north-eastern Europe around the Baltic, especially the Wends, the original Prussians, and the Livs of Lithuania. The kings of Denmark and Scandinavia supported these wars, concentrating on raiding Estonia. Various Popes and churchmen, like St **Bernard of Clairvaux**, also encouraged them, and linked them to crusading, despite their lack of a pilgrimage element. The Baltic wars came to be dominated by German conqueror/settlers, and by the **Teutonic Knights**. Smaller, Templar-based **Military Orders** such as the **Sword Brethren** and the Knights of Dobrin were also involved during the early phases, and developed a harsh reputation.

**Honorius III** tried to encourage missionary activity in the Baltic, looking to the **Cistercians** and then the Mendicant Orders for this purpose. He also offered full **indulgences** to those who took up arms against the pagans. The Teutonic Knights had conquered most of Prussia by 1270, and laid the foundations for their own Order/state, where they would hold sovereignty. Though their official purpose was to convert the pagans, the more general policy seems to have been to rob, massacre and dispossess them. It was not all easy conquest, however. Swedish and German forces were defeated by Alexander Nevsky (a Russian Orthodox Christian) in the 1240s, and the fatal blow to the Teutonic Order's ambitions of conquering Slavic territories farther east came at Tannenberg in 1410, when they were defeated by a Catholic King of Poland. The Baltic wars were ongoing, and took the form of seasonal campaigns. They were motivated at least in part by colonial ambition and a desire to control trades such as the supply of furs, amber and timber. The Templars played little part in this theatre, perhaps considering it an inauthentic Crusade.

## Banking

The Templars, within a few decades of their foundation, developed an international bank, though this was a secondary activity. The Templars' financial services perhaps began as a practical measure to improve security for **pilgrims**. Hitherto pilgrims had needed to carry all their money with them, making them tempting targets for highway robbers. The Templars introduced a credit service where the pilgrims could deposit money at a local **Preceptory** and gain a coded receipt, which would allow them to draw out funds at Templar establishments along their way in exchange for a modest service fee. They developed a reputation as reliable and competent money handlers. Subsequently the Templars' financial services expanded, and they became treasurers to nobles and kings. Individually the Templars, being persons of religion, did not have private property or finance, but collectively they came to be responsible for large sums of money. They could also be approached for loans, and sometimes lent huge sums to monarchs, for example during the **Second Crusade**, where **Everard des Barres** raised large sums to loan to **Louis VII**.[64] Later they lent money to King **John** of **England** during periods where he faced financial difficulty. It seems **Philip the Fair** was in the Order's debt in the fourteenth century, and it is conceivable that he attacked them on fabricated charges rather than repay them.

The **Paris Temple** included among its staff a treasurer who was deeply involved with the finances of successive **Capetian** Kings. **Henry III** of England, meanwhile, at one stage transferred the crown jewels of England to the Paris Temple for security, during a period of turbulence at home. (The London Temple was obviously deemed somewhat less secure, and indeed was subjected to a raid by Henry's son soon afterwards.) The Paris establishment also operated to some extent as a modern bank, apparently having a cash desk, where clients made deposits, and where the Templar cashiers kept meticulous records, fragments of which survive. The ultimate fate of the Templars' bank, however, is a mystery.

## Bannockburn

Bannockburn, in 1314, was one of the major battles of **Scotland**'s struggle for independence from the Crown of **England**. **Robert the Bruce** and his outnumbered forces overcame a powerful English army under **Edward II**, near Stirling, partly by luring the English knights into a charge over hidden pits filled with sharpened stakes. According to a story originating from Scottish Freemasons in 1843, fugitive Templars lent assistance to the Bruce at this battle and that this accounts for the panicked English retreat. Robert the Bruce was an **excommunicant** at the time, after all, and it is suggested would probably have had had no inclination or incentive to arrest any Templars in his kingdom. Rather he would have had a motive to grant fugitive Templars sanctuary. The notion of any direct, organised Templar involvement at Bannockburn is difficult to credit, though. The English would have been sure to mention the fact and no medieval sources mention Templar participation.

## Baphomet

The name Baphomet was sometimes associated with the **idol** allegedly worshipped by the Templars. The name was not mentioned in all of the trials and did not appear in the official list of **accusations**. It is possible that Templars in **Carcassonne**, undergoing torture by the **Inquisition**, simply made up the name for something to tell their interrogators. The Templar Jean de Cassagne mentioned an idol resembling a man wearing a Dalmatic during the trials there, while other local Templars identified the bearded **head** or **skull** idol as Baphomet.[65] The name seems to defy interpretation or explanation, though there have been attempts to link it to **John the Baptist** and to Mohammed (or Mahomet), the Prophet of **Islam**. The worship of an idol would be inimical to Islam, so the idea that there can be any connection between the alleged Templar heresy and Mohammed seems a non-starter. (There remains the possibility that the Order's enemies invented the name Baphomet deliberately to evoke the name of Mohammed and imply apostasy on the part of the Knights Templar.) It was observed by Dr **Hugh Schonfield** that the word 'Baphomet' appears to convert to 'Sophia' when an ancient form of encryption known as the Atbash Cypher is applied to it, Sophia being Greek for 'Wisdom'. Sophia was also conceived of as a feminine embodiment of divine wisdom, regarded in **Gnosticism** as one of the Aeons. How the Templars might have known of this ancient code is unexplained.

There used to be displayed in museums carvings of an androgynous, pseudo-Egyptian figure, with a narrow beard and female breasts, sometimes identified as 'Baphomets' or 'Templar idols'. (The images on the **Coffret d'Essarois** are an example.) Their real origins are unknown, but they are almost certainly from a later period, despite the claims of the nineteenth century Orientalist **Joseph von Hammer-Purgstall**.[66] He seized upon the obscure name of Baphomet (despite it apparently only receiving mention at the Templars' trials in Carcassonne). He identified it as the Templars' mystical focus. He saw the head as a Gnostic symbol, possibly of **Egyptian** origin, and interpreted the name as *Baphe Metis* – 'Baptism into Wisdom'. Hammer-Purgstall regarded the wisdom in question as pagan and profane.

Descriptions of the form of Baphomet (or rather of the Templars' alleged idol) had varied during the Templar trials but none closely resembled the goat-headed and hoofed **demon** of popular imagination. This fanciful vision, with its black angel's wings, first appeared as an illustration in an occult work of 1854 by **Eliphas Levi**. He claimed it was based on a Gargoyle from a Templar Church at St Bris le Vineux. **Leo Taxil**, in his defamatory hoax, portrayed the **Freemasons** as worshippers of this demonic Baphomet. Since that time Baphomet has taken on a life of its own, becoming, among other things, a symbol of Satanism.

## *Barletta*

Barletta is a city in Apulia, southern Italy. A number of **grave slabs** from Templar **burials** were found there. These are mostly from the late thirteenth century, and, unusually, feature carved images of the knights in monastic dress. They also include inscriptions and family heraldry. One of them once covered the tomb of the Preceptor Simon de Quincey.

## *Barozzi* (twelfth–thirteenth century)

Brother Barozzi is one of very few Templars mentioned in connection with the **Fourth Crusade**. He was in the entourage of **Baldwin of Flanders**, who became the first Latin Emperor of **Constantinople** after the conquest of the city in 1204. He was apparently a **Venetian**, so may originally have joined the Fourth Crusade as part of Doge Enrico Dandolo's staff. He was charged with taking Baldwin's letter announcing the discreditable victory to Pope **Innocent III**. A papal letter mentioned him. According to the Pope's letter, Barozzi was also charged with delivering gifts from the **Frankish** conquerors of **Byzantium** to the Pope. These gifts (probably loot intended as bribes to bring the Pope on-side) included a precious jewel, an altar cloth and other gifts, as well as things that had been given to the Templars, including a portion of the **True Cross**, two Byzantine icons and some liturgical vessels. These treasures were stolen from Barozzi by some piratical merchants of Genoa, in the port of Mondone, in southern Greece.

## *Battles*

The Knights Templar were more often involved in sieges and skirmishes than full-scale pitched battles. However, on a number of occasions they augmented the cavalry of the Latin **Holy Land** and of western **Crusading** armies. The major pitched battles in which the Order was involved in the East included the Christian victories of **Montguisard**, and **Arsuf**, and the defeats of **Hattin** and **La Forbie**. They were also involved in significant sieges at **Acre**, **Damascus**, and **Damietta**.

## Batu Khan (1205–55)

Batu Khan was a grandson of the great **Mongol** conqueror Genghis Khan. Batu himself commanded the Mongol Horde that conquered most of Russia and Poland. He also conquered the **Kipchak Turks** and subsequently recruited many to his army. He ravaged Kiev in 1239. An army under Kadan and Baidar, Batu's lieutenants, defeated a Christian coalition and wiped out a contingent of Templars at the battle of **Liegnitz** in 1241.

## Baybars (1223–77)

Rukn al-Din Baybars al-Bunduqdari ibn Abdullah (also called Malik az-Zahir) was a **Mameluk** general and later Sultan of **Egypt**. He was known to the **Franks** as Benocdar. He contributed to a significant Egyptian victory over the **Mongols** and gained many others over the **Crusaders**. Like most Mameluks he was a **Kipchac Turk** and began life as a **slave**, captured probably in the Crimea region. He was sold cheaply in Syria to a Mameluk officer on account of having a white spot in one of his blue eyes, and this may have given him a sense of having something to prove.

Baybars was converted to **Islam** at an early age and trained as a bodyguard of as-Silah **Ayyub**, the Sultan of Egypt. He was already a commander by 1244, and may have played a part at the battle of **La Forbie**. Baybars was back in Egypt by the time of the **Seventh Crusade**, which invaded down the Nile. He led the Mameluks who decimated the Templars and the other Crusaders at the battle of **Mansourah** in 1250. Later that year he had a part in the murder of Sultan Ayyub's heir, **Turan Shah**. Some accounts name Baybars as the first to strike at the young Sultan. Eventually the Mameluk **Kutuz** rose to power as Sultan, Baybars having remained a power behind the scenes.

Baybars led the vanguard of Kutuz's army to victory over Kitbuqa and the Mongols at **Ain Jalut**. Subsequently Baybars asked to be rewarded for his services with the city of **Aleppo**. Kurtuz declined the request, also disagreeing with Baybars about pursuing a more hostile policy towards the vestigial **Kingdom of Jerusalem**. He took the army homeward, whereupon Baybars murdered him during a hare hunt and claimed the Sultanate for himself. He soon united Syria and Egypt under his rule, capturing **Damascus** and Aleppo after a swift campaign. The balance of power had shifted inexorably against the Crusaders. Baybars built up a mighty war machine. His intention was to punish Antioch, and to weaken if not destroy the vestigial

Kingdom.[67] His forces captured castles and cities, sometimes acting with great brutality and taking many into **slavery**. In 1265 he took **Caesarea**, followed by Haifa and **Arsuf**. A Muslim commentator said of Baybars that he never destroyed the hiding place of error (Christianity) 'without giving it to the flames and drenching it in blood'.[68]

Baybars deprived the Templars of their castle at **Saphet** (Safed) in Galilee, and beheaded every member of its garrison, which had surrendered on promise of safe passage. Next, in 1267, he besieged **Acre**, but without success. A truce was made and he withdrew his forces. The following year he renewed his campaign, taking first **Jaffa** and then the Templar castle of **Beaufort**. In May, Baybars besieged Antioch, breaking in after a four-day siege. He held the citizens in contempt because their Prince, **Bohemond VII**, had paid homage to the Mongols, and so massacred or enslaved them all.[69] Prince Bohemond had been absent at **Tripoli** (which he had expected Baybars to attack first). Baybars wrote to him from Antioch gloating over the savage acts that he had committed. He told Bohemond to be glad that he had not seen his churches demolished, his knights lying prostrate under the hooves of horses, his palaces plundered, his women and children sold in the slave markets, sold for a dinar a piece – a dinar, at that, taken from Bohemond's own hand.[70] Baybars also raided the **Armenians** in Cilicia, punishing King Hetoun who had also submitted to the Mongols. The remaining Franks in the Levant concluded a truce on Baybars' terms. In the opinion of Baybars' representative ibn Abd-al-Zahir, who concluded the truce, Baybars had more Frankish captives in Cairo than there were soldiers left in the Christian army.[71] Baybars mustered troops to fight for a second time against the Crusading **Louis IX**, but news of Louis's death in Carthage made this unnecessary. Baybars was free to conduct yet another campaign against Frankish Syria, and in 1271 crowned his career by capturing the mighty **Krak de Chevaliers** from the **Hospitallers**. Baybars died, probably of poisoning, in 1277 and was buried in a mausoleum in Damascus.

## Beaufort

Beaufort was a Crusader castle inland from **Tyre** and **Sidon**, commanding the Beka Valley. It consisted of upper and lower castles protected by a rock fosse. It was sold to the Order in 1260 by Simon, Lord of Sidon in the face of the **Mameluk** threat. Despite Templar attempts to strengthen the castle, it fell to **Baybars** after an overwhelming assault in 1268.[72]

## Beauseant

Beauseant was the name of the Templars' war banner. It was half black and half white, apparently signifying the two faces of the order, light and benevolent to Christians, dark and terrible to the enemies of the Church.

The name has been interpreted romantically (as *Beau seant)* to mean 'be fine!' and prosaically (as *bauçant*) to mean 'piebald' (i.e. two coloured). Beauseant could also mean 'well placed' or 'well seated'.[73] A deliberate multiple meaning could have been intended. The Gonfanier (or Balcanifer) was the Templars' standard bearer. He bore their banner Beauseant into battle. Sometimes the **Seneschal** of the Order may have performed this role. Illustrations by **Matthew Paris** show the flag black above and white below, while the frescoes in **San Bevignate** show the opposite configuration, with a cross in the white upper part.

## Bedford Castle, Siege of

The Templars tried to avoid getting caught up in secular, dynastic or domestic conflicts in Europe, but they failed in this when it came to the siege of Bedford Castle in 1224. The castle in **England** was the stronghold of the rebellious Lord Falkes de Breaute. Falkes' brother William had captured King **Henry III**'s Justice Henry de Braybroke, who was held prisoner in the castle. King Henry responded by laying a determined siege to the castle. The fighting was bloody, and after four vicious assaults the defenders began to waver, sending out Falkes' wife and the women of the castle, and releasing Henry de Braybroke. The siege continued, however, until the defenders capitulated and hoisted the king's banner over their battered tower. They remained there under the King's custody through the night. The next morning the defeated rebels were brought before the King. The King commanded the attendant bishops to lift the prisoners' **excommunication**, and he ordered them to be hanged. More than eighty were taken to the gallows, though at the behest of their leaders three Templars were spared so that they might serve God in the **Holy Land**. The chaplain of the castle was taken to face an ecclesiastical tribunal. It seems Falkes himself survived.

## Beguines

Beguines were members of lay communities of religious women, akin to convents, but without any vows being taken, so sisters could leave. The Beguines were devoted to prayer, study and good works. They flourished in the twelfth and thirteenth centuries in France and the Low Countries. Many women joined them on a temporary basis, for example when husbands were away fighting in the **Crusades**. Beguinages were autonomous, enclosed communities with their own walls, normally situated within towns. Some Beguines involved themselves in preaching, and in religious mysticism, possibly with **Gnostic** influences. At the time of **Clement V** the Beguines became suspected of **heresy**. Clement instructed the **Inquisition** to investigate 'this abominable sect of unfaithful women'.[74] (Their male counterparts, the Beghards, were also condemned for their association with the heresy of the Free Spirit.)

## Belbies

Belbies was a fortress town on the Nile Delta in **Egypt**. King **Amalric I** of **Jerusalem** took it in alliance with the **Hospitallers** under **Gilbert d'Assailly**, who had provided 500 knights and 500 **Turkopoles** for the expedition. The Hospitallers had been promised the town and occupied it for a while afterwards. The Franks were later forced to evacuate when **Nur ed-Din** sent a force to relieve the Egyptians, led by the General **Shirkuh** with some 8,000 horsemen. As the Templars had feared, the King's campaign failed to result in the capture of Egypt and only acted as a provocation – ultimately bringing **Fatimid** Egypt under Syrian Sunni rule.

## Bellator Rex

*Bellator Rex* was the term devised by **Crusade** theorists in the early thirteenth century for the leader of a unified **Military Order** called the Knights of Jerusalem. It is possible **Philip the Fair** aspired to this position, or that he wished to install one of his sons as the Grand Master of the conceived new kinghood following the amalgamation, the plan to merge the Military Orders **(merger scheme)**. The idea was somewhat unrealistic and would likely have been resisted by those mistrustful of the King's motives and wary of the expansion of **Capetian** power.

## Benedict, St (480–543)

St Benedict of Nursia, an Italian hermit, was the founder of the first Christian monastic Order in the West. He was canonised in 1220. His writings formed the basis for the **Rule** that governed the lives of monks through subsequent ages. St Benedict is credited with founding the **Benedictine Order**, whose earliest monastery was at Monte Cassino, south of **Rome**.

## Benedictine Order

The Benedictine Order was the first monastic brotherhood founded in the West. Benedictines were coenobitic monks (living in enclosed communities and under obedience to abbots) as opposed to anchorites (hermits) living in seclusion. They were followers of St **Benedict** and observed the **Rule** attributed to his hand, which governed these communities. Their earliest monastery was Monte Cassino in Italy, but by the beginning of the Crusading era the greatest Benedictine house was the Abbey of **Cluny**. The **Cistercians**, an offshoot of the Benedictine Order, adopted a purist approach to the Rule of St Benedict. Benedict's rule emphasised the virtues of unhesitating obedience, humility and silence. Monks were expected to renounce their personal will and private possessions, to be serious, to speak sparingly and calmly, and to confess sins and sinful thoughts. They were to be obedient to their Abbots and to each other. They were to devote themselves to daily prayers, and to hear religious readings while they ate. They were to perform manual labour in addition. They were to sleep still in their habits, in a dormitory where a light burned through the night. Such was to be the life of a Benedictine monk (or nun – there were many Benedictine convents ruled by abbesses). Many of these instructions were echoed in the Templars' **Rule of Life**.

## *Berengaria of Navarre (c. 1170–1230)*

Berengaria of Navarre was a princess who married **Richard the Lionheart** on **Cyprus** in 1291 (the princess having survived a shipwreck, along with Richard's sister Joan of Sicily, and both having been rescued from **Isaac Comnenus**). This marriage gained for Richard a useful ally in his bride's father, which strengthened Richard's holdings in southern France. However, it caused a rift between Richard and **Philip II Augustus** of **France** who had been insisting Richard make good on a pledge to marry Princess Alys (Philip's sister). Richard had backed out of this engagement, alleging that his father **Henry II, King of England** had deflowered Alys. The division between the two Crusader kings would simmer on.

## *Bernard de Tremelay (died 1153)*

Bernard de Tremelay was the fourth **Grand Master** of the Knights Templar. He was elected following the abdication of **Everard des Barres**, and led the Order in the aftermath of the unsuccessful **Second Crusade**. Bernard was probably a **Burgundian**, from a family originating near Dijon. Bernard and the Templars supported King **Baldwin III** of **Jerusalem** in his 1153 campaign against **Ascalon**, the only coastal town still in Muslim hands. A preliminary to this had been the strengthening of the castle at **Gaza**, which the Templars had taken over. This had severed Ascalon's land connection to Egypt. The Christians laid siege to Ascalon itself on 23 January 1153. Bernard de Tremelay had a wooden siege tower built and moved it close to the walls. The Egyptian defenders of the city succeeded in setting this on fire, but the wind changed direction, carrying the flames towards Ascalon. The walls themselves came crashing down. According to the chronicler **William of Tyre** (who was seldom one to ascribe the best motives to the Knights Templar) the Templars rushed into the breach without the King's knowledge, while Bernard de Tremelay prevented the other Crusaders from following, hoping to keep the greater part of the plunder.[75] If so it was foolish over-confidence, for the next day the Egyptians hung the beheaded bodies of the Grand Master and forty of his men over the ramparts. The Christians fought on and the city fell to Baldwin soon after. Meanwhile, **André de Montbard** succeeded as Grand Master of the Temple.

## Bernard of Clairvaux, St (1090–1153)

Bernard de Fontaines de Dijon, later known as St Bernard of Clairvaux, was the influential leader of the **Cistercian Order**. He was a great proponent of the Knights Templar and did much to ensure they were incorporated into the Church establishment.

Bernard was the son of the Burgundian knight Tiscelin Sorrel and of Aleth de Montbard. Aleth (the elder sister of the Templar **André de Montbard**) died when Bernard was in his teens. Bernard had a pious upbringing, which instilled a desire for purity. As a youth he supposedly jumped into a vat of cold water to combat his carnal passions.[76] Gaining military experience as a squire, he evidently formed a low opinion of the secular knighthood. He sought a refuge from the vainglory of aristocratic life and gravitated towards the Church. Riding from the siege of a castle called Grancey, he stopped in a roadside chapel and, while praying, felt the flame of religion igniting in his heart.[77] Bernard prayed before a wooden statue of **Mary, the Blessed Virgin** and received a vision of her, during which she let three drops of her divine milk fall into his mouth.[78] Bernard became a lifetime devotee of the Holy Mother, and promoted her veneration.

In 1113 Bernard joined the Cistercian house of Citeaux, which was then presided over by Abbott **Stephen Harding**. Bernard brought thirty other young Burgundian nobles, most members of his extended family, who also took the vows of Cistercian monks. His associates later helped him establish a new monastery at Clairvaux, where Bernard became Abbot. This was the first of over 100 daughter houses of the Cistercian Order to be founded within Bernard's lifetime, and Bernard himself is generally credited with this flowering. Though Clairvaux technically remained subordinate to Citeaux it became the hub of the growing Order on account of Bernard's presence.

At some point in the 1120s Bernard started to openly advocate the cause of the Knights Templar. He received a letter from **Baldwin II, King of Jerusalem** before 1126 telling of the Templars' mission and asking that Bernard use his influence to secure the Order's official recognition.[79] He had probably already heard of their activities from their shared patron Count **Hugh of Champagne**. Baldwin II's letter arrived with **Gondemer** and André de Montbard, so Bernard also had a family interest in promoting the Templars. The Abbot clearly agreed that the **Holy Land** was more in need of knights than monks, and it occurred to him that the Templars offered a way of reforming knighthood as an institution, of taking something vain, worldly and destructive and making it noble, holy and useful. Bernard also met **Hugues de Payens** when he returned to Europe, and at Hugues' request penned his famous polemical letter 'In Praise of the New Knighthood' – *De Laude Novae Militiae*, which portrayed the Templars as engaged in a spiritual and physical battle with forces of evil, and the Holy Land as a font of spiritual salvation. Bernard, though languishing with ill health, the result of his ascetic lifestyle, chaired the **Council of Troyes**, where he secured almost unanimous support for the concept of a **Military Order**, and oversaw the drafting of the Templars **Rule**, which was ratified by Pope Honorius II.

On Honorius II's death in 1130, a rift opened in the Church, with two rival **Popes** claiming legitimacy. Thanks to Bernard's intervention **Innocent II** won general recognition, while Anacletus II was widely dismissed as an antipope. Bernard probably favoured Innocent because he was a stauncher advocate of the Church's right to appoint its own clerics, and was also a fellow devotee of the Virgin Mary. Innocent, following Bernard's lead, was to exalt the Virgin as the Queen of Heaven and Mother of God.[80] Bernard, meanwhile, threw himself into other theological battles. A man of emotional mysticism and faith, Bernard was repelled by the rationalist approach to religion advocated by Peter Abelard of **Paris**. He fulminated against Abelard and accused him of **heresy**. Bernard also toured southern France preaching against those other heretics the **Cathars**, whose creed was beginning to take hold in the region. (Bernard shared the Cathars' anti-worldly view of life as a state of trial and exile, up to a point, and yet there was part of him that revered nature, and that found God's wisdom in rocks and trees). The Cistercian Order continued to flourish, meanwhile, and in 1145 one of Bernard's protégés was elected Pope, **Eugenius III**.

Bernard of Clairvaux has been accused of twisting the teachings of the New Testament, as one of the instigators of the **Second Crusade**.[81] After the fall of **Edessa**, the Pope asked Bernard to preach the Cross. This Bernard did at **Vezelay**, and other places in France and Germany. He argued that God had allowed Edessa to fall to the **Saracens** in order to give **Christendom**'s knights and nobles the opportunity to prove their devotion to the Christian cause by recovering it and safeguarding the Holy Land. He promised glory or martyrdom. He had a hand in persuading both King **Louis VII** of France and **Conrad III** of Germany to **take the Cross**. He is also credited with opposing the attacks on **Jews**, which tended to accompany crusading endeavours. Later, Bernard would attribute the failure of the Crusade to divine punishment for the sinfulness of the Christians. At the Council of **Chartres** in 1150 he would be asked to personally lead a new campaign. The other Cistercians opposed this idea though, and in any event Bernard died within three years. He was elevated to sainthood in 1174 and declared a Doctor of the Church in 1830.

## *Bernard Gui* (1261–1331)

Bernard Gui (or Bernardo Guidonis) was a monk of the **Dominican Order**. He was a prominent member of the **Inquisition** (an institution which he claimed was founded by St **Dominic** himself). Having served as Prior of Albi and of **Carcassonne**, Bernard became Inquisitor of Toulouse from 1307 until 1323. He wrote a manual codifying Inquisitorial methodology, and the relentless interrogation process that suspected heretics were to be subjected to. He also wrote on the various manifestations of 'heretical depravity' that existed, or were supposed to exist at the time. His description mixed rumour and superstition with credible accounts of alternative creeds. The **Waldensians**, for example, were supposed to have a demonic **cat** appear at their secret gatherings. Bernard Gui was mainly involved in persecuting the remnants of the **Cathar heresy**, and does not seem to have played a prominent part in the trials of the Templars. He also hunted **Waldensians**, **Beguines**, sorcerers and relapsed **Jewish** converts. Of the 900 guilty verdicts arrived at during his tenure, he condemned forty-nine souls to the flames.

## *Bernard Raymond Fabré-Palaprat* (died 1838)

Bernard Raymond Fabré-Palaprat was a Parisian doctor and former **Freemason** during the time of **Napoleon**. He was also a former **Catholic** clergyman, who had left the priesthood in order to marry. He was involved in the **Gnostic** revival movement, and also a founder of modern **neo-Templarism**. He produced the **Larmenius Charter**, a document allegedly proving that the Templars had continued until Fabré-Palaprat's time as a secret society. He claimed to be **Grand Master** himself and used the charter as the justification for his neo-Templar order. Fabré-Palaprat claimed that the Order of the Temple had survived as an aristocratic institution, but that many of its members had been killed during the **French Revolution**. Before his execution, the last alleged secret Grand Master, the Duc de Cossé-Brissac, had supposedly passed the Order's documents to one Radix de Chevillon, from whom Fabré-Palaprat apparently received the charter and the list of **clandestine Grand Masters**. Fabré-Palaprat publicly revived the Knights Templar in 1808. He was also in possession of a purported ancient Greek **Johannite** text, the **Evangelikon**, which he apparently picked up in a second-hand bookshop. Fabré-Palaprat would also found a Johannite Church. Meanwhile, it seems Fabré-Palaprat's brand of neo-Templarism took root, and he was succeeded as Grand Master by the English Admiral Sir **William Sydney Smith**.

## *Bertrand de Blanquefort* (1109–69)

Bertrand de Blanquefort (or Blanchefort/Blancfort) was elected as the sixth **Grand Master** of the Knights Templar in 1156. He presided during the reign of **Baldwin III**, and seems to have been one of the first Grand Masters to use the symbol of the two riders on his official **seal**. Blanquefort is known for extending and revising the Templars' **Rule**, adding a number of regulations dealing with specifically military situations and the hierarchy of the Order, which had by this time become more complex. (The original Rule had been primarily concerned with monastic living.)

In 1159 Bertrand de Blanquefort was **captured** by the Sultan **Nur ed-Din** of **Damascus**, after being ambushed by the **Saracens** in the Jordan Valley. He was released three years later, at **Byzantine** instigation, after the Emperor **Manuel I Comnenus** negotiated an alliance between Byzantium and Nur ed-Din against the **Turks** of Anatolia. Subsequently Bertrand de Blanquefort recommended to the King of **Jerusalem** that they should make an alliance with **Fatimid Egypt** against Nur ed-Din. **Amalric I**, the new king, instead preferred a policy of aggression against Egypt. Bertrand accompanied the King against Egypt in 1163. However, in 1168 Bertrand refused to allow any Templar involvement in Amalric's last invasion of the Nile, arguing that it violated a truce and probably fearing that the army's departure from the Kingdom would leave Jerusalem vulnerable. Blanquefort died the following year and was succeeded by **Philip de Milly of Nablus**.

## Bertrand de Sartiges (died *c.* 1310)
The knight Bertrand de Sartiges was the Preceptor of the Temple at Carlat, and a knight who had served in the East. He was one of the four defence spokesmen appointed at the Papal Commission during the Templar trials in **Paris**. The Cardinals appointed them as procurators or spokesmen though they were reluctant to become such without permission from **Jacques de Molay**.

## Bethlehem
Bethlehem was the site of the nativity – the birth of Christ, and is therefore considered a **Holy Place** by Christians (and to a lesser extent by **Muslims** also). The site of the stable was identified by St **Helena**, and the Church of the Nativity was built during the reign of her son **Constantine I**. The **Byzantine** Emperor **Justinian** subsequently enlarged the church. The church is one of the oldest in the world and the longest in continual use. Today it is shared by **Catholic** and Greek Orthodox clergy. The nave walls of the ancient basilica have the remnants of Byzantine-style mosaics featuring angels against a gold background, as well as images of domed buildings and organic patterns featuring foliage emerging from jugs and chalices. These mosaics are probably the work of Syrio-Palestinian artists, and date from the Crusaders' rule.

## Bisham Abbey
Bisham Abbey is a manor house in Buckinghamshire, **England**, parts of which are the remains of a Templar **Preceptory**. After the suppression of the Templars, **Edward II** gave the manor to his 'favourite', Hugh de Spencer. The house eventually passed to the Hoby family, the ghost of a lady of

which is supposed to haunt it, tormented with guilt for beating her young son to death for blotting his copybook. Bisham Abbey is now the home of the National Sports Council and is not open to the public.

## *Bisol* (eleventh–twelfth century)

Bisol (possibly Geoffroi Bisol) may have been a knight from Buxeuil in **Champagne**. He has been named as one of the **Nine Knights** involved in the foundation of the Order.

## *Black Madonna*

A Black Madonna (or Black Virgin) is a statue or icon of **Mary, the Blessed Virgin** that is darkly coloured. There were a number of these in Medieval Europe, especially in **France**. The Templars on Mallorca venerated a 'Black Maria'. It has been argued that there was a specific cult of the Black Madonna. Some have linked the image to the sacred mother and to the **Isis**, or to some primitive mother-earth goddess (whose colour reflects the fertile soil). Some, meanwhile, have associated them with **Mary Magdalene**, with the Queen of **Sheba** or with St **Sarah**.[82]

## *Blanche of Castile* (1188–1252)

Blanche of Castile was the daughter of Alfonso VIII of **Castile** and a grand-daughter of **Eleanor of Aquitaine**. In 1200 she was married to the future Louis VIII (r. 1223–6). After her husband's early death she served as regent for her son Louis IX, and even after transferring power to him in 1234 remained a powerful influence in the realm. During her first regency, Blanche received a petition from the Templars against the repossession of some of their estates in **Champagne** by Count Theobold IV. Blanche was a pious and domineering woman, who interfered in Louis' relationship with his wife Marguerite, and sought to keep them separate much of the time. Blanche again ruled as regent when Louis embarked on the **Seventh Crusade**. She frustrated attempts to foment rebellion, among barons who thought that 'a woman should not govern so great a thing as the Kingdom of France'. On occasion she even headed royal armies.[83] She ensured governmental continuity during her son's absence, and news of her death was one of the things that persuaded him to return from the East.

## *Bogomils*

The Bogomils were a medieval Dualist sect akin to the **Cathars**, present in Bosnia, Macedonia, Thrace and Bulgaria.[84] An unfavourable account of them appears in the writings of Anna Comnena. (The founder of the sect was said to be a Bulgarian called Bogomil, who lived in the tenth century). It is possible the Bogomils were indirectly influenced by Persian Zoroastrianism and by Manichaean **Gnosticism**. Some Gnostic/Dualist thought seems to have influenced the Paulician sect, which flourished in eastern Anatolia despite **Byzantine** persecution, and at some stage **Armenian** Paulicians were settled in Thrace, from whence they could have influenced the Bogomils of the Balkans. The Bogomils in turn seem to have had some contact with the Cathars. Bogomil missionaries carried their doctrines into Russian lands, but they were everywhere persecuted. The Bogomils' enemies sometimes accused members of the sect of deviant sexual practices. The name of the sect (in the West they were also called Bulgars) became the route word of *bougre* or 'bugger'. The perceived link of heresy and heretical groups with **sodomy** had a bearing on the scandalous **accusations** made against the Templars.

## *Bohemond III of Antioch* (1144–1201)

Bohemond III was Prince of **Antioch**. He was the son of **Raymond of Poitiers** and **Constance of Antioch**, and brother of Maria of Antioch, the wife of **Manuel I**. Bohemond's mother (then remarried to **Reynald de Chatillon**) acted as regent while her stammering son was underage, but was reluctant to concede power, a situation that escalated to caused a riot and tension between the **Armenians** (who supported Constance) and the **Kingdom of Jerusalem**. Once Bohemond was secure in power, he joined with **Raymond III** of Tripoli, and led his forces to battle at **Harim**, against **Nur ed-Din**. Sixty Templars died fighting alongside Bohemond's contingent.[85] Bohemond himself was captured and held to ransom. Following his release at the Emperor's behest, he visited Manuel in Constantinople and agreed to re-establish the Orthodox **Patriarch** in Antioch, causing tension with the **Catholics**. Bohemond earned more criticism later for abandoning his wife Theodora and marrying the alleged witch Sibylla. For this he was **excommunicated**. In 1180, Bohemond tried to exert influence in the **Kingdom of Jerusalem** with regard to the succession, supporting the faction of Raymond III and the Ibelins, who hoped to see **Sibylla of Jerusalem**, King **Baldwin V**'s sister, married to their candidate Baldwin of Ibelin. The spectre of **Saladin** loomed, meanwhile. Bohemond's son Raymond fought at **Hattin** but escaped with Raymond III of Tripoli. Bohemond, helped by Sicilian reinforcements, was able to prevent the Saracens from advancing far into his principality, and his subsequent policy of neutrality largely enabled Antioch to escape the fate of Jerusalem.

## *Bohemond VI of Antioch* (1237–75)

Bohemond VI was the last effective Latin Prince of **Antioch**. He inherited a territorial dispute with the Armeanians, which was happily ended when **Louis IX** negotiated Bohemond's marriage to Sibylla of Armenia. Unfortunately, meanwhile, Bohemond had erred on the side of the **Mongols** during their power struggle with the **Mameluks**. This meant that after the Mameluk triumph at **Ain Jalut**, Antioch became a target for Mameluk reprisals. **Baybars** took the city in 1268, writing to Bohemond (absent in **Tripoli**) to let him know of the atrocities committed against the Christian population by the victors.

## Bohemond VII of Antioch (1261–87)

Bohemond VII was Lord of **Tripoli** and nominal Prince of **Antioch**. He was raised in the **Armenian** Court, and was protected by Leo III of Cilicia. From shortly after Bohemond's accession in the mid-1270s he became embroiled in an internecine conflict with the Templars, under **Guillaume de Beaujeu**, who supported Bohemond's rivals.

During Bohemond's early reign, Tripoli had been governed by Bartholomew, Bishop of Tortosa. However, Bartholomew was challenged for the regency by Paul of Segni, Bishop of Tripoli, who was the leader of an anti-Armenian faction and was close to the Grand Master. When Bohemond himself came of age in 1277, it seems the Templars were already hostile to him. Later, the Templars supported Bohemond's rebellious vassal Guy II Embriaco, Lord of Gibelet, who had become a *confrere* of the Order in **Acre**. The political conflict degenerated into violence. Bohemond attacked the Templars' house in Tripoli and sent ships against their fortress in **Sidon**, while the Templars sent a fleet of their own against Tripoli. They also contributed thirty brothers to help Guy against Bohemond meanwhile, defying their long-standing principle of not fighting against fellow Christians. They joined battle near Botron. Later, Guy made an attempt to seize Tripoli, gaining entry and staying initially with the Templars there. He was made suspicious, however, by the absence of the local Preceptor, Reddecoeur, and moved on to the **Hospitaller** Commandery. Guy was soon forced to surrender to Bohemond, and was executed. At a time when the threat to the diminishing Latin territory from the **Mongols** and the **Mameluks** was dire, this sort of infighting amongst the Christians of Tripoli was considered scandalous and 'a great evil'.

## Bohemond of Taranto (1058–1111)

Bohemond (originally Miles) of Taranto (later Prince Bohemond I of **Antioch**) was a southern Italian warlord of Norman origin. He was a leader of the **First Crusade**. He had taken part in raids led by his father Robert Guiscard against the **Byzantine Empire**, before **taking the Cross** (along with his nephew **Tancred**) in a war partially justified by the defence of Byzantium. Anna Comnena, who met him in **Constantinople**, described his impressive appearance and evident warlike passions. Bohemond led the Norman contingent of Crusaders as they crossed Anatolia and was the first to invest Antioch. The city finally fell due to Bohemond recruiting an insider who admitted the Christian army. Bohemond took credit for the resulting victory and established himself as Prince of Antioch. Bohemond remained there, consolidating his power base, visiting Jerusalem only after it had fallen. In 1100 the Danishmend Turks of Sivas captured and held him for three years. Islamic and Byzantine incursions then threatened Bohemond's security in Antioch. He had himself smuggled back to Europe where he received a hero's welcome and the hand of Constance, daughter of Philip I of **France**. Bohemond's domed mausoleum in Canosa in Apulia shows distinct Middle Eastern influences.

## *Boniface VIII* (1235–1303)

Bernardetto Caetani, a member of a prominent aristocratic dynasty, was elected **Pope** in 1294, and took office as Boniface VIII. He replaced **Celestine V**, a simple hermit who had been chosen with the hope of restoring sanctity to the office. Celestine had proved unsuccessful and after five months became the first Pope ever to resign. Boniface VIII was a less spiritual and more political being, and was a keen advocate of **Papal Supremacy**. He made little distinction between spiritual and worldly power. (The Pope would sit on a throne and proclaimed himself Caesar in 1300, during the Holy Year celebrations in **Rome** when the city was crowded with pilgrims.) This set him at odds with the monarchs also claiming power by Divine right. In the late 1290s Boniface became embroiled in a feud with **Philip the Fair**, regarding the latter's right to tax the clergy in France. Philip resorted to cutting off all French tithes to Rome. Boniface asserted absolute and universal Papal Sovereignty in *Unam Sanctam*, an uncompromising **Papal Bull** of 1302. Philip repudiated the bull and was consequently **excommunicated**. Philip responded by accusing the Pope of corruption, simony, sorcery, **heresy**, blasphemy and causing the death of Celestine V (who had indeed died in Boniface's custody at the age of 81). The French Templars, under the governance of **Hugues de Pairaud**, did not oppose the King's stance and were careful not to be seen to cross him.

In September 1303, Philip sent **Guillaume de Nogaret** with a squadron of French soldiers to seize Boniface from his palace in **Anagni**. The French party met with their Italian co-conspirators under **Sciarra Colonna**, the head of a family long antagonistic to Boniface's Caetani clan. In a move that provoked widespread outrage, they invaded the palace and held the Pope under house arrest. Guillaume de Nogaret intended to drag Boniface back to France to stand trial on the trumped-up charges. Colonna, it is said, wanted to execute Boniface there and then and at one point struck the Pope's face. The argument between de Nogaret and Colonna gave the Pope's supporters in the town the opportunity to conduct a rescue. The episode had left Boniface badly shaken and he died within the month.

Boniface's short-lived successor, Benedict XI, excommunicated Guillaume de Nogaret for the outrage at Anagni, but cleared King Philip of involvement. De Nogaret continued to exert influence from the shadows, however. He and the King continued to circulate rumours blackening Boniface's reputation. Subsequently Philip the Fair sought to discredit the deceased Pontiff by inaugurating a posthumous trial to investigate Boniface's alleged crimes. As well as being accused of simony and sorcery, Boniface, the embodiment of Papal Supremacy, was alleged to have secretly held that Christianity contained many false doctrines. The King pressed for a posthumous condemnation, something **Clement V** resisted, knowing the impact such a trial and condemnation would have on the Church's reputation, but was ultimately obliged to vindicate the **Capetian** version of events.[86] Philip also wished to see Boniface's body disinterred from the magnificent tomb the Pope had commissioned for himself and burned. The threat of resurrecting the posthumous trial of Boniface VIII was another lever Philip used to get his way over the Templar **suppression**.

## Boniface of Montferrat (c. 1152–1207)

Boniface, Marquis of Montferrat was a Piedmont noble, and leader of the **Fourth Crusade**, which sacked Constantinople in 1204. He was a son of **William V of Montferrat** and younger brother of **Conrad of Montferrat**. Boniface became the head of the Fourth Crusade in 1201 after the death of its original leader Theobald III, Count of Champagne. When the participants got into debt, Boniface lost influence to Doge Enrico Dandolo of **Venice**. He made himself absent during the attack on Zara, perhaps to preserve his standing with Pope **Innocent III**.[87] After the capture of **Constantinople** it was decided to crown a Latin as Emperor. The Venetians vetoed Boniface, in favour of **Baldwin of Flanders**. Boniface went on to capture Thessalonica and much of central **Greece** and to establish his own lordship there, justifying himself by claiming that Manuel I had once granted Thessalonica to his brother Renier. Boniface made some property grants to the Templars during his short rule there, or at least his successors did after Boniface died in a skirmish with the Bulgarians in September 1207.

## Brian de Jay (died 1298)

Brian de Jay was the Master or **Grand Preceptor** of the Temple in **England**. He was also in charge of the Templars in **Scotland**. He possibly came from the village of Jay in Shropshire. He apparently visited **Cyprus** briefly in the early 1290s, and consulted with the **Grand Master**. However, he soon returned to the British Isles. He was a close ally of **Edward I**, and swore fealty to the King at Edinburgh Castle in 1291. He later died fighting for Edward against **William Wallace** and the Scots at the Battle of **Falkirk**. This was in contravention of the Templars' **Rule**, which technically forbade the brethren to fight other Christians. Brian fought in an individual capacity, however, and led Welsh mercenaries rather than a detachment of Templars. According to one version of events, Brian was among the English knights who pursued the fleeing Scots, who turned to fight a rearguard action in the Woods of Callander, and it is then that he was killed, perhaps by Wallace himself.

Brian de Jay had a cruel reputation in Scotland, where he had served as Master. A later document of 1354 recorded that when a tenant of the Templars died in 1295, the Templars had gone to evict the widow, Christaine of Esperton, from the estate of the property in Midlothian. She had refused to go and had clung to the doorframe. (She probably had the right, as the property had come to her and the Templars' only claim was that her husband had died a corrodan or pensioner of the Order in **Balantradoch**.) De Jay ordered his men to drag Christaine away, and one of them drew his sword and cut off her fingers where they held the door. For the Scots, the episode became a metaphor for the English occupation. Brian de Jay was mentioned at the **trials** in the testimony of **Thomas de Thoroldeby**. Thoroldeby claimed that Brian had treated the poor with contempt and on one occasion when begged for alms for the love of the Virgin, had tossed a farthing into the mud so the paupers had to grovel for it.[88]

## Bristol

Bristol is a port city in the west of **England**. It was chartered as a city in 1155, and was a key maritime centre in the medieval period, famous for being the starting place of Giovanni Caboto's (John Cabot's) voyage of discovery of 1497, which reached **America**. The Templars were active in Bristol to judge by the many street names there containing the world 'Temple'. They had a **Preceptory** there with a **round church**. To this building (called the Temple or Holy Church) was added a chapel dedicated to St **Catherine**, which was used by the weavers' guild. Wool was the basis of Bristol's prosperity. The Templars exported wool from their estates as part of their internal trade with their continental brethren, and imported wine and other goods from **La Rochelle**. Bristol was also an embarkation point for **Crusades**. The excavated foundations of the round church can be seen within the ruins of the later church built on the site. The later church, a grand building in the Perpendicular style of **Gothic**, was built by the **Hospitallers**. It features a tower that not only leans but bends in the middle, the process of subsidence having begun half way through its building. The church has been in ruins since being bombed during the Second World War.

## Bruer, Temple

Temple Bruer was a significant agricultural **Preceptory** in Lincolnshire, **England**. The last remnant of the Templar buildings is an oblong tower. It was one of two attached to a **round church**. The site was excavated in

Victorian times by one Dr Oliver. Oliver claimed to have discovered underground chambers containing human remains showing signs of violent death. No such bones were found in subsequent excavations. Bruer was the home of at least one literary Templar, Brother **Henry d'Arcy**, who commissioned or wrote at least four poetical theological tracts in Norman French. It is said the Templars used to hold jousts and tournaments at nearby Byards Leap. If so then they were hardly keeping to their rule, though it could have been a training ground. Temple Bruer received a licence to crenellate in 1306, suggesting that the Templars remained in favour with the English monarchy until the eve of their downfall.[89]

## Burgundy

Burgundy (Bourgogne), neighbouring **Champagne**, was the region of **France** from which many of the original Templars came. Burgundy is famous for wine production, and the Templars, in their **Rule**, were permitted to partake of a little alcohol, though not to drink to excess. In the early medieval period, the region was effectively independent of the Kingdom of **France**. It lay between the spheres of influence of the **Capetian** monarchs and the **Holy Roman Emperors**. Burgundy was the home of the first **Grand Master**, **Hugues de Payens**, and of the Order's patron, Abbot **Bernard of Clairvaux**. It was also where the Templars received some of their earliest grants of land.[90] The last Grand Master, **Jacques de Molay**, was initiated there at Beaune.

## Buri (died 1132)

Taj al-Muluk Buri was the ruler of **Damascus**. He was the son of Tughtigin, who had contributed forces to the battle of the **Field of Blood**. Buri took ruthless measures to rid Damascus of the **Assassins** and their supporters. In late 1129 he fended off an attack on Damascus by **Baldwin II**, the lords of **Antioch** and **Tripoli**, the early Templars and western **pilgrims**. The Crusader force grew demoralised and withdrew after a foraging party was wiped out by Buri's men.[91] Buri was later fatally wounded by two Assassins who had infiltrated his bodyguard.

## Burials (Templar)

The Papal decree *Omne Datum Optimum* gave the Templars the right to bury their own dead in ground adjoining their own churches. They also had their own **priests** to preside at these funerals. Templar brothers were often buried in stone coffins, the hollowed-out receptacle for the body being shaped around the shoulders with a niche for the head. (Such coffins can be seen emerging eerily from the ground at the ruined Preceptory at **Penhill** in Yorkshire.) The **grave slab** that formed the lid sometimes remained exposed above ground and was sometimes carved with Templar symbols, such as a sword and/or an elongated **Calvary cross**. Sometimes the figure of the deceased Templar was carved into it, as may be seen on the slabs from **Barletta**. These slabs also feature inscriptions and heraldry. It does not seem that any of the tombs of the **Grand Masters** are known to survive. These were probably destroyed after the loss of the **Holy Land**. It is known, however, that the Grand Masters received elaborate funerals, attended by the leading prelates and nobles of the land. The event was marked by a great lighting of candles, and over the following seven days the brethren would recite 200 *paternosters*. According to their statutes they also gave **charity** to 100 paupers in honour of the deceased leader.[92]

Some have claimed that on occasion Templars were buried in a peculiar way, with the head cut off and placed on the chest, and the legs dislocated at the hips and crossed over the torso.[93] There does not seem to be any evidence for this bizarre notion, however. Templar burials were in accordance with orthodox practices of the day, and the stone coffins surviving at **Temple Church, London**, and at Penhill provide clear evidence of conventional monastic burial (They are nearly the same as stone monks' coffins found at Whitby Abbey and various other such locations.) The Christian dead, whenever possible, were interred intact, orientated with the head at the west so that on the Day of Judgement they would resurrect facing east towards **Jerusalem** (perhaps not if they were buried east of Jerusalem). Priests were buried with crosiers and liturgical chalices and were laid the other way, ready to administer to the flock.

## Burning, Execution by

Burning was, in the thirteenth century, becoming the accepted method of execution for convicted **heretics**. The revival of Roman law seems to have been a factor in this. The most common method was burning at the stake, whereby the victim would be chained to a sturdy upright post at the centre of a platform of logs and kindling, which would then be lighted under their feet. An even crueller method was suspending the victim above the flames. This way the death would usually be slower. As the victim died, a **priest** would perform the last rites before them.

Burning became a particularly widespread form of execution during and after the **Albigensian Crusade**, when the **Inquisition** condemned hundreds of Cathars to this fate, releasing them to the secular authorities for the sentence to be carried out. The object of this method of execution was to terrorise others into submission. If someone confessed to heresy and then was found to have returned to their previous beliefs, they were to be considered a relapsed heretic, and could be consigned to the flames. The sting in the tail was that if a suspect confessed to heresy under **torture** (or through fear thereof), and subsequently protested their innocence, then they were also to be considered relapsed heretics and to suffer the same fate. Thus it came to pass that hundreds of Templars were burned for claiming to be loyal **Catholics**. Unlike the **Cathars**, who were happy to embrace **martyrdom** for an alternative creed, not a single Templar died defending his alleged heresy. The Templars died protesting their fidelity to the Church.

The **trials** of the Templars in Paris seemed to be about to unravel when hundreds of Templars began to defend their innocence, their most effective spokesman being **Pierre de Bologna**. Those who wished to destroy the Order therefore convened the Council of **Sens**, where the royalist Archbishop, **Philip de Marigny**, began to convict as relapsed heretics those who had previously confessed and who now retracted their confessions. Defendants were taken away from the Papal Commission trials to face condemnation before de Marigny. The appeals the other Templars made to the **Gilles Aicelin** and the Papal Commission were in vain, and on 30 May 1310, fifty-four Templars were carted to a field outside Paris, near the Convent of St Antoine. Still protesting their innocence they were burnt to death.[94] More Templars, probably dozens more, followed them into the flames in Paris and elsewhere in the **Capetian** domain. The last two victims were the **Grand Master Jacques De Molay** and the Preceptor of Normandy **Geoffroi de Charney**, who were immolated in 1314.

## Byzantine Empire/Byzantium

Byzantium was an ancient city on the Bosphoros, where the Balkans meet Asia Minor. During the reign of **Constantine I**, it was re-founded as the Second **Rome**. It became known as Constantinople, the Queen of Cities. Today it is Istanbul. Byzantium was also a term for the Byzantine or Eastern Roman Empire, which in the twelfth century, though on the retreat, covered **Greece**, western Anatolia, **Cyprus** and various Mediterranean islands. The Byzantines called themselves Romans but their culture was purely Greek. Government was in the hands of a semi-divine Emperor, or *Basileus*, assisted by an extensive civil bureaucracy. The religion of Byzantium was Orthodox Christian, with a spiritual leader in the Orthodox **Patriarch** in Constantinople. (The Eastern Church and the Roman **Catholic** Church had split as a result of the Great Schism of 1054, disagreeing over doctrinal minutiae.) Still, the Latin and Greek Churches considered each other sisters, and there was a broad sense of Christian solidarity. The **Crusades** were set in motion in part to aid Byzantium against the **Seljuk Turks**. After Manzikert the Turks had advanced almost to the gates of Constantinople.

The Byzantine Imperium and the **First Crusaders** cooperated, at first. Their relationship grew strained after the Emperor **Alexius I Comnenus** failed to reinforce the **Franks** at **Antioch**. The Franks considered that this dereliction invalidated the oaths of allegiance that they had been obliged to swear to the Emperor. Vindicating the mistrust of Anna Comnena, Bohemond of Taranto later tried to organise a Crusade against the Empire, but was defeated and obliged to accept Byzantine suzerainty at the treaty of Devol. The succeeding Emperors **John II** and **Manuel I Comnenus** would seek to assert their authority over Antioch with little real effect, and also to establish influence over the **Kingdom of Jerusalem**. Military alliances achieved little, but Byzantine involvement contributed to a cultural flowering, as the jointly organised restoration of the **Holy Sepulchre** exemplified during the reign of **Amalric I**. The **Hospitallers** were established in Constantinople during the reign of Manuel I and operated a hospital dedicated to St John. The Emperor also used the Hospitaller brother Petrus Aleman as an envoy. The Greek Church found the idea of **Military Orders** alien, but the Hospitallers had a more conventional primary purpose and were probably, therefore, more acceptable.

The relationship between the Franks and the Greeks deteriorated in the late twelfth century, especially during the reign of **Andronicus I Comnenus**. There were attacks on the Latin communities in the capital, including a massacre of those westerners in the Hospital of St John. At the beginning of the thirteenth century, Byzantium itself fell victim to the **Fourth Crusade**. The core of the Empire fell under Frankish and **Venetian** occupation. In 1261 the Greeks, under **Michael VIII Palaeologus** of Nicæa, recovered Constantinople, but the Empire never recovered its former prestige. It was gradually swallowed up from the east. Constantinople fell to the **Ottomans** in May 1453. The last Emperor, Constantine XI, died on the walls fighting against an army perhaps fifty times greater in size than his own.[95] The loss of Constantinople to **Islam** was felt as a great blow to **Christendom**.

# C

## *Cabbalah*

The Cabbalah (or the Kabbalah or Qabbalah) is a religious mystical system from the **Jewish** tradition. It purports to offer initiates some insight into the mind of God or even union with the divine. The term came to refer specifically to the esoteric traditions concerning the way to God and understanding of the universe. One aspect of Cabbalism is a symbol called the Tree of Life. It is a diagram expressing the cosmology of the Cabalists. The diagram has twenty-two paths connecting ten spheres, one below and nine above (it looks rather like a model of an atom). The spheres are called *sephirot*. They are said to represent different levels of spiritual awareness, the highest is where one communes with the divine. Cabbalism flourished during the medieval era, being studied by learned rabbis in Spain, and also in southern **France** (Narbonne and Lunel). The enigmatic, patterned circles on the ceiling of the Templar church at **Montsaunes** seem to reflect the Sephirot of the Tree of Life, and possibly hint that the Templars were influenced by this esoteric Judaic speculation.[96]

## Caesarea

Caesarea Palestina was a port founded in ancient Judea, by King Herod the Great. It was the administrative and cultural centre of the Roman province. The city, important to early Christianity, fell to the **Arabs** after AD 638. In 1101 it was captured by the **Franks** under **Baldwin I**. Its mosque was converted into the cathedral of St Peter, the seat of a new Latin Archbishopric. At around this time, a hexagonal, emerald (or green glass) chalice was found, which some identified as the **Holy Grail**. This relic found its way to Genoa. Caesarea was lost to **Saladin** in 1187, but recovered by the Christians during the **Third Crusade**. During the **Fifth Crusade**, when the Franks were preoccupied in **Damietta**, Caesarea was stormed by al-Muazzam of **Damascus**. This prompted the Templars to return to Palestine from **Egypt** for a time, in order to recover the city and to safeguard other places. In 1251–2, after the **Seventh Crusade**, **Louis IX** refortified Caesarea. It was here that Louis disciplined the Templars and banished Brother **Hugues de Jouy** for negotiating over land with the Sultan of Damascus without the King's assent. Caesarea fell again in 1265, this time to **Baybars**. The city was abandoned thereafter, later to be re-established under the Ottoman Empire.

## Calatrava, Order of

The Order of Calatrava was a Spanish **Military Order**, under **Cistercian** tutelage. Pope Alexander III recognised the Order in 1164. It played a prominent role in the **Reconquista** of the **Iberian** Peninsula, along with the orders of Alcantara and **Santiago**. Their **dress** was similar to that of the Templars. Their red cross was distinctive in having fleurs-de-lis at the ends of its arms, the outer petals of which curved back making an 'm' shape, possibly a reference to **Mary, the Blessed Virgin**. The Order of Calatrava had been in existence some time before it was officially recognised as a **Catholic** Order. Calatrava was a castle recovered in 1147 from the **Moors** by Alfonso VII of Castile, in the south of his territory. The name derives from *Qalat Rawaah* meaning 'Castle of War'. The king gave the castle to the Templars, hoping that they would use it to defend the approach to Toledo against **Muslim** raiders. The Templars, however, soon relinquished the castle, feeling it too much trouble to retain and wishing to direct their energies elsewhere.

The Cistercian Ramon Sierra, Abbot of Santa Maria de Fietero, went to the king and offered to raise a band of men to garrison Calatrava. Ramon transferred his monks there and also recruited soldiers. Subsequently the Order took on more of a military character, though the knights were still affiliated with Citeaux. Calatrava was originally under the auspices of the Cistercian monastery of Morimond in Burgundy, which appointed its Grand Priors. The Order gained more land and castles, and developed its structure. It spread through Castile and Leon. The Order won initial successes. In 1195, though, the Order in Castile was decimated at the battle of Alarcos against invading Moors from North Africa, the **Almohades**. It temporarily lost control of Calatrava itself. The knights subsequently based themselves in the castle of Salvatiere, until that too fell in 1209. The Order's fortunes picked up in 1212 when it regained Calatrava and contributed to a victorious coalition at the Battle of **Las Navas de Tolosa**. The Order continued to play a part in the ongoing wars of the Reconquista, though it fragmented. Eventually, like other Iberian Military Orders, it lost much of its religious character and became embroiled in the secular strife of dynastic struggles.

## Calf Worship

During the trials of the Templars in **England**, some witnesses mentioned hearing that the brethren worshipped a calf. Templars from Temple **Hirst** were accused of this. There does not seem to be any basis for the rumour. The Biblical episode (Exodus 32:1–21), where Aaron made a golden calf that the Hebrews worshipped during the absence of **Moses**, was probably the only form of **idolatry** the medieval Christians had heard of; thus it came to mind with the talk of the Templars worshipping idols.

## Calvary Crosses

A cross with a stepped base is called a Calvary Cross. It was a popular **Byzantine** symbol, often appearing on coins. In many castle dungeons where the last Templars were held, similar Calvary Crosses can be seen carved into the walls. The imprisoned Templars themselves apparently left these carvings. Such crosses can be seen in castles at **Chinon** in **France**, and at **Warwick** and **Lincoln** in **England**. Stepped base crosses are also familiar from Templar **grave slabs**.

## Cambridge

Cambridge Castle is where the Templars from the eastern counties of **England** were held in 1308 after the **arrests**. Only the castle mound remains, in the grounds of Shire Hall above the River Cam. The **Round Church** in Cambridge, named after **the Holy Sepulchre**, is somewhat similar in appearance to **Temple Church, London.** It is earlier in date and its round nave has eight thick **Romanesque** pillars with round arches supporting the central section (as opposed to Temple Church's six **Gothic** arches). The Cambridge church was built between 1114 and 1130. The building was much altered later, being given late Gothic windows and an extension to its central tower. Victorian restorers (directed by the Camden Society) returned it to the early Norman style in the 1840s. The piers supporting the ribs of the restored interior dome rise from carved heads, which may or not be original features. This church may originally have belonged to the **Order of the Holy Sepulchre** rather than the Templars, but the two groups were closely connected (if not one and the same institution) during the Templars' early phase.

## Canons Regular of the Holy Sepulchre

The Canons Regular of the **Holy Sepulchre** were an **Augustinian** Order of priest-monks, founded in **Jerusalem** soon after the **First Crusade.** Pope Celestine III ratified their institution, but they were clearly around long before this time. It is said that they were instituted by **Geoffroi de Bouillon** to serve in the Church of the **Holy Sepulchre.** They had other possessions in the **Holy Land** and some in Western Europe. The Canons of the Holy Sepulchre also seem to have been given custody of the **Dome of the Rock** where they were known as the Canons of the Temple of the Lord. The Chronicler **William of Tyre** recorded that they granted the early Templars the court on **Temple Mount.** They also staffed the **Abbey of Zion,** and a shrine on the Mount of Olives. The Canons seem to have been closely linked to an elusive **Military Order,** the **Order of the Holy Sepulchre.** As there is little reference to it after the 1120s, it seems likely that these Knights of the Holy Sepulchre effectively *became* the Knights Templar. The closeness of the Canons of the Holy Sepulchre to the Templars and **Hospitallers** is made clear in the will of **Alfonso I of Aragon,** who left his entire realm to these three institutions. There was an associated Order of Canonesses. Relations were not always so smooth, however. William of Tyre recorded an incident where the Canons of the Holy Sepulchre and the Hospitallers fell out over some issue, and where the Hospitallers shot arrows into the Canons' cloister.[97] The Canons of the Holy Sepulchre fragmented on national lines following the loss of the Holy Land. In 1489 Pope Innocent VIII attempted to merge them with the Hospitallers, but the merger was only fully implemented in Italy.

## Capetian Dynasty

The Capetian dynasty was the royal family ruling **France** through much of the early medieval period. The line was founded in 987 when Hugh Capet, the Count of **Paris** was elected king by an assembly of nobles convened by the archbishop of **Reims**, replacing the defunct Carolingian dynasty. The greatest kings of the house of Capet were probably **Philip II Augustus** and the sainted **Louis IX**. During the Capetian era the royal realm had grown from a small region around Paris (the *Ile-de-France*) to cover much of the modern state of France. At the end of the thirteenth century the Capetians gained control of the Templar heartland of **Champagne** by uniting with the Royal house of Navarre. The dynasty also began to foster belief in divinely sanctioned monarchy.

The male Capetian line died out in 1328 with Charles IV, the third son of **Philip the Fair**. French law (as recently rewritten) forbade Charles IV's daughters inheriting the throne so it ultimately passed to Philip of Valois, (the Valois being a branch of the Capetians descending from a younger son of Philip III). They retained the royal arms, which consisted of a blue shield with gold fleurs-de-lis. In the mid-1260s, meanwhile, another cadet branch of the Capetian dynasty had become rulers of Naples (originally Sicily too) when the papacy offered **Charles of Anjou** that crown in exchange for championing the **Guelf** cause against the **Hohenstaufen**. The heads of this branch were also Counts of Provence and sometimes titular kings of **Jerusalem**. The Templars were on the whole supporters of the Capetian dynasty and flourished in the Capetian domains, where they were most extensively established. It would also be in the Capetian realms that the Order was most ruthlessly suppressed.

## Capitalism

It has been claimed that the Templars were pioneers of the capitalist economic system, because they were involved in **banking** activity. This theoretically helped to overthrow the **Catholic** Church's long-standing attitude that usury (lending money for interest) was sinful and unworthy of Christians. The Templars had some things in common with a multinational business corporation, and have even been described as 'Templar Inc.'[98] It could as well be said that they were socialists, or even communists, as they lived communally, held property collectively, adopted an internationalist outlook and ran their estates as a planned/controlled economy.

## Captivity

Captivity was an occupational hazard for **Crusaders** and for Latin settlers in the **Holy Land**. For the rich and powerful it normally meant a spell in tolerable conditions of imprisonment awaiting the payment of ransom, for the rest it might mean **slavery** or death. Many captives were prisoners of war, taken in battle. Prominent Crusaders who spent long periods in enemy custody included **Bohemond of Taranto**, **Baldwin II**, **Raymond III of Tripoli** and **Reynald de Chatillon**. Templar **Grand Masters** who experienced captivity by the **Muslims** included **Bertrand de Blanquefort**, **Odo de St Amand**, **Gerard de Ridefort**, and possibly **Armand de Perigord**. Odo apparently died in chains in a Muslim prison, and this may also have been the fate of Armand. The Templars themselves never executed prisoners, as a rule, and were sometimes reluctant to give them up, valuing their skills too highly.

## Caput LVIIIm

*Caput LVIIIm* was presumably a **holy relic**, venerated by the Knights Templar. It was found by Guillaume Pidoyne, the royal official given custody of the **Paris Temple**, after a search of the Templars' buildings. As the Papal Commission heard, it was a beautiful silver gilt **head**, shaped like that of a woman. Inside were the bones of a fragmented skull, rolled up and stitched in red and white cloth. This bore a label reading *Caput LVIIIm* (Head 58m). The bones were identified as those of a small woman, and it was said to be the head of one of the **11,000 virgins**.[99] Similar reliquaries have survived, and it is likely this one was a real object. The reliquary does not seem connected to the head that was supposedly at the centre of the Templars' unholy worship.

## Carcassonne

Carcassonne is a city in the Languedoc, famous for its well-preserved medieval walls, with many towers and turrets. These were extensively restored in the nineteenth century by the architect Eugene Voillet-le-Duc. Carcassonne suffered during the **Albigensian Crusade** in 1209, when it was captured by **Simon de Montfort** and the **Catholic** host. The Viscount Raymond-Roger Trencavel was deposed and died in prison, while the people, stripped of all their possessions, were driven out through the gates. Before the Albigensian Crusade, Carcassonne had been a safe and tolerant city for **Cathars**. After the war it became a notorious centre of the **Inquisition**. The Templars in Carcassonne, after the **arrests** in 1307, were tortured into confessing **idol worship** and it seems to have been here that the name **Baphomet** emerged. Carcassonne's troubles were not over. In later years Edward the Black Prince, the son of **Edward III** of **England**, took the lower town and let his men pillage and burn all but the churches.

## Carmelites

The Order of Our Lady of Mount Carmel, known as the Carmelite Order, was a **Catholic**, contemplative, monastic Order. It was founded during the Crusades on Mount Carmel in the **Holy Land**. Like the Templars they were devoted to the **Virgin Mary**. The Order was founded by the little-known Italian, St Berthold, who died in the 1180s. However, it traced its origins farther back through the generations of hermits, from the Old Testament Elijah who has previously occupied the mountain. In the Bible, Mount Carmel is where Elijah defeats the priests of Baal in a test of who has the real god (1 Kings 18, 19–20). The Carmelite monastery became a popular pilgrim destination in its own right.

## Carthusian Order

The Carthusians, founded by St Bruno in 1084, were the strictest of the medieval monastic Orders. Semi-hermitic, the white-clad monks and nuns of the order confined themselves to small, austere cells for most of the time and only came together for prayer. Their centre was *la Grande Chartreuse*, situated amid the mountains in the former province of the Dauphine (south-eastern France). The Carthusian Order's much-respected fifth Prior, Guigo (d. 1136), wrote to **Hugues de Payens** in about 1130 advising that the fighting monks of the Order of the Temple should not neglect the internal, spiritual struggle. In the medieval **Catholic** Church, monks were technically only permitted to transfer to stricter orders than the one they had joined, and Carthusian discipline was considered the harshest of all. The Templar **Adam de Wallaincourt** joined them for a short time before returning to the Order of the Temple, having found the Carthusian Order's severity unbearable.

## Castles

The Templars were given castles from the 1130s onwards, and began to build their own shortly after that. Templar castles, including **Baghras,** were clustered in the north around **Antioch** and in the south around **Ascalon,** defending the frontier facing **Aleppo** and **Egypt.** Others were positioned along the roads traversed by **pilgrims,** between the coast and the heartland of **Jerusalem.** The greatest Templar Castles were at **Acre,** Atlit/**Pilgrim's Castle, Saphet** in Galilee and **Chastel Blanc** in Syria. The major castles were substantial, enclosed fortresses, containing the garrison's chapel, refectory, halls, stables, dormitories and various other vaulted chambers, some capable of storing tons of provisions to withstand lengthy sieges.[100] Others might be simple towers serving as patrol bases and places of refuge on the pilgrim road. As the thirteenth century wore on, the **Military Orders** received an increasing number of castles from Latin nobles inclined to abandon the vestiges of the **Kingdom of Jerusalem.** The Military Orders were deemed better able to defend them. Other magnificent Crusader castles that survive include the **Hospitallers' Krak des Chevaliers** and the nobles' strongholds of **Kerak,** Beaufort and Saone. Saone is remarkable for its deep fosse ditch, with a tall pinnacle of rock left in place that once supported a bridge above the deep drop.

The Templars built castles in the Iberian Peninsula as defences against the Muslim **Moors**. These included **Tomar** and **Almoural** in **Portugal**, **Miravet**, **Monzon** and **Peñíscola** in **Aragon**, and **Grañena** and Barbarã in the county of Barcelona.[101] In **France** and **England**, where the Order avoided participation in dynastic warfare, Templar Preceptories might have some fortifications as a precaution, but full-scale castles were rare. The **Paris Temple** might have resembled a castle but it was not a fortress to compare to the Order's strongholds in Syria/Palestine. Castles, in both the East and West, were a source of power and prestige, but a drain on finances. They also obviously required garrisons to man them, and if these were depleted to make up armies (as was the case at the time of **Hattin**) and the castles were left under-manned, then they almost inevitably fell.

## Cat Worship

The allegation that the Templars worshipped a cat appears alongside **head worship** in the **accusations** against the Order. This bizarre accusation was probably included so that the popular mind would associate the Templars with other heretical groups, especially the **Cathars**, who had previously been accused of revering a cat, and sometimes of placing obscene kisses on the rear of a satanic cat.[102] Though there had been a cat goddess in ancient **Egypt**, Bast, and though Freya the Norse fertility goddess was sometimes associated with cats, there is little to suggest these cults survived, or any reason to think either the Cathars or Templars would have had any reason to worship cats. Cats were already becoming associated with witchcraft and the devil in the minds of more paranoid members of the clergy, however, and their place in certain pagan religions had probably not been completely forgotten.

## Catalan Rule of the Temple

The Catalan Rule of the Temple was a translation into the Catalan dialect. It was similar in form to the standard Rule, but some of the clauses had been rearranged into a more rational order. It describes the proceedings of **chapter** meetings, including the punishments given to **penitents**. The rule also contained revised regulations, and examples of various problems and issues that had arisen, and how they were to be dealt with. Case studies established, for example, that brothers who left the Order and returned to it could be considered to have lost honour, and thus lost privileges, such as the right to a vote in the election of new Masters.[103]

## Cathars

The Cathars were a religious sect of the twelfth and thirteenth centuries, prevalent in the **Languedoc**. They were particularly strong in the town of Albi, hence they were sometimes called Albigensians. They considered themselves *Good Christians*, but the **Catholic** Church condemned their dualist beliefs as **heresy**. The Cathars believed the material world to belong to a dark, impostor god, analogous with the Devil. In their view, only the soul was the creation of the good and true God. The fallen angel had lured other heavenly spirits into the fleshly bodies he had created, so that they would be his captives.

The Manichaean view that the flesh was evil had made some inroads into Christianity, partly as a result of the teachings of **St Augustine**: consider the Templars' rule that God would be with them if they 'promise to despise the deceitful world in perpetual love of God and scorn the temptations of the body'.[104] Cathar preachers mirrored Catholic ascetics in their rejection of worldly things and their commitment to **chastity**. The sect differed notably from the mainstream religion though, in that it allowed both sexes to be ordained as spiritual leaders. These *Parfaits* (Perfect Ones) lived austerely, ministering to *Credentes* (believers). They preached that no violence was just and that social rank was irrelevant. They believed in reincarnation and practised strict vegetarianism. Their one sacrament was the *consolamentum*, which conferred the sanctified status of a *Parfait*. Having renounced corrupt matter, they believed death would release the spirit back to paradise from its material snare.[105]

The Cathars had links to a sect in the Balkans known as the **Bogomils**. Their anti-materialism was supposedly so extreme that they regarded having children as sinful. They were also accused of believing that (among *Credentes*) indiscriminate fornication was no worse than sex within marriage, and that **sodomy** was preferable because it did not lead to conception and trap more souls in a world created by the Devil. The Cathars had a particular reverence for the Gospel of **John the Evangelist**. However, according to **Inquisition** records they held that all the fathers of the Old Testament were damned; and that **John the Baptist** was one of the greater **demons**. They repudiated this John because he baptised people with water, which, being material – ergo tainted – could not truly wash away sins.[106] Some even denied that the true **Christ** had taken physical flesh (a standpoint called Docetism). The anti-Cathar writers Ermegaud de Béziers and Durand de la Huesca alleged that some of the Cathars secretly taught that **Mary Magdalene** was the wife or concubine of the man Jesus, and also (less controversially) that she was the woman 'taken in adultery' (John 8: 3–7).

As Catharism grew in popularity, the Catholic hierarchy started to lose its influence on religious life in the Languedoc. Pope **Innocent III** urged the local nobility to prosecute the heretics. When they proved reticent, the Pope instigated the **Albigensian Crusade**. The southern nobility, who resented northern French and papal attempts to dominate Occitania, sometimes sheltered the Cathars. Many atrocities were committed over the ensuing decades. The last Cathar castle, **Montsegur**, fell in March 1244. Two hundred and thirty Cathars and Cathar sympathisers, including their leader Bertrand Marty, refused to recant and were **burnt** alive. Catharism, though driven underground, continued to exist. **Inquisitors** continued to work to root out Cathars and their sympathisers from the community up to the turn of the fourteenth century. Cathars were also hunted beyond the Languedoc. In May 1239, on another **Friday 13th**, the Inquisitor **Robert le Bougre** burned 180 alleged Cathars in Mont-Aimé in the county of **Champagne**.[107]

The word *Cathar* may derive from the Greek for 'Pure Ones'. The word, however, seems only to have been used by the sect's enemies, and may relate to the spurious accusations of **cat worship**. Alternately it may be a version of 'Kaffir' the Arabic for Infidel.[108] Pope Innocent III spoke of the Cathars as worse than the **Saracens** – they were a poison in society, ulcers needing to be cut out with the knife. Some have claimed that, because of some supposed shared **Gnostic** heritage, or through family ties, the Templars offered shelter to fugitive Cathars during the persecution of the sect, and that the Templars subsequently embraced many Cathar doctrines, hence among other things their alleged repudiation of the Cross and the sacraments. A mysterious treasure smuggled from *Montsegur* before its fall by four *Parfaits* may also have had something to do with this.

Another possible connection between the fate of the Templars and that of the Cathars presents itself. **Guillaume of Nogaret**, the chief minister of **Philip the Fair** and architect of the Templars' destruction, was a native of the Cathar heartland. His relatives were apparently burned for heresy. His attack on the Templars may have had something to do with his background. It also emerges that **Esquin de Floyran** was from Béziers, the first target of the Albigensian Crusade. With the two initiators of the move against the Templars having at least tenuous links to the Cathars, some sort of anticlerical revenge conspiracy seems at least possible. The trouble with this hypothesis is that the attack on the Templars strengthened the **Dominican Order** and its notorious arm the **Inquisition**, which had been the real nemesis of the Cathars.

## Catherine of Alexandria, St

St Catherine of **Alexandria** was a legendary early Christian **martyr** who was persecuted by pagans. It was believed that she was put to death by **torture**, and broken on a spiked wheel. The wheel thus became her symbol. Alternatively it is said that the wheel itself broke miraculously when she touched it, so she was instead beheaded. Catherine was venerated in the Eastern Church, especially at the great monastery dedicated to her on the Sinai Peninsula, where her cult took root in the ninth century. One pilgrim to this monastery was apparently **Philip de Milly of Nablus**, the future Templar **Grand Master**. St Catherine became better known in the West after the **Crusades**, but was dropped from the list of officially recognised **saints** in the 1960s. The Templars seem to have revered St Catherine, presumably because of her association with purity, courage and martyrdom. The Crusaders won a victory at Ramlah on St Catherine's day, 25 November 1177. The Templars were involved and this may be another reason they adopted her as a patron saint. An image of the saint holding her wheel appears among the dungeon carvings left by the Templar prisoners at **Chinon**. Another appears in a faded fresco at the Templar chapel in **Metz** in the Lorraine. Yet another appears amid the carvings at **Royston Cave**.

## Catholic Church

In medieval times, most of Western Europe owed its allegiance to the Roman Catholic Church and its head the **Pope**. The phrase 'Catholic Church' was first used by St Ignatius of **Antioch**, in the early second century AD. Catholic meant universal, but it came to refer to what was considered the true or authentic Church, as opposed to those groups considered schismatic or heretical. After the great schism of 1054 the Roman Church became dominant in the West, and its adherents were called Roman Catholics. They were known also as **Latin** Christians because Latin, the language of Imperial **Rome**, had become the language of the Church of the Apostles. The Vulgate Bible (the translation of St Jerome from Hebrew and Greek) was the only version generally allowed, and the service of the Mass was likewise in Latin. There were also Latin churches in the East, those affiliated and in communion with the Roman Church. After the Schism the Latin Church was separated from the Orthodox Church, which remained the state religion in the **Byzantine Empire**. The doctrinal difference was over a split hair – the variation of a single word in the versions of the Nicaean Creed used by the two Churches (the *Filioque* controversy).[109] The real divide was over political power – the authority of the Pope.

## Celestine II, Pope (died 1144)

Celestine II, formerly Gaudio de Castello, became **Pope** in September 1143. He is one of the Popes who helped the Templars to establish themselves as part of the Church. Before his death in March 1144 he issued the papal bull *Milites Templi*. This granted certain privileges to the Templars. It also urged prelates and princes to support these liberators and defenders of the Eastern Church, and to make collections for them.

## Celestine III, Pope (1106–98)

Celestine III, formerly Giacinto Boboni, was elected **Pope** in March 1191. He **excommunicated** the German Emperor Henry IV for imprisoning **Richard the Lionheart**. Celestine also feared Henry's power in Italy and is said to have sent an assassin. The assassin was caught and executed by having a red-hot crown nailed to his head.[110] Celestine also recognised the **Teutonic Order**. In 1196 he rebuked the Templars for breaking their promise to divide tithes with the **Canons of the Holy Sepulchre**. He was succeeded by **Innocent III**.

## Celestine V, Pope (1215–96)

Celestine V, originally Pietro del Morrone, was **Pope** for a short period from 7 July to 13 December 1294. He was the only medieval Pope to resign the office. Of humble origins, he had been a **Benedictine** monk and hermit, and had spent many years living in a cave on Mount Morrone. In 1292, on the death of Pope Nicolas, he appealed to the dithering cardinals to elect a successor quickly. To his surprise they responded by electing him, and all but forced him to accept the papacy. Soon he resigned, unable to cope and wishing to retreat back to his cave. His successor, **Boniface VIII**, had Celestine V seized and imprisoned in a castle near Ferentino in south-east Italy. There Celestine died, under suspicious circumstances. This, at any rate, was one of the charges that **Philip the Fair** made against Boniface. Philip kept pressure on **Clement V** throughout the proceedings against the Templars with the threat of exposing the scandal of the previous Pope's conduct. Philip also lobbied for the canonization of Celestine.

## Celibacy

The monastic vow of chastity was understood to mean abstinence from sexual activity. It was required of all monks and nuns, usually along with **poverty** and **obedience**. From the early Middle Ages celibacy was also required of regular **priests**. This was justified by the assumption that **Christ** had been celibate. It was also argued that celibate and unmarried priests were free to devote themselves entirely to the care of Christ's flock. Compulsory celibacy also guarded against priestly dynasties being formed and meant the Church as an institution retained its possessions.

The Templars were also required to take such vows. The **cord** that the brothers wore was to remind them of their bond to chastity. There are suggestions that not all Templars managed to keep this vow, but most probably persevered. Bernard of Clairvaux opined that 'to be always with a woman and not to have intercourse with her is more difficult than to raise the dead'.[169] It has been observed that the male priesthood's concern for celibacy translated sometimes into hostility towards women. The Templars' rule advised that it could be dangerous to look at a woman and forbade kissing even female relatives. Ironically though, in one copy of the rule, a romantic love ballad to a 'worthy lady' appears written by an unknown hand on the blank last page. It is possibly the work of a late thirteenth century Templar of Dourges – one who may have been reconsidering his commitment to abstinence?[111]

## Celts/Celtic Culture

The Celts were a tribal culture that dominated much of Europe before the ascent of **Rome**. They were guided by a priestly class called the Druids, and valued ornament, honour and poetry. Celtic myths of magic cauldrons possibly inspired the medieval romances of the **Holy Grail**. Another Celtic tradition was a cult of **heads**. The Celtic tradition is reflected in the proliferation of carved heads around **Romanesque** and **Gothic** churches, including the **round churches** of the Templars. The artistic convention of carving heads on buildings perhaps recalled shadowy times when real severed heads were set into niches in walls and on standing stones

Celtic culture did not die out on the fringes of the British Isles, and an independent form of Christianity survived there. Called Celtic or Culdeean Christianity, it was somewhat at odds with the Roman version, possibly less hierarchical and with a greater reverence for nature. Irish monks continued to decorate their Bibles and liturgical chalices with intricate knot patterns (knot patterns curiously similar to those found on **Armenian** monuments) and Welsh monks wrote down Celtic legends.

## Cernunnos

Cernunnos was an ancient **Celtic** fertility god, usually shown as a man with horns or antlers. His image, sometimes sitting crossed-legged, has been compared to **Baphomet**, as envisaged by **Eliphas Levi**. It has also been compared to a carved **head** in the Templar church at **Garway**, which resembles a horned **green man**.

## Champagne

The county of Champagne was a prosperous region to the north of **Burgundy**, covering parts of modern **France** and Belgium. Its capital was at **Troyes**. The region was also noted for its vineyards and for the **Champagne fairs**. Champagne was important to the early history of the Knights Templar in Europe, and also of the **Cistercian** Order. The Count of Champagne was one of their earliest aristocratic supporters of both institutions, and his successors would carry on a **Crusading** tradition. After the 1280s, Champagne became part of the **Capetian** realm.

## Champagne Fairs

The Champagne Fairs were large cloth markets, which flourished in the twelfth and thirteenth centuries. Large, vibrant commercial events accompanied by various entertainments, they were held six times annually in the county of **Champagne**, at venues including **Troyes**, Provins and Lagny. Luxury items, including finely woven cloth, attracted merchants and customers from as far afield as Italy. Products of the Templars' own estates were probably sold in these fairs too. To keep up the standards of products on offer, special agents were authorised to confiscate any shoddy merchandise they found. Precious metals were also traded at the Fairs, and here one of the earliest standard measure was used, the 'Troy' weight. The weight system was supposedly brought back from **Egypt** by the **Crusaders**. For the first time in Europe a system of promissory letters of credit came into use at these fairs.

This could have been influenced by the **banking** practices of the Templars, whose European heartland lay in and around Champagne. The Templars were granted various taxes on the Champagne fairs, to raise money for their cause. At Provins, where they had two **Preceptories**, they had the right to charge a toll on all goods entering the town. Naturally enough it caused some grumbling among the merchants.

## Chansons de Geste

*Chansons de Geste* (songs of heroic deeds) were epic poems, popular among medieval **Franks**, especially appealing to the warrior nobility. They were often what inspired the **Crusaders** in their quests for glory, and were largely concerned with exalting warfare, especially the earlier versions. One of the most popular early *Chansons de Geste* was the *Song of Roland*, concerning a Frankish warrior of Charlemagne who died heroically in battle against the **Moors** at Roncesvaux. (The real engagement at Roncesvaux had been against native Basque raiders, not the Muslims, but an epic story of struggle against the Infidel better suited eleventh-century tastes.) Other favoured themes included the adventures of King **Arthur** and his knights, and fantastical accounts of the exploits of Alexander the Great. Monsters, magicians, enchanted swords and mythical creatures came increasingly to feature. The Crusades also inspired such works, including the *Chanson d'Antioch*, written shortly before the **Third Crusade**, but concerning the events of the **First**.

## Chapter

A chapter was a formal meeting held in a monastic community, for purposes other than worship. The general chapter was the ruling institution. These meetings were held for discussions on organizational matters, to hear complaints, to punish transgressors and to reach decisions on various matters. It seems that in the Templars, offenders against the **rule** were punished before the brethren at chapter meetings. Chapter meetings were not religious services, as such, though they might commence and finish with prayers.

## Charity

The Templars were both the recipients and the bestowers of charity. Their charitable activities involved defending pilgrims and giving alms to paupers.

## Charles of Anjou (Charles I of Sicily and Naples) (1227–85)

Charles of Anjou was a younger brother of **Louis IX** of **France**. (He was created Count of Anjou by Louis, and was not related to the **Angevin** Plantagenets.) Charles took part in the **Seventh Crusade** and fought alongside the Templars at **Damietta** and **Mansourah**. Ruthless and ambitious, he was interested in self-aggrandisement and the expansion of **Capetian** power. In 1266, at the invitation of Pope Urban IV, Charles invaded Italy from his lands in Provence. He took Sicily and Naples from the **Ghibellines**, on behalf of the **Guelfs**. Charles killed **Manfred** at the battle of Benevento in 1266, and executed **Conradin** after capturing him in 1268. It was the end of the **Hohenstaufen** dynasty.

Charles then sought conquest in **Greece**. He first took Corfu, and many other Aegean islands. He wrangled with the displaced **Frankish** princes who had been driven out of Constantinople by resurgent **Byzantine** Greeks, securing a claim to the title of Latin Emperor for his dynasty with various marriage alliances for his children. Louis was preparing to embark on the Eighth Crusade at this time. Charles was preoccupied making plans of his own – against Constantinople. Charles suggested Louis divert to Tunis, and set out to join him. By the time Charles arrived, Louis had died, and sickness had taken a toll throughout the camp. Charles took over and fought a few skirmishes before withdrawing to Sicily. In 1271 he invaded Albania. His ambitions of taking Constantinople would be thwarted though. The Pope was in talks with the Byzantine Emperor **Michael VIII Palaeologus** and preferred to direct Charles against the **Holy Land** at this time. Meanwhile, Maria of **Antioch** (the only living grandchild of **Isabella of Jerusalem**) sold to Charles her claim to the Crown of the vestigial **Kingdom of Jerusalem**. This only created tension in **Acre** because most of the Barons and the **Hospitallers** rejected the claim and recognised Hugh III de Lusignan of **Cyprus**. Charles sent his agent Roger of Sanseverino to Acre, who muscled his way into power with the help of the Templars. The Grand Master of the Templars, **Guillaume de Beaujeu,** showed himself to be an obsequious crony of Charles, which compromised the Order's reputation.

Charles's lieutenants' harsh rule of Sicily was unpopular and in 1282 there was a violent insurrection there known as the **Sicilian Vespers**. King Peter III of **Aragon** took advantage of the situation and seized the island, though Charles of Anjou retained control of Naples. Subsequently, Pope **Martin IV**, a French partisan, continued to support Charles and called a 'Crusade' against the Aragonese and Sicilians. This latest phase of the interminable Guelf/Ghibelline wars paralysed Europe just when the Holy Land was desperate for aid against the **Mameluks**. The futile war dragged on until Charles' death in 1285, and peace was only effectively restored in 1302. Charles had maintained good relations with the Templars, for example permitting Baldwin, Master of Apulia to export provisions and horses from his ports to the Holy Land free of duties.[176] However, Charles's activities distracted attention from the Holy Land.

## Charles G. Addison (nineteenth century)

Charles G. Addison was a lawyer of the **Inner Temple** the Inns of Court, who in 1842 wrote *The History of the Knights Templars, the Temple Church, and the Temple*. He argued for the innocence of the Order and sought to rehabilitate the Templars' name. He dismissed **Joseph von Hammer Purgstall**'s theories and argued that the Templars were plundered and persecuted by those who should have been their defenders and supporters. He also told the later history of the **New Temple** in London. He mentions some Templar traditions that survived among the societies of the Inner Temple and **Middle Temple** in his day.

## Charles II of Anjou (died 1309)

Charles 'the Lame' of Salerno was the son of Charles of Anjou. He was a devotee of Saint Mary Magdalene, and presided over a 'rediscovery' of her relics in 1280 in Provence. As king of Naples, he persecuted the Fraticelli.

## Charles Louis Cadet-Gassicourt (1769–1821)

Charles Louis Cadet-Gassicourt was a Parisian writer, initially hostile to **Freemasonry**, later a member of the fraternity. He wrote the tract *Le Tombeau de Jacques de Molay* in 1794, revealing a **conspiracy theory** that the Templar-Freemasons were behind all revolutionary activity in Europe, especially the **French Revolution**, and that they were sworn to avenge **Jacques de Molay** and massacre the kings of Europe and to form a 'universal republic'. He also alleged that the Templars had been contaminated by doctrines derived from the **Assassins**, that the last **Grand Master**, having been 'thrown into the Bastile', had instituted four secret Lodges (based at Edinburgh, Stockholm, Naples and Paris) to keep the Order's secrets and to conspire against monarchy and the papacy. He claimed that after de Molay's burning, the clandestine Templars 'disguised as bricklayers' had recovered his ashes, and fifteen days later assassinated **Esquin de Floyran**. After de Floyran's burial in Avignon, they had secretly stolen his body and replaced it in his tomb with the Grand Master's ashes. Cadet-Gassicourt's far-fetched work was translated anonymously into English as *The Tomb of James Molai*, and published in Boston, USA. His theory was similar to that of his contemporary, the Abbé Barruel, who suspected the Freemasons of conspiring wth the Illuminati.

## Charles of Valois (1270–1325)

Charles, Count of Valois was the younger brother of **Philip the Fair**. In the course of the war between **Guelfs and Ghibelines**, which had escalated in the Mediterranean, Pope **Martin IV** offered Charles the crown of **Aragon** as a Papal vassal; all he had to do first was invade it. Charles also claimed the crowns of Sicily and **Byzantium**. Charles' son, Philip VI, became the first king of the Valois dynasty. Charles had been put forward as a candidate for the office of **Holy Roman Emperor**, but Clement V resisted this and crowned instead Henry of Luxembourg. If Charles had obtained the Imperial rank it would have meant total domination of the Church by the **Capetian** dynasty. Charles also claimed the Imperial title of the Eastern Empire, through his wife Catherine de Courtenay, who was a granddaughter of Baldwin II of the Latin Empire of **Constantinople**. Clement V supported Charles' plans in the years before 1310 to lead a Crusade against Andronicus II, but nothing came of this scheme.[112] Meanwhile, Charles went with Philip to meet Clement at **Poitiers,** after the Estates General at **Tours**, to put pressure on the Pope over the matter of the Templars. This led to the reopening of the **trials**. Charles was also present at the **Council of Vienne**, again supporting his brother in his bid to ensure the abolition of the Knights Templar.

## Charles Warren (1840–1927)

Sir Charles Warren was a British general and also a pioneer of archaeology in the **Holy Land**. Born in Bangor, Wales, he joined the Royal Engineers. He was initiated as a **Freemason** while serving in Gibraltar. In 1867 he led an excavation in **Jerusalem**, for the Palestine Exploration Fund. He gained permission from the **Ottoman** authorities to dig around the Old City. With Charles Wilson, he uncovered extensive networks of passages and chambers. Trouble arouse when his team started to clear a **tunnel** passing north from the southern wall of **Temple Mount**, under the Stables of Solomon. They disturbed the **Muslims** praying in the **Al Aqsa Mosque** above and soon a violent protest broke out. The diggers were driven off, and the Turkish governor halted the dig. Warren was thwarted. His expedition was of greater value in other areas, mapping the ground plan of the Second Temple and various wells, aqueducts, cisterns and passages under the city.

Warren later went to **Egypt**, searching for the lost expedition of Professor Edward Palmer. Then, following a failed attempt to enter politics in **London**, Warren returned to Africa, as part of the expedition to relieve General Gordon at Khartoum. He was promoted to General during the Boer War. Warren was a keen Freemason and this probably had a connection to his interest in the site of the **Temple of Solomon**. In London he was the founder of the Quatuor Coronati Lodge #2076, which was devoted to Masonic research. His Masonic connections and strange behaviour when

Commissioner of the Metropolitan Police during the Ripper investigation also caused him to feature in various **conspiracy theories**.

## Chartres

Chartres is a town in **France**, fifty miles to the south of **Paris**, famous for its cathedral. It was within the domain of the Counts of **Champagne** for a time. It was the venue of the Council of Chartres in 1150, at which **Bernard of Clairvaux** was asked to lead a new **Crusade** (though this never came to fruition). Chartres was also probably the home of the **Grand Master** of the Templars **Guillaume de Chartres**. The Cathedral of *Notre-Dame de Chartres* was dedicated to the **Virgin Mary** and housed the relic of her robe. This relic survived a fire, which destroyed a newly completed cathedral in 1194. The people of Chartres rebuilt the cathedral even grander than it had been before, completing the body of the building by 1220. It was one of the earliest **Gothic** cathedrals. The cathedral's entrances are surrounded by sculpture. One of these seems to depict the **Ark of the Covenant** in transit. The west façade, all that survived the original fire, is dominated by a central rose window shaped like a flower of twelve petals, and by two soaring towers, one much later in date and more ornate in style than the other. The interior of the cathedral is famous for its stained-glass windows. One features a pane of glass that sends a beam down to illuminate a brass pin in the floor when the sun shines through on the Summer Solstice. Also on the floor, under the central crossing, is the famous labyrinth.

## Chastel Blanc

Chastel Blanc, also called Burj Safitha, was a Templar stronghold located between the port of **Tortosa** and the **Hospitaller** Castle of **Krak des Chevaliers**. It dominates the town of Safitha. The castle fell to the **Mameluks** under **Qalawun** in 1289. Only the great limestone keep called the white tower remains of the once extensive fortress, but this is still impressive. The keep is one of the best-preserved Crusader edifices in Syria.[113]

## Chess

The Templars' rule instructed that the Templars were not supposed to play games like chess and backgammon. The evidence that the Templars sometimes did indulge in the game of chess comes from a manuscript of King Alfonso X of Castile, *Liro de Ajedrez, dados y tables*. The manuscript contains an illustration of two Templar knights in their monastic **dress** sat facing each other across a large chessboard, playing the game. The game of chess is very ancient, and has been known in Europe at least since the dark ages. It was probably invented in the Orient. The phrase 'checkmate' is said to derive from the Persian *Shah mat*, meaning 'the King is defeated'. The black and white chequered pattern of the chessboard reflected the Templars' banner **Beauseant**, and centuries later it became customary for **Masonic** lodges to include black and white chequered floors. The chessboard is also a metaphor in the **Holy Grail** literature of **Wolfram von Eschenbach**.[114]

## Children's Crusade

The children's Crusade was a semi-legendary event in AD 1212, a manifestation of impractical popular piety. It is said that a shepherd boy claimed to have received visions of **Jesus**, and preached that where sinful adults had failed to liberate **Jerusalem**, innocent children would succeed by God's grace. The idea seems to have spread in both **France** and **Germany**. It was said that thousands of children ran away from home to join the Crusade. Unscrupulous sea captains, perhaps **Genoese**, allegedly promised to deliver the young pilgrims to the **Holy Land** but sold them into **slavery** instead.

## Chinon, Château

Chinon is a town in west-central **France** dominated by its castle, which sprawls on a hillside above the River Loire. The castle was enlarged by **Henry II, King of England** and **Philip II Augustus** in turn. (Henry II died there in 1189.) It was also the place where Joan of Arc met the Dauphin in 1429. Some sixty Templars were imprisoned in Chinon for a time in 1308. These included the five most important Templars to be arrested in France, namely **Jacques de Molay**, the **Grand Master**, and the senior dignitaries **Raymbaud de Caron**, **Hugues de Pairaud**, **Geoffroi de Gonneville**, and **Geoffroi de Charney**. They were imprisoned in a keep called the Tour de Coudray. There they were visited and questioned by three cardinals sent by **Pope Clement V**. The lead Templars made limited confessions and said that they made them freely (at least according to the **Chinon Parchment**, which records them). This seems unlikely given that another Templar held at Chinon reputedly perished under torture.

The castle survives in a ruinous state. Its dungeons contain carvings left by the Templar prisoners. These include strange geometric symbols including a **Star of David**, figures of **saints** including **St Catherine of Alexandria**, disembodied **heads**, grids divided into squares and triangles, hearts and crosses including **Calvary crosses**. There is also an inscription in the dungeons at Chinon, apparently left by the Templar detainees. It claims that Geoffroi de Charney had been warned by **Gilles Aicelin**, the Archbishop of Narbonne, on the day of Holy Cross (a month before the **arrests**) that the King of France (**Philip the Fair**) would start and win a trial of the Order of the Temple, and so as not to participate in the crime Aicelin had resigned as Keeper of the Seals and come to warn the preceptor what was being planned.[115]

## Chinon Parchment

The Chinon Parchment is a document recently brought to light in the **Vatican Secret Archives** by researcher Dr Barbara Frale, who interpreted it as evidence that the Church secretly pardoned the Templars. Much of the document's contents are familiar from the trial records. Three Cardinals sent by Pope Clement V questioned the five senior Templars over three days in August 1108. These were Bérengar, Cardinal presbyter of St Nerus and Archelius, Stephanus, cardinal presbyter of St Ciriacus in Therminis, and Landolf, cardinal deacon of St Angel. They interviewed the Templars individually – first **Raymbaud de Caron**, then **Geoffroi de Charney**, followed by **Geoffroi de Gonneville**, then **Hugues de Pairaud** and finally **Jacques de Molay**. Their testimonies varied only slightly. Each said he had undergone a reception decades before, with nothing initially untoward. After receiving his cappa, each said he was led aside, and shown a cross (a picture in a book in de Gonneville's account) and told to denounce the one on the cross. All but de Caron said they had been instructed to spit on the cross in addition to denying the crucified one. All also said they had denied Christ with the mouth but not the heart.

Raymbaud de Caron said he had been told that it was better to be chaste, but if he must sin it was better to sin secretly. He knew nothing of **sodomy** being practised within the Order apart from that three brothers had been imprisoned for it in **Pilgrims' Castle**. All five senior Templars were vague regarding knowledge of what happened at other receptions but most denied knowledge of the **head**, or of **idolatry**, obscene kisses or sodomy. De Caron and de Charney said they had confessed soon after denying Christ. De Caron said he was absolved by a kinsman, the Bishop of Carpentras, and de Charney said that he had been pardoned by the **Patriarch** of **Jerusalem**. Most claimed they were received only with a kiss to the mouth, though de Charney also mentioned a kiss to the stomach. Both de Gonneville and de Pairaud said they had been initiated in the **New Temple, London**. De Gonneville claimed that he had refused to deny the cross or spit at its image, even to spit at the receptor's hand on top of the cross. He said his receptor had let him off on the condition that if any Brother had asked him about it, he would tell them that he had done as required.

Hugues Pairaud said his own father, Humbert de Pairaud, had presided at his initiation. He said that he himself had gone on to perform more receptions than any other Templar, and made postulants kiss the base of his spine, his stomach and his mouth – something he supposedly had not had to undergo himself, curiously. He alone confessed to knowing of the head. Jacques de Molay said he had been received at Beune in Autun (**Burgundy**), and that there he had been compelled to make the denial and spit at a crucifix, but had only spat near it. Each Templar agreed that they were now confessing willingly and not through fear of **torture**. At the end of each interview the cardinals absolved the Templars of their sins, and reconciled them with the

**Catholic** Church. The testimony was written down by Robert de Condet, the church notary of Sissons and witnessed by other notaries and clerics.

The Templars evidently thought they had to confess something, and agreed a story between them. Hugues de Pairaud's confession was especially full of contradictions. It seems as though he intended them to read as nonsense. He stated, for example, that he encouraged initiates to commit sodomy, but that no Templars actually followed this supposed injunction except the three imprisoned *for it* in the East. He also stated that the denial of Christ was a Templar tradition, which he wished to see ended, when supposedly he was the one perpetuating it. The Templar chiefs probably made these token confessions for fear of reprisals which the king's men would have carried out against brethren imprisoned elsewhere, had they denied every single thing at that point. Some have interpreted the Chinon parchment as showing that the Templars were secretly exonerated by the Church (or found innocent, the spitting on the cross etc. explained as some preparation for what the Templars may be compelled to do if captured by the Saracens). In fact, the parchment shows only that the Templars repeated their limited confessions and were absolved. De Molay and de Charney would make themselves 'relapsed heretics' by retracting these confessions in 1314.

## Chi-Rho
The Chi-Rho (or Labarum) resembles a letter 'P' overlaid with an 'X'. It is usually interpreted as a Christian symbol, 'X' (Chi) and 'P' (Rho) being the first two letters of the Greek word for **Christ**. Such a symbol appears carved at the Templar **Preceptory** at **Montsaunes**. Often the first and last letters of the Greek Alphabet, *Alpha* and *Omega* ('A' and 'Ω') are also incorporated into the symbol, signifying Christ's statement that he was the beginning and the end. The Templars' **seal** incorporated Chi and Rho in the composite word '**Xpisiti**'.

## Chivalry
Chivalry could be a collective term for the **knights** (*Chevaliers* in French), the mounted warrior elite of medieval Europe. It also came to denote an ethos of honour, valour, loyalty, service, piety and courtesy, which noblemen were encouraged to aspire to as an ideal. Chivalry, though far from pacifist, became associated with Christianity, in so far as it implied that the great and mighty should serve the weak, protect the innocent and uphold the faith. Ideas and ideals relating to chivalry suffused medieval literature, in *Chansons de Geste* and in the romances of King **Arthur** and his knights on the quest for the **Holy Grail.** The Order of the Temple was seen by churchmen like St **Bernard of Clairvaux** as a means by which the real-life knightly class could be taught virtue, being either redeemed within the fraternity or inspired by its example. The **Crusades** came to be seen as the ultimate expression of Chivalry and test of knightly merit.

Being gentle and respectful to ladies and defending their honour also became important aspects of the ethos. Troubadours, minstrels and *trouvères* entertained aristocratic households with ballads on the theme of courtly love. The **Rule** of the Templars may be seen as less than chivalrous in this regard, though in practice the Templars may have had a more chivalrous approach. Medieval romances of chivalry did not show the Templars as misogynists, and sometimes had them lending assistance to lovers.[116]

## *Chretien de Troyes* (died c. 1190)

Chretien de **Troyes** was a *trouvère*, the northern French equivalent of a troubadour. From the 1160s he was associated with the cultured court of the Countess **Marie of Champagne**. Chretien composed many romances, mainly set in the mythical Court of King **Arthur**, and also began translating the *Metamorphosis*, a work of the ancient Roman poet Ovid. In Chretien's stories are found the earliest mentions of Sir Lancelot and his love affair with Queen Guinevere. Chretien is often credited, moreover, with inventing the **Holy Grail**. In his later years Chretien moved to the Court of the Count of **Philip of Alsace, Count of Flanders.** Philip was Chretien's patron while he wrote his last work, *Perceval, le Conte du Graal* (Perceval, the story of the Grail). Regrettably, the poet died before he could complete it or explain what the Grail was. It was left to later writers, such as **Wolfram von Eschenbach,** to finish the story.[117]

## *Christendom*

Christendom meant all the lands where Christians lived, or which were predominantly Christian. In the centuries before the Protestant Reformation there was a sense that these were united by common cause and common religion – a Christian Republic, as it was termed, under a heavenly king. The concept of Christendom was gradually deteriorating through the thirteenth century, as the age of faith giving way to the epoch of Nationalism. In some ways Christendom was the equivalent of the *darl al Islam* or *ummah*, which was the pan-Islamist concept of a global nation of the Muslim faithful. (Neither conglomeration was without its internal divisions, of course.) Christendom was divided between the **Catholic** West and the **Byzantine,** Orthodox East. The West was also plagued by an intermittent power struggle between the **Pope** and the **Holy Roman Emperor,** who both sought to be recognised as the leaders of the Christian world. Muslim expansionism was felt to be a threat to Christendom as a whole. The international **Military Orders** were an expression of a unified response to this threat. The destruction of the Templars and the fragmentation along national lines of the other Orders were a symptom of the disintegration of Christendom, and dissatisfaction with internationalism.

## Christopher da Gama (died *c.* 1542)

Don Christopher (Cristovão) da Gama was the younger son of **Vasco da Gama** and a member of the **Order of Christ**. Don Christopher served under his brother Estovão (who was Viceroy of India) in a naval campaign against the **Ottoman** Turks in the Red Sea. After that he commanded a Portuguese mission to **Ethiopia** in 1541, taking 450 men including musketeers. This force lent assistance to the Christian Emperors of Ethiopia, then beset by **Muslim** invaders under Ahmed Gragn. It is said da Gama's band saved the Christian civilization of Ethiopia. Da Gama led his men to numerous victories but was eventually captured and beheaded. A year later the surviving Portuguese and the Ethiopians defeated the Muslim forces in a battle near Lake Tana. Not long after, however, the Christian Emperor expelled the Portuguese, perhaps fearing their colonial ambitions. Writer Graham Hancock has speculated that the Knights of Christ inherited a long-standing Templar interest in the land of Ethiopia, possibly related to their awareness that the **Ark of the Covenant** lay there.

## Churches

After **castles**, the Templars' churches were the Order's most significant contribution to **architecture** (though their agricultural buildings were also impressive). The Templars gained the right to build their own churches and maintain their own priests from Pope **Innocent II**, with the issuing of the Papal Bull *Omne Datum Optimum*. They built many types of churches, including oblong, cruciform, octagonal, polygonal and **round churches** (or rather circular-naved, which became something of a trademark). They built both parish churches and chapels serving **Preceptories**. In their own chapels the brethren could worship without coming into contact with females.

Templar churches were often built with great precision. Anomalies have been noticed in the **alignment of Templar churches**. Sometimes Templars were donated already existing churches, along with the tithes from their lands. Bishop Henry of Lebus (**Germany**) donated them the Church of Tempelberg in 1244, for example.

## Cistercian Order

The Cistercians were a strict Order of monks who wore white habits. They were founded in **Burgundy** by Abbot Robert (1027–1111), a **Benedictine** monk who wished to establish a more austere community. He felt that the Benedictines had grown somewhat lax, no longer working the land themselves for example and living a little too comfortably for true servants of God.

Robert had been a monk at Montier-la-Celle, and then Abbot of St Michel de Tonnerre, which he endeavoured in vain to reform. He then became Prior of St Aiyoul. In around 1075, Robert left this monastery and, accompanied by a number of hermits, who had chosen him as their leader, established a monastery amid forests at Molesme. He insisted on the monastic Rule of St Benedict being obeyed to the letter. He led Molesme until about 1097 when he felt moved to found an even stricter community. This he did near Dijon at Citeaux (the origin of the name Cistercian). The monks and patrons of Molesme protested at Robert's abandoning them and eventually persuaded him to return. Citeaux passed to Abbot Alberic, and then to **Stephen Harding**, a monk of English origin.

In about 1112 Harding's Cistercian community was joined by Bernard of Fontaines and thirty other young nobles, an influx that re-energised the community. Bernard subsequently founded the first daughter house of the Cistercians at Clairvaux, on land granted by Count **Hugh of Champagne**. This was the first of many Cistercian foundations that would spring up across Europe during Bernard's time as Abbot. Bernard became tremendously influential and would eventually be canonised as St **Bernard of Clairvaux**. Bernard conceived of the Cistercians as spiritual soldiers, fighting a battle against their own weak flesh and against demonic temptations. Their weapons were to be discipline, prayer, work, abnegation of the individual will and mortification of the flesh. The monks ate no meat and dined in silence, while hearing Bible readings.

The Cistercians favoured remote locations for their settlements; however, their leaders were deeply involved in political and sometimes military affairs. Bernard was a supporter of the early Templars, and the Cistercians had a strong influence on the early Military Order, possibly inspiring their white clothing. A Cistercian monk, Jean Michael, wrote down the **Rule** of the Knights Templar after the Order was recognised at the **Council of Troyes**, where St Bernard presided. A later Pope, **Eugenius III**, was a former Cistercian monk. Eugenius persuaded Bernard to help preach the **Second Crusade**. There was no expectation, however, that the monks would actually participate in the Crusade, and they were discouraged even from **pilgrimage**. In 1147, Bernard wrote to his brother abbots, advising them to prohibit their monks from joining the expedition. Monks were expected to seek salvation in their monasteries.

In the twelfth and thirteenth centuries the Cistercian Order expanded exponentially. It became very rich and powerful as a land-owning organisation. (Cistercian nunneries were also founded.) Every year the Abbots of the Cistercian Order, including those from **Scotland** and northern **England**, met for a General **Chapter**, held at Citeaux. The Abbot of Citeaux presided over the chapter and was the head of the Order. Parts of these meetings may have been secret, though others were open and attended by secular nobles, for example Boniface of Montferrat attended at Citeaux on the eve of the **Fourth Crusade**, and the Crusade was preached there. After the Fourth

Crusade a number of Cistercian establishments were founded in Latin-occupied Greece. Cistercians like the uncompromising **Arnaud Aumery** also played a part in the **Albigensian Crusade**.

The Cistercians admitted 'lay brothers' who took responsibility for the working of the land and looking after the vast flocks of sheep kept by a number of monasteries. The choir monks no longer did manual labour themselves. Their standards of simplicity, apostolic poverty and discipline were adversely affected by this development, and though the order survived it was somewhat superseded as a spiritual force by the **Franciscan** and **Dominican** Orders. Later the Protestant Reformation in Britain and **French Revolution** diminished the Cistercian Order's power and influence. Many Cistercian Abbeys survive, however, intact or in ruins. Some Cistercian buildings incorporate a degree of symbolism in common with Templar ones. Kirkstead was an Abbey of the Cistercian Order in Lincolnshire. The pilgrims' chapel there, called St Leonards Without, contains a roof boss featuring the **Agnus Dei** holding a flowery cross of a kind popular with the Templars. There is also the tomb effigy of a knight that has lost its lower legs. The effigy dates from around 1250 and is unusual in that the knight is wearing his great helm, which masks his face.

## *Clandestine Grand Masters*

The Clandestine Grand Masters were those that **Bernard Raymond Fabré-Palaprat** claimed succeeded **Jacques de Molay** and secretly preserved the Templar tradition. This is the list of those who allegedly led the Templars over the five centuries following the suppression:

| | |
|---|---|
| 1313–24 | **Jean-Marc Larmenius** |
| 1324–40 | Thomas Theobald of Alexandria |
| 1340–49 | Arnaud de Braque |
| 1349–57 | Jean de Claremont |
| 1357–81 | Bertrand du Guesclin |
| 1381–92 | Bernard Arminiacus |
| 1419–51 | Jean Arminiacus |
| 1451–72 | Jean de Croy |
| 1472–78 | Bernard Imbault |
| 1478–97 | Robert Leononcourt |
| 1497–1516 | Galeatius de Salazar |
| 1516–44 | Phillippe Chabot |
| 1544–74 | Gaspard de Galtiaco Tavanensis |
| 1574–1615 | Henri de Montmorency |
| 1615–51 | Charles de Valois |
| 1651–81 | Jacques Ruxellius de Granceio |

| 1681–1705 | Jacques Henri Duc de Duras |
| 1705–24 | Phillippe, Duc d'Orleans (**Philip II, Duke of Orleans**) |
| 1724–37 | Louis Augustus Bourbon |
| 1737–41 | Louis Henri Bourbon Conde |
| 1741–76 | Louis-Francois Bourbon Conti |
| 1776–92 | Louis-Hercule Timoleon, Duc de Cosse Brissac (executed during the French Revolution) |
| 1792–1804 | Claude-Mathieu Radix de Chavillon |
| 1804–38 | **Bernard Raymond Fabre-Palaprat** |

The names up to Phillipe Duc d'Orleans are apparently signed on the controversial **Larmenius Charter**. There was an alternative list of Clandestine Grand Masters, promulgated fifty years earlier than Bernard Raymond Fabré-Palaprat's, by the **Karl, Baron von Hund**, a German **Freemason**. Von Hund claimed that the Order of the Temple had survived secretly in **Scotland** rather than France, and that Jacques de Molay had passed his authority to a Templar called Pierre d'Aumont rather than Jean-Marc Larmenius. He claimed to derive his knowledge from exiled **Jacobites**.

## Clement V (1264–1314)

Clement V was the **Pope** who, with initial reluctance, presided over the demolition of the Order of the Temple. He was also the Pope who imposed **excommunication** on **Robert the Bruce**, and who removed the Holy See from Rome to **Avignon**. His reign began in 1305, two years after the outrage committed against **Boniface VIII**. Originally Bernard de Got, Archbishop of Bordeaux he owed his elevation to **Philip the Fair**, King of **France**, and also to the support of the influential cardinal **Napoleone Orsisi** (who later became a critic of Clement's pontificate).[196] According to a rumour reported by the Florentine chronicler Giovanni Villani, Clement had secretly promised Philip that he would be the king's bondsman. At any rate Clement never obtained the resources to resist the king.

King Philip and his brother **Charles of Valois** were foremost among other princes who attended Clements's coronation in the church of St Just in Lyons, which technically lay just outside the Kingdom of France at that time. After the solemnities, the papal procession passed through the streets. A section of wall suddenly toppled under the weight of spectators on a rooftop. The Duke of Brittany was mortally injured, Charles of Valois badly hurt and the Pope was thrown from his white horse. It was not the best of omens.[118]

Clement V remained in France despite the consternation of Italian ecclesiastics. His early years as Pope were dominated by his deteriorating health. One of his first acts was to increase the number of cardinals by eighteen, of whom ten were French (including the three who later would interrogate the Templars at **Chinon**). Several of these were receiving pensions from King Philip; French control of the Curia was quite entrenched. Clement did not push the doctrine of Papal Supremacy, which Boniface had taken to extremes. He shelved **Unam Sanctum**, and exonerated the Colonnas who had been allies of the French during the **Anagni** incident. In 1306, Clement summoned from Cyprus the **Grand Masters** of the two main Military Orders to discuss the prospect of a new Crusade, and the **scheme to merge the Military Orders**. Jacques de Molay of the Templars made clear his feeling that the plan had more potential drawbacks than advantages. **Fulk de Villaret** of the **Hospitallers** was more taciturn but no more positive. Clement also sought to establish peace between the Kingdoms of France and England as a preliminary to the launching of a new Crusade.

It is unclear how much Clement knew of Philip the Fair's plan to attack the Knights Templar. The Pope and King had discussed the Templars the previous summer, but the King had not gained the Pope's permission to proceed. By the time Clement became aware of the **arrests** (October 1307) the campaign was already a *fait accompli*. **Confessions** had already been secured by means of **torture**. Nonetheless, the Pope expressed indignation at Philip's insolence and at first seemed sceptical regarding the **accusations against the Order**. Moreover, from the Pope's standpoint the arrest of members of an exempt Order (and their treatment 'without due leniency') was a flagrant assault on ecclesiastical jurisdiction. The involvement of the excommunicated **Guillaume de Nogaret** made this new assault on Papal authority even worse.

By this time, though, confessions were already being produced from **Jacques de Molay** and other leading Templars, and the king was enflaming the population with anti-Templar propaganda. Under pressure, Clement issued the bull *Pastoralis Praeeminentiae*, ordering the arrest of the Templars in every country where they were found, and the sequestering of their land in the Church's name. Clement continued to be displeased with Philip however, especially with the King's refusal to transfer the Templar prisoners into ecclesiastical custody. In February 1308 Clement suspended the Inquisition's activities against the Order in France.

Philip kept the pressure on Clement. During the ecclesiastical assembly at **Poitiers**, the royal Jurist **Guillaume de Plaisians** denounced the Templars, raving against their heretical depravity. He harangued Clement on the urgency of the matter and all but threatened the Pope with destruction if he failed to act against the Order. Evidently it became easier for the Pope to convince himself of the Templars' guilt and to become an active agent in their persecution than to risk continuing to be remotely critical of **Capetian** policy. (The fate of Boniface VIII no doubt played on Clement's mind.) After Poitiers he agreed to establish hearings into the Templars' guilt collectively and individually. As time went by the Pope began to press for torture to be used against the Templars in those lands where confessions were not forthcoming. He seems to have convinced himself that only the use of torture (euphemistically termed *ecclesiastical procedure*) would get to the truth.

At the **Council of Vienne** in 1312 he delivered the decree ***Vox in Excelso***, having imposed silence on the assembly on pain of excommunication so that none might speak out against it. The only concession the Pope won was retaining the Templars' land for the Church and passing it to the Hospitallers (though Philip and his heirs extorted huge sums of money from the Hospitallers over the years in 'costs'). Like the King, it is likely that Clement V profited richly from the plundering of the Temple, but if so, neither lived long to enjoy the spoils: Clement died of stomach or bowel cancer soon after the burning of Jacques de Molay.

## Clifford's Tower

Clifford's Tower is a quatrefoil-shaped shell keep standing in ruins atop a mound (motte) in **York**, northern **England**. It is the last remaining part of York Castle, which was built soon after the Norman Conquest. There was formerly a wooden fortress on the spot, which was burned down in 1190 by local mobs when it became a place of short-lived refuge to a number of **Jews**, of whom 150 perished. It is said some of the Jewish leaders killed themselves and their families, rather than fall into the hands of the rioters. The stone tower dates to the mid-thirteenth century, when the castle was rebuilt by **Henry III**. York Castle was one of the places where the English Templars from the regions were imprisoned. (They were possibly kept in a part of the castle since demolished.) Clifford's Tower received its name after 1322, when Roger de Clifford was executed for supporting an unsuccessful rebellion against **Edward II**. His body was hung in chains from the tower.

## Cluny

The Abbey of Cluny was a **Benedictine** foundation that came to prominence in the eleventh century, having been founded in the late tenth. It was the leading monastic institution of the time, originally founded with a reforming mission. It came to boast the largest **Romanesque** abbey church of the time, with numerous towers, wings and side chapels. Only one tower and transept remain after the greater part of the building was despoiled during the **French Revolution**. The **Cistercian Order** was an offshoot of the Benedictine Order, and Citeaux, a humbler place, was established some fifty miles north of the great monastery. The motive for this move was to recapture the original simplicity and asceticism of the

Benedictine movement. The founder Cistercians, principally Robert of Molesme, deemed Cluniac monasticism to have become too grand and formalised, and the monks had taken to employing tenants and servants to do the menial or hard work.

## Coffret d'Essarois

The Coffret d'Essarois is a stone casket of dubious provenance, speculatively attributed to the Templars, and decorated with scenes and symbols of an occult or alchemical character. These include (on the lid) a hermaphrodite figure (**Baphomet**) holding staffs capped with the moon and sun, above a seven-pointed star, a **skull** and a **pentagram**. Strange Arabic-style script surrounds this.

## Confessions

Confession in a religious context is a sacrament of the Catholic Church whereby the believer admits his sins to a priest hoping for absolution. In a legal context it is admitting to having committed a crime. These definitions began to fuse when the **Inquisition** strove to secure confessions of **heresy** from suspects. Roman law tended to require confessions before sentences could be passed. In the Templars' case, torture was used to force confessions to the items in the **accusations against the Order**.

## Confraters/Confreres

Confraters were honorary members or associate brothers of the Temple. Many were men of status who protected the Order and donated land or money (or pledged property in their wills) in order to share in the spiritual benefits that they believed would be bestowed on the Templars.[119] Prominent Confraters included **Fulk V, Count of Anjou**, Alfonso Henriques of Portugal, Ramon Berengeur III of Portugal and **William Marshall, Earl of Pembroke**. Some joined the Order on their deathbeds.

## Conrad III of Germany (1093–1152)

Conrad III was the first **Hohenstaufen** King of **Germany**, although he was never crowned **Holy Roman Emperor**. He was the son of Frederick of Hohenstaufen, Duke of Swabia. Conrad led the German contingent of the **Second Crusade**, having been persuaded to take the cross by **Bernard of Clairvaux**. Conrad arrived at **Constantinople** in December 1146, some time before the French forces led by **Louis VII**, which included the Templars. The Germans has come into conflict with the Greeks during their passage. Conrad and the Byzantine Emperor **Manual I Comnenus** had exchanged antagonistic messages, and below Constantinople the Germans found themselves confronting a Byzantine army that included Turkish mercenaries. Eventually crossing into Anatolia, Conrad's army was bloodily mauled by the **Seljuks** at **Dorylaeum** (where in 1197 the **First Crusade** had gained a victory). Conrad returned to Constantinople to make peace with Manuel, and later sailed to the **Holy Land**. He achieved nothing of note and returned to Germany disillusioned after the failed siege of **Damascus**. He had more success defeating his **Guelf** rivals at home.

## *Conrad IV/Conrad II of Jerusalem* (1228–54)

Conrad IV of **Hohenstaufen** was the son of the Emperor **Frederick II** and of **Yolande of Jerusalem**. He was recognised as Conrad II of Jerusalem, inheriting the throne from his mother who died shortly after his birth. He was also King of Germany from 1237 and of Sicily from 1250 until his death. Conrad was dragged into his dynasty's struggle against the papacy. In 1245, Pope **Innocent IV** sought to depose Conrad in Germany, and warfare ensued against the papal candidate Henry Raspe. Conrad held on in Germany and also defeated the Pope's next ally William of Holland. Conrad succeeded his father in 1250 in Sicily and the **Guelf-Ghibelline** wars carried on. He came to Italy, continuing the struggle there, in alliance with **Manfred** his half-brother, who would succeed him. He died in 1253 of malaria, leaving one young son, **Conradin**, by his wife Elizabeth of Bavaria. Conrad was an absentee ruler as far as the **Kingdom of Jerusalem** was concerned.

## *Conrad of Montferrat/Conrad I of Jerusalem* (*c.* 1145–92)

Conrad was the second son of **William V, Marquis of Montferrat**. Conrad had been engaged in the service of the **Byzantine Empire**, but embarked for the **Holy Land** after reputedly committing a murder in Constantinople, abandoning a wife, a niece of the Emperor, in the process.[120] In 1187, Conrad sailed to the Levant, only to find that the **Kingdom of Jerusalem** was almost completely lost to the forces of **Saladin**. When Conrad arrived in **Tyre**, the port was on the point of surrendering. Conrad took over the defence and put a stop to any defeatist talk. For the next two years, Conrad fended off repeated attacks, not even wavering when Saladin paraded the Marquis, his captured father, below the walls. (Conrad said he would kill the old man himself rather than surrender the city.) During this period, Conrad also won an impressive naval victory over an Egyptian fleet, just off shore, with the help of the Templars and **Hospitallers**. The Christian fleet captured eleven Muslim galleys.

In 1189, Saladin released **Guy de Lusignan**. Conrad refused to recognise Guy's authority, claiming that he had lost any legitimacy at **Hattin**, and that anyway, his coronation had violated the will of **Baldwin IV**. He turned Guy away from the walls of Tyre. Guy took his followers north to commence the siege of Acre. Conrad later joined forces with Guy outside Acre, but still refused to recognise him, especially after **Sibylla** and her two daughters perished. The majority of Barons wanted to make Conrad the new king and to that end married him to the young Queen **Isabella of Jerusalem**, having first forced her to put aside her inconvenient husband **Humphrey of Toron**. (Everyone seemed to have forgotten about Conrad's jilted Greek wife.) Thus Conrad claimed the title King of Jerusalem. His most significant opponent was **Richard the Lionheart,** who persisted in recognising Guy's claim. (The Templars seem to have remained aloof durung this round of dynastic struggles, having paid a price for their involvement under **Gerard de Ridefort** in the last round.)

Conrad helped negotiate the surrender of Acre and led the Crusaders into the city. New squabbles over the Kingship of Jerusalem followed and Conrad was persuaded to agree to Guy's reinstatement in exchange for being named his heir and for being given control of a number of cities, including Tyre and **Sidon**. In 1192 a new referendum among the barons finally rejected Guy's claim to the throne, and Conrad was officially recognised, much to Richard's annoyance. On 28 April, four days after learning of his restoration as titular King of Jerusalem, Conrad was slain by Syrian **Assassins** disguised as monks. It seems the Assassins were put up to the murder, but by whom has always been a matter of debate. Much suspicion was attached to Richard at the time, but Saladin also had an interest in depriving the Christians of a strong leader. Alternatively, the Assassins could have had their own private grudge against Conrad. Conrad's pregnant widow was hastily married off to **Henry II, Count of Champagne.**

## *Conradin* (1256–68)

Conradin was the Duke of Swabia and rightful heir to the crowns of Sicily and **Jerusalem** (where he was recognised as Conrad III). He was the son of **Conrad IV** of Germany/II of Jerusalem (d. 1254), and the grandson and last descendant of **Frederick II** and of **Yolande of Jerusalem**. Thus he was the last of the houses of **Hohenstaufen** and Rethel (the dynasty descending from **Baldwin II**). Conradin's authority in Sicily was usurped during his childhood by his uncle **Manfred**. After Manfred's death at Benevento at the hands of **Charles of Anjou**, Conradin, aged fifteen, came to take up the baton of the **Ghibelline** cause. Conradin met with enthusiastic support from Italians sick of the Papal-Angevin yoke. After initial successes, he met Charles's forces at Tagliacozzo, where the **Guelf**/French forces ultimately triumphed. Conradin was captured while making for Sicily and beheaded in Naples. His death caused arguments over the succession to the title of Jerusalem. Ironically, one of his female relations, Mary of **Antioch**, sold her claim to the title to Conradin's implacable enemy Charles of Anjou, who was subsequently recognised by the **Pope** and by the Templars.

## Consorores

Consorores were female honorary associates of the Order of the Temple. Sometimes women became consorores when their husbands became **confraters**. They made an annual donation to the Order and on their deaths were buried in the Order's churchyard. Some consorores (or *Donatae*) might even receive the habit of the Order and live within the precincts of the **Preceptories**. One such seems to have been Açalidis, a woman of Rousillon who, for the good of her soul and those of her parents, gave her property in the region, as well as her body and soul, to God and the Templars. Other women seem to have become full **Sisters of the Order**, vowing obedience to the Master, despite the **Rule's** forbidding of the admission of females.[121]

## Conspiracy Theories

The Templar **trials** were among the biggest ever held. The allegations all implied that the brethren were part of an unholy conspiracy to undermine **Christendom** from within. If there was truth behind the accusations then the Templars were perpetrators of one of the greatest conspiracies in history. If they were innocent, they were the victims of no less audacious a conspiracy on the part of **Philip the Fair**, his ministers, the **Inquisition** and senior **Catholic** clergy.

Since their demise, the Templars have been associated with multifarious other conspiracies, feeding the literary genre of 'Templarism'. Many of these theories rely upon the idea of Templars having **continuity** as a secret society, and being the guardians of some great **treasure** or powerful secret knowledge. The Templars have been linked to Ancient **Egypt**,[122] the **Cathars** and **Gnostics**,[123] the **Essenes**,[124] the **Assassins**,[125] the Alchemists, the **Rosicrucians**, the Illuminati, and the **Priory of Sion**.[126] They have been identified as the guardians of the **Ark of the Covenant**, or the **Holy Grail**,[127] or even of the embalmed head of **Jesus Christ**.[128] They have been said to engage in diabolical occult rituals or enlightened **goddess veneration**,[129] and to possess ancient wisdom relating to sacred geometry. They are said to have left clues and codes in documents and paintings, in the details of buildings and the placement of those monuments in the landscape.[130] They have been cast as the originators of **Freemasonry** and the group behind the **French Revolution**.[131] Indeed, they have been associated with powerful, shadowy forces operating in the world to this day.

Many Templarist conspiracy theories associate the order with **Rennes le Château** or with **Rosslyn Chapel**. Conspiracy theories are, by nature, based on circumstantial evidence and conjecture. The Templars came into being somewhat mysteriously, and rose to power with relative rapidity. Their demise was also sudden and strange, and in the interim they were generally secretive about their internal affairs. This has made it easy for theorists to attach them to all sorts of notions.

## Constance of Antioch (1127– c. 63)

Princess Constance of **Antioch** was the only child of Bohemond II of **Antioch** and of Alice of Antioch. Her father was killed while she was an infant. Her grandfather, **Baldwin II of Jerusalem**, acted as regent but was resisted by Alice, who went so far as to seek an alliance with **Zenghi**. Baldwin prevented this and Alice was exiled. In 1136, King **Fulk** invited **Raymond of Poitiers** to Antioch to become the new ruler. It seems Alice was led to believe that she was to be his bride, but instead he was married to Constance. In 1149, Raymond was killed at Inab. Constance and the Patriarch helped organise a determined defence of Antioch, which was soon heavily besieged by **Nur ed-Din**'s forces. The city held out until a relief force led by **Baldwin III of Jerusalem** and the Templars arrived to drive off the enemy. Four years later, Constance married **Reynald de Chatillon**. Constance's eldest son from her first marriage was to become **Bohemond III, Prince of Antioch**. Constance would die in exile, having been forced by civil unrest to install her son as prince in around 1161.

## Constantine I, Emperor (272–337)

Constantine I, later called Constantine the Great, was proclaimed Emperor of Rome in AD 306. He was the first Emperor to legalise Christian worship, which he did in AD 313. He also presided over the Council of Nicæa in AD 325, where representatives of the various Christian sects argued over the nature of God and **Christ**, and where those advocating the doctrine of the Holy Trinity won out (also imposing the view that Christ was coeternal with God, and of the same substance, and denouncing the Arians who thought otherwise).

Constantine's mother, the Empress **Helena**, was a Christian, and attributed to her are the discovery of the sites of the **Holy Sepulchre** in **Jerusalem**, and the Grotto of the Nativity in **Bethlehem**. Constantine built the first Basilica of St Peter in Rome, and founded a New Rome at **Byzantium**, which became Constantinople. Constantine supposedly converted to Christianity after the miracle associated with his victory over his rival Maxentius at the Battle of Milivian Bridge. (He is said to have seen the **Chi-Rho** in a dream, and been told 'in this sign conquer'. He had his legionaries paint the symbol on their shields and they went on to win.) Constantine donated to the Pope not only buildings in Rome but also sovereignty over the Western Empire. In the eighth century the Church produced a document called the '**Donation of Constantine**'. It was denounced as a forgery by the secular claimant to Constantine's legacy, the Holy Roman Emperor Otto III.

## Continuity (Alleged Templar)

Certain people, including some in modern **neo-Templar** groups, advance the idea that the historical Knights Templar were not extinguished, but that after the **suppression** the surviving brethren regrouped in secret. The **conspiracy theory** has it that the Templars survived as a secret society for five centuries, before resurfacing in **Paris** during the regime of **Napoleon Bonaparte**. Advocates of the idea are tempted to take seriously the claims of **Bernard Raymond Fabré-Palaprat** and accept the **Larmenius Charter** and the list of **clandestine Grand Masters** as authentic. This version of events supposes secret continuity within **France**. The alternative speculation is that the Templars found sanctuary in **Scotland**, where they became mixed up with guilds of stonemasons, and eventually created the fraternity of **Freemasonry** to preserve their secrets.

A mystery surrounds the disappearance of fifty to 100 Templars from France, a probably greater number from **England** and **Ireland** and seemingly nearly all of them from Scotland (where only two were arrested in the English-controlled lowlands). However, there followed nearly 500 years during which there was little hint that the Templars were still in existence. While the probability of the Templars existing undetected for such a length of time seems remote, it is possible there was some Templar networking in the decades immediately following the suppression. There may have been a low-key association of mutual support among former brethren, both within the scattered monasteries in which many former Templars found themselves and in the wider world where others were living as fugitives. The idea of the Templars quietly continuing as an entity is supported by an obscure reference to an unnamed **Master of the Temple in England** with the assent of the brethren releasing from his vows one **William de Grafton**, the last Preceptor of Grafton. This occurred in 1331, twenty years after the suppression (during which time William had been living at **Selby Abbey**). The implication seems to be that there was still a coherent Templar Order in England, in defiance of *vox in excelso*, and that at least one Master may have succeeded **William de la More**.[132]

That an underground society of former Templars would have continued for more than a generation and would have gone on recruiting new members seems unlikely. Who would have joined it when it conferred no dignity and served no obvious purpose? The preservation of esoteric, secret knowledge of some sort is one of the few motives the Templars could have had for seeking to survive as an underground movement after they had lost everything else – all their land, privileges, public respectability, their ability to perform their **Crusading** mission, even the right to openly exist; but no-one has proved that the Templars ever possessed such knowledge.

## Copper Scroll

The Copper scroll is one of the **Dead Sea Scrolls**. It contains, engraved on a rolled sheet of copper, an inventory of various hidden **treasures**, possibly those of the Jewish Temple. It proves that there were treasures secreted around the **Holy Land**. The scroll also provides directions for the recovery of these treasures, but they have proved difficult to interpret. Among the things listed are ingots of gold and silver talents, hidden in tombs and caves and down cisterns. The Templars reputedly discovered some buried coins by accident during the construction of **Pilgrim's Castle**. Perhaps these relate to the caches described in the Copper Scroll.

## Coptic Christians

The Coptic Church was the indigenous Christian population of **Egypt**, owing allegiance to the **Patriarch** of **Alexandria**. In medieval times they were a much more substantial minority than they are now. The **Ethiopian** Orthodox Church was affiliated to the Coptic Church, and under the direction of Alexandria. Coptic Christians were Monosyphites, believing Christ to have a single, divine nature (in this belief they split from the rest of the Church after the Council of Chalcedon in AD 451). There was also a Coptic language, related to Ancient Egyptian but written in the Greek Alphabet. Both Ethiopian and Egyptian Copts had a religious presence in **Jerusalem** in the period of the Crusades. The Copts were suspected by their **Muslim** rulers of sympathy with the **Franks** and after the **Seventh Crusade** were subjected to greater persecution.

## Cords

The **accusations against the Order** stated that the Templars were made to wear cords around their middles, which had beforehand been wrapped around their **idol**, the **head** they worshipped. These implicitly kept them in its snare by means of sinister forces. The Templars nowhere denied wearing cords, but denied any such sinister associations. Some maintained that the cord was a sign of purity. The Templars were told never to remove these cords. Richard de Colingham, the Preceptor of Sandford, Oxfordshire, **England**, called the cord belt the 'girdle of chastity'.

Cords were also significant to the **Cathars** and were known to be a sign that one had received the *Consolamentum* rite. Of course this could be evidence of Templar links to the Cathars, but it could only be an attempt by the accusers to make it look that way. Many monks, including **Franciscans**, wore cord belts about their habits, although not directly against their skin, as it was claimed the Templars did.

## Council of Clermont

The Council of Clermont, in November 1095, was the symbolic beginning of the crusading era. It was a grand Church assembly called by Pope **Urban II** and attended by many nobles, at which the Pope preached the **First**

**Crusade**. After the episcopal council in the cathedral, Urban II addressed a massed crowd of people in a field outside the city. He called on them to put aside their disputes and unite to fight for Christ, to **take the cross**, and win absolution and salvation (and possibly riches) fighting to liberate **Jerusalem** and the Eastern Church from the infidel. The crowd responded enthusiastically with shouts of 'God wills it!'

## Council of Troyes

The Council of Troyes was an ecclesiastical council convened during the Papacy of Honorius II. It was convened in January 1129, at **Troyes** in **Champagne** (north-eastern **France**). It was attended by the host, Count **Theobald of Champagne**, and presided over by the Papal Legate Matthew, Cardinal-Bishop of Albano. **Hugues de Payens** and five of the Templars then in Europe also attended, as well as Abbots **Stephen Harding** and **Bernard of Clairvaux** of the **Cistercians**, and various other prelates including the Archbishops of **Reims** and Sens and the Bishops of **Paris** and Troyes. The scribe was the Cistercian monk **Jean Michel**. Hugues de Payens (who had recently been travelling though the West advancing his Order's cause) addressed the Council, outlining the Templars' purpose and their mode of life. Despite some lingering doubts concerning the morality of crusading among certain attendees, the council came out in favour of recognizing the new Order of the Temple. The influential St Bernard's support doubtless swayed things in the Templars' favour. The Templar Order was endorsed and given its Latin **Rule**, which was drawn up in the course of the council. These events went in tandem with a drive to recruit new members for the order and new lay **Crusaders** to assist the Holy Land.[221]

## Council of Vienne

The Council of Vienne was a general ecclesiastical council, attended by many prelates. It had been planned since 1308 and was finally convened on 16 December 1311. It was held in Vienne Cathedral, above the Rhône. It was organised with three items on the agenda, namely Church reform, plans for a new **Crusade** and dealing with the Templars. The first items were farcical, considering that **Clement V**, the **Pope** presiding, was notorious for his nepotism. The only significant secular ruler who deigned to attend the Council was **Philip the Fair**. Philip arrived six months into the proceedings, and then only to force his way over the matter of the Templars.

Selective summaries of the Templar **trials** and lurid confessions were read out. As a formality, Clement called for any Templar who might wish to give a final defence of the Order's reputation to present himself. Surprisingly, seven did exactly that and claimed many more of their brethren were on their way. The guards were called and the Templars removed. The French clergy, clearly afraid of the King, favoured the immediate suppression of the Order of the Temple. All the rest had grave misgivings, and stood by the Templars. The English deputy, **Walter of Hemmingborough**, recorded the widespread feeling that the King of France was the source of all this scandal.

The king again convened his parliament, the Estates General, at nearby Lyons, and from there put pressure on Clement to comply with his agenda. Finally, the king and his formidable retinue arrived to force the issue. On 22 March, the clerics and delegates were summoned to the Cathedral where the Pope sat enthroned between **Philip the Fair** and Philip's son, the King of Navarre. The Pope imposed silence on the assembly, on pain of **excommunication**, and read out the fateful bull, *Vox in excelso*, which officially ended the existence of the Knights Templar. This was done not through vote or due legal process but by the Pope's personal authority. Two months later the Pope issued the bull *AD Providam*, bestowing most of the Templars' land on the Knights **Hospitaller**. It seems King Philip had been persuaded to relent on this matter, but only after being paid off with a great deal of Templars' and Hospitallers' wealth for his troubles. The Council of Vienne withdrew the Templars' Papal protection and denied their right to exist. The council also absolved the King of any wrongdoing in his dealings with **Boniface VIII**. A new Crusade was discussed, meanwhile, and taxes introduced to fund it, but the King would keep all the money from these for himself.

## Creslow

Creslow was a village near Aylesbury in Buckinghamshire, **England**, which was eventually depopulated. Its manor, which belonged to the Templars, survived until Victorian times, and was said to be haunted by a mysterious lady ghost. The village church was converted into a coach house and now survives as part of farm outbuildings. After the **suppression** of the Templars, the manor passed to the **Hospitallers**, and the estate became royal pastureland. The land passed into the hands of Cornelius Holland, one of the Parliamentarians who signed the death warrant of King Charles I.

## Cressac

Cressac sur Charente was a Preceptory in southern **France**. The Preceptory, known as the Dognon, was on land donated in the 1150s by the lord of Chatigniers. Only the Templar chapel survives. It suffered degradation during the **French Revolution** and was used as a barn for a time, but it has now been restored. The chapel is oblong and solidly built. It is classical in proportion, with a shallow pitched roof recalling Roman temple architecture. The church is entered through a **Romanesque** door in the west wall. The chapel contains original twelfth-century **wall paintings**. On one side above the door St **George** on foot protects the princess from the dragon. On the other side a mounted knight (or king) tramples a man under his horses' hooves, before another regal lady. To the left of a quatrefoil window – an engrailed cross within a circle. Within the upper two segments of the circle are a star formed of eight lines radiating from a central point and a letter 'A'. The lower two segments contain circles with dots in their centres. One of the side walls, meanwhile, has two friezes of mounted knights. On the upper register they ride out from a fortified city. More riders in white adorn the lower frieze, though strangely the tops of their heads are lost under the decorated border dividing the two scenes.

## Cressing Temple

Cressing Temple in Essex, south-east **England**, was an agricultural manor belonging to the Order. Two timber-framed barns survive there, each an impressive monument to the scale of the Templars farming operations. The estate was one of the earliest donated to the Order in England. It was granted by Matilda of Boulogne, the wife of King **Stephen**.

## Cresson, Battle of

The Battle of the Springs of Cresson was a military débâcle into which the **Grand Master** of the Templars, **Gerard de Ridefort**, according to one version, steered a force under his command. It took place near Nazareth. In retaliation for a raid on a Muslim caravan by **Reynald de Chatillon**, **Saladin** sent a large scouting party across the county of **Tripoli**, reconnoitring south of Tiberias with the permission of **Raymond III of Tripoli**. The Muslim force was led by al-Afdal, one of Saladin's sons. Gerard de Ridefort at the time was on his way to attempt to negotiate with Raymond, to try to persuade him to abandon his truce with Saladin and reconcile with **Guy de Lusignan**, the upstart who had become King of **Jerusalem**.

When Gerard de Ridefort learned of the **Muslim** incursion, he decided to attack the Saracens who were then passing homeward towards Syria. With Gerard were ninety warrior monks, including the **Hospitaller** Grand Master, **Roger de Moulins**, as well as some forty or fifty secular knights. On 1 May 1187, Ridefort's 140 knights intercepted the 7,000 Muslim warriors at the Springs of Cresson, north of Nazareth. The Marshal of the Templars, **Jacquelyn de Mailly**, and Roger de Moulins both supposedly protested against Gerard's reckless command to attack, but were goaded into following by de Ridefort's accusations of cowardice. The knights charged. The Muslims parted before them, and then closed in from the sides. The Templars were virtually wiped out, losing sixty knights. Jacquelyn de Mailly fought with particular valour, but was eventually overwhelmed. Only Gerard de Ridefort and two others managed to escape. Roger de Moulins and his Hospitallers were also killed. A party under **Balian of Ibelin** had been following Gerard de Ridefort. Balian found the castle of la Feve emptied of its garrison, which Ridefort had summoned to augment his meagre force. Later, Balian learned of the disaster. The battle was a blow to the Kingdom of Jerusalem, although it shamed Raymond into reconciling with Guy. It formed a prelude to **Hattin.**

**Ibn al-Athir** gave a different version of events. Al-Afdal's force had been plundering and laying waste the region of **Acre.** They left by night and in the morning attacked Sephoria in Galilee. A body of Templars and Hospitallers and others came out of the city to repulse them and a terrible battle followed. The Muslims gained the upper hand and put the Franks to flight. Some were killed and the rest captured.[133]

## Criticism of the Templars

Though the Templars had many admirers, and were praised by Abbot **Bernard of Clairvaux,** various **Popes** and men of power, they also had their critics, including prominent clerics. Clerical chroniclers like **William of Tyre** and **Walter Map** in the twelfth century, and **Matthew Paris** in the thirteenth, sometimes gave a negative account of the Templars' actions and motives. Peter the Venerable, Abbot of **Cluny,** had his doubts about the Templars, and whether knighthood and religious life could be compatible; and Guigo, a **Carthusian** Prior, wrote to **Hugues de Payens** that spiritual, internal battles had to be won before external enemies could be defeated.[134] John of Salisbury also criticised the Order's Papal privileges.

Bernard's *De laude Novae Militiae* was in part a response to pacifist criticism of the concept of a **Military Order.** Meanwhile, Bernard's support did not prevent the **Cistercian** theologian Isaac of Étoile criticizing the new knighthood as being from the 'fifth gospel' (i.e. heretical) because it was set up to force conversions through lances and cudgels and could freely despoil and kill those who were not Christians, and because it accounted as martyrs those who fell in battle. Some of these criticisms were valid, others less so. The Templars, unlike the later **Teutonic Knights,** did not actually force unbelievers into the Christian faith. Some of the opprobrium the Order attracted evidently came from Churchmen jealous of the Order's privileges, including its right to collect tithes and its independence from Episcopal jurisdiction. The **Hospitallers** also received censure for abusing privileges. **Jacques de Vitry,** for example, accused them of carrying off bodies for **burial** in their own cemeteries, so that they could collect the burial fees and deprive the parish churches of this income. The arguments between the Templars and Hospitallers, which sometimes escalated into open hostility, also caused criticism. De Vitry did, however, defend the vocation of the Military Orders in principle, and generally praised the Templars.

## Crosses (Templar)

The *Croix Pattée*, with flaring arms of equal length, was a characteristic Templar symbol, but not unique to the Order, much as round churches were a characteristic but not uniquely Templar architectural form. Pope Eugenius III granted the Templars the privilege of wearing a red cross on their white mantles or cloaks on the eve of the Second Crusade, but the exact type of cross was not stipulated. Some depictions show them wearing a cross with straight arms of equal length (a Greek cross). The Templars used other forms of cross besides, including the stepped-based **Calvary Cross**, the cross within a circle, and the cross with the diamond-shaped opening at its centre. At **Garway** there are also carvings of a **Maltese Cross** and a cross with a serpent entwined around it, but these may not be original Templar features. The order may also have used the double-barred **Patriarchal Cross** and the **Jerusalem Cross** with its four crosslets.

## Crusades

Describing the rise of the Crusades, Gibbon wrote that by the late eleventh century 'a new spirit had arisen of religious **chivalry** and Papal domination; a nerve was touched of exquisite feeling; and the sensation vibrated to the heart of Europe'.[135] This mysterious impetus led to the formation of mass volunteer armies forming an international coalition. They travelled far to fight the **Muslims**, in a campaign that resulted in the seizure or recovery of territory in the **Holy Land** and the establishment of the **Latin** states of **Edessa**, **Antioch**, **Tripoli** and the **Kingdom of Jerusalem**.

There are three main historical standpoints concerning the Crusades. The 'traditionalist' view holds that a distinct movement was born at the **Council of Clermont**, and that only the expeditions directed eastward, with the purpose of recovering or succouring **Jerusalem**, count as genuine Crusades. (The most significant of these are the conventionally numbered examples, the **First Crusade** to the **Seventh Crusade**.)[136] The 'pluralist' view, meanwhile, classes a Crusade as any campaign orchestrated by the **Pope**, where the Church offered remission of sins to those who vowed to participate. (These additional campaigns included the wars of the **Reconquista** in **Spain**, the **Albigensian** and **Baltic Crusades** against **heretics** and pagans, and the wars against the papacy's political enemies, such as those against the **excommunicated Hohenstaufen**, against **Byzantium** and against **Aragon**.) Finally, the 'generalist' view places the Crusades in a long-standing tradition of Holy War, and argues against their having a distinctive or novel character.

Ostensibly the First Crusade was a response to appeals for aid for the Eastern Christians and the **Byzantine Empire**. **Alexius I Comnenus** called for military support against the **Turks**. The West's response went beyond anything the Emperor had envisaged. It is possible **Urban II** fostered the crusading movement, seeing it as a way to unite in a common venture the fractious **Frankish**, feudal aristocracy. The Crusade would both reconcile and remove this troublesome element, at least temporarily, while at the same time bringing these volatile forces theoretically under the Church's authority. That may have been so but the long-term absence from their estates of so many lords potentially resulted in as much instability, hence the need for the 'peace of God' movement and the Church's pledge to protect the lands and dependants of those who embarked.

Guibert of Nogent (1053–1124), the **Benedictine** chronicler, saw crusading as a new path to salvation, allowing laymen to earn redemption without changing their status and becoming monks.[137] The romantic image of a Crusader is of a **knight** inspired by a sort of mystical fervour, fighting for salvation in the **Holy Land**. However, individuals of all classes and ages and of both sexes took part. (**Jonathan Riley-Smith** compared the First Crusade to a military monastery on the move, but it surely resembled a whole society in migration.) Those who swore to go on Crusade 'took the Cross', literally sewing a cloth cross onto their clothing, the cross having been given to them by a priest. This alluded to the biblical passage about taking up the cross and following Jesus. For noblemen, serving as a Crusader became almost a ritualistic activity. After 'taking the Cross' the Crusader would settle his accounts in the world and hear and redress grievances from his vassals. Then a priest would ceremonially bestow the scrip (pouch) and staff of a pilgrim. The Crusader might then make a tour of local pilgrimage shrines before taking final leave of home and kin and embarking by whatever means on the long and often lethal adventure. The enterprise itself would be punctuated by religious observances, such as fasts and processions. It has been argued that the **Military Orders** were not themselves technically Crusaders, although their fate was bound up with the Crusading movement. A Crusader was a layperson who had made a vow to go on a Crusade, which was conceived of as an armed **pilgrimage**, and generally a temporary condition. For the Military Orders, fighting the Saracens was more an extension of the spiritual battles waged by ordinary monks.

The Pope's offer of indulgence helped motivate the Crusaders. Crusaders believed their struggles were to do with the liberation of 'Christ's patrimony' from 'pagan' oppression. Not everyone, therefore, accepted the directing of the Crusades to places other than the Holy Land, as happened increasingly from the pontificate of **Innocent III** onwards.[138] The Templars' general reluctance to participate in the internal Crusades reflects their prioritisation of the cause of **Outremer**. The **Sixth Crusade** proved that a Crusade could succeed without ecclesiastical support. It became clear, subsequently, that many were unimpressed with the Popes for misusing spiritual armament by calling

Crusades against their temporal enemies, thereby bringing crusading into disrepute. According to **Matthew Paris**, the English knights accompanying the Crusade of **Richard of Cornwall** in 1240 swore publicly to proceed to the Holy Land, lest they be prevented from fulfilling their vows by the delaying tactics of the Roman Church or be turned aside to shed the blood of Christians in Greece or Italy.[139]

## Curse

Legend has it that **Jacques de Molay**, at his execution, placed a deadly curse on those responsible for the persecution of the Templars, especially Pope **Clement V** and King **Philip the Fair**. Clement died after much suffering less than a month later, while Philip perished after a hunting accident seven months after. It may be noted that strife also beset his three sons, who reigned in turn, and that none produced an heir, so that within a generation Philip's line was at an end. Meanwhile in **England** it happened that **Edward II**, who had presided over the Temple's destruction, also ended his reign in the most miserable circumstances. His fortunes, in fact, deteriorated sharply from the time of the **suppression** onwards. Certain Italian chroniclers recorded the story of a Templars' curse. Ferratto of Vicenza told a variant of it where a Neapolitan Templar, brought before the Pope, denounced Clement's unjust doings, and as he was about to be executed summoned the Pope and the King of France to answer for their crimes in God's presence within the year. Both **Guillaume de Nogaret** and **Guillaume de Plaisians** were apparently dead before the execution of the last **Grand Master**.

## Custos Chapellae

The Custos Chapellae was the guardian of a portable chapel tent that travelled with the Templars' camp in times of war.

## Cutting of the Elm

The 'Cutting of the Elm' was an event of 1188, supposedly occurring during a meeting of the Kings of **France** and **England**, in a field near **Gisors** in Normandy. It seems **Philip II Augustus** and **Henry II** found themselves in irreconcilable disagreement over some matter, and the elm tree that marked the spot of the discussions was felled on Philip's orders to mark the fact. The nature of the disagreement is unclear, but there does not appear to have been any mention that it involved the Templars, or their leadership, diverging from another body. Therefore the idea that the Cutting of the Elm signified the point where the Templars separated from a supposed **Priory of Sion** is in all likelihood a modern myth.

## Cyprus

Cyprus is an island in the **Levant**, and the third largest in the Mediterranean. Up until the late twelfth century it was a possession of the **Byzantine Empire**, and though it suffered Arab invasions and brief occupations, its population remained predominantly Greek Orthodox Christians. The destiny of the island was greatly affected by the coming of the **Crusades**.

In 1156, Cyprus suffered a raid by **Reynald de Châtillon** in which he committed atrocities against the local population, naturally turning them against the **Franks**.[140] The island subsequently became a dominion of the rebel Byzantine Prince **Isaac Ducas Comnenus**, who styled himself Emperor of Cyprus. Isaac took prisoner some troops shipwrecked there in 1291 on their way to take part in the **Third Crusade**; thus prompting **Richard the Lionheart** to overthrow Isaac, with the help of **Guy de Lusignan**, and to claim the island for himself. Richard subsequently sold it to the Knights Templar for 100,000 Saracen bezants (the equivalent of the cost of maintaining 330 knights for a year).[141]

The Templars made an initial payment of 40,000 and promised to raise the rest from the islanders. Templar rule on Cyprus was thus doomed to unpopularity. The island was entrusted to a Templar force consisting of only fourteen knights, twenty-nine mounted sergeants and seventy-four foot soldiers. This small, inexperienced garrison imposed heavy taxes. On Easter Day 1192 the Templars discovered that Cypriot conspirators were plotting against them. The Templars withdrew to their citadel in Nicosia, where the Cypriot rebels soon besieged them. After failing to negotiate a passage from the island, the Templars sallied out into the streets in a surprise dawn attack on the Cypriots. They crushed the rebellion, but subsequently decided the island was unmanageable and returned it to Richard. The knights returned to Syria, although they retained certain estates on Cyprus, which were probably part of the settlement. The island was ultimately given to **Guy de Lusignan** as compensation for surrendering his claim to the title King of **Jerusalem** (though his Cypriot descendants would revive the claim).[142] His brother Amalric inherited and his descendants ruled the island until 1474.

The Templars may have come to regret yielding up Cyprus, which could have served as an Order state where they could be masters and relatively safe from monarchs who might turn against them. Unlike the **Hospitallers**, who seized **Rhodes**, they never had the opportunity to create such a haven. It is possible they could have been attempting to consolidate their power on Cyprus with a view to eventually taking over when they assisted in the overthrow of **Henry II of Cyprus** in favour of his brother **Amaury de Lusignan**. In the event it was too late for any such plot. In obedience to Pope **Clement V**, Amaury had the Knights Templar on the island arrested. The **Marshal** of the Templars, **Ayme d'Oselier**, organised an abortive resistance, and was besieged in the castle at Limassol at the end of May 1308. He was persuaded to surrender. Afterwards 120,000 white *besants* were found by those making an inventory of the fortress, but apparently the Templars had hidden a much greater **treasure** elsewhere.[143] Seventy-four Templars were ultimately brought to trial before two papal legates, Bartholomew, Abbot of Alet and Thomas, Arch-priest of St John of Rieti. Twenty-one secular witnesses including sixteen knights also made statements. None were overtly hostile to the Order. Jacques de Plany testified to the courage of the Templars who had fought at **Acre**, Renaud de Soissons to their religious devotion. **Raymond de Bethno** had seen a miracle, which for him proved the Templars' innocence. The Templars themselves denied all the **accusations against the Order**.

Though the charges of **heresy** and depravity did not stand up, the situation worsened for the Templars after June 1310, when Henry II of Cyprus regained the throne. The Templars on Cyprus had been younger than their counterparts in France, as might be expected (only one was over fifty and only two had joined the Order before the fall of **Acre**). They had resisted arrest with greater vigour but had ultimately had no choice but to submit to the authorities. In August 1311, Clement V ordered a new trial for the Templars, and this time no **torture** was to be spared. The Templars were handed to an **inquisition** under the Papal legate Pierre de Plaine-Cassagne. In 1316, Ayme d'Oselier, and many other Templar prisoners, perished while imprisoned in the castle at **Kerynia**. Cyprus was governed by **Venice** from 1489, and fell to the **Ottoman** Empire in 1571. Surviving Crusader era buildings include two adjoining churches in Famagusta (in the eastern part of north Cyprus), which belonged to the Templars and Hospitallers.

# D

## *Dagobert II, King* (650–79)

Dagobert II was a King of the **Merovingian** dynasty, rulers of the 'Dark Ages' Frankish Kingdom of Austrasia. He was murdered near Stenay in December 679, leading to the rise of the Carolingian dynasty. He is linked tenuously to the Templars in a **conspiracy theory** propagated in *The Holy Blood and the Holy Grail*.

## *Damascus*

Damascus was the greatest city in Syria, as well as one of the most ancient. It was a rich and important caravan city on the silk road from China to the West. The city was famed for producing silk and highly refined steel blades.

The Caliph **Omar I** conquered Damascus from **Byzantium** for **Islam** in AD 636, the year before he took **Jerusalem**. Byzantine mosaic artists were employed to decorate the new Great Mosque. Damascus became the centre of the Islamic Empire under the **Umayyad** dynasty, whose armies subjugated territories from **Spain** to India. Under the succeeding **Abbasids**, Damascus lost prominence and was subordinated to **Baghdad**. The city subsequently changed hands between the Abbasids, the Fatimids and **Turkish** warlords. Just before the coming of the **Crusades**, the city became the centre of an independent Turkish emirate under the Burid dynasty. Damascus sometimes allied to the Crusaders, especially against the common enemy **Zenghi** of **Aleppo**. Even so, the Crusaders twice attacked Damascus. **Baldwin II** failed in an attempt to capture it in 1129, in what was probably the first major operation in which Templar Knights participated. In 1147 the forces of the **Second Crusade** again besieged the city, but were driven off by the governor **Unur**.

Damascus was always wary of Aleppan domination, and was prepared to renew its alliance with the Crusaders, even after the Second Crusade. Nonetheless, it fell under the rule of **Nur ed-Din** in 1154. Nur ed-Din had made himself the personification of the *Jihad* and taking Damascus was a major step in uniting **Muslim** Syria against the Latin **Kingdom of Jerusalem**. After Nur ed-Din's death, **Saladin** seized control of Damascus, uniting it with **Egypt** and encircling the Frankish Kingdom. From Damascus he launched out to destroy the Christians at **Hattin** and to take Jerusalem. Subsequently, Saladin's heirs, the Ayyubid Sultans, held power in Damascus and Egypt, though they were as often divided against each other as united against the Crusaders. Damascus would later fall under **Mongol** domination, and then under the domination of the **Mameluks**; nor were these the last ruthless conquerors to pass that way.

## Damietta

Damietta was a city in **Egypt**, at the eastern mouth of the River Nile. It was considered the key to Egypt and controlled a chain across the Nile Delta. It was the focus of two major attempts by crusading armies to conquer the country and safeguard **Jerusalem** from future threat from Egypt. Both the **Fifth Crusade** in 1219 and the **Seventh Crusade** in 1249 stormed Damietta. Both times they captured the city, after a long siege in the first instance, more rapidly in the second. The leaders of both Crusades were reluctant to relinquish Damietta, even when the **Ayyubids** offered to exchange it for **Jerusalem**. On both occasions they intended to occupy it on a permanent basis. They converted the city's mosques into churches and even started introducing Latin settlers. Both times the Crusaders were forced to surrender Damietta after facing defeat farther south, near **Mansourah**. The **Mameluks** later demolished it and rebuilt it farther inland, where it would be less at risk of siege.

## Dante (1265–1321)

Dante Alighieri was a Florentine poet who wrote in Italian. His most famous work was *La Divina Comedia* (*The Divine Comedy*). It described an odyssey of the soul through Hell, Purgatory and Heaven, encountering various other souls along the way. Dante's guide through Hell and Purgatory, in the poem, was the ghost of Virgil, the pagan Roman poet. In Paradise he encountered an idealised conception of his lost love Beatrice, a maiden whom he had met only twice in real life but who haunted his dreams forever. Dante was involved with the more worldly politics of his times. (He took a delight in placing his political opponents in his imagined hell.) He spent much time in exile from his home city, first in **Rome** as a virtual hostage of Pope **Boniface VIII** and later in Verona and Ravenna, where he was to die. His faction, known as the 'White Guelfs', who were suspicious of Papal power and aspired to civic autonomy, had lost power in Florence to the 'Black Guelfs', who were Papal loyalists. Had Dante gone back to Florence he would have been killed. When it came to the Suppression of the Knights Templar, meanwhile, Dante did not believe the **accusations against the Order**. He saw King **Philip the Fair** as a great wrong-doer, and once alluded to him as a 'new cruel Pilate'.

## Darbessaq

Darbessaq was a fortress in the north of the Crusader States, in the principality of **Antioch**. It was besieged in 1188 by **Saladin**'s armies. When the walls were breached the Templars astonished the **Muslims** by standing as still and quiet as statues in the breach. They resisted for a fortnight before capitulating. Later, Darbessaq was the place where the Templars from Baghras joined with Armenian forces under King Hethoum's sons, the princes Thoros and Lavon, to confront the **Mameluk** invaders. The Mameluks were again victorious.

## David (King of Israel) (c. 1000–960 BC)

King David, supposedly a former shepherd boy and giant slayer (I Samuel 17: 46–50), was the Biblical King of the **Jews** who took **Jerusalem** from the Jebusites. He was a successful general, as well as a musician and poet. Many of the Bible's psalms are attributed to him. He was also the one who brought the **Ark of the Covenant** to the Holy City. David was the founder of the Davidic line from which the Jews believed the messiah would come, and he was said to be the ancestor of **Jesus Christ**. King David's alleged tomb was later located in Jerusalem, in the basement of the same building that boasts the supposed room of the Last Supper on the upper floor.

## David I (King of Scotland) (c. 1084–1153)

King David I of **Scotland** was the fourth son of Malcolm Canmore and the sainted Queen Margaret. He was raised from the age of nine in the

Norman-dominated court of William II (Rufus) of **England**. He was given lands in Scotland, south of the River Clyde, on the death of his brother Edgar, while his brother Alexander I retained the north. David also had many lands in England, including Cumbria and Northumbria. He succeeded to the whole Kingdom of Scotland when Alexander died in 1224. He brought many Anglo-Norman courtiers with him and used them to set up a feudal system in Scotland. He also warmly received **Hugues de Payens** in 1228, having invited him north. David donated lands in Midlothian for the nascent Order of the Temple, some of the earliest grants it received. These lands became the **Preceptory** of **Balantradoch**. Hugues, during his brief stay, became David's trusted advisor and it is said almost persuaded him to come on Crusade.

David attempted to extend his kingdom south following the death of **Henry I, King of England**. (David had paid homage to Henry, Henry being the husband of his sister Matilda.) David was forced to withdraw from the Battle of the Standards in 1139, but the following year secured both recognition of Scotland's sovereignty and the ceding of Northumbria from King **Stephen**. The rest of David's reign was without major upheaval, and he died peacefully in Carlisle in 1153.

## Da Vinci Code

*The Da Vinci Code* is a 2003 novel by US author Dan Brown. The Templars feature in the plot, much as they do in the pages of *The Holy Blood and the Holy Grail*. In 2006 the novel was adapted into a feature film, directed by Ron Howard and starring Tom Hanks, Audrey Tatou and Sir Ian McKellen.

The plot follows the escapades of 'symbologist' Robert Langdon following the murder in the Louvre of curator Jacques Saunière – whose body was found arranged in a circle as the *Vitruvian Man*, with a **pentagram** drawn in blood on his chest. Langdon is whisked from the crime scene by cryptologist Sophie Nouveau, who is revealed as Saunière's estranged granddaughter. They have stumbled into a secret war. The **Catholic** Church is engaged in a struggle with the **Priory of Sion**, who are the secret guardians of the **Holy Grail**. The Catholic organization **Opus Dei**, in the form of the **flagellant** albino monk Silas, has murdered four leaders of the Priory. Saunière was the last, but he left clues for Langdon and Nouveau to follow to whatever it was he died protecting. The Templars come into the equation when Langdon explains that the Order discovered the Grail under the **Temple of Solomon** after the **First Crusade**. They found a secret which enabled them to blackmail the **Pope** and ascend to power, but which also resulted in their downfall. At length the pair arrive at the mansion of eccentric historian Leigh Teabing. Teabing reveals the Grail secret is that **Jesus Christ** and **Mary Magdalene** were married and had a daughter. Mary Magdalene *is* the Grail, hidden in the painting of the Last Supper by **Leonardo Da Vinci**. The Priory of Sion protected this secret and created the Templars in order to recover the sarcophagus of Mary Magdalene and the documents proving the bloodline from Jerusalem, to save them from a Church which was busy painting Mary out of history and hunting down her descendants. More twists and turns lead the characters to Britain, through **Temple Church,** and Westminster Abbey in London. The *denouement* takes place at **Rosslyn Chapel.** The book caused strident protests from religious groups. The *Da Vinci Code*'s central theme, the alleged relationship between Christ and Mary Magdalene, naturally caused the most controversy.

## Dead Sea Scrolls

The Dead Sea Scrolls were a cache of ancient writings discovered in a cave at Qumran near the Dead Sea between 1947 and 1956. They are some of the oldest known Biblical documents. Some were written on parchment, others papyrus, and one concerning buired treasure was of copper. Most are in Hebrew and date from around the first century. Some of the hundreds of scrolls may be the work of the **Essenes,** others could be from the archives of the Temple in **Jerusalem,** possibly hidden to save them from the Romans during the Jewish Revolt. The authors of some of the scrolls seem to have regarded themselves as the living embodiment of the Temple, a concept echoed in the way the Templars spoke of themselves. Some have speculated that the Templars might have found more such scrolls as these, and that these changed their belief system. This is something that could relate, remotely, to the accusation they faced that they taught that **Jesus Christ** the man was not God.

## Defence of the Order (at the Paris Trials)

The Templars gathered in **Paris** began to defend their reputation in an organised way during the Papal Commission, under the Archbishop of Narbonne, **Gilles Aicelin,** which convened in late 1309. Leadership did not come from the **Grand Master** or any of the high dignitaries of the Order, who were not prepared to commit themselves. In this respect **Jacques de Molay, Hugues de Pairaud** and the others let down the brethren who looked to them. De Molay, in an agitated state, did assert his willingness to defend the Order, but claimed it was difficult because he was in the King's custody, and he had nothing to spend on the defence. He also denied the confession he had supposedly made at **Chinon** when confronted with his testimony (the **Chinon Parchment**). However, de Molay later prevaricated, clearly hoping to gain a private audience with Pope **Clement V** to put forward his case personally. Other Templars also seemed fearful of defending the Order initially, having suffered much in custody. They began to admit, though, that **torture** had made them say things that were not true. **Ponsard de Gizy** was the first Templar to strenuously deny the accusations against the Order. He said thirty-six others had already perished under torture and described some of the things he had endured. Ponsard's credibility as a witness was undermined, however, when he was confronted with a letter he himself had allegedly written, complaining of various corrupt practices within the Order.

King **Philip the Fair** ordered all the Templars from the provinces who wished to defend the Order to be sent to the capital, probably not anticipating any coherent defence from the rank and file without leadership from the Grand Master. After a recess the Templars began to be called. In early 1310 many rallied to the Order's defence. A meeting of those willing to defend the Order was allowed. Five hundred and thirty-four Templars were assembled in the gardens of the Episcopal Palace, and the accusations were read to them. The commissioners required the Templar defendants to choose representatives or procurators. **Renaud de Provins** and **Pierre de Bologna** emerged as the Templars' spokesmen, later joined by the knights **Guillaume de Chambonnet** and **Bertrand de Sartiges**, though they were reluctant to become official procurators without the Grand Master's say so.

The defenders lodged a complaint over the conditions in which the brethren had been held – chained up, abused, and denied the sacraments. Bologna called the accusations shameful, wicked, and unreasonable things, and the invention of lying enemies. He argued that **confessions** already made should not prejudice the Order as they were made under tortures or through fear thereof. Provins requested access to the Order's confiscated funds so that they could mount a proper defence, and that the brethren be released from the custody of the king's men, so that they need no longer fear persecution (things the commission had no power or inclination to grant). Provins also used legal arguments, calling for the accuser to come forward, and be ready to pay restitution if it were found he had brought the case unjustly. If the Order had been denounced from within, meanwhile, then that evidence should not be admitted, as grievances should have been taken through the chain of command, and no such complaints had been raised within the Order.

The defence of the Order was gaining ground, and Philip the Fair decided to take drastic action to quash it. The king had his appointee **Philip de Marigny**, the Archbishop of Sens, reopen the inquest into the individual Templars in his jurisdiction, which happened to include the capital. On 10 May 1309 de Marigny convened a court to proceed against them. Bologna recognised this as an attempt to undermine the Papal commission, and appealed to the Archbishop of Narbonne to stop this. Aicelin simply bowed out, with some feeble excuse. The rest of the commission decided it had no authority to prevent the removal of the defendants to the court of Sens. When next the Papal commission convened, it was after the **burn-**

**ing** alive of fifty-four Templars in a field outside Paris, on the orders of the Archbishop of Sens, on the grounds that claiming innocence made them relapsed **heretics**. Others, who had never confessed, were condemned to life imprisonment. These were not the last burnings, and their effect was to terrorise the Templars appearing at the Council of Sens, who mostly returned to making confessions of guilt. At least one defendant, Aimery de Villiers le-Duc, maintained that the Order was innocent, but pleaded with the commission not to tell the king's agents what he was saying because they would have him burnt.

## De Laude Novae Militiae

*De Laude Novae Militiae* ('In Praise of the New Knighthood') was an open letter written by St **Bernard of Clairvaux**, at the request of **Hugues de Payens**, some time around the convening of the **Council of Troyes**. It was an endorsement of the Knights Templar. It conveyed in dramatic, rhetorical speech Bernard's vision of the Templars as embodiments of a knighthood reformed and spiritually purified, and turned to the service of God.[144] It contrasted these spiritual new **knights**, covered with the dust and grime of the desert, with their vain and worldly secular counterparts, who delighted in ornamental and, in Bernard's eyes, effeminate trappings.

Bernard referred to a 'new kind of knighthood, unknown to the ages gone by'. The life of meditation in the cloisters and tumult of warfare had been seen as opposites, traditionally. St Bernard, though, saw monasticism as a kind of warfare, monks fought against vice, temptation and **demonic** forces. The Templars would combine this spiritual battle with physical battle with flesh and blood enemies. They were to be as gentle as **lambs** but as ferocious as **lions**. When they killed it would not be a sin, because they were not striking down men but evil itself. This sanctified violence, however, was only justified when there was no other way of preventing the pagans from persecuting the faithful.

The tract became more mystical in tone as it went on. It spoke of the Temple in **Jerusalem**, the façade adorned with weapons, in place of the jewels of the old Temple. It spoke of the other holy sites in the **Holy Land** (which Bernard never saw, but where the Templars would act as guides and guardians to **pilgrims**) and explained the deeper significance of these places. It exalted Jerusalem and a promised land flowing with healing grace and vital sustenance for the whole world. 'Glorious things are spoken of you, city of God.' The tract evidently succeeded in encouraging many spiritually minded knights to seek admission to the Templars. It also set up an ideal image of Christian knighthood, bringing with it such high expectations that inevitably they would be hard for the Templars to live up to.

## De Molay International

De Molay International is a US-based group for young men between ages twelve and twenty-one. It was originally called the Order of De Molay, and is affiliated with **Freemasonry**. The group was founded in 1919 in Kansas City. It took **Jacques de Molay** as an example of **chivalry** and leadership, the qualities the founder, Frank S. Land, sought to promote in members.

## Demons

Demons are supposed supernatural spirits, malevolent in nature, in the service of the Devil and having certain powers in the world. Demons could be visible or invisible. Christian monks believed that they did battle against these external forces of spiritual evil when they devoted themselves to lives of purity and prayer. **Heretics** and **witches** were accused of consorting with physically manifested demons, and to be involved in **Devil worship**. It was implied that the **head** and the **cat** in the **accusations** against the Templars might be demonic in nature. At some trials the suggestion also arose that the Templars consorted with demons in female form. **Peter of La Palud** had heard a story that the rear rider of the Templar's **seal** was the devil disguised in human form.

## Denial of Christ

Denial of **Christ** was one of the main **accusations against the Order**. The Templars were accused of denying or renouncing Christ (three times according to some versions of events), as well as denying God and **Mary the Blessed Virgin**. The accusations had it that denying Christ was confirmed by the spitting on the Cross. Many of the Templars in France, including the **Grand Master** and the other leading **Preceptors**, originally **confessed** to this, under **torture**, but later retracted their confessions. It was sometimes alleged that the Templars thought Christ's claim to divinity was false and an affront to a true God who existed in heaven. Sometimes it was suggested that the Templars put forward their **idol**, the bearded **head**, as an alternate saviour.

Denial of Christ and spitting on the Cross (or other abuses of the Cross) were conventional accusations against **heretics**. Such things would be heard of again in later **witchcraft** trials. Many Templars swore that they had never denied Christ, in whose name Templars had fought and died in the **Holy Land** for two centuries, while proudly wearing the sign of the cross. There was never any satisfactory explanation why the Templars should have started renouncing Christ or abusing the cross at their reception ceremonies, and given that the imprisoned Templars seem to have obsessively carved crosses in their dungeon walls it is unlikely they would have dreamt of spitting on the symbol, or of denying Christ.

## Denny Abbey

Denny Abbey (formerly Temple Denny) in Cambridgeshire, between Cambridge and Ely, is a well-preserved Templar **Preceptory**, a rare survival in England. The estate covered marsh and fenland, with meadows and fisheries, while the Preceptory itself was built on a gravel island. The site was occupied first by **Benedictine** Monks from Ely, then by the Knights Templar, and then by **Franciscan** Nuns, the Order of Poor Clares. The surviving building resembles a large oblong house, three storeys high. However, a two-storey in-filled **Romanesque** arch in the wall and a pilaster intersecting another bricked-up arch show that it had taken other forms in the past. The larger arch resembles part of the central crossing of a cruciform church.

Denny became a Templar possession in 1176. It served as a hospital for members of the Order. Templars retired here when they became sick or elderly. (There were two such institutions in England, the other being **Eagle** in Lincolnshire.) Whereas many secular knights entering old age went on a last penitential **Crusade** to die in the **Holy Land**, Templars who gave their lives to the Holy Land, if they survived, returned to die in their homelands.

Most of the Templars arrested at Denny in 1307 were quite elderly, including the Preceptor William de La Ford, who had served forty-two years and previously been the Preceptor of Eagle. One, John de Hauteville, was described as insane. Two died before coming to trial. There were also three lay pensioners or corrodians on the site. There was a chapel where rich altar furnishings and gilt liturgical chalices were found. Templar graves there have been excavated in which the skeletons have shown signs of senescent conditions such as arthritis. After the suppression of the Templars, the property passed to Mary of Valence, Countess of Pembroke, who established the nunnery. The nuns continued to foster agriculture on the site.

## Devil Worship

Devil worship was believed to be a practice of medieval **heretics** and early-modern **witches**. It was alleged that at their gatherings the Devil or a **demon** would appear, possibly in animal form, to receive the adoration of the unchristian sect. Satanic services were supposed to involve **denial of Christ** and spitting on or otherwise abusing the Cross. The Devil might appear to be kissed beneath his tail by his worshippers, who might sacrifice infants to him and afterwards engage in 'bloodstained orgies and abominable banquets' (as **Eliphas Levi** put it).

This concept of Devil worship is now widely dismissed as a dark fantasy transmitted through the ages by the **Inquisition** and the persecuting authorities. **Konrad von Marburg** was one of the first Inquisitors to **burn** people on the basis of unsupported accusations of Devil worship and the attendance of satanic orgies. Confessions secured through **torture** fed belief that it was a real practice. The **suppression** of the Templars, though politically and economically motivated, was made possible to some extent by society's readiness to believe in Satanic conspiracies. The association of the Templars with diabolical worship has endured in the imagination of many. It has been central to many slurs against **Freemasonry** including the **Taxil Hoax**. Self-styled Satanists themselves have also invoked the name of the Templars. **Aleister Crowley** adopted the name of **Baphomet**, while Anton Szandor LaVey (1930–1997), the American founder of the Church of Satan and author of the Satanic Bible, claimed that some of the rituals used in his brand of Satanism originated in the Knights Templar. The claims are unfounded, and LaVey's precepts of self-indulgence are entirely at odds with the Templar ethos of self-sacrifice.

### Dieudonné, Abbot of Lagny (thirteenth/fourteenth century)

Dieudonné, Abbot of Lagny in the diocese of **Paris**, was one of two French clerics sent as inquisitors to England to interrogate the English Templars, who had hitherto pleaded innocent. (The other Inquisitor was Sicard de Vaour, a canon of Narbonne.) They arrived with their staff in England in September 1309. **Edward II** received them and ordered that they be protected from injury and molestation wherever they might wish to travel in the realm (a clue to how his subjects might feel about the encroachment of the **Inquisition** onto British shores, this being the only time this ever happened).

Various English prelates, including the Bishop of **London**, joined the Inquisitors on their mission to convert ostensibly loyal **Catholics** into penitent **heretics**. They presided over a trial at **Holy Trinity Church, London**. When no confessions or reliable witness testimony was forthcoming, the Inquisitors approached the Provincial Council of Canterbury, which was held in London in November. They pressed for permission to use **torture** on the Templars, something which was outside the English legal system. Pressured by the Pope, King Edward reluctantly permitted it. In April and May 1310 the Inquisitors questioned the Templars held in **York** and **Lincoln**, but again confessions were not forthcoming before heavy pressure and torture were applied. The Templar prisoner **Thomas de Thoroldeby**, who had fled and been recaptured, said that when at Lincoln he had been asked by Dieudonné if he wished to confess and had replied that he had nothing to say unless he would admit falsehood. At this Dieudonné had seized him and sworn that he would deliver his confession before he escaped from his hands.[145]

### Diniz, King of Portugal (1261–1325)

King Diniz (Denis) was the ruler of **Portugal**. He succeeded in 1279 and was on the throne at the time of the **suppression** of the Knights Templar.

Diniz's reign was prosperous and largely peaceful (the **Reconquista** having driven the **Moors** from Portugal) and was only marred by some tension with neighbouring Castile. Diniz built new towns and castles and promoted maritime trade. When it came to the suppression of the Knights Templar, Diniz founded a new Portuguese order to inherit their land. They were called the Military Order of Christ, or the **Knights of Christ**. Diniz secured recognition for the new Order from Pope **John XXII**, the successor to **Clement V**.

## Dinsley, Temple

Temple Dinsley was a major Preceptory in Hertfordshire, **England**. The land was probably granted in the time of King **Stephen**. It was one of the most important English Templar houses outside of **London**. Fragments from Templar **grave slabs** from Dinsley can be seen in St Mary's Church, Hitchen, but the original Templar halls and chapel are lost. The estate attached to Dinsley was farmed by hired labourers.

Provincial **chapters** of the **Langue** of England were routinely held at Dinsley. The remote, heavily wooded location of the Preceptory was useful for maintaining **secrecy**. One such chapter was held in 1270 in the presence of the **Visitor** of the Order, **Hugues de Pairaud**. It was also the scene of many initiation ceremonies. The Templars at Dinsley had various privileges and powers, including the right to erect a gallows. They hanged at least three men including two who stole liturgical silverware from their chapel and one man who abducted and mistreated a woman. An air of mystery grew to surround Temple Dinsley after the suppression of the Templars. The Preceptory was rumoured to have a complex of underground passages and **treasure** was said to be concealed in these. **Edward III** even sent a commission to dig there, to see if they could unearth the supposed buried riches. The site is now occupied by the Princess Helena College for Girls.

## Dome of the Rock

The Dome of the Rock is an **Islamic** shrine in **Jerusalem**, completed in AD 691. It was built by the Caliph Abdul Malik ibn Marwan. It was sometimes called the Mosque of **Omar**, after the first Muslim Conqueror of Jerusalem, who had prayed on the site. A beautifully proportioned shrine, it has a gold-covered, slightly pointed dome above a circular drum within an encompassing octagon. The pillared interior was richly decorated with mosaics by Byzantine artists.

It is located in the centre of **Temple Mount**, which Muslims call the *Haram al-Sharif* (Noble Sanctuary), and covers the probable site of the ancient **Temple of Solomon**. The rock it is built around was said to be the foundation stone of the **Jewish** Temple. It was also said to be the site of the aborted sacrifice by **Abraham** of Isaac (although Islam has it that the elder son Ismail was to be the sacrifice). Islamic tradition also has it that this is the site from which Mohammed ascended in spirit during his 'night flight' to commune with Allah, but Jerusalem is not in fact named in the Koran. (The Koran speaks of his journey from Mecca to the 'farthest mosque' but there were no mosques in Jerusalem at the time.) After the conquest of Jerusalem by the **First Crusade**, the Dome of the Rock (called the 'Temple of the Lord' by the Crusaders) was converted into a church and given to **Augustinian** canons, probably linked to the **Canons of the Holy Sepulchre**. These canons donated the court to the Knights Templar, who based themselves in the adjacent **Al-Aqsa Mosque**. After **Saladin**'s conquest, both buildings were restored as mosques. The exterior walls of the Dome of the Rock were decorated with blue glazed tiles during the later Ottoman era.

## Dominic, St (1170–1221)

Domingo de Guzmán was a Spanish monk and eventual founder of the **Dominican Order**. He was a former **Augustinian** canon commissioned by Pope **Innocent III** to preach against the **Cathars** in the **Languedoc**. Born into the Castilian nobility, he was to become a leader of great faith and conviction. When he arrived in the regions 'infested' with **heresy** in 1206, he was struck by the contrast between the apostolic poverty of the Cathar leaders, the *Parfaits*, and the splendour of the **Catholic** Bishops and the **Cistercian** Papal legates with their trains of servants and retainers. Dominic saw that if the Roman Catholic Church was ever to win back souls from the Cathars, then its preachers had to appear as austere and holy as the *Parfaits* themselves.

He began to preach against the heretics, and also debated with them, at first accompanied by his bishop Diego. Near **Carcassonne**, Dominic set up a convent, a refuge for young women who had formerly inhabited Cathar communes. He gathered male companions, meanwhile, and received permission to preach more widely by Bishop Fulk of Toulouse. In late 1216, Dominic visited **Rome** and secured official recognition for his band, which became known as the Order of Preachers, or the **Dominican Order**. Preaching against the Cathars was only successful up to a point. Dominic and his followers accompanied the 'Crusaders' in the **Albigensian Crusade**, when the Church decided to resort to force to quash dissent. Dominic died in Bologna in 1221. He was made a saint in 1233.

## Dominican Order

The Order of Friars Preachers, more commonly known as the Dominican Order, was a society of monks who concentrated on preaching in the wider world rather than seeking seclusion in **monasteries** as monastic orders had hitherto done. There were sixty Dominican houses by the death of their founder, St **Dominic**. Fifteen years later there were 600.

Dominican Friars followed a rule based on that of St **Augustine**. They wore a distinctive black **cappa** (hooded cloak) over a white habit. Their Order was founded to preach against the **Cathars** and their **heresy** in the Languedoc. The Friars of the Order soon took it upon themselves to be the sentinels of **Catholic** Orthodoxy and the hounds of heresy. The name Dominicans was punned as *Domini canes* – 'the dogs of God'. The **Inquisition** was largely drawn from the Dominican Order, especially in **France**. Alhough the Dominican Order spread to **England** and became prominent, they never took on inquisitorial activities there. In both France and England, Dominicans became politically influential, and gained positions as royal confessors. The Dominican Order's relationship to the their fellow Mendicants, the **Franciscan Order**, was much like the Templars' relationship to the **Hospitallers**, in that they were partners and sometimes rivals. Both the Dominicans and Franciscans subsequently were used as Papal tax collectors, missionaries and envoys, and both were also present at the tribunals before which the Templars appeared. The Dominican Order still flourishes today.

## Domme

Domme is a village and castle in the Dordogne, **France**. The castle is said to contain **dungeon carvings** left by Templar prisoners. The carvings show strange symbols and figures. They include crucifixes and crosses with triangular or pyramidal bases. There is also a figure holding a staff or spear, and an abstract design that may be related to the tree of life of the **Cabbalah**.[146]

## Donation of Constantine

The Donation of Constantine was purported to be an edict issued by the Roman Emperor **Constantine I**. In it the Emperor transferred temporal authority over the city of **Rome** and the Western Roman Empire to the **Pope** and the 'successors of St Peter'. The document appeared in the eighth century, about 400 years after the supposed event. It was denounced as a forgery by the secular claimant of Constantine's imperial legacy, the **Holy Roman Emperor** Otto III, but it entered the Church's mythology, and was a building block of the doctrine of **Papal Supremacy**. From the late Middle Ages onward, the Church accepted that the 'Donation' was not genuine, so clearly it was not essential to the doctrine.

## Dorylaeum

Dorylaeum in Anatolia was the site of two major battles during the **Crusades**. The first was during the **First Crusade**, when the **Franks** routed the **Seljuk Turks**; the second was during the **Second Crusade**, when the Turks decimated a German army.

## Dover

Dover is a major port in Kent, **England**, famous for its white cliffs, and dominated by its medieval castle. On the heights above Dover, to the west of the town, may also be seen the flint foundations of a small round Templar chapel with an oblong chancel attached. It is possible the **round church** doubled as a watchtower. It also may have been used by Templars about to embark for the **Holy Land**. The Preceptory in Dover (or possibly nearby Temple **Ewell**) played host to a meeting between the Papal legate Pandulph and the **excommunicated** King **John** in 1209. Two Templars mediated in the negotiations between the hostile parties who at first refused to meet face to face. The outcome of the negotiations was the lifting of the King's excommunication at the heavy cost of surrendering the Kingdom to the **Pope** and paying homage.

## Dress (Templar)

Pope **Eugenius III** granted the Templars the privilege of wearing a red **cross** on their white mantles or their cappas (cloaks) on the eve of the **Second Crusade**. However, the exact type of cross was not stipulated. Some thirteenth-century images of Templars, for example tomb figures from Italy and a carving from Villasirpa, Palencia, show the brothers in their monastic dress. They wear white cappas over long, darker coloured habits. On the left shoulder of the cloak is a simple cross with straight arms of equal length (a Greek cross). Other illustrations show a *Croix Pattée*.

The colour white is said to stand for purity, the red for martyrdom. **Sergeants**, lower-class members of the Order, must have been deemed less pure than the more aristocratic brethren in that case, as they wore black or brown instead. The Templar knights were protective about their white finery, and resented the offshoot Order the **Teutonic Knights** adopting the same dress, albeit with a black cross instead of red. The Templars do not seem to have developed a system of rank insignia but their **Grand Master** was identified by the ceremonial staff he carried, called a **baculus**. The Templars also wore cord belts as a sign, as they claimed, of chastity.

# E

## Eagle

Eagle in Lincolnshire was one of two known hospitals maintained by the Templars for sick and elderly brethren in **England** (the other being **Denny** in Cambridgeshire). Templars from Eagle were initially imprisoned and tried in **Lincoln** during the **suppression**.

## Earls Bu

Earls Bu was a manor (or drinking hall) at Orphir, Orkney. Near the site is the ruin of the **round church** of St Nicholas, built in about 1123. A section of the outer wall and an apse with a small window remain. It was built by one Earl Håkon, on return from a Crusade, which he went on in penance for ordering the murder of one Earl Magnus. It is probably the medieval round church the greatest distance from the **Holy Sepulchre**.

## Edessa

Edessa (known by the **Franks** as Rohais) was an ancient city in northern Mesopotamia. It was re-founded in 303 BC by the Macedonian general Seleucus, and named after a city in Greece. The city subsequently fell under the influence of Parthian, Armenian and Roman, Persian and **Byzantine** power. The Arabs conquered it in AD 637. It remained a primarily Christian city, however, housing **Holy Relics** such as the **Mandylion** (although this was transferred to Constantinople in 944). Edessa itself was restored to Byzantium in 1031. It was taken by the **Seljuk Turks** in 1087 and then taken by the **Crusaders** under Baldwin of Boulogne (**Baldwin I**), who entered the city with only eighty knights in 1098. Initially allied to (and adopted as a son by) the local Armenian governor, Baldwin took power himself and established the first Latin State in the East, with Edessa as its capital. The county of Edessa was the most vulnerable of the Latin possessions, being isolated in the north-east, and away from **Jerusalem**, which drew the most pilgrims, defenders and settlers. Edessa was constantly raided by its hostile Muslim neighbours, especially the **Seljuk Turks**.

Edessa passed to **Baldwin II**, and then to **Joscelin I de Courtenay**. The Templars do not seem to have become a significant presence in the county of Edessa or in the city. Edessa was besieged by a **Muslim** army under **Zenghi** of **Aleppo**, while Joscelin II was absent, having been out-manoeuvred by Zenghi.[147] The civilian population and a garrison of mercenaries resisted for four weeks but were unable to prevent a breach of the walls. The Muslims burst through on Christmas Eve 1144. They people fled to the citadel, but many were slaughtered before they reached it or killed in the crush. The citadel itself offered no refuge, moreover, as the Latin Archbishop Hugh had forbidden the opening of its doors without his order, and by this time he was no longer alive to give it. Zenghi ordered the killing or enslavement of the Frankish population, but was showed clemency to the Syrian and Armenian inhabitants. He also brought in **Jewish** settlers, whom he considered likely to be more loyal. Joscelin II returned to try to recapture Edessa in 1146, but was driven out by **Nur ed-Din**, who had succeeded his father Zenghi, and who subsequently exiled the entire Christian population. The fall of Edessa was regarded as a catastrophe by the Western Christians. It prompted Pope **Eugenius II** to call the

**Second Crusade**. This Crusade brought the Templars to military prominence but it never restored Edessa to Christian rule.

## Edward I (1239–1307)

Edward I was a King of **England** known for his ruthlessly conducted military campaigns, especially against the Welsh and the Scots. Edward I was the Son of **Henry III** and the nephew of **Richard of Cornwall**. As Prince, Edward, fought for his father against the rebellious **Simon de Montfort, 6th Earl of Leicester**. Early in the wars the Lord Edward (as he was known) returned from fortifying **Dover** Castle to find his father in a moribund state in the **Tower of London**, beset by enemies and lacking funds. Edward proposed an armed raid on the **New Temple, London**, the Templars headquarter and the centre of their **banking** industry, with its vaults full of **treasure**. With a body of knights, Edward descended on the Temple and requisitioned the necessary funds. The episode showed Edward's decisive and ruthless nature (something which would enable him to keep the barons in check during his own reign). However, it could be that the raid was something of a charade to cover Templar support for the royalist cause. Edward would go on to be a leading light in the war against de Montfort, and would vanquish him at the battle of Evesham.

At fifteen, Edward had visited Spain where he was knighted by King Alfonso X of Castile and married the Infanta (princess) Eleanor (1241–90), who was to become the love of his life. In 1270 she accompanied him on Crusade to **Acre**. This expedition is sometimes called the 'Ninth Crusade'. It is said Edward survived an attack by an **Assassin** (he fought off his attacker) and that Eleanor tended him and sucked poison from his wound. While at Acre she also gave birth to a daughter, subsequently known as Joan of Acre (not to be confused with Joan of Arc). Edward and Eleanor of Castile were to remain a loyal couple. The Prince had not been able to muster a large army for his Crusade, however, and since **Louis IX** had died in Tunis and the French contingent (sometimes called the 'Eighth Crusade') had never reached the East, Edward could do little in Acre besides negotiate with the **Mongols**, hoping to lay the ground for an alliance against the **Mameluks**. This came to nothing. Edward saw action defending Acre from the forces of **Baybars**, and initiated a few abortive raids. He exhausted his financial resources before negotiated a truce with the Mameluks. Meanwhile, Henry III died while Edward was on his way back from the East, and Edward and Eleanor were crowned on their return in 1274.

Edward reformed English government and encouraged the institution of Parliament. He embarked on a series of military campaigns, crushing the Welsh and seeking to do the same in **Scotland**. In Wales he built a number of great castles, including Caernarfon, which may have been inspired by the walls of **Constantinople**. It is said that Edward's rule became sterner after the death of his beloved Eleanor in 1290 (he built the famous 'Eleanor Crosses' as monuments to her.) Edward's harsh deeds include expelling all **Jews** from England in the same year. He was married again in 1299 to Margaret (1282–1317), a young sister of **Philip the Fair.** Edward had in common with Philip a policy of centralizing power, and reining in ecclesiastical independence. In 1296, Edward secured oaths of allegiance from **Brian de Jay**, the **Master of the Temple in England**, as well as from the Master of the English **Hospitallers**, which were sworn at Edinburgh Castle. Brian de Jay subsequently fought for Edward against the Scottish independence fighter **William Wallace** at the Battle of **Falkirk** (1298). This broke the **Military Orders'** long-standing tradition of neutrality in conflicts between Christian states within Europe and of acknowledging no allegiance to secular power. No other Templars seem to have been involved in the fighting, however.

Edward fathered fifteen children from his first marriage and three from his second. He produced more legitimate offspring than any other English king. In 1307 the King was struck down with illness while campaigning in the north. The throne passed to his thirteenth child (according to most estimates), who became **Edward II**.

## Edward II (1284–1327)

Edward of Carnarvon, son of **Edward I**, and the first English Prince of Wales, succeeded to the English throne on 8 July 1307. He was thus new to power when news came of the **arrests** of the Templars in France. Before this his father had arranged his betrothal to **Isabella (the she-wolf of France)**, the daughter of **Philip the Fair.** Edward went to Boulogne for his marriage in January 1308, leaving the realm in the care of his Gascon 'favourite' Piers Gaveston. Gaveston was the first of Edward's male favourites who would antagonise his wife and the barons and eventually cause Edward's downfall.

When French envoys brought the charges against the Templars to Edward's court, the King did not believe them, and (despite being **Philip the Fair's** future son-in-law) even wrote letters to the **Pope** and to the crowned heads of Europe defending the Order, which he had always found to be loyal and worthy. However, when Pope **Clement V**'s instructions arrived for the arrest of the Templars in England (*Pastoralis praeeminentiae*), Edward had little choice but to act. He ordered all his county sheriffs to take the Templars into custody. This was done without the ruthless efficiency of the French operation, and the Templars were not subjected to the same harsh treatment at first. If Edward demonstrated no initial animosity to the Templars, he clearly came to see their confiscated **Preceptories** as desirable. Almost at once he began to use Templar lands as staging posts and supply bases for renewed campaigns against **Scotland**.

Edward received the French representatives of the **Inquisition** with courtesy, but only reluctantly permitted them to use torture on the Templars. In December 1310 the Pope wrote to Edward suggesting that torture was still not being used extensively enough, and proposing to move the trial to Poitou where it could be used unsparingly. (The Pope even offered remission of sins if the King allowed this.)

In the event, most of the Templars in England agreed to a compromise solution, and made ambiguous public declarations of disgrace at the accusations, before being reconciled with the Church and going into exile around scattered monasteries. The king, meanwhile, was reluctant to turn the confiscated Templar lands over to the **Hospitallers** and it was some time before he was compelled to do so.

Edward's reign began to unravel with the ignominious English defeat at **Bannockburn**. A new royal favourite, Hugh de Spencer, and his father, Hugh 'the elder', gained much power in the land, and again Edward was suspected of rewarding his male lovers. The de Spencers intrigued against the Queen, persuading Edward to deprive his wife of her estates in 1324. She left for France, where she allied with Sir Roger Mortimer, a Welsh warlord (who ironically had been knighted at the **New Temple, London**). Mortimer became the Queen's lover. They raised an army, which invaded England in 1326. They captured and executed the de Spencers and had Edward deposed in favour of his young son **Edward III** and imprisoned in Berkeley Castle in Gloucestershire. There, the king who had allowed the Inquisition into England met a ghastly death at the hands of his jailers. A hot iron was thrust up his backside, passing into his entrails through a hollow horn, so that no external sign of injury was left. Edward was subsequently thought of with more sympathy and his tomb in Gloucester cathedral became something of an object of pilgrimage.

## *Edward III* (1312–77)

Edward III was proclaimed king by his mother **Isabella (the she-wolf of France)** after her rebellion against his father **Edward II**. After the extinction of the direct male **Capetian** line in 1340, Edward claimed the throne of **France** through his mother, though the French rejected this claim, not by that stage recognizing inheritance through the female line. Edward subsequently went to war in France to assert his claim, winning notable victories at Crecy in 1346 and at Poitiers in 1356, where the English longbowmen decimated the French knights. Edward captured Calais in 1347. Edward III's son Edward, 'the Black Prince', also distinguished himself in these campaigns, as well as leading campaigns in the south where he ravaged **Carcassonne**, among other places. Later reverses such as a naval battle at **La Rochelle** diminished Edward's grasp on the Continent and England's control of the Channel.

Meanwhile, the terrible plague known as the Black Death had spread through Europe and both England and France were hard hit from 1348.

This was also the year in which Edward III founded the **Order of the Garter**. Although this was an Order for secular knights, in some respects it filled a gulf left by the Templars. Like the Order of the Temple, the Order of the Garter was dedicated to **Mary, the Blessed Virgin** and to St **George**. They also used the device of red cross on white, which became the national flag.

## Egypt

Egypt, in north-east Africa, borders the Red Sea and the Mediterranean. It is connected to the **Holy Land** by the Sinai Peninsula. Its ancient civilization was said to be the gift of the River Nile, the annual inundations of which created a strip of fertile land through the desert. The country was rich in gold and in grain. It was considered the breadbasket of the Roman and then the **Islamic** world. Egypt's unique civilization endured from more than 3,000 years before the time of **Christ** until a century after. Its ancient religion encompassed the worship of many gods. Amon-Ra, the sun god, was chief of these. Other significant deities included Osiris, the god of fertility and of death, **Isis**, the mother goddess and patroness of magic, sister and consort of Osiris, and mother of the sky god Horus. Some have supposed that the Christian image of **Mary, the blessed Virgin** sitting enthroned with the Christ Child reflects ancient Egyptian depictions of Isis and Horus. (The legend of the **Skull of Sidon** may also have been a muddling of the Isis/Osiris myth.)

Egyptian culture and religion survived Assyrian and Greek occupation. **Jewish** scripture vilified the Egyptians, and yet Egypt was a land of sanctuary as much as a land of slavery and oppression. It sheltered the infant Christ from Herod's persecution. Egypt was governed by ma'at, the principle of justice personified as a goddess. The land was eventually converted to Christianity under the Romans in the third century. Egypt (in particular the city of **Alexandria**) was important to early Christianity, producing some of the earliest theologians and the pioneers of monasticism. The **Arabs** conquered Egypt in the seventh century, bringing **Islam**. By the time of the **Crusades** a **Fatimid** Caliph was ruling the land, governing as the Pharaohs had with the aid of a powerful minister called the vizier. Egypt's indigenous **Coptic** Christian Community survived and Alexandria continued to be the seat of a **Patriarch**.

The Crusaders from early times aspired to the conquest of Egypt. This was justified as a measure to make the **Kingdom of Jerusalem** more secure from Muslim attack. **Amalric I** invaded Egypt three times; in the last incursion the Templars refused to take part. It was in Egypt that **Saladin** first fought the Crusaders. Saladin would eventually seize power there for himself and establish the **Ayyubid** dynasty. The Templars took part in the invasion of Ayyubid Egypt during the **Fifth Crusade**, and the repeat performance that was the **Seventh Crusade**. Soon after the latter débâcle the ruthless **Mameluks** seized power, and from there launched out to destroy first the **Mongols** and then the Kingdom of Jerusalem. The Mameluks held sway in Egypt until **Napoleon**'s arrival.

Some **conspiracy theories** have it that lost Egyptian knowledge somehow found its way into the inner circle of the Knights Templar. There has been speculation that this knowledge was transmitted via **Moses** and **Solomon**, and that hypothetical discoveries made by the Templars while excavating **Temple Mount** revealed this lost wisdom to them.[148] Respectable proof of such connections is lacking. Egypt was an important sphere of military activity for the Templars, and they probably had some interaction with the Egyptian Christians. Muslim rulers, especially **Ayyub** and **Baybars**, initiated persecutions of the Copts, suspecting them of sympathising with the Franks.

## Eleanor of Aquitaine (1122–1204)

Eleanor, Duchess of Aquitaine was a prominent figure during the **crusading** era. She accompanied her first husband **Louis VII** of **France** on the **Second Crusade**, having **taken the Cross** in her own right before St **Bernard of Clairvaux**. She was accompanied by her ladies in waiting and 300 of her vassals from Aquitaine. Louis, who has been judged something of a prig, was jealous of Eleanor, and suspected her of having an affair with **Raymond of Poitiers**, Prince of **Antioch**, during their stay there in 1147.[149] Still, Eleanor and Louis's marriage produced two daughters, **Marie of Champagne** and Alix of France. Louis, wanting a son and mistakenly deeming Eleanor incapable of producing one, divorced her, conveniently citing consanguinity. In 1152, Eleanor promptly married the future **Henry II** of England. It was to be a tempestuous union. She bore Henry (who was some years her junior) eight children, of whom two sons (namely **Richard the Lionheart** and **John**) would survive to inherit the English throne.

Henry may have been an unfaithful husband. At any rate Eleanor often backed her sons when they revolted against their father, first the Young Henry in the 1170s (until he died in 1183), and then Richard. By the time of Henry II's death he had been keeping his wife a prisoner for fifteen years. Eleanor rose to prominence again early in the reign of Richard, and was instrumental in his marriage to **Berengaria of Navarre**, whom she escorted as far as Sicily. During Richard's captivity in Austria after the **Third Crusade**, Eleanor appealed on his behalf to the **Pope**, securing the **excommunication** of his captors. At the time of her death Eleanor was supporting John in a brewing conflict with **Philip II Augustus**. Eleanor was famously cultured and learned, her effigy is carved reading a book. Both she and her daughter Marie were great patrons of troubadours and poets of 'courtly love'. Eleanor was also a supporter of the Templars, either granting or renewing their exemption from paying harbour tax in **La Rochelle**, and giving them the windmills she owned in the town. She succeeded, meanwhile, in keeping Aquitaine a separate domain from both France and England. She was buried at Fontevraud Abbey, close to Henry and Richard.

## Eleven Thousand Virgins

The Eleven Thousand Virgins, according to Christian myth, were pious handmaidens who followed St Ursula of Cornwall on a **pilgrimage** to **Rome** during the Dark Ages. They passed Cologne on the way back, where they were set upon and slain by pagan Huns. The maidens were all beheaded while St Ursula was shot with arrows. A **Holy Relic**, labelled **Caput LVIIIm**, was found at the **Paris Temple** during a search by the royal custodian of the site. The Papal Commission heard that this head was said to be one of the eleven thousand virgin martyrs. Cologne was famous for holding the **Holy Relics** of the Magi, the three Kings who visited the infant **Christ**. This would have been what drew Ursula there. The cult of female virgin martyrs also seems to have taken hold early on there, though the original number may actually have been nearer to eleven than eleven thousand.

## Eliphas Levi (1810–75)

Eliphas Levi (Alphonse Louis Constant) was a French occultist and self-styled magician. He had originally trained in a seminary as a **Catholic** priest, but left for romantic reasons and was never ordained. He became interested in **Rosicrucianism** and the **Cabbalah**. He was somewhat influenced by the eccentric English novelist Edward Bulwer-Lytton. Levi claimed that behind all the esoteric secret societies and the religions of the ancient civilizations was a singular secret doctrine. Levi's eclectic approach to the 'occult sciences' would later influence **Aleister Crowley**. At some of the medieval trials of the Templars, the Order's alleged **idol** was named as **Baphomet**. Since the nineteenth century this name has become associated with the image dreamed up by Eliphas Levi. This devilish Baphomet, with black wings and the head and legs of a goat, first appeared as an illustration from Levi's 1855 work *Transcendental Magic, its Doctrine and Ritual*. It has hermaphroditic elements and is seen as representing the union of opposites. Eliphas spuriously linked this Baphomet to the goat of Mendes, supposedly an Ancient **Egyptian** deity (which was actually a ram).

## Elizabeth of Hungary, St (1207–31)

Elizabeth of Hungary was the daughter of King Andrew II of Hungary (who had taken part in the **Fifth Crusade**). She was raised in **Germany**, being betrothed as a child to Ludwig, Count of Thuringia, whom she married at the age of thirteen. She developed a reputation for her generosity and kindness to the poor, building hospitals and distributing alms. She eventually fell under the control of her harsh confessor **Konrad of Marburg**. Elizabeth (while pregnant with her third child) was widowed by the **Sixth Crusade**, and died herself in 1231. She was declared a saint in 1234. Marburg became a centre of the **Teutonic Knights**, for whom Elizabeth became an important patron saint.

## England

England, under the Norman and **Angevin** Kings, was moving from the periphery to the political centre of Europe, particularly because she also ruled a not inconsiderable portion of what is now **France**. English forces would play a part in most of the **Crusades**. The Templars were present in England from the time of **Henry I** and **Hugues de Payens** himself apparently established the first Templar Headquarters in the **Old Temple, London**. In the time of King **Stephen** the Templars received numerous grants of land and established their presence throughout the realm as landlords, farmers and monks. England constituted a Langue or **province** of the internationally organised Order. The **Masters of the Temple in England** also had authority over the Masters of **Scotland** and **Ireland**.

The Order rose to prominence in the time of **Henry II**, when they gained positions as royal ambassadors, advisors, diplomats and treasurers. They were also used as tax collectors, gathering the **Saladin tithe** to fund the planned **Third Crusade**. The Order in England reached its apex in the time of **Henry III**, when such was their high standing that the King planned originally to be buried at **Temple Church, London**, which was extended for the purpose. The Norman Conquest of 1066 had grafted the **feudal** system onto England and the Conquest led to a French-speaking ruling class coming to control almost all the land and to hold almost all power, secular or spiritual. The knightly class would have been steeped in the Frankish culture of the conquerors, and of the Templars probably only the sergeants were English speaking, at least up until the last years of the Order's history. Society was becoming more unified and a national identity was emerging by the 1300s. English became the language of court during the reign of **Edward III**.

Henry III's reign degenerated into civil war after a baronial revolt fomented by **Simon de Montford, Sixth Earl of Leicester**. Henry's successor, **Edward I**, brought the barons to heel, and attempted similarly to dominate Wales and Scotland. He also secured an oath of allegiance from **Brian de Jay** the **Master of the Temple in England**, and indeed the Order gave the monarchy no reason to doubt its faith or loyalty to the realm. **Edward II** was initially reluctant to believe the **accusations** against the Templars. He obeyed the Papal order to **arrest** them, but went by the book and ordered his county sheriffs to take inventories of the Templars' properties. The sheriffs were to hold the Templars securely but not to put them in any hard or vile prison, and they were not to be deprived of sustenance. In the event only about 153 Templars, of whom only fifteen were full knights, were arrested in England, including the Master of England, **William de la More** (plus fifteen in Ireland and two in Scotland). Other Templars must have gone on the run in the meantime. Conditions worsened for the Templar prisoners after the two French **Inquisitors** secured the King's grudging permission to proceed with the use of torture, which was against the conventions of English law.

In the end most of the Templars in England were reconciled and released to other monastic institutions after giving a public declaration of being disgraced by the accusations and admitting the error of believing in illicit lay absolution – the most minor and least humiliating of the **accusations**. They were mostly reconciled during ceremonies in St Paul's Cathedral, London. It was seen as a decent compromise, which saved some face for all sides. However, **William de la More**, the last Master of England, defended the Order's innocence to his last breath and died languishing in chains in the Tower. There are hints that there may have been some degree of Templar **continuity** in England, at least for a couple of decades after the Order's official dispersal.

## Equestrian Order of the Holy Sepulchre

The Equestrian Order of the Holy Sepulchre of Jerusalem is an existing Roman **Catholic** Order. It consists of knights and dames as well as **priests**. The Order's badge is a red **Jerusalem Cross**, worn on white cloaks by knights and black robes by dames. Its role includes charitable work in the **Holy Land** and preserving the Catholic faith in Palestine. The Order claims to have some 23,000 members in fifty countries, being under the authority of a Cardinal **Grand Master** and a Governor General based in **Rome**. It traces its (spiritual) ancestry to the historical **Canons of the Holy Sepulchre** and also bases itself somewhat on the supposed Military **Order of the Holy Sepulchre**, which may have been the original form of the Order of the Temple (although no Templar link is acknowledged). The present Equestrian Order seems to date from 1847, when **Pope** Pius IX revived the Latin Patriarchate of Jerusalem. The modern Order stresses its loyalty to the Pope.[150]

## Esquin de Floyran (died c. 1316)

Esquin (or Esquieu) de Floyran was the man attributed with bringing the **accusations** against the Templars to the attention of King **Philip the Fair** of **France**. De Floyran may have been a renegade Templar, formerly the Preceptor of Montfaucon. His name implies links with Florence, but a Templar, **Ponsard de Gizy**, named an Esquin de Floyran of Béziers (**Languedoc**) among the enemies who had persecuted the Templars. Punished by the **Grand Master** for some crime, Esquin seems to have developed a bitter grudge against the Order of the Temple. The Florentine chronicler Giovanni Villani described how Esquin and one Noffro Dei conspired against the Templars, and took their allegations to the King of France. The King, moved by avarice, then made plans with the **Pope** to destroy the Templars.

There is some doubt about Esquin's role, and other sources for the rumours against the Templars are sometimes mentioned. However, it seems Esquin de Floyran had also approached **James II** of **Aragon** with his scandalous reports of the Templars' secret, **heretical** activities. James seems to have disbelieved the accusations. Esquin de Floyran subsequently wrote to him reminding the king of a promise he had allegedly made to pay him money if the charges should prove to be true. What became of Esquin is unclear. He seems to have had a role in the **torture** and interrogation of some of the Templars held in France. It is possible that he was rewarded with money and land for his part in the conspiracy.

## Ernoul (twelfth century)
Squire of **Balian of Ibelin** and author of a chronicle critical of **Gerard de Ridefort**, blaming the **Grand Master** for the defeat of **Cresson**.

## Essenes
The Essenes were one of various mystical sects on the fringes of **Judaism**, who lived in Judea from the second century BC to the first century AD. Some believe Essenes were settled at Qumran and were the authors of the **Dead Sea Scrolls**. They were ascetics, who anticipated the imminent arrival of the **Messiah**, the anointed one. They expected an apocalyptic battle between the forces of light and darkness. Unlike other Jews, the Essenes, also called Nazareans, did not offer animal sacrifices. Like the later **Cathars,** the Essenes seem to have esteemed celibacy, ate no meat and repudiated the swearing of oaths. If they likewise believed in the immortality of the soul and the cycle of reincarnation then it may have been as a result of influence from Greek Orphism. The Essenes may also be regarded as pioneers of Christian monasticism. There has been speculation that the Templars may have rediscovered Essene ideas during their sojourn in the Holy Land. The evidence for this is so far lacking.

## Etienne de Troyes (thirteenth–fourteenth century)
Etienne de Troyes was a former Templar serving brother. Early on during the **suppression** he agreed to **confess** to the **accusations against the Order.** He was among those Templars willing to testify before **Clement V** at **Poitiers** that the accusations were true. Seeing that the King intended to push the affair strongly, Etienne had previously confessed before secular officials including **Guillaume de Martigny**, and also before the Bishops of Bayeux and Coutances. He claimed that at his reception he had been compelled at swordpoint to deny Christ and all the saints. He said he had been made to spit three times at the cross, but had spat on the ground, and then had been made to

strip naked before receiving the receptor's kisses on the base of the spine, the navel and the mouth. Then, he claimed to have had a **cord** tied about him, which had been wrapped around the mysterious **head**, an **idol**, and that the Order held the head to be their holy saviour. He described the appearance of the head at general **chapter** meetings (which he claimed were held annually on 24 June, **St John the Baptist's** Day). At midnight a priest carried the head to an altar, flanked by two brothers carrying candles. The head had bluish skin, and a black beard flaked with white. He claimed the **Visitor** of the Order, **Hugues de Pairaud**, had announced that the head was to be worshipped.

Etienne claimed that after the chapter meeting he had been dispatched to the East, but had subsequently returned to France. He said he had been pestered for sexual favours by another Templar and had suffered a broken jaw for refusing. He had taken the matter to the **Visitor**, only for Pairaud to say that he should not have denied him. Etienne had also alleged that there was a secret **Rule** within the Order. Subsequently he had tried to leave the Templars, on account of the 'evil and shameful things' that he had witnessed and at the prompting of his brother. He had taken refuge with the Count of Brittany, and returned to secular life. After visiting his mother he claimed he had been snatched by his erstwhile brethren, and not released until his mother had deliverer a payment of gold.

## Et in Arcadia Ego

*Et in Arcadia Ego* (and in Arcadia I) is a Latin phrase appearing in a painting also known as *Les Bergers d'Arcadie* (Shepherds of Arcadia) by Nicolas Poussin (1549–1665). The painting is in the Louvre. The pastoral scene features three Greek 'shepherds' and a shepherdess or nymph contemplating a tomb in a landscape. The theme is probably the presence of death even in the idyllic Arcadian countryside. The painting has more recently become associated with the **Rennes le Chateau** mystery, and the **Priory of Sion**.

## Ethiopia

Ethiopia lies in the horn of Africa, south of **Egypt** and the Sudan. With its ancient capital at **Axum**, it had historical links to southern Arabia and was at one time part of a common kingdom (**Sheba**). Legend has it that monotheism was introduced to Ethiopia by the Queen of Sheba, and that the **Ark of the Covenant** was later brought there by **Menelik I**, the son born to the Queen and King **Solomon**. Subsequent rulers claimed descent from this branch of the Davidic line. Christianity was later brought by St Frumentius, one of two companions of a merchant of **Tyre** who was captured on a return voyage from India. Frumentius gained a place of honour at the Axumite court and became regent for the boy king Ezana at the behest of the queen mother. Frumentius went to Alexandria to ask the **Patriarch** to appoint a bishop. The Patriarch chose Frumentius himself. The kingdom was converted in AD 331.

Ethiopia maintained close ties to the **Coptic Church** and with the **Holy Land**, even after the forces of **Islam** overwhelmed Egypt and the Middle East. There are some accounts of Ethiopian embassies to Europe, and Ethiopia may have fed the '**Prester John**' myth. Graham Hancock has theorised that the Templars could have come to Ethiopia during the time of King **Lalibela**, perhaps on account of having discovered the rumour of the Ark being there. Support for this has been cited in apparent Templar symbols found in the sunken churches carved out of the rock in a city Lalibela founded in Ethiopia on his return from exile in **Jerusalem**. There is also an account by the geographer Abu Silah (a Christian **Arab**) which speaks of the Ark being carried in Ethiopia by men who were white and red in complexion, with red hair.[151] The interest shown in Ethiopia by the Templars' Portuguese successors, the **Knights of Christ**, also hints that there may be something to the theory that the Templars had dealings in that land. According to the Coptic monks who claim to be its guardians, the Ark remains in Ethiopia.

## *Eugenius III, Pope* (died 1153)
Bernardo dei Paganelli di Montemagno of **Pisa** was elected as **Pope** Eugenius III in 1145. He was a friend and former pupil of St **Bernard of Clairvaux** and had likewise been a **Cistercian** Abbot. He spent much of his reign in exile from **Rome** because of the resistance of its citizens to Papal claims of temporal sovereignty (**Papal Supremacy**). Eugenius called the **Second Crusade** in late 1145, after the fall of **Edessa** the year before. He called on **Louis VII** of **France** to lead it, and also appealed to **Germany** and its ruler **Conrad III**. In a papal letter encouraging the young knights of Europe to **take the cross**, he said that it would be seen as a great sign of nobility and uprightness if the places taken by the efforts and valour of their fathers could be vigorously defended by the sons, but if, God forbid, it came to pass differently, then the bravest of the fathers would be shown to have diminished in the sons. Eugenius called on St Bernard to assist with the preaching of the Crusade. He also issued the Papal Bull **Militia Dei**, consolidating the rights and privileges of the Knights Templar, and granting them the honour of wearing the red **cross** on their white mantles.

## *Euphemia, St* (fourth century)
Euphemia of Chalcedon was a female saint, apparently martyred by pagans in Asia Minor in about AD 303. She was better known in the Eastern Church. During the **trial** of the Templars on **Cyprus**, the Drapier of the Order and two knights mentioned that the Templars were the custodians of Euphemia's embalmed **head**. The relics of the saint had apparently previously been kept at **Pilgrim's Castle**, and were attributed with miraculous powers.

## Evangelikon

The Evangelicon or Levitikon is said to be a **Gnostic** or **Johannite** version of the Gospel of St **John**, differing in many ways from the accepted version. A version entered in the possession of **Bernard Raymond Fabré-Palaprat**.

## Everard des Barres (died 1174)

Everard des Barres was the third **Grand Master** of the Knights Templar. From an aristocratic family of Meaux, **Champagne**, he entered the Order in his teens, and by 1143 had risen to the rank of **Grand Preceptor** of **France**. He was close to King **Louis VII** of France and accompanied him on the **Second Crusade**, soon after his elevation, in 1147. The embarkation followed a chapter meeting held in **Paris**, attended by King Louis, by Pope **Eugenius III** and by 120 Knights of the Temple, including some summoned by Everard from Spain. It was probably at this meeting that the Order received the right to wear the red **cross** of **martyrdom** on their white habits.

Everard des Barres was one of those sent ahead of Louis to **Constantinople**, where he met with **Manuel I Comnenus**. Subsequently, Templar discipline and courage saved Louis' army from destruction, fending off the attacking **Turks** amid the Cadmus Mountains in Anatolia. Odo of Deuil praised Everard for his piety and for the wise example he offered up to the others. The Grand Master later assisted Louis with a substantial loan of 2,000 silver marks. He also took part in the ill-fated campaign against **Damascus**, which may have planted a seed of disillusionment in him. Everard returned to France with the King after the ignominious end of the Crusade, apparently stricken with guilt over the failure of the venture. He resigned from the Templars in around 1151, and joined the **Cistercian Order** at **Clairvaux** in order to do penance.

## Ewell, Temple

Temple Ewell was a **Preceptory** in Kent, south-east **England**, acquired in 1163 from William, the brother of **Henry II**, and from the Constable of Dover Castle. The local church, which the Templars rebuilt, is dedicated to Sts Peter and Paul, and contains a probable Templar **grave slab**. The last Preceptor of Temple Ewell was Ralph de Malton. Little remains of the Preceptory, which was occupied by the **Hospitallers** until the Reformation.

## Excavations (of Temple Mount)

**Temple Mount** has been excavated at various times through history. It is said that the Templars may have conducted one of the first such digs at the site. Although there is no historical record, it has been suggested that **Hugues de Payens** and his patrons and associates may have learned of lost **treasure** or **Holy Relics** buried under the site of the Temple. Alternatively, the Templars could simply have stumbled across pre-existing tunnels and ancient underground chambers during the course of their occupation of the site, perhaps while they were constructing their buildings adjoining the **Al Aqsa Mosque**. They probably unearthed the vaulted, artificial caverns known as the Stables of Solomon (they may have been the first to use them as stables). It is also claimed that Crusader artefacts, including a sword hilt, spear tip and spurs, were found in a **tunnel** under these caverns, leading towards the centre of the mount.[152] The Temple platform was excavated in the 1860s by **Charles Warren** and Charles Wilson, and again in 1910 by **Montagu Brownlow Parker**. Parker was actively seeking the **Ark of the Covenant**, and caused outrage and bloody riots by sneaking into the **Dome of the Rock** at night and trying to cut his way through the rock.

In 1968, Israeli archaeologist Meir Ben-Dov excavated the periphery of Temple Mount, rediscovering the entrance to the tunnel leading under the Stables of Solomon, but was unable to clear the whole length of it. The Haram al-Sharif remains a religiously sensitive location and little archaeological work has been permitted within the sacred enclosure in more recent times.

## Excommunication

Excommunication was a religious sanction. One who was excommunicated by the **Pope** or a Bishop was theoretically cast out of the Christian community. Christians were expected to have no dealings with the excommunicated person, and if they died without being reconciled then they would be deprived of a Christian burial and considered damned. If a king was excommunicated, so the Church declared, then his subjects were released from any obligation of allegiance to that king. Excommunication could thus be used as an instrument of **Papal supremacy**. In the thirteenth century the Popes used excommunication a little too liberally, in an attempt to control or isolate their political enemies, and it began to lose some of its force. Related to excommunication was **interdict**, where the Church withdrew the sacraments from a whole town, region or even country. No church services could be performed and no divine grace received. All of **England** was under interdict when **Innocent III** excommunicated King **John**. When the excommunicated Emperor **Frederick II** took **Jerusalem** without a fight and crowned himself in the **Holy Sepulchre**, the **Patriarch** Gerold placed the entire Holy City under interdict.

In the case of King John at least, the Templars still rendered service to the King, despite his being excommunicated, and they played a part in the negotiations that resulted in his reconciliation with the Pope. When the Templars were finally suppressed and abolished by Pope **Clement V**, the bull outlawed the Order of the Temple and excommunicated anyone who presumed to join the Order or act as a Templar.

## *Exemen de Lenda* (thirteenth–fourteenth century)

Exemen de Lenda was the Templar **Grand Preceptor** of **Aragon**. He was one of those seized by the agents of **James II** in December 1307. Exemen had clearly been worried that trouble was brewing for the Order since receiving news of the arrests in **France**, and had advised the **Preceptors** under him to put a guard on their **castles**. In the end, the Templars of Aragon had little spirit to resist attack from the forces of their own king, although some Templar castles held out under siege for up to a year.

# F

## *Faciens Misericordiam*

*Faciens Misericordiam* was a **papal bull** of 12 August 1308, sent to the international authorities responsible for arresting the Templars. It detailed the history of the proceedings against the Temple, and how **Clement V** had come to believe the **accusations** against the Templars. It alleged that the brethren were guilty of an unspeakable, wicked apostasy, 'the vice of detestable idolatry and the execrable acts of sodomites and various heretics'. The edict excused the conduct of **Philip the Fair**, who had acted (initiated the **suppression**) not from greed but 'with the fervour of the orthodox faith'. The Pope therefore ordered provincial councils to be set up to try the Templars throughout the Catholic world, and established the **Cardinals' Commission** to investigate the guilt of the Order as a whole.

## *Fakhr al-Din* (died 1250)

Fakhr al-Din Yusuf Ibn al Shaykh was a prominent Emir in **Egypt** in late **Ayyubid** times. He served **al-Kamil** as an envoy to **Frederick II** in Palermo on the eve of the **Sixth Crusade**, and soon became a friend and confidant of the Emperor.[153] He was an intermediary between the Emperor and the Sultan in the **Holy Land**, and played a part in the ruse that enabled Frederic to recover **Jerusalem**, apart from **Temple Mount**, having enacted a charade of threatening it militarily. Later, Fakhr al-Din was given charge of **Damietta** by the Sultan as-Silah **Ayyub**, but abandoned it on the arrival of the army of the **Seventh Crusade** in 1249. He narrowly escaped execution by the ailing Sultan on reaching **Mansourah** because of his dereliction of duty. He manoeuvred closer to power and allied with the Sultana Shaijar al-Durr at the time of Ayyub's death and before the arrival of **Turan-shah**, and took charge of the army. He was caught by surprise during the Crusader attack on his camp, led by the Templars and **Robert, Count of Artois**. It is said that he leapt from the bath and rode out unarmed to rally his men, but was cut down by the Franks.

## Falkirk, Battle of

The bloody Battle of Falkirk was fought in **Scotland** on 22 July 1298. It was a victory for **Edward I** of **England** over the Scots under **William Wallace** who resisted English rule. Edward had been forced to conclude a truce with **Philip the Fair** and hurry back from battle in Flanders, following news of Wallace's victory at Stirling Bridge. Edward mustered an army of 2,000 knights and 12,000 infantrymen in **York**, and from there commenced his second invasion of Scotland. The invasion was hampered by Wallace's scorched earth tactics, and Edward was on the point of withdrawing when he learned of Wallace's position in the woods of Callendar near Falkirk.

Wallace's Scots were formed in three schiltrons (formations of foot soldiers armed with long spears). Between them were archers under Sir John Steward. A cavalry force was deployed behind. Edward's heavy cavalry charged, being led by the Bishop of Durham and the Earl of Norfolk. The Scots' cavalry soon abandoned the field and the Scottish bowmen were slaughtered in the English cavalry onslaught. The schiltrons, bristling with spear points, proved tougher nuts to crack however, and after the English cavalry made several unsuccessful charges, Edward ordered his knights back and brought his longbow archers forward. The archers wore down the schiltrons. When the formations broke, Edward sent his knights back in to finish them. The Scots army broke up and fled into the woods, pursued by Edward's Welsh mercenaries under Brian **de Jay**, the **Master of the Temple in England**. William Wallace fought a rearguard action, during which Brian de Jay was slain. Wallace escaped to fight another day. He continued to wage war with scorched earth, and the hungry and disease-afflicted English forces had little chance of consolidating their victory.

## Fatimids

The Fatimid Caliphs were a dynasty of religious and political leaders of Shi'ite **Islam**. Originally holding power in Tunisia, they conquered Egypt in about AD 970, and founded the new city of Cairo as their capital. The dynasty was named after Fatima, the Daughter of the Prophet Mohammed, from whom the Caliphs claimed descent. To some extent their influence extended into the **Holy Land** also, and it was from the Fatimids that the **First Crusade** took **Jerusalem**. The Fatimid Caliphs were finally deposed by **Saladin**, in 1169. Saladin founded the **Ayyubid** dynasty, and recognised the Sunni **Abbasid** Caliph in **Baghdad**.

## Fernando Campello Pinto Pereira de Sousa Fontes (present day)

The Portuguese Conde Don Fernando Campello Pinto Pereira de Sousa Fontes is said to be the present Prince Regent and **Grand Master** of the **OSMTH**, and has been since 1960 (although not universally recognised within the fragmented Order). It is not known if he is still alive.

## Fiction

The Templars have appeared in and influenced works of fiction since their own times, for example the **Holy Grail** romances. In the nineteenth century they appeared as villains in *Ivanhoe* and *The Talisman* by Sir **Walter Scott**. Umberto Eco parodied Templar **conspiracy theories** in his novel *Foucault's Pendulum*, while Dan Brown incorporated the Templar/**Priory of Sion** idea into his thriller *The Da Vinci Code*. The latter made the subject particularly popular and inspired several derivatives including Raymond Khoury's *The Last Templar*. The Templars (or similar knights) have also featured in popular motion pictures, including: *Revelation, National Treasure, Indiana Jones and the Last Crusade,* and *Kingdom of Heaven*, and in video games such as 'Assassin's Creed'.

## Field of Blood (battle)

The Battle of the Field of Blood, or *Ager Sanguinis*, was fought early in the reign of **Baldwin II** of **Jerusalem**. In 1119, **Il-ghazi** led the combined forces of **Aleppo** and **Damascus** against knights from the principality of **Antioch**. Though Baldwin II hastened to the city's aid, by then the Prince of Antioch, **Roger of Salerno**, a famed warrior, had led his forces out without waiting for his allies to arrive. His force, comprising 700 knights, 3,000 foot soldiers and an assortment of 10,000 civilian followers, took up a position in a mountain pass. Their camp was surrounded during the night by 40,000–80,000 Muslim warriors, largely **Seljuks**, under Il-ghazi. The battle the following day was savage, and was interrupted by a whirlwind. Roger was killed by a sword while most of his men and their horses were mown down in a crossfire of arrows. Afterwards most of the Frankish prisoners were slaughtered.[154] Il-ghazi failed to capitalise on this victory, however.

## Fifth Crusade

The Fifth Crusade was called by Pope **Innocent III** in the bull *Quia Maior*, in 1213. Innocent called on the faithful to aid the **Holy Land**, and organised preparations through Europe. He encouraged men to take the cross, if need be without permission from their **feudal** lords or even from their wives. He tried to suspend the **Albigensian Crusade**, acknowledging that it was absorbing the energies of the French aristocracy. The Fifth Crusade was on the agenda of the **Fourth Lateran Council**, which Innocent convened in 1215. The expedition only got underway in 1217, a year after Innocent's death. It would last four years and not end well.[155]

The Christian armies assembled in the East, including **Hospitallers**, **Teutonic Knights** and Templars under their Grand Master **Guillaume de Chartres**.

Other crusading contingents were led by Andrew II, King of Hungary, by Hugh I, King of **Cyprus**, and by Leopold VI, Duke of Austria. In **Acre** they joined with forces led by **John of Brienne**, titular king of **Jerusalem**, and with Bohemond IV of **Antioch**. They conducted indecisive campaigns in the **Holy Land**, including a raid into Galilee and an operation to reduce Muslim fortifications on **Mount Tabor**, which had threatened Acre. Andrew then returned to Hungary, while Hugh of Cyprus died. The rest sailed to attack **Damietta** in the Nile Delta. The attack on **Egypt**, the centre of **Ayyubid** power, was supposedly a prelude to recovering **Jerusalem**.

Damietta controlled the eastern mouth of the Nile. Its strong fortifications included a separate tower on an island in the river, and a connecting chain preventing the passage of ships. The Crusaders besieged the city fiercely from May 1218 onwards. They were accompanied by clergy, including **Jacques de Vitry** and Raoul de Merencourt, the **Patriarch** of Jerusalem, who carried another portion of the **True Cross** in barefoot processions outside the walls and prayed for victory for the Crusaders. (St **Francis of Assisi** also visited the Crusade.) The Templars were in the thick of the fighting, and took many casualties, as **Oliver of Paderborn** recorded, both on land and on ships on the river. During one episode a crippled Templar ship was swept towards the enemy's side and boarded. The boarders descended upon the Templars, and a long fight ensued. The ship was holed, by whom was not clear, and sank, 'drowning Egyptians with Christians ... and as Samson killed many more in death than he had in life, so also those martyrs dragged into the abyss ... more than they could have killed with the sword.'[156] Harried by Muslim forces from without, the Crusaders pressed the siege. A Frisian contingent stormed the chain tower on the river from a siege engine straddling two ships lashed together, which survived a barrage of Greek fire. Meanwhile, Sultan **al-Adil** died and was succeeded in Egypt by **al-Kamil** and in **Damascus** by al-Muazzam. At around the same time, Cardinal-Bishop **Pelagius of Albano**, the legate of Pope **Honorius III**, arrived to take charge of the Crusade.

Al-Kamil offered to restore Jerusalem to Christian rule, along with the True Cross taken at **Hattin**, and nearly all the former Latin **Kingdom of Jerusalem**, if the Crusaders would agree to withdraw from Damietta. The papal legate dismissed the offer. What Pelagius evidently wanted was conquest by force, control of Egypt's wealth and the crushing of Muslim power. The representatives of the Italian **maritime republics**, and also the **Military Orders**, supported the Patriarch's stance. Meanwhile, Guillaume de Chartres died and was succeeded as Grand Master of the Templars by **Pierre de Montaigu**. In November 1219, after months of siege, the starving Damietta submitted to the Crusaders. The Christians established themselves there, repairing the city's fortifications and converting its mosque into a church. However, they experienced problems with division, indiscipline and disease. The intransigent Pelagius again turned down the Sultan's proposals, and continued to exasperate John of Brienne and other Christians who had more experience of the East. Though sporadic reinforcements continued to arrive, there were as many desertions. John of Brienne abandoned Damietta for a time, to press his interests in Cilicia. The Templars, who had helped secure the environs of Damietta including Tanis, also withdrew for a time to reinforce the newly built **Pilgrim's Castle**, which had in the meantime come under attack from **al Muazzam** of **Damascus**. Al Muazzam had already captured **Caesarea**.

Throughout 1220, the remaining Crusaders dug in at Damietta, awaiting the return of John of Brienne and the arrival of the Emperor **Frederick II** and his promised reinforcements. Some anticipated deliverance by the fabled **Prester John**, on account of garbled reports of the **Mongol** advance, or put their faith in spurious prophetic writings which had been discovered. Frederick never came, but a few hundred Imperial knights eventually arrived in late spring 1221, under Duke Ludwig of Bavaria who was keen to fight the **Saracens**. Soon the annual inundation of the Nile would make it impossible to march towards Cairo, as the Delta would become impassable. John of Brienne, lately returned, advised that it was already too late to move out. Al-Kamil made a third offer of peace. Pelagius, even so, ordered the Crusaders in Damietta to mobilise.

The army ran into grave trouble that July, approaching Mansourah, as the river flooded. Pelagius marched them into a bottleneck formed by the Nile and the canal from Mansourah to Lake Manzalah. The Egyptians breeched the flood barriers of a second channel behind. This trapped the Crusaders with the rising waters, which swept away their baggage train. Pelagius ordered a retreat, which was a shambles, mitigated only by the disciplined Templar rearguard fending off two attacks from the Sultan's Nubian infantry.[157] This was insufficient, however, to alter the course of events. Al-Kamil, now reinforced from Syria and Jazira by his brothers, was clearly in a position to overwhelm the Crusaders. Pelagius was now forced to accept terms, which, though lenient, were nothing like as favourable as those he had been offered before. Damietta was surrendered in exchange for the release of prisoners, and the Fifth Crusade was abandoned. The French commentator Guillaume le Clerc wrote that 'because of the Legate who led the Christians, we lost that city through folly and sin. Greatly should Rome be humiliated by the loss of Damietta.'[158]

## First Crusade

The First Crusade began as a response to a call for assistance against the encroaching Turks, made by the **Byzantine** Emperor **Alexius I Comnenus** to **Pope Urban II**. At the **Council of Clermont in 1095**, Urban preached a Holy War, placing as much stress on liberating the **Holy Places** of **Jerusalem** from the Infidel as the liberation of the eastern Christians from the cruel **Turks**.

The campaign would restore **Christ**'s kingdom and win salvation for its participants. Most of those participations came from Normandy and **France**, the **Languedoc**, the Lorraine, Flanders and Norman Italy.

The **Crusade** began with disorderly masses of ordinary poor people following a visionary leader called **Peter the Hermit**, who had entranced them with his preaching. Most of this starry-eyed rabble was slaughtered as soon as it crossed into **Muslim** territory from Constantinople, or perished later through famine and pestilence. The more orderly armies of the great nobles – **Godfroi de Bouillon**, Baldwin of Boulogne (**Baldwin I**), Baldwin of le Bourg (**Baldwin II**), **Raymond of Toulouse, Bohemond of Taranto, Tancred de Hauteville** and the rest achieved greater success, though the Crusading armies continued to be accompanied by ragged holy beggars called Taffurs, often spurring the others on with their visions of saints. The Crusaders defeated the Turks at **Nicæa** and **Dorylaeum**, captured **Edessa** and **Antioch** against all odds, and finally took **Jerusalem** in 1099. There ensued an appalling massacre of the non-Christian inhabitants, which failed to taint the miraculous achievement in the eyes of most western commentators at the time.[159]

## Flagellants

The flagellants were a cult on the fringes of medieval Christian orthodoxy, who processed from place to place whipping their own backs in atonement for sins. They came into being particularly in **France** and **Germany** after the Black Death (1348), which they attributed to divine punishment for society's sinfulness. There were earlier manifestations of the movement, however, for example in Italy, some of which incurred Papal disapproval. Some flagellants wore hooded robes, like those of monks but cut away at the backs, baring the flesh to the leather flails they used. There was a history of flagellation being used as a form of punishment in monastic communities. Flogging was also used as a **penance**, and there are accounts of penitent Templars enduring flogging at the hands of the Preceptor during chapter meetings. A cult of penitential flagellation was also associated with the Templars' church of **San Bevignate** in Perugia, and a group of flagellants (*disciplinati*) feature among the murals there. Self-flagellation is also practised within Shi'ite **Islam**.

## Fonts

Fonts are stone receptacles for water used in Christian baptism. It is interesting that Templar **churches** and chapels appear always to have contained fonts (old fonts survive in **Balsall**, **Rothley** and **Temple Church, London,** among other places). Templar churches were generally built to serve self-contained communities of **celibate** men, so one would not expect there to be many babies being born in these **Preceptories** requiring baptism (if there were any female servants, these were generally expected to be too old to be a temptation, and therefore past child-bearing age). There is no evidence that the Templars practised adult baptism, though, and there is no particular reason to suspect that these fonts were installed after the time of the Templars, so infant baptism, presumably in the presence of the children's' mothers, must have taken place in these churches. Sometimes the Templars may have shared their churches with local parishioners, which may explain the presence of fonts.

## Foundation of the Order

The origins of the Knights Templar are shrouded in mystery. **William of Tyre**, writing in the 1180s, stated that the Order was founded in **Jerusalem** in 1118, by **Hugues de Payens**, **Godfroi de St Omer** and several other companions. These pious knights placed themselves in the hands of the Patriarch (Warmund of Piquigny) for the service of **Christ**, professing the wish to live as regular canons and to take monastic vows. King **Baldwin II** gave the knights a temporary house in his palace (formerly the **Al Aqsa Mosque**) on **Temple Mount**. The **Canons of the Temple of the Lord** ceded to them the adjacent square, for the celebration of their offices. Other grants followed from these benefactors and others. The Patriarch and the bishops imposed on the knights, for the remission of their sins, the duty of guarding **pilgrims** against the attacks of bandits and marauders. After nine years there were still only **nine knights**, but after the **Council of Troyes** the Order expanded exponentially, and gained its distinctive **dress**. At first the Templars performed their duties satisfactorily and remained faithful to their vows, but later, in William's judgement, they were corrupted by wealth and power, forgetting their humility and their debt of obedience to the Patriarch.[160]

Many modern historians prefer to think the Templars were founded in 1119, in response to a major attack on pilgrims when 300 were massacred, on the basis of other statements made in the records of the Council of Troyes, and in a donation charter made by Thierry, Count of Flanders.[161] A monk of **Cluny**, Richard of Poitiers, dated the Templars' foundation even earlier, however, claiming that the Order was founded in 1108 or 1109. It is possible, then, that the first Templars were veterans of the **First Crusade** who remained in the **Holy Land**.

William of Tyre's report that there were originally only nine Templars seems an incredibly small number given their allotted task. **Michael the Syrian** wrote that there were thirty founding Templars, which seems more realistic. Perhaps there were nine knights and a number of additional sergeants or serving brothers who were deemed too lowly to warrant mention. Albert of Aachen mentioned the Patriarch of the Holy Sepulchre being obliged to pay for the upkeep of thirty knights. These could be the same band Michael referred to. (In that case, the early Order of the Temple could have been the same thing as the elusive Military **Order of the Holy Sepulchre.**)[162] According to Bernard the Treasurer, the group of knights who would become the Templars went to Jerusalem from 'all lands' and originally obeyed the Prior of the Holy Sepulchre. After a period of indolence, they chose a leader and asked the King for permission to fight the infidel. They secured release from their obedience to the Prior, and grants of land and castles.

The powerful **Hugh, Count of Champagne** was also a pivotal figure in the foundation of the Order. He may have prepared the ground for the Templars during his earlier sojourns in Jerusalem. (Hugh apparently abandoned his wife in order to join the 'Knights of Christ' in about 1308.) **Fulk V, Count of Anjou** also supported them. The original knights secured the approval of the clergy, first at the Council of Nablus in 1120 and especially the Council of Troyes in 1129, where they were supported by St **Bernard of Clairvaux**, himself a nephew of one of the early Templars, **André de Montbard**. The 'new knighthood' became a recognised institution and generally the toast of **Christendom**, though some churchmen had their reservations.

## Fourth Crusade

The Fourth Crusade was the first **Crusading** project of Pope **Innocent III**. It was originally planned that the Crusaders would attack **Alexandria** and conquer **Egypt**, as a prelude to recovering the **Holy Land**. The leadership kept this plan from the rank-and-file volunteers, allowing them to believe that they would go directly to **Jerusalem**.[163] The Frankish barons lost control over the Crusade's intention to the **Venetians**, under Doge Enrico Dandolo, however, and as a result the Crusade was destined not to attack any Muslim nation. Instead, in 1203 the army captured and ravaged **Constantinople**. This has widely been seen as a terrible tragedy. It is probably to the credit of the **Military Orders** that they played virtually no part in the Fourth Crusade – at least they are not mentioned in accounts of military action, though they were involved in preaching the Crusade.[164] They probably mistrusted the financial and mercantile ambitions of the Venetian Republic, and suspected that they would subvert the Crusade if they could. Another explanation is that they were already in the **Holy Land** and would have planned to join an attack on Egypt from there.

The Crusade was primarily a French enterprise, led by Counts Theobald III of Champagne, Louis of Blois, **Boniface of Montferrat** and **Baldwin of Flanders**. Boniface assumed leadership after the death of Theobald in 1201. Unwisely, the leaders delegated authority to envoys that they dispatched to Venice to charter transport. Overestimating the numbers of ships needed, the envoys promised the Doge far more money than the Crusaders could afford to pay. The Crusaders, when they arrived in Venice, found themselves heavily in debt. The Venetians offered to reduce the debt if the Crusaders would help them capture the city of Zara in Croatia from the Hungarians.

Some Crusaders, including **Simon de Montfort, 5th Earl of Leicester,** were appalled by the idea of attacking Christians and abandoned the Crusade. Pope Innocent, on hearing of the storming of Zara in November 1202, **excommunicated** the whole army temporarily. While at Zara the Crusaders were approached by the Byzantine Prince Alexius, the son of the Emperor **Isaac II Angelus.** Isaac Angelus had been deposed, blinded and imprisoned by his brother, now reigning as Emperor Alexius III. Prince Alexius made extravagant promises in order to secure the Crusaders' help in reclaiming his father's throne. The restoration of Isaac and the Prince provided the pretext for the move against **Byzantium.** Several more knights deserted the Crusade meanwhile, dismayed with the direction it was taking. The **Cistercian** Abbot Guy de Vaux-Cernay became the spokesman for a party within the army opposed to the idea of yet again attacking fellow Christians, but his protestations were disregarded.[165]

The Crusade reached Constantinople in June 1203 and attacked it by land and sea. The usurper Alexius III fled. Hoping to appease the Crusaders, the Greeks put Isaac back on the throne, along with his son who was soon crowned as Alexius IV. However, the terms that Alexius IV had agreed – surrendering a fortune and submitting to the **Catholic** Church – proved too much for the citizens of Constantinople, and they rebelled. A palace advisor, Murtzuphlus, seized Alexius IV and had him first imprisoned, then strangled. In April 1204 the Venetians and the Crusaders responded by seizing Constantinople once more, ransacking it and dividing the loot between them. Soldiers were allowed three days of pillage, churches were divested of treasures and **Holy Relics,** and civilians were murdered. Subsequently the heartland of Byzantium was divided between the Venetians and the **Frankish** chiefs, with Baldwin of Flanders being crowned the first Latin 'Emperor of Constantinople'.

An Italian Templar called Brother **Barozzi** acted as messenger between Baldwin of Flanders and the Pope. Though the Templars were not active militarily in the Fourth Crusade, the pillagers of Byzantium apparently made certain gifts of to the Templars from their loot, including icons and relics. This may have been in order to win Templar support for the occupation and make it seem more like part of a legitimate Crusade.

Some of the Military Orders also received grants of land in occupied **Greece,** but their presence seems to have been short-lived and left little trace. The Greeks meanwhile established the substitute 'Empire' of Nicæa. In the 1260s they would recover Constantinople and expel the Latins. However, Byzantium was fatally undermined and never recovered its former power. The Crusaders' controversial victory of 1204 left a legacy of bitterness and ultimately assisted the cause of the **Ottoman Turks**.

## Fourth Lateran Council

The Fourth Lateran Council followed on from the **Fourth Crusade** and formed a prelude to the **Fifth Crusade**. Held in 1215, it was a grand summit of the **Catholic** Church presided over by Pope **Innocent III**. It was attended by 71 Patriarchs, 412 bishops and some 800–900 heads of monastic institutions. The **Grand Masters** of the Knights Templar and **Hospitaller** and many of the brethren also attended.

Outcomes of the council included the recognition of the **Dominican Order** and the definition of various measures to be taken against **heresy**, in part laying the groundwork for the creation of the **Inquisition**. **Confession** was made obligatory. The doctrines of transubstantiation and **Papal supremacy** were also enshrined. Standards were laid out for the behaviour of clergy and measures taken against secular interference in ecclesiastical appointments. It was also decided that non-Christians should be marked by special badges on their clothing, which they would be forced to wear. Taxes were instituted for new Crusades, and 'indulgences' (promises of spiritual rewards) were offered, not just to anyone who would personally **take the Cross**, but also to anyone who would pay mercenaries to fight in the Crusades.

## France

France was the continental heartland of the Knights Templar. The Templars' European headquarters was at the **Paris Temple**, a fortified **Preceptory** that was also the centre of the Templars' continental **banking** activities. The Kingdom of France comprised a relatively small area of the modern country in the early Middle Ages, being only the region around **Paris**. However, throughout the Crusading era the **Capetian** monarchy extended its influence over the vassal states surrounding. **Burgundy** and **Champagne**, where the earliest Templars originated, were gradually incorporated into the French Kingdom, and Toulouse and the **Languedoc**, where the Templars were also well established, were brought under the direct control of the Capetian dynasty after the vicious **Albigensian Crusade**. **Philip II Augustus** extended his control over much of the territory in the west of France, from Normandy to Gascony, which had formerly been part of the English/**Angevin** domain.

## Franciscan Order

The Franciscan Order was a brotherhood of Monks founded in 1209 by St **Francis of Assisi**. They were also known as the Friars Minor. They were sometimes known as Grey friars on account of their simple grey habits.

A preaching Mendicant Order, dependent on charity, the original Franciscans made a cult of poverty and worked to regenerate the spirituality of the Church. Pope **Innocent III** gave them support, apparently after receiving a dream of Francis holding up a toppling church. There was also an order of Franciscan nuns, known as the Poor Clares, after St Clare of Assisi who was inspired to found them after hearing Francis preach.

Later the Franciscans became an institution of the Church, sometimes used as papal tax collectors, along with the **Dominicans**. They were also used as Crusade preachers, and as envoys and missionaries. In the course of the thirteenth century the Franciscans lost some of their original humility. It is said of their Minister General (as their leader was styled), Elias of Cortona, that his head was so turned by power that he would appear in public only on horseback. Like the Dominicans, some Franciscans would be involved in the **Inquisition**. Franciscans were also present at the **trials** of the Templars. Some time after the loss of the Holy Land, meanwhile, Franciscan brothers were appointed to represent the Catholic Church in the **Holy Sepulchre** in **Jerusalem**, and at other sacred sites, where the **Islamic** authorities allowed them to install themselves. Some Franciscans friars would become Bishops, and even **Popes**. A Franciscan splinter group, the Fraticelli, took the Franciscan esteem for poverty a stage further. They argued that the Church, to be Holy, should be without material possessions. They were denounced as **heretics** in 1318 and subsequently persecuted.

## Francis of Assisi, St (1182–1226)

Francis of Assisi was a holy man from Assisi in Umbria, Italy, who founded what was to become the **Franciscan Order**. He was the well-educated son of a rich cloth merchant, and before his spiritual conversion took part in a military expedition against Puglia, subsequently spending a year as a captive. Later, Francis gravitated away from worldly things and towards a religious life. He received a vision where an icon of **Christ** before which he prayed spoke to him, telling him to rebuild Christ's house. He subsequently renounced worldly wealth and comfort and spoke of being wedded to sacred **poverty**. He embarked on a preaching campaign, barefoot and clad in a ragged habit. He attracted followers, who adopted his lifestyle, originally inhabiting an abandoned Leper hospital near Assisi. Francis became famous for his personal austerity, for his compassion for all creatures, and for his preaching to Popes, peasants, birds and Sultans. Francis appeared before Pope **Innocent III**, and gained support for his mission. He attended the **Fourth Lateran Council**, and probably encountered St **Dominic** as well as the Grand Masters of the **Military Orders**. In 1219, Francis went to **Egypt** during the **Fifth Crusade** and tried in vain to convert the Sultan **Al-Kamil** to Christianity. Francis went on to visit the **Holy Land**. He then returned to Italy to oversee the growth of the Franciscan Order. After experiencing another vision in 1223, he was said to have miraculously incorporated the Stigmata (the wounds of Christ on his hands and feet). He was canonised by Pope **Gregory IX** as St Francis in 1228, only two years after his death.

## François Raynouard (1761–1836)

François-Juste-Marie Raynouard was a French playwright, lawyer and historian. Following **Napoleon**'s conquests in Italy, some of the **Vatican Archives** were brought to **France** where Raynouard spent some years scouring them for references to the Templars. He found no conclusive evidence regarding secret **Gnostic** doctrines or mystical practices. Raynouard wrote a historical work called *Monuments Historiques Relatifs a la Condamnation des Chevaliers du Temple*, one of the earliest histories to vindicate the Templars.

## Franks

The Franks were a Germanic race that settled in and around what is now northern **France**, supplanting or mixing with the indigenous **Celtic** Gauls. The Franks were possibly descended from the ancient Sicambri tribe. France was originally described as West Frankia, parts of **Germany** as East Frankia, each having once formed part of the empire of Charlemagne. The Frankish aristocracy considered themselves distinct from the people they ruled and were proud of their status as a vigorous and warlike elite. Broadly the Normans also counted as part of this group, having a similar culture and ethnicity. In the Crusading era, 'Franks' was also a generic term for western European **Catholic** Christians. They were sometimes also referred to as **Latins**. Palestinian Franks were their descendants in the **Holy Land**.

## Frederick I Barbarossa (Emperor) (c. 1122–1290)

Frederick I was the King of **Germany** from 1152, succeeding **Conrad III**. He was elected **Holy Roman Emperor** in 1155. He was of the **Hohenstaufen** dynasty and was known as Barbarossa, after his red beard. He was a veteran of the **Second Crusade** having been Duke of Swabia at the time. His desire to extend his power in Italy led to a struggle with the **Pope**, and Pope Alexander III **excommunicated** Frederick in 1160. Frederick initially supported rival claimants to the Papacy (antipopes). He led three campaigns into Italy against the Church-backed Lombard League, but defeat at the Battle of Legnano in 1176 finally compelled him to come to terms with Alexander. Frederick I intended to be a leader of the **Third Crusade**. He **took the Cross** in Mainz Cathedral, and in 1189 led a mighty German army across Anatolia, overcoming **Turkish** opposition. In June 1190, while crossing the Saleph River, Frederick was thrown from his horse and drowned. To **Saladin** and the **Muslims** of Syria, who had dreaded Frederick's approach, it seemed a divine intervention.

## Frederick II (Emperor) (1194–1250)

Frederick II of Hohenstaufen was the King of both **Germany** and Sicily. He held the title **Holy Roman Emperor** and during the course of the **Sixth Crusade** he restored **Jerusalem** to Christian rule without bloodshed.[166] However, the deed was little appreciated by the **Catholic** Church. Frederick had been **excommunicated** for delaying his embarkation, and shortly after his triumph the Latin **Patriarch** Gerold put Jerusalem under **interdict**.

Frederick II, known as 'stupor mundi' (the wonder of the world), was the son of the Holy Roman Emperor Henry IV and of Constance of Sicily. After his parents' deaths, Pope **Innocent III** acted as Frederick's guardian. Frederick, already King of Sicily (and much of southern Italy), was elected undisputed King of Germany after the defeat of Otto of Brunswick at Bouvines and his fall from power. In 1216, **Honorius III** crowned Frederick as Emperor. Frederick subsequently spent little time in Germany. He was, nonetheless, loyally supported by the **Teutonic Knights** under their *Hochmeister* **Herman von Salza**, who became a trusted advisor to the Emperor. Frederick **took the Cross** while the **Fifth Crusade** was under way, but did not depart for the East before the Crusade's disintegration. He had been distracted by a **Muslim** revolt on Sicily. Having overcome the rebels, he forced the Sicilian Muslims to resettle in Lucera in Apulia, after which they became dependable subjects. Frederick knew Arabic and had read the Koran, and had a respect for **Islam**. Even so, he was serious about embarking on Crusade.

In 1225, Frederick II obtained a claim to the throne of Jerusalem by marrying **Yolande of Jerusalem**. Yolande died in 1227 shortly after bearing Frederick's son, **Conrad IV**. The **Sixth Crusade** got under way in 1228. It had an inauspicious start, for **Gregory IX** excommunicated Frederick for delaying his embarkation due to illness. Prior to this, Frederick had negotiated with **Al-Kamil**, the Sultan of **Egypt**, who had promised him the return of Jerusalem (as well as Nazareth and **Bethlehem**) in exchange for assistance against his Syrian enemies, especially his rebellious brother **al-Muazzam**. Ignoring the papal ban, Frederick made his way to the **Holy Land**, via **Cyprus**. In a diplomatic tour de force, the Emperor held the Sultan to the arrangement, even though his military assistance proved to be no longer necessary, al-Muazzam having died. **Fakhr al-Din** acted as a go-between, and played a part in devising the scheme, whereby Frederick postured as though he intended to take the city by force, and al-Kamil spread the impression that Islam was in for a long and bloody war for survival. Thus the Sultan was able to present the surrender of Jerusalem as a bid to spare Muslim lives. Jerusalem, bar the Islamic Holy sites, was given to Frederick in February 1229, along with **Bethlehem** and Nazareth. Frederick regretted pressing for so much and told al-Kamil he would not have done so were it not vital for his prestige in Europe.

On the way to Jerusalem the Templars and **Hospitallers**, obedient to the Pope, had refused to ride in the same army as an excommunicant (they followed some miles behind) and they took orders in the name of **Christ** rather than from Frederick. Their Grand Masters were further offended when the Emperor ratified his treaty without their seals. The Templar **Pierre de Montaigu** doubtless resented the clause that left **Temple Mount** under Muslim control. Only the Teutonic Knights supported the Emperor as he entered Jerusalem, although the Templars and Hospitallers were with the army. Frederick was also unpopular with some of the local Christian barons, notably John of Beirut, who resisted his authority. Frederick conducted a crown-wearing ceremony in the **Holy Sepulchre**, symbolising Hohenstaufen sovereignty there. He made a conciliatory speech and invited the **Military Orders** to help restore certain fortifications in Jerusalem. His attitude to his opponents within the Catholic establishment hardened, though, after he heard of the interdict imposed from **Acre** by the Patriarch. His relationship with the Templars went into particularly sharp decline. In the meantime he had visited Temple Mount as a guest of the Qadi of Nablus, and had roughly driven off a Catholic priest he caught trying to enter the **al-Aqsa Mosque**.[167] He refused to stay long in the city, supposedly owing to fear of the Templars.

According to **Matthew Paris**, the Templars, motivated by envy of the Emperor's achievements, and knowing of the Pope's hatred for him, began to intrigue against Frederick. They wrote telling the Sultan that Frederick proposed to visit the River Jordan. Frederick would go in secret, unarmed and with few companions, so the Sultan could easily capture or kill him there if he wished. The allegation that the Templars were involved in setting up ambushes was a damning indictment of an Order that had been created precisely to protect such pilgrims from Muslim ambush. According to Paris the plan backfired, for al-Kamil was disgusted by the suggestion and promptly forwarded the Templars' letter to Frederick, complete with the Order's **seal**. (It may be noted that this seems a rather clumsy plot. Paris does not acknowledge the possibility that the Emperor could have forged the letter and colluded with al-Kamil to discredit their common enemy, the Templars.) Some of Frederick's other propaganda against the Order, including the old accusation that they secretly sought to undermine the Crusades in order to safeguard their own martial role, gained wider circulation.

Frederick resorted to laying siege to the Templars in their fortress at Acre. He was forced to return from the **Holy Land**, however, having heard of threats to his realm in Italy from papal mercenaries under **John of Brienne**. In the 1230s, Frederick confiscated Templar properties in Apulia, despite a temporary reconciliation with the Papacy. In 1239 a renewed dispute over power in northern Italy broke out. Gregory issued a new excommunication and warfare broke out afresh. At the Council of **Lyons**, Pope **Innocent**

IV, who had fled from Italy, declared the Emperor deposed and called for a Crusade *against* him. Frederick maintained his good relations with the Ayyubid regime in Cairo, meanwhile. In a letter to **Richard of Cornwall**, Frederick blamed the Templars under **Armand de Perigord** for wrecking the settlement in the Holy Land by breaking the truce with Egypt and forcing the Sultan as-Silah **Ayyub** to call on the **Khoresmians**, bringing about Jerusalem's downfall. Frederick further denounced them for lavishly entertaining their Muslim allies, and of permitting Islamic rituals and secular delights within the walls of the Temple, in the run up to **La Forbie**. This sort of accusation would be echoed at the time of the **suppression**.

Frederick was in no position to intervene in the Middle East by the 1240s. The war of **Guelfs and Ghibellines** would continue after his death and exhaust both parties. It made little difference that Frederick died penitent in the habit of a **Cistercian**. Frederick's sons **Conrad IV** and **Manfred** inherited the Papacy's wrath and the line would finally be ended when his grandson **Conradin** was beheaded by **Charles of Anjou**.

## *Frederick von Salm* (thirteenth–fourteenth century)

Frederick von Salm was a **German** Templar. He was Preceptor of the Rhine provinces at the time of the suppression. He was the brother of **Hugh von Salm**. He had been a Templar for twelve years by 1310, had served in the East and knew **Jacques de Molay**. When he appeared before the council of the Archbishop of Mainz, investigating the Order in the diocese, Frederick offered to undergo trial by red-hot iron to prove the Order's innocence.

## *Freemasonry*

Freemasonry is an international fraternity. Its members are required, in most rites, to profess a belief in a Supreme Being. Also, like members of religious Orders (including the Templars), Freemasons sometimes refer to each other as brother. Freemasonry is an esoteric society, introducing its philosophies to its initiates through a progressive series of rituals. Some of these are shrouded in mystery and Freemasonry has been at times a very secretive society. The 'craft' (as Freemasonry is sometimes called) imparts its moral and philosophical teachings using the tools and practices of stonemasons as symbols and metaphors. Freemasons meet in halls usually called Lodges, which represent **Solomon's Temple**. They wear aprons and use the symbol of the square and compasses. Some of the rituals are based around the foundation myth of Hiram Abiff (the legendary architect of the Temple, who was murdered by three jealous apprentices for refusing to surrender the secrets of the craft). The official governing bodies of Freemasonry are called Grand Lodges. Lodges generally do not admit women (those co-Masonic Lodges that do are not officially recognised).

The Grand Lodge of England was constituted in AD 1717. The fraternity's history is somewhat vague before that time. It originated in medieval stonemasons guilds. If so, then how and when it evolved from a trade association of operative craftsmen into what is termed 'Speculative Freemasonry' (a fraternity drawn almost exclusively from the aristocracy and the middle classes and performing elaborate mystical rituals) is a mystery. Freemasonry is, in principle, apolitical and open to all men of good character who believe in God, whom Freemasons call the Supreme Architect. (The French *Grand Orient* rite is the exception, as it admits atheists.) Freemasonry set out to be acceptable to all members of monotheistic religions. Formerly, however, it may have had an anti-Catholic bias. (Pope Clement XII condemned Freemasonry in a **Papal Bull** of 1738.) Though the fraternity was predominantly a conservative force in England, it had a more radical character elsewhere, and Freemasons had a part in the **Jacobite** rebellion, the American War of Independence and the **French Revolution**. French Freemasonry for a time came under the influence of the Bavarian **Illuminati**. Catherine the Great of Russia was first an admirer and then a scourge of the brotherhood.

Freemasonry's nature, with its outlandish rituals involving swords, nooses and blindfolds, and with its deadly oaths and secret passwords and handshakes, has made it a target of criticism and the subject of **conspiracy theories**. Freemasonry has thus been linked with everything from **Devil worship** (thanks to **Léo Taxil**) to the Jack the Ripper murders (owing to the involvement of **Charles Warren**). It has also been linked to **Zionism**. Both Augustin Barruel and **Charles Louis Cadet-Gassicourt** wrote that a secret society of Templar-Masons was fomenting revolutions and conspiring to bring down Europe's monarchies in order to avenge **Jacques de Molay**.[168]

The suggestion that Freemasonry had anything to do with the Knights Templar seems to have arisen in **France** in the late eighteenth century. A Masonic, neo-Templar tradition gained some ground even before **Bernard Raymond Fabré-Palaprat** made the movement public in 1804. It perhaps could be traced back to **Andrew Michael Ramsay**, but came to prominence during and after the **French Revolution**. (The anti-clericism and anti-royalism of the Revolutionary period caused a re-evaluation of the Knights Templar, who had suffered at the hands of these institutions nearly five centuries previously.) Also during this period, **Napoleon Bonaparte**'s expedition awoke a popular fascination with Ancient **Egypt**, and certain strands of Freemasonry accrued pseudo-Egyptian elements. In this milieu it was not long before the Templars began to be seen as mystics attributed with ancient wisdom.

Fabré-Palaprat's pseudo-Templar Order went on to become the non-Masonic **OSMTH**. Meanwhile, within 'York Rite' Freemasonry there continued a Masonic Knights Templar tradition. This brand of Freemasonry is now most popular in the United States. 'Scottish Rite' Freemasonry has an equivalent Rose-Croix degree, implying links to **Rosicrucianism**.

An alternative version of events would have it that fugitive Knights Templar arrived in the **Scotland** of the excommunicant **Robert the Bruce**, at the time of the suppression, and there reorganised themselves into a secret society which became Freemasonry, aided by the **St Clair** dynasty. It is often suggested that the carvings at **Rosslyn Chapel** show a transition between Templar and Masonic imagery.

## French Revolution

The French Revolution began in 1789. The revolutionaries overthrew the autocratic monarchy of Louis XVI in the name of liberty, equality and brotherhood – *Liberté, égalité, fraternité*. The monarchy was abolished and a republic declared. The idealism of the Revolution soon gave way to the reign of terror, where not just members of the old ruling class but any critic of the ruling revolutionary council was imprisoned and executed. The Revolution also witnessed attacks on the **Catholic** Church and the desecration of its buildings. Meanwhile, monastic institutions within **France**, including the **Hospitallers**, were suppressed and their lands sequestered.

The publications of the Jesuit exile Augustin Barruel (1741–1820) expressed his **conspiracy theory** that the Freemasons and the Bavarian Illuminati were behind the Revolution. **Charles Louis Cadet-Gassicourt** thought along similar lines and saw the events in the context of a Masonic plot to avenge their supposed Templar ancestors. A number of **Freemasons** were indeed involved in the French Revolution (some were nobles, like Louis Philippe, the Duke of Orleans, trying to manipulate events to serve their own interests, until they themselves fell foul of the terror). There was a myth that the attacks on the Church and the monarchy formed some sort of Templar revenge. It is even alleged that as Louis XVI was beheaded in the Place de la Concorde, a man shouted '**Jacques de Molay**, thus you are avenged!'[169] It is hard to say whether this truly happened. The terror continued, meanwhile, and the people's suffering only worsened. Robespierre himself was guillotined in 1794, and government passed to five 'Directors', notoriously corrupt and ineffective. Eventually the Revolution led to near anarchy, which was replaced by military dictatorship under **Napoleon Bonaparte**, who seized power in 1799.

## Friday the 13th

Superstition has it that the thirteenth day of any month is unlucky if it falls on a Friday. It certainly was for the French Templars in October 1307, the day of the **arrests**, when they were seized by the crown agents in the name of the **Inquisition**. Some believe that this event is the source of belief in Friday the 13th being the accursed day.

## *Fulk de Villaret* (died 1319)

Fulk (or Foulques) de Villaret was the **Grand Master** of the Knights **Hospitaller** at the time of the **suppression** of the Templars. He was elected in 1305, succeeding his brother Guillaume, having served as the Order's Admiral. Fulk wrote to **Clement V** at about this time, offering ideas on how a new **Crusade** might be organised to recover the **Holy Land**. He advised that the passage should be begun 'well and prudently', envisaging a large-scale expedition of the kind launched by **Urban II**. The kings should also be instructed to forbid baronial interference with the three leading **Military Orders** or to impede the export of supplies and equipment. Fulk also advocated measures to stop 'wicked Christians' (i.e. **Venice**) selling war materials to the **Muslims**. The fleets of the **Military Orders** and the Kingdom of **Cyprus** should be used to enforce an embargo on **Alexandria**. He also proposed taxing the **Jews** to fund the proposed Crusade.[170]

Fulk de Villaret and **Jacques de Molay** met the **Pope** in 1306 to discuss the future of crusading and the **scheme to merge** the Military Orders. Fulk de Villaret opposed the amalgamation, but in a less outspoken way than Jacques de Molay. (Fulk may have been regarded as a possible candidate to head the combined Order.)[171] Subsequently, he presided over the capture of **Rhodes** and the transition of his Order from the Knights Hospitaller to the Knights of Rhodes. This seizure secured the Order's future, gaining it an independent power base. Fulk convinced Pope Clement V to bestow upon his Order the lands of the abolished Order of the Temple. Fulk's last days were less auspicious. He became excessively dictatorial and morally lax, allegedly indulging in drinking and womanising. In 1317 he was moved against by rebellious brethren led by an elderly commander named Maurice de Pagnac, and had to flee from Rhodes to the castle of the acropolis of Lindos. He was deposed, and in 1319 compelled to retire to a Commandery in the **Languedoc**, where he died.

## *Fulk, King of Jerusalem/Fulk V, Count of Anjou* (*c.* 1090–1143)

Fulk V, Count of Anjou was the son of Fulk IV 'the Rude' of Anjou and Bertrande de Montfort. (Bertrande had subsequently caused scandal by deserting Fulk IV and bigamously marrying King Philip I of **France**, resulting in the King's **excommunication**.) Fulk V succeeded as Count of Anjou in 1109. He would become one of the most powerful and well-connected barons in Europe, and would sire two dynasties of kings. Fulk was an enthusiastic pilgrim. In 1120 he went to **Jerusalem**, and became a close associate of **Baldwin II** as well as of **Hugues de Payens** and the Templars. He may have become the first **confrater** of the nascent Templar Order and certainly supported their mission.

In 1127, Fulk's son by his first marriage, Geoffrey V 'the Fair' Plantagenet, married the Empress **Matilda**, the daughter of **Henry I** of England, giving rise to the **Angevin** Plantagenet dynasty which would hold the English throne for several centuries. Shortly after this, Fulk, by then widowed, received Baldwin II's invitation for him to return to Jerusalem to marry the princess **Melisende**, and become co-heir to the **Kingdom of Jerusalem**. Baldwin probably saw this as a way of thwarting the ambitions of the other Frankish barons in the **Holy Land**. Baldwin also knew that Fulk was rich and powerful and would bring much needed men and money to the kingdom. Fulk agreed, on condition he inherit full authority, and the wedding took place. Before Baldwin II's death in 1131, however, the old king changed the arrangement, bequeathing sovereignty jointly to Fulk, Melisende and the infant **Baldwin III** instead of exclusively to Fulk.[172]

As king, Fulk fought various campaigns intended to secure the realm. He launched an unsuccessful campaign against **Damascus**, but did capture **Banyans**. Later he allied with **Unur** of Damascus against **Zenghi** of **Aleppo**. In 1137, Fulk and his army, including a Templar contingent, went to relieve Barin (Montferrand to the Franks), north-east of **Tripoli**, which Zenghi was besieging. A bitter battle ensued and the Franks were defeated. Fulk and the other survivors took refuge in the fortress. They were reduced to eating their own horses, but were eventually permitted to depart after promising Zenghi a ransom.[173] Shortly afterwards, a **Byzantine** relief force showed up, much to the chagrin of Fulk, who subsequently snubbed the Emperor **John II Comnenus** in Jerusalem, wary of Byzantine aspirations to turn the Latin Kingdom into a client state.

Fulk had to contend with rebellions by Alice of Antioch and Pons of **Tripoli**, and by Hugh II, Count of **Jaffa**. As **William of Tyre** portrayed it, Fulk, through jealousy, unjustly accused Hugh of Jaffa of being too close to Melisende and of plotting against him. Hugh responded by rebelling in league with Muslim **Ascalon**, but eventually accepted exile to Sicily, although not before surviving an assassination attempt by a knight seeking to please the King. Fulk was reconciled with his wife in the latter years of his reign. He died during a hunting accident while they were staying in **Acre**. His body was interred in the Church of the **Holy Sepulchre** in Jerusalem. He was succeeded by Melisende, and eventually in turn by their sons Baldwin III and **Amalric I**.

# G

## *Galcerand de Teus* (thirteenth–fourteenth century)

Galcerand de Teus was a Templar who was received in Catalonia. During the **suppression** he was arrested in the Kingdom of Naples. He confessed that absolution was a common practice within the Order. The Master in **Chapter** would pray God that he would pardon the sins of the recipient of absolution 'as he pardoned them to St **Mary Magdalene** and the thief who was put on the cross'. It was implied that this 'thief' meant **Jesus Christ** (not the thief who was saved), whom the Templars were accused of denying as the saviour. Galcerand could well have made up his entire confession under torture. (The King, Charles II of Naples, was an uncle of **Philip the Fair** and may therefore have ordered torture to be used on the Templars in his realm. This is one of the few places outside France where confessions were forthcoming.) If these are the real words used in a Templar absolution, the thief being referred to, obviously, could be the penitent criminal crucified alongside Christ.

## *Garway*

Temple Garway was a Templar **Preceptory** in Herefordshire, **England**, on the Welsh Marches. This was an unstable region and the Preceptory with its fortified tower held a commanding position. The Preceptory was founded in the 1180s. There was originally a **round church** at Garway with an oblong chancel. The Templars replaced the round section of the church in the thirteenth century with an oblong nave, though the round foundations were rediscovered in the 1920s. There are some original carvings in the church at Garway (which is dedicated to St Michael). These including a horned **green male** face emerging from a capital on one side of the Norman **Romanesque** Chancel arch. On the church's exterior are carvings including a hand, more **heads**, various kinds of crosses and an **Agnus Dei**, though some of these may be later additions (they are carved into individual stones, and in no way seem part of an original decorative scheme). Inside, the **font** has carvings of upwards and downwards pointing triangles around its rim as well as a carving of a serpent entwined around a red cross, but these again may be later additions (they resemble symbols from **Freemasonry**). More certainly authentic are the fragments of Templar **grave slabs**, bearing the elongated **baculus** cross. There is also a Templar cross, originally from the top of a gable, with a diamond shaped opening in the centre and a carving of a hand making the sign of blessing. There is also a **piscina**. Above this are graffiti carvings of a fish, a snake or eel, and a cross within a circle at the tip of a triangle like a pyramid. Near the church at Garway is a medieval dovecote. Spookily, this antique roost contains 666 pigeonholes.

## Gaza

Gaza was an ancient Phoenician city in southern Palestine, near the border with Egypt. By the era of the **Crusades**, it had fallen into ruins due to the unstable times. The city was partially rebuilt by the **Franks** in the time of **Baldwin III**. The castle on the hill was committed by general agreement of the barons to the custody of the Templars. It was one of the first major fortifications that the Order gained in the **Kingdom of Jerusalem**, one of several Crusader strongholds established to place a stranglehold on **Ascalon**, ten miles to the north (the last coastal city still in Muslim hands, and a thorn in the side of the Christians). The 'brave men and valiant warriors' of the Order (as **William of Tyre** wrote with unusual approbation) had guarded Gaza faithfully and wisely ever since.[174] The city would be resettled under their tutelage, and also served as a bastion for the Kingdom against Egypt. In 1150 the Templars withstood a determined attempt by the Egyptians to retake Gaza. Three years later it served as a base for the conquest of Ascalon. Its Templar garrison also contributed to the victory over **Saladin** at **Montguissard**. Both Gaza and Ascalon fell to the Sultan in 1187.

## Geoffrey, Brother (Almoner to Henry III)

The Templar brother Geoffrey served as Royal **Almoner** during the reign of **Henry III, King of England**. It was a position of trust and honour, with many duties. Geoffrey was in charge of distributing moneys for the king, feeding and clothing the poor, managing hospitality in royal households, transporting royal robes and regalia when required by the King on state occasions in various places, equipping military expeditions and keeping the accounts for all this. Geoffrey was also responsible for collecting a tax imposed on the **Jews**. **Matthew Paris** said that Geoffrey was unpopular at court and was dismissed because he was too subservient to **Rome**, but another reason may have been his refusal to sign a writ giving an uncle of the Queen a toll of 4*d* on every sack of wool exported from England to Flanders.[175] It was the giving of such privileges to Henry's foreign courtiers that later provoked the other barons to rebel under **Simon de Montfort, the 6th Earl of Leicester**.

## Geoffrey de Mandeville (died 1144)

Geoffrey de Mandeville, First Earl of Essex, was a noble patron of the Order of the Temple in England. His dour effigy can be found in **Temple Church, London**. The effigy's present battered state is a result of bomb damage from the Blitz. Geoffrey was a warlord who capitalised on the strife surrounding the civil wars between King **Stephen** and the Empress **Matilda** to seize lands for himself – mostly lands lost by his father William, the former constable of the **Tower of London**, who had fallen out of favour with **Henry I**. Stephen shifted sides as seemed expedient during the civil wars known as 'the anarchy'. Subsequently he created his own power base around Ely, controversially raiding Ramsey Abbey and afterwards using it as a headquarters. (He had been **excommunicated** for this.) Geoffrey died of an arrow wound incurred in a skirmish against King Stephen at the siege of Burwell Castle in Cambridgeshire. He must have bestowed endowments upon the Templars presumably for the sake of his soul. The brethren cast the mantle of a Templar over his body and took him for burial – apparently in the **Old Temple, London**. However, they could not bury him in consecrated ground as he was excommunicated, so sealed his body in lead and kept it, either hung from a tree in their orchard or in a ditch by the graveyard, until the excommunication was posthumously lifted in 1163. They then buried him in the **New Temple, London**.

## *Geoffrey Fulcher* (mid-twelfth century)

Geoffrey Fulcher was a prominent Templar Preceptor in the **Holy Land**. He accompanied Hugh, Lord of **Caesarea** on a mission to negotiate a treaty with the Vizier Sharwah of **Egypt** against **Nur ed-Din** on behalf of **Amalric I of Jerusalem**. His name also appeared with that of **Bertrand de Blanquefort** on a royal charter granting rights for the **Pisans** in **Acre** in return for assisting Amalric against **Alexandria**, although the Templars would afterwards distance themselves from this scheme.[300] Later, he wrote to **Louis VII** of France detailing events in the East, such as the loss of a number of Templars at **Harim**, where they had fought alongside the forces of **Antioch**. Geoffrey returned to Europe and became **Visitor** of the Houses in the West.

## *Geoffroi de Charney* (c. 1252–1314)

Geoffroi (sometimes Guy?) de Charney was a senior Templar dignitary, the Preceptor of Normandy. He was initiated by **Amaury de la Roche** at Étamps near Sens. After the arrests, he was held at **Chinon** in 1308, where he was questioned by the visiting Cardinals about his reception ceremony. He said he was received by Amaury de la Roche at Etamps near Sens. He confessed to being made to deny **Christ**. De Charney was subsequently returned to **Paris**, along with **Jacques de Molay**, and the other Templar dignitaries (apart from **Raymbaud de Caron**, who apparently perished.)

In 1314, De Charney, along with the three other surviving high officials of the Temple, was brought before the Papal representative and the gathered crowds in Paris to hear his sentence, which was one of life imprisonment. He joined with Jacques de Molay in making a surprise retraction of his confession, and consequently died alongside the **Grand Master**, burning at the stake.

## *Geoffroi de Charny* (c. 1300–56)

Geoffroi de Charny of Lirey was a French knight famed for his piety and for his gallant conduct during the Hundred Years War and in other campaigns. He was the son of Jean de Charny and Marguerite de Joinville (the daughter of

Jean de Joinville) Geoffroi epitomised **Chivalry**. He was probably the nephew of his near-namesake, **Geoffroi de Charney**, who had been the Templar Preceptor of Normandy. He fought at Hainault and in Flanders, and in a crusading expedition against the Turks in Eastern Europe in the 1340s. He had the distinction of carrying the French war banner, the **Oriflamme**. He was captured at Calais in 1350 and held prisoner in England until ransomed by his king (Jean II) the following year. Geoffroi was later killed fighting the English at the Battle of **Poitiers**. It appears Geoffroi had at some stage came into possession of the **Holy Shroud** (later called the Turin Shroud), which was passed to his widow Jeanne de Vergy, who had it exhibited in public at a church in Lirey. The family connection possibly indicates some link between the Templars and the Shroud.

### Geoffroi de Gonneville (born *c.* 1260)
Geoffroi de Gonneville was a senior Templar, the Preceptor of Aquitaine and Poitou. He was among those who were questioned by the Cardinals at **Chinon**. According to his testimony on the **Chinon Parchment**, he had served for twenty-six years having been received in the **Temple Church, London**, by Preceptor Robert de Torreville. He confessed that after his reception ceremony he had been shown a picture of a cross in a book and called to deny he who was on the Cross. However, he claims he refused to do this or to spit at the image. In 1314, Geoffroi de Gonneville, like **Hugues de Pairaud**, declined to join **Jacques de Molay** in repudiating previous confessions and declaring the Order innocent. He thus escaped condemnation to the flames and was returned to prison, where he presumable spent the remainder of his days.

### Geoffroi de Sargines (thirteenth century)
Geoffroi de Sargines was Seneschal and *bailli* of the **Kingdom of Jerusalem** (reduced to **Acre** and its environs by **Mameluk** advances) about 1254–67. He, like **Oliver of Termes**, was a veteran of the **Seventh Crusade** and was one of the knights maintained in the East with the support of **Louis IX of France**, also acting as the king's representative.

### George, St (*c.* 280–1303)
St George was a third-century Christian **saint**. Like St Maurice, he was a Roman army officer who was **martyred**. He refused to carry out an imperial order to persecute Christians and was consequently tortured and beheaded. His martyrdom encouraged others to convert to Christianity. George was venerated at Lydda in the **Holy Land**. The church devoted to him was rebuilt by the **Crusaders**, for whom, as a warrior saint, he was something of a patron. The church was destroyed by the forces of **Saladin**. The legend of St George slaying a dragon dates to the ninth century. This episode was supposed to have taken place in Lebanon. By the Age of **Chivalry**, George had become an

embodiment of the virtues of a Christian **knight**, generally shown in armour and mounted on a white horse, rescuing a princess from a ferocious dragon. St George was often shown wearing a white mantle with a red cross and looking rather like a Templar. Only a wall painting of the saint in the Templar chapel of **Cressac** indicates that the Templars themselves venerated St George. George was also venerated in Georgia and Genoa, and regarded as a patron by the Order of the **Garter**, the **Teutonic Knights** and the **Freemasons**.

## *Gerard de Ridefort* (died 1189)

Gerard de Ridefort (or van Ruddervoorde) was the tenth **Grand Master** of the Knights Templar. He presided at the time of the disasters that befell the **Kingdom of Jerusalem** in and around 1187. He was an ally of **Guy de Lusignan**, Queen **Sibylla** and **Reynald de Chatillon**. Gerard has been portrayed as a sinister firebrand and a warmonger of the same cast as Reynald, pursuing policies and tactics inconsistent with the best interests of the Kingdom. From this distance it is hard to trace any military or political wisdom in his actions. He did not seem to lack personal courage, however, and perhaps if he had been blessed with more luck he would be better thought of. Still, given his clearly immoderate nature, it is difficult to account to his rise to the top of the Order of the Temple, especially considering that he was not a career Templar.

Gerard was probably of Flemish extraction. Like Reynald he may have been a member of the **Second Crusade**, who chose to remain in the East. Gerard took service as a secular knight under **Raymond III of Tripoli**, on the understanding that he would be rewarded with a grant of land and the hand of the heiress Lucia of Botrun. Raymond later reneged on the arrangement, and Gerard joined the Templars, nursing a bitter grudge against Raymond. (Gerard's rival was a **Pisan** merchant named Plivano. It seems Plivano had offered Lucia's weight in gold to Raymond in order to claim the heiress's hand and power in Botrun.) Gerard's rise within the Order of the Temple may be attributed to 'driving ambition and aggressive self-confidence'.[176] He became **Seneschal** in 1183, and had reached the top by 1185. The following year the death of the boy king **Baldwin V** plunged the Kingdom of Jerusalem into crisis. Raymond III led the barons opposed to the accession of Sibylla and Guy de Lusignan. Gerard supported Guy and Sibylla, perhaps as much to spite Raymond as for any other reason. The support of the Knights Templar (who were sworn to obey their master whatever the cost) swung events in favour of the de Lusignan faction, and facilitated Guy's coronation as co-ruler.

Gerard seems to have believed in his own invincibility. In May 1387 a 7,000-strong Muslim force scouted into Crusader Galilee. Gerard, with around 130 knights including ninety Templars, heard of it, and intercepted it on its return journey at **Cresson**. He decided to attack, despite the objections of more judicious companions including the **Hospitaller** Grand Master **Roger de Moulins** and the **Marshal** of the Temple **Jacques de Mailly**. (Gerard may not have been so rash, however. **Ibn al-Athir** presents the Templars' action not as an unprovoked charge but as a defence of Sephoria, which was under attack from al-Afdal's forces, and the battle seems to have been a close-run thing.) At any rate it seems only Gerard and a couple of others escaped death or capture. Al-Athir's army finished sacked and pillaging the land, then returned safely to spread the 'joyful news'. They considered it a great accomplishment, for the **Military Orders** were the 'backbone of the Frankish army'.[177]

Later that year, **Saladin**'s full host (some 40,000–60,000 warriors) crossed the Jordan and beset Tiberias. The army of **Jerusalem** assembled, perhaps 20,000 including about 600 of the Knights of the Temple and the Hospital. Raymond advised Guy not to take the army to Tiberias but to force Saladin to come to them. Again, Gerard (along with Reynald) advocated the opposite policy. Gerard visited Guy in the night to persuade him to advance across the blazing desert, even though Raymond had warned that such a march would drastically weaken the army and leave Jerusalem itself vulnerable. Gerard pronounced Raymond a traitor, and persuaded Guy that if as king he failed to act decisively against Saladin and to save Tiberias, then he would seem weak and unworthy.

So came to pass the Battle of **Hattin**. The weary and parched Christians fought bravely but under the circumstances victory was impossible. The Templars and Hospitallers who had been taken prisoner were beheaded. Saladin spared only Gerard de Ridefort and kept him for ransom, though given the sequence of disasters he had precipitated, it is a wonder anyone wanted him back. The Templar Brother **Terric** led the Order in the meantime. Gerard was finally released in May 1189. He went on to lead the Templars again at the Siege of **Acre**. And once again he led his companions in an excessively bold charge, ending in their slaughter. This time, it is recorded, he declined the chance to save himself lest it bring shame and scandal on the Templars, and he fell with the slain.[178]

## Gérard de Sède (1921–2004)
Gérard de Sède was a French writer who played a part in creating the **Priory of Sion** hoax, apparently as a sort of surrealist joke. An associate of **Pierre Plantard**, his book *Le Trésor Maudit de Rennes-le-Château* (The Cursed Treasure of **Rennes le Château**) popularised the mystery surrounding that location, and introduced the coded documents later mentioned in *The Holy Blood and the Holy Grail*.

## Gérard de Villiers (thirteenth–fourteenth century)
Gérard de Villiers was the last Templar **Grand Preceptor** of **France**. He fled before the arrests in 1307. He was never found. During the trials it was

alleged that some of the brethren had held him responsible for the loss of **Arwad**, the island off **Tortosa** in Syria, and for the deaths of those stationed there. The Templar **Raoul de Gizy**, in his testimony before the trials, also associated de Villiers with the **head** idol that was supposedly brought out at the chapter meetings, and accused de Villiers of reducing the alms given by the Order to the poor. Anyone who crossed de Villiers was placed in a pit-like dungeon at **Merlan**, according to the testimony of the serving brother Jean de Châlons. Jean de Châlons also said that de Villiers had received prior warning of the **arrests**, and had fled with fifty horses, and apparently slipped away with eighteen galleys, while another fugitive, Hugh de Châlons, had made off with the treasure of **Hugues de Pairaud**.

### Gerard Thom (Gerard the Hospitaller) (1040–1120)
Gerard Thom, known later as the Blessed Gerard, was the effective founder of the Knights **Hospitaller**. He is said to have been a merchant from Amalfi, Italy, who went on a **pilgrimage** to **Jerusalem**, possibly just before the **First Crusade**, and created the Order of the Hospital of St John of Jerusalem as a **Catholic**, monastic institution caring for Christian Pilgrims. This received official recognition as early as 1113, although it did not become also a **Military Order** for another couple of decades.

### Germany
Medieval Germany formed the heart of the **Holy Roman Empire**. It was a quasi-elective monarchy, and its king was usually also recognised also as Emperor. Germans contributed significantly to the **Crusades**, both in the **Holy Land** and also in the **Baltic**. The Templars were not extensively established in Germany, where most religious knights would have gravitated to the **Teutonic Order** after its foundation. They did, however, have Preceptories there, and they were neither systematically **suppressed** nor convicted of **heresy**. The German Preceptor of Supplingenberg, Otto of Brunswick, remained a powerful lord of the place after the **suppression** for example, and only after his death did the property pass to the **Hospitallers**. It is quite possible that many German Templars went on to serve in the Teutonic Order, which followed a near identical **Rule** of Life, despite there having been tension between the two Orders in the past.

### Gilbert d'Assailly (died 1170)
Gilbert d'Assailly was **Grand Master** of the **Hospitallers** in the time of **Amalric I** of **Jerusalem**. He was elected in 1163. He supported the King's last expedition into Egypt in 1168, which the Templars under **Bertrand de Blanquefort** had refused to be a part of. Gilbert's tenure saw the Knights Hospitaller come of age as a **Military Order**. The Templars were reluctant to take part without

the promised **Byzantine** aid materialising. Besides, it breached a treaty and left the Kingdom vulnerable to attack from the north-east. Gilbert, however, offered Amalric the services of 1,000 knights and Turkopoles in exchange for possession of the city of **Belbies**. The expedition was ultimately futile. It saw the capture of Belbies and the massacre of its people, but after the Egyptians called for Syrian aid and **Nur ed-Din** sent his general **Shirkuh**, Amalric and the Hospitallers were forced to abandon the town.

The defeat adversely affected the Order of the Hospital's finances, as well as its Grand Master's mental equilibrium: in 1170 he abandoned the Order to dwell in a cave as a hermit. He was persuaded to return, but soon afterwards drowned while crossing the sea to England.

## Gilbert Erail (or Horal) (1152–1200)

Gilbert Erail (or Erill or Horal) was a Templar from **Aragon**. He had joined in his teens and risen to be Master of the Temple in Aragon and Provence, and had seen action in the **Reconquista** as well as in the **Holy Land**. He became the twelfth **Grand Master** succeeding **Robert de Sable** around 1194. Unlike **Gerard de Ridefort**, Gilbert Erail favoured peaceful relations with the Muslims. This caused tension between the Templars and the **Hospitallers,** who at this time were the more militant party. Gilbert's conciliatory policy towards the Muslims also set him at odds with Pope **Innocent III** and the more militant of the **Catholic** clergy who wanted eternal war against the infidel. The Bishop of Sidon excommunicated Gilbert. However, the **Pope** overturned this **excommunication**, on the basis that only Popes had the authority to excommunicate a Templar. Gilbert died in December 1200.

## Gilles Aicelin, Archbishop of Narbonne (thirteenth–fourteenth century)

Cardinal Gilles Aicelin, Archbishop of Narbonne was the chair of the Papal Commission, convened by **Clement V** to investigate whether the Order of the Temple as a whole was guilty of institutionalised **heretical** depravity. He could hardly be considered the most impartial judge, given that he was on **Philip the Fair**'s Royal Council and had spoken against the Templars (along with **Guillaume de Plaisians**) at the assembly in **Poitiers**. During the sessions of the Papal Commission, the Archbishop was repeatedly absent on royal business. Even so, Aicelin was a moderate compared to Guillaume de Plaisians, **Guillaume de Nogaret** or **Philip of Martigny**, the Archbishop of Sens. Aicelin had been uneasy about the regime's treatment of Bernard de Saisset, the Bishop of Pamiers, and also of the action against **Boniface VIII**. He trod an uneasy path between his conscience and towing the royal line.

There is some suggestion the Archbishop of Narbonne may initially have sympathised with the Templars, and even resigned as Keeper of the Seals (the title he supposedly held before de Nogaret assumed it) on learning of the King's design to attack the Templars. However, in the end Aicelin did nothing to save the Templars from their fate.

When the Templars started to be **burned** as relapsed heretics by order of the Archbishop of **Sens**, and the other defendants appealed to Aicelin to intervene to stop this, Aicelin absented himself from the trials. He was unwilling to jeopardise his standing with the court (or indeed his own security) by speaking openly in the Templars' defence.

## *Giovanni da Carignano* (died *c.* 1329)

Giovanni da Carignano was a cartographer from Genoa. He was apparently the first to assert that **Prester John** was an African rather than Asiatic king. Apparently Carignano had encountered an embassy of thirty men from **Ethiopia** passing back from an audience with Pope **Clement V** in 1306. It seems poor sailing conditions had detained the Ethiopians in Genoa, and Carignano had some time to question them about their homeland. Carignano's writings have been lost and are only alluded to in a later source. If such a diplomatic mission did meet with the Pope in that year, it would have been sent by the Emperor Wedem Ara'ad. It has been speculated that the timing of the mission was significant to the fate of the Templars, who may have been present in Ethiopia and may have over-stayed their welcome.[179]

## *Gisors*

Gisors is a castle in the old Vexin region of Normandy. The Templars were made temporarily guardians of the castle in 1158 when it formed part of the dowry of Marguerite, the infant daughter of King **Louis VII** of **France** who was betrothed to Henry, the infant son of **Henry II of England** (later known as 'Henry the Young King', one of the famous 'devil's brood' who would grow up to rebel against their father). Henry II brought the wedding date forward, and took over the castle in 1164. The handing over of the castle irritated Louis, who expelled from France the three Templars responsible, namely Robert de Pirou, Tostes de St Omer and **Richard Hastings, the Master of the Temple in England**. The Vexin remained a vassal state of **England** until the castle fell to the French in 1129. The magnificent castle is now ruinous, dominated by a circular keep on a mound at is centre.

There has been stories of a Templar **treasure** being hidden somewhere at Gisors, but if it is there no one has found it. Unless, that is, one believes the claims made by one Roger Lhomoy to **Gérard de Sède** in the 1960s, when de Sède employed him on his pig farm. Lhomoy claimed that during the 1940s he had been employed as a caretaker of Gisors Castle. He had taken it upon himself to carry out surreptitious excavations, looking for rumoured treasure. After digging one of his tunnels, Lhomoy claimed to have found a hidden vault thirty metres long, with statues of Christ and the apostles on corbels on the walls, and with an altar, sarcophagi and thirty great metal trunks on the floor. Lhomoy may have amused himself digging up Gisors Castle, but did not find the Templars' treasure there. As mentioned, the Templars were only in custody of the castle (along with another at Neafle) for a short time before handing it into the custody of Henry II. It seems unlikely they would bury their treasure in a castle that they were about to relinquish.

## Glastonbury

Glastonbury Abbey in Somerset was one of the richest monastic institutions in **England**. It had housed a community of monks at least since Anglo-Saxon times. It was associated in legend with **Joseph of Arimathea** who was said to have brought the **Holy Grail** to Britain, and planted the famous Glastonbury Thorn – which grew from where he laid his staff, and which miraculously flowered not only in May but at Christmas. Pilgrimage to Glastonbury increased after 1191 when the supposed graves of **King Arthur** and Queen Guinevere were found in the grounds, along with a leaden cross naming Arthur. The Abbott Henry de Blois commissioned the search for the bodies. Glastonbury, with its nearby Tor, had become associated with the Isle of Avalon from Arthurian myth. The relics he found drew pilgrims and helped pay for the completion of the new abbey. The skeletons were reburied amid great pomp near the high altar by **Edward I** in 1278. It seems that after the Templars were disbanded at least one lived out his days as a penitent in Glastonbury Abbey. Glastonbury survived as a rich and powerful institution until it was plundered by Henry VIII. The last Abbot was hanged on Glastonbury Tor.

## Gnosticism

Gnosticism was an early **heresy**, flourishing in the second and third centuries AD. One of their characteristic doctrines was salvation through knowledge (Gnosis). A Gnostic usually claimed to have received some personal insight into or connection with divinity, which somehow freed their soul. This esoteric but intuitive approach differed greatly from the orthodox teaching that salvation derived from faith, and through the medium of the established Church and its **priests**. There were a great variety of Gnostic sects, existing from around the time of Christ to the fifth century and beyond. Some of them were more conventionally Christian than others. All claimed to preserve the true teachings of Christ, as passed to whichever disciple they particularly favoured, be it **Mary Magdalene, John the Baptist** or even Judas Iscariot. Some Gnostics made stone charms carved with the **Abraxas** and other magical and astrological symbols. Some, including the later **Bogomils,** held that God had two sons, Sataniel/Satan and the Archangel Michael/Jesus Christ. The former, the eldest, became a rebel against God and the creator of the earth and the lower Heavens, the latter became the saviour of souls.

There was a strong dualist strand in Gnosticism, particularly that of the Manichaean-influenced sects (named after the pre-Christian Persian prophet Mani). Matter was viewed as degraded and distant from the pure spirit that is God. Such ideas resurfaced among the **Cathars**. The material world was created by a lesser divinity, the Demiurgos, as a prison for souls, which should belong in a spiritual realm of light. That realm of light was supposed to be inhabited by beings of light called Aeons, very like angels, but described as emanations of God, and somehow aspects of the divine rather than independent entities. The Aeons were sometimes said to come in pairs, male and female, and together to form the 'fullness' of God. One pair was named as **Christ** and his heavenly bride Sophia. Certain Gnostic Gospels, such as the *Pistis Sophia*, one of the texts found at **Nag Hammadi**, have the resurrected Jesus delivering teachings concerning this Gnostic cosmology to his disciples. The established Christian Church anathematised such accounts. The Nicæan Creed was devised largely to counter Gnostic doctrines.

Eighteenth-century **Freemasons** claimed that the Templars were the guardians of secret Gnostic wisdom, and that an inner core within the Order formed a Gnostic secret society. **Joseph von Hammer-Purgstall** alleged something similar, though disparagingly. Tenuous evidence for this **conspiracy theory** include the Order's use of the Abraxas seal, the alleged relationship of the word **Baphomet** to Sophia, and the limited nature of Templar involvement with the **Albigensian Crusade**, although the latter may be accounted for more simply as reluctance to see Crusades directed other than to **Outremer.**

## Goddess Veneration

It has been argued that the characteristics of pagan goddesses such as **Isis** and Diana were sublimated into those of the **Virgin Mary** and other female **Catholic** saints. The Templars' **Rule** was inimical to living women, reflecting the common attitude among churchmen at the time that they were a source of temptation that could lead men astray from the way to salvation. None of these churchmen, least of all **Bernard of Clairvaux**, saw any contradiction between their distrust of women and their reverence for the Madonna, whom Bernard exalted as the Queen of Heaven.

The trials of the Templars heard little of veneration for the sacred feminine. The **accusations** actually suggested that the Templars repudiated the Holy Virgin as well as Christ. This seems extraordinary given the Order's well-known and perfectly orthodox devotion to the Virgin. There are clues that the Templars revered sanctified femininity in various other manifestations.

These clues include the object found in the **Paris Temple**, a beautiful silver gilt reliquary shaped like a woman's head, called **Caput LVIIIm**, said to contain the skull of a virgin martyr. The Brethren on Cyprus also claimed to be the custodians of the head of **St Euphemia**, another female martyr. Yet another, St **Catherine of Alexandria**, seems to have been important to the Templars. They also invoked St **Mary Magdalene** when forgiving sins of penitent brethren at **chapter** meetings. Though none of this equated to goddess worship.

Recently, especially since the popularisation of **conspiracy theories**, attempts have been made to link the Templars (and the **Holy Grail**) to a supposed secret tradition of exalting this 'sacred feminine' but this strays a long way from verifiable history.

## *Godfroi de Bouillon* (1061–1100)

Godfroi (or Godfrey) de Bouillon was the Duke of the Lower Lorraine. In 1905 he sold his castle and estates and embarked on the **First Crusade**, clearly without any intention of returning. Godfroi was the brother of Baldwin of Boulogne (**Baldwin I**). Godfroi, with his Brothers Eustace and Baldwin, led the first of the 'professional' Crusader forces to pass through **Constantinople**. He was reluctant to swear allegiance to **Alexius I Comnenus**, but eventually complied. He subsequently fought in all the major battles of the Crusade and was active in the conquest of **Jerusalem** in 1099. Members of Godfroi's contingent were the first over the walls of the Holy City, scrambling across from Godfroi's siege tower. Therefore (and as **Raymond IV of Toulouse** had apparently declined the throne) the Crusader barons elected Godfroi to rule the conquered city. Godfroi assumed the title of *Advocatus Sancti Sepulchri* (Defender of the **Holy Sepulchre**), deeming it unsuitable to wear a kingly crown where **Jesus Christ** had worn a crown of thorns. As the conqueror and first Crusader ruler of Jerusalem, Godfroi soon entered legend as a pious Christian hero and in later times his fame would eclipse that of the other leaders of the enterprise. Godfroi subsequently defended the fledgling **Kingdom of Jerusalem** from **Turkish** and **Egyptian** attack, and fended off the theocratic ambitions of the **Patriarch** Daimbert of Pisa. Godfroi laid the groundwork for the codified legal system that became known as the *Assizes of Jerusalem*. He was also associated with the formation of the **Order of the Holy Sepulchre** (linked to the Augustinian **Canons of the Holy Sepulchre**) who in turn were influential over the earliest Templars. After Godfroi's death in 1100, control of Jerusalem passed to Baldwin I, who had no problem with the title of King.

## *Godfroi de St Omer* (eleventh–twelfth century)

Godfroi (sometimes Godfrey, or Geoffrey) de St Omer is mentioned by the chronicler **William of Tyre** along with **Hugues de Payens** as one of the leaders of the original Templars. He was probably from the family occupying the castle of St Omer in Picardy (northern France/Flanders). He may have been a relation (perhaps son or brother) of Hugh de St Omer, a noble who participated in the **First Crusade**, and who subsequently held an important fief in Galilee. William (Guillaume), Lord of St Omer (Hugh's father) also participated in the Crusade. The St Omer links to the Templars and the **Crusades** continued. William II, castellan between 1128 and 1145, made grants to the Templars, along with his son Osto, who subsequently joined the Order. This William de St Omer possibly later joined the **Cistercian Order** at **Clairvaux**.[180] William's other son, Walter (Gautier), went on Crusade and was present at the capture of **Ascalon** in 1152. He married the heiress Eschiva of Bures and came to hold the same fief as had been occupied by Hugh. Godfroi de St Omer returned with Hugues de Payens to the West in the late 1120s, promoting the new Templar order, receiving grants and donations, and attending the **Council of Troyes**.

## *Godfrey Wedderburn* (unknown date during the existence of the Order)

Godfrey Wedderburn features in a legend attached to **Maryculter** in eastern **Scotland**. A folklorist named Henderson recorded this story in 1892.[181] It is unclear whether it has any historical basis. Godfrey Wedderburn was a Templar from the Preceptory Maryculter. He went to the **Holy Land,** where, during a battle with the **Saracens**, he came up against a great Emir and was severely wounded and left for dead. After the battle he crawled to a well, where he lost consciousness. He awoke again to see a beautiful Saracen maiden watching him, the daughter of the man he had fought.

She bore the Templar to a cave, where she tended his wounds, and gave him a golden ring as a healing charm. Eventually, Wedderburn remembered his vows though, and left the maiden, eventually returning home to Scotland. The heartbroken Saracen maid followed him and gained entrance to the Preceptory at Maryculter. The Master discovered her there and had her roughly ejected. Wedderburn saw this and knocked his superior to the ground. For this mutiny he was sentenced to death.

His brethren led him outside to the place of execution, and stabbed him to death with his own dagger. As he fell a terrible scream resounded around the valley. The Saracen maid appeared and cradled Wedderburn's body. She drew the gold ring from his dead finger and challenged the **Master** to put it on if he dared. As the Master slid it on, a bolt of blue fire struck him down dead. The Saracen maid then drew her dead lover's dagger and killed herself. Subsequently, blue light was seen hovering over the accursed field and the Templars never ventured there again. Wedderburn was buried in the Templars' chapel where the bloodless ghost of the Saracen maid could be seen afterwards, floating over his tomb. The ghost of the knight could be seen riding through the glens in full armour, and the ghostly, raven-haired eastern maid could be seen sitting by the beds of the dying in the county.

## Golden Spurs (Battle of the)

In 1300, King of France, **Philip the Fair** decided to stamp his mastery on Flanders. He sent troops in, took the Count Guijde (Guy) van Dampierre (Philip's own godfather) and his sons hostage, and appointed a noble named Jacques de Chatillon governor of the region. French rule was harsh and unpopular and two years later exiled citizens of Belgian towns, led by Pieter de Coninc, leader of the Brugge trade guilds, returned. They stirred up a revolt and slew any Frenchmen they could find. King Philip sent an army of 10,000, including a large contingent of secular knights under Count Robert II of Artois, to stamp out the revolt and to take revenge on the Flemish. (Robert II was the son of **Robert, Count of Artois** whose impetuosity cost the Christians the battle of **Mansourah** during the **Seventh Crusade**.) They met opposition at the town of Kortrijk, defended by a ramshackle rebel force, led by de Coninc and by Willelm van Gullik, the grandson of Count van Dampierre.

The French failed to take the town and joined battle with the rebel force (which was primarily comprised of tradesmen and farmers) on a field below the walls. The topography favoured the Flemish, and the French cavalry were hindered by their own poorly deployed infantry, by dead horses in their path, and by the streams that crossed the field, which the rebels used to their advantage. The French knights were beaten and forced onto the retreat. They were chased by the Flemish forces, who took no prisoners. The engagement was remembered as 'The Battle of the Golden Spurs' from the number of these taken from dead French knights by the victorious Flanders army. The conflict is often interpreted as an early nationalist struggle, though some towns, notably Ghent, took no part in the uprising and had favoured the French. The Battle of the Golden Spurs was costly for France and disastrous for Philip's prestige. The King himself led a new army to try to reverse the verdict of this battle the following year. Again, the French sustained heavy losses, but forced the rebels to withdraw and to hand certain cities to French garrisons. In terms of cost the Flanders campaign were hardly worthwhile and contributed to the King's financial problems, providing a major motive for his subsequent attack on the Templars.

## Gorgon Medusa

The Gorgon Medusa was a female monster in Greek mythology, who had writhing snakes instead of hair. She turned whoever saw her to stone. She was beheaded by the hero Perseus. This legend may have survived in a confused form in the **Levant** and influenced the story of the **Skull of Sidon**.

Both severed heads were said to have been thrown into the gulf of Satalia, causing the whirlpools perilous to shipping in that area.

## Gothic Architecture

Gothic architecture evolved in Europe during the period of the Crusades. Its defining characteristic is the pointed arch. In cathedrals other common features were soaring columns and stone ribbed vaults, tall, stained-glass windows (including circular rose windows with fine stone mullions and tracery), flying buttresses, spires and pinnacles. Pointed arches and ribbed vaults appeared at Durham Cathedral, which was begun before the Crusades. Continental gothic architecture began in northern France in about 1140. Abbot **Suger of St Denis**, loyal advisor to **Louis VII**, had much to do with introducing the style when he rebuilt the Abbey of St Denis, near Paris, which served as the royal mausoleum for the Kings of France. The glorious new style served to exalt and sanctify the Capetian dynasty as well as the Catholic Faith. **Chartres Cathedral** developed the style. The age of high gothic architecture corresponded to the Crusading heyday, with around eighty cathedrals being built in France alone between 1180 and 1270. St **Bernard of Clairvaux** would have advocated greater simplicity in architecture, without unnecessary ornamentation. This was the tradition the early Templars followed. Their buildings like **Temple Church, London**, show that they were abreast of architectural fashion and very sophisticated builders, still they preserved an element of **Cistercian** austerity. It is unclear what involvement the Templars had in the building of the great cathedrals – their main endeavour was castle building – they sent their revenues to support the military effort in the East and did not spend extravagantly on ecclesiastical architecture in Europe, which would have been perceived as a distraction from their true purpose.

## Grand Preceptor

A Grand Preceptor/Grand Commander was usually the **Master** of a **Province** or administrative district of the Knights Templar (also called **Langue**, as the provinces were loosely based on languages spoken). He was superior to the **masters** of the individual **Preceptories** in these provinces. The **Master of the Temple in England** might also be called the Grand Preceptor of England, to make clearer his higher rank than the Master or Preceptor of, say **Denny** or **Garway**. The most important and senior Grand Preceptor, one of the most important dignitaries under the **Grand Master**, was the Grand Preceptor of the **Kingdom of Jerusalem**, who was sometimes known as *the* Grand Preceptor. Known Grand Preceptors of Jerusalem include:

| | |
|---|---|
| Odon | 1156 |
| **Gilbert Erail** | 1183 |

| | |
|---|---|
| **Jean de Terric** (also acting **Grand Master**) | 1188 |
| Gerbert | 1190 |
| William Payne | 1194 |
| Irmengaud | 1198 |
| Barthélemy de Moret | 1240 |
| Pierre de Saint-Romain | 1241 |
| Gilles | 1250 (February) |
| Étienne d'Outricourt | 1250 (May) |
| Amaury de la Roche | 1262 (May) |
| Guillaume de Montignane | 1262 (December) |
| Simon de la Tour | (unknown) |
| G. de Salvaing | 1273 |
| Arnaud de Châteauneuf | 1277–80 |
| **Theobald Gaudin** | before 1291[182] |

## Grand Masters

The Grand Masters were the leaders of the Knights Templar. The **Hospitallers** were also under a Grand Master, as were other **Military Orders** (the alternative term Grand Prior was sometimes used by the Hospitallers, and the term 'General Master' was also used). The leader of the **Teutonic Knights** was called the Hochmeister.

The Grand Master was the spiritual, political and military leader of the Order. He was chosen by a complex electoral system similar to that used in **Venice** to elect the Doge. The Preceptors in the **Holy Land** would usually choose a provisional leader until an electoral college, drawn from the international Order's chapters, could be established. Eventually, after a whittling down process, the next Grand Master, who was in theory supposed to be an experienced, professed brother of the Order, and not an outsider, was chosen. The Grand Master was supposed to be beyond the influence of kings, and to answer only to the **Pope**.

The Grand Master presided from **Jerusalem**, and subsequently from **Acre** (and from **Cyprus** in the final years). He was normally installed for life, though there was precedent for a Grand Master's resigning. The Grand Master did not quite have autocratic powers within the Order, despite the emphasis on obedience as a sacred duty. He could not access the Order's treasury on his own; one key was retained by the Commander of Jerusalem, who was also the Treasurer. He in theory ruled with the advice of a council, the **Chapter**, and rather as in an important monastic institution, important decisions were usually made at chapter meetings. The Chapter had to approve any decision to make war or to accept peace treaties. Moreover the Grand Master's power seems to have been somewhat limited when it came to appointing regional preceptors. The local brethren were able to have a say in this.

The Grand Masters frequently toured Europe seeking aid for the **Holy Land** from the western sovereigns, and also visiting regional Preceptories. In his absence, a deputy called the Visitor had the task of inspecting regional Templar establishments, to ensure they were maintaining standards and supplying the required men, money and provisions to the East. The Grand Master was an important figure during the heyday of the Order, afforded the honours due to a prince. The latter Grand Masters lived in a palatial residence in **Acre** and travelled with a host of servants and retainers. The list of Templar Grand Masters is somewhat controversial regarding exact dates, but it is generally thought to be as follows:

| | |
|---|---|
| **Hugues de Payens** | 1118–36/7 |
| **Robert de Craon** | 1136/7–46 |
| **Everard des Barres** | 1146–9 |
| **Bernard de Tremelay** | 1149–53 |
| **André de Montbard** | 1153–6 |
| **Bertrand de Blanquefort** | 1156–69 |
| **Philip de Milly of Nablus** | 1169–71 |
| **Odo de St Amand** | 1171–9 |
| **Arnold de Tarroja** | 1179–84 |
| **Gerard de Ridefort\*** | 1185–9 |
| **Robert de Sable** | 1191–3 |
| **Gilbert Erail** | 1193–1200 |
| **Philip de Plessiez** | 1201–8 |
| **Guillaume de Chartres** | 1209–19 |
| **Peter de Montaigu** | 1219–30 |
| **Armand de Perigord** | 1230–44 |
| Richard de Bures\*\* | 1245–7 |
| **Guillaume de Sonnac** | 1247–50 |
| **Reynald de Vichiers** | 1250–6 |
| **Thomas Berard** | 1256–73 |
| **Guillaume de Beaujeu** | 1273–91 |
| **Tibald Gaudin** | 1291–3 |
| **Jacques de Molay** | 1293–1314 |

\*With the Capture of Gerard de Ridefort in 1187 one Brother **Terric** took over as acting Grand Master. He used the title, but is usually not counted as an official Grand Master.
\*\*Some lists omit Richard de Bures. This period of the Order's history is not well documented, and the central **archives** of the Order, which would doubtless clarify much, have not survived.

## Grave Slabs

Many Templar **burials** were marked by flat slabs of stone laid along the top of the grave. The Templars' stone coffins at **Temple Church, London,** are plain. Those within the church, carved with effigies, covered the tombs of donors and patrons of the Order rather than Templar brothers. Templar grave slabs generally do not carry effigies, coats of arms or inscriptions. A device which frequently takes their place is an elongated cross with a stepped base. Sometimes the **cross** reflects the **Grand Master**'s **baculus**. Sometimes, though, the circular part at the head contains a flowery cross, with eight arms like spokes finishing in fleurs-de-lis. Sometimes the head of the cross opens in the centre into a curved-sided diamond shape (there are examples at Temple **Ewell** and at **Westerdale**). A head can be carved above the cross (an example being at **South Witham**). Often a broadsword is carved alongside the cross, and on occasion tools testifying to the craft of the deceased are also shown. Plain or decorated Templar grave slabs and stone coffins can be seen at various Templar burial sites across the British Isles and Europe. (There are also curious examples of miniature, Templar-style grave slabs, including those found at **Rosslyn Chapel** and **Hexham Abbey.**) The ornate grave slabs at **Kilmartin** and **Kilmory** in **Scotland** may also be Templar.

## Greece

Greece, during the Crusade period, was the heartland of the **Byzantine Empire**. It was coveted by certain Norman and **Frankish** powers and by **Venice,** all of which made inroads even before the fall of **Constantinople** in 1204 to the **Fourth Crusade**. The conquered land having been divided between the Franks and Venetians, the western conquerors established the Empire of Constantinople. The Venetians took parts of Greece including Crete and most of the islands, and also kept control of a large part of Constantinople itself. **Baldwin of Flanders** and his successors were, however, acknowledged emperors.

The Latin Empire was beset by enemies. The Bulgarians almost immediately defeated and captured Baldwin at Adrianople. There was also resistance from Epirus in the Balkans and Nicæa in Asia Minor, the latter the origins of the Emperor **Michael VIII Palaeologus**, who recovered Constantinople in 1261. **Charles of Anjou** aspired to recapture the city. Attempts to link the defence and then the recovery of the Latin Empire to the Crusades were less than successful, especially as the Latin Empire was widely seen to harm the vestigial **Kingdom of Jerusalem** by drawing away men and resources. Some parts of mainland Greece remained under Latin control. The **Military Orders** had been granted a few properties. The Templars were given some estates and knights fees, but these were mostly not kept long and of little significance. The small Templar presence survived until the time of the **suppression**, though there do not seem to have been trials in Greece. The Catalan Company, a mercenary band that had formed around **Roger de Flor**, the renegade Templar, seized power in the Duchy of Athens. The **Hospitallers** continued as a power elsewhere in the region, especially after establishing their control of **Rhodes**. The Venetians, meanwhile, held on to Crete and other islands until the seventeenth century, when they were lost to the **Ottoman Empire**. Greece was overwhelmed by the Ottomans in the fourteenth and fifteenth centuries.

## Green Man

The green man is the name often given to a sculptural motif that appears in many medieval churches. This is the **head** of a man, who either has foliage growing from his mouth or has hair and a beard made up of leaves. These foliate heads crop up in Templar churches in Britain quite often; twelve of them decorate the exterior of the Norman door at **Temple Church, London**. A horned example leers from one side of the chancel arch at **Garway**. The later **Rosslyn Chapel** also contains numerous examples.

The motif appeared long before the time of the Templars and was still being carved long after the Order's **suppression**. However, given that the Templars were accused of worshiping a head that not only gave them riches but also had the power to make the trees flower and land germinate, one cannot help but wonder if the accusation was related to the motif of the green man. The leafy head is sometimes associated with paganism, for example with the **Celtic** god **Cernunnos**, or the Roman Sylvanus or Faunus. However, verified examples from before the eleventh century are rare, and the motif occurs most frequently in medieval Christian sculpture.

## Gregory VIII (1100–87)

Albert de Mora, a former **Cistercian**, was elected **Pope** on 25 October 1187 and reigned as Gregory VIII until his death on 17 December the same year. His single notable act was issuing the **papal bull** *Auditia tremendi*, proclaiming the **Third Crusade**. It described the disaster at **Hattin**, mentioning the beheading of the Templars. It quoted the psalm 'Oh God, the heathens are come into thy inheritance', and summoned Christians to repentance, described the Crusade as a divine test. It offered full **indulgences** to the Crusaders and placed them and theirs under the Church's protection.[183] The worse news of the fall of **Jerusalem** only arrived later.

## Gregory IX (1143–1241)

Pope Gregory IX succeeded Honorius III in 1227. Originally called Ugolino di Conti, he was a nephew of **Innocent III**. Like his uncle he was an uncompromising advocate of **Papal supremacy**, and his reign was dominated by a feud with **Frederick II** and a power struggle for mastery in Italy and ascendancy in the Christian world. It was a bitter, underhand and unseemly struggle. One of Gregory's first acts was to **excommunicate** Frederick for his delay in embarking on the **Sixth Crusade**. Subsequently, Gregory exploited Frederick's absence to attack the Emperor's lands, having recruited mercenaries for this purpose. Frederick returned, having regained **Jerusalem**, and defeated the **Guelf** forces. Hermann von Salza negotiated a peace between the Pope and the Emperor. When Gregory again excommunicated Frederick the feud began anew. Gregory IX, meanwhile, also presided over the canonization of the founders of the Mendicant Orders, **Dominic** Guzman and **Francis of Assisi**. In 1135 he also saw the establishment of the **Inquisition** throughout France, under the auspices of **Robert le Bougre**, and in Germany under **Konrad von Marburg**. Gregory was keen for it to become a permanent Papal institution in the fight against suspected **heresy**, although the excesses of Konrad astonished even the Pope.[184]

## Gregory X (1210–76)

Theobald Visconti, the Archdeacon of Liege, was elected **Pope** in 1271, and took office as Gregory X. He was in **Acre** with **Edward I** when he heard of his election. (Gregory had been elected by a College of Cardinals that had been wrangling for three years. The Cardinals had only reached a verdict when the exasperated authorities of Viterbo, where they were meeting, had removed the roof from the hall – exposing dignitaries to the elements – and locked them in with only bread and water to live on until they had decided.) Gregory was crowned in Rome the following year.

Gregory X was committed to the cause of the **Holy Land**, and at once called a council at **Lyons** (the second Council of Lyons) to discuss a new **Crusade**. The council convened in 1274, attended by the **Grand Masters** of the **Military Orders**, the Templars being represented by **Guillaume de Beaujeu**. To the Pope's disappointment, Europe had lost its appetite for crusading, especially after the second disastrous Crusade of **Louis IX**, which had cost the French King's life in Tunis, and there was little enthusiasm for the enterprise.

## Gregory the Priest (died c. 1162)

Gregory the Priest was the continuer of the **Armenian** chronicle of Matthew of Edessa, covering the years 1137–62. He may have been Matthew's pupil. He mentioned the Templars several times, showing great admiration for their courage and faith. He described how, in about 1157, the 'wicked and malicious' Turkish general Ya'qub had been sent by the Sultan to ravage the Armenian lands and encroach against **Antioch**. The 'Christ-like' Templars had appeared 'as if sent by heaven' and allied with the Armenian general Stephen had attacked a contingent of 3,000 infidels, annihilating them to a man. Gregory also described the Templars courage at the capture of **Ascalon**, and their role as mediators between the Armenians and the **Byzantine** Emperor **Manuel I**.

## Gréoux-les-Bains

Gréoux-les-Bains is a town in Provence, **France**, not far from Aix. It has a Templar **castle**, which is one of the Order's biggest in Europe.

## Gualdim Pais (1118–95)

Gualdim Pais became the Templar **Grand Preceptor** of **Portugal**. He had been **knighted** on the battlefield of Ourique in 1139 by King Alfonso Henriques, after the Portuguese had gained a great victory over the Andalusian **Muslims** and the Amoravids. Thereafter Gualdim went on **Crusade** to the **Holy Land**. He joined the Templars while in the East, probably participating in the battle of **Montguisard**. He returned and took part in campaigns against the Muslims in Portugal. He became Master of the Province in 1145. In the 1160s he oversaw the building of the fortress in **Tomar**, the new headquarters of the Order, and led a successful defence against the **Moors** who besieged it in 1190. He died after presiding over the Temple in Portugal for fifty years and was buried in the Church of Santa Maria do Olival in Tomar.

## Guelfs and Ghibellines

Guelfs and Ghibellines were the names of the supporters of the **Pope** and their temporal rivals (especially the **Holy Roman Emperors**) respectively, in the conflicts that raged in Italy intermittently in the medieval period, especially in the thirteenth century. The Popes increasingly sought, however, to define the war against the Ghibellines as a **Crusade**, and later would attempt to link Ghibellinism with **heresy**.

The north Italian city states were divided between the two factions, with Florence and Genoa being predominantly Guelf, and Siena and **Pisa** tending to favour the Ghibellines. The Guelf/Ghibelline division was reflected in the Latin territory in the **Holy Land**, especially after the **Sixth Crusade**. Those who resented the pretensions of **Frederick II**, including the Templars, tended to fall into the Guelf camp.

The Pope's claim to suzerainty over Sicily was at the heart of these Italian Crusades. Papal forces fought against Frederick and his son **Conrad IV**, and then after a hiatus, against **Manfred**, Conrad's half-brother. The Popes tried to recruit English support, but in the end it was **Charles of Anjou**, the **Capetian** ruler of Provence, who became the champion of Guelfism, being proclaimed by the Pope as King of Sicily and Naples. Charles defeated and killed Manfred at the battle of Benevento in 1266, and defeated and executed the last **Hohenstaufen**, the young **Conradin**, soon afterwards. He also managed to extend his power over Rome, to the extent that when Sicily revolted against Charles' exacting rule (the Sicilian Vespers), Pope Martin IV preached a new Crusade against the rebels, as well as against the King of **Aragon**, Pedro III, who had chosen to champion the revolt and to push his own claim to Sicily. The controversial Crusade escalated, with Capetian forces invading **Aragon**, (which the Pope promised to Charles of Valois). The invasion was a failure, however, costing the life of Philip III, the father of **Philip the Fair**. By the time of **Boniface VIII**, though, the Guelfs had triumphed in Italy, and some settlement over Sicily was in sight. The Guelfs then split into Black Guelfs who supported **Papal Supremacy** and White Guelfs, who were more suspicious of ecclesiastical power and who sought regional autonomy. Meanwhile, **Capetian** influence became stronger, taking the place of the old Imperial threat to Papal autonomy.

The Templars and **Hospitallers** did not participate actively in the Italian Crusades, and were more or less exempt from the taxes imposed on the Church to fund these wars.[185] Some Templars, however, showed their Guelf credentials, notably Brother Bonvicino, who made himself indispensable to the Pope in Perugia during the struggle against Frederick and his heirs, and **Guillaume de Beaujeu**, who became Grand Master, having been a close ally of Charles of Anjou. Other Templars, notably **Ricaut Bonomel**, were highly critical of these European wars against Christians, which the Papacy packaged as Crusades, seeing them as detrimental to the cause of the Holy Land.

## *Guichard de Marsillac* (thirteenth–fourteenth century)

Guichard de Marsillac was a former *sénéchal* of Toulouse and a witness at a Templar **trial** at the Papal Commission. His house in **Paris** was also one of the private properties where Templar prisoners were kept. Guichard was involved in the **torture** process. Not surprisingly he was hostile towards the Order in his testimony. He claimed that he had heard stories about the Templars' rite of obscene kisses over the past forty years in various places, in the south and in Paris. Something called 'article number 30', perhaps of a Secret **Rule,** was supposed to concern this.

Guichard also spoke of a relative of his named Hugues, who had joined the Templars. Apparently Hugues had been received in the Toulouse Preceptory, and then taken into a room where something had happened behind closed doors to cause him to look very pale as though disturbed and stupefied when he emerged in Templar habit.[186] Hugues was subsequently supposed to have made a personal seal bearing the legend *Sigillum Hugonis Perditi* (the seal of Hugues the lost).

This Hugues had apparently never spoken of his secret, but had returned to his family, fallen ill and died. Guichard had to concede that Hugues' problem could have been the austerity of the Templars (which new members were warned of in no uncertain terms at their **reception ceremonies**) rather than being party to heretical depravity, and could come up with no more incriminating evidence.

## *Guillaume de Beaujeu* (*c.* 1230–91)

Guillaume de Beaujeu was the twenty-first **Grand Master** of the Knights Templar and the last to preside in the **Holy Land**. He was elected in 1273, on the death of **Thomas Bérard**. Guillaume had been a long-serving Templar Knight. In 1261 he had been captured in a raid and then ransomed. He had also gone on to serve as Preceptor of the county of **Tripoli** and then of Sicily. He was a distant relation of the **Capetian** monarchy, and was suspected by many of being too much a partisan of the **French** cause.

As Grand Master, Guillaume attended Pope **Gregory X**'s Council of **Lyons** in 1274, and advocated a *passagium particulare*, with professional troops being mustered to reinforce **Acre**, and also proposed a blockade of **Egypt** to weaken it economically. He also argued that the Crusaders would need to establish their own fleets so that they did not depend on the **Maritime Republics** of Genoa and **Venice**, which were only interested in making money from trading with the **Muslims**. (The Venetians, at the time, were evens selling swords to the **Mameluks**.) After touring the Order's European Preceptories, Guillaume de Beaujeu returned to the **Holy Land**. His closeness to the Capetians compromised his position among the Palestinian-Frankish barons of the **Holy Land**, who saw him as an agent of **Charles of Anjou** (who claimed the throne of **Jerusalem**). Indeed, the Templars under de Beaujeu had thwarted King Hugh of **Cyprus** in his attempts to assert his rival claim. The Templars were involved in another quarrel besides, with **Bohemond VII of Antioch**, which weakened Christian unity at a time when it was desirable. (Little had changed in a century in that respect.)[320] When the war broke out over control of Sicily between **Aragon** and Charles of Anjou, it ended all hope of western relief materialising for the Holy Land.

By 1180, **Baybars** had been succeeded as Sultan by the Mameluk General **Qalawun**. Qalawun sent armies to further reduce the Frankish presence in the Holy Land. Guillaume de Beaujeu learned from a paid informer, the Emir al-Fakhri, that the Mameluks planned to attack Tripoli, and wrote to warn the citizens. Unfortunately the leaders of Tripoli neither trusted the Grand Master nor believed his warning, and consequently the Mameluks found Tripoli unprepared and took the city with relative ease. Guillaume's informer also told him of Qalawun's planned attack on Acre, but again Guillaume's warning went unheeded. Guillaume then tried to arrange a payment to buy off the Mameluk assault but this was rejected by the **Haute Cour** in Acre, who accused Guillaume of treachery.

Qalawun mustered his massive armies in 1290, but fell ill and died before he reached Acre. The campaign was carried on, however, by his son **al-Ashraf**

**Khalil**. The defenders were severely outnumbered, but made a determined and courageous resistance. Guillaume de Beaujeu fought valiantly, leading the Templars in a sortie against the Mameluk camp. He combined with the Hospitallers to defend St Anthony's gate, pushing the Mameluks back over the walls. The moats filled with bodies as the Mameluks pressed their attack. The city's great defensive towers began to crumble, undermined by Muslim siege engineers. When de Beaujeu learned that the Muslims had taken the Accursed Tower he rushed to counter-attack, but was wounded and driven back. He was carried to the Templar fortress by the sea, where he died of his wounds. The Templars battled on but the end was nigh.

## Guillaume de Chambonnet (died c. 1310)
Guillaume de Chambonnet was a Templar Knight, prominent during the defence of the Order before the Papal Commission. He was made one of the four procurators (spokesmen). The others were the priests **Pierre de Bologna** and Renaud de Provins and another knight, Bertrand de Sartiges.

## Guillaume de Chartres (died 1219)
Guillaume de Chartres became the fourteenth **Grand Master** of the Knights Templar in 1209. He was probably born into the nobility of the **Champagne** region, and became a Templar in Sours, near **Chartres**, in about 1200. As Grand Master he was best known for building the impregnable fortress known as **Pilgrims' Castle**. He died of fever in 1219 during the Crusaders' siege of **Damietta** in **Egypt**, the first major engagement of the **Fifth Crusade**. He was succeeded by **Peter de Montaigu**.

## Guillaume de Nogaret (c. 1360–13)
Guillaume de Nogaret, a secular lawyer, was one of the most important ministers in the Royal Council of King **Philip the Fair** of **France**. From 1307 he held the position of Keeper of the Seals. He was born near Toulouse, and it is possible some of his family had been executed as **Cathars**.

Guillaume became a close advisor of the king and retained his influence despite being an **excommunicant** as a result of his part in the 'outrage' against Pope **Boniface VIII** in 1303. De Nogaret had led a party of French troops and assorted allies including mercenaries raised by **Sciarra Colonna**, to seize the **Pope** at his palace in **Anagni**, Italy. De Nogaret's intention was to bring Boniface back to France to face an unprecedented trial on various trumped up charges, including **heresy**, simony, **sodomy** and murder. The move against the Pope was probably ordered and certainly authorised by the King, but Guillaume may have persuaded Philip to go through with it.

The coup failed when the Boniface's allies in the town rallied to rescue him, but the shaken Pope died soon afterwards. Although excommunicated,

Guillaume de Nogaret continued to wield power in France, though where the Church was concerned he was obliged to operate from behind the scenes. Though Benedict XI absolved King Philip of blame in the affair, he refused to absolve de Nogaret. De Nogaret claimed Pope Benedict's untimely death vindicated his cause. (Some have suspected more sinister reasons for Benedict's demise.)

De Nogaret became a driving force in the **suppression** of the Templars. The full list of **accusations** has been attributed to de Nogaret's hand. He and King Philip used the threat of reopening the proceedings against Boniface VIII to ensure cooperation from **Clement V** and used other coercive measures to ensure that the Pope went along with the action. De Nogaret was involved in the trial of Guichard, Bishop of Troyes, which possibly hinted at what might befall Clement himself if he resisted the will of the King too strongly.

Guillaume de Nogaret, being held in odium by the Church, did not present himself at the **Poitiers** assembly, but his influence is clear in the address given by another of Philip's ministers, **Guillaume de Plaisians**. Both ministers had access to the trials of the Templars (both interfered in the interrogation of **Jacques De Molay**) and both reported goings on to the king. It may even have been de Nogaret's suggestion to begin the tribunal of the Council of Sens, under the cooperative Bishop of Sens, **Philip de Marigny**, and initiate the **burnings** of the Templars. De Nogaret lived to see the Templars suppressed but not to hear **Jacques De Molay** revoke his confession. Meanwhile, de Nogaret had eventually been absolved and reconciled with the Church on condition that he **took the Cross**. Whether Guillaume was sincere when he undertook to go on Crusade is open to question, but he was the author of a treatise, in around 1310, on how the **Holy Land** might be recovered. Like Pierre Dubois he sought to portray the attack on the Templars as a component of this strategy.

If Guillaume secretly held Cathar sympathies then it is unlikely he would have been a serious supporter of the Crusading movement. Guillaume de Nogaret was born in St Felix de Carman near Toulouse. In 1162, St Felix de Carman had hosted to a Cathar council. In the 1240s several Cathars were burned alive in St Felix, and it is possible Guillaume de Nogaret's close relations were amongst them. De Nogaret may have grown up nursing a grudge against the Roman Catholic Church. His part in the destruction of the Templars may have been personal vengeance. If this was Guillaume de Nogaret's motive then the irony is remarkable. The son of heretics engineered it so that the Pope would destroy his own Catholic foot soldiers. Clement V apparently detested Guillaume de Nogaret, perhaps aware of what he was doing.

## *Guillaume de Paris* (thirteenth–fourteenth century)
Guillaume Imbert de Paris was the shadowy head of the **Inquisition** in **France**. He held the title 'Grand Inquisitor', which seems to have been

created for him by King **Philip the Fair**. Guillaume was a member of the **Dominican Order**, and was a Papal inquisitor, holding his authority as a deputy of the **Pope**. However, he was also the King's personal confessor.

Under Guillaume's tenure the Inquisition had become more an instrument of Royal than Papal authority. Guillaume de Paris was certainly party to the King's confederation against the Templars, and helped him preserve some semblance of legality throughout the affair. Guillaume enabled Philip to present the arrest of the Templars as something done at the Inquisition's behest. He instructed his fellow inquisitors in the **Languedoc** to show no mercy to the Templars, whose alleged crimes he denounced as a 'burning shame to heaven'.

He instructed that the Templars' confessions were to be recorded and sent sealed to Paris, claiming to be too busy and infirm to come south himself. Guillaume subsequently presided at Paris tribunals, hearing Templars confess. His inquisitorial powers were suspended by **Clement V** through the first half of 1308 but eventually restored.

## *Guillaume de Plaisians* (died *c.* 1313)
Guillaume de Plaisians was a minister serving in the Government of **Philip the Fair**. Like **Guillaume de Nogaret**, he was a master political propagandist. He is most noted for addressing Pope **Clement V** at the assembly of clergy at **Poitiers**. He gave two thunderous speeches denouncing the Templars for their terrible crimes and **heresies**. To the other **accusations against the Order**, he added the charges of treachery against the **Crusades** and conspiracy with the **Muslims**.[187]

He delivered veiled threats to the **Pope**, during these speeches, where the attack on the Templars was presented as an act in defence of **Catholic** faith. Plaisians was also present for a period during the second interrogation of **Jacques de Molay** at the Papal Commission. De Molay, in his confused state, appealed to Plaisians, of all men, for advice and support. Plaisians was good enough to warn de Molay to mind he did not perish in a noose of his own making.

## *Guillaume de Sonnac* (died 1250)
Guillaume de Sonnac became the eighteenth **Grand Master** of the Knights Templar. He was elected in a general chapter held in **Pilgrim's Castle** in 1247. He led the Order during the **Seventh Crusade**, under **King Louis IX**. He and the Templars rode in the vanguard of the Crusade as it moved south from captured **Damietta**, ahead of the main body of the Crusade, along with **Robert, Count of Artois** and an English detachment under **William Longespee**.

The advance party attacked a Muslim camp under **Fakhr al-Din** and routed the defenders. Then, over-confident, the Count of Artois decided to pursue the enemy into the town of **Mansourah** itself without waiting for the rest of the Crusaders. De Sonnac and Longespee counselled against it (according to the version of events recorded by **Matthew Paris**)[188] but Count Robert goaded them with accusations of cowardice and treachery and then charged against the town. De Sonnac and Longespee followed.

The **Mameluks** used a variation of their standard tactic – feigning a retreat and then springing an ambush. They fell back through the narrow streets. When the Crusaders followed, the Muslims shut off their escape route then sprang on them from the side streets. The knights were unable to manoeuvre to defend themselves. Longespee and the Count of Artois and some 300 other knights were killed in the ensuing bloodbath. De Sonnac and one other Templar made it out alive, though the de Sonnac had been wounded and lost an eye.

By this time Louis arrived and after fierce fighting drove the Mameluks back into the town. Over the following weeks they established a fortified camp below Mansourah, making a rampart from captured Egyptian siege engines. The Mameluks launched out in a sortie against the Crusaders' camp, supported by numerous archers and catapults throwing Greek fire on the Crusaders' wooden bastion, which was set alight. Seeing that the Templars were few in number the Mameluks dashed through the collapsing structure. Though they were repelled, Guillaume de Sonnac, leading the remaining Templars, lost his remaining eye and then his life.

### *Guillaume Pidoyne* (thirteenth–fourteenth century)
Guillaume Pidoyne was the royal custodian of the goods of the Temple, which were confiscated by the Crown after the **arrest** of the Templars in **France** on 13 October 1307. He took charge of the **Paris Temple** and conducted the search that resulted in the finding of **Caput LVIIIm**.

### *Guiot de Provins* (died *c.* 1208)
Guiot de Provins was a *trouvère* poet turned **Cluniac** monk. He was from Provins in **Champagne**. He wrote of the Templars mentioning their boldness – how they were held in great honour in the East, and how they never fled in battle and were thus greatly feared by the Saracens. He thought the Templars were rather too doughty for his liking though. He would not have wanted to join them, as he thought it preferable to be alive and a coward than dead and the most admired man in the world. Guiot travelled to the East and may have taken part in the **Third Crusade**.

### *Guy de Foresta* (died *c.* 1275)
Guy de Foresta was **Master of the Temple in England**, known to be presiding in 1273–1274. He was mentioned later at the **trials** by the witness Robert de Dorturner, a London notary. Robert claimed that he had once escaped from Guy who had wished to seize him for **sodomy**.

## *Guy de Lusignan* (1150–94)

Guy de Lusignan was the controversial King of **Jerusalem**, best known for leading the army of the **Kingdom of Jerusalem** to defeat at the Battle of **Hattin**, which resulted in the subsequent loss of Jerusalem to **Saladin**. Along with **Reynald de Chatillon** and **Gerard de Ridefort**, he usually bears the bulk of the blame for the disaster that befell the kingdom.

Guy was a younger son of Count Hugh of Lusignan, then under the Duchy of Aquitaine. This made him a vassal of **Eleanor of Aquitaine** and of her son **Richard the Lionheart**. Some time after 1168 Guy and his brother Amalric left France for the **Holy Land**, apparently after being banished. They eventually gained entrance to the royal court of **Baldwin IV**. Amalric married a daughter of the Lord of **Ibelin** and also charmed the Queen Mother **Agnes of Courtenay**. Agnes encouraged her daughter **Sibylla** to marry Guy (following the untimely death of Sibylla's first husband, William of Montferrat, known as 'Long-Sword'). On the marriage Guy became Count of **Jaffa** and **Ascalon**. The faction of Agnes de Courtenay was aligned against that of **Raymond III of Tripoli**, and that made them allies of **Gerard de Ridefort**, who had become **Grand Master** of the Templars. Baldwin IV himself lost faith in Guy, after he displayed a lack of leadership during the siege of **Kerak**. The King sought to have his sister's marriage dissolved. However, when Baldwin IV died from leprosy, followed within the year by **Baldwin V** (Sibylla's sickly son by William of Montferrat), Agnes de Courtenay and Gerard de Ridefort supported Guy and Sibylla in the palace coup that saw the couple hurriedly crowned as rulers of Jerusalem. (This in defiance of the will of Baldwin IV, which had stated that the succession was to be decided by **Pope** and the kings of Europe.)

Many were astonished to see the upstart Guy on the throne (the crown was placed on his head by Sibylla herself). His own brother Amalric deemed him unworthy and allegedly said 'if they would make Guy a king they should make me a God!' Still, Sibylla had chosen Guy and Guy was king. Three weeks later Reynald de Chatillon raided a **Muslim** caravan, setting in motion the chain of events that led to the Battle of Hattin. Guy initially followed the cautious advice of Raymond III, but was goaded into action by Reynald and Gerard, with disastrous consequences. Guy was captured and imprisoned for a while in **Damascus**. Later he was released, at Sibylla's behest, but by then both Guy's credibility and the Kingdom itself were in tatters. **Conrad de Montferrat** refused Guy entry to **Tyre**, the last Christian city holding out, claiming that Guy's incompetence had caused the present disaster, and that he had forfeited his position. Guy therefore took his followers to commence what would become the epic siege of **Acre**.

During the **Third Crusade**, Guy met Richard the Lionheart on **Cyprus**. He assisted in Richard's campaign against **Isaac Comnenus** and swore fealty to him. Consequently Richard would try to uphold Guy's right to the title of

King of Jerusalem, in face of objections from Conrad and **Balian of Ibelin**. However, by this time Sibylla and her infant daughters by Guy had both perished in the plague that had decimated the Christian camp, further diminishing Guy's claim, and Guy was without support among the Latin Barons. In a vote they rejected Guy's claim outright and elected Conrad as king, marrying him to Sibylla's half-sister **Isabella of Jerusalem**. Even so, Guy redeemed his reputation somewhat in these years. His initiative in laying siege to Acre facilitated the partial recovery of the Latin Kingdom, which began there, and during the fighting he also saved Conrad's life, despite Conrad's snubbing him at Tyre. Guy also fought at **Arsuf**. Richard gave Guy a new domain in Cyprus, which the Templars had briefly occupied. Guy died without issue but was succeeded by his brother who had also married Isabella of Jerusalem (as her fourth husband, following the deaths of Conrad and of **Henry of Champagne**, her third husband). The de Lusignan dynasty would endure as rulers of Cyprus and titular kings of Jerusalem for centuries to come.

# H

## Hanseatic League
The Hanseatic League was a powerful medieval trading federation formed of countries bordering the North Sea and the Baltic. The Hansas were mercantile guilds, established across a wide area from London and Brugge through Hamburg and Lubeck to Riga in Latvia. They established a monopoly on maritime trade in this area, and had links with the **Teutonic Knights**.

## Harim, Battle of
The Battle of Harim was an engagement in August 1164 between **Bohemond III of Antioch** and the Sultan **Nur ed-Din**, who had killed Bohemond's father, **Raymond of Poitiers**, at **Inab**. The sultan was capitalising on King **Amalric I**'s absence on campaign in **Egypt**, which had left **Outremer** vulnerable. The Muslims' attack on **Tripoli** had been thwarted by the **Hospitallers** near **Krak des Chevaliers** a year previously. Nur ed-Din now took a force drawn from his substantial empire and beyond, to besiege the castle of Harim in the principality of Antioch. Bohemond III came to relieve the castle's hard-pressed lord, Reginald of St Valery, along with **Raymond III of Tripoli**, Joscelin II de Courtenay and other Christian allies. Nur ed-Din feigned retreat, then turned on the pursuing Christians and launched a strong counter-attack. Bohemond's army was supported by a Templar contingent of sixty-seven; all but seven were wiped out. Bohemond was taken prisoner, as were Raymond and Joscelin. Nur ed-Din, victorious, returned to Harim and took the fortress, and then went on to take **Baniyas**.

## Harran

Harran is a site in south-eastern Turkey. It was an ancient city, which had become part of the **Muslim** world. **Baldwin II**, while still Count of **Edessa**, was captured by the **Seljuk Turks** in a battle near Harran in 1104. During his captivity he was abducted by another Turkish warlord who felt his share of the booty was not great enough. Baldwin was only released in 1108. The **Crusaders** never took Harran. The defeat there weakened the **Frankish** grip on Edessa and enabled the **Byzantine Empire** to assert its authority over **Antioch**. Being the first major setback the Franks had suffered, it also dispelled the myth among the Muslims that the Frankish knights were invincible.

## Hassan-i-Sabbah (1024–1124)

Hassan-i-Sabbah was the Persian founder of the sect that became known to the **Crusaders** as the **Assassins**, and which cast a long shadow over the Middle East. He converted many Shi'ite Muslims to the obscure Nizari Ismaili branch, including the garrison of the great castle of Alamut, which became the sect's headquarters, and from whence Sabbah, who became known as the first 'Old Man of the Mountains', exercised his power.

## Hattin, Battle of

The Battle of Hattin was fought on 4 July 1187. It was a decisive victory for **Saladin** and his **Muslim** army over King **Guy de Lusignan** and the Christian army of the **Kingdom of Jerusalem**. **Gerard de Ridefort**, the **Grand Master** of the Templars, and **Reynald de Chatillon**, the bellicose old baron, had goaded King Guy into taking his army out to confront Saladin and to relieve the besieged town of Tiberias on Lake Galilee, against which Saladin had mustered some 30,000 infantry and 12,000 cavalry.[189] He had come up from the vicinity of Kerak to rendezvous with the force under al-Afdal that had dealt a blow to the **Military Orders** at **Cresson**.

The strategy of advancing against Tiberias, as advocated by Gerard, entailed a harrowing march across arid desert from Sephoria. It was just what the Muslims had hoped the Christians would do.[329] Saladin's men had poisoned all the water sources along the way and his advance parties of mounted archers harried the Christians as they marched, with the Templars forming the rearguard. **Raymond III of Tripoli**, who had opposed the strategy, reluctantly accompanied the army, which comprised no more than 20,000 in total. The mustered army of the Kingdom of Jerusalem was augmented by about 300 Knights Templar, and around the same number of **Hospitallers**. The Templars bore the brunt of the harassment on the march. When the king agreed to a request to rest for the night, Raymond is said to have declared, 'Lord God, the war is over, we are dead men, the

Kingdom is finished!' (The contention is the Christians could have hacked their way through to the lake if they'd attacked immediately rather than resting. After all, the benefit of the extra rest was probably countered by the extended period of suffering from thirst.)

Without water the army camped on a barren hill, with twin peaks known as the Horns of Hattin. Below was the glistening lake of Tiberias, and in the way the massive Muslim army. The Christians passed the night tormented with thirst, hearing their enemies' confident shouts of 'Allah akbar'. As the Franks attacked early the next day, Saladin ordered the dry scrub between the armies to be set on fire. The prevailing wind carried the smoke into the faces and dry throats of the Christians. The Templars charged but the rest of the Franks failed to support them, and surrounded, the Templars were killed or captured. Muslim archers targeted the horses of the Franks. The battle raged relentlessly. Count Raymond and his knights cut their way back though their own ranks and fled the field. Eventually Guy's party, having failed to fight their way through to the lake, were driven back up the slope. They rallied for one final charge, sending the Muslims reeling back towards Saladin's position, as al-Afdal remembered. Saladin pulled his beard in desperation but managed to organise a counter-attack, pushing the Franks back up the hill. Again the Franks charged with 'undiminished ardour' but again were driven back. Guy fought on bravely, but was ultimately captured, as were Reynald de Chatillon and Gerard de Ridefort. The **True Cross** was also lost. The Franks had never suffered such a defeat.[330]

The Frankish leaders, wretchedly exhausted and thirsty, were brought to Saladin's tent afterwards. Saladin offered a cup of water to Guy, indicating that he would be spared. Guy passed it to Reynald. Saladin remarked that he had not offered the cup, and Reynald, the most hated enemy of the Muslims, was not under his protection. Saladin then castigated Reynald for his catalogue of outrages against **Islam**. Reynald disdained to feign penitence and was at once beheaded.

The next day the citadel of Tiberias surrendered to Saladin, and the sultan permitted the Countess and her children to leave unmolested. Meanwhile, those of his men who had captured members of the Military Orders he paid handsomely to hand over their prisoners. He brought together 200–300 Templar and **Hospitaller** captives, and ordered them killed. All refused to apostatise to save their lives, and all were beheaded by the **Sufis** accompanying the Muslim army. According to Saladin's secretary **Imad ad-Din**, the Sultan was determined to 'purify the land of these two impure races'.[190] The military monks had to be killed, according to **Ibn al-Athir**, because they were the fiercest of all the Frankish warriors, a verdict echoed by the author of the *Itinerarium Peregrinorum et Gesta Regis Ricardi*.[191] Sufis, on the other hand, were supposed to be a pious religious brotherhood, men of the law, savants, devoted to peaceful mysticism. It is unclear why Saladin issued the Sufis with the task of carrying out these executions. His purpose may also have been to show that **jihad** was a duty even to usually non-combatant Muslims. It was all too much for some of the bookish Sufis, who recoiled from the task, though it seems many of the warriors found it an amusing spectacle.[192] The Templars, for their part, are said to have faced what they saw as martyrdom with a grim eagerness. One, named Nicolas, supposedly encouraged the others, so that they competed to be first in line for martyrdom, and afterwards a divine light shone down on the bodies.[193]

The Christians had carried a relic of the True Cross into Battle at Hattin, in a great golden reliquary. This time it had failed to bring victory. The loss of this had, if anything, a more demoralizing effect than the capture of the King and the great barons of the realm. Many thought that God had abandoned them. Raymond III of Tripoli was certainly crushed with such thoughts, and died soon after escaping from Hattin. The King, the **Grand Master** and other prisoners were sent to **Damascus**. **Terric**, one of the few senior Templars to escape, wrote to the West to tell of the great disaster. Meanwhile, the cities and castles of the kingdom had been stripped of their garrisons for the disastrous battle, and in its aftermath fell in rapid succession to the Muslim forces.

## Haute Cour

The Haute Cour (high court) of **Jerusalem** was a parliament of nobles, which had executive authority in the Latin **Kingdom of Jerusalem**. It had law-making and judicial powers, and also decided on affairs of state such as the validity of royal marriages and the correct military and political alliances and strategies to pursue. It also judged major criminal cases concerning the nobility and decided upon levels of taxation. The court was attended by the monarch, by the feudal aristocracy, by leading clerics, and by the **Grand Masters** of the Knights Templar and **Hospitaller**.

## Heads, Worship of

According to the **accusations against the Order**, in every province the Templars had **idols**, namely heads, of which some had three faces, some one, and some had a human **skull**. This was supposed to be regarded as a saviour by the Templars, and as something that made the trees grow and the land germinate. Many Templars in **France** were induced to confess to worshipping or having seen a head during the Order's **chapter** meetings. Descriptions of it varied; most described it as frightening; some seemed to describe a real embalmed, severed head with a straggly black beard. It was sometimes said to be encased at the neck in a gold reliquary with three or four legs. Other variants were black, gold or red, and some were said to be horned. The only head actually found in the **Paris Temple** was the skull fragments in the head-shaped reliquary labelled **Caput LVIIIm**. The Templars on Cyprus also said they possessed the head of **St Euphemia**. Most other Templars, though, especially outside France where torture was not rigorously pressed, said they knew nothing of any heretical head and had never engaged in anything but Christian worship. (Merely possessing and venerating the head of a **saint** would not have been deemed heretical in that time. **Holy Relics** were an accepted part of worship, and the Church actively encouraged belief in their spiritual powers.)

Severed heads appear in myths and legends, including some with **Celtic** origins. Peredur, in a Welsh legend associated with the Mabinogion, is the inspiration of Perceval in the **Holy Grail** romance written by **Chretien de Troyes**. Peredur encounters a severed head on a platter in place of the Grail. In another British legend the head of the God/King/Giant Bran the Blessed was attributed with magical powers, and was buried under Tower Green near the **Tower of London**, facing towards the Continent and acting as a protection against invasion. In England a former Templar called John de Donyngton gave evidence at the Templar Trials. By then he had become a **Franciscan** Friar. He claimed that he had heard of four heads in the Templars' possession, in **London**, **Bisham Abbey**, **Bruer** and another somewhere in the north. None of these were ever found. However, a medieval panel showing a bearded head, hidden in medieval times, was discovered (in the mid-twentieth century) in **Templecombe**, Somerset, an enigmatic object hinting that there may have been some substance to the **accusation** of revering a bearded head after all.[194]

In many **Romanesque** and **Gothic** churches, including those associated with the Templars, there are a profusion of carved heads. These often form corbels or roof bosses. **Temple Church, London** has curious animal, human and **demon** heads spaced around its internal arcade and **green man** heads sprouting foliage from their mouths above its original entrance, on the exterior. Another 'green man' head, this one with horns, may be found on the chancel arch of Temple **Garway** church. Carved heads may also be found at Temple **Bruer** and Temple Guiting, and on many Templar churches on the Continent.

## Hebron

Hebron is in southern Judea, Palestine. It was once a great city of the **Holy Land**. It houses the Tomb of the **Patriarchs**, also known as the Cave of the Machpelah. This is believed to be the burial place of the Old Testament Patriarchs and Matriarchs: **Abraham**, Sarah, Isaac, Rebecca, Jacob and Leah. Much of the standing shrine was built by King Herod and gives a clue to the appearance of the lost Temple that once occupied **Temple Mount**. The building was added to by the **Byzantines**, the **Muslims** and the **Crusaders**, and was held sacred by all three faiths that looked to the God of Abraham. **Godfroi de Bouillon** took Hebron in 1099. It does seem the Crusaders subsequently permitted **Jews** and Muslims to continue to visit the site, much as the Templars permitted privileged Muslims to pray on **Temple Mount**. However, Jewish visitors (one such being the famous Jewish rabbi and physician Moses Maimonides of Córdoba) were horrified by the Christian icons installed within the Tomb of the Patriarchs, which they saw as **idolatrous**. Hebron was conquered by **Saladin** but recovered by the Crusaders during the **Third Crusade**. It fell to **Baybars** and the **Mameluks** in 1260. For many years thereafter, only Muslims were permitted to enter the Tomb of the Patriarchs.

## Helena (Empress, St) (240–329)

St Helena was the Christian mother of the Emperor **Constantine**.[195] Late in life she visited **Jerusalem** searching for the **Holy Sepulchre**. She was directed to a site that has been converted by Hadrian to a temple of Venus, and had it cleared away. She discovered the cave, which was said to be the tomb of **Christ**, and, according to legend, a nearby cistern containing three crosses, taken to be the Cross of Christ and the crosses of the two criminals crucified alongside him. Not knowing which cross was that of Jesus, all three, so a version of the story goes, were taken to a sick woman, and the one that healed her was recognised as the authentic **True Cross**. Elsewhere, Helena identified the site of the Ascension, and in **Bethlehem** the site of the stable where Christ was born. She had the earliest Church of the Resurrection built around the tomb in Jerusalem (also called the Holy Sepulchre), and the Church of the Nativity built around the stable/cave in Bethlehem.[196] Helena was subsequently canonised. Some of her relics were apparently held by the Templars, and along with those of other saints and some pieces of the cross were sent to London by **Thomas Bérard**.[197]

## Hellfire Club

The Hellfire Club was a hedonistic secret society founded in eighteenth-century **England** by Sir Francis Dashwood (1708–81). The Club mockingly styled itself after a religious order. Its other titles were the Friars of St Francis of Wycombe, the Monks of Medmenham and the Order of the **Knights** of West Wycombe. The club met first in a former **Cistercian** abbey at Medmenham and then in caves and caverns (the Hellfire Caves), which Dashwood had excavated under a hill adjoining his estate, near High Wycombe in Buckinghamshire. Dashwood was a prankster and apparently a dabbler in the occult. The Hellfire Club's underground meetings involved the performance of rituals (either diabolical or mock-**Catholic**), between sessions of drinking and wenching. They adopted from Thelema the motto *Fay ce que voudras* (Do what thou will), which would become also the motto of **Aleister Crowley**. Sir Francis Dashwood was an MP and many powerful men were part of the club. He was also said to have been a **Jacobite**, and an initiate of **Rosicrucianism** and of **Freemasonry**. The Hellfire Club was primarily an excuse for theatrical tomfoolery and possibly blackmail, but it may also have absorbed elements of the Templarist mysticism that was starting to surround Masonic circles in Europe. Coincidentally, the Knights Templar had possessed land at Wycombe.

## Helmets

The protective headgear of medieval knights evolved gradually during the **Crusade** period. The Norman style helmet, a metal skull-cap with a nose guard (worn over a chain mail hood) was by the late twelfth century given a face mask to protect the wearer's mouth and cheeks. Slits were left for the eyes, and holes or a grille pierced the front to enable the wearer to breathe. By the mid-thirteenth century this had become the fully enclosed great helm, with two reinforcing bands forming a cross at the front serving both a practical and symbolic function. Flat topped and pointed-dome topped helmets were in use, but the pointed ones probably deflected blows better. By the end of that century such helmets were better shaped to the head, and soon hinging, pointed visors replaced the flat front and the cross bands (the quaintly named 'pig-faced bassinet' was in use by the fifteenth century). Mantling (a decorative cloth cover) helped prevent the wearer overheating in sunny climes and was probably an innovation of the Crusaders. Another popular medieval helmet type was called variously the war hat, kettle hat, or *chapel de fer*. It had a wide brim and was similar in shape to British army helmets from the First World War. In the case of the Templars, the Knights probably favoured the enclosed great helm, while the sergeants and foot soldiers wore the open version with the brim.

## Henry Charles Lea (1825–1909)

Henry Charles Lea was a nineteenth-century American historian. He was the author of various medievalist works, including *The History of the Inquisition in the Middle Ages*. In this work he examined the processes of the **Inquisition** and, in the third volume, established the Templars' probable innocence of **heresy**.

## Henry I, Count of Champagne/Henry the Liberal (died 1181)

Henry I, Count of **Champagne**, known as 'Henry the Liberal', was the son of Theobald, Count of Champagne and Blois. Henry took part in the **Second Crusade** under **Louis VII**, and was present at the Council of War in **Acre**. Back in Europe, Henry married **Marie of Champagne**, the daughter of **Louis VII** of **France** and of **Eleanor of Aquitaine**, and their court in **Troyes** became a centre of culture. The chronicler **Walter Map** and the poet and **Holy Grail** romancer **Chretien de Troyes** flourished there. Henry also instituted the **Champagne Fairs**. In 1179 Henry returned to the **Holy Land**, shortly before the battle of **Jacob's Ford**. He was captured by the **Turks** in Anatolia on his return journey, and died soon after being ransomed.

## Henry II, Count of Champagne/Henry I of Jerusalem (1166–97)

Henry II, Count of **Champagne** was the son of **Henry I, Count of Champagne**. He embarked for the **Holy Land**, having secured the promise of his vassals that they would recognise his younger brother Theobald as Count. Young and able, he was a popular figure among the Latin Barons during the **Third Crusade**. He fought at the Siege of **Acre** and was wounded in action. When **Assassin** agents murdered **Conrad of Montferrat** in 1192, Henry was chosen to replace him as king. He was acceptable to **Richard the Lionheart** because he was the son of Richard's half-sister **Marie of Champagne**. (Henry was also a nephew of **Philip II Augustus**, therefore acceptable to the French.) A week after Conrad's death, Queen **Isabella of Jerusalem** was married to Henry. The Kingdom itself now consisted of a narrow strip of coast, ninety miles long and scarcely ten miles wide, and Jerusalem was only a title. In September 1197 Henry died when he fell from a window, possibly the result of a collapsing balcony. It seems a dwarf servant tried to stop him falling but ended up falling after him and landing on top. If foul play was involved, it is possible **Pisan** merchants had a hand in it, as after discovering a Pisan plot to capture **Tyre** and reinstate **Guy de Lusignan** as king, Henry had deprived the Pisans of their trading privileges in **Acre**.

There is a legend that Henry, during his reign in **Outremer**, sought an alliance with the **Assassins**, and visited their castle at al-Khaf. The successor of **Sinan** entertained Henry cordially, and laid on a demonstration of the devotion of his followers. The sheik called forward a couple of members of the sect, and on his word they went to the ramparts and stepped off to their deaths. He offered to repeat the demonstration and asked whether any of Henry's followers were so loyal. Henry excused himself from the presence of these fanatics and returned to Acre, little suspecting that he himself would soon likewise fall to his death.

## Henry d'Arcy (died 1174)

Brother Henry d'Arcy was the Templar Preceptor of Temple **Bruer**, Lincolnshire, **England**, from 1161 until 1174. He was something of a patron of literature (if not a poet himself). He commissioned (or wrote) religious poems in Norman French, including 'Lives of the Fathers' on the early desert Church fathers, and 'Thaïs' on a prostitute who became a saint. There was a work on the **Antichrist** and another 'The Descent of St Paul into Hell' based on the fourth-century apocryphal scripture 'The Apocalypse of Paul'. In this, St Paul descends into Hell and witnesses the suffering of the damned. Moved by it, and supported by angels, he pleads for God's mercy on their behalf, causing God to allow the damned respite on Sundays.

## Henry II de Lusignan of Cyprus (1271–1324)

Henry II was one of the de Lusignan kings who reigned on **Cyprus** but also claimed the title of **Kingdom of Jerusalem**. He was the son of Hugh III, and possibly epileptic. He succeeded his brother, John I of Cyprus, in 1285, John reputedly having been poisoned. Henry II forcibly recovered **Acre** for his realm, ejecting the officials sent by **Charles of Anjou**, who had pushed his own claim to the throne of Jerusalem. He had a second coronation in Acre and was the last Christian king to be crowned in the **Holy Land**. Henry returned to the city and fought for a while at the final siege of Acre in 1291, but withdrew to Cyprus once the situation became hopeless.

Henry's Kingdom of Cyprus played host to the refugee Franks of the Holy Land, and also became the headquarters of the **Military Orders**, who hoped one day to launch a new **Crusade** from the island, possibly with the **Mongols** as allies. The King apparently shared this hope and tried to stop the **Genoese** from trading with the Mameluks in an attempt to weaken them economically. Little came of these plans and soon the Templars, bereft of their original purpose, became embroiled in political scheming on Cyprus. **Jacques De Molay** had never been very friendly with Henry II. Henry wrote to the Pope complaining about the Templars continuing hostility towards the crown. The Templars in turn seem to have questioned Henry's ability to defend the island or administer justice. In 1303, Henry had his brother Guy executed for conspiring against him. In 1306, when Henry II forbade the Templars from adding to their holdings on the island, the Templars allied with the King's other brother **Amaury de Lusignan, of Cyprus** and deposed Henry, imprisoning him in **Armenia** in the custody of King Oshin. Amaury was proclaimed governor.

Despite having been installed with Templar help, Amaury felt obliged to obey Pope **Clement V**'s orders to arrest the Templars. The Templars were eventually compelled to appear before tribunals, though little evidence of heresy was heard. Many of the nobles called as witnesses at the trials were supporters of the exiled Henry, including Aygue de Bessan, who said he knew nothing about the accusations against the Order and, on his soul, had heard nothing but good, while others testified to their courage in battle. Even so it is possible that some of these nobles, gathered for the trials, used the occasion to plan a counter-coup to reinstate Henry II. On 5 June 1310, Amaury de Lusignan was murdered in his palace, paving the way for Henry's restoration. The **Hospitallers** (by now safely established as masters of **Rhodes**) also supported Henry's return to Cyprus. In August 1310 Clement V issued orders for The Templars on Cyprus to face a new trial, and Henry II seems to have been happy to oblige and to implement **torture**. The Templars languished in dungeons while their property passed to the Hospitallers. King Henry died in Strovolos near Nicosia in August 1324.

## *Henry II, Duke of Silezia* (died 1241)

Henry (or Henryk) II, Duke of Silezia, known as Henry the Pious, was one of the most powerful Polish nobles. He was killed leading an army of Polish and Bavarian knights, including Templars, against the invading **Mongols** at the battle of **Liegnitz**.

## *Henry I of England* (c. 1068–1135)

Henry I, the youngest son of William the Conqueror, was the third of the Norman kings of **England**. He was known as Henry Beauclerk (fine clerk), on account of his scholarly character. He was not resigned to a clerical vocation, however; and moved quickly to secure his succession – he was crowned four days after the death in a hunting accident of his brother William Rufus in 1100. Henry's elder brother Robert of Normandy was then in the process of returning from the **First Crusade**. Henry secured the support of the Barons for his own claim by issuing the Charter of Liberties. Henry travelled much between England and Normandy (Robert had been overthrown and much of Normandy fell under Henry's rule). His only legitimate son, Prince William, was drowned when the *White Ship* was lost with all hands while returning from Normandy in 1120. After this loss, Henry reputedly never smiled again. Henry's daughter and heiress **Matilda** (known as the Empress Matilda) had previously been married to the German Emperor Henry V. After the emperor's death she was married to Geoffroi, the son of **Fulk V, Count of Anjou**, thus establishing the **Angevin** line of English monarchs. King Henry welcomed **Hugues de Payens** in Normandy in the late 1120s, and permitted him to visit England and establish a branch of the Knights Templar there. The meeting was recorded in the **Anglo Saxon Chronicle**. Later Henry ratified the grant to them of their first headquarters (the **Old Temple**) in **London**, at Holborn. Henry died near **Gisors** in 1135, probably from food poisoning.

## *Henry II of England* (1133–89)

Henry, the first of the **Angevin** or Plantagenet Kings of **England**, did much to restore stability after the years of anarchy and civil war fought between his mother, the Empress **Matilda**, and her cousin **Stephen**. Henry's reign is unfortunately remembered for the fiery King's acrimonious feuds with those who were once close to him, his former friend Thomas à Becket, with his estranged wife **Eleanor of Aquitaine** and his rebellious sons, the 'Devil's brood'.

During the civil wars in England, Henry's father, Geoffrey of Anjou, had capitalised on the situation by taking Normandy and in 1150 invested Henry as Duke. The following year Geoffrey died and Henry became Duke of Anjou and Maine. In 1152 Henry married the newly divorced Eleanor of Aquitaine, though a decade younger than her (Henry's father had also been a decade younger than his mother so it may not have seemed too odd to him). The next year Stephen conceded Henry's claim to the throne. Henry succeeded Stephen in 1154 and thus became one of the most powerful magnates in Europe.

Henry restored law and order to England, ably assisted by his chief minister Thomas à Becket. Henry restored the northern counties to English rule from **Scotland**, campaigned in Wales and in **France** to uphold Eleanor of Aquitaine's claim to Toulouse. On his return in 1163 the famous quarrel broke out between the King and Thomas à Becket, whom Henry had made Archbishop of Canterbury. Becket became a stubborn defender of the rights of the church – both spiritual and temporal. He refused to accept the principle that priests could be subject to secular justice. In 1164 Becket was forced to flee England. He stayed with the continental **Cistercians** and solicited Papal support. Eventually, thanks partially to the mediation of the Templar **Richard of Hastings**, the King and Becket met in Normandy and were reconciled. Becket returned to England. It wasn't long before the Archbishop again provoked the King's anger. In the end, Becket was murdered by four **knights** who attacked him in Canterbury Cathedral, believing they did the King's will.

The Church at once elevated Becket as a **martyr**. The King was obliged to make a humiliating public display of penitence, while the murderous knights were obliged to go on pilgrimage to the **Holy Land** and possibly joined the Templars. In 1172, Henry **took the Cross**. In 1185 Henry met the **Patriarch Heraclius**, who came to raise support for the threatened **Kingdom of Jerusalem** and while in England consecrated the newly finished **Temple Church London**. Henry's Parliament was unwilling to allow the King to leave to fulfil his Crusading vows when he was needed at home to defend England, but did grant permission to embark to any nobles or prelates willing to **take the Cross**. Henry meanwhile raised a substantial sum and donated it for the defence of **Jerusalem**. This treasure was given to the Templars and **Hospitallers**, who conveyed it to Jerusalem. He even accompanied Heraclius to a meeting with **Philip II Augustus**, but the Crusade was not yet to materialise.

Henry had always been on good terms with the Templars, one of whom, a Brother Roger, served as his Councillor. Henry also instituted the '**Saladin Tithe**' to fund the planned Crusade. He would never be able to fulfil his ambition of fighting for Jerusalem. The situation deteriorated with **Philip II Augustus**, and Henry's disloyal sons who had allied with Philip against their father. Defeated and embittered, Henry died at **Chinon** Castle, cursing his remaining progeny.

## *Henry III of England* (1207–72)

Henry III was the son of King **John** and the grandson of **Henry II** of **England**. At the time of his accession at the tender age of nine, the realm had been invaded by the French, who had the support of much of the baronial class. Only the loyal support of the elderly but still doughty **William Marshal**, Earl of Pembroke, rescued the throne for Henry. William and the loyalists began to expel the French prince Louis and the rebel barons. Marshal served as regent in Henry's early years. **Magna Carta** was reissued, winning back much baronial support. The Templars, given their links to William Marshal, no doubt also supported Henry, though it is unlikely they were involved in the fighting at this time. **Hubert de Burgh** later effectively succeeded William Marshal as regent.

Henry III grew to be very pious and spent lavishly rebuilding Westminster Abbey as a shrine to his royal patron **saint**, Edward the Confessor. Henry also saw the chancel of **Temple Church, London**, rebuilt on a grand scale. In 1231 he had made it known that he intended to be buried there, and made donations to support three chaplains to pray for his soul. However, he would finally decide to be buried in Westminster. Still, the remodelled Temple Church stands as testimony to the esteem in which Henry held the Templars, at least in the first half of his reign. Henry employed a Templar, Brother **Geoffrey**, as his **almoner**, a position of great trust with many responsibilities. Henry also amassed treasure, some of which he stored at the **New Temple, London**. Henry raised money by confiscating property from **Jews** and also – despite his famous piety – by imposing a levy on monastic institutions, which were forced to pay to have their confiscated charters and suspended privileges renewed. (Even the Templars themselves had to pay for the reaffirmation of their rights.)

During Henry's reign a small party of Templar and **Hospitaller** knights arrived from the **Holy Land** bearing a vial of **Christ**'s blood, which was enshrined in Westminster. The **Military Orders** no doubt hoped to raise awareness of the cause of the **Holy Land** during the accompanying ceremonies. In 1250, during the **Seventh Crusade**, Henry III **took the cross**, but never got around to embarking on Crusade. Four years later the Pope attempted to drag Henry into the war with Frederick II by 'converting' Henry's Crusader vow and enlisting the King as an ally against the Emperor. In the event the Pope raised **Guelf** armies and sent them against Frederick. He then attempted to bill Henry for it when the venture failed – the bill amounting to three times the annual revenue. Henry was told to pay for this war not of his making or face **excommunication**.

Henry was suspected of autocratic tendencies. A baronial opposition party arose under the leadership of the King's brother-in-law, **Simon de Montfort, 6th Earl of Leicester**. Henry was forced into submission and consented to summon a parliament and to govern with the advice of the Barons. When Henry tried to reassert royal authority, civil war broke out.

Simon de Montfort defeated the royalists and captured the King at the Battle of Lewis. Henry and his son Lord Edward (Later **Edward I**) were kept under arrest while De Montfort established something like a parliamentary system, though retaining great power himself. Subsequently, Lord Edward escaped and took the lead in the opposition to de Montfort and defeated him at the battle of Evesham in 1265. Edward restored his father to power, though Henry was diminished by the affair.

### *Henry VI, Holy Roman Emperor* (1165–97)
Henry VI was the **Holy Roman Emperor** from 1191 until his death in 1197. He was the son of **Frederick I** (Barbarossa), the husband of Constance of Sicily and the father of **Frederick II**. The union of the Empire (Germany in effect, and some of northern Italy) and the Kingdom of Sicily (which, after Henry defeated his rivals, included Naples and parts of southern Italy) rendered the Papacy in **Rome** fearful of encirclement. Henry VI was the overlord of Leopold of Austria and took charge of his prisoner **Richard the Lionheart**, King of **England**, whom Leopold had seized during Richard's return from the **Third Crusade**. Henry demanded a massive ransom of 150,000 silver marks from the English.

### *Henry St Clair, Lord of Roslin* (1297–1331)
Henry St Clair was a Scottish aristocrat of Norman ancestry. He and relation William gave evidence against the two Templars arrested in **Scotland**, who were Walter Clifton, Preceptor of **Balantradoch** and William Middleton of **Maryculter**. Henry and his sons, John and **William St Clair**, apparently went on to fight at **Bannockburn** under **Robert the Bruce**, and he was a signatory of the declaration of Arbroath, which justified and asserted Scottish independence to Pope **John XXII**.

### *Henry St Clair, 1st Earl of Orkney* (c. 1345–1400)
Earl Henry St Clair (or Sinclair) was the Earl of Orkney, Shetland and Roslin. He is supposed to have been a great mariner who in 1398 sailed to Nova Scotia, or at least to Greenland. Some **conspiracy theorists** have written about the possibility that some latter-day Knights Templar may have accompanied him on this supposed mission to the New World (**America**), perhaps taking the **Grail** with them. Henry's reputation as an explorer stems from his being identified with a Prince Zichmni who appears in the accounts of Nicolas Zino of **Venice** (c.1558) as the leader of a voyage in the North Atlantic. Zino's account was supposedly based on letters and a map produced by his ancestors, brothers Nicolo and Antonio Zino, who were part of the voyage. The identification is a highly speculative notion, needless to say. Henry's grandson **William St Clair** (1401–84) was the builder of **Rosslyn Chapel**. Some of the

carvings there are claimed to represent indigenous American plants, though this notion too is controversial.[198]

## Henry the Navigator (1394–1460)

Henry (Henrique) the Navigator was a Portuguese prince. He was the son of King John (João) I of **Portugal** (founder of the Avis dynasty) and the English Philippa of Lancaster (daughter of John of Gaunt and granddaughter of **Edward III**) Prince Henry was a knight both of the **Order of the Garter** and the **Order of Christ**, of which he was **Grand Master**.With the help of the Order of Christ, Henry did much to promote Portuguese maritime trade, exploration and colonization, and was a great patron of cartographers, and also of Jewish doctors and astronomers. Based in the Sagres peninsula in the Algarve, he sponsored missions exploring the coast of Africa, the Madeira Islands, the Azores and the Canaries. Some of this activity was a result of a fascination with the continent of Africa, born when Henry was part of the conquest of Ceuta, a city in Morocco. Part of Henry's motivation seems to have been the search for civilization beyond the **Muslim**-controlled regions, which might form an ally in renewed **Crusades**. In particular he was interested in the legend of **Prester John**, the semi-mythical Christian Emperor. He has been accused, however, of profiteering from a nascent African slave trade.

## Heraclius, Patriarch of Jerusalem (c. 1128– c. 90)

Heraclius (or Eraclius) was the Latin **Patriarch** of **Jerusalem**, rising to prominence during the reign of **Baldwin IV**. Heraclius was born in the Auvergne. He became a leading prelate in the **Holy Land** though his name was sometimes associated with scandal. He owed his promotion in around 1180 from the archbishopric of **Caesarea** to the intervention of the queen mother **Agnes of Courtenay**. This earned Heraclius the enmity of the Archbishop **William of Tyre**, who himself had evidently hoped for the title of Patriarch. William of Tyre in his chronicle was critical of Heraclius's performance, as was the author of a continuation chronicle. The chronicle depicts Heraclius as Queen Agnes's lover, and also the keeper of a concubine, a merchant's wife from Nablus known as 'Madame le patriarchesse'. Heraclius had William of Tyre **excommunicated**, for reasons unclear.

In 1185 Heraclius toured Europe, accompanied by Templars and **Hospitallers** (the Grand Master of the Templars, **Arnold de Tarroja** died in Verona on the way). The company met **Henry II, King of England** at Reading, and fell on their knees begging for aid on behalf of **Jerusalem**, which was under dire threat from **Saladin**. They even offered Henry the keys to the Citadel and the royal banner of the Kingdom. The King and his companions were much moved, it is said, and promised to bring the matter before parliament. Heraclius, meanwhile, visited the **New Temple**, and consecrated **Temple Church, London**. He failed to persuade Henry to come at once to the aid of Jerusalem, but did secure a donation of enough money to support 200 knights for a year. He was also with the King later in Normandy, at a meeting with **Philip II of France**, but nothing came of this.

Heraclius returned to Jerusalem. He found Baldwin IV dead and the infant **Baldwin V** on the throne. Soon afterwards the child too succumbed, and Heraclius crowned his mother **Sibylla** as Queen of Jerusalem. She in turn crowned her husband **Guy de Lusignan** as king. There swiftly followed the debacle of **Hattin**. Heraclius was called on to bear the **True Cross** into the battle, but he proved not up to it, and abdicated the role to the bishop of **Acre**. Heraclius remained in Jerusalem, and met **Balian of Ibelin**, who arrived to collect his family, having been permitted so to do by Saladin on the condition that he would not stay to fight. The Patriarch begged Balian to remain. Heraclius himself remained throughout the siege, along with the Queen. Finally after a stiff defence Balian negotiated the surrender of the city and the ransom of its inhabitants. A Muslim source scornfully described how Heraclius carried off a cartload of Church treasure rather than ransom the poor Christians of the city who could not afford their ransoms. Heraclius bore the same name as the Byzantine Emperor who had recovered the Holy Land from the Persians. As William of Tyre had supposedly predicted, under this namesake the Kingdom was lost.

## Hereford
Hereford is a provincial cathedral city in the west of **England**. The Templars had a Preceptory there with a **round church**, now vanished. The tomb of St **Thomas Cantilupe** in Hereford Cathedral is surrounded by carvings of Knights, possibly Templars, in attitudes of mourning.

## Heresy
Heresy (from *hairesis*, the Greek for 'choice') is defined as a belief contrary to the received doctrines of the Christian Church – especially the Roman **Catholic** Church. To count as a heretic, in the Christian sense, one has to hold views at variance with orthodoxy, and yet profess to be a Christian. Most historical heretics were those who defined the nature of God or Christ in different ways. Many beliefs, or interpretations of scripture, were not clearly defined as heretical until Church councils decided one way or the other. From early times heretics were ruthlessly persecuted, the official justification for this being that heretical ideas threatened to corrupt the Church's dogmas. Heresy was defined as a spiritual crime, linked to blasphemy, and dealt with as a political one. It was presented as treason against God, thus the powers felt justified in condemning convicted heretics not only to **excommunication**, but to imprisonment and even death.

The task of tackling heresy originally lay in the hands of the bishops, aided by the secular authorities. Early movements denounced as heretical included Arianism, Pelagianism and **Gnosticism**. In the fourteenth century the **Cathar** heresy was perceived as the greatest threat to Catholic Orthodoxy. To combat the heresy, the Church brought about the **Albigensian Crusade**, and eventually set up the **Inquisition**, which served to terrorise many dissenters into submission. By then public **burning** was becoming the standard mode of execution for those convicted. It also started to use **torture** to produce the requisite **confessions**. Clearly the process of denunciation was open to abuse. As time went on it perhaps became expedient for the powerful to accuse their political enemies of heresy. Such ulterior motives evidently lay behind the **suppression** of the Templars.

### Hermann von Salza (1179–1239)

Hermann von Salza, a Thuringian noble, was Grand Master (Hochmeister) of the **Teutonic Knights**, from 1209. In 1211 he led an expedition against the Cuman Turks in Transylvania, at the behest of King Andrew Hungary, but his Order was suspected by the Hungarian barons of seeking to aggrandise itself, and was subsequently expelled. Hermann was a close ally of **Frederick II** and supported him throughout the **Sixth Crusade**. He helped recruit Crusaders in Germany, and helped preserve some semblance of unity among the army once the irregular Crusade was under way.

The Teutonic Knights escorted Frederick into **Jerusalem** and attended at his crown-wearing in the **Holy Sepulchre**. Hermann read out Frederick's on the whole conciliatory speech translated into German and French.[199] Hermann later had the difficult task of representing Frederick to the hostile Papal Curia of **Gregory IX** where he endeavoured to have Frederick's **excommunication** lifted. Hermann also presided over the establishment of the Order's territory in the **Baltic**. Hermann's more difficult task was trying to serve two masters faithfully, and to act as a bridge between the mutually hostile courts of the Pope and the Emperor. His diplomatic efforts finally failed on Palm Sunday 1239, when Frederick was again excommunicated. On the same day Hermann died.[200]

### Hermits

Hermits were religious recluses who lived in the wilderness, away from the temptations of the world (or as anchorites in cells attached to churches) devoting themselves to prayer and subjecting themselves to corporal **mortification**. Some developed a reputation for wisdom and holiness. **Peter the Hermit** became a leader of the **First Crusade**. A number of veterans took to living as hermits in remoter parts of the **Holy Land**, such as around **Mount Tabor**. Some took to semi-communal living along monastic lines. Gerard of

Nazareth wrote about the hermits, including one named Bartholomew, who came East as a **pilgrim**, then became a Templar, then cared for **lepers** and finally joined the hermits.

## Hertford

Hertford is the county town of Hertfordshire in the south-east of **England**. It had a castle of which the fifteenth-century gatehouse and Norman earthworks remain. **Conspiracy theories**, and dubious stories reported in the press, link supposed **tunnels** under Hertford to the Knights Templar. Some papers, including *The Times* and the *Guardian*, repeated claims linking the 'Templar tunnels' to the **Holy Grail**.[201] The stories also allude to Templar **continuity** in the town and mention the modern 'Hertford Templars' requesting an apology from the **Pope** for the persecution of the medieval Order. The story of the Hertford Templars seems to be a hoax, though, emanating from a singular individual. The historical Templars had various settlements in Hertfordshire, including Temple **Dinsley** and the town of **Baldock**. They may also have been the creators of **Royston Cave** but are not known to have dug or occupied tunnels in Hertford itself.

## Hexham Abbey

Hexham Abbey is a great church in Hexham, Northumbria, **England**. It was originally a **Benedictine** monastery (the crypt dates to AD 674) and then became an **Augustinian** Priory. The choir is primarily twelfth century, while the transepts are thirteenth century work. The nave was rebuilt in 1908. Set into the walls are historic stones including fragments of Templar-style **grave slabs**. One shows a shield with a *Croix Pattée*, above a broadsword.

## Hieros Gamos

*Hieros Gamos* (Greek for 'Holy Wedding') was a supposedly widespread pagan practice of seeking religious experience through sexual intercourse, or to channel the energies of a god and **goddess** thereby. The concept was revived, if only symbolically, with the advent of the Wiccan movement, as the 'great rite'. In the medieval and early-modern periods, suspects of **heresy** and **witchcraft** were often accused of conducting rituals accompanied by sexual practices. Margaret Murray theorised that the accusations were a distorted reflection of reality, and that an ancient pagan fertility cult lived on in defiance of the Church.[202] However, Norman Cohn and others rejected this, seeing the lurid notion as an unfounded but self-perpetuating fantasy within the **Inquisition**.[203] Such notions were adapted in the **accusations** against the Templars, where **sodomy** was emphasised. However one fragmentary trial record from the **Vatican Archives** speaks of the Templars consorting carnally with maidens at their rite – in some cases allegedly **demons** in female form.[204]

## Hildegard von Bingen (1098–1179)

Hildegard von Bingen was a **Benedictine** nun, raised within the church. She became the Abbess of a nunnery at Bingen in **Germany**, which she founded in about 1147. A relation of The Emperor **Frederick I**, she gained a reputation for wisdom. She corresponded with Pope **Eugenius III**, with Abbot **Suger of St Denis**, and with St **Bernard of Clairvaux** among others. In her youth and beyond, she received illuminating mystical visions, which she eventually wrote down in three volumes, which the local Bishop approved as authentic and orthodox. She also wrote on theology, science, medicine and ethics, and composed religious poetry and music. Her music was for nuns to sing during services. The 'Order of the Virtues' had a single male role, that of the Devil.

Hildegard's prophetic works contained exquisite illustrations, including mystic diagrams. Hildegard was a moralist and a staunch advocate of chastity. In her latter days the canons and Bishop of Mainz placed her convent under **Interdict** when the Abbess refused to have disinterred from its graveyard the body of a young man who they claimed had died an **excommunicant**. She defended her position and eventually the interdict was raised. After her death she was widely regarded as a **saint**.

## Hirst, Temple

Temple Hirst was a Templar **Preceptory** in Yorkshire, attached to a major sheep rearing estate. It exported wool to the Continent from the port of Faxfleet. The land was donated in 1152 by Ralph, brother of **Richard de Hastings**. Parts of the Templar Preceptory are incorporated into a later manor, including a **Romanesque** archway and an octagonal brick tower.

## Hohenstaufen Dynasty

The Hohenstaufens were a German princely family of Swabian (south-west German) origin, to which belonged the Kings of Germany and **Holy Roman Emperors** from 1138–1254. The greatest Hohenstaufen ruler of the thirteenth century was **Frederick II**, who also ruled Sicily and much of Italy. The conflict between Frederick and his heirs and the Papacy for supremacy in Italy ultimately resulted in the wiping out of the dynasty by **Charles of Anjou**.

## Holy Blood and the Holy Grail, The

*The Holy Blood and the Holy Grail* was a best-selling work of popular history by Michael Baigent, Richard Leigh and Henry Lincoln. Published in 1982, it was written after Lincoln developed a fascination with the **Rennes le Château** mystery. He discovered the writings of **Gérard de Sède**, telling how Bérenger Saunière, the priest of the remote village in the French Pyrenees, had become suddenly and mysteriously rich. There was speculation that in 1891 Saunière had found a treasure or a secret that enabled him to fund his lavish building projects . He gained enough to remodel the Church of St **Mary Magdalene**, to build a neo-gothic folly, the *Tour Magdala* and to build a fine house for himself and his housekeeper/mistress. De Sède claimed that Saunière had found parchments hidden in a hollow pillar supporting the altar in his church, containing codes alluding to Poussin, to a treasure belonging to King **Dagobert II**.

It seems the authors were the victims of a hoax, originating from de Sède and **Pierre Plantard**, claiming that there existed a secret organization called the **Priory of Sion**, originating from the mysterious monks of **Orval**. They were the guardians of the 'Davidic Line', the secret descendants of **Jesus Christ** and Mary Magdalene. This supposed royal line had flowed into the **Merovingian** monarchs of Dark Ages **France** and survived a Church-sponsored usurpation. **Godfroi de Bouillon** was supposed to have belonged to this secret lineage. The authors cast the Templars as the guardians of this secret bloodline, being under the same leadership as the Priory of Sion until the **Cutting of the Elm**. The authors alleged that the Templars were suppressed by the Church because they knew the secret of the bloodline. The authors also involve the **Cathars** in the conspiracy, and reinterpreted the **Holy Grail** legends as allegories alluding to the existence of the sacred royal family (turning *San Greal* (Holy Grail) into *Sang Real* (Royal Blood)). They supposed that the purpose of the Priory of Sion was to restore the line to the throne of a united kingdom of Europe, which would be a sort of second coming.

## Holy Grail

The Holy Grail is a mysterious object, or **Holy Relic**, which appears in medieval literature as the object of the one true quest. It first appeared in *Perceval, le Conte du Graal* by **Chretien de Troyes**. It was carried by a beautiful damsel and was described as a vessel of pure gold set with jewels, shining with such radiance that the candles lost their brilliance. The questing **knight**, Perceval, encountered the Grail procession (which also included a bleeding lance) in the ghostly castle of a maimed sovereign called the Fisher King, whose realm lies within a wilderness. The next morning all had vanished. Perceval later learns from a hag who appears at Camelot that his failure to ask the meaning of the Grail, and whom it serves, had somehow meant missing an opportunity to heal the Fisher King and his blighted land. She sets **Arthur's** knights on the quest for the Grail. The narrative digresses then to the adventures of Sir Gawain, before returning to Perceval. Earlier, Perceval has rescued the noble maiden Blanchefleur, defeating the besiegers of her castle. His having to be parted from his lady to pursue the Grail Quest is another element of the romance. After his own adventures the knight encountered a hermit, who imparts some spiritual wisdom. Shortly after that the original narrative ends. Chretien died before he could complete the story.

The German poet **Wolfram von Eschenbach** based his Epic *Parzival* closely on Chretien's earlier work, though he expands the scope and gives Parzival a Saracen half-brother. The story follows Parzival's stumbling path from an unsophisticated youth kept ignorant of the ways of the world and of knighthood, through love and loss, triumph and disgrace, to atonement and enlightenment. In Wolram's version the Grail is a stone, possibly an emerald that fell from the crown of Lucifer. It is attributed with the power to greatly prolong life. Guardians of the Grail shrine called *Templeisen* feature in Wolfram's work, seemingly as a reference to the Knights Templar. Parzival's family connections to most of the main characters makes evident the significance of a 'Grail family', divinely appointed to have a leading role in world affairs. The Biblical character **Joseph of Arimathea** was brought into the Grail mythology by the romancer Robert de Boron.

Templar-like characters crop up in other Grail stories, which became a staple of medieval literature. Later Grail stories, such as that of Mallory, follow de Boron in describing the Grail vessel as the cup of the Last Supper, the same cup as that in which Joseph of Arimathea (according to the apocryphal tradition) caught **Christ**'s blood at the Crucifixion. An anonymous **Cistercian** monk penned a Grail story, the *Queste del Saint Graal*, in which Galahad is the main hero, and receives a white shield with a red cross. He is also revealed to descend from King **Solomon**.[205] The Templars had common patrons with the authors of the Grail romances, but do not seem to have had a direct input into the genre. In more recent times, the Grail stories have been linked to various **conspiracy theories**, sometimes related to the Templars' **treasure** and/or **Gnostic** knowledge, and the belief that the stories obscure some deeper meaning.

## Holy Land

Holy Places, to medieval Christians, were usually sites attached to the stories of **Jesus Christ**, the Apostles, martyrs and the **saints**, which attracted **pilgrims**. Significant holy places in Europe included **Rome**, Santiago de Compostella, and Canterbury, but none quite rivalled those in the Holy Land. Nearly all of the Holy Land was occupied by the **Crusaders**, and formed parts of the **Kingdom of Jerusalem**. (The Latin Kingdom roughly corresponds to modern Israel and occupied Palestine, Lebanon and south-eastern Syria.)

The Franks sometimes called the land 'Outremer' meaning overseas. The Holy Land was also sacred territory for the **Jews** who regarded this as the Promised Land of God's Chosen People. It roughly equates to ancient Canaan, or Judah, or Judea. **Jerusalem** was the heart of the Holy Land. While it stood, Jews were obliged to perform annual **pilgrimages** to the Temple in Jerusalem, and places elsewhere in the region, like the Tomb of the Patriarchs in **Hebron**, were also scenes of Jewish veneration.

Early Christianity was hostile to the notion of **holy places** and objects. Origen (an early Greek Christian theologian who died in **Caesarea** in about AD 250) argued that the holy place is the pure soul. Meanwhile according to Clement of **Alexandria** (another theologian from slightly earlier) the Temple was the assembly of Christian people. It wasn't long before the faithful began to wish for a more tangible focus for their devotions, however. It seems natural that the earliest Christians, despite believing in God's omnipresence, would have remembered sites where **Jesus Christ**'s passion (the events of his last days) has been played out, and would have regarded them as significant.

To the Christians the most sacred places were where Jesus had walked, and where the earliest Christian churches were built. Jerusalem had the **Holy Sepulchre** (believed to include both the site of the crucifixion and the tomb where he resurrected). There was also the room of the Last Supper, and the church of the Ascension, among other holy sites. **Temple Mount** itself was sacred to Christians, too (for there Jesus has questioned the priests as a boy and expelled the money lenders as a man). **Bethlehem**, meanwhile, had the Church of the Nativity, the scene of Christ's birth in a stable. Nazareth and Galilee were Christ's homeland, the River Jordan, where he had been baptised. Pilgrims could dip in the water and take some away with them, believing in its healing properties. They could also visit a cave where **John the Baptist** had supposedly lived. Sephoria was thought to be the childhood home of the **Virgin Mary**, while the earliest altar dedicated to her was found in Tortosa, where 'Our Lady performed many great miracles' including driving **demons** from the possessed.[356] Lydda, meanwhile, was the burial place of St **George**. Various scenes of Christ's ministry could also be venerated, and Old Testament sites such as the Tomb of the Patriarchs in Hebron were on the Christian Pilgrim trail. (Even the setting for the parable of the Good Samaritan was located!)[206] Mount Carmel was another sacred site, one of the most venerable of monasteries. Crusader architectural additions could be seen at the churches and shrines in many of these places. Many of these churches contained various **Holy Relics**, along with works of art in the **Byzantine** tradition. The Templars were founded to protect pilgrims visiting these shrines from all sorts of raiders and bandits.

## Holy Relics

Holy relics were objects relating to Biblical episodes or to Christian **saints**. They often included the bodies or dispersed bones of saints. The most sacred relics related to **Jesus Christ** himself. These relics were regarded as conduits for divine power, and credited with the ability to heal illnesses, grant prayers and secure military success. Relics were often the objects of **pilgrimage**. The relics were normally kept in churches in reliquaries, often of gold and precious stones. The Crusaders were zealously devoted to a large fragment of the **True Cross**, which they found in **Jerusalem**, and lost at the battle of **Hattin** in 1185.

Other supposed relics from the Passion of Christ were important to Medieval **Catholics** too. There were various places boasting Holy Nails. The Veil of Veronica (**Mandylion**) was a cloth reputedly marked with the face of Jesus, after St Veronica wiped his face with it on the path to Golgotha. There was a contender for the **Holy Lance** of Longinus (that pierced Jesus' side) at **Constantinople**, while another Holy Lance was unearthed by the knights of the **First Crusade** at **Antioch**. **Louis IX** of France, meanwhile, would purchase the Crown of Thorns from a cash-strapped Latin Emperor of Constantinople. Many other relics would be removed westwards from Constantinople, including possibly the **Holy Shroud**. Some are likely to have found their way into the possession of the Templars.

## Holy Roman Empire

The Holy Roman Empire (*Heiliges Römisches Reich* in German) was the misleading name of a confederation of states under a Holy Roman Emperor, who was usually also the hereditary king of the Germans. Technically, however, the Emperor was chosen by regional princes designated Electors, and was confirmed by the **Pope**, who crowned him. The 'Empire' was a somewhat nebulous concept. It was dominated by the German states but extended beyond, from Belgium to Austria, and also included parts of northern Italy. Beyond the German heartland the Emperor presided more as a figurehead than an absolute ruler. During the heyday of the **Hohenstaufen**, the Empire also included the Kingdom of Sicily, including Naples and Apulia.

The Holy Roman Emperors, though **Catholics**, sometimes came into conflict with the Papacy, as both Pope and Emperor claimed to have inherited the authority of the Caesars of Ancient **Rome**. Each presumed to be the leader of the Christian world and protector of the Western Church. Ironically the feud between the Papacy and the Hohenstaufen Holy Roman Empire did more to damage Western Christendom than probably anything else in the thirteenth century (**Guelfs and Ghibellines**). With the defeat and destruction of the heirs of **Frederick II**, an interregnum followed, from which the Habsburg dynasty emerged supreme. The institution of the Holy Roman Empire was disbanded in 1806 by **Napoleon Bonaparte**.

## Holy Sepulchre

The Holy Sepulchre in **Jerusalem** is the supposed tomb of **Christ** and the scene of his rising from the dead. It is contained within a grand rotunda called the *Anastasis*, which is the main component of the Church of the Resurrection. The tomb itself lies under a smaller structure called the Edicule, under the great dome of the outer church. Extending from the rotunda is a nave and apse largely built by the **Crusaders** on **Byzantine** foundations, with various side chapels and auxiliary shrines. This also covers the supposed spot of the crucifixion.

The church is situated within the old city walls, leading some to question its authenticity, given that the gospels place Golgotha, the site of Christ's crucifixion and burial, outside the city. However there is evidence that a new wall was built around an enlarged city by Herod Agrippa, in the 40s AD, which brought the site within the walls. The site, moreover, seems to have been venerated by early Jerusalem Christians. After the Jewish revolt of 135 AD, the Emperor Hadrian sought to obliterate the tomb and built over it a temple dedicated to Venus. Excavations in the AD 320s, presided over by the Empress **Helena**, mother of the Emperor **Constantine I**, and by the Bishop Macarius, saw the rediscovery of the tomb. A basilica was built, famed for its beauty and boasting relics including portions of the **True Cross** and the Titulus, the plaque that was placed above, which were shown to pilgrims on special occasions. It was also the venue for the supposed miracle of the Holy Fire.

The building was ransacked in 614 by Persians, but restored by the Byzantine Emperor Heraclius. The **Muslim** conquerors, later in the seventh century, initially respected the sanctity of the church. However in 1009, al-Hakim, the **Fatimid** Caliph of **Egypt**, a persecutor of Christians, ordered it to be destroyed. Subsequently the Byzantine Emperors gained permission to carry out limited rebuilding work. The Holy Sepulchre, also the seat of the Christian **Patriarch** of Jerusalem, was the main draw for Christian **pilgrims**, and to liberate it from Muslim hands was the declared objective of the Crusaders. The barons of the **First Crusade** gave thanks there in the aftermath of their bloody victory. **Godfroi de Bouillon** associated himself closely with the building and rather than 'King of Jerusalem' styled himself the 'Defender of the Holy Sepulchre'. The church, gradually restored to something approaching its former glory, became the seat of a Latin Patriarch, supported by Canons of the Holy Sepulchre drawn from the Augustinian **Order**. It was a venue for knighting ceremonies, and the first Templars swore their monastic vows there, on Christmas day 1119. There is a possibility some of the early Templars were veterans of the First Crusade who remained based at the Holy Sepulchre as guardians of the building, under a personal vow to the Patriarch. These original **Knights of the Holy Sepulchre** could have been the proto-Knights Templar.

The Holy Sepulchre was also the place for the coronation and burial of the Crusader Kings. The church did not suffer too much with **Saladin**'s conquest and was restored to the Eastern Christians. Later **Frederick II** won it back for the Franks (by diplomacy) and crowned himself there, but in 1244 it was ransacked by the **Khoresmians**. The **Latin** Christians were subsequently excluded from Jerusalem. They only regained a presence in the Holy Sepulchre in the 1300s when the **Franciscan Order** was permitted to found a community there, sharing the building with the rival Greek Orthodox and **Armenian** clergy. As they proved not to be very good at sharing, the main door key was kept by a Muslim guardian of the Nuseibeh family.

## Holy Spear (or Lance)

The holy spear is said to be the remains of the weapon that pierced **Christ**'s side at the Crucifixion. Legend says it was held by a blind Roman centurion named Longinus, whose sight was restored when he was splashed by Holy Blood. Longinus thus became the first Christian convert. A contender for the holy spear already existed in Constantinople when the Crusaders discovered another at Antioch.

Another holy spear was later revered at Nuremberg, and is now in Vienna. This was originally thought to be a spear belonging to St Maurice (another Christian Roman officer, the commander of the Theban Legion, who was martyred for refusing to kill other Christians in Gaul). This holy spear came into the possession of Charlemagne. It has a hollow centre and in it is inserted a supposed nail from the Crucifixion of Christ. In literature, a Holy Spear sometimes featured in the **Holy Grail** legends, being carried in the mystic procession, and miraculously dripping blood from its tip.

## Holy Shroud

The relic in Turin has long been venerated as the burial shroud of **Christ**. The linen shroud bears the faint image of a man, 6ft tall and well built, with long hair and a short beard, and bearing the marks of crucifixion. It shows the full length of the man's body; front and back, as if the cloth had been folded over his head. In 1988 a small sample of the shroud was carbon dated between AD 1260 and 1390. The shroud indeed came to light in the mid-fourteenth century, when **Geoffroi de Charny**, a French noble, had it exhibited in Lirey. In 1389 the Bishop of **Troyes** denounced the shroud as a fake, which he alleged was painted in about 1355. The shroud, however, does not seem to be a painting. There are no brush-marks, no pigments are in evidence, nor any medieval stylisations. The shroud was first photographed in 1898. The photographic negative showed the shroud with a three-dimensional positive image. The shroud itself is therefore a perfect negative.

Authors Christopher Knight and Robert Lomas have theorised that the Knights Templar revived an **Essene** ritual involving symbolic resurrection of the dead, and incorporated it into their secret rites. The authors speculated that while searching the **Paris Temple** after arresting its occupants in 1307, **Guillaume de Paris** found the shroud the Templars used in the rite, perhaps in some secret shrine. The **Inquisitor** at once had his men crucify **Jacques de**

**Molay**, then enfolded him in the shroud. This was the real, forgotten origin of the Turin Shroud.[207] The only evidence in favour of this theory is that the shroud emerged in 1357 in the possession of Geoffroi de Charny. Another, earlier **Geoffroi de Charney** had been the Templar Preceptor of Normandy and there could be a family link. However there is in fact evidence neither of the Templars using shrouds in their rituals, nor that Jacques de Molay was crucified. If he had been, then de Molay would surely have mentioned it in his last defiant speech.

The Shroud emerged in 1357, and it was taken to Chambéry some time after 1453. In 1578 it was taken to its present home. At various times it has been shown publicly, during religious festivals. Controversy over the relic has not been settled by the carbon dating results, which can be explained by contamination of the sample. There is some evidence that it existed before the 1350s. A psalter in Budapest, the Pray Codex, dating to the 1190s, shows Christ being taken down from the cross and placed in a shroud. The shroud in the illustration features a distinctive group of four small round holes in an 'L' formation. The same holes may be seen in the Turin Shroud.

Claims have been made for and against the authenticity of the Shroud, which apparently contains pollens from Turkey and dust from Palestine. It has also been linked to the *Sudarium*, the supposed headcloth from the tomb, presently in Oviedo Cathedral in Spain; which has provenance at least to AD 570, and which was apparently brought West via Alexandria. Some associate the Turin Shroud with a **Byzantine** relic called the Mandylion. According to a letter written by one Theodore Ducas Angelus to Pope **Innocent III** in the aftermath of the **Fourth Crusade**, the Crusaders' loot included the linen in which Jesus was wrapped after his death and before his resurrection. Theodore hinted that the Shroud had been taken to Athens. There is no record of the Knights Templar possessing the Shroud, though there are hints at a Templar, Brother **Barozzi**, being linked to the removal of other Byzantine relics and treasures, so the possibility that the Shroud passed through Templar hands cannot be ruled out.

## Holy Trinity Church, London

The Church of the Holy Trinity in London was an Augustinian Priory in medieval times. From 1220 to about 1248 its Prior was Richard de Templo, possibly a former Templar and translator from French of the *Intinerarium Peregrinorum et Gesta Regis Ricardi*. Holy Trinity later became the venue for the most important of the Templars' trials in Britain. The French Inquisitors, **Dieudonné** and **Sicard de Vaour and the Bishop of London** questioned the defendants, including **Imbert Blanke** and **William Raven**. The defendants denied all of the **accusations**.

## Holy War

Holy War is war waged in the name of God or religion. It possibly had its origin in the Hebrew conquest of Canaan, where the followers of Joshua believed they were doing God's will. The Muslim concept of *Jihad* (war against non-believers to defend or extend the empire of Islam), and the Christian concept of the **Crusade** (war to return **Christ**'s kingdom to Christian rule) are both examples of the doctrine of Holy War. St **Augustine** argued that Christians could fight without sinning provided the conflict met the criteria for a just war. The notion of Holy War was largely an aberration within Christianity, and it was not fully accepted, even at the height of the Crusading era.

## Honorius III, Pope (1148–1227)

Cencio Savelli, a Roman, and formerly a tutor to the Emperor **Frederick II**, was elected Pope in 1215, succeeding **Innocent III**, and would reign as Honorius III. Honorius presided over the launch of the **Fifth Crusade** in 1217, in which the Templars were major participants. He bore some share of the blame for its failure, for having been seen to sanction the decisions made by his legate **Pilagius of Albano**. The Pope also continued to support the controversial **Albigensian Crusade**, and confirmed **Simon de Montfort, 5th Earl of Leicester**, as Count of Toulouse. Honorius was generally a conciliatory figure, who sought to establish cooperation between the Papacy and the Empire for the greater good of Christianity. In 1220 he crowned Frederick as **Holy Roman Emperor** and encouraged him to take the Cross. The Pope also helped to bring about the Emperor's marriage to **Yolande** (also called Isabella), the daughter of **John of Brienne** and heiress to the **Kingdom of Jerusalem**. This followed a meeting between the parties concerned and representatives of the Military Orders in Ferentino in 1223, where the future of Crusading dominated the agenda. Honorius persuaded Frederick to embark on the **Sixth Crusade** but grew frustrated with Frederick's delaying. He died in 1127, and his successor **Gregory IX** promptly **excommunicated** Frederick.

## Horses

The Templars prized their horses and were known for how well they cared for them. Odo of Deuil recorded admiringly how the Templars managed to keep their horses alive during the arduous passage of the **Second Crusade** through Anatolia, where many of the secular knights lost theirs due to the harsh conditions. Medieval knights went into battle on heavy warhorses (destriers), no doubt strong and heavy, but probably not the enormous Shire or Percheron type later used as draft horses. Templar Knights typically had three horses, a warhorse and two lighter horses for general transportation. A palfrey was defined as one with a smooth gait, a more comfortable type to ride for long distances at some speed. Templar horses may have had cloth liveries called caparisons, coloured half black and half white and displaying red crosses. The Templars would have needed at least 4,000 horses for their ongoing work in the **Holy Land**, and more than this during major Crusades. Most horses were reared and trained on the Order's estates in the West, and brought over by sea. Joinville describes them being brought into the bays of ships below the water line, the doors of which were then corked closed. Sometimes the horses were secured in cradles suspended from the upper decks during transport.

## *Hospitallers*

The Hospitallers were a **Military Order** akin to the Templars, and founded in **Jerusalem**, to defend the faith and assist the poor. They had the additional role of looking after sick **pilgrims**. They were variously known as the Knights Hospitaller, the Order of the Hospital, and the Order of St John. They were later known as the Knights of Rhodes and as the Knights of Malta. They survive today with the official title of the Sovereign Military Hospitaller Order of Saint John of Jerusalem of Rhodes and of Malta (happily shortened to SMOM).

The Hospitallers, during the Crusades, were counterparts and sometimes rivals of the Templars. The two military/religious Orders were in competition for patronage, influence and glory. The Order traces its origins to a hospital caring for pilgrims in Jerusalem, predating the **First Crusade**. It was strongly associated with merchants from Amalfi in Italy. The Hospital was dedicated to **St John the Baptist**, although its original patron saint was the more obscure St John the Almoner.[208] The hospital was staffed by **Benedictine** monks, as well as by sisters of the Order, who cared for female pilgrims.

After the First Crusade, the hospital was reorganised by a merchant turned pilgrim/monk called Brother Gerard (**Gerard Thom**). He secured recognition for the Hospitaller Order in 1113. He was succeeded by **Raymond du Puy**, who oversaw the Order's expansion. Perhaps following the lead of the Templars, the Hospitaller monks started to admit knight brothers, and soon evolved as a partially militarised Order, escorting pilgrims and contributing cavalry to the **Kingdom of Jerusalem**'s army in defence of the Christian lands against Muslim raiders. However they also continued their Hospitaller role. During the era of the Templars, the Grand Masters of the Order of Hospital were:

| Grand Master | Tenure |
|---|---|
| Gerard Thom | 1099–1120 |
| Raymond du Puy | 1120–60 |
| Auger de Balben | 1160–62 |
| Arnaud de Comps | 1162–63 |
| **Gilbert d'Aissailly** | 1163–70 |
| Gaston de Murols | 1170–72 |

| | |
|---|---|
| Jobert of Syria | 1172–77 |
| **Roger de Moulins** | 1177–87 |
| Armengol de Aspa | 1187–90 (Provisional) |
| Garnier de Nablus | 1190–92 |
| Geoffroy de Donjon | 1193–1202 |
| Alfonse of Portugal | 1203–06 |
| Geoffrey le Rat | 1206–07 |
| Garin de Montaigu | 1207–28 |
| Bertrand de Thercy | 1228–31 |
| Guerin de Montacute | 1231–36 |
| Bertrand de Comps | 1236–40 |
| Pierre de Vielle-Bride | 1240–42 |
| Guillaume de Châteauneuf | 1242–58 |
| Hugues de Revel | 1258–77 |
| Nicolas Lorgne | 1277–84 |
| Jean de Villiers | 1284–94 |
| Odon de Pins | 1294–96 |
| Guillaume de Villaret | 1296–1305 |
| **Fulk de Villaret** | 1305–19 |

The expansion of the Knights Hospitaller mirrored that of the Templars. Like them they established **Commanderies** across Christendom, sometimes served by **round churches**. The Hospitallers, however wore a white cross on their cloaks, which were black (later they adopted red mantles, but retained black monastic dress). The Hospitallers' banner was red with a white cross. Later they adopted the eight-pointed Maltese Cross as their defining symbol. Like the Templars the Hospitallers were influential at royal courts, and held many **castles** in the **Holy Land**. In battle the Templars and Hospitallers normally cooperated. They took it in turns to guard the fore and rear of Crusading armies. The two Orders fought together, in the East and elsewhere against **Saracens**, **Moors**, **Mameluks**, and **Mongols**, at great battles including **Hattin**, **Arsuf**, **La Forbie**, **Las Navas de Tolosa** and **Liegnitz**. The brotherhoods were usually held in equal esteem when they fought bravely for the Christian cause, and equal scorn when in later times they feuded with one another. The Orders were reunited as comrades in arms in 1291, at the last stand of the Christians in the Holy Land, at **Acre**, against the Mameluks. Both Orders withdrew to **Cyprus**. The Hospitallers then went their independent way and established themselves as rulers of **Rhodes**. This project made them more secure, in that they were not reliant on the good will of host sovereigns but were a sovereign power themselves. Fulk de Villaret presided over the conquest of the island.

Meanwhile after the **suppression** of the Templars, **Clement V** secured most of the Templar estates for the Hospitallers at the **Council of Vienne** in

1312. The Hospitallers had restructured their Order so that it became more a federation of national Priories (Langues). This made a French takeover more difficult. Now styled Knights of Rhodes, the Order continued to wage **Holy War**, normally by attacking **Muslim** shipping. They built a fleet and also strong fortifications on their island possessions as well as at Bodrum on the Turkish mainland. They beat off two major sieges from Rhodes, one in 1444, and one in 1480, from the Sultan Mehmed II, the **Ottoman** conqueror of **Constantinople**. In 1522 the Sultan Suleiman the Magnificent landed 200,000 Turkish troops, outnumbering the defenders by almost thirty to one. After six months of siege the surviving Knights of Rhodes were permitted to depart with their lives. In 1530 the Knights were compensated with the small islands of Malta and Gozo by the Emperor Charles V, for the token rent of a Maltese falcon given annually to the Emperor's viceroy on Sicily.

As the Knights of Malta, the brethren continued to serve as a bastion against Ottoman sea power and a defence against Barbary piracy. The Ottomans soon tried to dislodge the Knights from Malta, but were repulsed against the odds by the Knights under their **Grand Master** Jean Parisot de la Valette, who subsequently founded the capital Valetta. Later they contributed ships to the Christian maritime victory at Lepanto. The Order remained in control of Malta until 1798 when it was ejected by **Napoleon Bonaparte**. Vestiges of the Order continued in Europe and do to this day, though the Order has abandoned all military activities. Through most of the nineteenth century it was without a Grand Master, and came for a time strongly under Russian influence (having previously established ties with the Tsars). In the 1830s, the Order became based in **Rome**, which remains its home. As well as preserving the humanitarian Hospitaller tradition it remains a bastion of hereditary nobility. The Order has Priories around the world.

## Hubert de Burgh (1165–1243)

Hubert de Burgh was a leading baron during the reigns of Kings **John** and **Henry III** of **England**. Starting as a squire of Norfolk, he joined the court and rose to become chamberlain and then justiciar, the chief of the judicial system of England. He amassed great wealth and many manors.

During the wars against **Philip II Augustus** in France in the early part of John's reign, King John captured his nephew Arthur of Brittany, and Arthur's sister Eleanor. De Burgh was made their jailor at Rouen. At some point Arthur died under suspicious circumstances. De Burgh's role in the affair is not clear. Later, John made de Burgh castellan of **Chinon** on the Loire. De Burgh was besieged there and subsequently made a prisoner by the French. He returned to England in 1207 and began to recover his standing. He remained loyal to King John through the barons' revolt, but advised the King to sign **Magna Carta**. He was also one of the twenty-five named who would see the charter was implemented. The last years of John's reign saw a French invasion of England, with Louis (later **Louis VIII**), the son of Philip II Augustus, landing in the south-east. Hubert defended **Dover** Castle through the middle months of 1216, and eventually drove the French off. He subsequently defeated them in naval engagements at Dover and Sandwich.

Hubert de Burgh became practically the regent in the early years of Henry III's reign, especially after the death of **William Marshal** in 1219. He was made Earl of Kent. However he had made enemies. In 1232 the Bishop of Winchester, Peter des Roches decided to bring him down. He accused Hubert, among other things, of amassing a great hoard of treasure, deposited at the **New Temple, London**, which included items that rightly belonged to King Henry III. He also charged De Burgh with giving the King bad counsel, plotting with the **Pope** against the realm, abducting and marrying Margaret, the daughter of William the Lion, King of **Scotland**, wasting money and being responsible for the loss of **La Rochelle**. Hubert was consigned to the **Tower of London**. King Henry, persuaded of Hubert's guilt, summoned Brother Robert, the Master of the London Temple. Robert said that it was true Hubert had deposited treasure at the Temple, but he did not know how much and anyway, the key was held by the client and moreover he did not have authority to hand anything over without de Burgh's consent. By whatever means, de Burgh was persuaded to produce his key and was moved from the Tower to a more comfortable prison in Devizes castle. The King and the Bishop got their hands on de Burgh's treasure chest. Its contents included gold and jewellery with bejewelled rings, crowns and brooches, gold and silver cups including a great cup with figures in relief, crosses, **holy relics** a 'gryphon's egg cup' a fortune in coins, silk girdles and a silver porringer. Two years later Hubert was reconciled with the King, through the mediation of Edmund Rich, the Archbishop of Canterbury.

## Hugh, Bishop of Lincoln, St (c. 1135–1200)

Hugh, Bishop of **Lincoln**, was born at the Castle of Avalon, in south-eastern **France**. His widowed father brought him up from the age of eight in a monastery. Hugh eventually rose high in the **Carthusian Order**, and was invited to England by **Henry II** to be prior of the first Carthusian foundation or Charterhouse at Witham, Somerset, near the Templar **Preceptory**. Hugh became bishop of **Lincoln** in 1179. He had some quarrels with the King over ecclesiastical independence, but was more diplomatic and less turbulent than **Thomas à Becket**. He also developed a reputation for **charity** and humanity, for example protecting **Jews** during the persecutions accompanying the calling of the **Third Crusade**. He was an able diplomat and trusted as an envoy to France by **Richard the Lionheart** and by King **John**. Hugh commenced the rebuilding of **Lincoln Cathedral** in 1185. On one of his visits to France he is said to have indulged in some pious theft, carrying away in his mouth a finger of St **Mary Magdalene** to install as a **Holy Relic** in his grand new cathedral. Hugh was raised to sainthood himself in 1220.

## Hugh, Count of Champagne (c. 1074–1132)

Hugh (or Hughes) de Champagne was the powerful Count of **Champagne**, with his capital at **Troyes**. **Hugues de Payens** was his vassal and a close associate. Hugh was the son of Theobald I of Champagne and succeeded on the death of his older brother in about 1092. He apparently visited the **Holy Land** in the company of Hugues de Payens, in 1104–8 and in 1114/1115. Hugh was married to Constance, the daughter of King Philip I of **France**, but it seemed they divorced without having produced children, and that she was remarried to **Bohemond of Taranto**, when Bohemond came West to raise support for his controversial projected campaign against the **Byzantine Empire**. Hugh's second marriage was to Elizabeth of Varadis, but he did not recognise Eudes, the son she bore, as his own. Hugh was subsequently criticised by the Bishop of Chartres for abandoning his wife and avowing himself to the Knighthood of Christ. Hugh returned to the Holy Land in 1125, five years after the Council of Nablus, becoming a member of the Knights Templar. He swore allegiance to Hugues de Payens, the Master of the Temple, who had previously been his vassal. Hugh was not only the most important early backer of the Templars. He was also a patron of the **Cistercian Order**, with links to St **Bernard of Clairvaux**.

## Hugh III of Cyprus (1235–1284)

Hugh III of Cyprus was King of **Cyprus** from 1267 and titular King of Jerusalem from 1268, and was a grandson of Bohemond IV of **Antioch**. Hugh claimed the succession of **Jerusalem** on the execution of **Conradin** by **Charles of Anjou**. His claim was disputed by Mary of Antioch, a closer relation of Conradin. Hugh's claim was upheld by the *Haute Cour*. Mary of Antioch subsequently sold her claim to the Crown of Jerusalem to Charles of Anjou, who sent Roger of San Severino as his bailli, ejecting Hugh's officials from parts of the kingdom. The Templars also supported the Angevin claim. Roger of San Severino and the Templars prevented King Hugh from asserting his authority in **Acre**. This brought the Order into conflict with members of the indigenous nobility, including the d'Ibelin clan, who supported Hugh's claim. The Templars undermined attempts by the Cypriot King to assert his rule in **Tyre** and **Beirut**. Hugh felt compelled to return to Cyprus and retaliated by attacking the Templars' establishments there, including the Preceptories in Limassol and Paphos and the castle at Gastria, which he demolished. Hugh was succeeded by his son John, and then by a younger son **Henry II of Cyprus**.

## Hugh Schonfield (1901–88)

Hugh Schonfield was a British Bible scholar and a **Jewish** Christian (he considered himself a Nazarene). He was the author of many books on Early Christianity including *The Passover Plot*. He argued that **Jesus Christ** deliberately set out to fulfil the prophecies in order to be the Messiah, believing himself a descendant of King **David**. When Jesus was crucified his closest disciples supposedly supplied him a drug so that he would appear to have died, intending afterwards to be revived by his followers. Jesus would then have presented himself as the Messiah and reigned as priest-king of Israel. The plot went wrong, however, when the Roman centurion unexpectedly stabbed Christ's side, causing him to die from that injury. The idea was speculative and naturally controversial. Schonfield also thought that Jesus' original message had been corrupted by St **Paul of Tarsus**. Schonfield studied the **Dead Sea Scrolls**, and wrote 'The **Essene** Odyssey'. In it he observed that the name of the alleged Templar idol, '**Baphomet**', when encrypted via an ancient Jewish code called the Atbash Cipher, became 'Sophia', the Greek word for 'wisdom', and in **Gnosticism** a goddess-like angel or *Aeon* personifying divine wisdom and regarded as a heavenly counterpart of Christ. (The Atbash cipher was a simple code used in Biblical times where the letters from the Hebrew alphabet as written right to left were substituted for the letters as written left to right.) Since then some have speculated that the Templars had links to the Essenes, or to Jewish practitioners of the **Cabbalah**, wherein the Atbash Cipher is also supposedly used.

## Hugh von Salm (thirteenth–fourteenth century)

Hugh von Salm was the Templar Preceptor of Grumbach in **Germany**, at the time of the **Suppression**. In May 1310, fully armed and accompanied by twenty fellow Templars, Hugh burst in on the session of the Archbishop of Mainz, Peter of Aspelt. Hugh declared that he knew the council had been convened on the orders of the **Pope** with a view to destroying the Knights Templar, and that the Order had been **accused** of outrageous **heresy**. He protested against the harsh and intolerable treatment that the Order had received, with them being condemned without due process, and with the brethren in **France** who proclaimed their innocence being burned alive. He claimed that God had shown their innocence, for the red crosses that the executed men wore would not burn. The frightened archbishop promised to take the matter up with the Pope. The council dispersed and did not reconvene for nearly a month.

## Hugo Peccator (eleventh–twelfth century)

Hugo Peccator (Hugh the Sinner) was the author of an undated letter to the early Templars apparently intended to raise their spirits in the face of criticism from members of the Church establishment and others who questioned the validity of their vocation as warrior monks. The brethren evidently felt that they were striving thanklessly. The criticism they received was that Christians should not hate their foes or take booty in battle. Hugh reminded the Templars that were it not for them the Christians would be overwhelmed by a storm from the East, that they lived spiritually when not fighting, and that when fighting they had good reason to hate – they were hating evil, not men, and that they plundered only to fund the defence of the Holy Places. God had not abandoned them, Hugh promised, and if their worth was not recognised by their fellow Christians then it would be recognised by God. Some theorise that the 'Hugh Peccator' was none other than **Hugues de Payens** himself. **Hugh, Count of Champagne** (who renounced his title to join the brethren) is another possible identification, as is Hugh of St Victor, **Augustinian** abbot of **Paris**.

### *Hugues de Jouy* (thirteenth century)

Hugues de Jouy became the **Marshal** of the Temple during the later phases of the **Seventh Crusade**. After a dispute, King **Louis IX** compelled **Reynald de Vichiers**, the **Grand Master**, to exile Hugues from the **Holy Land**. The King accused the Templars of being 'over bold' in negotiating with the Sultan of **Damascus** on their own behalf, after the Grand Master has sent de Jouy to settle a land dispute with the Sultan. Hugues was made the scapegoat, in what must have been a rather humiliating episode for the Order. The Grand Master, meanwhile was compelled to kneel barefoot before the King offering public apology.

### *Hugues d'Empuries* (died *c.* 1303)

Hugues d'Empuries (or Hugh of Dampierre) was a Templar Knight captured by the Muslims at the siege of **Tripoli** in 1289. He was subsequently released and rejoined the Order. He presided over the surrender of the island of **Arwad**/Ruad after its siege by the Mameluks. He arranged safe conduct away from the island for his men, but the Mameluks reneged on their agreement and the Templars were taken captive. Hugues was beheaded.

### *Hugues de Pairaud* (born *c.* 1244)

Hugues de Pairaud (or Hugo de Pérraud) was the second highest official in the Knights Templar in the last years of the Order's existence. He was the **Visitor** of the Temple in France and Poitou and the deputy of the **Grand Master**. He and about sixteen companions were arrested in Poitiers while awaiting an audience with the **Pope**. He was held and interrogated at **Chinon** with the other grandees, and made a slightly more extensive confession than them, albeit one full of contradictions. Hugues said he had been received into the Order at the **New Temple, London**, by his own father Humbert de

Pairaud. This was forty-six years before, when he had been eighteen years old. He said he had been taken aside by a brother John, later Preceptor of La Muce. He said he was menaced into denouncing **Christ** but refused to spit. He said he had many times presided at initiations, more than any other. He had made the initiates kiss him at the bottom of his back, his navel and his mouth. He had told them to abstain from women and that if they must sate their lusts to do it with one another. However, he said that despite his instructions he knew of no cases of **sodomy** within the Order besides the two or three brothers that had been imprisoned for it in **Pilgrims' Castle**.

Hugues claimed that he had been shown the **head** idol by Preceptor Peter Alemandin in Montpellier. He said that he wished the errors could be done away with, and had only participated because they were traditions of the Order. (This testimony seems nonsensical, given that Hugues had introduced the kisses to the body to the rite of reception himself.) One may guess that Pairaud was deliberately confessing absurdities in an attempt to show that the allegations against the Order were all nonsense. Hugues de Pairaud was brought out to hear his sentence of perpetual imprisonment in 1314, along with the three other surviving former high officials of the Templar Order. He and **Geoffroi de Gonneville** did not demur, and escaped the fate of **Jacques de Molay** and **Geoffroi de Charney**. Pairaud was still alive in 1321, when he was again interrogated about the whereabouts of his vanished treasure.[209]

## Hugues de Payens (*c.* 1170–36)

Hugues de Payens (or Payns) was the presumed founder and first **Grand Master** of the Knights Templar. He was a **Knight** from Payens, ten miles from **Troyes**, a vassal of **Hugh, Count of Champagne**, and a relative of the Lords of Montigny. **Walter Map** wrote of how the knight from Payns in Burgundy took pity on his fellow Christian travellers, who were frequently attacked by pagans at a cistern outside Jerusalem. He defending them to the best of his ability, setting ambushes for the saracens. A man of energy and conviction, he lived poorly dressed and ill fed, spending everything he had on horses and arms, and recruiting fellow pilgrim-soldiers to his cause. He forged links with the **Canons of the Holy Sepulchre**. In 1118 or 1119 Hugues, with **Godfroi de St Omer** and the others, approached **Baldwin II** in **Jerusalem** and won royal approval for their new military/religious Order, originally known as the Militia (or the Poor Fellow Soldiers) of **Christ**. They were probably endorsed at the Council of Nablus (1120) and soon given quarters in the former **Al Aqsa Mosque** on **Temple Mount**. The knights swore religious vows before the **Patriarch** in the **Holy Sepulchre** and pledged their swords to the defence of pilgrims and the realm. By 1123 Hugh was being referred to as the Master of the Knights of the Temple (*Magister Militum Templi*). **William of Tyre** claims that after nine years there were still just **nine knights**, another source, **Michael the Syrian**, mentions thirty founding companions.

Hugues de Payens returned to Europe in 1127 seeking support for his new brotherhood and recruiting volunteers to aid the **Kingdom of Jerusalem**. He won the support of the influential Abbot **Bernard of Clairvaux**, and after three requests received from the Abbot a missive endorsing the Order, titled *De Laude Novae Militiae* (In Praise of the New Knighthood). Armed with this (assuming it originated from this period) Hugh toured **France**, Flanders, **England** and **Scotland**, having gained the favour of the rulers of these lands. He also met **Fulk V, Count of Anjou**, who would become one of the first honorary associates and a great supporter of the Order in the Holy Land. Hugues addressed the ecclesiastical **Council of Troyes** in 1129, giving an account of the Templars purpose and way of life. He had an input into the Latin **Rule**, which was produced and ratified at the council, making the Knights Templar an official arm of the **Catholic** Church. Hugues returned to the **Holy Land**, and saw action in Baldwin's unsuccessful campaign against **Damascus**. He apparently died peacefully seven years later, and was succeeded by **Robert de Caron**.

## *Hulagu* (1217–65)

Hulagu Khan was the grandson of Genghis Khan and the commander of the **Mongol** force that decimated much of the **Muslim** world in the Middle East. He enjoyed a fearful reputation. The **Assassins** surrendered **Alamut** to him on the basis of it. This was even before his greatest atrocity, the massacre of 80,000 in **Baghdad**, including the last **Abbasid** Caliph. Hulagu went on to capture **Aleppo** in 1260, again killing thousands. The Ayyubid ruler of **Damascus** capitulated soon after. Hulagu's approach also terrified the Palestinian **Franks**. The Prince of **Antioch** and the **Armenian** king Hethoum submitted to Mongol suzerainty, and Nablus and **Gaza** fell to Hulagu's advancing forces. It was the **Mameluks** that were mainly left to deal with the Mongol threat.

## *Humphrey II of Toron* (1117–79)

Humphrey II, Lord of Toron and Banyas and Castellan of **Hebron**, served as Constable of the **Kingdom of Jerusalem** from 1153. Humphrey II was given the position of Constable by **Baldwin III** in gratitude for his support in the power struggle against **Melisende**. Humphrey gained much respect through his career. He fought alongside the King and the Templars at the capture of **Ascalon**. Humphrey was a loyal supporter of **Baldwin IV**, and an ally of the Regent **Raymond III of Tripoli**. In 1179 he mediated in a dispute between the Templars and **Hospitallers**. In the same year he was mortally wounded while saving the leper King's life after Baldwin was unhorsed in a skirmish near Banyas.

## Humphrey IV of Toron (1166–97)

Humphrey IV of Toron succeeded his grandfather **Humphrey II of Toron.** Humphrey IV, a good-looking young man, lacked a warlike nature and thus fell short of the expectations of the Crusader barons, who considered him effete. Humphrey was a marked contrast to **Reynald de Chatillon** who became his stepfather when Reynald married Humphrey's mother Stephanie de Milly, thus gaining the lordship of Transjordan. In 1172 Humphrey was married to **Isabella of Jerusalem** in the castle of **Kerak.** A legend has it that at the time the castle was being besieged by **Saladin.** Humphrey's mother sent some cake out for the Sultan, who showed his gratitude by not bombarding the honeymoon tower. Humphrey was a consistent supporter of **Guy de Lusignan,** before and after the loss of **Jerusalem.** Though Humphrey was no warrior, he made himself useful during the **Third Crusade** as a negotiator with the **Arabs,** being fluent in Arabic.

# I

## Ibelin

Ibelin was a fortress in the south of the Latin Kingdom of **Jerusalem.** It was one of the castles built to counteract the threat from **Ascalon,** then still in Egyptian hands and a base for frequent raids into Christian territory. The Lords of Ibelin (the d'Ibelin dynasty) became influential nobles in the Latin Kingdom, and subsequently in the Kingdom of **Cyprus** under the de Lusignan kings. The Castle was given to the first of the dynasty, Barisan in 1141 by King **Fulk.** Barisan was also constable of **Jaffa.** The d'Ibelins became partisans of **Raymond III of Tripoli** during the court factionalism that broke out in the reign of **Baldwin IV.** They were opposed to **Guy de Lusignan** and his succession.

A younger son of Barisan's, **Balian of Ibelin,** would become famous as the defender of **Jerusalem** against the overwhelming forces of **Saladin. John d'Ibelin** of Beirut, the son of Balian, allied with the Templars against **Frederick II.** The family later came into conflict with the Order when the Templars supported the claim to the throne of **Charles of Anjou.** Another Balian d'Ibelin, titular Prince of Galilee, oversaw the arrest of the Templars on Cyprus during the suppression.[373]

## Iberia

The Iberian Peninsula was a frontier of Christianity and **Islam** in medieval times. The south, called al-Andalus, was controlled by the Muslim Moors, linked to North Africa. In the north-west was **Portugal,** then the Spanish kingdoms: Castile in the centre, and Navarre and **Aragon** in the north-east. The Christian states were fighting the Muslims in the adjunct to the

Crusades known as the **Reconquista**. The Templars were granted castles from the 1130s, especially in Portugal and Aragon, and encouraged to play a part in the ongoing push southward.

## *Ibn al-Athir* (1160–1233)

Arab chronicler, author of *The Perfect History*, running to thirteen volumes and including many events from the Crusades.

## *Ibn al-Qalanisi* (1073–1160)

Ibn al-Qalanisi was a **Muslim** historian based at **Damascus**. He wrote one of the earliest Syrian accounts of the **Crusades**, including the defeat of the **Second Crusade**.

## *Idolatry*

Idolatry is the worship of images, statues or objects, and is generally considered sinful within the monotheistic faiths. It is against the second commandment given to Moses and is also forbidden in the Koran. It is rare to find depictions of living creatures in **Jewish** or **Islamic** art. Various Christian groups, from the **Byzantine** Iconoclasts and the **Cathars** to Puritan Protestants have also regarded figurative imagery, especially in a religious context, to be idolatrous. However Roman **Catholicism** and Eastern Orthodoxy both endorsed worship with images. The veneration of statues of **saints** and of **Holy Relics** was accepted, as they were supposed to be a focus for devotion or as conduit through which divine power was channelled. Thus when in 1307 the Templars were accused of idol worship it implied that they were going beyond the veneration of a relic and, according to the **accusations**, thought their idol was their saviour and had powers in its own right. The Templars' idol was usually described as a **head**, and at the trials in **Carcassonne** it became associated with the name **Baphomet**.

## *Il-ghazi (died 1122)*

Najm ad-Din Il-ghazi ibn Artuq was the **Turkish** former governor of **Jerusalem**. He had a taste for wine, according to the **Muslim** chronicler ibn Al Qalanisi, but was also an early proponent of Jihad as a counter-Crusade against the Franks. When ousted by the Fatimid Egyptians Il-ghazi sought his fortune in the northern regions. He eventually became ruler of Mardin (now in southern Turkey), from where he sometimes made alliances with the Crusader barons. In 1117 Il-ghazi gained control of **Aleppo**, extending his power base. Two years later he turned against the Crusaders and defeated Roger of Salerno of **Antioch** at the battle of the **Field of Blood.** Walter the Chancellor, the Antiochene chronicler, described how Il-ghazi delighted in torturing and executing his Frankish prisoners.[210] Il-ghazi's forces were driven back by the arrival of **Baldwin II**, but the following year Il-ghazi was again able to raid around **Edessa**, as well as into **Armenia** and Georgia. Defeated in Georgia, Il-ghazi returned to troubling the Crusaders. With his nephew Balak he captured **Joscelin I de Courtenay** of Edessa in battle. Shortly afterwards Il-ghazi died and Aleppo passed to Balak.

## Illuminati

The Bavarian Illuminati was a secret society founded in 1776 by the radical philosopher Adam Weishaupt. Based on **Freemasonry**, it was a curious combination of 'enlightenment' rationalism and esoteric mysticism, with an agenda to bring about a world republic without priests and princes. The Illuminati's reputation probably outstripped its real influence. The Illuminati has been linked with **conspiracy theories** since the **French Revolution**.

## Imad ad-Din al-Isfahani (1123–1201)

Imad ad-Din al-Isfahani, was the secretary of **Nur ed-Din** and then of **Saladin** and a **Muslim** chronicler. He wrote with a dramatic and rhetorical style, and was fond of colourful metaphors. He saw the Templars and **Hospitallers** as a danger to **Islam**, 'rebels, demons and evil men' with castles on inaccessible crags, which were like the lairs of wild beasts. He described with glee the execution of the Templar and Hospitaller prisoners by the **Sufis** after **Hattin**, which he witnessed. Imad ad-Din also described with notable excitement the shipment of 300 beautiful and depraved Frankish harlots that he believed had arrived to service the Crusaders at **Acre**.[376]

## Imbert Blanke (c. 1250–1314)

Imbert Blanke was the Templar Preceptor of the Auvergne. He was visiting **England** at the time of the **arrests**, and after being arrested there played a prominent role in the defence of the Order in that country. He had been a Templar for thirty-eight years, and fought under **Guillaume de Beaujeu** who had died at **Acre** in 1291. Questioned at **Holy Trinity Church, London**, Imbert attested that the Order was innocent, and that any secrecy was on account of foolishness. The **Inquisitors** confronted him with incriminating confessions secured in **France**, made by other Templars who claimed that Imbert had presided at **heretical** receptions. He denied it. Imbert refused to confess anything, or even to make the declaration that he had been defamed by the accusations, which enabled most of the Templars to end their suffering, be reconciled and retire to various monasteries. Even after being incarcerated in chains and probably being subjected to **torture** Imbert continued to assert the Order's innocence, and probably perished in prison.

## Inab (Battle of)

The Battle of Inab took place on 29 June 1149. Capitalising on the departure of the **Second Crusade**, the Sultan **Nur ed-Din** had decided to renew his attacks on the principality of **Antioch** from **Aleppo**. He defeated a large Christian force led by **Raymond of Poitiers**, who was slain. The Muslims were prevented from gaining permanent control of the principality by a relief force led north by **Baldwin III of Jerusalem** and including a substantial Templar contingent. The Sultan's siege of Antioch was broken and his forces, which had been pillaging the land at will, were forced to withdraw.

## Indiana Jones and the Last Crusade

*Indiana Jones and the Last Crusade* was an action adventure film directed by Steven Spielberg in 1989. Set in the 1930s, it starred Harrison Ford as maverick archaeologist hero Indiana Jones and Sean Connery as his Arthurian scholar father. They are on a race against the Nazis to discover the **Holy Grail**. A Templar-esque immortal **knight** features as the guardian of the Grail, which is finally discovered. An ancient temple called the 'treasury' in Petra, Jordan, was used for the exterior of the lost Holy Temple in the film. The film does not reflect genuine Grail mythology but is an entertaining caper that stands the test of time.

## Indulgence

An indulgence was a spiritual pardon or absolution offered by the **Pope** for past sins. It was offered to Crusaders as an encouragement to engage in penitential/Holy warfare to defend the Church, and it was one of the features that defined a Crusade. Joining the **Military Orders** seems to have been considered equivalent of receiving an indulgence in terms of spiritual benefit.

## Initiation Ceremony

According to the **accusations against the Order**, the Templars were initiated amid blasphemous and **heretical** rituals. Those who denied the charges, however, described more sober and orthodox methods of reception. Aspirant Knights Templar had to prove that they were already of knightly class and were expected to have already received military training. The reception ceremony was customarily held with only members of the Order present. Sometimes several initiates were received at a time. It was all very sombre. Originally, candidates for the Templars underwent a probation period to prove their commitment. At the initiation, the candidate would be asked if he sought membership of the Order of the Temple. He would then be told that he sought a great thing, for he did not know the harsh rules observed within the Order. He had seen the Order from the outside, well **dressed** and with fine **horses**, but could not know the austerities within. When he wished to be on one side of the sea they would be sent beyond it and vice versa. When he wished to sleep he would be obliged to be awake, and when he wished to eat to go hungry. He was asked if he could sustain all this for the honour of God and the safety of his soul. He then had to affirm that he was of noble and legitimate birth, of **Catholic** faith, not **excommunicated**, unmarried, not of another Order, and without debts or dependants. He had to attest also to having no secret illnesses and to being fit to fight.

After answering satisfactorily, he was led into the chapel, and invited to pray to God, the **Virgin** and the **saints** about his decision to seek admittance. The initiate would then be taken to the presiding receptor, and kneeling, he would ask for admission to the Order. He would be invited to give himself to serve the Order in perpetuity, and renounce his individual will. The receptor would explain that his decision meant entering into a life of sacrifice, **poverty**, **chastity** and **obedience**, protecting Christians and fighting for **Jerusalem**, and that no brother could leave without the permission of his superiors. The initiate would then be received, and given the white mantle (if a knight) and the blessing of the priest who was present. The receptor then gave the initiate the kiss of peace (on the mouth). The Master then told the initiate to be glad because the Lord had led him to so noble an Order. There followed a lecture on Templar customs. The Master outlined the **Rule** and warned that there were things that might cause the brother to lose his habit, or to be punished in other ways.

## Inner Temple and Middle Temple

The Inner Temple and the Middle Temple are the societies of lawyers who took over the site of the **New Temple, London**, following the suppression of the Knights Templar in **England**. The societies were first mentioned by name in 1388, and were probably originally tenants of the **Hospitallers**. They took their names from the positions they occupied on the former Templar site (there was no law society of the Outer Temple). The societies constitute two of the four 'Inns of Court', the others being Lincoln's Inn and Gray's Inn, serving as residences for members of the legal profession. Members include judges, barristers and students. Those lawyers who completed their training were 'called to the bar' (Temple Bar) and became barristers. In later centuries the two societies built grand new halls. They also built the classical buildings that replaced the medieval Temple after the Great Fire of London. **Temple Church, London**, miraculously survived the Great Fire, and to some extent the Blitz. It remains in use by the two societies.

## Innocent II, Pope (died 1143)

Innocent II, formerly Gregorio Papareschi, became **Pope** in 1130. He was the Pope who granted the Templars extensive freedoms and privileges in the Papal Bull *Omne Datum Optimum*. Innocent's early reign was dominated by a struggle against a rival claimant to the Papacy, the antipope Anacletus II. Innocent was recognised more widely as the legitimate pope on account of the support of St **Bernard of Clairvaux**.

## Innocent III, Pope (1160–1216)

Lotario de Conti was an aristocratic Roman Cardinal Deacon, well versed in Canon law. Born in Segni and educated in Paris and Bologna, he was elected **Pope** soon after the death of Celestine III, reigning as Innocent III. At only thirty-seven, he was a strong personality, committed to the doctrine of **Papal Supremacy**. He affirmed that he was not only the successor of St Peter but the Vicar of **Jesus Christ** himself. He would assert Papal ascendancy over Emperors, Kings and lords alike. One of his first acts was to impose Papal sovereignty in **Rome**. He also consolidated the Papal States. He was a vigorous proponent of **crusading**, regarding it as a means of bringing international armies under ecclesiastical authority, and as a weapon that could be used against the Church's internal enemies as well as against **Muslims** and Pagans on the fringes of Catholic Europe. His first Crusade was preached against Markward of Anweiler in Italy, setting the tone for the later territorial wars between **Guelfs and Ghibellines**. He also appealed for aid for the **Holy Land** but the only one of Innocent's Crusades to engage Islam effectively during the Pope's lifetime was the campaign in Iberia that culminated at **las Navas de Tolosa**.

Innocent organised the **Fourth Crusade**, with the intention of conquering **Alexandria** as a prelude to the liberation of **Jerusalem**. When in 1204 the Crusaders took and ravaged **Constantinople**, and passed no farther, Innocent was originally incensed. His wrath, it seems, was mollified by gifts of plundered treasure, and the knowledge that the conquest of **Constantinople** had finally established the dominance of the **Latin** Church over the Greek. The Templars were not directly involved in this campaign, though at least one of them, brother **Barozzi**, was present, and acted as a messenger between the Crusader barons of the new Latin Empire and the Papal curia. This Templar also had the duty of bearing valuables from Constantinople to the Pope. Innocent meanwhile called on the King of Denmark to take the cross against the inhabitants of the Baltic, and promised him indulgences for expiating the errors of the pagans and spreading the boundaries of Christendom.[211]

Innocent had sent legates to harangue Count **Raymond VI of Toulouse** whom he accused of not doing enough to suppress the **heresy** of the **Cathars** in his lands. The Pope lost patience with the Count, and in 1108 instigated the **Albigensian Crusade**. He promised the same **indulgences** to the northern French knights who gathered to subdue the rebellious southerners as had been offered to those who had fought to recover the Holy Land (ignoring protests against this policy from representatives of Latin Syria/Palestine whose cause it undermined).[212] He approved **Simon de Montfort's** subsequent seizure of power in the **Languedoc.** At the same time he sent St **Dominic** to preach against the heretics, and paved the way for the inception of the **Dominican Order** and the **Inquisition.**

During the dispute between Leo of Armenia and **Bohemond III** and Bohemond's allies the Templars over **Antioch,** Innocent switched sides. He favoured first the former and then the latter party, and in 1211 **excommunicated** Leo. Other sovereigns also felt the force of the Pope's spiritual sanctions. Innocent had become the guardian of the young **Frederick II,** thus re-establishing Church influence in Sicily. The Pope excommunicated and sought to depose the **Holy Roman Emperor** Otto IV, and backed **Philip II Augustus** of **France** against Otto at the battle of Bouvines (1214), eventually seeing Frederick II installed as King of Germany. Innocent also excommunicated King **John** and put **England** under interdict, after a dispute over rival candidates for the Archbishopric of Canterbury got out of hand. The English Templars mediated between the King and the Papal legates in **Dover,** where the King agreed to Innocent's humiliating terms, recognizing the Pope as his overlord and paying homage for the kingdom. Innocent's pontificate was crowned when he presided over the grand assembly of the **Fourth Lateran Council.** After this, preparations were made for the **Fifth Crusade,** but Innocent would not live to see it embark. He died of a sudden fever in Perugia on 16 July 1216, on the fourth anniversary of las Navas de Tolosa.[213]

## Innocent IV, Pope (c. 1180–1254)

Sinobaldo di Fiesci was elected **Pope** in 1243 and reigned as Innocent IV. His tenure was dominated by the ongoing feud with **Frederick II.** The Pope pursued Frederick with great enmity. Innocent presided over the First Council of **Lyons** in 1245, where he approved the **Seventh Crusade** in response to the crisis in the **Holy Land. Jerusalem** had been lost the year before to the **Khoresmians.** Innocent IV also used the Council to declare the Emperor **Frederick II** deposed, and to call Crusades against him. The Pope created a conflict of interests, refusing to allow **Louis IX** to make peace with the Emperor, even though this would have it made safer for Louis to leave **France** for Egypt. The feud between the Papacy and the **Hohenstaufen** continued after Frederick's death in 1250. Innocent continued to scheme to overthrow Frederick's successor Conrad. Meanwhile in 1252 Innocent issued the **Papal Bull** titled *Ad Extripanda,* which permitted the **Inquisition** to use **torture** on suspected **heretics.** In 1254, Innocent permitted the **Teutonic Knights** to recruit for **Baltic Crusades** without specific papal authorisation each time, facilitating an ongoing campaign in the region.

## Inquisition

The Inquisition was an official Papal institution, also known as the Holy Office, or the Inquisition into Heretical Depravity. It was formed as a weapon in the **Catholic** Church's war against **heresy**. At stake were people's souls, and in order to save souls, members of the thirteenth-century **Catholic** clergy felt they had the right to rob individuals of their privacy, liberty and property, to terrorise and **torture** them, and in the end to condemn them to death. In earlier times the task of investigating heresy was allotted to local Bishops. **Excommunication** was the traditional sentence for those found to be heretics. This, however, by the twelfth century, was losing its force as a spiritual sanction. Excommunication meant banishment from the Church and community, but when heretics formed their own community and support networks, excommunicating them was bound to be futile. Harsher methods were deemed necessary.

After the **Albigensian Crusade**, in 1231, Pope **Gregory IX** recognised a permanent Inquisition, staffed mostly by friars of the **Dominican Order**, but (after 1233) also by **Franciscans**. The Inquisition was created to systematically suppress the **Cathar** movement in the **Languedoc** and elsewhere. It also targeted groups like the **Waldensians** and **Beguines**. Toulouse and **Carcassonne** became its centres. It created a climate of fear and denunciation there, condemning heretics to **burning**, and even exhuming and burning the bodies of people posthumously condemned, and dispossessing their heirs. Inquisitors routinely toured their territory, with contingents of guards. They called for heretics to come forward, repent, and receive penance. They also called on the population to inform on any heretics they knew of, while securing the cooperation of parish priests in rounding up the inhabitants to make declarations of loyalty to the Church. Defendants at the Inquisition's tribunals had little legal resort. All they could do was list their enemies in the hope the names matched their accusers. They were subjected to relentless interrogation backed up by the fear if not the reality of **torture**, and urged to confess and to denounce others. The Inquisition's questioning techniques were designed to counter the most cunning of suspects, but likely to draw incriminating answers from simple **Catholics** too. Confinement, fear, disorientation and detachment from the outside had the effect of torture.[214] The Inquisition officially received the right to apply physical torture in 1252, in the **papal bull** *Ad Extripanda*, issued by Pope **Innocent IV**. The Inquisition might impose any sentence from **penance** and the wearing of a yellow cross, to life imprisonment (on the bread of sorrow and the water of tribulation) or even to death by burning. Sentences were not much milder for those who merely sheltered heretics.

The institution became established throughout **France** and the continent. (Torquemada's famous Spanish Inquisition was a later manifestation however.) Notorious inquisitors included **Konrad von Marburg** in **Germany** and **Bernard Gui** in Toulouse. They also include one Inquisitor Ferrer, who presided over the burning of the 200 Cathars after the fall of **Montsegur**. From May 1245–August 1246, inquisitors Bernart de Caux and Jean de Saint-Pierre subjected more than 5,000 people to interrogation in Toulouse. **Robert le Bougre**, meanwhile, oversaw the Inquisition's establishment in northern **France**. The Papal Inquisition never operated in **England** (except during the period when two representatives, **Sicard de Vaour** and **Dieudonné of Lagny** arrived from France to investigate the Templars). However, having become close to the King of France, the Inquisition under the Dominican 'Grand Inquisitor' **Guillaume de Paris** was **Philip the Fair**'s confessor and cooperated closely with the King's *baillis* and *sénéchaux*. Inquisitor monks were involved alongside the royal agents in the interrogation and torture of the Templar prisoners.

The Inquisition continued to exist, flourishing in Spain in particular during the fifteenth and sixteenth century, where it particularly targeted **Jews** who had been forced to convert to Christianity, and who were suspected of secretly adhering to their original faith, and later it persecuted Protestants.[215] It also extended its scope to involve action against alleged practitioners of sorcery and **witchcraft**. It lost much of its power over life and death in the late eighteenth century, but continues to exist to this day under the name of the Congregation for the Doctrine of the Faith. It is still dominated by members of the Dominican Order, and is still charged with upholding Catholic doctrine and morality.

## Interdict

An interdict was a spiritual sanction imposed on regions by the Pope or a bishop or papal Legate. In interdicted regions church services could not be performed, nor burials, nor baptisms, and effectively the imagined doors of heaven were shut against the people. If the pope imposed **excommunication** on a ruler, he might also put his land under interdict, as a measure to turn the people against the lord who had incurred ecclesiastical wrath. The Templars had the privilege of performing one church service a year in a region under interdict while collecting funds for the **Crusades**.

## Ireland

By the fourteenth century the Templars had obtained a number of profitable estates in Ireland. The earliest Templar recorded in Ireland was one Matthew the Templar who witnessed a charter in 1171. However the first grants of land were given after 1187 by **Henry II** of England. These included houses at St. Congal, Clontarf (Dublin), Croke (Waterford), and Kilbarry. The king also gave mills and a church in Wexford. (Most of their estates lay along the east coast, and were donated by Anglo-Norman conquerors.) The Templars themselves in Ireland were usually Anglo-Norman or French, using local labour on their farmland. On these estates they tended to convert grazing lands into more profitable wheat fields. They also bred **horses** in Clonaul, probably for military purposes.

The **Hospitallers** were also prominent in Ireland, as servants of the English crown, and some brothers of the Order assumed leading roles in the colonial government. As in England the Military Orders sometimes served as diplomats and mediators. In 1234 the Templars mediated between royal officials and the rebel baron Richard Marshal, but were unable to prevent the outbreak of violence.[216] The **Master** of the Temple in Ireland was subordinate to the Master and **Chapter** in England. A Templar Master of Ireland, **Walter Bacheler**, was taken to the **New Temple, London** on charges of appropriating the Order's property and died in custody. However Templar **Preceptories** in Ireland were just as prosperous as those in England. The chapel of the Preceptory in Kilcogan was found to contain silver dishes and cups and priestly vestments of silk. Other Preceptories were found to contain arms and **armour**, and the manor at Ballymean was strongly fortified. The Templars were arrested in 1307–8, and tried in Dublin. Of the fourteen arrests, three appeared to be from Ireland, nine from Britain, and two were of unknown origin. An inventory of their properties was held, meanwhile, and their movable goods were brought by Royal agents to Dublin.

## *Isaac II Angelus* (1156–1204)

Isaac II Angelus came to power as **Byzantine Emperor** after a revolt overthrew **Andronicus Comnenus** in 1185. Isaac strengthened his position by marrying his sister to **Conrad of Montferrat**, who became a defender of Isaac's regime. It proved a sound strategy when the Byzantine general Branas, who had successfully driven off the Norman/Sicilian invaders in the Balkans, turned against the Emperor instead of suppressing a Bulgarian revolt. Conrad defeated Branas, later departing for the Holy Land on the eve of the **Third Crusade**.

The Emperor Isaac earned the contempt of Western **Christendom** when he made an alliance with **Saladin**, and impeded the progress of **Frederick I Barbarossa** through Byzantine territory at the commencement of the Crusade. Meanwhile in 1195 Isaac's brother Alexius seized power as Alexius III, and had Isaac blinded and imprisoned. Isaac was briefly reinstated eight years later after the intervention of the **Fourth Crusade** and his son Alexius IV. Discontent rose, with the Crusaders demanding Isaac and (his now co-ruler) Alexius IV make good on the promise to deliver treasure and church reunification. The palace coup by Murtzuphlus (who claimed the throne as Alexius V) saw Isaac again deposed. Isaac perished in prison while his son was strangled.

## Isaac Comnenus of Cyprus (1155–96)

Isaac Ducas Comnenus, a renegade **Byzantine** prince, was the despot of **Cyprus** and an ally of **Saladin**. When some Crusaders were shipwrecked on the island Isaac had them taken prisoner. When **Richard the Lionheart** arrived, with the other ships, he ordered the prisoners' release. Isaac refused. Richard went to war, took Isaac's castle and deposed him with the help of a newly arrived **Guy de Lusignan**. Isaac surrendered on the condition he not be put in iron chains, which was his personal phobia. Cyprus became Richard's possession, later sold to the Templars. Isaac became a prisoner in silver chains. He was handed to the **Hospitallers** who kept him captive for several years before his release.

## Isabella of Jerusalem (1172–1205)

Described as exceedingly fair and lovely, Isabella of **Jerusalem** became the ultimate pawn in the power politics of the Crusader barons after the fall of Jerusalem and the death of **Sibylla**. Isabella was the daughter of **Amalric I** and Maria Comnena, the younger half-sister of **Baldwin VI** and **Sibylla**, and the stepdaughter of **Balian of Ibelin**. At **Tyre**, those who wished to depose **Guy de Lusignan** recognised Isabella as the rightful Queen. They forced her to divorce her husband **Humphrey IV of Toron** and to marry **Conrad of Montferrat**. Humphrey was a stepson of **Reynald de Chatillon**, whom she had married in castle **Kerak**, then besieged by **Saladin** (who had courteously directed his artillery to avoid the tower containing the honeymoon suite). Humphrey was a good enough husband to Isabella, but was no soldier and any way loyal to Guy de Lusignan, so the barons decided he had to be sidelined. Conrad married Isabella in November 1191, and claimed the kingship. The fact that the kingdom was all but lost by then didn't stop the factionalism however. The following year Conrad was murdered in **Acre** by **Assassins**. Two days later Isabella, pregnant with Conrad's daughter Maria, was betrothed to Count **Henry II of Champagne**. Henry in turn died after falling from a window in 1196, whereupon Isabella married her last husband Amalric de Lusignan, the King of **Cyprus**.

## Isabella (the 'she-wolf of France') (c. 1296–1358)

Isabella of **France** was the **Capetian** wife of **Edward II** of **England** and the daughter of **Philip the Fair** of France. Her son **Edward III** would claim the throne of France, although the French did not recognise female succession. This was one of the causes of the Hundred Years War. Promised since infancy, Isabella married Edward II in 1308. Philip became Edward's father in law, a factor that may have worsened things for the Templars in England. It was not a happy marriage for Edward neglected Isabella in favour of his male favourites, first Piers Gaveston and then the De Spencers, who undermined the Queen's position. Isabella found solace in Sir Roger Mortimer, a rebellious Welsh baron that she first encountered in the **Tower of London**. She arranged his escape from a death sentence. In September 1125 she joined Mortimer in **Paris** and year later they invaded England, landing at Harwich, deposing Edward II by 1127 (he was murdered later at Berkeley Castle). Later Edward III had Mortimer executed at Tyburn, and obliged his mother to live a virtual prisoner in Castle Rising, Norfolk, almost until her death.

## Isis

Isis was the Ancient Egyptian goddess of magic, featuring in mythology as the original Queen, the sister/wife of Osiris, whom she restored to life after his murder by Set, in order to conceive the royal sky god Horus. Isis was depicted as a woman, sometimes with wings, and sometimes carrying a solar disk, or her throne hieroglyph atop her head. She was a popular goddess whose worship spread beyond **Egypt** to the Middle East and also through the Roman Empire. Her image, enthroned, suckling the infant god-king Horus prefigured the Christian icon of the Madonna and Child (and **Mary, the Blessed Virgin** inherited one of Isis's titles, that of 'Queen of Heaven'). Isis was also a figure of interest within **Freemasonry**. At least since the publication of *The **Holy Blood and the Holy Grail***, there have been attempts to link the Templars to **goddess veneration** and to Isis. There is no concrete evidence for this, but the mention of 'Yse' in the story of the **Skull of Sidon** possibly indicates that some of the myths of Isis survived in folklore in the East.

## Islam

Islam is the religion of the Muslims. It was founded by the **Arab** Prophet Mohammed (AD 571–632). 'Muslim' means one who submits (i.e. to God). The Holy book of Islam is the Koran, which Muslims believe was transmitted to Mohammed from God via the angel Gabriel. The religion is based on five 'pillars':

> *Shahadah* (acceptance of there being no god but Allah and Mohammed is his prophet
> *Salat* (praying five times a day)
> *Zakat* (giving **charity** to the poor)
> *Sawm* (fasting during the daylight hours during the month of Ramadan)
> *Hajj* (making a pilgrimage to the holy city of Mecca)

*Jihad* (striving) was another principal of Islam, which could be interpreted as **Holy War** to defend and extend the Faith. In AD 622, Mohammed and his followers (the *Muhajirun*) were expelled from Mecca, following the death of Abu Talib,

Mohammed's uncle and protector. The first mosque was Mohammed's house in Medina, where he became chief, gaining many Arab recruits to his new faith (the *Ansar*). In 625 these Muslims clashed violently with Median's **Jews**, killing many. The Muslims of Medina also fought against Mecca. Mohammed himself took up arms and Islam was well on the way to becoming a theocratic empire while he lived. In 630 Mecca submitted and Mohammed had the Ka'ba shrine purged of idols. The early expansion of Islam was achieved by active *Jihad*, but subsequently the concept became less prominent. *Jihad* was resurrected as a reaction to the **Crusades**. Some of the Muslim warriors who fought the Crusaders believed that if they died in battle they would be **martyrs** and receive heavenly rewards. Their conception of paradise had the added sensuous attraction of houri brides. Houris, alluded to in the Koran, were conceived of as beautiful, black-eyed virgins, untouched by man or *jinn* (spirit) who would be wedded in paradise to worthy Muslim men.

The Main schism in the Islamic world occurred after Mohammed's death, and focussed on which branch of the Prophet's family inherited Mohammed's spiritual authority. There was a bloody civil war between the Shiat' Ali (party of Ali, also known as Shi'ites) and the initially dominant Sunni faction (from *Sunnah* – path). The main doctrinal difference is that the Sunnis observe the *hadiths* (teachings and sayings of Mohammed and the first three Caliphs) as law, while the Shi'ites have their own legal tradition and a doctrine of an infallible Imam. Sunni Islam became the prevailing orthodoxy under the successive **Umayyad** and **Abbasid** Caliphs of **Damascus** and **Baghdad**. A branch of the Shi'ites meanwhile established the **Fatimid** Caliphate in **Egypt**. There were other schisms within Shi'ite (or Shi'a) Islam, concerning the identity of the Imam. One such schism produced the Nizari Ismailis, which produced the **Assassin** sect.

The Crusades were in part a belated response to Islamic imperialism (which had spread Islam across North Africa and into **Iberia** to the west and as far as India to the east). Muslims, however, had a capacity for infighting probably exceeding even that of the Christians. These internal divisions somewhat neutralised the supposed Islamic menace. (It became quite common for the Crusaders to ally with one Muslim power against another, and even to involve Muslim forces in their own internal conflicts.) The early Crusaders were, meanwhile, generally ignorant of the basic tenets of Islam and accused the Muslims of **idolatry** (where in fact Islam forbids religious imagery). Doubtless, close contact over the years enabled them to gain a better understanding. There is evidence that some of the Frankish Barons and leading Templars learned Arabic, and many Muslims lived within or passed through the Crusader States (notably **Usama Ibn Munqidh**). It is likely that after things settled down after the **First Crusade**, many Muslim refugees returned to the land.

It has been suggested that some of the **accusations** against the Templars were intended to show Islamic influence, what with the alleged denial of the divinity of **Christ** and the spitting and urinating on the cross (indeed it was not unknown for Muslim troops to taunt Christian enemies by abusing the cross in this way).[217] It has even been thought that the alleged Templar idol was linked to Islam, and that **Baphomet** was a version of the name Mohammed. This seems inherently unlikely; if anyone would have known that the Muslims abhorred idols, it was the Templars. The Templars understood Islam but for the most part they refused to embrace it, even to save their lives – for example after **Hattin**. Meanwhile the **Benedictine** Abbot of **Cluny**, Peter the Venerable (1092–1156) had commissioned a translation of the Koran into Latin in 1143, so any educated individual in the Europe of 1307 would have understood the tenets of the Muslim religion.

## *Intinerarium Peregrinorum et Gesta Regis Ricardi*
This is a chronicle of the **Third Crusade**, beginning with the defeat of the **Latin Kingdom of Jerusalem** by **Saladin**. The chronicle then describes the course of the Crusade, particularly praising the courage of **Richard the Lionheart**, and is quite favourable to the Knights Templar. It mentions the gallant death of **Jacquelin de Mailly** at **Cresson**, and presents the Templars executed after **Hattin** as being grimly eager for death and **martyrdom**. Its authorship is unclear but it seems to have been written not long after the events described. It seems the chronicle was translated from French by Richard de Templo, **Augustinian** prior of **Holy Trinity, London** from 1220, who may have been a former Templar. There has been speculation that the original version of the chronicle was also produced by a Templar or someone close to the Order.

## *Ivanhoe*
*Ivanhoe* is a historical novel, written by Sir **Walter Scott** in 1819. Its hero is a disinherited Saxon knight and **Crusade** veteran called Wilfred of Ivanhoe. One of the main villains is the Templar Brian de Bois Guilbert. Scott generally portrays Templars (and the other Norman characters) as haughty, cruel and corrupt. Robin Hood also makes an appearance. At one point the Templars conduct a sorcery trial for one of the heroines, the Jewess Rebecca, where a fictional **Grand Master**, accuses her of bewitching Brian de Bois Guilbert, and causing him to break his vow of chastity. Brian had abducted her and taken her to a Norman lord's castle, and the attempts of the heroes to rescue her are the main sources of action. At the end, after Ivanhoe has defeated Brian and rescued Rebecca, **Richard the Lionheart** arrives and sends the Templars on their way. Much of the story is historically inaccurate, as Richard was actually a great ally of the Templars, and they were not given to conducting **witchcraft** trials (although they did have the authority to try and execute

other accused criminals on their lands). The Templar in *Ivanhoe* also takes part in a joust, which would also have been against their rules. In the classic 1952 film *Ivanhoe*, Sir Brian is not a Templar but a secular knight. Elizabeth Taylor's Rebecca is tried before Prince John instead of the Grand Master, and Richard arrives at the end escorted by a cavalcade of Templars. Evidently a decision was made at some stage to diverge from the literary source and treat the Knights Templar favourably. (It was probably a conspiracy.)

# J

## *Jacobins*

The monasteries of the **Dominican Order** in Toulouse and in **Paris** were both called the Jacobins. Hence the medieval Dominican friars who persecuted the Templars were sometimes called Jacobins. The Paris Jacobins building, in the late eighteenth century, became a meeting place for revolutionary society, which would also adopt the name Jacobins. However they had nothing in common with the Dominicans except that they took over the building – and that they were remarkably single-minded in pursuit of their aims. **Charles Louis Cadet-Gassicourt** identified the revolutionary Jacobins with a secret republican elite within **Freemasonry**, preserving the secrets and the vengeful, anti-monarchist agenda of the Templars.[218]

## *Jacobites (Supporters of the House of Stuart)*

Jacobites were the supporters of the exiled royal house of Stuart and its claim to the British throne. The name derives from Iacobius, the Latin form of James (James VII of Scotland and II of England) who was deposed in 1688 for his **Catholic** beliefs and perceived absolutism. The Protestant parliamentarians, known as the Whigs, who organised the coup (which they called the Glorious Revolution) replaced James with his Protestant daughter Mary and her Dutch husband William of Orange. William defeated the original Jacobites in Ireland at the battle of the Boyne. Meanwhile Jacobite highlanders won a victory in Scotland at Killiecrankie over forces loyal to William, but then Jacobite leader John Graham of Clavenham (later romanticised as 'Bonnie Dundee') was killed and the battle has little lasting effect. (Legend has it that Bonnie Dundee was a latter-day Templar.)

William and Mary produced no heirs, neither did Mary's sister Queen Anne, and thus the Hanoverian George I was brought in. Many Jacobites, meanwhile, especially Scots, found themselves exiles in Europe. In Georgian times, their hope was invested in Charles Edward Stuart, 'Bonnie Prince Charlie', the son of James VIII and III (as his supporters hailed him), or 'the Old Pretender' (as his enemies dismissed him). James was the son of James VII/II and his second wife the Catholic Mary of Modena. Prince Charles

Edward landed in Glenfinnan, Scotland, rousing the clans in a rebellion. The Jacobites gained spectacular success before being crushed at the Battle of Culloden in 1746. Charles was forced to flee.

Both **Templarism** and **Freemasonry** seem to have been popular among exiled Jacobites in France. The 'Chevalier' **Andrew Michael Ramsey** who drew a connection between Freemasonry and the Crusaders had been a tutor to the prince, and **Karl, Baron von Hund** claimed to have been initiated as a Templar Mason by Jacobites.

## Jacobites (Syrian Orthodox Christians)

The **Crusades** in the **Holy Land** encountered Syrian Christians known as Jacobites (after Jacobus Baradaeus, a Monophysite Bishop (d. 578). The Syrian Church was centred in **Antioch**, and preserved Syriac Aramaic as its liturgical language. The **Catholic** Bishop of **Acre, Jacques de Vitry** described the medieval Jacobites as practising circumcision and having no rite of **confession**. He attempted to steer them from these and other practices into a more conformist mode of worship. He also suspected them of being Monophysites, believing in the single nature of **Christ** contrary to the Council of Chalcedon in AD 451. The Jacobites were allowed freedom of worship under Frankish rule.

## Jacob's Ford

Jacob's Ford (Vadum Iacob) was a short-lived Templar/**Crusader** Castle. Its construction was begun in October 1178 by **Baldwin IV** to guard the only place where the River Jordan (which formed the border between the Christian territory and Muslim Syria) could be forded, between the Sea of Galilee and Lake Huleh. It was supposed to be the place where Jacob had wrestled with an angel. (Genesis 32:17–32). The Templars had convinced the King that a castle there would be a necessary defence for the Latin Kingdom. **Saladin** considered its construction to be provocative and to threaten the security of Damascus. He offered Baldwin a large sum in gold coins to cease construction, but the King declined. Saladin was preoccupied at the time and could not bring his forces into the region until June the following year, which he did, ravaging the area as far as **Sidon**.[219] The skirmishers were driven back but Saladin's main army then defeated a Christian force under **Raymond III of Tripoli** and **Odo de St Amand**, the **Grand Master** of the Templars. The Sultan forced the former to withdraw, and captured the latter. By then, the newly built castle was fully enclosed – an oblong fortress on a high rise of ground above the river. However, only the inner of the two planned walls had been completed. Saladin first forced Baldwin to withdraw to Tiberias, after several heated skirmishes.

On 24 August 1179, having been reinforced with fresh **Muslim** troops, Saladin attacked. He subjected the Templar-led defenders of Jacob's Ford to a storm of arrows from the east and west. He then brought his engineers to tunnel under the walls in order to bring a section crashing down. Saladin sent his forces through the breech, and they eventually overwhelmed the defenders, killing 800 and taking the remaining 700 prisoner. Captured crossbowmen and apostates from **Islam** were immediately executed.[220] Baldwin and his reinforcements, including **Henry I, Count of Champagne**, delayed at Tiberias for a day, and were later to find that the castle was fallen, and there was nothing to do but retire. Afterwards, the Muslims demolished the castle and poisoned its well by filling it with the dead bodies of the Christians. (This may have backfired and caused the plague that subsequently swept through Saladin's ranks.)

## *Jacquelyn de Mailly* (died 1187)

Jacquelyn de Mailly was the **Marshal** of the Knights Templar, and a knight of Touraine. In May 1187 he rode with **Gerard de Ridefort**'s small force and intercepted the great **Muslim** army returning from a reconnaissance through Galilee at the Springs of **Cresson**. The force included a contingent of Templars, the Master of the Hospitallers **Roger de Moulins**, and some secular knights. A chronicle the *Intinerarium Peregrinorum et Gesta Regis Ricardi* records Jacquelyn's particularly gallant death as a **martyrdom**. When his companions had been killed or captured, he fought on alone against many battalions. His courage won his enemies admiration and they urged his surrender, but he was not afraid to die for Christ. At last he was overwhelmed, 'crushed rather than conquered by spear, stones and lances'. De Mailly finally fell above a pile of Muslims that he had slain. Because of his white armour, horse and weapons, the Saracens 'who knew that **St George** had this appearance in battle, boasted that they had killed the Knight of Shining Armour, the protector of the Christians.'[221]

## *Jacques de Molay* (c. 1245–1314)

Jacques de Molay (or Molai) was the twenty-third and last **Grand Master** of the Knights Templar, and is one of the best known on account of the circumstances of his death in **Paris**. De Molay was a relation of the Lords of Longwy in Franche-Comté. He was initiated into the Order in around 1266, in the Preceptory of Beune near Autun, according to his **Chinon** confession, and was received by Humbert de Pairaud (the father of **Hugues de Pairaud**). In 1291 he possibly fought at the siege of **Acre**, and two years later on **Cyprus** was elected Grand Master. De Molay was one of the foremost advocates of action to recover the **Holy Land**. In 1294 he visited **Rome**, Paris and **London**, raising support and gathering a new Templar force. Back in the Levant he sought alliances with the **Mongols** and **Armenians**, and strengthened the garrison on the island of **Arwad**. De Molay even purchased six war galleys from **Venice** with a view to invading **Tortosa**, and re-establishing a Christian foothold in Syria. The operation ended in costly failure, though, when Arwad itself was lost to a **Mameluk** invasion fleet of sixteen galleys.

In 1306 de Molay was summoned from Cyprus by Pope **Clement V**. He and **Fulk de Villaret**, his opposite number in the **Hospitallers**, were invited to discuss plans for a new **Crusade**, and also a proposal to amalgamate the Orders of the Temple and the Hospital. De Molay prepared a paper on the subject, conceding that there would be some advantages to the proposed **merger**, but that on the whole it was a bad idea because the rivalry between the two orders was healthy and spurred them on to greater efforts in the Christian cause. Fulk kept quiet on the matter, but apparently felt the same. Meanwhile on the matter of a new Crusade both Grand Masters expressed the view that only a large scale *Passagium generale* would succeed in re-establishing the Christian kingdom in the **Holy Land**.

De Molay went next to the **Paris Temple**. On 13 October 1307 he and his brethren were arrested there. This was in accordance with orders secretly issued a month beforehand by King **Philip the Fair**, accusing the Templars of blasphemous crimes and **heresy**. De Molay had attended the funeral of the King's sister-in-law as a pallbearer only the day before the **arrests** however, and seems to have been taken by surprise when the raid came. De Molay was interrogated by Royal agents and the **Inquisition**, probably being held in the Templars' own dungeons at the Paris Temple. He was probably subjected to **torture**. On 24 October he confessed to some of the **accusations** – namely spitting on the Cross and **denial of Christ**. He would not, however, confess to homosexual practices. He was obliged to repeat his confession publicly the following day to the masters of the University of Paris, and also to urge his brethren likewise to confess. The Grand Master's early capitulation, forced as it may have been, did much to undermine the **defence of the Order** and was a propaganda coup for the **Capetian** authorities. It prejudiced the wider world against the Templars and lent credence to the astonishing accusations. It also made it impossible for the Pope to continue in a critical stance regarding the King's actions.

With the other leading Templars that had been captured, (**Raymbaud de Caron**, Hugues de Pairaud, **Geoffroi de Charney** and **Geoffroi de Gonneville**), Jacques De Molay was moved to the castle of **Chinon**. There these Templars again gave a partial confession to three Cardinals sent by the Pope, who afterwards bestowed absolution on them. All the Templar dignitaries except de Caron were subsequently brought back to Paris to testify at the tribunal called the Papal Commission.

Jacques de Molay retracted his confession at the end of the year. Over the following years, he wavered, evidently worn down by his captivity. He offered little leadership to the Templars wishing to defend the Order, but at times seemed willing to assert the Order's honourable nature. He apparently remained imprisoned throughout 1310 when the Archbishop of Sens, **Philip de Marigny** incapacitated the Templars' defence at the Papal Commission by taking and **burning** fifty-four Templars, and through 1312 when the **Council of Vienne** abolished the Order of the Temple and consigned it to oblivion. He and the three other dignitaries of the late Order were eventually brought out before an assembly of prelates (including Cardinal Arnold Novelli and Archbishop de Marigny), lawyers, university theologians and the public on 18 March 1314, to hear their sentence of perpetual imprisonment. Hugues de Pairaud and Geoffroi de Gonneville persisted in their confessions and accepted their fate. Jacques De Molay, though, stunned his persecutors by making a lucid and passionate last-minute defence of the Order. He was supported by Geoffroi de Charney.

The rebellious Templars were passed to the prévôt of Paris and flung back into jail. When the King learned what had happened, he went into a rage, and ordered the two Templars to be condemned as relapsed **heretics**. Before night fell they were taken to the Ille des Javiaux in the Seine, and burned to death. It was recorded that their courage and constancy impressed and surprised the onlookers. The next day, recorded the Chronicler Giovanni Villani, came friars and other religious persons, who gathered up the ashes of the Templar **martyrs** and carried them away to holy places.

## *Jacques de Vitry* (died 1240)

Jacques de Vitry was Bishop of **Acre** from 1216 to 1228. A Frenchman, educated in **Paris**, he was also a man of letters. He was zealous and well meaning, but prejudiced against the Syrian Christians and suspicious of their indigenous practices. He was shocked by the moral decrepitude of Acre's citizens. He also criticised the Italian merchants for being 'indifferent to the word of God'.[222] He however reported that his preaching often had the desired effect. He visited **Tyre**, **Sidon**, and **Tripoli**, ministering to the faithful, preaching to the **Saracens** (even converting a couple), and passing at some risk through the land of the **Assassins**. He visited the Templars at **Castel Blank**, after which the Templars escorted him on his way to Tortosa.

Jacques de Vitry encouraged the Templars to take heart from the prospect of **martyrdom**. He accompanied the **Fifth Crusade** to **Damietta**. He later became Cardinal Bishop of Tusculum.

## *Jaffa*

Jaffa (or Joppa) is an ancient port city in the **Holy Land**, famous for its oranges. Today it is a district of Tel Aviv in Israel. It is mentioned in the Bible as the port through which the Cedars of Lebanon were brought for the furnishing of **Solomon's Temple**, and where St Peter brought back to life the widow Tabitha.

Under Islamic rule from 636, Jaffa served as a port for **Ramlah**. The Crusaders captured it in 1099, and it became the seat of a Latin Count, a vassal of the King of **Jerusalem**. For a time it was a seat of the d'**Ibelin** family. Jaffa was one of the main ports used by western pilgrims passing to Jerusalem, and the Templars had a house there. Jaffa fell to **Saladin** in 1187 and was largely destroyed, but was recovered during the **Third Crusade**, and was the scene of a daring relief operation by **Richard the Lionheart** in 1192. It was rebuilt, only to be lost with the rise of the **Mameluks**. The Mameluks destroyed the port as a precaution against the Crusaders returning.

## James II of Aragon (1267–1327)

James (Jaime) II succeeded to **Aragon** in 1281. He had previously ruled Sicily, but relinquished it after signing a peace treaty with Charles II of Naples and **Boniface VIII**. Boniface saw James as a potential Crusade leader, and offered 100,000 silver marks as a dowry for James's Angevin bride (Blanche of Anjou), as compensation for surrendering his claim to Sicily, and as an inducement to lead the Crusade (which would possibly have been aimed at **Constantinople**). The Templar and **Hospitaller** possessions in Aragon and Valencia were to be used as security for the payment. In January 1296 James was made 'standard-bearer, captain, and admiral general of the Church' with a view to the new Crusade, but little came of it. James was the first monarch to whom **Esquin de Floyran** took his allegations against the Templars. James was so unconvinced (as it seems from a later letter to him from Esquin) that he offered to reward the would-be whistleblower with lands and money should the **accusations** prove to have any foundation. On 16 October **Philip the Fair** of **France** wrote to James II, telling him of the arrests, and inviting him to take similar action. Like **Edward II** of England, James II of Aragon originally seemed of a mind to defend the Templars, but then turned against them, and began to move against the Order even before Pope **Clement V**'s bull arrived (*Pastoralis praeeminentiae*). James confiscated the Templars' properties in Aragon and took their castles after some resistance. The **trials** in Aragon were inconclusive. Following the **Council of Vienne**, James resisted the Papal demand to transfer the Templar lands to the **Hospitallers**, and secured permission instead to bestow them on the order of **Calatrava**. James understood that the Hospitallers could become too powerful in Aragon if they obtained the Templars' fortresses, but a smaller order like Calatrava could more easily be kept under royal control.

## Jean de Gisors (1133–1220)

Jean de Gisors was a Norman lord who also had estates in **England**. He founded the city of Portsmouth, the Cathedral of which began as an **Augustinian** Chapel, which Jean founded in honour of the recently **mar-**

**tyred** Archbishop **Thomas à Becket**. Jean's castle in **Gisors**, in the Norman Vixen, was taken over by **Henry II of England**, but Jean had other land in the area, part of which was a traditional meeting place of the English and French Kings. He owned the land where the '**Cutting of the Elm**' event occurred. **Conspiracy theory** also makes him an early **Grand Master** of the **Priory of Sion**. He has links to the Templars in that they had been guardians of the castle of Gisors for a short while before 1164.

## Jean de Joinville (c. 1224–1317)

Jean, Lord de Joinville was the Seneschal of Champagne. He was a key participant in the **Seventh Crusade**, during which he became a friend and trusted advisor to King **Louis IX**. In later life he gave testimony to help ensure Louis's recognition as a **saint**. He also began writing his *Life of Saint Louis* (in which he portrayed the King as valiant and virtuous but human) at the behest of Queen **Jeanne de Navarre**. De Joinville was the heir to a family tradition of crusading, which possibly included at least one Templar.[223] He generally wrote admiringly of the Templars' courage in battle, which he witnessed in **Egypt**. De Joinville and his knights were in the thick of the fighting at **Mansourah**. Subsequently the Crusade unravelled. The Muslims moved a fleet to cut the Crusaders' supply lines, and after suffering much attrition through disease, hunger and enemy action, the Crusaders decided to abandon camp and retreat to Damietta as best they could by land and water. King Louis was captured, having refused to abandon his army. Joinville was captured separately during an encounter with Muslim ships that had intercepted his on the Nile, and might have been butchered on the deck but for the fortunate intervention of the Saracen captain. The Sultan – and after the Sultan's murder the **Mameluks** – demanded a great ransom, as well as the surrender of **Damietta** in exchange for the King's life. Damietta was duly returned and the King, his brother and certain nobles including de Joinville were released (though many others remained in captivity, some of whom were killed). The money was still owed, meanwhile, and the King did not have adequate funds. Jean de Joinville suggested obtaining it from the Templars. The Order's commander, Stephen of Otricourt, refused to hand over money from the Templars' custody on the grounds that he could only release it with the permission of those who had deposited it. The Templars may have been concerned about protecting their credibility as bankers as well as being naturally loath to hand to the **Muslims** money that had been raised to fight them.

The situation reached an angry impasse until the new **Grand Master** of the Templars, **Reynald de Vichiers**, intimated that although the Templars could not possibly *give* Louis the money, if de Joinville took it by force on the King's behalf they couldn't really do anything about it. At any rate, Jean de Joinville boarded the Templars' ship on which the money was stored and confronted the Templar treasurer with an axe. Reynald de Vichiers, who was a friend of de Joinville's, advised the treasurer to surrender the money. Having sailed with the King to the relative the safety of **Acre**, Jean de Joinville urged Louis to stay in the **Holy Land** to strengthen the defences of the Christian settlements. De Joinville witnessed the disciplining of the Templars by Louis after they negotiated a land treaty with the Sultan of Damascus without the King's consent, after which Louis exiled brother **Hugues de Jouy**. He also fought alongside the Templars in several skirmishes with the Muslims, such as that at Banyas. De Joinville however did not participate in Louis's second Crusade, apparently having his doubts about the venture.[224]

## Jean de Montréal (thirteenth–fourteenth century)

Jean de Montréal was one of the French Templars who spoke in defence of the Order before the Papal Commission in early 1310. Jean presented a document in French, telling of the Order's honest foundation, and how it had continued to be orthodox and innocent of **heresy**. He claimed that Templar brothers had long been afforded positions of trust and honour by great Kings and lords. He also spoke of the Order's deeds in the **Holy Land** and **Spain.**

## Jean de Terric (late twelfth century)

The Templar Brother Terric (or Thierry) was a Templar **Grand Commander** of **Jerusalem**. He may have been the only Templar besides **Gerard de Ridefort,** the **Grand Master**, to escape the Battle of **Cresson**. He evidently took charge of the Order during Gerard de Ridefort's captivity, and the slaughter of the knights at the disastrous battle of **Hattin**. He seems to have been one those who escaped the 'dreadful field' along with **Raymond III of Tripoli**. Terric referred to himself as the 'so-called Grand Master of the impoverished house of the Temple … and that brotherhood all but annihilated'. He wrote letters to the Templar leaders of Europe, telling of the great calamities that had overwhelmed the **Holy Land** and appealing for immediate aid. He detailed the catastrophic defeat at Hattin and how afterwards, the Saracens, revelling in the blood of Christians, had marched on **Acre** and taken it by storm. Knights of the **Military Orders** brought Terric's letter to Pope **Urban III**, who subsequently died of sorrow at the news.

## Jean de Tours (late thirteenth century)

Jean de Tours was a late Treasurer of the **Paris Temple**. A few days after the mass burnings of the Templars by the Archbishop of Sens, **Philip de Marigny,** the body of Jean de Tours was exhumed from its grave and burnt with four other Templars, though the others had the greater misfortune of still being alive at the time.

## *Jean-Marc Larmenius* (early fourteenth century)

Jean-Marc Larmenius was a Palestinian-born Templar to whom **Jacques De Molay** supposedly passed the reins of the Knights Templar in early 1314. Larmenius is said to have gone on to lead the Temple, which continued undercover, until his death. In 1324 he created what became known as the **Larmenius Charter**, or the *Carta Transmissionis*. There is no evidence of Larmenius and his charter before the time of **Bernard Raymond Fabré-Palaprat**.

## *Jeanne de Navarre, Queen* (1271–1305)

Queen Jeanne de Navarre was the wife of **Philip the Fair** of France, and Queen of Navarre in her own right. She was also the Countess of **Champagne**, inheriting these lands from her father Henry I of Navarre upon his death in 1274. Her mother acted as regent, and brought her up at the French royal court. She was married to Philip in 1284, a year before his succession. This brought Champagne into the French royal domain. Jeanne would have seven children, of whom four surviving sons would reign in France (none producing heirs). Her daughter **Isabella, the 'she-wolf of France'** would be Queen Consort to **Edward II** of **England**. Jeanne died under mysterious circumstances. Philip accused Guichard, Bishop of Troyes of poisoning her or using black magic. At least one chronicler suspected Philip himself of such murderous deeds.

## *Jerusalem*

Jerusalem has long been religiously significant within **Judaism**, Christianity and **Islam**. The Jews regarded it as the capital of their Promised Land. The ancient Hebrews, under King **David**, conquered Jerusalem from the Jebusites in about 1000 BC The city would house the **Temple of Solomon**, which in 600 BC was destroyed by the Babylonians, who took the Jews into seven decades of servitude and exile. They returned, led by Zerubbabel. Jerubabbel's second Temple, enlarged by Herod, survived until AD 70 when the Romans destroyed it during the harsh suppression of the Jewish Revolt. (Jerusalem had been conquered by Alexander the Great and subsequently by the Greeks' successors the Seleucids, who dominated much of the Middle East. Jewish independence was regained under the **Maccabees**, but soon lost as **Rome** established its domination.) After the failed revolt, only the Western Wall, (the 'Wailing Wall') of the Temple compound remained, and it was a focus of melancholy Jewish devotion. After a second Jewish revolt all but a few Jews were banished from the city.

Jerusalem, under the auspices of the **Byzantine Empire**, became a sacred site for Christians, meanwhile, who regarded it touched by the divine presence of **Jesus Christ**; being the scene of his suffering, burial and resurrection. The **Holy Sepulchre** and **True Cross** would become a magnet for Christian **pil-**

grims and the basilica also became the seat of a Christian **Patriarch**. In 614 Jerusalem fell to the Persian Khuso II, but the city and the stolen True Cross were recovered by the Byzantine Emperor Heraclius (610–41).

**Islam**, from its conception, also regarded Jerusalem as *al Quds* (the Holy), if not the most holy city. In Islam, Mecca had become the most holy place. The Muslim **Arabs** under the Caliph **Omar** conquered Jerusalem in AD 638. Umar cleared the **Temple Mount**, where his successors built the **Dome of the Rock** and the **Al Aqsa Mosque**. Muslim rule was initially tolerant of other faiths for the most part, but in 1109 the **Fatimid** Caliph al Hakim destroyed the Holy Sepulchre and persecuted the Christians. Conditions for Christians again worsened when the **Seljuk Turks** took control in 1073.

The **First Crusade**, under **Godfroi de Bouillon** and **Raymond of Toulouse**, burst into Jerusalem in July 1099, after a difficult siege, and a massacre of the non-Christian inhabitants ensued. After this bloody 'liberation' Jerusalem became the capital of the nascent **Kingdom of Jerusalem**, and the nucleus of the Crusader states. **Godfroi de Bouillon** ruled for a year, and was then succeeded by **Baldwin I** and **Baldwin II** in turn, who struggled to ensure the realm's survival. Baldwin II granted **Hugues de Payens** and the original Templars custody of the **Al Aqsa mosque** on **Temple Mount** as a base from which to protect pilgrims and aid the defence of the kingdom. Jerusalem remained in Christian hands, until (despite a gallant resistance led by **Balian of Ibelin**) it fell to **Saladin** in the wake of **Hattin** in 1187. The Latin Christians either withdrew as part of Saladin's amnesty, or were taken into slavery, but there was no comparable massacre. **Frederick II** regained the city peacefully in 1229, but in 1244 the **Khoresmians** Turks, at the behest of the Egyptians, swept into the city and this time there was slaughter of Christians. By then the Crusades had lost their sense of direction. The remains of the Latin Kingdom were gradually worn away. The Muslims (the **Mameluks** and then the **Ottoman Turks**) remained in control of the Holy City until the twentieth century.

## Jerusalem Cross
The Jerusalem Cross is a symbol closely associated with the **Crusaders**. It is formed of five crosses, possibly referring to the five wounds of the crucified Christ. The large central cross has 'T' shaped ends, and four smaller 'crosslets' are positioned between these. The symbol appeared on the coat of arms of the **Latin** Kings of **Jerusalem**, and also became the badge of the **Order of the Holy Sepulchre**. It was also used by the de Lusignan kings of **Cyprus**.

## Jesus Christ (c. 0–30)
The word 'Christ' is based on the Greek equivalent of the Hebrew 'Messiah', meaning anointed one. It is the usual epithet of Jesus of Nazareth, whom

Christians recognised as the saviour and King of the **Jews** whose coming was foretold by the prophets. The Templars were dedicated to Christ, being called in full the Poor Knights of Christ and the Temple of Solomon. They regarded Christ as their King, as St **Bernard of Clairvaux** stated. Their successors in **Portugal** were simply called the **Knights of Christ**.

Medieval Christians saw Jesus as the divine Son of God, (as well as being one with God and a co-eternal aspect of the Holy Trinity). He was also regarded as a heavenly ruler, to whom Christians owed devotion and service as vassals to a Lord. **Crusaders** all fought in the name of Christ. They wore his cross and believed themselves to be about his business, liberating his earthly kingdom, and winning a place in his heavenly kingdom for themselves. The Templars, like other religious groups, also imposed **chastity, obedience, poverty** and sometimes corporal **mortification** upon themselves, believing that by doing so they emulated Christ (*Imitatio Christi*). In many monastic institutions, the chapter consisted of a master/abbot and twelve brothers, representing Christ and the twelve disciples.

The **Popes** claimed to be Christ's envoy on earth, and the heirs to the authority that he bestowed on St Peter. Ironically at the same time they also claimed to be the heirs to the Caesars, and the concept of **Christendom** and the Roman Empire had become confused. Christ had been executed by the pagan Romans as a seditionist in the first century. A little over 1,000 years later **Rome** (i.e. the papacy) sent armies to the same place in the name of Christ. The Templars who had died and killed in Christ's name were eventually accused by **Philip the Fair** of **denying Christ**.

## *Jihad*

Jihad in **Islam** is the concept of 'striving' against unbelief. It can have an internal or external application. In the latter case it is understood to mean waging **Holy War**. The concept was ever present, and turned Islam into a religion of conquest. It gained new life as reaction to the **Crusades**, especially after the Muslims were emboldened by the capture of **Edessa** by **Zenghi**. **Nur ed-Din** and **Saladin** summoned Muslims to fulfil the 'obligation' of military Jihad. Later the **Mameluks** took up the mantle of Jihad, seeing it as their duty to defend Islam from the Crusaders and the **Mongols**.

## *Johannes Michaelensis* (early twelfth century)

Johannes Michaelensis (or Jean Michel) was the scribe at the **Council of Troyes**. He recorded the presence there of the founding Templars, St **Bernard of Clairvaux**, Abbot **Stephen Harding**, the Archbishops of Sens and **Reims**, Count **Theobald of Champagne** and 'several others whom it would be tedious to record'. He also wrote down the **Rule** of the Templars, possibly under direction from St Bernard.

## Johannites

Johannites were **Gnostic** sects believing that **John the Baptist** was a more important prophet than **Jesus**. In the Middle East the **Mandaean** community continued in this ancient Gnostic tradition. The Neo-Templar **Bernard Raymond Fabré-Palaprat** was also a Johannite.

## John II Comnenus (1087–1143)

John II Comnenus was a **Byzantine** Emperor, the son of **Alexius I** and brother of Anna Comnena. John defeated the Pechenegs (a nomadic Turkic group) in Bulgaria and also led successful campaigns against the Turks in Anatolia and Armenian Cilicia. He hoped also to ally with the Franks and to expand Christian territory into Syria at the expense of the Muslims. However the Franks failed to cooperate, mistrusting the Emperor's ambition of restoring **Antioch** to **Byzantine** rule. John had been enraged that Antioch had chosen a new western prince (**Raymond of Poitiers**) without seeking his consent.[225] He was determined to assert Byzantine suzerainty, and after conquering Cilicia brought a great army and besieged the city. Raymond's forces, which seem to have included detachments of Templars and **Hospitallers**, resisted.[226] However Raymond was eventually persuaded to recognise John as his overlord, and agreed to hand Antioch back to direct imperial rule once Aleppo and Shaizar had fallen into Christian hands. The understanding was that Raymond would hold these new conquests as an imperial fief. The emperor commenced his Syrian campaign, but it was sabotaged by his supposed allies, Raymond of Poitiers, Prince of Antioch and Joscelin II de Courtenay. They famously demonstrated their indifference by fooling around and playing dice throughout the abortive siege of Shaizar. Evidently there was little love lost. John's Eastern ambitions remained unfulfilled when he was killed during a hunting expedition in Cilicia in April 1143.

## John de Eure (thirteenth–fourteenth century)

Sir John de Eure was the sheriff of **York**. He gave testimony against the Templars at the **trials** in northern **England**. (He was also acting as their jailor at the time.) He claimed that six years before, after a banquet the Templar Preceptor of Westdall (**Westerdale**), **William de la Fenne**, had leant to his wife, the Lady de Eure, a book to read. She found in it a loose sheet, on which were written heretical notions that **Christ** was not the son of a Virgin, nor the Son of God, and that he was a false prophet crucified for his sins. William de la Fenne was called in and asked about this. He remembered lending the book (evidence if nothing else that the Templar **rule** forbidding social contact with females was not strictly observed) but knew nothing of any page fastened in it.

## John de Stoke (born *c.* 1269)

John de Stoke was a Templar priest questioned by the **Inquisitors** visiting **England** in 1309. He was one of the three Templars in England who made any sort of confession relating to the more serious **accusations against the Order**. He had originally received an orthodox **initiation ceremony** when inducted into the Order eighteen years previously. However he said he had undergone another ritual a year after that at **Garway**, in the presence of **Jacques de Molay**. The Templars had allegedly shown John a crucifix and asked him whom it represented. He had said **Jesus Christ**, the saviour. De Molay had allegedly replied that this was false: that this was the son of a certain woman who was crucified for claiming to be the Son of God. He allegedly called on John to renounce Christ, threatening to imprison him if he did not comply. John was forced to do so at sword point. The inquisitors asked what de Molay had told John to believe in if not in Christ. John said that de Molay had told him instead to believe in a great omnipotent God, who created heaven and earth, but not in the Crucifixion. John was formally absolved by the Church in St Paul's Cathedral in July 1309.

## John (King of England) (1167–1216)

King John was a **Plantagenet** King of **England**, the youngest son of **Henry II** and **Eleanor of Aquitaine** (and the favourite of both). He was known as John Lackland, as his elder brothers beat him to the possession of all available patrimonies. In 1185 Prince John was made viceroy of **Ireland** but he achieved little success there and he withdrew after eight months. John came to power in England when his brother King **Richard the Lionheart** was absent leading the **Third Crusade**. John overthrew the unpopular regent, the bishop of Ely Guillaume de Longchamp, who was also Chancellor of the realm. (One dubious story has it that when John marched on London, the Bishop fled to **Dover** disguised as a woman. The attentions of an amorous sailor discovered him. John was so amused on hearing of this that he let Guillaume go free.)

The extent of John's complicity in the imprisonment of Richard in Austria is unclear. At any rate Richard forgave John on his return. John was made Duke of Normandy, and later acceded to the throne of England. Hostilities broke out with the French, and John pioneered the creation of a new Royal Navy. Subsequently, John was implicated in the murder of his nephew Arthur of Brittany, the son of John's late brother Geoffrey and a rival to the throne. Arthur was killed at Rouen in 1203, while in the custody of **Hubert de Burgh**, an English baron close to John. **Philip II Augustus** drew new justification from this to invade John's continental possessions of Brittany and Normandy, gradually demolishing the **Angevin** empire on the continent. John meanwhile had divorced his first wife and remarried the young Isabella of Angoulême, who would become the mother of **Henry III**, **Richard of Cornwall** and three daughters.

In 1205 John entered into a feud with Pope **Innocent III** when he opposed the Pope's candidate for Archbishop of Canterbury (Stephen Langton) and backed instead John Bishop of Norwich. Innocent **excommunicated** John and placed England under **interdict**. The Templars remained loyal to the king, however, and at Dover mediated between John and the Papal legates who eventually forced John not only to capitulate but to resign his Kingdom to the Pope and receive it back as a vassal state of the papacy. Soon afterwards John's allies on the continent were defeated at Bouvines. John retained some allies in Poitou partly by paying pensions, the money being channelled via the Templar **Preceptory** at **La Rochelle**. Discontent spread at home, meanwhile. The barons, encouraged by Langton, brought their grievances to John on 15 June 1215 at the famous meeting at Runnymede by the Thames, near Windsor, compelling him to sign the bill of rights known as **Magna Carta**. Several Templars were mentioned in the document.

John attempted to renege on the agreement, causing a renewed baronial revolt. The French capitalised on the situation. Philip II Augustus's son Louis invaded, backed by some of the rebel barons, and claiming the English throne. John's problems were compounded when he lost his treasure in the Wash. He took ill and died at Newark Castle, and was buried in Worcester Cathedral. The French were still at large but were subsequently driven off by **William Marshal**, who championed the cause of the young Henry III.

## John of Brienne (1148–1237)

John (Jean) Count of Brienne was a French noble who came to prominence in later life. He held the title King of **Jerusalem** and also became **Latin** Emperor of **Constantinople**. In 1208 the barons of the vestigial **Kingdom of Jerusalem** delivered a request to **Philip II Augustus**, asking that he send a French noble to marry the heiress Maria, the daughter of **Isabella of Jerusalem** and **Conrad of Montferrat**, and become King of Jerusalem. Philip sent John of Brienne, despite his being fourty-four years older than Maria. They married in 1210. John's coronation in Acre was arranged and attended by the **Grand Master** of the Templars, **Guillaume de Chartres**. Two years later Maria died shortly after giving birth to the union's only child, the Princess **Yolande**.

John, retaining his title, took a lead in the **Fifth Crusade**, fighting alongside the Templars. Unfortunately, however, ultimate control lay with the Papal Legate **Pelagius of Albano**, who steered the enterprise into a disaster. Subsequently John toured Europe. He met with Pope **Honorius III** and with the Emperor **Frederick II**, and promised the Emperor the hand of Yolande in exchange for a guarantee of support in the **Holy Land**. Then in **Spain** John took another young wife, Berengaria of Castile. Meanwhile Frederick II took

Yolande (who herself died after childbirth). Frederick subsequently sought to deprive John of his title King of Jerusalem, claiming it for himself, and later on behalf of the infant Conrad. John gained revenge by leading the **Guelf** armies against Frederick's lands in southern Italy while the Emperor was engaged in the **Holy Land** on the **Sixth Crusade**. In 1229 John, though aged, was invited to Constantinople to take the throne as Latin Emperor by the Frankish barons who had clung to power there since the **Fourth Crusade**. John held the throne for the remainder of his life, and succeeded in successfully holding off Greek forces from Nicæa who attempted to retake the city.

## John of Nevers (1371–1419)

John (Jean), Count of Nevers, later Duke of **Burgundy**, was one of the latter-day **Crusaders**. In 1396 he took a predominantly French army with a smaller English contingent to ally with Transylvanian forces under Sigismund, King of Hungary, in response to the westward expansion of the **Ottoman Empire** under Beyezid I. The Christian and **Muslim** forces met at the battle of Nicopolis in Bulgaria. John earned the nickname 'the fearless', but was eventually captured in the unsuccessful campaign and held for ransom. The Eastern European states were left to stand alone against the Turks after this.

## John of Plano Carpini (c. 1180–1252)

John of Plano Carpini (Giovanni da Pian del Carpine) was a **Franciscan** Friar. He became the first European envoy to reach the court of the **Mongol** Emperor. In 1245, Pope **Innocent IV** chose him for this epic journey, despite John's age and corpulence. John left **Lyons** and travelled to Kiev, where he saw the strewn bones of the Mongols' victims, and from there to the camp of the Mongol warlord **Batu**, on the Volga. Batu permitted him to carry on, and over the following months John and his companion Friar Benedict the Pole rode the 3,000 miles to the imperial encampment near Karakorum, the Mongol capital. They were present at the coronation of Khan Guyuk, who received homage from 4,000 envoys including princes from Russia and Georgia and representatives of the Caliph of **Baghdad**. John's account told of the barren homeland of Mongols, and its perilous extremes of weather. He described the Mongols' customs and way of life. He described their history, too, including a sometimes fanciful account of the conquests of Genghis Khan. (Elsewhere he mentioned being told of a race of people with hoofed feet and dogs' faces, who broke into barking at intervals.) He described how envoys to the Mongols had to pass between two fires in a purification ritual, and how the Russian Duke Michael of Chernigov was beheaded at Batu's court for refusing to prostrate himself before a representation of the late Genghis.

The new Khan showed no interested in converting to Christianity but rather seemed intent on invading **Christendom**. The letter he gave the

Franciscans to take back asserted his status as King of Kings and scourge of God, and demanded submission. John concluded that the Mongols were 'exceedingly grasping and avaricious ... They consider the slaughter of other people as nothing.' John survived to deliver the message to the Pope. He also made some recommendations on how Europe must unite to combat them. John was appointed to the archbishopric of Antivardi in Dalmatia.

## John XXII, Pope (1249–1334)

John XXII (formerly Jacques d'Euse) was the **Pope** who succeeded **Clement V**, being elected in 1316, two years after Clement's death. He was the second of the **Avignon** Popes, and began the construction of the Papal palace there. He is best known for condemning as heretics the Spiritual **Franciscans** or Fraticelli, who insisted on churchmen embracing apostolic poverty. He also presided over the final settlement of the Templars lands, seeing it transferred to the **Hospitallers** or granted to smaller Orders in **Iberia**.

## John the Baptist, St (first century)

John the Baptist features in the New Testament as a prophet and preacher who dwelled in the wild, and who baptised people in the River Jordan to wash away their sins. He was usually represented in Christian art with unkempt hair and beard and wearing animal skins. He was a cousin of **Jesus Christ** and baptised him on the eve of his ministry. He was regarded as the one who paved the way for the Messiah (though certain Gnostics like the Mandaeans actually thought him the Messiah). He is sometimes shown holding the *Agnus Dei* because he announced Christ to be the Lamb of God, come to take away the world's sins. John's preaching against the Pharisees and Saducees (the established priesthood) disturbed the authorities, and King Herod Antipas had him imprisoned, later to be beheaded at the behest of Queen Herodias, whose daughter Salome beguiled Herod with her dancing. (John had angered Herodias by claiming that her marriage to Herod was adultery because she was the king's brother's widow, thus Herodias wanted his head on a platter.) The Knights **Hospitaller** especially revered John the Baptist, and adopted him as their patron saint. The Templars also venerated John and his head sometimes featured on their seal.

## Joscelin I de Courtenay (Joscelin of Edessa) (died 1131)

Joscelin de Courtenay was a French Crusader who arrived in the **Holy Land** in 1101. He served under Baldwin of le Bourg of **Edessa** (**Baldwin II**) and was captured in battle at **Harran**. He was released before Baldwin in 1108, and helped secure Baldwin's release, thereafter apparently being instrumental in procuring forces from **Muslim** Mosul to support Baldwin against **Tancred**, who was reluctant to relinquish power in the county. On Baldwin II's accession to the throne of **Jerusalem** in 1118, the King named Joscelin as the new Count of Edessa, to take his place. Joscelin took part in the battle of **Azaz**, and continued to defend the territory of Edessa from the Danishmends and the Seljuks of **Aleppo**. He died in 1131 after being wounded while conducting a siege against a fortress near **Aleppo**, when the tunnel they were excavating under the walls collapsed.

## *Joscius, Archbishop of Tyre* (died 1202)

Joscius was the Archbishop of **Tyre** succeeding **William of Tyre**. He was part of the party sent for talks with **Raymond III of Tripoli** after the coronation of **Sibylla** and **Guy de Lusignan** to make peace between them and end Raymond's alliance with **Saladin**. Joscius was held back with **Balian of Ibelin** while **Gerard de Ridefort** led his contingent into disaster at **Cresson**, attacking a much larger force. Things went from bad to worse for the **Kingdom of Jerusalem**, and after the fall of Jerusalem Joscius travelled Europe appealing for aid. He met **Philip II Augustus** of France and **Henry II** in 1182 at **Gisors**, attempted to make peace between them, and persuaded them both to **take the Cross**. Joscius returned to the Holy Land, and was present at the formation of the **Teutonic Order** during the **Third Crusade**.

## *Joseph of Arimathea, St* (first century)

Joseph of Arimathea is mentioned in the Bible as a rich man who had become a disciple of Jesus, and who donated his own tomb to receive **Christ**'s body after the crucifixion, in the presence of **Mary Magdalene** and others (Matt 27:56–61). Joseph pleaded with Pontius Pilate, the Roman Governor, to secure the release of Jesus' body. He and one Nicodemus took charge of the hurried burial. Joseph was mentioned more prominently in apocryphal scriptures than in the accepted gospels. The apocryphal 'Gospel of Nicodemus' (also known as the 'Acts of Pilate') has Joseph being subsequently imprisoned by the Jewish elders and escaping miraculously through the risen Christ's intervention. Later Joseph became part of Grail lore, appearing in Robert de Boron's *Joseph d'Armimathie* at the end of the twelfth century. De Boron had Joseph catching Christ's blood at the crucifixion in the **Holy Grail.** On Joseph's release from prison, Joseph left and voyaged to Avalon where he became the first in a dynasty of Grail guardians. **English** myths have it that Joseph brought Christianity to the British Isles and founded a church at **Glastonbury**, and that the Holy Thorn there grew from where he set his staff down. Joseph's travels to the West are also mentioned in the medieval Golden Legend.

## *Joseph von Hammer Purgstall* (1774–1852)

Joseph von Hammer Purgstall was an Austrian orientalist who had served in the embassy to **Constantinople** (Istanbul) and taken part in action against the French, during the **Napoleonic** Wars. He translated various Arabic and Turkish works, and later wrote histories unfavourable to the Templars, portraying them as a **Gnostic** secret society. In 'The Mystery of **Baphomet** Revealed' He hypothesised that the word *Baphomet* derived from the Greek for 'baptism into wisdom', and that this referred to the Templars' occult initiation.

## Judaism

Judaism, the religion of the Jews, had its origin in the **Patriarch Abraham**. Abraham received a covenant with God that singled out his descendants as the chosen people. Jews became marked out by following the Law of **Moses**. Sacred authority is embodied in the *Tanakh*, the Old Testament, while the *Talmud* holds additional rabbinical writings. Jews observe dietary restrictions, the rite of circumcision and the holiness of the Sabbath. **Jerusalem** became the sacred capital of the Jews, where the **Temple of Solomon** was built, housing the **Ark of the Covenant**. By the medieval period, however, misfortunes had befallen the Jews. They had been exiled from the 'promised land', first by the Babylonians and then by the Romans. Jews were scattered among the gentiles (the Diaspora). They had lost their Temple, but for a fragment of its Western Wall, and they were subjected to varying degrees of persecution from Christian and **Muslim** rulers. Rabbis had replaced priests as the guardians of the religious tradition and scattered synagogues stood in for the lost Temple.

The medieval **Catholic** Church forbade Christians to practise usury. Jews, meanwhile, were allowed by their own law to lend at interest to non-Jews. At times during the Crusades, Jews suffered heightened persecution. The rabble elements of the **First Crusade** pillaged and murdered Jews in the Rhineland and along the Danube, and also in Jerusalem after it fell. Jews were subjected to pogroms in **France** around the launch of the **Second Crusade** and in **England** around the launch of the **Third Crusade**. Both **Philip the Fair** of France and **Edward I** of England expelled all the Jews from their realms and confiscated their wealth. The Templars on the whole were not involved in persecuting Jews. Neither on the whole were the early **Cistercians**. **Bernard of Clairvaux** had condemned anti-Semitic violence. Jews were a living symbol of the Passion of **Christ**, to Bernard's eyes, and their punishment was primarily their dispersal. He believed they would ultimately be converted, but that this could not be achieved if they were ground down. It is said that the Abbot **Stephen Harding** used rabbis to assist in translating scripture just before the time the Templars were formed, in order to better understand the word of God. The Templars as bankers may have learned from the Jews. (The Order began to erode the Church's attitude towards usury, being able to justify profiting, or profiteering, from financial transactions in order to help support their pious work in the East.) It is possible the Templars also took an interest in the **Cabbalah**, which mystic Jewish rabbis saw as a key to spiritual enlightenment. The Templars had financial dealings with Jews in their capacity as **bankers**, and as landlords.

# K

## *Karl, Baron von Hund* (eighteenth century)

**Karl, Gotthelf von Hund** was an aristocrat of north-east Saxony who in the 1750s created the Masonic Rite of Strict Observance. This contained many Templar-inspired elements; indeed Karl expressly claimed that the Templars had been the originators of Freemasonry. The Rite also had more occult and mystical elements than earlier forms of the Craft. He claimed to have been inspired by exiled **Jacobite** Freemasons that he encountered in **Paris**, and that had supposedly initiated him into their secrets. The Baron produced a list of **clandestine Grand Masters** differing from that later produced by **Bernard Raymond Fabré-Palaprat** (the so called **Larmenius Charter**). Von Hund claimed the Order had survived in **Scotland** (The Isle of Mull) rather than **France**, and that **Jacques de Molay** had passed his authority to one Pierre d'Aumont. This Pierre, Karl alleged, had reconstituted the Order of the Temple using the symbols and customs of masonry as a cover. Hund presided over the expansion of a system with seven grades up to 'Eques Professus', supposedly with a requirement of nobility and with interests in alchemy. He styled himself 'Provincial Grand Master', but claimed that the Order was headed by 'Unknown Superiors'.

## *Kerak*

Kerak (or Kerak des Moabites) is a forbidding hilltop castle dominating a town south of Amman in Jordan, and overlooking the Dead Sea. It was built by the **Crusaders** in the 1140s. It was the centre of the Crusader region known as Oultrejordian, virtually autonomous from the **Kingdom of Jerusalem**.[227] Many of the subjects of the region were Bedouin tribesmen. The castle was later captured by the **Muslims** and remained in their hands. The **Ayyubids** came to regard it as an essential stronghold, one they were never prepared to restore to the Crusaders.

## *Kerynia*

Kerynia (or Kyrenia) is an old coastal town in northern **Cyprus**. It possessed a castle, which was enlarged during the de Lusignan era. Here, in the dungeons, perished a number of the Templars held on Cyprus, including the last **Marshal** of the Order, **Ayme d'Oselier**. The castle still stands, though it was later strengthened and much altered by the **Venetians**.

## Khoresmians

The Khoresmians (or Khwarazmians) were **Turks** from Central Asia around modern Uzbekistan, who made a brief and bloody entry into the narrative of the **Crusades**. In the 1220s they were displaced from their homeland by the advance of the **Mongol** conquest, and spilled towards Palestine. At the instigation of Sultan as-Silah **Ayyub** of **Egypt**, they attacked **Jerusalem** which was undefended, its walls having been demolished previously in accordance with a treaty. Ayyub had been provoked by the forging of a pact between the Franks and the Damascenes. His mercenaries stormed through Damascene territory, bypassing **Damascus** (perhaps this was their original target but it was too well fortified) and set upon the soft target of the Holy City on 11 July 1244. The Christians had only recently reoccupied Jerusalem and their army was deployed elsewhere with their new Damascene allies. After meeting in council, the Christians in Jerusalem decided to evacuate to Joppa. Thus the civilians departed, escorted by **Hospitallers** under Guillaume de Châteauneuf. Many, however, were lured back by the sight of Frankish flags over the city. It was a trap. The 'barbarous and perverse' Khoresmians were waiting and a massacre ensued. The Khoresmians then sacked the city, slaying the **priests** who remained in the **Holy Sepulchre** and despoiling the building. Only about 300 Christians escaped.[228] The Khoresmians subsequently linked up with Ayyub's army and went on to decimate the Crusaders at the Battle of **La Forbie**.

## Kilmartin

Kilmartin in Argyll and Bute is a remote and rocky spot on the west coast of **Scotland**. A graveyard there contains, among later graves, some medieval **grave slabs**. These are carved with swords, organic and Celtic knot patterns, figures of **knights**, lions, six-leaf patterns within circles and pattée crosses. Eighteen miles to the south, similar slabs can be found in the abandoned churchyard of Kilmory, also featuring carvings of long ships and apparently Templar crosses. Again there are slabs with Celtic patterns on, as well as effigies of medieval knights in armour. The knights wear casque helmets, chain mail hoods and padded hauberks (no mantles or cloaks). These sites have fed speculation that some of the Knights Templar found a refuge in the isolated Scottish Highlands during or after the **suppression** – the carvings of ships perhaps hint at the destination of the Templar fleet from **La Rochelle**. The earliest of the grave slabs is said to date from around 1300. Some of the slabs also feature carvings of tools such as sheep shears, hammers and tongs. As at **Balantradoch**, (and at **Melrose** Abbey) there are also many later gravestones at these Argyll sites, some carved with the **Skull and Crossbones**.

## *Kingdom of Heaven* (film)

*Kingdom of Heaven* is a 2005 feature film about the **Crusades**, directed by Ridley Scott. It stars Orlando Bloom as **Balian of Ibelin**, leading the heroic defence of **Jerusalem**. The film, which also stars Jeremy Irons as Lord Tiberias (**Raymond III of Tripoli**) and Eva Green as Queen **Sibylla**, brings to life the last years of the Latin **Kingdom of Jerusalem** during the reign of **Baldwin IV** (played movingly by a masked Edward Norton). The villains of the piece are **Reynald de Chatillon** (played by Brendan Gleeson) and **Guy de Lusignan** (played by Marton Csokas). A subtle **Saladin** is played by the Syrian actor Ghassan Massoud. Some elements are fictionalised, especially Balian of Ibelin's background and his relationship with Queen Sibylla. In the film, Balian is a blacksmith in **France**, whose long-lost father the Baron of **Ibelin** (played by Liam Neeson), collects him and makes him a **knight** just before dying from a wound received in an ambush. Balian retires to France with Sibylla, returning to the simple life. The historical Balian was born in the nobility of the Kingdom of Jerusalem, and continued to play a political role in the rump of the Latin state while Sibylla died at the Siege of **Acre**. The real Guy de Lusignan was probably not the villain presented in the film and he and Sibylla were actually a very close partnership. Other parts of the film are fairly accurate, such as the aftermath of the Battle of **Hattin** and the execution of Reynald. The armour and heraldry of the Crusaders is also accurately represented. The film has been criticised (for example by **Jonathan Riley-Smith**)[229] for distorting events – portraying the **Catholic** Church as bigoted, cowardly and greedy, and the Templars as cruel and fanatical warmongers. **Gerard de Ridefort** is not featured by name, and the Templars come across more as a private militia of Reynald de Chatillon. The **Hospitallers** (as represented by a character played by David Thewlis) are made to seem more enlightened. Under the direction of Gerard de Ridefort the Templars were indeed a militant party aligned with Reynald de Chatillon. Some of the actions of the **Patriarch** in the film (played by Jon Finch) do reflect accounts of **Heraclius's** conduct.

## *Kingdom of Jerusalem*

The Kingdom of Jerusalem was the most southerly, and in religious and political terms, the most significant of the **Latin** states created in the **Holy Land** by the **Crusaders**. **Jerusalem** was its capital, while it remained in Christian hands, and while they survived the other Crusader states of **Tripoli, Edessa** and **Antioch** generally accepted the **Kings and Queens of Jerusalem** as their overlords. Through most of the thirteenth century **Acre** served as the capital of the kingdom. The disputed title survived even after every inch of the kingdom was lost.

## Kings and Queens of Jerusalem, Crusader

The Title 'King of Jerusalem' was first used by Baldwin I, who succeeded his brother Godfroi de Bouillon, who had called himself Advocate or Defender of the **Holy Sepulchre**. The dynasty and thus the kingdom was weakened by the misfortune of **Baldwin IV** being a sufferer of leprosy, and by the subsequent periods when there was no male heir, and factionalism, with ambitious outsiders marrying heiresses and laying claim to the throne. The monarchs (effective and titular) of Latin Jerusalem were:

| *Sovereign* | *Reign* |
| --- | --- |
| **Godfroi de Bouillon** | 1099–1100 |
| **Baldwin I** | 1100–18 |
| **Baldwin II** | 1118–31 |
| **Melisende of Jerusalem** | 1131–53 |
| and **Fulk V Count of Anjou** | |
| **Baldwin III** | 1153–62 |
| **Amalric** | 1162–74 |
| **Baldwin IV** | 1174–85 |
| **Baldwin V** | 1185–6 |
| **Sibylla of Jerusalem** | 1186–90 |
| and **Guy de Lusignan** | |
| **Isabella of Jerusalem** | 1192–1205 |
| and (1) **Conrad of Montferrat**, | |
| (2) **Henry of Champagne**, | |
| (3) Amalric de Lusignan | |
| Maria de Montferrat | 1205–12 |
| and **John of Brienne** | |
| **Yolande of Jerusalem** | 1212–28 |
| and **Frederick II** | 1228 |
| Conrad II Hohenstaufen | 1228–54 |
| Conrad III | 1254–68 |
| Hugh I/**Hugh III of Cyprus** (disputed) | 1268–84 |
| **Charles of Anjou** (disputed) | 1277–85 |
| John II (disputed) | 1284–85 |
| **Henry II of Cyprus** | 1285–91 |

The Knights Templar had a special relationship with all the Kings of Jerusalem from at least the time of Baldwin II. Sometimes their relationship was very close, while at other times there were serious disagreements and disputes. The crown was weakened by outside factions during the thirteenth century because there was no strong, undisputed central monarchy, as there had been during the twelfth. This was a factor that contributed to the demise of the Kingdom. The Kingdom of Jerusalem ceased to be in 1291 and was never restored. The de Lusignan Kings of Cyprus continued to identify themselves as Kings of Jerusalem, however, and maintained a tradition of having dual coronations. The Angevin Kings of Naples meanwhile continued to assert their own claim to the title (following the purchase of it from a female claimant by Charles of Anjou). Through that line it became a secondary title of the sovereign of Spain, presently King Juan Carlos I.

## Knights

Knights were mounted warriors steeped in the culture and code of **Chivalry**. A superiority of social class was implicit. To be made a knight was considered a great honour, as it was not (in theory) a hereditary status but something conferred. Knights started off as pages, and then became squires, being trained for the profession of arms from an early age. To become a knight was to join an honorary fraternity, but not necessarily an Order. Not all knights were great nobles. It was considered an honour even for a Duke or Prince to be knighted.

Knighthood could be bestowed on the battlefield, or during a pageant arranged for the purpose. One of the last pageants held at the **New Temple, London** was the dubbing of a number of aspirant nobles as secular knights – one of them being Sir Robert Mortimer who would later cause such trouble for **Edward II**. Knighthood could be conferred by established knights as well as by kings. In the medieval period knighthood developed a sacred and ritual aspect. Those being made knights kept a prayerful vigil, normally in a chapel, through the night before their dubbing, to purify their soul. They would then take a ceremonial bath (hence the Order of the Bath), and be clad in white. The dubbing itself would usually take place in the open, after a religious mass. The new knight would be reminded of his oath to be a true knight and to be courageous in the face of his enemies; to be brave and upright that God might love him. He would then be given a hard blow to the face called a *colée*, to help him remember. After that he would receive his arms, armour and steed, and then tilt at a quintaine or take part in jousts and other war games.

Knights were at the centre of a warlike cult during the Age of Chivalry. The Provencal poet Bertrand de Boron glorified warfare, writing how he loved to see knights and horses in battle array, tents and pavilions spread out in the meadows and shields that would be riven and shattered when the fight begins. Not everyone took a positive view of secular knights, and the Italian poet **Dante** placed Bertrand in Hell, in his *Divine Comedy*, for encouraging war between feudal Lords by thus over-glamourising conflict. St **Bernard of Clairvaux** had viewed their vainglory and love of pomp with disdain, and thought the secular knights were heading for Hell. He viewed the Templars as a medium for reforming Knighthood as an institution by their influence, much as the **Cistercians** functioned to reform monasticism.

## Knights of Christ

(1) The Military Order of Christ was a national Order founded in **Portugal** after the suppression of the Knights Templar. It inherited all the Templars' Portuguese properties including their old headquarters at Tomar (which became the Order of Christ's headquarters after 1357). What is not so clear is how many former Templars carried on in the Order of Christ – whether it was business as usual for the Knights Templar under a modified name or whether the personnel was thoroughly replaced.

The new Order was founded by **Diniz, King of Portugal**. Pope **John XXII** officially recognised it in 1319. The first **Grand Master** of the Order of Christ was Dom Gil Martinez, who had served in another Knightly fraternity, the Order of Aviz. Knights of Christ were originally sworn to Poverty and Chastity, and wore a red cross with a hollow centre and widening ends. The main difference between the Order of Christ and the Order of the Temple was that the Knights of Christ swore allegiance to the King of Portugal.

Like other Iberian monarchs, Diniz wanted the Templars' assets to go to Orders more under the control of the crown than the church, and without the independence the larger, international **Military Orders** exercised. The Order found a purpose in maritime activity. One of its Grand Masters was the famous Prince **Henry the Navigator**, who supported numerous voyages of discovery. In 1460 the Order received the right to take a levy on all imports from the new African trading colonies. After Henry's time the Order continued to be led by members of the royal family, and gradually secularised. By the 1490s brethren were no longer expected to take vows of chastity, and in 1505 they jettisoned the vow of poverty. The Order became more a royal, honorary association, like the **Order of the Garter** (to which Prince Henry had belonged), though Knights of Christ were still obliged to donate a third of their wealth to the Order. **Manuel I** of Portugal became Grand Master in the early sixteenth century. Other famed members of the Order included **Vasco da Gama**, the first European mariner to sail to India, and **Christopher da Gama**, his son, who died fighting the **Muslims** in **Ethiopia**.

Knights were expected to be Catholics of noble birth and (in the case of Portuguese brethren) to have served at sea or in Africa. At some stage the religious and lay members of the Order split, after brother Antonius of Lisbon attempted to reform the Order and restore its monastic character. The religious brethren were thereafter separated from the Knights who had abandoned all pretences of pursuing a religious vocation. In 1789 the Order was officially secularised. It lost its properties in the mid-nineteenth century, and was abolished in 1910 when Portugal became a republic. It was subsequently revised as an honorary Order of merit.

(2) The terms *Knights of Christ* or *Knight of the Cross* could be generic terms for those involved in waging **Crusades** during the medieval era. These Soldiers of God (as they could also be called) need not necessarily belong to any military-religious Order, but could be secular warriors who had **taken the cross**.

## Konrad von Marburg (died 1233)

Konrad von Marburg, initially a crusade preacher, became a notorious German **Inquisitor**. He was involved in persecuting the **Cathars** in the **Languedoc**, in the wake of the **Albigensian Crusade**, and afterwards returned to **Germany**. With little basis, he began to accuse various inhabitants of Thuringia and Hesse, including nobles, of **heresy**, **Devil worship** and attending orgies. He condemned his victims to death by **burning**. One of those Konrad accused was Heinrich, Count of Sayn, whom Konrad pursued even after the local bishops had declared him innocent. Heinrich probably arranged Konrad's murder on the road by a group of knights, which ended Konrad's reign of terror.

Konrad had become personal confessor to **Elizabeth of Hungary**, the pious young widow of Count Ludwig of Thuringia. Konrad dominated Elizabeth, held her to impossible standards of saintliness, beat her and kept her from her children when she fell short, possibly precipitating her early death.

## Krak des Chevaliers

Krak des Chevaliers is a **Crusader Castle** in Syria. It was the largest castle belonging to the Knights **Hospitaller**, and is one of the best-preserved fortresses from the Crusading era. There was an **Arab** castle on the site, which fell to the **First Crusade**. It is still known in Arabic as *Hisn al-Akrad* (Castle of the Kurds) after its original garrison. It is set on an isolated hill called the Jubal Khali, overlooking a wide pass between the mountains of Lebanon and the ranges of the Jubal Ans Ariyya. Thus it defended the route from **Muslim** Syria to the central area of the county of **Tripoli**.

The Knights Hospitaller built most of the present castle, probably in the early thirteenth century, after earthquakes damaged the previous fortress (the Hospitallers took over the site in 1142). The castle contained halls, storage vaults, passages, a **gothic** chapel and cloisters, all within gargantuan walls with thirteen towers. Homs was the nearest Muslim outpost to Krak des Chevaliers, and was on the receiving end of numerous Hospitaller raids. Conversely the castle was one of several built to counter the threat Homs posed to Christian Tripoli. The Hospitallers successfully defended the castle when it was besieged in turn by **Nur ed-Din** and by **Saladin**. It is said that in the latter battle Saladin captured the Hospitaller Commander, and instructed him to go below the gates and order his brethren to surrender. The Commander shouted an order in Arabic to surrender and in French to battle on to the end. The Castle has double walls, ten metres thick in places. The lower parts of the walls sloped to prevent siege towers being brought up against the ramparts. The Castle was finally taken by **Baybars** in 1271.

## *Kurtuz* (died 1260)

Kurtuz (or Qutuz) was a **Mameluk** general who became a sultan of **Egypt** in around AD 1259, some years after the Mameluks had turned against the **Ayyubid** Sultans. The **Mongol** conqueror of the Middle East, **Hulagu**, sent an ambassador to Kurtuz demanding Egypt's homage. Kurtuz, by way of reply, sent back the envoy's severed head. Kurtuz made an arrangement with the **Franks**, whereby the Christians allowed the Mameluk army to cross their territory to confront the Mongols. The Christians allowed this, though were divided on how far to go with the alliance. Kurtuz led the Mameluks to victory subsequently over the Mongols at **Ain Jalut**. Kurtuz's subordinate **Baybars**, who had been prominent in the battle, demanded to be made governor of Aleppo as a reward. Kurtuz refused, and took the army back towards Cairo. Baybars murdered him during a hare hunt, and was soon afterwards acclaimed as the new Sultan.

# L

## *La Cavelerie*

La Cavelerie is a town in Aveyron, in the old **Languedoc** of southern **France**. It is not far from **St Eulalie de Cernon**, another major Templar centre. La Cavelerie was founded by the Templars and contains a Templar **church** as well as **Hospitaller** fortifications.

## *La Fève*

La Fève was a key Templar **castle** in the **Holy Land**. It guarded the crossroads in the Jexreel valley, where the route from Tiberias to **Jerusalem** and that from **Acre** to Baisan intersected. It was built by the Order atop a mound dating back to the Bronze Age. The castle had a garrison of some fifty or sixty knights.

## *La Forbie, Battle of*

The battle of **La Forbie** (also called Harbiyah) was remembered as the worst **Frankish** defeat in the **Holy Land** since **Hattin**. The battle was fought between the **Kingdom of Jerusalem** and the Sultanate of **Egypt**. The Christians had allied with the forces of **Damascus**; the Egyptians had joined up with the **Khoresmians**, who were fresh from ravaging **Jerusalem** at the behest of the Egyptian Sultan as-Silah **Ayyub**. The battle was fought near **Gaza** on 17 and 18 October 1244. The Christians of **Acre** had been slow responding to the threat and many of the Latins of Jerusalem had been massacred.

The Christian army was commanded by **Walter IV of Brienne** and **Philip de Montfort**. They put into the field just over 1,000 knights including brethren of the **Military Orders**, with the Templars under **Armand de Perigord**, the sixteenth **Grand Master**. They also had some 6,000 infantrymen. Their allies, the Damascenes, were under the Emir of Homs, al-Mansor Ibrahim, who had brought 2,000 horsemen, and an-Nasir, the Muslim lord of Kerak had also brought a contingent of Bedouin. The Egyptian/Khoresmian force, meanwhile, was of roughly equal size and dominated by the **Mameluks**, a military elite on the rise. The combatants met near the village of la Forbie. Al-Mansur advised his Frankish allies to adopt a cautious approach, but Walter of Brienne was keen to attack.

The Frankish and Damascene cavalry charged at the Egyptians, but the Egyptian line held. The next morning Ayyub sent his Khoresmian horsemen to attack his enemies' flanks, with deadly result. The few surviving warriors from Damascus and the Bedouins fled the field, abandoning the Christians to their doom. Thousands were killed and 800 taken prisoner to Cairo. Among them were Armand de Perigord and Walter of Brienne, both of whom would perish in captivity (some accounts say Armand was killed in the fighting). Guillaume de Châteauneuf, the Grand Master of the **Hospitallers**, was also captured. Of the Military Orders only 36 out of 348 Templars and only 26 of 351 hospitallers survived.[230] The Frankish Kingdom would never recover from La Forbie. The disaster motivated the launch of the **Seventh Crusade**, but this only led to further defeat.

## *Lalibela* (died *c.* 1229)

Gebrel Mesque Lalibela of the Zagwe dynasty was a medieval ruler of **Ethiopia**, who gave his name Lalibela to the city he re-founded in northern Ethiopia, with its great sunken churches carved out of the rock. A tradition has it that Lalibela spent some time in exile in **Jerusalem**, before returning to Ethiopia in the late 1180s to overthrow his despotic brother Harbay, and build (or rather excavate) the city of Lalibela (formerly called Roha). The monolithic churches of Lalibela have been considered an attempt to remake the Holy City in Ethiopia. The most famous is the Church of St **George**, a three-storey high (or rather deep) cruciform church that appears to stand within a great pit, all carved out of the bedrock. Graham Hancock wrote that Prince Lalibela could have encountered the Templars in the **Holy Land** and persuaded them to assist him in overthrowing Harbay, perhaps in exchange for access to the **Ark of the Covenant**, believed to be in Ethiopia. Hancock also discerned Templar iconography in Ethiopian churches, and speculated that the Templars helped build these monuments.

## Languedoc

The Languedoc is a region of south-western **France**. The name, Langue d'Oc refers to the Language of Oc, or Occitan. In this now scarcely spoken language, 'Oc' rather than 'Oui' means 'yes'. The wider region where the language was spoken was sometimes called Occitania – therefore encompassing Toulouse. The Languedoc was where the belief system labelled the **Cathar** heresy took root. It was the land ravaged during the **Albigensian Crusade**. It was an area where the Templars were well established.

## La Rochelle

La Rochelle is a port city on the west coast of **France**, with a fortified medieval harbour. The Templars had ships and trading concessions there, some of which were granted or confirmed by **Eleanor of Aquitaine**. They exported wine to **England** and probably imported wool. Their ships in La Rochelle apparently facilitated the escape of a number of Templars at the time of the **arrests**. It was reported that the **Grand Preceptor** of France escaped with the treasure of the **Visitor, Hugues de Pairaud** and that fifty Templars from Paris rode to La Rochelle and escaped on eighteen galleys. What became of them is a mystery. **Scotland** and **Portugal** have been suggested as possible places of refuge.

## Larmenius Charter

The Larmenius Charter was a document supposedly written after **Jacques de Molay**, during his last days, transferred authority to one **Jean-Marc Larmenius**. This was so that Larmenius could continue the Order of the Temple in secret, thus inaugurating a second phase of Templar existence as a clandestine society. The document is also known as the 'Charter of Transition' or *Carta Transmissionis*. In the Charter, Larmenius entrusts the secret Order to one Franciscus Theobaldus. Associated with the charter is a list of subsequent **clandestine Grand Masters** of the Temple extending right into the late eighteenth century. The list and the charter are of questionable provenance, being associated with **Bernard Raymond Fabré-Palaprat**.

## Las Navas de Tolosa, Battle of

The Battle of Las Navas de Tolosa (or *Hisn al-Uqab*) was an engagement between Christian forces and **Muslim** Almohad invaders (known as the **Moors**) in southern **Spain**, fought on 6 July 1212. It was a defining moment in the wars of the *Reconquista*. The Almohad Caliph Mohammed al-Nasir was the ruler of an extensive empire in North Africa (the Mahgreb). He brought a formidable army across the Strait of Gibraltar, hoping to consolidate the Muslim victory over Alfonso VIII of **Castile** at Alarcos in 1195, which had resulted in the Almohads gaining much ground. Alfonso VIII managed to draw together a Christian coalition to meet the threat, and was joined by

Sancho VII of Navarre, Alfonso II of **Portugal** and **Pedro II of Aragon**. They were also joined by contingents of Templars, **Hospitallers** and Knights of **Santiago** and **Calatrava**, and by French and Italian Crusaders. The armies mustered in Toledo, and marched out behind the Cross, beginning their campaign by recovering Calatrava.

The Moors made a camp in a secure position, defended by apparently impassable mountains. The Christians, however, managed to manoeuvre around these and attack the ill-prepared invaders. Though initially beaten back, the Christians eventually triumphed. The battle was a rout and (it is claimed) a 100,000 Moors were slain. The heroes of the battle were Pedro of Aragon and Sancho of Navarre, who stormed the Caliph's tent, cutting his way through Mohammed's bodyguards who were chained together making a barrier (to commemorate this, Sancho incorporated the captured gold chains into the royal arms of Navarre).

Somehow the Caliph himself escaped. The Christians had won a great victory even so, suffering relatively slight losses – the bulk of those being born by the **Military Orders**. The Caliph meanwhile made it back to Marrakech, but died soon after. *Las Naves de Tolosa* precipitated the collapse of the Almohad power. In Spain a number of cities were regained within a few decades, including Seville, Córdoba and Cadiz.

## Latin Christians

The Latin Christians were those loyal to the **Pope** and the Roman **Catholic** Church and attended the Latin Mass. They were mostly from Western Europe and (in the context of the crusades) the term *Latins* is usually synonymous with **Franks**. The Latins had an increasingly strained relationship with the Greek Orthodox Christians of **Byzantium** during the era of the **Crusades**. Those Latin Christians born in the **Kingdom of Jerusalem** were sometimes nicknamed Poulains, akin to beginners, or debutants.

## Le Bèzu

Le Bèzu was a castle in the **Languedoc**, above the Blanque River, near **Rennes le Chateau**. It is sometimes named as a Templar fortress, though it has stronger links to the **Cathars**. The lords of Le Bezu were the Sermon family, scions of the Aniorts, Viscounts of Plateau de Salut. The castle was a place of refuge to fugitive Cathars, but surrendered to the **Catholic** forces of the **Albigensian Crusade** in 1210, after the fall of Termes Castle demoralised its garrison. One earlier Lord of the Castle, Bernard Sermon I du Bèzu had been associated with the Templars. He had joined the Order, probably as a **Confrere** in 1151, and donated money. Other local legends claim that the Templers operated gold mines in the area, and/or hid some of their bullion in the castle.[231]

## Leonardo da Vinci (1453–1519)

Leonardo da Vinci was a great Florentine artist during the Renaissance, and also a scientist, inventor, anatomist and probably the finest *uomo universale*. He has no real connection to the Templars though certain **conspiracy theories** link him to the topic. The spurious '*Dossiers Secrets*' named him as a Grand Master of the secret society the **Priory of Sion**. (There is no evidence that da Vinci was involved in any such group.)

## Léo Taxil (1854–1907)

Léo Taxil (Gabriel Jogdan) was a French journalist and hoaxer. After an early career producing sordid anti-**Catholic** material he joined the **Freemasons**, but was soon expelled for being a pornographer and plagiarist. He never passed beyond the Entered Apprentice degree. Subsequently he feigned a conversion to Catholicism and (like a latter-day **Esquin de Floyran**) started putting about the suggestion that the Freemasons were involved in heretical depravity and unholy worship of Lucifer in a secret and sinister cult within the movement called 'Palladism'. Some of the forged material he disseminated contained imagery obviously based on the **Baphomet** drawing of **Eliphas Levi**.

In 1887 Taxil even convinced Pope Leo XIII of his spurious claims (the Pope had already denounced Freemasons as leaders in the Kingdom of Satan). Taxil kept up the hoax for twelve years, supported by Catholic clerics whom he was also intent on making fools of. With a collaborator he wrote 'The Devil in the Nineteenth Century,' describing the secret degree of Palladism and its dualist/Luciferian creed. He later used a female associate, Diana Vaughan, who was in on the caper, to back up his tall story. She was presented as having been involved in the Masonic **Devil worship**, supposedly holding the position 'Mistress Templar'. Taxil revealed his practical joke at a press conference in 1895. The audience did not see the funny side and Taxil was lucky to escape without serious injury.

## Lepers/Leprosy

Leprosy (Hansens Disease) is a chronic skin disease, causing debilitation and terrible disfigurement. In medieval times it was incurable, and being deemed highly contagious, those infected were isolated from society in leper colonies. These were often built outside city walls, administered along monastic lines and termed 'Lazar Houses'. In the **Holy Land, knights** who contracted the disease joined the **Order of St Lazarus**, which had both military and **Hospitaller** functions. The disease carried great stigma and must have seemed a living death. The achievements of **Baldwin IV of Jerusalem** seem the more impressive considering that he was a sufferer.

## Les Grandes Chroniques de France

*Les Grandes Chroniques de France* were official accounts in French of the reigns of the **Capetian** Kings. They presented the establishment's version of events. The chronicles mentioned the suppression of the Templars and repeated the list of **accusations**, describing the idol as a head with hollow, carbuncled eyes that glowed. They allege that the Templars were traitors against the **Crusades**. They also add the gruesome embellishment that the child of a Templar and a maiden was burnt and the fat used to anoint the **idol**, while new Templars were fed the powdered remains of their dead comrades.

## Liegnitz

Liegnitz, or Legnica was a battle that took place in Poland on 9 April 1241. A Christian coalition including small detachments from the three main **Military Orders** fought against a vast invading **Mongol** army. The Mongols advanced behind their totem of the nine yaks tails, tightly packed in formation so the Europeans underestimated their strength. The Christians, with Templars, **Hospitallers** and **Teutonic Knights** present, inflicted unexpectedly heavy casualties on the Mongols, but were themselves all but wiped out. **Henry II, Duke of Silesia**, the commander of the combined German and Polish army, was captured and his head was carried off on a lance. Baidar and Kadan, the Mongol commanders, took seven sacks of severed ears to present to their overlord **Batu Khan**.[232]

Fortunately for the Christians the death of the Mongolian Emperor, Ogodai Khan, spared them, as on hearing of it Batu was obliged to return to Mongolia, taking most of his men. Meanwhile the Christians who escaped the terrible battle of Liegnitz attributed their defeat to the demonic power of the Mongols' yak tail totem – misinterpreted as the head of a dreadful demon with a long flowing beard.

## Lincoln

Lincoln is a city in the East Midlands of **England**, on the River Witham. It was at the centre of the county where some of the largest Templar estates were located. They had large sheep farms in Lincolnshire and also bred and trained horses in the area. Local **Preceptories** included **Temple Bruer**, South Witham, **Eagle** and Willoughton (one of the largest in the country). The Templars owned property in Lincoln itself, including the **Jew**'s House on Steep Hill, which stands today as a rare survival of an early medieval stone town house in England (if such is the same house as the Order leased to one Aaron the Jew, a well-known money lender in the mid-twelfth century with royal and ecclesiastical clients).[233]

The Castle in Lincoln was begun in Norman times, as the high mound testifies. The Castle became the prison of the Templars arrested in the county in 1307. They appear to have been confined in a tower in Cobb Hall.

Twenty-one brothers in all were held at Lincoln. Three probably infirm brothers from the Templar hospital at Eagle would perish in captivity. Crude carvings, scratched into the stone, may still be seen in the tower cells, including a number of stepped based crosses (**Calvary Crosses**) a crucifix, a St Christopher figure and a human figure with a raised arm. These carvings were probably made by the Templar prisoners and are comparable to those seen in **Chinon, Royston Cave** and **Warwick Castle**.

The Templars held here were interrogated at a tribunal held nearby in the chapter house of the Cathedral. The tribunal heard no confessions to the **accusations against the Order**. One Templar, Henry de la Wold, confirmed that the Master had kissed him on the mouth on his **initiation** (not that this was illicit). Another, Robert de Hamilton, admitted to wearing a cord girdle that had touched a column in Nazareth. The Lincoln tribunal wound up in March 1311, when the defendants were removed to **London**.

## Lions

The Templars' rules contains a curious clause (clause 56) permitting them to hunt lions. The prohibition from hunting did not include lions, for the lion 'comes encircling and searching for what he can devour'. It is not clear how many wild lions the Templars encountered in the **Holy Land**, or if they ever really hunted lions. The clause may be intended as a metaphor. The lion became something of a symbol for the Templars, the fiercer alternative to the **Lamb of God**, representing the other side of their nature. A lion appeared on the **seal** used by the Templars in **England**. Lions were also associated with King **Solomon**.

## London

London was already well established as the capital of **England** by the time of the Norman Conquest. By 1300 its population was around 800,000, making it by far the biggest city in the British Isles. Most were crammed within the old Roman walls, under the shadow of old St Paul's Cathedral. The Templars settled early in London and established their first base at Holborn (**Old Temple, London**). They later moved to a more substantial complex at the **New Temple, London**, in a suburb to the east. After 1307 and the arrests, the Council of Canterbury tried the Templars in London, while in the end all the Templars from England were eventually bought for trial in the capital, kept in the Tower of London, at jails attached to the city gates, and in private houses. Most of the Templars were ultimately absolved in St Paul's.

## Louis VII (1120–80)

Louis VII was the **Capetian** king of **France** whose reign saw the Templars grow into a powerful institution in the Kingdom. Louis was crowned in

1137 and at the same time married **Eleanor of Aquitaine**. He was famously pious and more like a monk than a king in the eyes of his first wife. They had two daughters, **Maria of Champagne** and Alix of France. Louis meanwhile came into conflict with **Theobald II of Champagne** and ultimately invaded the region. He sacked Vitry, during which 1,000 refugees were burned alive in a church.

Perhaps through guilt over this, Louis **took the Cross**, encouraged by St **Bernard of Clairvaux**. Louis and Eleanor both embarked on the **Second Crusade**, taking the land route for the **Holy Land**. In Anatolia the French Army was mauled in an ambush by the **Turks**. The King was lucky to escape capture and only strong Templar leadership held the Crusader force together. Louis's ability to continue the Crusade was also dependent on his receiving loans from the Templars. Having arrived in the **Kingdom of Jerusalem**, Louis joined with Conrad III of Germany and **Baldwin III** of Jerusalem and went to besiege **Damascus**. It was a costly failure.

Back in Europe after the Crusade, Louis's marriage to Eleanor continued to deteriorate, and was annulled in 1152, partly because Louis deemed Eleanor incapable of giving him a son. To his chagrin she soon married his rival **Henry II of England**, and produced a brood of children including four sons who survived to adulthood, two of whom reigned as kings. Louis remarried Constance of Castile, meanwhile, who gave him two daughters, Marguerite and Alys. After her death in childbirth he married again to Adèle de Champagne, who produced his son and heir, **Philip II Augustus**, as well as a daughter Agnes, who was sent to **Constantinople** and ended up being claimed by the Emperor **Andronicus**.

## Louis VIII (1187–1226)

Louis VIII was the son of **Philip II Augustus** of **France**. As prince he was remarkable for invading **England** to support the rebel barons against King **John**, and for being proclaimed King of England in **London** in 1216. (He later abandoned his claim when his allies were defeated and when he was paid off.) Meanwhile he also took part in the ongoing **Albigensian Crusade**.

In 1219 he was responsible for massacring the 7,000 inhabitants of Marmande in the **Languedoc**.[234] He succeeded to the French throne in 1223, and renewed the Albigensian Crusade in 1225. He laid siege to **Avignon** and then Montpellier, but fell ill with dysentery, and died in November 1226.

## Louis IX (1215–70)

Louis IX was the **Capetian** King of **France** who led the ill-fated **Seventh Crusade**, one of the last major expeditions launched from Europe against the Eastern **Muslims** in the thirteenth century. Louis was brave and committed, but was let down by his inability to impose his authority on his arrogant barons, especially on his brother **Robert, Count of Artois**. His early reign was spent under the shadow of his devout mother **Blanche of Castile**, who presided as regent until Louis came of age, and again while he was absent on **Crusade**. Louis would be a popular king, generally known for his piety, humility and approachability.

He married the fair **Marguerite of Provence**, who would accompany him on the Crusade, and prove a devoted and supportive queen. Louis had long intended to lead a Crusade to the East, and to that end tried to bring closure to the **Albigensian Crusade** and to make some sort of peace with **Frederick II**, the latter against Papal objections. His piety also manifested in his building of the beautiful shrine the *Sainte Chapelle*, where he installed Holy Relics including the Crown of Thorns purchased at great expense from a **Latin** Emperor of **Constantinople**, Baldwin II. Louis swore, while seriously ill, that if he recovered, he would embark on Crusade, and in 1248 he fulfilled his vow. Louis's Crusade in **Egypt** began with success at **Damietta**, but crumbled after Robert of Artois and the Templars under **Guillaume de Sonnac** rode into **Baybars'** trap at **Mansourah**. Later the Muslim **Mameluks** captured Louis himself, and the King had to agree to restore Damietta to them and to deliver a hefty ransom. Louis's pregnant wife Marguerite had to plead with the Italian contingent in the meantime to dissuade them from abandoning the city. **Jean de Joinville** practically had to force the reluctant Templars to contribute to the payment.

After the less than glorious Egyptian campaign, Louis went to **Acre** and tried to strengthen the defences of the rump **Kingdom of Jerusalem**, where he would surely have been better off going in the first place. He sent ambassadors to the **Mongols** and negotiated with the **Assassins** trying to win friends against the new Mameluk power in Egypt (which his disastrous intervention had helped to bring into being). The Mongols and Assassins proved less than friendly and each demanded Louis's submission. Louis took out some of his frustration on the Templars, punishing the new Grand Master **Reynald de Vichiers** for negotiating with the Damascenes without his permission.

After four years Louis returned to France, but swore to lead another Crusade. He embarked on the Eighth Crusade in 1270, with the intention of succouring the Holy Land. He diverted to Tunis for obscure reasons, perhaps related to the ambitions of **Charles of Anjou**, his brother. Disease broke out almost as soon as the French force landed, and before long Louis died, along with his son John Tristan, who had been born at Damietta during the darkest phase of the Seventh Crusade. Louis was succeeded by **Philip III**. He was canonised as St Louis in 1297.

## Ludolph of Sudheim (fourteenth century)

Ludolph of Sudheim was a German **priest** and **pilgrim** who visited the **Holy Land** from 1336 to 1341 and left an account of his journey, dedicated to Baldwin, Bishop of Paderborn. The end of the Crusades did not entirely put a stop to the practice of Christian pilgrimage to the region. Ludolph discovered two old men who had been Templars, captured at the fall of **Acre** in 1291. They had survived in isolation, in the service of the Sultan, had taken families, and were unaware of the fate of the Order in the West. The men, from Toulouse and **Burgundy**, were brought back to Europe, received with honour, and allowed to end their days in peace. Ludolph also witnessed the great collection of **Holy Relics** held by the **Hospitallers** on **Rhodes**, some of which they had inherited from the Templars. These included a cross supposedly made from the bowl Christ had used to wash the feet of the disciples.[235]

## Lyons

Lyons (Lyon) is a city in east-central **France**. It was the scene of two ecclesiastical councils where **Crusading** expeditions were discussed. At the First Council of Lyons in 1245, **Innocent IV** approved the **Seventh Crusade**, in response to the loss of **Jerusalem** to the **Khoresmians** in 1244. This Crusade, however, seemed a secondary priority to Innocent, who was more concerned with preaching a war against **Frederick II**. The Pope declared the Emperor deposed at the council. Other items on the council's agenda included aid to the Latin Empire of **Constantinople** and **Christendom**'s response to the arrival in Eastern Europe of the **Mongols**. At the Second Council of Lyons, in 1274, **Gregory X** presided. A new **Holy Land** Crusade was proposed, though many delegates proved apathetic regarding any future commitment to the Holy Land. It was also attended by **Guillaume de Beaujeu** and James I of **Aragon**, who was keen to support the crusading cause. The Templars themselves seemed less enthusiastic, perhaps because de Beaujeu wished to see the Crusade led by **Charles of Anjou** rather than by James.[441]

# M

## Macbenac

Macbenac or *MacBenach* is a word significant in **Freemasonry**. Its meaning is unknown. Some interpret it as the Gaelic for 'Blessed Son'.[236] A Turkish Masonic magazine (*Mimar Sinan*) mentioned a Templar who allegedly escaped to Scotland in the fourteenth century, called Mabaignac. Other interpretations have 'mac' as the Hebrew for 'to smite'. The word/name has also been linked with the legendary **Pierre d'Aumont**. **Charles Louis Cadet-Gassicourt** mentioned the word as part of the 'counter-sign' or 'word of order' of the supposed secret Templar chapters within eighteenth-century Freemasonry

(Jakin-Boaz, Mac-benach, Adonai 1314', standing for 'Jacobus Burgundus Molai, Beat Anno-domini 1314').

## Maccabees

The Maccabee clan were leaders of a **Jewish** revolt against Hellenistic/Seleucid rule. They established the Hasmonean dynasty, which ruled an independent Judea immediately before the Roman era. The First and Second 'Book of Maccabees' were sometimes considered part of the authentic Old Testament and were know by medieval Christians. The Templars sometimes saw themselves as the new Maccabees, as holy warriors defending the Temple. The Papal bull **Milites Templi** referred to the Templars as 'New Maccabees'.

## Magna Carta

The Magna Carta was an important document, theoretically limiting royal authority in **England**. King **John** was obliged to sign it by the barons who met him on 15 June 1215, in the meadow of Runnymede by the Thames, between Windsor and Staines. It defined the freedom of the Church to appoint its own bishops, and defined the rights of the barons and the people, to some extent. Rather than stating guiding principles of liberty, it lists various concessions dealing with such things as inheritance rights on lands. The Magna Carta ended arbitrary exactions of money by the king, and ruled that no one was to be punished except in accordance with the law. The charter was reissued a number of times, though most of its clauses were subsequently repealed or replaced. Brother Aymeric (Aymer St Mawer), **Master of the Temple in England**, is mentioned in the preamble along with Stephen, Archbishop of Canterbury, **Hugh, Bishop of Lincoln**, **William Marshal**, and **Hubert de Burgh**, among others who had advised the king to adopt the charter. Four medieval copies of the original Magna Carta survive, two in **London**, one in **Lincoln** and one in Salisbury.

## Malih (died 1175)

Malih (or Mileh) was a brother of Thoros II of Armenia. He was described by **William of Tyre** as a most wicked man, who hoped to dispossess his brother's heirs, and who allied with the **Muslims** to achieve this. **Nur ed-Din** gave him use of a cavalry force with which Malih usurped power. He seems to have been an oppressive ruler. He was apparently an ex-Templar, but turned against the Order and confiscated their possessions bordering Cilicia, which they only recovered after his death.[445]

## Malta

Malta is a small island, or rather an archipelago of three islands in the Mediterranean Sea, south of Sicily. It has been inhabited since prehistoric times and boasts some enigmatic and impressive megalithic temples. It was colonised by the Romans and visited by St Paul, and occupied by the **Arabs** from AD 870–1091. The Arab occupation's effect was leaving Malta the only Christian country with a largely Semitic language. Malta was captured by the Sicilian Normans and subsequently its fate was tied to that of Sicily. In 1530 the island was given to the Knights **Hospitaller** by the Emperor Charles V, in compensation for the loss of **Rhodes**. The Hospitallers became known as the Knights of Malta. The Order repulsed two **Ottoman Turkish** invasions and was only deprived of the Island by **Napoleon Bonaparte** in 1798. Napoleon introduced Republican government, chiselled the Knights' escutcheons from their fort and suppressed the **Inquisition**. The Maltese later rose against the French with British help. The Knights of Malta sought to have Malta restored to them, but the British retained it as a military base. It gained independence in 1964. Valletta, the capital, contains various Hospitaller remnants including extensive harbour fortifications, Baroque churches and the **Grand Master**'s palace with its armoury.

## Maltese Cross

The Maltese cross is a symbol formed of four swallow-tailed, wedge shapes (like 'V's), meeting in the centre. It has eight external points. A white Maltese cross was the badge worn (on black or red robes) by the Knights **Hospitaller**. Their ordinary flag was a straight white cross on a red field. (Incidentally the cross on the modern flag of Malta is not a Maltese cross but a representation of the George Cross Medal, which was awarded to the Islanders as a whole for their courage during the Second World War.) The Maltese cross is also used as an emblem by the modern Orders of St John, and by the St John's Ambulance Brigade. Some Neo-Templars also wear a red Maltese cross on white robes. A plain Greek cross or a flaring *Croix Pattée* would probably be more authentic.

## Mameluks

Mameluks were originally a corps of slave bodyguards used by the Caliphs and Sultans of **Egypt**. Many were Circasians or Kipchack Turks, bought as slaves as young boys, brought up as **Muslims** and trained as elite soldiers. **Saladin** and his **Ayyubid** successors used Mameluks as bodyguards and shock troops. The Mameluks became a military elite in **Egypt**, and were prominent in the Muslim response to the **Seventh Crusade**. Ibn Wasil, contemporary Muslim writer, called the Mameluks 'Islam's Templars', when describing their ferocious pursuit of the Crusaders retreating from **Mansourah** in 1250. Soon after their victory over **Louis IX**, however, the Mameluks, fearful of losing their privileged position, murdered the young Sultan Turan-Shah. Abetted by Shaijar al-Durr, a wife of the late Sultan as-Silah, the Mameluk Emirs seized power, and commenced their own rule in Egypt, the first Mameluk sultan being Aybeg, who married Shaijar. They governed together for another seven years. Then, as one version of events has it, the Sultana stabbed Aybeg while bathing him, having learned that he preferred a fourteen-year-old concubine to her. The murder was discovered by one of Aybeg's sons, and Shaijar died while being pursued by the palace guards. Aybeg was succeeded by **Kurtuz**. A **Mongol** envoy soon appeared at the court of Kurtuz, and demanded Egypt's submission in the name of Hulagu, whose armies had swept all before them and reached as far as **Gaza**. The Mameluks beheaded the envoy and prepared for war.

The Mameluks were subsequently responsible for halting the progress of the Mongols in the Middle East, when they defeated them at **Ain Jalut** in Nazareth in September 1260. One of the leading Mameluks was **Baybars**, who ultimately killed Kurtuz and seized power himself. In the following years, the Mameluks turned on the Christians. Baybars and his successors **Qalawun** and **al-Ashraf Khalil**, wiped out the vestiges of the Crusader **Kingdom of Jerusalem**. These were brutal times. The Mameluks captured castles and massacred surrendering garrisons. They destroyed ancient cities, killed thousands and took hundreds of slaves. At this time Europe was distracted by the papal-imperial wars in Italy and Sicily, and little help (aside from that sent by Louis IX) materialised to help the Latin East in the face of this ruthless onslaught. The Mameluks were later defeated by the **Ottoman Turks**, but retained power in Egypt as client rulers within the Ottoman Empire. Their rule, which saw Egypt's stagnation, would last until 1798 when the country was invaded by **Napoleon Bonaparte**.

## Mandylion

The Mandylion was a **Holy Relic**, a cloth marked with the face of **Christ**. It was supposedly the Veil of St Veronica, which touched the face of Jesus face during his passage to Calvary. The relic was recorded as being in **Edessa** in the AD 500s. The face in the **Holy Shroud** somewhat resemble various copies of the lost Mandylion. The Mandylion was taken to **Constantinople** in 944, and probably looted from there after the **Fourth Crusade** took the city. The Templars took no direct part in the plundering of Byzantium, but some speculate that the Mandylion found its way into their hands. The bearded **head** panel found in Templecombe bears a resemblance to the Mandylion, and could be evidence that the Templars venerated this relic.

## Manfred (1232–66)

Manfred of Hohenstaufen, King of Sicily was the son of **Frederick II** by Bianca Lancia, who may have married Frederick just before her death. Manfred was, however, generally considered illegitimate. Despite this he was given positions of authority. Manfred seized power in Sicily in 1258. He succeeded his half-brother **Conrad IV** in 1354 in Sicily (ostensibly as regent for the young **Conradin**) and inherited their father's struggle against the Papacy, but Hohenstaufen relations with the Templars thawed somewhat. Manfred forbade interference with the Order's property and placed them under his protection. Manfred had been helped to power by Albert of Canelli, the Templar Preceptor of Apulai. Manfred was an effective ruler. He was **excommunicated** in 1254 for refusing to surrender Sicily to the Pope, and became the object of a papal Crusade in 1255. He defeated **Guelf** forces and papal mercenaries under a Florentine cardinal that marched against him in Lucera (where the Muslim inhabitants supported Manfred). In 1258 the triumphant Manfred was crowned in Palermo. Successive Popes sought wider support for the war against Manfred, and eventually recruited **Charles of Anjou**. Charles defeated and killed Manfred at Benevento (26 February 1266) and with papal backing assumed the throne of Sicily. After this the Templars aligned firmly with the **Capetian** Angevin power.

## Mansourah

Al-Mansourah was a town in the Nile Delta in Egypt, some way inland. The army of the **Fifth Crusade** came to a halt near there in 1221 when they were trapped by the flooding river, having foolishly advanced during the season of the annual inundation, and when **Muslim** troops cut off their escape. In 1250 Mansourah became the scene of a significant Muslim victory during the **Seventh Crusade**.

The Crusaders' second defeat at Mansourah owed much to the rashness of the Christian commander **Robert, Count of Artois** and something to the cunning of the **Mameluk** commander **Baybars**. King **Louis IX** and his army moved out from the captured **Damietta**, moving south towards Cairo. The cavalry vanguard was led by the Templars under **Guillaume de Sonnac**, with other knights under the king's brother Robert of Artois, and an English contingent under **William Longespee**. They achieved initial success and the Count of Artois was all for riding into Mansourah to gain the glory of taking the town before the main army could cross the river to link up with them. The Templars (according to the version of events recorded by **Matthew Paris**) counselled against it, as did **William Longespee**, whereon the Count mocked them and accused them of treachery and cowardice.[238] Thus goaded, against their better judgement they followed him into the town, where hundreds of waiting Mameluks set them upon from the side street. Trapped in the narrow alleys by beams thrown down from the rooftops, the **knights** were slaughtered. **Jean de Joinville** reported the same sorry outcome in his account of the Crusade. However he claimed that the Templars, rather than protesting the Count's rash advance, had been keen to assert their position at the fore of the Crusader cavalry.[239]

Guillaume de Sonnac lost an eye. Only he and one other Templar survived out of nearly 300 and Longespee and the Count of Artois were both killed. King Louis arrived in time to drive the Mameluks back in to the town after a fierce battle, but too late to do anything for those his brother has led to their deaths. In the fighting that raged over the following days the Crusader camp was assailed with Greek fire and a hail of arrows. Guillaume de Sonnac lost his other eye and then was killed amid the burning stockades. Disaster overcame the Christians when the Mameluks cut their supply line with Damietta by transporting a prefabricated fleet of warships to the river across the desert. Hunger and disease eventually took a toll in the Crusaders. They were forced to attempt to withdraw, although many, including Louis (who had refused to abandon his army) were captured.

## Manuel I Comnenus (1118–80)

Manuel I Comnenus was a **Byzantine** Emperor who managed to restore some of the Empire's prestige during his eventful reign. He was the younger son but designated heir of the Emperor **John II**, and succeeded in 1143. Manuel met **Louis VII** of **France** and **Conrad III** of **Germany**, and managed the passage of the **Second Crusade** through Byzantium. (He probably met the Templars who came ahead of Louis VII to negotiate passage.) Manuel generally pursued a pro-western policy, but relations were somewhat strained at this time as the rapacious armies passed through the Byzantine Empire.

In 1156, **Reynald de Chatillon**, the lord of **Antioch**, one of the Crusaders who remained behind, took it upon himself to conduct a barbaric raid against **Cyprus**. Manuel responded to this attack on Byzantine territory by taking his army towards Antioch, punishing Reynald's **Armenian** allies along the way, and bringing Cilicia under his control. Reynald made a grovelling submission before the Emperor, after which Manuel rode in triumph into Antioch, restoring Byzantine hegemony. In 1161 Manuel married Maria of Antioch, stepdaughter of Reynald and cousin of **Amalric I, King of Jerusalem**. Manuel established good relations with Amalric (thanks in part to the diplomacy of **William of Tyre**), funding some restorations and new mosaic works in Bethlehem and in the **Holy Sepulchre**, and securing the rights of the Greek clergy to operate there as well as the **Latin**. In 1168 Manuel allied with Amalric for a combined assault on **Egypt**, for which the Greeks provided a substantial fleet. The campaign proved fruitless, in the event. Manual has been criticised for concentrating on far-flung campaigns in Egypt, Armenian Cilicia and southern Italy, and neglecting to deal with the Turks in Anatolia. While Manuel was distracted, the Turkish leader Kilij Arslan II, based at Konya, was consolidating his power and building up the Turkish war machine. In 1179 Manuel did bring an army against the Turks. However Kilij Arslan sprung an ambush in the mountains, inflicting a grievous blow on the Manuel's forces at Myriocephalum, ending any Byzantine hope of regaining the Anatolian hinterland. To the Greeks it was the greatest calamity since Manzikert.

Internal struggles followed Manuel's death, and **Andronicus Comnenus** soon ascended to power, murdering many of Manuel's relations and former supporters in the process. His reign would prove disastrous for relations between Byzantium and the **Franks**.

## Manuel I, King of Portugal (1469–1521)

Manuel (or Manoel) I was a King of **Portugal** and a **Grand Master** of the **Knights of Christ**. He succeeded to the crown in 1495. Like Prince **Henry the Navigator**, he was a patron of maritime explorers, and including the voyage of **Vasco da Gama**, a fellow Knight of Christ. Manuel also gave his name to the flamboyant late gothic of architecture popular in Portugal called the **Manueline** style. Following the lead of zealously **Catholic** Spain, and in order to secure marriage to a Spanish princess, Manuel ordered the expulsion or conversion to Christianity of all of Portugal's **Jews**. Some were prevented from leaving and forced into conversion.

## Manueline Architecture

Manueline architecture is an ornate and exotic late **gothic** style of building, predominant in Portugal in the early 1500s. It was named after King **Manuel I** of Portugal. The extension of the Convento de Cristo in **Tomar** is a good example, and bears a certain similarity to the style of the slightly earlier **Rosslyn Chapel in Scotland**. The style contrasts to the relatively austere **round church** of the older Templar Convento. The Manueline style became a trademark of the **Knights of Christ**, who had become great mariners. Manueline decoration often incorporates nautical and navigational motifs such as roped and astrolabes. The Order of Christ's cross is also often incorporated into the rich carving. Other buildings in the style include the Jerónimos Monastery and the Belém Tower in Lisbon.

## Marguerite of Provence (Queen of France) (1221–95)

Marguerite was one of the famously beautiful daughters of Count Raymond Bérenger V of Provence. She was married to **Louis IX** of France. Her three sisters were married to **Henry III** of **England**, to his brother **Richard of Cornwall**, and to **Charles of Anjou**. Queen Marguerite accompanied Louis on the **Seventh Crusade**, remaining at **Damietta** when he passed south to **Mansourah**. After Louis was capture by the **Mameluks,** Marguerite collected his ransom, and persuaded the Italian merchant fleets not to desert the **Crusaders**. She accompanied Louis and the remains of his army to the **Holy Land**, and there gave birth to a son, (one of a total of eleven children that she bore him between 1243 and 1260).

## Marie of Champagne (1145–98)

Marie of Champagne was one of the two daughters of **Louis VII** of **France** and **Eleanor of Aquitaine**. By her mother she was half sister of **Richard the**

Lionheart and **King John**, and by her father half sister of **Philip II Augustus**. She was married in 1164 to **Henry I, Count of Champagne**. She was the mother of **Henry II, Count of Champagne** who became titular King of **Jerusalem**. Maria ruled Champagne as regent during her husband's absence in the **Holy Land**, and after his death, while her sons were infants. She was a patron of the arts including of the poet **Chretien de Troyes** who later wrote one of the earliest **Holy Grail** Romances. She is also said to have been sympathetic to **Cathar** ideas.

## Maritime Republics

The Marine Republics, during the **Crusading** era, were the self-governing or semi-self-governing Italian city-states of **Venice**, Genoa, **Amalfi** and **Pisa**. These vied for economic dominance in the Eastern Mediterranean, trading with **Byzantium**, the **Levant** and **Egypt**. Their interests sometimes coincided with those of the Crusaders and sometimes went against them.

## Maronites

Maronites are a Christian sect living in the Middle East, speaking Arabic, with Aramaic as their sacred language. They are mostly found in Lebanon, and are in communion with the Roman **Catholic** Church. They were originally the followers of fourth/fifth century hermit from **Antioch** called St Maron. They established mountain communities in Lebanon, safe from Monophysite, **Byzantine** and **Arab** persecution. They were allies of the **Crusaders** during the **Frankish** rule and suffered persecution from the **Mameluks** once the Franks were expelled from the region. It is possible that in the mean time some Maronites or half Maronites may have joined the Templars, or served as **Turkopoles**.

## Married Brothers

The Rule of the Templars made provision for married men to join the Order. However these *fratres conjugati* were technically not supposed to wear the white habit of a full brother, and their wives were supposedly expected to live apart, also having taken religious vows. Generally married brothers (who could only join with their wives' consent) donated all their property to the order, with provisions made for their wives. Motivation for joining in this capacity might be to benefit the soul, and to ensure the provision of welfare in old age. Whether wives became **sisters of the Order** is not always clear, but there is some evidence that they did. One prominent married brother was Hugh de Bourbouton, a noble who joined the Preceptory of Richerenches in 1139, and who eventually became **Preceptor**. He, as he put it, surrendered himself to the Order, along with his wife and his son Nicolas, who also became a Templar in the course of time.

## Marseille

Marseille is a port city in the south of **France**. In 1212 Roncelin, Count of Marseille, granted the Templar **Master** of Provence Deodat de Brissac, the right to operate ships from the harbour. The Templars and Hospitallers subsequently used the port to transport troops, supplies and pilgrims to the **Holy Land**. However, the merchants of the port grew jealous of the Military Orders' expanding share in this market, and in 1233 the consuls of Marseille restricted the Templars to two annual sailings, at Easter and in August.

## Marshal

The Marshal of the Knights Templar was an important dignitary, responsible for the military side of the Order's activities. Known Marshals include:

| | |
|---|---|
| Hugues de Quilioco | 1154 |
| Robert Franiel | 1186 |
| **Jacques de Mailly** | 1187 |
| Geoffroy Morin | 1188 |
| Adam | 1198 |
| Guillaume d'Arguillières | 1201 |
| Hugues de Montlaur | 1244 |
| **Reynald de Vichiers** | 1250 |
| **Hugues de Jouy** | 1252 |
| Étienne de Saisi | 1260 |
| Guillaume de Molay | 1262 |
| Gimblard | 1270 |
| Guy de Foresta (Forêt) | 1277 |
| **Pierre de Sevrey** | 1291 |
| Barthélémy | 1302 |
| **Ayme d'Oselier** | 1309 |

## Martim Martins (thirteenth century)

Martim Martins was Master of the Knights Templar in **Portugal**, and a childhood friend of King Sancho II (1223–45). He supported Sancho when Sancho's brother Alfonso of Boulogne led a revolt. Despite this the revolt was successful. Sancho was overthrown, causing the Templars' position in the realm to suffer for a time.

## Martin IV (Pope) (1210–1285)

Born Simon de Brion, Martin IV was a French pope. In support of **Charles of Anjou**, he called a crusade against sicilian rebels and their supporter, Peter III of Aragon. Pope Martin ordered funds held in the Paris Temple, intended for the Holy Land, to be diverted to this cause.

## Martyrdom

A martyr is one who suffers persecution and/or dies for their religious beliefs. Those who share the martyr's faith will tend to believe that their spirit is richly rewarded in the afterlife. In the Christian tradition, to be a martyr generally meant refusing to give up the faith in the face of oppression and torture by pagans. Many Christian **saints** were also martyrs, but not all martyrs were elevated to sainthood. Martyrs revered by the early church included St Stephen (the first martyr, who was stoned to death). **St Catherine of Alexandria**, and **St Euphemia** were female martyrs revered by the Templars. A martyr, originally, could not be one who harmed others, his or her courage had to manifest in peaceful ways according with the teachings of **Christ** and following his example of sacrifice. Only during the **Crusades** was this idea temporarily suspended, so that **knights of Christ** who died in battle could be considered martyrs. Christians spoke of their martyrs receiving crowns in heaven.

The Templars were described by the commentator Orderic Vitalis as admirable knights who devote themselves to the physical and spiritual service of God, who rejected all things of this world and faced martyrdom daily. Often the Templars who died bravely in the **Holy Land** (such as **Jacquelyn de Mailly**) were hailed as particularly blessed martyrs. Perhaps those who perished in dungeons in Europe (like **William de la More**) or at the stake (like **Jacques de Molay**) while defending the Order's innocence and orthodoxy would be recognised as Christian martyrs if they had been persecuted by any agency other than the Church itself.

## Maryculter

Maryculter was a Templar **Preceptory** near Aberdeen in **Scotland**, comprising about 8,000 acres, donated to the Order in the late twelfth century by William 'the Lion' of Scotland. It is the setting for a ghost story relating to the Order, that concerning **Godfrey Wedderburn**, who may or may not have actually existed. The last historical Preceptor of Maryculter, William Middleton, was one of only two Templars arrested and tried in Scotland (the other being Walter Clifton of **Balantradoch**).

## Mary Magdalene (AD first century)

Mary Magdalene was a female follower of **Jesus Christ**, and one of the closer disciples to him outside the twelve. According to the gospels, Christ cast out of her seven **demons** (Luke 8: 1–3). She was also present at the crucifixion, and afterwards had a part in preparing Christ's body for burial, along with **Joseph of Arimathea**. The gospels all name her as the one who discovered the empty tomb of Christ, and who told the disciples of it, also mentioning encounters with angels. The Gospel of John (20:15–17) has it that Mary was the first one to whom the risen Christ appeared.

In 591, Pope Gregory the Great identified the Magdalene with Mary the sister of Martha and Lazarus of Bethany, who anointed Christ's feet, and whom Jesus defended from the disciples' criticism (John 11: 2, 12: 2–8). He identified her as the woman who was a sinner. Bede, likewise, identified her with the unnamed woman 'taken in adultery' whom Jesus rescued from stoning (John 8: 3–11). The identification was somewhat supported by Mary's apparent exorcism of demons, which could be interpreted metaphorically. This became the standard medieval **Catholic** opinion, whereas the Greek Orthodox teaching was that Mary Magdalene, the unnamed adulteress and Mary of Bethany were different women.

There are a few passages in **Gnostic** gospels (including the 'Gospel of Philip', discovered at **Nag Hammadi**) that show a closer relationship between Jesus and the Magdalene and imply a jealous hostility towards her on the part of St Peter and others. It was perhaps in the interest of the **Popes** who claimed to derive their authority from St Peter (and who excluded women from the clergy) to downplay Mary Magdalene's significance. However Mary's relationship with Christ is presented as close and loving even in a **Dominican** source, the Golden Legend. She was honoured as one of the foremost saints. During the Crusades Gerard of Nazareth argued in favour of the Catholic identification against the Greek. Gerard's position supported the veneration of Mary Magdalene at Bethany. The **Jacobites** (Syrian Orthodox) Christians, maintained a church in **Jerusalem** which they claimed stood on the site of Simon the Leper, where (on another occasion, it seems) Mary had anointed the feet of Christ. They preserved some of her hair as a **holy relic**.

The medieval Catholic idea of Mary Magdalene as a sinner redeemed by Christ was a useful archetype. It provided a positive model for those who had strayed from the light and hoped to return. This was how the Templars viewed her. Those receiving absolution in **Chapter** would hear the words 'And I pray God and ask him, through his mercy, to pardon your sins, as he pardoned them to St Mary Magdalene.' Magdalon, Mary's supposed birthplace, was in the region of Galilee safeguarded by the Templar castle of **Saphet**. The Eastern Church believed that Mary Magdalene had been buried at Ephesus in Anatolia. A separate tradition associated her with southern **France**. The Golden Legend (which also records that Mary may originally have been betrothed to **John the Evangelist**) tells of her miraculous deliverance by boat to **Marseilles** with Sts Lazarus and Maximin, where they preached, converted and worked miracles. It has her spending her final thirty years as a **hermit** and being daily lifted up by angels to be sustained by heavenly foods. (Another curious legend went that after the Crucifixion, Mary had visited the Emperor Tiberius, and that after miraculously making an egg turn red she had inspired him to punish those responsible for ordering Christ's death.) Rival shrines of the Magdalene existed in

Aix-en-Provence and **Vezelay**, the latter claiming that her relics had been transplanted from the former in 771. Alternative relics were later discovered near Aix (at Saint-Maximin-la-Saint-Baume), and her cult reverted to its supposed original locale. **Louis IX** and **Jean de Joinville** visited her supposed Provencal sepulchre on their return from the **Seventh Crusade**, and also looked at the mountain cave where she was said to have lived.[240]

Mary Magdalene was mentioned in the Templars' **Rule** among a number of other saints whose feasts the brethren were to observe and her image appears among the frescoes of their church at **San Bevignate**. She was occasionally mentioned during the trials, in the context of absolution. A **conspiracy theory** holds that the Templars, exploring in Jerusalem, may have uncovered proof that Jesus and Mary Magdalene were married, that they used this knowledge to blackmail the Pope, and that this secret somehow both secured the Order's sudden rise to power and provoked its sudden destruction. Though there is no proof of this, there is some evidence that the **Cathars** held unorthodox views on the issue.

## Mary, The Blessed Virgin

The Blessed Mary, (or the Madonna) the mother of **Jesus Christ**, was a figure held in deep reverence by Medieval Christians, Roman **Catholic** and Eastern Orthodox alike. St **Bernard of Clairvaux** was an especial devotee of hers in **France**, regarding her as a channel of God's grace. She was an important figure for the **Crusaders**, and the **Franks** of the **Kingdom of Jerusalem**. **Pilgrims** visited the rebuilt shrine containing her tomb in the Kidron Valley, which also became the preferred place of burial for the Queens of Jerusalem, notably **Melisende**.

The Templars were also dedicated to the Blessed Mary, and told initiates that in her honour the Order was founded and in her honour it would end when God pleased. Many of their churches were dedicated to her. The Biblical Mary by that time had been transmogrified into a semi-divine and wholly pure being, sometimes called the Queen of Heaven and the Mother of God. The Eastern Church used the term Theotokos, or 'God bearer'. St Jerome advanced the article of faith that Mary had remained perpetually a virgin, despite there being several Biblical references to Jesus' siblings (e.g. Luke 8:20). It also became a Catholic doctrine that Mary herself was immaculately conceived (although this was still an unresolved issue in the thirteenth century). Many also held that Mary, like Christ, was assumed, bodily, into Heaven. The Eastern Orthodox equivalent of this doctrine was the Dormition of the Theotokos, holding that she died and that her body was taken up three days afterwards. (Byzantine representations of the event showed Christ holding Mary's soul in the form of a child above her body, one such appears in the Psalter of **Melisende**.) It was believed to have taken place on Mount **Zion** in **Jerusalem**. As late as 1950 Pope Pius XII defined the Assumption as dogma.

Mary was believed to have the power to intercede with Christ on behalf of those who prayed to her. Most churches contained a statue or icon of the Madonna and Child, while most cathedrals had special 'lady chapels' devoted to her. The **Teutonic Knights**, meanwhile, were also especially devoted to the Virgin Mary, who was their foremost patron saint. They dedicated their Baltic conquests to her and turned her into an unlikely war-goddess. The cult of Mary occasionally came under criticism for being close to **idolatry**. It was condemned by the **Cathars**, for example, and by the later Protestants.

## Mas Deu

Mas Deu was a major Templar Preceptory in Rousillon (French Catalonia). Much of it was destroyed during the Second World War, though a tower and a ruined chapel survive. The last Preceptor of Mas Dieu was **Ramon sa Guardia**, who led the Templars resistance in **Aragon** and was besieged for a year at the castle of **Miravet**.

## Mass

Mass was the Christian Church service considered to be spiritually nourishing (a sacrament conveying divine Grace). It involved the celebration of the Eucharist (thanks giving), the symbolic re-enactment of the Last Supper, where **Christ** shared the bread and wine with his disciples, saying to do it in remembrance of him, for it was his body and his blood. The Roman **Catholic** view, especially after the **Fourth Lateran Council** formalised the doctrine of transubstantiation, was that the bread and wine transformed invisibly (in the hands of the presiding **priest**) into the actual body and blood of Christ. The anti-materialist **Cathars** had obviously rejected such a view. They asked how divinity could be present in substances that entered the body and came to a foul end. The Protestants would later re-evaluate the Eucharist as a symbolic affair, without a literal transformation of substance taking place. In medieval times the Roman Catholic mass was performed in **Latin**, the language of the Church. One of the **accusations** against the Knights Templar was that their priests omitted certain words from the mass, thus invalidating the sacrament. This accusation was included, as Malcolm Barber interpreted it, to make it seem as though the Templars had been defrauding their patrons who donated to the order for the sake of their departed kin, who were presumed to benefit on the other side from the prayers said by monks. Unlike other monastic Orders, the Templars did not have a standard liturgy in their European chapels, tending to base the rites of each newly founded Templar community on those of the nearest ecclesiastical institution.

## Master of the Temple

(1) At first the overall leader of the Knights Templar was known as the Master. St **Bernard of Clairvaux** addressed **Hugues de Payens** as the 'Master of the Chivalry of Christ'. Later the overall leader became known as the **Grand Master**, while the heads of individual houses of the Order (**Preceptories**) became known as Masters. The Masters of whole **provinces** were sometimes called **Grand Preceptors**.

(2) In **England**, after the **suppression** of the Knights Templar, the clergyman attached to **Temple Church, London** (in its capacity as a 'Royal Peculiar' serving the **Inner** and **Middle Temple**) became known as the 'Master of the Temple'. Under the Templars, such a priest would probably have been called the *Custos*.

## Master of the Temple in England

The Knights Templar in **England** were managed by the **Grand Preceptor** or **Master** of England. The holder of this post was also the senior Templars in the British Isles. He was based at the **New Temple, London**. The known Masters of the Knights Templar in England were:

| Master of England | Period (known to be presiding) |
|---|---|
| Hugh of Argentin | 1140–50 |
| Osto | 1150–5 |
| **Richard de Hastings** | 1155–64 |
| Geoffrey fitz-Stephen | 1180–5 |
| William de Newham | 1185–1200 |
| Aymer St Mawer * | 1200–18 |
| **Alan Martel** | 1218–28 |
| Robert de Dandford | 1219–48 |
| **Amadeus de Morestello** | 1259–60 |
| Ambesard | 1264–73 |
| **Guy de Foresta** | 1273–4 |
| Robert de Turville | 1276–90 |
| Guy de Foresta | 1291–5 |
| **Brian de Jay** | 1296–8 |
| **William de la More** | 1298–1312 |

*Aymer de Mawer is referred to as brother Aymeric in the **Magna Carta**. Some accounts mention Humbert de Pairaud as 'Master of England' presumably because he presided over initiations at the London Temple. However Humbert seems to have been the **Visitor** of the Order, responsible for the running of the Order in the West.

## Matilda of Boulogne (1105–52)

Matilda, Countess of Boulogne (Queen Matilda of **England**, not to be confused with her contemporary 'Empress' **Matilda**) was the wife of King **Stephen** of England, the Daughter of Eustace III of Boulogne and the niece of **Godfroi de Bouillon** and **Baldwin I** of **Jerusalem**. Perhaps influenced by her family association to the **Holy Land**, she bestowed upon the Templars estates including **Cressing** in Essex in 1131. She also donated land at Cowley in Oxfordshire to the Order.

## Matilda, the Empress (1101–67)

Also known as Maud, Matilda was the daughter and designated heiress of **Henry I** of **England**. Via her mother, Maud of Scotland, Matilda restored the Anglo-Saxon bloodline to the English throne (though Matilda herself only spoke French, **Latin** and German, thus was never seen as very English). She was known as Empress on account of her first marriage in 1114 to the short-lived **Holy Roman Emperor** Henry V. She was married to Geoffrey Plantagenet, the son of **Fulk V, Count of Anjou**, in 1127 and thereafter became the mother of the future **Henry II** of England. Henry I made the English barons swear allegiance to Matilda as his successor. However, on the King's death in 1135, Matilda was challenged for the throne by her cousin, **Stephen**, the son of **Stephen of Blois**. Stephen and his supporters did not like the idea of a regnant queen. There ensued a civil war, known as the 'anarchy'. Matilda's main champion was Robert, Earl of Gloucester.

Both the Empress Matilda, King Stephen and their supporters donated land to the Templars, as did Stephen's queen consort, **Matilda of Boulogne**. The Empress donated grazing rites in Shotover Forest. The civil wars were ended when Matilda agreed to renounce the throne on condition that her son **Henry II** was named as Stephen's heir. She spent her last days in Rouen in **France**.

## Matthew Paris (died 1259)

Brother Matthew Paris was a monk at St Albans Abbey, during the reign of **Henry III** of **England**, who left an extensive account of his time. Many of his entries relate to local events. He was also well informed of wider happenings, and included details of events in Europe and beyond, including the **Seventh Crusade**, led by **Louis IX**. He related the acrimonious feud between the Emperor **Frederick II** and the **Pope**, including an attempt by the Pope to poison the Emperor. Paris evinces a grudging admiration for the Emperor and is not always favourable towards the Pope, who was resented for demanding money and seen as corrupt. Paris recorded reports of the **Mongols** (Tartars) and their barbaric deeds. He also recorded the arrival at Westminster of Templars and **Hospitallers** bringing a vial of **Christ**'s blood to be enshrined there. Paris was sometimes critical of the **Military Orders**' conduct in the

**Holy Land,** however. His chronicle is enlivened by the wit of the opinion-ated author and by the characterful illustrations, also by Paris's hand. The many illustrations include Maps of the Orient with camels, religious and battle scenes, Louis IX **taking the cross** on his sickbed, heraldry and banners, including the Templars' **Beauseant,** and an image of two Templars on one horse, reflecting the design on the Order's **seal.**[241]

## Mazères

The Templar chapel of Mazères is in Haute Garonne, southern **France.** It was a dependency of **Montsaunes.** The chapel stands intact but derelict. It is aus-tere and almost windowless, but for a few narrow Romanesque windows in the apse where the altar would have been.

## Mecca

Mecca is the holiest city in the religion of **Islam.** Muslims are expected to make at least one pilgrimage there in their lifetime to process around a pre-Islamic, cube-shaped shrine called the Ka ba. During the **Crusading** era, **Reynald de Chatillon** earned the outrage of the Muslim world by raiding ships taking pil-grims making the Hajj to Mecca on the Red Sea.

## Melisende, Queen of Jerusalem (1105–61)

Melisende of **Jerusalem** was the eldest daughter of **Baldwin II** and the **Armenian** princess Morphia. For many years she reigned as Queen in Jerusalem, earning the respect and support of many, including prominent clerics. Her father invited **Fulk V, Count of Anjou** to Jerusalem in order to marry Melisende, having promised that Fulk would thus become heir to the kingdom. As the old king lay dying, however, he decided not to leave care of the realm exclusively to Fulk but to Melisende and their infant son Baldwin (**Baldwin III**) as well.[242] Fulk and Melisende were crowned in 1131. Another son, Amalric (**Amalric I**) followed. Melisende seemed to attract the particu-lar loyalty of barons disaffected with her husband, and her sympathies were evidently with Hugh II of **Jaffa,** even after his rebellion. She reserved her wrath for those nobles whom she blamed for turning the King against Hugh, her second cousin, to the extent that they considered it dangerous to appear at court. Later it seems she and Fulk were reconciled, and in his final years he was, as **William of Tyre** put it, 'uxorious', taking no decisions without her consent. After Fulk's death in 1143 Melisende reigned either in her own right or as regent for their oldest son, supported by the Constable, Manasses of Hierges. Melisende was a supporter of the arts and the Church, richly endowing the convent of Bethany where her sister Jovita was abbess. She was also the probable patron of an exquisite manuscript known as the Melisende Psalter, preserved in the British Library and probably produced in the **Holy Sepulchre**. Images in the psalter show a mixture of **Byzantine** and western styles, and include representations of **Mary Magdalene**.

Melisende had a taste for power, which she was reluctant to yield up to her son when he came of age, considering herself rightfully queen and her father's intended heiress. Her son Baldwin grew more and more impatient to assume the reins of government. Baldwin eventually extracted the right to a solo coronation and a share of the kingdom, but Melisende maintained control of Jerusalem and Nablus. In around 1152, Baldwin invaded his mother's territory, expelling Manasses, and besieging the Queen in the **Citadel of David**. Melisende agreed to surrender control of Jerusalem but retained Nablus. This was the first major outbreak of court factionalism among the Franks that the Templars in the East had to deal with. Initially **André de Montbard** may have favoured Melisende; however, the order retained its favoured position after Baldwin had achieved power. Afterwards Melisende and Baldwin likewise seem to have been reconciled. Melisende was an able ruler, whom William of Tyre wrote of with general approbation, in contrast to her sister Alice of Antioch, whom he condemned in no uncertain terms.

## Melrose Abbey

Melrose Abbey, near Edinburgh, was one of the earliest **Cistercian** foundations in **Scotland**. It survives in magnificent ruins. Melrose was donated to the monks by King **David I**, who also invited the Knights Templar into the kingdom. (An older, **Celtic** Christian monastery of Melrose had existed nearby since c. 650, and was associated with St Cuthbert.) The first Cistercians arrived from Rievaulx, Yorkshire, in 1136, and founded the new Melrose.[243] Waltheof, the King's stepson, became one of the first Abbots. His body was reputed never to have decayed, and he was afterwards revered as a **saint**. Melrose, meanwhile, became the centre of an extensive estate. Most of the standing ruins postdate an attack on the Abbey by the soldiers of Richard II of **England** in about 1385. A contrite Richard sponsored the rebuilding, which carried on for over a century. Melrose Abbey is reputedly the burial place of the heart of King **Robert the Bruce**. Grave slabs have also been found at Melrose, including some carved with the sword and elongated **Calvary cross** often associated with Templar burials.

## Menelik I (c. 900 BC?)

Menelik I was a prince of **Ethiopia**. He was the purported product of the assignation in **Jerusalem** between King **Solomon** and the Queen of **Sheba**, whom the lore claims as an Ethiopian Queen called Makida. The *Kebra Nagast* (Glory of Kings), which had been written down by the thirteenth century, describes how at the age of the age of twenty, Menelik visited Jerusalem, and with the blessing of the priests stole the **Ark of the Covenant** away to Ethiopia. Menelik was the first Emperor of the Solomonic dynasty. The Solomonic tradition survived into the modern age, only ending with the death of Haile Selassie in 1975.

## Merger Scheme (scheme to merge the Military Orders)

The scheme to merge the two leading **Military Orders** had been mooted for some time even before the loss of the **Holy Land**. It seems **Louis IX** had favoured a merger of the Orders and **Raymond Lull** saw such a merger as vital for the future of the **Crusades**. The rivalry, and sometimes hostility between the Templars and **Hospitallers** was seen as hampering the Christian cause, as well as duplicating expenses. The Call for the merger of the Orders grew louder after the fall of **Acre**. To a degree it could have been a ploy to secure **Capetian** control over the proposed new Order, and to deflect blame for the collapse of the **Kingdom of Jerusalem** onto the Military Orders. Pope **Clement V** summoned from Cyprus the **Grand Masters** of the two Orders affected by the proposal in 1306. Discussions were held in April 1307. **Fulk de Villaret** withheld his opinion. **Jacques de Molay** conceded that the proposal had some potential advantages, but drawbacks too, for sometimes the competition between the Orders was productive. In the event the Templars were formally suppressed in 1312 at the **Council of Vienne**, and the Papal Bull *Ad Providam* transferred their goods, buildings and lands in most of Europe to the Knights Hospitaller (a transfer achieved after the Hospitallers paid extensive 'expenses' to the French monarchy). Some former Templars may have found their way into the Order of the Hospital at the same time, so in some sense the merger of the Orders was achieved.

## Merlan

The Templar house at Merlan was said to house a harsh prison operated by the Templars and is spoken of in several testimonies at the trials. It was said to be a terrible place from which no one came out, and where no one was able to live long. Supposedly fear of being put in this prison caused the Templars to go along with the things mentioned in the **accusations against the Order**.

## Merovingians

The Merovingians were the enigmatic rulers of a shifting **Frankish** kingdom centred on **France**. They held sway from the fifth to eighth century AD. They were originally warlike leaders and were known as the 'long haired kings.' They were descended from one Merovetch, the grandfather of the king who brought the dynasty to real prominence, Clovis I (466–511) who defeated the Romans and other tribes including the Visigoths of Toulouse. It was also he who adopted **Catholic** Christianity. Owing to the custom of dividing legacies between sons, there were often several kings at a time in the Merovingian realm, though sometimes-fratricidal civil wars brought the realm under single leadership. The kings eventually lost power to the chief officials, the Mayors of the Palace, rather as the **Fatimid** Caliphs would to their Viziers. At length they became little more than figureheads. One such Mayor was Charles Martel, whose victory over invading **Moors** at the battle of Tours halted **Islam**'s expansion into Europe. Martel's son Pepin (known as Pepin the Short) became the first of the Carolingian kings, with Papal support. Pepin deposed the last Merovingian king, Childeric III (died *c.* 754). Childeric was shaven of his long hair and banished to a monastery. Thereafter the Merovingians were largely consigned to history.

There is little reason to think the Knights Templar were interested in a Merovingian restoration, even accepting the unlikely scenario of the line secretly surviving from **Dagobert II**. The Merovingians never claimed descent from **Jesus Christ** and **Mary Magdalene**. There was a legend, however, attributing the dynasty with an equally outlandish origin. The mother of Merovetch, already pregnant by his father King Clodio, went swimming in the sea and was re-impregnated by a sea monster 'like a Quinotaur', thus Merovetch was born of two fathers and with magical attributes. A certain aura continued to surround these early kings. The tomb of Childeric I (Father of Clovis I) was discovered in 1651. Its treasures, now lost, included coins, jewellery, a gold bull's head and many small gold bees. Later **Napoleon** would have gold bees sewn into his robes when he had himself crowned Emperor, linking himself to a mythical past.

## Metz

The town of Metz is located in the Lorraine in Eastern **France**, near the German border. Its association with the **Crusades** began inauspiciously when armed bands comprising part of the **First Crusade** attacked the town's **Jewish** inhabitants. There is a Templar chapel surviving at Metz.

## Michael VIII Palaeologus (1224–82)

Michael VIII Palaeologus was the **Byzantine Emperor** who in 1261 liberated **Constantinople** and effectively ended the **Latin** Empire that had been centred there since the **Fourth Crusade**. He allied with Genoa, granting its merchants duty-free trading rights throughout his realm in exchange for their support, and he successfully resisted the invading forces of **Charles of Anjou**.

## Michael the Syrian (1126–99)

Michael the Syrian was a native of the **Holy Land** who chronicled the **Crusades** from an Eastern Christian perspective. He was the **Jacobite (Syrian Christian) Patriarch** of **Antioch** from 1166. He gave an ambiguous account of the **foundation** and statutes of the Templars.

According to Michael the Syrian, **Hugues de Payens** came east intending to remain as a monk, which he did after helping in the King's wars for three years. The King persuaded Hugues and his thirty companions to become guardians of the road. Hugh and his brethren lived without wives, possessions or bathing. Kings and princes joined their spiritual fraternity. Candidate Templars served a year on probation before being admitted. After that anyone who took the vows and fell short of their promises was killed by the sword without mercy. The Templars said forty masses for their dead and gave alms to forty paupers for forty days in their name. Any dead brother who was found to have kept secrets or held back personal possessions from the Order was denied burial. They were friendly and charitable to Christians, looked after **Pilgrims** and buried any who died. The Masters distributed a tenth of the Order's goods (such as bread corn and wine) to the poor. Although the Templars' original task was escorting pilgrims, they participated in battles with the **Turks**, built **castles**, having grown in numbers and wealth, while remaining individually poor and detached from things.

## Milicia Dei

*Milicia Dei* (Army of God) was a **Papal bull** issued by Eugenius III in April 1145, confirming the Templars' right to recruit their own priests, build their own **churches** and bury their dead in their churchyards. It mentioned how mingling with men and meeting women could imperil the souls of religious brethren.

## Military Orders

The Military Orders were the brotherhoods of warrior monks, which were recognised by the **Catholic** Church at the time of the **Crusades**. Most were in theory committed to **Holy War** against the enemies of Christianity, either in the **Holy Land**, on the frontiers of north-eastern Europe (the **Baltic Crusade**) or in Spain (the *Reconquista*). The most significant Military Orders were the Templars and **Hospitallers**, who were involved in fighting to defend **Jerusalem** and the **pilgrims** venturing there. Offshoot orders included the **Order of St Lazarus**, which cared for **lepers**, and the **Teutonic Knights**, a German Order. Some new Military Orders were created in **Iberia** after the suppression of the Templars, for example the **Knights of Christ**. The orders of Avis and **Calatrava** were also enriched.

## Milites Templi

*Milites Templi* (Soldiers of the Temple) was a **Papal bull** issued in March 1144. It described the Templars as the agents of God's liberation of the eastern church, willing to die defending pilgrims from the attacks of pagans. It awarded indulgences to patrons who donated to the Templars and also permitted the Order to perform the **Mass** even in regions placed under **interdict** when collecting donations of its cause there. The bull was issued during the brief papacy of **Celestine II**.

## Militi Templi Scotia

The *Militi Templi Scotia* (Scottish Knights Templar) is a Scottish **Neo-Templar** organization. Henry Lincoln, one of the authors of *The Holy Blood and the Holy Grail* has apparently been invested as an honorary member. They may be loosely affiliated to **OSMTH**.

## Miravet

Miravet was a Templar **castle** in **Aragon**. Its ruins still stand in good condition. The original **Moorish** castle was captured by Ramon Berenguer IV, Count of Barcelona, in 1153, and given to the Templars. The Templars subsequently enlarged and strengthened the castle. In early 1308 King **James II** of Aragon besieged the Templars there, led by **Ramon sa Guardia**, the Preceptor of **Mas Deu**. Ramon sa Guardia defended the castle for nearly a year, with sixty or seventy companions, all the while protesting the Order's innocence and defending its honour.

## Mongols

The Mongols (sometimes known in Europe as the Tartars) were a nation of conquerors who burst into the Middle East and Eastern Europe in the mid-thirteenth century. Stocky and broad-faced, they were mostly pagans guided by shamans, but their subjects included Buddhists and Nestorian Christians (followers of a heretical patriarch of Constantinople who had been expelled and whose teachings had taken hold in the East). The Mongols' dwellings were portable domed tents made of felt. Their drink was kousmiss, fermented mares' milk. They began as a disparate group of pastoral nomads, divided into tribes caught in a cycle of tribal wars and blood feuds in the steppes of Central-East Asia. Genghis Khan changed this, as he was highly successful at defeating rival warlords and enlisting their warriors in his own war band. He became convinced of his people's manifest destiny to rule the world. By 1206 he had built the nation of Mongolia and amassed a vast army based on mounted archers. Known as the horde, this cavalry force attacked in two waves, the first only killing, the second harvesting the plunder and enslaving any survivors. Their weapons were speed, organisation, discipline and an apparent imperviousness to suffering, as well as deceit, intimidation and ruthlessness. Genghis Khan conquered a large part of China and much of Asia besides. The Mongols continued to travel over extraordinary distances, enlisting **Turkic** warriors into their horde and offering every civilization they encountered the choice of surrender or death.

The **Khoresmian** Turks were conquered by the Mongols, having provoked the Khan's fury by killing his envoys. The Mongol hordes pressed towards

Persia. One and a half million Khoresmians were slaughtered according to one estimate. Other Khoresmians were assimilated, while others were displaced, and became bandits or mercenaries – it was these that sacked **Jerusalem** in 1244. The Mongols themselves were not far behind, and were already threatening Mesopotamia. Another prong of the Mongol advance, meanwhile, having subdued Russia, had struck into Eastern Europe, reaching Poland and Hungary. It was met by a Christian force, including a handful of Templars, at **Liegnitz** in 1241. The Christians were annihilated. Only the timely death of Ogedai Khan (the successor of Genghis) and the Mongol commander Batu's resultant withdrawal (to be present when the succession was decided) saved Europe from a Mongol invasion.

For the Western Christians, at first, the Mongols were a completely unknown factor. Reports of their bloody victories over Muslim lands provoked a mixture of anxiety and hope. Missions to their territory by the Friars, beginning with **John of Plano Carpini**, enabled a clearer picture to emerge concerning their nature. Plano Carpini confirmed that the Mongols held a credo that they were never to make peace with any nation that had not submitted to them, and that the new Khan, Guyuk, had Western Christendom in his sights.[244] Despite such intelligence, the pious **Louis IX**, whilst on Crusade, sent envoys of his own to the Mongols, along with the gift of an elaborate chapel tent, apparently interested in the possibility of converting them to Christianity and gaining allies against Islam.

The Mongols, though little interested in conversion, had also been planning the invasion of Persia and the Middle East anyway. Their General **Hulagu** soon advanced with a mighty army, including Chinese siege specialists. He swept all before him (making short work of the **Assassins**). In 1258, he took **Baghdad** and massacred the Muslim population, including the Caliph. He then marched on Syria, receiving the surrender of the **Ayyubids** of **Damascus** and **Aleppo**, and the homage of the **Armenians** and the **Frankish** Prince Bohemond VI of **Antioch**. Hulagu withdrew to Mongolia, however, on the death of Mongke Khan (Guyuk's successor) – and again the death of a Khan offered a respite to those in the path of the Mongol juggernaut. The empire effectively fragmented into four Khanates, one of which, the Il-Khanate, Hulagu took.

Meanwhile the Franks in the vestigial **Kingdom of Jerusalem** permitted the **Mameluks** to cross their territory to engage the Mongol army that Hulagu had left in the **Holy Land**. They nervously stood back awaiting the outcome. In the event the Mameluks triumphed in 1260 at the Battle of **Ain Jalut**. The Mongol threat in the region was over, for the time being, and replaced by a Mameluk one. Elsewhere, Mongol conquest lost momentum, and internal rivalries caused the break up of the far-flung empire. In Mongolia the spread of Buddhism undermined the race's warlike ideology, while in China the Mongols were gradually absorbed into the existing culture.

## *Montagu Brownlow Parker* (born 1878)

Montagu Brownlow Parker, son of the Earl of Morley, and former Grenadier Guards captain, was the leader of an irregular British excavation of **Temple Mount** in Jerusalem in 1909–1911. He was following in the footsteps of Sir **Charles Warren**. However, unlike Warren, Parker was openly looking for the **Ark of the Covenant**.

Parker was an associate of Finnish mystic Valter H. Juvelius, who claimed to have calculated the Ark's hiding place under the ruins of **Solomon's Temple** via secret codes in the Bible.[245] Convinced by Juvelius, Parker raised funds from British and American investors whom he promised a stake in the discovery of the treasure. He set up camp on the Mount of Olives in August 1909, and began his **excavations** around the Temple. The team was joined by an engineer called Johan Millen. He built on Warren's work, clearing the tunnels from the Pool of Siloam and rediscovering the Springs of Gihone. When it came to Temple Mount, however, protests by locals and poor weather postponed the excavations until the following summer.

In 1911, Baron Edmond de Rothschild (the wealthy French **Zionist**) became a leading opponent of Parker's activities. He bought land surrounding Parker's excavations from which to thwart him. Parker resorted to bribing the **Ottoman** governor, Amzey Bey Pasha, and the Arab guardian of the **Dome of the Rock**, Sheik Khalil who allowed them to enter the sacred enclosure, to conduct explorations at the dead of night. One night Parker's team entered the Dome of the Rock itself, lowering themselves into the undercroft, the 'Well of Souls' from ropes tied around the sacred rock (the **Shetiyyah**). They began to hack at the floor. They were then discovered by another mosque attendant, who raised the alarm. Parker and company fled for **Jaffa**, and a full-blown riot flared up in their wake, which resulted in the death of Sheik Khalil. Amzey Bey Pasha, feeling the heat, ordered Parker's arrest. The police in Jaffa arrested Parker and his associates and impounded their belongings. However the foreigners eventually were able to board Parker's motor yacht, and sailed homeward amid unfounded rumours that they had made off with the Ark of the Covenant.

## *Montesa*

The Order of Montesa was a **Military Order** in **Aragon** and Valencia, founded by **King James II of Argon**. It was based at St George of Montesa. It was granted the lands of the Templars and **Hospitallers** from the region of Montesa, while the rest of the Temple' lands went to the Hospital. In territorial terms it was therefore a new entity, rather than a continuation of the Order of the Temple. Pope **John XXII** officially approved the new Order in 1317. The Order was somewhat subordinate to the Order of **Calatrava**, from which its personnel were originally drawn.

The Order was involved in the conquest of Sardinia. It had little subsequent involvement with fighting the Moors, who were on the retreat by this time and had been pushed beyond the borders of Aragon. After 1586 the Grand Masters of the Order were always the Aragonese sovereigns.

## Montguisard

Montguisard (or Mont Guisard) was a victory gained by the young **Baldwin IV** over **Saladin**'s forces invading the southern part of the Latin Kingdom. In November 1177, Saladin brought a massive army (27,000 strong according to **William of Tyre**) and was so confident of victory that he let his troops disperse to ravage the land. Baldwin mustered around 370 knights including eighty Templars, and, accompanied by **Odo de Saint-Amand** and **Reynald de Châtillon**, rode down to **Ascalon**, bearing the **True Cross** with him (carried by Albert, Bishop of Bethlehem). Baldwin also had a few hundred hastily mustered foot soldiers, and deemed it wiser to hazard a battle than to leave the people exposed to fire, rapine and massacre.

This feeble force apparently of fewer than 400 caught Saladin by surprise in the rear before the scattered Muslim forces could regroup. A Templar charge clinched the victory. Odo spurred his men all together as one. Recognizing the section in which Saladin commanded, they charged and penetrated it, knocking down, striking, crushing and scattering their opponents. Saladin, however, escaped thanks to the devotion of his **Mameluk** bodyguards, who were virtually wiped out. The remnants of Saladin's army were compelled to retreat after a terrible slaughter.

Baldwin's men pursued them for over 12 miles from Montguisard to the swamp called Cannaie des Etrouneaux. The **Muslims** abandoned their armour in order to escape more quickly, and cast their arms into the waters. They were only saved by the onset of night. The victory, due largely to Baldwin's valour and effective leadership, and the Templars' discipline, was regarded as miraculous salvation for the **Kingdom of Jerusalem** and set back Saladin's plans by a decade. Christian losses were minimal, and much loot in the form of valuable weapons and armour was taken from the fleeing enemy or recovered from the swamp.

## Montjoie

Montjoie was the hill in the **Holy Land** from which the Crusaders first sighted the Holy City of **Jerusalem**. They gave it this name, which means 'mount joy.' A **Military Order** of Montjoie was founded in the Holy Land in about 1180, by one count Rodrigo of the Order of **Santiago**. The Order of Montjoie was a mainly Spanish Order, with a **Cistercian** constitution. In 1221 it merged with the Order of **Calatrava**.

## Montricoux

Montricoux, a town in Tarn et Garonne, southern France, was dominated by a major Templar **Preceptory**, donated probably by Raymond V, Count of

Toulouse, before 1179. There are some impressive buildings remaining including a towering keep and a church containing, among other things, a statue of St Peter and a roof boss containing a Tao cross. It seems that after the **arrests** of the Templars, King **Philip the Fair** gave it to **Esquin de Floyran**. It was subsequently given to the **Hospitallers**.

## Montsaunes

The twelfth-century Parish Church of Montsaunes in the Haute Garonne, southern **France** is an impressive example of surviving Templar **architecture**. The land was donated to the Templars by the Count of Comminges. The church at Montsaunes is an oblong building made of both stone and the pinkish bricks which defined the Toulouse region's medieval architecture. It is a large church with a semi-circular apse at the east end and a steeple with five openings for bells above the west facade. The steeple is capped by a **Maltese Cross**, an addition presumably of the **Hospitallers** who would have taken over the site. Below the steeple is a rose window of twelve petals, and below that a richly carved Romanesque doorway, with carvings seeming to depict the raising of Lazarus and the upside-down crucifixion of **St Peter** in its capitals. The band around the arch contains fifty-two carved human heads. Above the arch is inserted a carving of a Chi-Rho within a circle, held by two angels.

Inside the church there are mysterious **wall paintings**. The ceiling is painted with stars and strange, wheel-like symbols. A reccurring device is a circle containing six leaf shapes, meeting in the centre, formed of six intersecting semi-circles, a pattern easily drawn with compasses. This wheel pattern features in other Templar and **Cistercian** buildings. Templar crosses and other patterns within circles also appear there, as well as, at the centre, a strange composition incorporating a cross, an archway, and various interlocking triangles. Some of the wall murals echo those at **Cressac**. There are many fleurs-de-lis. There are also more figurative images, including saints and a huntsman centaur with a dog. All the designs are in a brownish-red pigment, the other colours apparently having faded away. Some of the abstract designs painted at Montsaunes may hint at the Templars having knowledge of and interest in the **Cabbalah**, and have been interpreted as illustrations of the sephirotic spheres. If the Templars did have a propensity for such mysticism, they would have had to investigate it in secret to avoid suspicion of **heresy**.

## Montségur

Montségur is famous for its castle perched on a steep-sided mountain in the foothills of the Pyrenees, in the Ariege region of southern **France**. It was the last major stronghold of the **Cathars**, filled with refugees from the **Inquisition**. The present ruin is of a later fortress. The original castle (subsequently destroyed) was the scene of some of the last dramatic events of the **Albigensian Crusade** from 1243 to 1244. Previously some knights from Montségur had ridden to Avignonet and ambushed a party of the Inquisition, killing the Inquisitors and destroying the list of names they had extracted from those they had interrogated. It may have been intended in the context of a new regional revolt against French/Roman **Catholic** domination. The castle was considered impregnable, but it had only a few hundred defenders, most of whom were non-combatant Cathar parfaits, led by Bertrand Marty, the Cathar 'bishop' and families of Cathar believers. The castellan Peire-Roger de Mirepoix commanded fewer than 100 soldiers. They were besieged by up to 10,000 royal troops, mainly from Gascony and Aquitaine, led by Peter Amiel, the Archbishop of Narbonne.

The siege lasted for nine months. The mountain made it impossible for the attackers to encircle the castle or bring in siege engines. In the end a lower bastion was scaled and captured during the night by Gascon mountain men, precipitating the capitulation of Montségur itself, as the besiegers could use the position to bombard the castle. The besiegers allowed the defenders a period of grace before coming down from the fortress. Those that recanted and submitted to interrogation by the Inquisition would be spared, while those who persisted in the heresy would be **burned**. Four of the last parfaits, under cover of darkness, had been sent to smuggle their **treasure** (whatever it was), down the mountainside and away to safety. The 200 remaining parfaits, meanwhile, prepared themselves to embrace **martyrdom**. Twenty-one others from the castle, who could have walked away, chose instead to receive the consolamentum, and to share the fate of their spiritual leaders. Ten days after the surrender, therefore, they were all burned alive together in a glade below the mountain. Some have identified the Cathar treasure, salvaged from the doomed castle, with the **Holy Grail**. It remains a mystery, but one possible explanation could be that the treasure was the lives of the escaping Parfaits themselves, who would preserve the faith and the chain of spiritual baptism, which they believed was the one thing which could save human souls from the diabolical snare of the material world. They probably also took as much gold and silver as they could carry to sustain them in their future ministry, secretly rebuilding the sect in hiding.

## Monzon

Monzon is a Templar castle in Huesca, **Aragon**. It was donated by Ramon Berengeur IV Count of Barcelona in 1143 after his accession to the Aragonese throne, and became the Order's chief establishment in the region. At the time of the **suppression**, the Templar garrison withstood a two-year siege before falling by treachery to royal forces in 1309.

## Moors

The Moors were the North African **Muslims**. They came primarily from Morocco and Algeria, and were a mixture of **Arabs**, Negroes and Berbers. Their African homeland was called the Maghreb. They invaded Spain from AD 711 and conquered the whole peninsula, even crossing the Pyrenees. The Franks under Charles Martel checked their advance in 1137. They were gradually driven back south during the medieval wars of the *Reconquista*, in which the Templars and various other Christian **Military Orders** often took part. The Moors occupied the southern territory, known as al-Andalus, until 1492. After that they were either forced from Spain or compelled to become **Catholic** converts, these converts being subject to the scrutiny of the revived **Inquisition**.

## Mortification

Mortification of the flesh was the practice of punishing one's body for spiritual gain, or as a means of **penance**. It was practised by **monks**, nuns, **hermits** and other religious ascetics, including the Templars and **Cistercians**. It took forms ranging from fasting and denial of worldy pleasures, to inflicting discomfort and pain on oneself by means of wearing coarse hair shirts and performing **flagellation**.

## Moses (*c.* thirteenth century BC)

Moses was the Biblical prophet who led the **Jews** in the Exodus from **Egypt**. He led them for forty years of wandering following the crossing of the Red Sea (which miraculously parted) preparing them for the conquest of the promised land of Canaan. On Mount Ararat he received the Ten Commandments from God, which he smashed in anger on finding the Hebrews worshipping a gold **calf**, made by Aaron. Moses was believed to be the only man to commune with God face to face. He later commissioned the making of the **Ark of the Covenant**, wherein God was somehow thought to reside. The fearful power of Moses' God, manifested through the Ark, enabled Moses to maintain his control over the Hebrews. Moses transmitted God's commandments, which became the basis of the law within **Judaism**. Moses' monotheism may have been inspired by Atenism, the solar cult of the unorthodox Pharaoh Akhenaten.

## Mount of Olives

The Mount of Olives lies to the east of **Jerusalem**. It is believed to be the site of the garden of Gethsemane and the Ascension of **Christ**. The shrine of the Ascension is a domed, octagonal building reconstructed in Crusader times. Nearby, in the Kidron Valley is the Church of the Tomb of the Virgin, where several Queens of Jerusalem including **Melisende** were buried. The Mount of Olives is also a traditional **Jewish** place of burial.

## Mount Tabor

The majestic Mount Tabor, situated in Galilee, was believed by some to be an alternative site of the Transfiguration of **Christ**. It was inhabited by **Benedictine** monks at least until the region was lost after **Hattin**. **Al-Muazzam** built fortifications there, which were stormed abortively by the forces of the **Fifth Crusade** in 1217. Many Templars and **Hospitallers** were wounded in the assault.

# N

## Nag Hammadi

Nag Hammadi, in central **Egypt**, was the site where a cache of buried writings was discovered in 1945. They were discovered in terracotta pots, by two brothers digging for fertilizer. Some they sold privately, while unfortunately their mother burned others, fearing they might have dangerous effects. The other documents subsequently found their way into museum keeping. They consisted of papyrus books, including early **Gnostic** Christian gospels, and hermetic and platonic texts. The texts were probably hidden in the fourth century by monks of the **Coptic** monastery of St Pachomius, rather than comply with an Episcopal order to destroy them, after such writings were denounced as **heretical**. Among the texts rediscovered at Nag Hammadi was the *Gospel of Thomas*, with its 'secret sayings of Jesus', the *Gospel of Philip*, the *Gospel of Truth* and the *Sophia of Jesus Christ*. The Gospel of Philip, among other things, contained the precept not to fear the essence of the flesh, nor to love it. It referred to the Holy Spirit as a female entity, and to **Mary Magdalene** as the 'companion' of **Christ**, whom he kissed on the (mouth, presumably, though the text is fragmentary).

## Napoleon Bonaparte (1765–1821)

Napoleon Bonaparte was an artillery officer from the minor nobility of Corsica who rose to become Emperor of the French. Napoleon attended military academy near **Troyes** on a scholarship from the King of **France**. He developed an interest in the **Crusades** and read avidly about the exploits of **Godfroi de Bouillon**. The Corsican developed an ambition to achieve similar greatness. Supporting the **French Revolution**, Napoleon rose to become a general, and his first major successes were gained in Italy. He subdued the north of the country and among other things occupied **Venice**, abolishing the ancient republic, and melting down some of the **Byzantine** treasures surviving from the time of the **Fourth Crusade** to pay his troops. Other treasures were sent to France, including the four horses which had been installed on St Mark's Basilica. Napoleon returned to France in glory, and proposed the ambitious project to invade **Egypt**. In 1198 he embarked with a mighty fleet, consciously following the path of **Louis IX**.

Many of Napoleon's officers professed themselves atheists. Napoleon believed in destiny, but his approach to religion was pragmatic. In Europe he was a Christian, in **Egypt** a **Muslim**.[246] Meanwhile on the way he took **Malta** from the Knights **Hospitaller**, and made off with their **treasure**. Arriving in Egypt, Napoleon captured Alexandria, and subsequently defeated the **Mameluks** at the Battle of the Pyramids. He set up a regime in Cairo and sent an army down the Nile to pursue the defiant Mameluks. Meanwhile Nelson destroyed Napoleon's fleet at the Battle of the Nile, leaving Napoleon's army stranded. (It seems the treasure of the Knights of Malta was sunk with the French flagship *Orient*.) Napoleon subsequently marched on **Acre**, where his army was mauled by Turkish and British forces under **William Sidney Smith**. He limped back to Egypt, and then escaped through the British blockade, abandoning his stranded army. Back in France, Napoleon orchestrated a takeover of power. In 1799 he became First Consul.

Napoleon restored some stability. His Concordat of 1801 restored recognition of the **Catholic** Church in France, although clergy were still to owe allegiance to the State. In 1804 he assumed the title Emperor, and summoned the **Pope** to **Paris** for his coronation. Napoleon placed the crown on his own head, however. Freedom of religion was still insisted upon, and it was around this time that the **Neo-Templars** of **Bernard Raymond Fabré-Palaprat** emerged, and that **Francois Rayounard** published his tragic play about the Templars, which portrayed King **Philip the Fair** as a villain and also served as anti-Royalist propaganda. Napoleon meanwhile demolished the **Paris Temple**, ironically, because it had become a shrine for Royalists. Napoleon fought more campaigns, defeating the Austrians again in Italy and elsewhere. His armies conquered Spain, Italy and **Germany**, and only at sea was France defeated. Soon his ambition resulted in the disastrous campaign into Russia. The rest needs no retelling.

It does not seem that Napoleon was a member of the Neo-Templar groups that sprung up during his reign. He may have taken an interest, though. When invading Egypt he took pains not to present himself as a Crusader. He told the **Arabs** that he had humbled the Pope and defeated their old enemies the Knights of Malta. He claimed to come as a friend of Islam and as a saviour from Mameluk oppression. But for the off-putting requirement of circumcision, he might have had his army converted to Islam to make them more acceptable. However, the Egyptians were not taken in by Napoleon's professed philanthropic motives, and still regarded him as an infidel.

## *Nasr al-Din* (died *c.* 1155)

Nasr al-Din was an Egyptian **Muslim** wanted along with his father, the Vizier Abbas, for the murder of a **Fatimid** Caliph. Abbas and his supporters found their palace surrounded by an angry mob. They threw jewels from the window to divert the people's attention, and then made for the border, hoping to reach **Ascalon**. In June 1154 the Visier's rich caravan was apprehended by a Christian force, mostly made up of Templars. Abbas was killed, and Nasr whose 'very name was dreaded in the region', was captured. Many slaves and spoils were also taken. The Templars took Nasr into custody, and eventually handed him back to face his fate in exchange for 60,000 gold pieces. Having been taken back to **Egypt** in chains, in a cage on a camel's back, Nasr was cruelly executed by the mob in Cairo.

## Neo-Templarism

Today there are a number of organisations calling themselves Templar. Most are fraternal and charitable organizations with either an ecumenical Christian or a **Freemasonic** foundation. Some of these Neo-Templar Orders must trace their origins back to the circle of **Bernard Raymond Fabré-Palaprat**, in **Paris** during the time of **Napoleon**. Most do not give particular credence to the idea of a secret continuity of the medieval Order, and accept that they represent a revival rather than a survival of the Templar tradition. Neo-Templars are predominantly members of **SMOTJ/OSMTH**, or of side orders of certain branches of Freemasonry, or of similar revivalist societies or re-enactment groups. They almost certainly have no connection to the medieval Templars, and are more like social clubs than military/monastic Orders. SMOTJ is an ecumenical Christian society but it is not a genuine Order of Chivalry. It is also neither sovereign nor military (though the US branch has many retired armed forces officers among its membership). There is little compelling evidence for organised **continuity** of the Knights Templar in any capacity – military, religious, social or political, at least beyond the generation living through the **suppression**. After their suppression it doesn't seem that anyone was recruited as a Templar until the pseudo-Templar movements appeared about 500 years later, and they certainly never fought in any more wars as an identifiable body.

## New Temple (London)

The New Temple in London was the headquarters of the Order in the British Isles, and could be called the Grand **Preceptory** of **England**. The Templars moved there from their original settlement the Old Temple, in about 1160. The New Temple is situated off the Strand, near where the Order owned two forges, and was originally a self-contained suburb just outside the old Roman walls of London. A river gate connected the New Temple to the Thames, the main highway of the medieval city. It was well placed for communication, and the Templars had their own pier for mooring boats and unloading goods.

The Temple would have been an enclosed, monastic establishment. Little of the medieval building survives aside from the impressive **Temple Church, London**. Apart from the fine church there would have been cloisters, an additional chapel, a hall and dormitory, the **Master**'s lodgings, lodgings for the other senior Templars, training and exercise grounds, stables, a brewery, kitchens, store rooms and service buildings and a strong house for keeping **treasure**. The New Temple was a centre of the Templars' **banking** activities, and at times guarded the Royal treasury of England. The staff included a resident stonemason, including one named Adam in 1308, whose task was probably to maintain the buildings. There were also half a dozen other servants, as well as a porter and a gardener.

The last **Master of the Temple in England** to preside from the New Temple was **William de la More**, who met a tragic end in prison. The site now belongs to the law societies known as the Inns of Court, the **Inner Temple and Middle Temple**, who occupy the elegant classical buildings that were built on the site in later centuries. Secular lawyers moved into the site soon after the demise of the Templars, and remained subsequently, apparently as tenants originally of the **Hospitallers**.

## Nicholas IV (1227–92)

Girolamo Masci, a former Master General of the **Franciscan Order**, was elected **Pope** in 1288, and reigned as Nicholas IV. Nicholas IV was a strong supporter of **Charles of Anjou** and his claim to Sicily. He supported a '**Crusade**' against the Kingdom of **Aragon**. In the meantime **Acre**, the last Christian bastion in the **Holy Land**, fell to the might of the **Mameluks**. According to Bartholomew of Neocastro, in 1289 Nicholas IV was accused by a Templar messenger of leaving the Holy Land to its fate, preferring to attack a Christian king and the Christian Sicilians. There was probably some truth in the accusation, if indeed a Templar had been so outspoken as to make it. Were it not for Nicholas's Aragonese war there would surely have been more assistance for the Holy Land. After the fall of Acre, Nicholas IV convened provincial Church councils to respond to the disaster, and proposed a trade embargo against **Egypt**, intended to weaken the country economically as a prelude to a new Crusade. Nothing came of such plans.

## Nine Knights

It was mentioned by **William of Tyre** that at the time of the **foundation of the Order** (and for nine years) the Templars numbered only nine, **Hugues de Payens**, **Godfroi de St Omer** and seven other **knights**.[247] The others are sometimes named as Archembaud de St-Amand, **Payen de Montdidier** (both relations of the ruling family of Flanders), **André de Montbard**, Gondamer, Rosal and Godfroi and Geoffrey Bisol. It seems unlikely that such a small Order could have had any impact in the **Kingdom of Jerusalem**, or could have suddenly become regarded as the champions of **Christendom**. **Michael the Syrian** mentions that there were originally thirty companions with

Hugues, which seems a more believable number. The Order may have been coalescing in **Jerusalem** some years before 1118, the year, according to William, that the Hugh and his associates approached King **Baldwin II**.

## Non Nobis

A Latin prayer derived from Psalm 113:9 of the vulgate Bible went: '*Non nobis non nobis Domine, Sed tuo da Gloriam.*' (Not unto us oh Lord but to thy name give glory.) The Templars were said to sing this on the eve of battle.

## Normans

The Normans were a warlike race descended from the Vikings, who settled in Normandy in northern **France** in the early tenth century. By the end of the century they had conquered **England**. Norman adventurers had also invaded southern Italy, and taken Sicily, and were threatening the **Byzantine Empire**. However the Normans were not a united force. Normans from Normandy, England and Italy (**Bohemond of Taranto** and **Tancred** in the latter case), played a major part in the **First Crusade**, and established their own power base in **Antioch**.

## Northampton Round Church

The **round church** at Northampton was apparently built by an Earl of Northampton, Simon de Senlis, on his return from the **First Crusade**. It is called 'Holy Sepulchre' and may therefore have been given to the **Augustinian** Canons (like the round church at **Cambridge** that has the same name seemingly was). Interestingly the Northampton church in its present form is an inversion of the **Dome of the Rock**, having an octagonal centre and a round perimeter. It predates the formation of the Templars but shows the trend they tapped in to with their **architecture**.

## Numbers of Templars

There are no exact figures for the number of Templars in the Order at any particular time. At their foundation there may have been between nine and thirty or perhaps more. The Order expanded rapidly, and was becoming a substantial international force by the time of the **Second Crusade**. They formed a key part of the permanent defence forces of the **Kingdom of Jerusalem**. It has been estimated that the kingdom could muster around 670 **knights**, and several thousand foot. The Templars could usually contribute a cavalry force of around 300 knights, and the **Hospitallers** about the same. The largest castles might have had a garrison of fifty or sixty knights, and several hundred other members of the Order. Knights formed an elite minority of the Order's membership. At its height, the Order possibly totalled around 15,000 brethren including 1,500 knights, widely dispersed across the lands where the Order operated. At the **Paris** trials, of the 138 Templars initially interrogated, only fourteen were full knights.[248] There may have been around 2,000 Templars altogether in **France**, of whom a minority escaped. The surprisingly small numbers arrested in Britain also suggest that many escaped. Only 153 Templars were arrested in **England**, fifteen in **Ireland** and two in **Scotland**. Of all the Templars arrested in the British Isles, only fifteen were knights.[249]

## *Nur ed-Din* (1118–74)

Nur ed-Din, the son of **Zenghi** of **Aleppo**, was a powerful Turkish ruler of Muslim Syria. He was a devout adherent of **Islam** and a committed practitioner of *Jihad*. On Zenghi's death, Nur ed-Din succeeded as ruler of Aleppo, while his older brother Saif ed-Din took Mosul.

Nur ed-Din began his reign by thwarting Joscelin II de Courtenay's attempt to recover **Edessa**, and subsequently expelled the entire Christian population. He also sought to extend his influence over **Damascus** and married the daughter of Unur its governor, hoping to steer Unur away from traditional alliances with the **Franks**. During the **Second Crusade** the Franks rather inexplicably attacked Damascus, playing into Nur ed-Din's hands. However, the siege failed before Nur ed-Din's forces arrived to support the Damascenes. When the western Crusaders had dispersed, the Sultan attacked the principality of **Antioch**, defeating a Frankish army at the battle of **Inab**, in which **Raymond of Poitiers** was killed. Nur ed-Din sent Raymond's head to the **Abbasid** Caliph in **Baghdad**. He then progressed to the coast for a swim in the Mediterranean, to demonstrate his power over all Syria. Later he allied with the Sultan of Rum (Anatolia) and deprived Antioch of yet more territory. He captured the wretched Joscelin II and kept him imprisoned until his death.

The Franks under **Baldwin III** (who had Nur ed-Din's grudging respect) captured **Ascalon** in AD 1153. This was a major setback to Nur ed-Din's dream of Muslim unity, as it cut off **Egypt** from Syria. Nur ed-Din grew frustrated with Mujir, Unur's successor in Damascus, who persisted in the policy of allying with the **Latins**. The following year Nur ed-Din overthrew Mujir with the support of the people of Damascus, annexing the territory to his emerging empire. Nur ed-Din adopted the title of Sultan. In 1157 he besieged the Knights **Hospitaller** in **Banias**, and after that defeated another Frankish army. The **Grand Master** of the Templars, **Bertrand de Blanquefort**, was also captured there. **Reynald de Chatillon**, the new Prince of Antioch, likewise became a prisoner of the Sultan at this time, and remained one for sixteen years.

In the 1160s the Sultan's forces were involved in a series of confrontations with **Amalric I**, centred on Egypt, where the **Fatimid** regime was in terminal decline. An ousted Vizier of the Fatimid court, Sharwah, appeared before Nur ed-Din, requesting the Sultan's aid to recover his position. Nur ed-Din obliged and sent an army under his trusty Kurdish general **Shirkuh**. Once reinstated, Vizier Sharwah sought to expel General Shirkuh's army and requested Amalric's aid in achieving this. Amalric and the Hospitallers besieged General Shirkuh in **Belbies** but any success was short-lived and both Amalric and Shirkuh withdrew from Egypt. Nur ed-Din had meanwhile launched another attack on the **Holy Land**. He had taken Tripoli briefly before being beaten back by the Templars at al-Buqaia. However in August 1164 the Sultan defeated a Frankish force at the battle of Harenc (or Harim). He captured several Frankish barons including **Raymond III of Tripoli**. He subsequently captured the castle of Harenc, which he had been laying siege to when the Frankish forces had arrived. He then captured Banias. Amalric returned just in time to prevent any farther gains.

In 1166 Nur ed-Din sent General Shirkuh back to Egypt, and a year later Amalric made another attempt at invading the Nile Delta, before being again forced to return. The **Byzantine**-Crusader alliance against Egypt resulted in a repeat of the situation, with Nur ed Din's forces in the Nile region again being led by Shirkuh, this time accompanied by Shirkuh's young nephew **Saladin**. This time Shirkuh remained, and deposed and executed the Vizier Sharwah. Without Templar support Amalric again tried to intervene, but it was a fiasco, and he was obliged to retreat. Egypt fell into Saladin's hands on Shirkuh's death, in March 1169. Nur ed-Din found that he had a loose cannon in Saladin, for soon the young Kurd began to assert his independence. Nur ed-Din was at the point of invading Egypt to recover it from Saladin when he fell ill and died in 1179. The path was open for Saladin to fulfil Nur ed-Din's ambition of uniting the Muslims in *Jihad* against the Christian Franks. Nur ed-Din had commissioned a Nimbar, a preaching pulpit, intending it for in Al-Aqsa Mosque once **Jerusalem** was recovered for Islam (from those who had recovered the city for Christianity). Saladin would see it installed. He would also deprive Nur ed-Din's short-lived young son of his inheritance.

# O

## *Obedience*

The Templars' **Rule** required that brethren give absolute obedience to their **Masters**. Everything they commanded should be obeyed without demur as if the command came from Jesus Christ himself. Brothers were expected to give up their own free will. This was a central idea within monasticism, and one of the most difficult things for men who were use to being their own masters to come to terms with, as the Templars made clear to potential initiates.

The cult of obedience doubtless was a strength for the Templars in that it limited internal factionalism. It helped the Order preserve its internal unity over two difficult centuries. Obedience was also a mainstay of the Order's famous discipline. On the other hand it was a weakness, as it meant the Order was only as effective or competent as its incumbent **Grand Master**. Pragmatic Knights like **Jacquelyn de Mailly** might advise against a suicidal tactic or dubious policy, but if the Master insisted then they had to obey whatever the cost. The cult of obedience meant subordinates were not free to act on their initiative. Templars were not allowed to leave camp to forage without permission, for example. The Templars' institutional reliance on direction from superiors was also a hindrance in the last days when those wishing to defend the Order were compromised by the general lack of leadership offered by **Jacques de Molay** the **Grand Master**, and other leading dignitaries of the Order.

## Odo de St Armand (died 1180)

Odo de St Amand hailed from an aristocratic family of Limousin. He came east and served as Marshal of **Jerusalem**, before joining the Knights Templar. Odo went on to become the eighth **Grand Master** of the Templars in 1171, during the reign of **Amalric I** of Jerusalem. He succeeded **Bertrand de Blanquefort**, with whom he apparently had been captured and held prisoner after the battle of Banyas against **Nur ed-Din**. Relations between the Order and the King continued to be difficult, and the troubles came to a head in 1172, when the Templar **Walter de Mesnil** ambushed an envoy of the **Assassin** sect, returning to Syria from negotiations with Amalric. According to a disapproving **William of Tyre**, Odo refused to hand over de Mesnil to royal justice, asserting the Temple's independence, but claiming that he would send Walter for judgement in **Rome**. Amalric seized de Mesnil, in the event, and was considering pressing his case against the Templars when he died.

Under Amalric's son, **Baldwin IV**, relations between the crown and the Order improved. In 1177 Odo and the Templars supported Baldwin and played a critical part in his victory over **Saladin** at **Montguisard**. Odo also defeated an army of Saladin's at Ramlah.[250] The Grand Master was less lucky in 1179, when he was captured in battle a few months before the fall of the castle of **Jacobs Ford**. William of Tyre, recording his capture, expressed little sympathy, and condemned Odo as an evil man, full of pride and arrogance 'in whose nostrils dwelt the spirit of fury'. He also claimed that many held Odo responsible for the military disaster.[251] Odo refused to be ransomed, in accordance with the **Rule**, and died in chains in prison the following year.

## Old Man of the Mountains (Sheikh al-Jebel)

The Old Man of the Mountains was the name by which the Crusaders knew the master of the **Assassins**. The original Old Man was **Hassan I-Sabbah** who reigned in **Alamut** in Persia. Later there was an Old Man of the Mountains leading the sect in the Jebel al-Sariya region of Syria, who was a wily and dangerous neighbour. At the time of **Saladin**, this was **Sinan**.

## Old Temple, London

The Old Temple, situated at High Holborn, in the Parish of St Andrew, was the Templars' headquarters in **London** in their earliest times. It was probably granted around the time of the visit by **Hugues de Payens** in the late 1120s, and was definitely in the Order's possession by the time of death of **Henry I** of **England**. (It was situated near the north end of the present Chancery Lane.) There was a small **round church** there and various other buildings. The Templars subsequently moved to the **New Temple**, off the Strand, and in 1161 sold the Old Temple site to the Bishop of **Lincoln**. The buildings apparently survived until 1595.

## Oliver of Paderborn (died 1227)

Oliver 'Scholasticus' of Paderborn was a preacher and chronicler of the **Fifth Crusade**. Originally a teaching cleric in the cathedral school of Cologne, he accompanied the Crusade to the **Holy Land** and to **Egypt**. He is credited with designing the floating siege engine that made possible the capture of the chain tower on the Nile delta and ultimately the city of **Damietta**. He recorded the tribulations of the long siege in which the Templars participated actively. Oliver was a supporter of the Papal legate **Pelagius of Albano**, and recorded how (at least to begin with) the **Military Orders** supported the legate's controversial decision to reject the Sultan's offer to restore **Jerusalem** and most of the lost territories of the **Kingdom of Jerusalem** in exchange for the Crusaders' withdrawal from Damietta. He was critical of **John of Brienne** for abandoning the 'camp of the faithful'.[252] After the failure of the Fifth Crusade and the loss of Damietta, Oliver returned to Europe, but continued to preach Crusade. He rose to be Bishop of Paderborn and then Cardinal of St Sabrina.

## Oliver of Termes (c. 1204–74)

Oliver of Termes was a noble from the **Languedoc**, whose family had **Cathar** connections. Initially he sided with the rebels against French and Catholic authority, and was part of an attempt to recover **Carcassonne** for the Trencavels. He played a part in successive revolts, and sheltered Cathars and other dissidents in his castle of Queribus, for which he was **excommunicated**. Later, however, he was reconciled with **Catholicism** and the **Capetian** monarchy, and became a participant in the **Seventh Crusade**. He remained in the **Holy Land** until 1255 and made subsequent visits in 1264, 1266–70 and from 1273. He became famed for his gallantry as a Crusader and his newfound loyalty to **Louis IX**. He had links to the Templars having sold them property in order to fund one of his crusading ventures. He also fought alongside the Templars in the East. He commanded the French garrison at **Acre**, where he died.

## Omar (Caliph) (581–644)

Omar was the second Sunni Caliph of **Islam**. It was also he who began the codification of Islamic law, and invented the Islamic calendar. Originally a leading Meccan of the Quraysh tribe who had opposed the early Muslims, he was apparently converted by his sister, and became a close companion of **Mohammed**. He was an advisor of the first Sunni Caliph Abu Bakir, and in 634 became Caliph himself. He went on to wage wars of conquest throughout the Middle East, taking **Damascus** in 636 and **Jerusalem** the following year. He defeated both **Byzantine** and **Persian** armies. He was stabbed to death in November 644 by a disgruntled **slave**.

## Omne Datum Optimum

*Omne Datum Optimum* (every best gift) was a **Papal bull** issued by **Innocent II** on 29 March 1139. It was addressed to 'our dear son' **Robert de Craon**, the second **Grand Master** of the Templars. The bull endorsed the rule of the Templars and placed the Order under Papal protection. It made the Templars independent of all ecclesiastical authority except for the **Pope** himself. It allowed the Templars to have their own **priests** and build their own **churches** and cemeteries, where they could bury their own dead as well as their patrons, confrates, servants, and any traveller who died on Templar land. They were entitled to receive tithes and exempted from paying them. The bull entitled the Templars to retain any spoils taken in battle and to dispose of them as they saw fit. Abbot **Bernard of Clairvaux** had supported Pope Innocent II's claim to the papacy over that of Innocent's rival who had styled himself Anacletus II. It is possible that Innocent II was so generous to the Templars as a way of repaying Bernard and the Cistercians for their support.

## Order of Lazarus

The Order of St Lazarus was a **Military Order** founded during the **Crusades**. The Lazarus whom **Christ** raised from the dead (John II: 38–42) was confused, it seems wilfully, with the other Lazarus, the beggar covered in sores, who features in a parable (Luke 16:19–35). The Order also revered **Mary Magdalene** (who was identified as the sister of the resurrected Lazarus, venerated at Bethany). The Order may have had its origin in the Leper hospital in **Jerusalem**, run by Greek or **Armenian** monks before the arrival of the **First Crusade**. Subsequently it became associated with the Knights **Hospitaller**, and switched from observing the Eastern **Rule** of St Basil to the **Latin** Rule of St Augustine. It was specifically concerned with caring for sufferers from leprosy. Knights of the Military Orders who contracted leprosy were obliged to leave, and it is likely they joined the Order of St Lazarus. Its first Master may have been **Gerard Thom** the Hospitaller, who may have contracted leprosy himself.

As the career of King **Baldwin IV** proves, leprosy (at least in its early stages) did not necessarily render men entirely incapable of fighting, and at least some **knights** of the Order of Lazarus still took part in military action. If anything they had an incentive to seek battlefield **martyrdom** before their bodies deteriorated. The Order had no castles, but brethren were present at the Battle of **La Forbie**, and also at the 1291 Siege of **Acre**, where twenty-five Knights of Lazarus fought. The Order also operated leper hospitals (Lazar houses) throughout Europe. (In England they had a hospital at Burton Lazarus in Leicestershire, donated by **Roger de Mowbray**, who was also a Templar patron.) Brethren wore black robes, with the later addition of a green **Maltese Cross**. The Order's history continued beyond the Crusading era, though it ceased to be a military or monastic organization, and it exists to this day.

## Order of St Thomas Acon

The Order of St Thomas of Canterbury at **Acre** (or Acon), also known as the Hospitallers of St Thomas, was a small English **Military Order** established during the **Third Crusade**. It was founded in honour of St **Thomas à Becket**. It is said that Becket's sister and her husband were among early patrons of the Order, possibly along with **Richard the Lionheart**. It was reorganised and militarised by the Bishop of Winchester, **Peter des Roches**, during the **Fifth Crusade**, being modelled on the **Teutonic Knights**. It played a minor role in the defence of the **Holy Land**, and was also involved in ransoming captives. After the fall of Acre it withdrew to **Cyprus** and became a purely Hospitaller Order (they also had houses in Naples and Sicily). After the 1370s it removed to its **London** headquarters, The Hospital of St Thomas of Acre, which had been founded in 1227 on the site where Becket was born. The Order was dissolved during the Reformation. Curiously it seems to have been revived in exiled Masonic **Jacobite** circles on the continent in the eighteenth century. Its badge was apparently a red Greek Cross with a hollow centre.

## Order of the Garter

The Most Noble Order of the Garter was an honorific **chivalrous** association created by **Edward III** of **England** in 1348. The Order was created to reward loyal barons and to secure their continuing loyalty, and soon became one of the foremost orders of chivalry. It consisted of the monarch, the Prince of Wales, and twenty-four knights. It had bases in Windsor dedicated to St **Mary, the Blessed Virgin**, and to St **George**, and was consciously inspired by King **Arthur**'s mythical knights of the round table. The Order's badge was a blue garter strap, buckled in a circle, with the obscure motto in gold letters '*Honi soit qui mal y pense*' (Shame on him who thinks ill of it). This has been interpreted as a cryptic allusion to Edward III's plan to assert his claim the throne of France. This garter sometimes contains a red cross on a white base.

## Order of the Hatchet

The Order of the Hatchet was a short-lived order of knighthood for women, founded by Count Raymond Berengar of Barcelona, honouring the women who had contributed valiantly to the defence of Tortosa in **Aragon** against a **Moorish** attack in 1149. These 'cavelleras' received various privileges and tax exemptions.

## Order of the Holy Sepulchre

The Order of the Holy Sepulchre of **Jerusalem** seems to have begun life as a company of lay-associate **knights** affiliated to the **Canons of the Holy Sepulchre**, for the specific purpose of defending the Church of the **Holy Sepulchre**. If such a group indeed existed, they were a **Military Order**, but never as widespread or well known as the Templars or **Hospitallers**. For a while in the fifteenth century the Canons of the Holy Sepulchre were merged with the Hospitallers, but the two groups seem to have split again subsequently. Today there is still an honorary **Catholic** Order of **Chivalry** going by this name (The **Equestrian Order of the Holy Sepulchre**) though this seems to be a nineteenth century creation. There is little primary evidence for a militarised Order of the Holy Sepulchre. That the Sepulchre was ranked along with the Temple and Hospital by **Alfonso I of Aragon** in his will perhaps implies that they were fulfilling a similar role, or were at least closely linked to the Military Orders. Some veterans of the **First Crusade** and other **pilgrim** knights evidently took religious vows before the **Patriarch** of Jerusalem and the Canons of the Holy Sepulchre, becoming guardians of the shrine. As there is little mention of any Military Order of the Holy Sepulchre after the 1120s, these Knights of the Holy Sepulchre may actually have been the nucleus of the Knights Templar before they gained their headquarters on Temple Mount. **Hugh, Count of Champagne**, could have joined them as early as 1104, during one of his earlier visits to Jerusalem. If so, then the Templars did not appear as suddenly as it seems they did. They existed for some time beforehand under a different name.

## Order of the New Templars

The Austrian Order of the New Templars (*Ordo Novi Templi*) was an obscure pseudo-Templar Order founded in 1907. Its founder was one Jörg Lanz von Liebenfels (born Adolf Josef Lanz), a former **Cistercian** monk. Lanz was influenced by neo-paganism, occultism and mysticism. He also absorbed the specious German racialist theories of the times, and developed his own in a book called *Theozoology or The Science of Sodom's Apelings and the Electrons of the*

*Gods.* Lanz and his followers bought the ruinous medieval castle of Werfensein as their first meeting place. The order survived until the late 1930s.[253]

## Order of the Trinity
The Order of the Trinity (or Trinitarians) was a religious society, founded at the end of the twelfth century, mainly concerned with the ransoming of Christian prisoners. It was also devoted to contemplating the mystery of the Holy Trinity, as well as to Hospitaller work.

## Ordo Templi Orientis (OTO)
The *Ordo Templi Orientis* (Order of the Eastern Temple) was a quasi-**Masonic**, neo-**Gnostic** society founded by Theodore Reuss and the Austrian industrialist Karl Keller in the early twentieth century. It became influenced by occultist **Aliester Crowley** and adopted his 'law' of Thelema. Initiates performed eclectic, mystical ceremonies, mostly invented by Crowley, some with Templar-esque elements.

## Ordo Supremus Militaris Templi Hierosolymitani (OSMTH)
The *Ordo Supremus Militaris Templi Hierosolymitani* (OSMTH) is the official Latin name of the **Neo-Templar** organization, which in English is 'Sovereign Military Order of the Temple of Jerusalem' (SMOTJ). The Order is an ecumenical Christian association, claiming to have over 5,000 members worldwide, being educated professionals, men and women (who term themselves knights and dames). A requirement of membership is the belief in **Christ** as the Messiah and in one God. The Order claims to be involved with humanitarian **charity** work in the **Holy Land** and elsewhere, and to seek the betterment of humanity through education, world brotherhood, chivalric principles, and civil behaviour. OSMTH seems to be the name used by the international body, whilst the 'Grand Priory' of the United States prefers SMOTJ. Despite its name, the Order is not sovereign, nor in its own capacity is it military, though former officers of the US armed forces appear to be prominent among the members.

The OSMTH had its origin in the Templar revival led by **Bernard Raymond Fabré-Palaprat** in 1804, in Napoleonic Paris. Fabré-Palaprat produced the **Larmenius Charter**, with its list of **clandestine Grand Masters** linking his Order to the historical Knights Templar. However the OSMTH does not officially claim continuity from the medieval Order. It is notable that after Bernard Raymond Fabré-Palaprat's death all **Johannite** and **Freemasonic** aspects of the Neo-Templar Order were apparently dropped.

It seems in more recent times the OSMTH suffered a schism over the leadership of Don Fernando Campello Pinto Pereira de Sousa Fontes, who had assumed the role unilaterally on the death of his father, claiming the title Grand Master and Prince Regent. The part of the Order loyal to Sousa Fontes ('regency' or 'loyalist' Templars) survives based in Portugal, while the other

Priories, wishing to elect a Grand Master, have broken away and become autonomous, though it seems they are mainly affiliated to the US Grand Priory, the SMOTJ. The latter group have UN recognition with 'Special Consultative Status'. There seems to be bad blood between the two factions, with the loyalists calling their rivals 'pretenders'. The Sousa Fontes group, which presents itself as the more purist of the two, use a double-barred red cross as its symbol, and is more likely to assert continuity from the original Knights Templar.

## Oriflamme

The Oriflamme was the war banner of **France**. It was a red flag with trailing tails, probably attached to a golden lance. The French carried it at great battles during the **Crusades** and later during the Hundred Years War. The flag was associated with the Frankish Kings and St Denis, the royal patron saint.

## Orval

Orval was an abbey situated by a spring in a valley in the Luxembourg region of southern Belgium. The widowed Countess Matilda of Tuscany (the aunt of **Godfroi de Bouillon**), according to legend, was at the fountain when her wedding ring accidentally fell into the water. She prayed to God, and a trout immediately swam to the surface holding the ring in its mouth and presented it. Matilda exclaimed 'truly this place is a Val d'Or!' (vale of gold). In gratitude she founded the monastery. The first monks settled at Orval from the Calabria region of Italy in around 1070. The local noble Arnold de Chiny donated land and the Italian monks began to build the first church on the site. About forty years later they suddenly moved away, mysteriously, leaving the abbey unfinished. Some have thought that they re-emerged in the **Holy Land**, taking over the **Abbey of Notre Dame de Mont Sion**.

Meanwhile at Orval, Othon the son of Arnold replaced the monks with a small community of canons, who completed the church (consecrated in 1125 by Henri de Winton, Bishop of Verdun). Before long these Canons seem to have fallen on hard times and were absorbed into the **Cistercian** Order. Abbot **Bernard of Clairvaux** sent seven Cistercian brothers under one Constantine, to join the community and entrusted the re-formation of Orval to the Abbot of Trois-Fontaines. The buildings were subsequently enlarged and new grants of land and property received, including forges where a steel industry developed. The Abbey's fortunes ebbed and flowed over the ensuing centuries.

## Ottoman Turks

The Ottoman, or Osmamli Empire began its rapid ascent to prominence in the early fourteenth century. The Ottoman Turks were those following the descendants of Osman I (1268–13). While Europe was busy turning against the Templars, the Ottoman Turks were gaining their first foothold in the Balkans.

They became the dominant power in the region and reduced **Byzantium** to a small area around Constantinople, which was a tributary state long before its eventual fall to Mehmed II and his overwhelming forces in 1453. Mehmed's elite troops were Janissaries, soldier-slaves modelled after the **Mameluks**.

The Ottoman Empire was founded on conquest, and expanded in all directions to exceed the extent of the Eastern Roman Empire, encompassing much of North Africa and **Greece**, the Balkans and Bulgaria to the west, **Egypt**, the Sudan and the coast of **Arabia** including Mecca to the south, Mesopotamia as far as the Persian Gulf to the east and Romania and the Crimea to the north. After tenacious battles the Turks ejected the **Hospitallers** from **Rhodes**, but could not defeat them on **Malta**. Ottoman sea power was reduced by a Christian league at the Battle of Lepanto. It was only in the nineteenth century that the Ottoman hold on Eastern Europe began to slacken, and only after the First World War that they lost control of Arabia and the **Holy Land**.

## Outremer

*Outremer* was a term for the **Holy Land** or the **Kingdom of Jerusalem**, in the Levant, used by **Franks** in the West. It meant 'overseas'. The sea voyage from Genoa to the Levant could take five weeks.

# P

## Papal Bull

A papal bull was any important decree, ruling or declaration issued by a **Pope**. These decrees were often intended to be read out in every major church in the Catholic world. The word comes from *bullum*, or seal. The Templars were awarded rights and privileges in papal bulls including *Omne Datum Optimum* (1139) *Milites Templi* (1144) and *Militia Dei* (1145). They were arrested throughout Europe as a result of the bull *Pastoralis Praeeminentiae* (1307) and they were tried as a result of *Faciens Misericordiam* (1308). They were condemned at the **Council of Vienne**, the assembling of which had been ordered in the bull *Regnans in Coelis*, and they ceased to be as a result of *Vox in Excelso* (1312).

## Papal Supremacy

Papal supremacy was the doctrine that the **Pope** had supreme spiritual authority on Earth. Thirteenth century Popes also claimed to have supreme temporal authority, and the power to create and depose lords, Kings and Emperors. The pretension to absolute authority had spurious justification in the '**Donation of Constantine**' and was most flagrantly expressed in a

**Papal Bull** of **Boniface VIII**, called *Unam Sanctum*. Anyone who wished to be saved had to submit to the Pope's authority.

## Paris

Paris, the Capital of **France**, was the traditional heart of the French royal domain. It first was a royal centre at the time of the **Merovingian** Clovis I. Centuries later, in 987 Hugh Capet, Count of Paris, was elected King, and founded the **Capetian** dynasty. The Capetians built the nation of France, and Paris remained their capital. Medieval Paris was dominated by the Cathedral of Notre Dame, and by the royal fortresses of the Louvre and the Concierge. The city experienced great growth under **Philip II Augustus**, who also extended and strengthened the city walls. Later **Louis IX** graced Paris with the exquisite Gothic chapel the Sainte Chapelle, within the royal palace opposite the cathedral on the island in the Seine, where he installed the **Holy Relics** he had obtained, thereby making Paris something of a sacred place. The main Templar headquarters in Europe was the **Paris Temple**. Paris was the main venue of the Templars' trials. The Inquisitor General examined 138 Templars, of whom fourteen were **knights**. Later 546 Templars were assembled for the General defence of the Order (of whom eighteen were knights). They met in the Episcopal gardens. Paris was also the scene of the burning of the last **Grand Master** of the Order **Jacques de Molay** along with **Geoffroi de Charney**. It was also one of the birthplaces of **Neo-Templarism** in the early nineteenth century.

## Paris Temple

The Templar enclave, the Paris Temple, was built just to the north of the walled city. Established by the time of the **Second Crusade**, it was a fortress in its own right, with a tall tower keep with four turrets and a pyramidal roof, and with conventual buildings within the outer walls. There was also a grand **round church**, dedicated to St Mary, the proportions of which reflected those of **Temple Church, London**. The walls around the Paris complex were probably sufficient to offer protection against rioting citizens, but were not designed to withstand a determined attack from an organised army. Indeed in 1306 the Templars of the Paris Temple offered shelter to King **Philip the Fair** when his economic policy provoked riots (The king devalued the coinage, which meant, among other things, that poor people's rents effectively trebled). The Paris Temple was also the centre of the Templars banking activities on the Continent, and it may have been at this time, when hiding from the angry mob, that the King observed the apparent wealth of the Templars, and began to formulate a plan to obtain it to alleviate his own financial difficulties. In October 1307 the King had the Templars arrested *en masse*. **Jacques de Molay**, the **Grand Master**, was among those seized in a dawn raid at the Paris temple. The brethren were soon confined there and subjected to interrogation and torture. The complex continued to serve as a prison for the Templars throughout the period of their trials. It subsequently passed into the possession of the **Hospitallers**, but was taken by the state during the **French Revolution**. The Templars fortress became a prison for King Louis XVI's family, while they awaited execution by the revolutionaries. The building subsequently became a shrine for monarchist supporters, and apparently on account of that **Napoleon Bonaparte** had the tower pulled down in 1808.

## Passagium Generale

*Passagium generale* was the term used by Crusade strategists for a large Crusade formed of massive, international, volunteer armies, in the manner of the **First Crusade**. This was opposed to the *passagium particulare*, which was a more limited exercise. In about 1300, **Jacques de Molay** advocated the mustering of a full scale *Passagium generale* to recover the **Holy Land**.

## Passagium particulare

*Passagium particulare* was the term used by **Crusade** strategists for a limited crusading expedition, formed of small scale, professional and committed troops.

## Pastoralis Praeeminentiae

*Pastoralis Praeeminentiae* was a **Papal bull** issued by **Clement V** on 24 November 1307. It ordered the arrest of all the Templars in every Catholic land where they were established, namely **England**, **Ireland**, **Portugal**, **Castile**, **Aragon**, **Germany**, **Italy** and **Cyprus**. The brethren were to be seized 'prudently, discretely, secretly', and kept in custody. Their properties were to be held in the name of the Church, pending the outcome of the ensuing trials. By this time confessions had already been extracted from many of the Templars in **France**, including leading dignitaries of the Order. Clement also praised the good faith of **Philip the Fair**, despite the fact that a month previously he had condemned the very actions that he was now condoning. This was a curious *volte-face*. It effectively internationalised what had been a unilateral move against the Templars. No other rulers before the issue of this edict had shown any signs of supporting the **Capetian** policy or of believing the **accusations against the Order**.

## Patriarch

A Patriarch is a leader assuming the role and authority of a father to those under him. **Abraham** was considered the great Patriarch of the Bible and father of the **Jewish** race. Isaac and Jacob were also considered Patriarchs. The early Christian Church was led by a number of high priests or Patriarchs, serving the most important centres of the religion. The original ecclesiastical patriarchs were the Bishops of **Constantinople**, **Antioch**, **Alexandria**, **Rome** and **Jerusalem**. The Patriarch of Rome was also the **Pope**, while the Patriarchs of Constantinople and Alexandria became the heads of the Eastern Orthodox and Coptic churches respectively. During the Crusades there were rival **Latin** and Eastern Orthodox Patriarchs of Antioch and Jerusalem.

## Patriarchal Cross

A Patriarchal Cross is a cross with two horizontal bars (similar to the Cross of Lorraine). The Portugal-based Neo-Templar group **OSMTH** uses it as a symbol. According to Bernard the Treasurer, the earliest Templars wore such a cross, which was associated with the **Holy Sepulchre**.[254] A number of reliquaries for pieces of the **True Cross** were produced there with this form. The patriarchal cross was also used by the **Hospitallers**. The upper bar is normally shorter than the lower, and may represent the *titulus* (the notice that was hung above **Christ**).

## Paul of Tarsus, St (died *c.* AD 68)

Paul of Tarsus, originally Saul from Tarsus, a Roman city in modern Turkey, became a tireless preacher of Christianity after his famous conversion on the road to **Damascus**. He preached also to gentiles, arguing that there was no requirement for them to observe **Jewish** customs such as dietary restrictions or physical circumcision, because **Christ** had brought the new Covenant and through him lay salvation. The Templars venerated St Paul. It seems that in 1863, in the site of a Templar Church in Florence dedicated to him, there were found items including an earthenware pot with the symbols of a sword and a snake and (as well as *fleurs-de-lis* and a **Maltese Cross**) with a scene of Paul dropping a serpent into flames. The motif referred to a biblical episode involving St Paul on Malta (Acts 28). An inscription read, 'in the name of St Paul, and by this stone, thou shalt drive out poison.' Also found was a medal with the image of a dragon and a similar inscription regarding St Paul's proof against poison.[255]

## Payen de Montdidier (eleventh–twelfth century)

Payen de Montdidier is named as one of the **founding** members of the Knights Templar (**nine knights**), who accompanied Hugues de **Payens to Jerusalem** at the time of King **Baldwin II**. Payen was apparently later put in charge of the Order of the Temple in northern **France**.

## Peace of God

The 'Peace of God' was a truce sworn between Christian lords, that they would not attack each other's territory while engaged in crusading (the concept actually slightly predated the **Crusades**). The Church initially undertook to safeguard the property of Crusaders during their absence. In practice, the peace was often broken.

## Peasants' Revolt

The Peasants' Revolt was a popular uprising in England in 1381. It was primarily provoked by harsh taxation. Its leader was Wat Tyler. During this insurrection, the **Hospitallers** were particularly targeted. Their Grand Prior, **Robert Hales**, had also been the Treasurer of the realm and was associated with a hated poll tax. He was seized by the rebels in the **Tower of London** and beheaded. Meanwhile many manors were raided by the rebelling peasants and their tax records were burnt. Templar records were probably among those destroyed at **Cressing** and **London**, being mixed up with the records of the taxes, which had brought such misery to the common people. According to John J. Robinson, the Knights Templar found refuge in Britain and went undercover as a secret society, and that this 'Great Society' lay behind the Peasants' Revolt, manipulating events in order to be avenged on the monarchy and the Hospitallers. This society, it is proposed, possibly evolved into **Freemasonry**.[256]

## Pedro II of Aragon (1178–1213)

Pedro II, 'the Catholic', was king of **Aragon**. In 1212 he was part of the victory over the **Moors** at **Las Navas de Tolosa**. The following year, accompanied by some Templars in his personal service, he intervened against **Simon de Montford** in the **Languedoc**, on behalf of his brother-in-law, **Raymond IV of Toulouse**. He was killed fighting at Muret.

## Pelagius of Albano (Papal Legate) (thirteenth century)

Pelagius, Cardinal-Bishop of Albano, was the Papal legate of **Honorius III**, who took charge of the armies of the **Fifth Crusade** in **Damietta** in 1219. He was probably a Spaniard, and had been close to **Innocent III**. He repeatedly rejected the Sultan **Al Kamil's** proposals to restore **Jerusalem** to the Christians in exchange for their leaving **Damietta**. The Templars initially supported this stance (before the capture of Damietta). Pelagius doggedly overruled **John of Brienne** and others, who thought it would be better to accept the Sultan's offer, renewed in June 1221, of all the land that had constituted the **Kingdom of Jerusalem**, bar the castles beyond the Jordan in exchange for Damietta. This time the Templars were for taking the deal, but Pelagius, putting his hope in spurious prophecies and the vain hope of succour from **Frederick II**, would not be moved. Even St **Francis of Assisi** could not persuade the Papal legate to negotiate.

Pelagus's leadership seems to have caused some disillusionment, and many Crusaders deserted. It was the Cardinal who ordered the attack down the Nile that same month, partly to appease Louis of Bavaria, the newly arrived leader of a contingent of Imperial troops, who was keen to fight the enemy. The Crusade ran headlong into disaster, when the army was trapped by rising water in the Nile Delta and when **Muslim** reinforcements arrived. Thus the Crusade failed and the arrogant Pelagius incurred much scorn. Pelagius seems to have stayed in the **Holy Land** after the debacle in Egypt. In October 1221 he mediated in a dispute between the Templars and **Hospitallers** over the town of Jabala, which he divided between them. He died in Monte Cassino, Italy.

## Penances

Penances were acts performed to atone for sins. Sacramental penances were imposed by **priests** following confession, and sometimes involved making **pilgrimages** or performing acts of corporal **mortification**. The Templars also imposed various penances as part of their disciplinary system of **punishment within the Order**. One brother **Adam de Wallaincourt** was subjected to harsh penances when he returned to the Order of the Temple humbly seeking readmittance after leaving to join the Carthusians. Some meanwhile joined the Templars or took **Crusading** vows in the first place as an act of penitence. In 1224, **Honorius III** instructed the Templars to receive a knight, Bertran, to serve seven years as penance for killing a bishop. The use of the Order as a place of rehabilitation for such violent criminals may not have gone down well with those who joined it for idealistic reasons. Some religious societies, meanwhile, devoted themselves to doing penance on behalf of the sins of others, such as the **Flagellants**.

## Penhill

Penhill is the site of a remote Templar outpost in Wensleydale, on the Yorkshire Moors, in northern England. Here it seems the Order bred and trained **horses**, including warhorses destined for service the East. They also reared flocks of **sheep**, following the example of the great **Cistercian** abbeys in the region, for which **wool** was a useful source of wealth. The land was donated to the Templars by **Roger de Mowbray**. The ruins of the Templar chapel at Penhill survive (though only at low level) and open stone coffins can be seen in a nearby field, resembling stone troughs.[257]

## Peñíscola

Peñíscola in Valencia is an old port on the Mediterranean coast of **Spain**. It was captured in 1233 by James I of **Aragon** and the Templars. Today it is dominated by a Templar **castle**, built on **Arab** foundations, atop a high, rocky crag. Almost an island, the town is connected to the mainland by a narrow isthmus. Forces of King **James II** of Aragon took the castle with little resistance in December 1307, along with most of the Templars' other possessions in the region of Valencia. After the suppression of the Templars the castle was given to the Order of **Montesa**.

## Pentagram

A pentagram is a five-pointed **star** formed of intersecting lines, usually drawn within a circle. Medieval stonemasons sometimes used the symbol as a mason's mark, in Europe and beyond. It was also used by the Templars, or at least their successors, being evident, for example, in the tracery of a round window in the Church of Santa Maria do Olivia, in **Tomar, Portugal**. The symbol has long been believed to have magical associations. It has been in use since ancient times and given different meanings. It has been said to represent Venus, or Lucifer (both called the Morning Star. It seems that every eight years the planet Venus traces the shape of a pentagram across the sky). The sign has been identified with King **Solomon**, with Sir Gawain, the legendary Knight, with the five wounds of **Christ**, with the five senses, and with the four elements plus spirit. The symbol is important in **Freemasonry**, and was passed on to Wicca. Nineteenth-century occultists also adopted the symbol. **Eliphas Levi** placed it on the brow of his **Baphomet** creature.

## Peter, Saint (first century)

Saint Peter was one of the twelve disciples of **Jesus**. The Popes regarded themselves as his successors, and inheritors of the authority passed to him by Christ. Warriors in the Church's service were called *beati sancti petri*. Peter's relics were venerated in Rome, where, according to the apocrypha, Peter has been crucified upside down. A carving of Peter's crucifixion appears at the Templar Church of **Montsaunes**.

## Peter of Aspelt (thirteenth–fourteenth century)

Peter of Aspelt was the Archbishop of Mainz in **Germany**. He was called by Pope **Clement V** to initiate a hearing into the Templars into the Archdiocese. This convened in 1310. The Templars, especially the brothers **Hugh** and **Frederick von Salm** forcefully protested their innocence. Thirty-seven Templar defendants were heard in all, along with twelve outside witnesses including nobles and clerics. A priest mentioned a time of famine in Masteire, when the Templars of the local Preceptory had given food to 1,000 paupers each day. Peter of Aspelt gave a favourable verdict on the Templars, but was overruled by Pope **Clement V**.

## Peter de Montaigu (died 1232)

Peter (Pierre, or Pedro) de Montaigu became the fifteenth **Grand Master** of the Knights Templar in 1219. Peter had been the **Master** of the Temple in Provence and **Aragon**, and had fought at the Battle of **Las Navas de Tolosa**. Peter de Montaigu was the brother of Garin de Montaigu, who was Grand Master of the **Hospitallers** from 1208–1228. This was the only time when two members of the same family presided over the two leading **Military Orders**. It secured some years of harmonious relations between them. During the **Sixth Crusade**, Peter became a bitter enemy of the Emperor **Frederick II** who ratified the return of Jerusalem in a treaty with **al Kamil** in a treaty without the Grand Masters' seal. Peter and the Templars were suspected of plotted against Frederick, who retaliated by besieging them in **Acre**.[258]

## Peter de Sevrey (died 1291)

Peter de Sevrey was the **Marshal** of the Temple who fought in the doomed defence of **Acre** in 1291. The Templars under de Sevrey held out for a week in their Citadel following the death of **Guillaume de Beaujeu**. De Sevrey at length negotiated their surrender to the **Mameluks**, and it was agreed that the defenders and the remaining refugees would be allowed to leave in safety. **Al-Ashraf** agreed, and the defenders allowed a detachment of Mameluks into their compound, who raised their standard. When the Mameluks began to molest the civilian refugees and rape the women the Templars attacked and killed them. De Sevrey afterwards went out to attempt to explain to the Sultan why his men had acted thus against the Mameluks, and to reopen the negotiations. The Sultan let the Marshal into the Muslim camp under a flag of truce and then had him beheaded.

## Peter des Roches (died 1238)

The Bishop of Winchester Peter des Roches was a powerful figure during the reigns of King **Richard the Lionheart**, King **John** and King **Henry III** of England. As bishop, he was one of the few prelates to support King John during his **excommunication**. He also took part in the battle of **Lincoln** in 1217 during the baronial wars. Peter was an enemy of **Hubert de Burgh**, and later persuaded Henry III to arrest Hubert and to seize his treasure from Templar keeping at the **New Temple, London**.

## Peter of La Palud (died 1342)

Peter of La Palud was a Dominican friar with a background in canon and civil law. He deposed at the **trial** of the Templars, expressing doubts about the **accusations against the order**. He attached more credence to those denying the charges than those who confessed, but believed some parts of the Order were corrupt. He later became a preacher of crusade and was appointed titular **Patriarch of Jerusalem**.

## Peter the Hermit (1050–1131)

Peter the Hermit was a charismatic preacher of the **First Crusade** and the leader of the mass migration known as the People's Crusade. A holy man of Amiens in Picardy, he evidently made an earlier pilgrimage and experienced rough treatment from the **Turks**. According to **William of Tyre**, in 1088, after some years in the **Holy Land**, Peter took a letter from Simeon, the Orthodox **Patriarch** of **Jerusalem**, telling of the privations suffered by the Christians in the East under Turkish rule, and has Peter promising that he would secure aid from the **Pope** and the Kings and princes of the West. Such a version of events would imply that it was Peter rather than **Alexius I Comnenus** who instigated the **Crusades**. On his return, and following Pope **Urban II**'s sermon at the **Council of Clermont**, Peter the Hermit toured **France** on his donkey, preaching. Evidently his message was especially appealing to the poor although there were knights also in the host that Peter mustered, and the force was co-led by a poor knight called Walter Sans-Avoir. They plundered their way across Eastern Europe to **Constantinople** and were given passage to Anatolia. Engaging the **Seljuk Turks**, most of the 'People's Crusade' was wiped out. At the time Peter was absent seeking aid from Alexius. He later joined the more organised Crusader armies. He retained some influence, even over the noble leaders of the Crusade, and had a place on their council. He continued with the Crusaders to the capture of Jerusalem. Peter subsequently became a legendary figure, and was an influence in the cult of sacred poverty, which was embraced by the early Templars.[9]

## *Philip II Augustus* (1165–1223)

Philip (Philippe) II Augustus was one of the most successful Kings of **France** in the medieval period. He was of the **Capetian** dynasty, the son of **Louis VII** and his third wife Adèle de **Champagne**. Louis was crowned in 1179 as co-king, a year before his father's death. His early reign was occupied by hostilities with **Henry II** of **England**. Philip's life's work would be the destruction of the **Angevin** empire in what is now western France. The **Crusades** would be a distraction from this, however. The Templars had continued to hold a position of trust in France, despite the affair over **Gisors** (a castle which Philip II would eventually recover). In 1190, before embarking on the **Third Crusade**, Philip arranged for all receipts from the royal demesne (the region around **Paris** which was the King's personal property) to be deposited in the **Paris Temple**.

After the fall of **Jerusalem**, Henry and Philip would arrange a truce while a new Crusade was planned. In the event Henry died before the Crusade embarked and his place was filled by **Richard the Lionheart**. The two kings met at **Vezelay** and planned the expedition together. They took different routes to the **Holy Land**, and Philip arrived at **Acre** months before Richard. They had once been close allies. There was a degree of rivalry between them though, which turned into enmity. Philip quarrelled with Richard over the leadership of the Crusade and over Richard's marriage (Richard had snubbed Philip's half sister). Philip also demanded to be given half of **Cyprus** (and was refused). He left the Holy Land, disillusioned, soon after the capture of Acre, and before Richard marched south. He left much of the French army in the East under Hugh III, Duke of **Burgundy**. Back in Europe, Philip sought to make political capital from his status as a Crusader, despite his having prematurely abandoned of the Crusade. He also besmirched Richard's name, and began to invade Richard's territory (in breach of the **Peace of God**). Philip II refused the Pope's invitation to lead the **Albigensian Crusade**, but permitted his barons (and later his son **Louis VIII**) to participate in it, seeing it as a vehicle for expanding Capetian dominance (Philip was on frosty terms with **Innocent III** as the Pope had refused to recognise the King's bigamous third marriage). Meanwhile Philip continued to assault the Angevin lands, depriving King **John** of England of most of his possessions in northern France, including Anjou, Normandy and Touraine. His victory at the Battle of Bouvines over John's German and Flemish allies sealed Philip's reputation in France.

## Philip II, Duke of Orleans (1674–1723)
Originally the Duke of **Chartres**, Duke Philip II of Orleans was a member of the Bourbon royal family and the regent for the young king Louis XV. He held great power in this role and was known for his taste for luxury. He features on the dubious list of **Clandestine Grand Masters** of the Knights Templar.

## Philip of Alsace, Count of Flanders (died 1191)
Philip of Alsace, a grandson of **Fulk V Count of Anjou**, was Count of Flanders from 1168. He embarked on an armed pilgrimage to the Holy Land in 1177, but failed to cooperate with his kinsman **Baldwin IV**, even though offered the regency of the **Kingdom of Jerusalem** and command of the armies. Having attempted to interfere in the remarriage of **Sibylla** and quarrelled with the Latin barons, he took his armies to campaign in the north, and did not contribute to the leper King's effort at **Montguisard**. On Philip's return to the West he became a patron of the poet **Chretien de Troyes**, and apparently he lent Chretien the mysterious book that inspired his **Holy Grail** romance. He also went to war with his former charge **Philip II Augustus**. Count and King having reconciled, both went on to participate in the **Third Crusade**. Count Philip died of the plague at the siege of **Acre**. He was buried in Clairvaux. He left no children, though twice married. On Philip's death Flanders passed to his sister Margaret and her husband Baldwin of Hainalt.

## Philip the Fair (Philip IV of France) (1268–1314)
Philip IV (*Philippe le Bel* as he was called) was the eleventh King of **France** of the **Capetian** line. He was the grandson of **Louis IX**, and the son of Philip III, who died during the unsuccessful Crusade against **Aragon** in 1285. A year before his accession, Philip IV had married the young Queen **Jeanne of Navarre**. Of their children, three sons would succeed as King of France, but none would produce a legitimate male heir. A daughter meanwhile would be Queen Consort of **England**, and produce a son who would ravage France.

Philip was crowned and anointed in the Cathedral of **Reims**. He would claim to be a zealous defender of the Christian Church, and was an advocate of something approaching the Divine Right of Kings. He consolidated his power, developing the professional state bureaucracy, and assisting secular lawyers into positions of authority. One such was his right-hand man **Guillaume de Nogaret**. Philip's reign witnessed wars with **England** and Flanders, disputes with the **Pope**, and domestic persecutions including the **suppression** of the Knights Templar. Philip was probably the man most responsible for the destruction of the Order. He was said to be handsome, but his effigy in the Abbey of St Denis shows him with a broad face, sly, narrow eyes and thin lips. His character was somewhat inscrutable and aloof.

Philip's true attitude towards the Eastern Crusades is unclear. It could be that he wished to sever the Capetian connection to Crusading; thus he attacked the Templars in order to destroy a reminder of the failed cause. On the other hand some have argued that Philip had grandiose plans for relaunching the Crusades under the aegis of the Capetian dynasty, and as a vehicle for the creation of a Capetian empire. If so, it is possible that he destroyed the Templars because they presented a barrier to this.[260]

Much of Philip's early reign was certainly devoted to attempting to extend Capetian authority. He had resorted to taxing the Church in France to finance his war of 1294–1298 against the English in Gascony. This measure put the King on a collision course with Pope **Boniface VIII**. (In 1296 Boniface's bull *Clericis Laicos* placed under **interdict** those who taxed the clergy without Papal permission.) Philip responded by cutting off all tithes to **Rome** from his realm. He also opposed and refuted the Pope's claims of **Papal supremacy**, as proclaimed in *Unam Sanctam*. The French Templars, under **Hugues de Pairaud**, tended to stand by Philip at this time. Philip also tried to raise funds, meanwhile, by imposing heavy taxes in Flanders, causing the Flemish, under Guy van Dampierre to rise up in support of England. When peace was achieved with England (cemented by the marriage of Prince Edward, later **Edward II**, to Philip's daughter **Isabella, the she-wolf of France**), Dampierre was isolated, and in 1300 Philip ordered the invasion of Flanders. In 1302, however, the Flemish again rebelled, in an uprising known as the Matins of Brugge. French forces suffered a major defeat at the Battle of the **Golden Spurs**, at the hands of the rebels. In 1304 Philip himself led a punitive expedition, fighting the Flemish to a standstill at Mons-en-Prévèle. Again the French suffered heavy losses, but the rebels were forced to retreat and the following year to agree to a treaty handing certain key towns to the French.

Philip's feud with Boniface VIII worsened until the King resorted to making scurrilous accusations against the Pope, whom he planned to arrest on charges of **heresy**, simony, blasphemy and **sodomy**. He sent Guillaume de Nogaret to seize Boniface at **Anagni**. The arrest was bungled and the Pope was rescued by his allies, but died soon after the incident, just before he could sign Philip's **excommunication**. Boniface's short-lived successor Benedict XI, cleared Philip of blame, but refused to lift an excommunication on de Nogaret. In 1305 Philip secured the election of Pope **Clement V**, a Frenchman whom he could expect to influence. Philip used as a lever the threat of reopening proceedings posthumously against the late Pope Boniface, whom he wished to have disinterred and burned. Such an unheard of event would have shattered the Papacy's credibility.

Meanwhile in the same year Jeanne de Navarre died, and it seems Philip's character hardened. The king was by now in something of a financial crisis, war having become a ruinously expensive business. To alleviate these difficulties he robbed and then expelled the **Jews** and the Lombard merchants. He also borrowed from the Templars and in 1306 devalued the coinage of the realm, provoking violent protests from an urban population who found that their rents had trebled. Philip was compelled to take refuge in the **Paris Temple**, while the riots raged. During his stay, he perhaps realised that the Templars might be a convenient source of wealth. Perhaps he conceived of them as a potential future threat, too, aware that they had recently been part of a plot against another anointed king, namely **Henry II** of **Cyprus**. It is unclear, though, whether Philip's plot against the Templars was germinating in the King's mind before the apparent denunciations of **Esquin de Floyran**.

Circumstances seemed to be in the King's favour by 1307. He held the Pope largely within his power. He had loyal men throughout the country, his *baillis* and *sénéchaux* and their foot soldiers. The head of the **Inquisition**, **Guillaume de Paris**, and many French bishops were also Philip's appointees. Crucially, it happened that **Jacques de Molay**, the **Grand Master** of the Templars and a number of other Templar dignitaries were staying in Paris, apparently oblivious to any threat. Philip and his ministers drew up their allegations and the King dispatched secret orders to his agents throughout the realm to arrest the Templars on the morning of **Friday 13** October. Jacques de Molay was lulled into a false sense of security by being afforded a place of honour at the funeral of the King's sister-in-law on the very day before the **arrests**. Philip's action against the Templars caused widespread dismay beyond France, though Philip's own subjects were conditioned to accept the charges against the Templars as a result of a sustained preaching campaign. Via the Estates-General at **Tours** and the direct intimidation of the Pope at **Poitiers**, Philip ensured the continuation of the **trial** proceedings. His ministers, Guillaume de Nogaret and **Guillaume de Plaisians**, kept him informed of events at the Papal Commission. When the defence started to gather momentum, Philip responded by having **Philip de Marigny**, the Archbishop of Sens, start to burn as 'relapsed heretics' those Templars who had retracted their earlier confessions.

Philip put heavy pressure on the Pope to ensure the formal suppression of the Order of the Temple at the **Council of Vienne**, and it was clear to many that he was driving the agenda. Philip and his son, the king of Navarre, sat on either side of Clement V as the Pope read out his bull *Vox in Excelso*. Philip was subsequently persuaded to allow the goods and lands of the Templars to be passed to the **Hospitallers** in exchange for a substantial pay-off. In 1314 Jacques de Molay came before an assembly of officials, clerics and citizens, to hear his sentence. Unexpectedly, he declared that the accusations were all false and that the Templars had always been innocent. **Geoffroi de Charney** showed solidarity with him. Philip was enraged, and without waiting for any ecclesiastical sanction, ordered the two Templars to be burned alive. They died that lingering death as the day, 18 March, drew to a close. Philip himself died on 29 November of the same year, apparently after a hunting accident.

## Philip de Milly of Nablus (died 1178)

Philip de Milly was the Lord of Nablus and then of Oultrejordan, holding the castle of **Kerak**. He would become a Templar **Grand Master**. Philip was son of Guy de Milly, a **Crusader** from Picardy. He was well connected, being a step-brother of the lord of Ramla, and brother in law of Barisan of **Ibelin**, who was married to his sister Helvis. Philip became an influential baron in the **Kingdom of Jerusalem**. He was loyal to Queen **Melisende**, and formed part of her response to the fall of **Edessa** in 1144, at a time when **Baldwin III** was being sidelined for political reasons.[261] Later, Philip fought alongside Baldwin and the Knights Templar at the capture of **Ascalon**. He is said to have been a gifted linguist, knowing French, Latin, Arabic and Armenian. At some point he also made a pilgrimage to the Monastery of St **Catherine of Alexandria** in the Sinai. He joined the Templars himself some time before 1166, probably after the death of his wife Isabella. In 1169 he was elected the Order's seventh **Grand Master**, succeeding **Bertrand de Blanquefort**. Philip was the first Grand Master to have been born in the orient. He probably led the Order during the defence of **Gaza** against an attack by **Saladin**. Philip resigned as Grand Master in 1171 for reasons unknown. In his place **Odo de St Amand** was elected. Philip then became a royal envoy to **Constantinople**.[262] Philip's daughter Stephanie de Milly was remarried to **Reynald de Châtillon**, upon his release from **Nur ed-Din**'s dungeons. Reynald thus became lord of Kerak.

## Philip de Marigny (born c. 1270)

Philip (Philippe) de Marigny was the Archbishop of Sens during the Trials of the Templars. He was the younger brother of the Royal Chamberlain Enguerrand de Marigny, and one eager to demonstrate his loyalty to the regime of King **Philip the Fair**. When the Papal Commission heard the Templars in Paris defending their Order with reasoned argument and conviction, there seemed to be a danger that they might be cleared of the **accusations** after all. The King's strategy was to reopen the Episcopal enquiries in the provinces, to examine the Templars as individuals, (as opposed to the Order as a body which was the remit of the Cardinals and the Archbishop of Narbonne). Philip de Marigny therefore convened the **Council of Sens**. By a quirk of administrative demarcation, it happened that Paris fell under the authority of Sens. Therefore the Archbishop of Sens was able to have the Templars taken from under the noses of the Papal Commission to be examined in at his own tribunal under less sympathetic conditions. Here those who had confessed under torture and then retracted their confessions were declared to be relapsed **heretics** and sentenced as such and were **burnt**. Those who had never admitted to the accusations and could not be judged relapsed were sentenced to life imprisonment.

## Philip de Montfort (died 1270)

Philip de Montfort, Constable of **Jerusalem**, was one of the Frankish leaders at the disastrous Battle of **La Forbie** in October 1244. He was a grandson of **Balian of Ibelin** via his mother Helvis, and of Simon de Montfort, 6th Earl of Leicester via his father Guy, who had died in the **Albigensian Crusade**. He escaped the battle and went on to become Lord of **Tyre**. He also participated in the **Seventh Crusade** under **Louis IX**. After that he quarrelled with the merchants of Venice and expelled them from Tyre, an event contributing to the **War of St Sabas**. He was ultimately stabbed in his chapel by an **Assassin** agent who had pretended to convert to Christianity.

## Philip de Plessiez (1165–1209)

Philip de Plessiez was a knight from the region of Anjou. He may have been born in the castle of Plessis-Macé near Angers. He participated in the **Third Crusade** as a secular **knight**, and at some point thereafter joined the Knights Templar. He became the thirteenth **Grand Master** in early 1201. Philip wrote to Abbot Arnaud Amalric of Citeaux in 1202, describing misfortunes in the East arising from Muslim encroachment, sandstorms and earthquakes.

## Philip de Voet (thirteenth–fourteenth century)

Philip de Voet was one of the jailors of the Templars in **Paris**. He had informed the tribunal how many of the imprisoned Templars, on the brink of death, had sworn that the **accusations against the Order** were false. He was sent by the Papal Commission to the Archbishop of Sens, **Philip de Marigny**, to request a postponement of the Templars sentenced to **burning**. This was ignored and the Templars were burned anyway, thus the **defence of the Order** was critically undermined.

## Pierre de Bologna (1270–1310?)

Pierre de Bologna was an educated Templar Priest and former representative of the Order to the Papal Curia. He was a leading spokesman in the defence of the Order before the Papal Commission trials, and seems to have been a skilful speaker. He was named as a procurator along with three others, **Guillaume de Chambonnet**, **Bertrand de Sartiges** and **Renaud de Provins**. He grudgingly accepted the position once it became clear that the **Grand Master** was unwilling or unable to lead the defence.

Provins highlighted procedural irregularities that exposed the action against the Templars as illegal. Bologna, meanwhile, concentrated on arguing that confessions secured under **torture** could not be held as incriminating or valid. He said the wonder was not that some had confessed lies, but that any had kept up to the truth, in face of the menaces and tribulations that befell those who denied the accusations, while the liars were promised favourable treatment. He denounced the accusations as shameful, impossible and outrageous, the work of false Christians motivated by greed and wickedness. (He said the King had been led astray by unscrupulous advisors, rather than implicating **Philip the Fair** directly.) He claimed initiates were received with 'the honest kiss of peace' and were devoted to **Christ**, whose cross they bore. The Papal Commission degenerated into a farce after the Archbishop of Sens, **Philip de Marigny**, in a separate trial, began to sentence Templars to be executed as relapsed **heretics**, and after **Gilles Aicelin** and the prelates of the Papal Commission proved themselves unwilling or unable to prevent this, despite Bologna's appeals. Bologna himself disappeared soon after. If he didn't escape, he may have been killed in prison.

## *Pierre Dubois* (born *c.* 1255)

Pierre Dubois was a lawyer, pamphleteer and propagandist for King **Philip the Fair**. At the time of the **suppression** of the Knights Templar or shortly before, he wrote a tract ostensibly concerned with future crusading strategy, called *Recuparatione Terre Sancte*. The ideas of Pierre Dubois were in tune with those of **Guillaume de Nogaret**.[263] His ideas would have placed **France** at the centre of any new crusading venture, and could be construed as little more than an attempt to transform the **Crusades** into a vehicle for **Capetian** supremacy. He advocated the destruction of the Knights Templar, and the sequestering of their resources for the new royal Crusade. He also proposed that vast amounts of Church money and the entire revenues of the surviving Military Orders be channelled into a Crusade treasury, which would implicitly be controlled by the king of France, who would have become emperor of east and west according to this vision. Dubois also spoke before the Estates General in Paris in 1308, condemning the Templars for **denial of Christ** and for **sodomy** (*bougrerie*).[264]

## *Pierre Plantard* (1920–2000)

Pierre Plantard, a French draftsman, originated the myth of the **Priory of Sion** as an ancient society. His claims formed the basis of *The Holy Blood and* *the Holy Grail*. Plantard also invented the extended name 'Plantard de **Saint-Clair**'. He was the son of a butler. He gravitated towards the political right, and during the Second World War wrote to Marshal Pétain about **Jewish/Freemasonic** conspiracies that he believed to exist. He also served some time in prison for fraud. In 1956, in Annemasse, with one André Donhome, he founded the **Prieuré de Sion** but it was short-lived and nothing like what it was later claimed to be (it was a group lobbying for cheap housing!). Plantard's outlook grew more mystical. He began to claim psychic abilities, and descent from the **Merovingian** Kings. He also took an interest in medieval **Gisors** and **Rennes le Château**. He reformed the Priory of Sion with two new associates, **Philippe de Chérisy** and **Gérard de Sède**. This time Plantard claimed that the Priory had been created by **Godfroi de Bouillon**. The three men also concocted the story of **Bérenger Saunière** discovering a treasure. Philippe de Chérisy faked the parchments, while Gérard de Sède published a book on the mystery of Rennes le Château, promising to share the profits with the other two. Plantard produced the list of **Grand Masters** for the 'Dossiers Secrets'. In 1984 researcher Jean-Luc Chaumeil expose Plantard's true past, prompting him to 'resign' as Grand Master of the supposed Priory of Sion and to retreat into obscurity. Plantard later changed his story and claimed that the Priory was something created in 1681, but by then the myth of the timeless secret society linked to the Knights Templar had captured people's imagination.

## Pilgrimage

The Knights Templar were originally formed to protect pilgrims from bandits, and to keep the roads safe, while the **Hospitallers** were originally responsible for caring for sick pilgrims. They saw it as a way of serving God by providing a service to his faithful. In ancient times **Jews** were required to perform pilgrimages to the **Temple of Solomon**. After the birth of **Islam**, Muslim men were required to perform pilgrimage to Mecca. Jerusalem remained the main focus of Christian pilgrimage, although there were shrines across **Christendom** that also drew pilgrims. These included Santiago de Compostella in Spain, **Rome** in Italy, **Vezelay** in France, Cologne in Germany, and **Constantinople**, the capital of the Byzantine Empire. The **Crusades** to the **Holy Land**, meanwhile, were originally presented as armed pilgrimages, with a penitential and devotional nature.

## Pilgrims' Castle

Pilgrims' Castle (also called Château Pelerin, or Atlit, or the Castle of Jesus Christ) was a Templar **castle** on the Palestinian coast, south of Haifa and north of **Caesarea**. The castle occupied a promontory jutting out into the sea. It was built from 1218 onwards, its construction having been ordered by **Guillaume de Chartres**, to replace the old tower-fortress of Destroit.

Hospitallers, pilgrims, Teutonic Knights, and Lord Walter of Avesnes also helped in the construction. During the construction, the Templars discovered a fresh water supply and a cache of ancient coins amid Phoenician foundations, which they put towards the building expenses.[265] The formidable defensive walls were protected by a fosse ditch, which made it impossible for enemies to undermine them (the tunnels would have been flooded). Inside was a fine polygonal church. The castle also had its own port. Atlit's garrison, under Peter de Montaigu, withstood a siege by the Ayyubid Sultan of Damascus, al-Muazzam in 1220. The large Syrian force came to put pressure on Frankish strongholds in the Holy Land while many of their defenders were absent during the Fifth Crusade. The few hundred Templars of Pilgrims' Castle managed to put the Damascene siege engines out of action, and to inflict heavy losses on the enemy, who after a number of months was forced to withdraw. The Emperor Frederick II beset the Templars in Pilgrims' Castle but failed to gain entrance. Later the castle withstood a siege by Baybars, and it never fell to enemy assault. It was only evacuated after the fall of Acre in 1191. The Mameluks then partially demolished it, though some ruins survive.

## Piscina

A piscina is a stone basin for rinsing the liturgical chalices etc. Piscinas are usually found in a niche in the church wall to the side of the altar. There are examples in the Templar churches of Garway, Dinsley and Temple Church, London. The name piscine was originally a Roman word for fish pond. Reflecting this, the carvings above the piscine at Garway include a fish.

## Poitiers

Poitiers is a town in west central France, near which the Muslim invaders were defeated in 732. Later, the city was developed and fortified by Eleanor of Aquitaine. It was also the centre of a Templar province. Poitiers may have been where Jacques de Molay met Pope Clement V after returning from Cyprus in late 1306. After the arrest of the Templars in 1307, Poitiers was also the venue for a meeting between King Philip the Fair and Pope Clement V in May and June 1308. After much debate the Pope agreed to set up two concurrent trials for the Templars, the Papal Commission, sitting in Paris, would examine the guilt or innocence of the Order as a whole, while provincial councils (tribunals) would try the Templars as individuals. Here it was also decided that a General Church Council would be held at Vienne (Council of Vienne), to deliver a verdict on the Order of the Temple. Pope Clement V had been harangued in two speeches, delivered by the King's minister Guillaume de Plaisians, which were laden with veiled menaces.

## Poitiers, Battle of
(1) The Battle of Poitiers (or Tours) of 732 was a victory for the Franks under Charles Martel over invading Arab forces that had crossed from Spain.
(2) The Battle of Poitiers of 1356 was a victory for the English under Edward the Black Prince (the son of Edward III) over superior French forces during the Hundred Years War. King Jean II of France was captured.

## Ponferrada
Ponferrada is in northern Spain. The castle there was the base of the Templar Master of Castle.

## Ponsard de Gizy (late thirteenth–early fourteenth century)
Ponsard de Gizy was the Preceptor of Payns (Champagne). He was a Templar heard at the Paris trials. He tentatively started to defend the Order's innocence. One strand of his defence was to name his known enemies. **Inquisitorial** procedure allowed this. Though the witness had no right to know by whom he was accused, if the names of his enemies matched the names he gave, this could be taken into account. Ponsard de Gizy named various persecutors, including Guillaume Robert, a monk who had subjected him to **torture**, and **Esquin de Floyran,** the man who had told tales of the order's **heresy** and who seems to have been present at some of the interrogations. He said that any confessions were on account of this torture.

It was found that Ponsard de Gizy had previously written a letter of complaint about various abuses in the Templar Order. He had among other things alleged that the Master swore in **sisters of the Order** as well as brothers, making the sisters promise poverty, chastity and obedience, but that once the sisters had entered, the masters deflowered them. Ponsard had clearly been disgruntled with the Order at the time of writing, and had also alleged that that the Order admitted the illegitimate offspring of these 'sisters' as well as all manner of criminals. However at the Cardinals' tribunal, Ponsard claimed that the Order was innocent of the things in the **accusations**. He had been harshly tortured before his earlier confession. He had been kept in a pit with his wrists bound so tightly the blood ran from his nails.

## Popes
The Popes were the heads of the Roman **Catholic** Church, with other titles including Vicar of **Christ**, Supreme Pontiff, Bishop of **Rome** and Prince of the Apostles. They were recognised by the Greek Orthodox Church as the **Patriarchs** of Rome, but not as universal ecclesiastical sovereigns. The Catholic claim is that the Popes are the successors of St Peter who received spiritual authority over the Church from **Christ** himself. In the Middle Ages the Popes asserted **Papal Supremacy**. The institution of the papacy was the Holy See.

The Papacy was sometimes disputed between two claimants. The loser in these often bitter struggles would be labelled an *antipope*. Because some antipopes were considered legitimate at the time this has sometimes caused confusion, especially in allocating regnal numbers. There were also periods when the position was vacant. The accepted Popes to reign around the time of the Templars were:

| Pope | Reign |
|---|---|
| **Urban II** | 1088–99 |
| Pascal II | 1099–1118 |
| Gelasius II | 1118–19 |
| Calixtus II | 1119–24 |
| Honorius II | 1124–30 |
| **Innocent II** | 1130–43 |
| **Celestine II** | 1143–4 |
| Lucius II | 1144–5 |
| **Eugenius III** | 1145–53 |
| Anastasius IV | 1153–4 |
| Adrian IV | 1154–9 |
| Alexander III | 1159–81 |
| Lucius II | 1181–5 |
| Urban III | 1185–87 |
| Gregory VIII | 1187–91 |
| **Celestine III** | 1191–98 |
| **Innocent III** | 1198–1216 |
| **Honorius III** | 1216–27 |
| **Gregory IX** | 1227–41 |
| Celestine IV | 1241 |
| Innocent IV | 1241–54 |
| **Alexander IV** | 1254–61 |
| Urban IV | 1261–4 |
| Clement IV | 1264–8 |
| **Gregory X** | 1271–6 |
| Innocent V | 1276 |
| Adrian V | 1276 |
| John XXI | 1276–7 |
| Nicolas III | 1277–80 |
| **Martin IV** | 1280–5 |
| Honorius IV | 1285–7 |
| **Nicolas IV** | 1288–92 |
| **Celestine V** | 1292–6 |
| **Boniface VIII** | 1294–1303 |

| Benedict XI | 1303–4 |
| **Clement V** | 1305–14 |
| **John XXII** | 1316–34 |

Catholic Christians in the twelfth and thirteenth century accepted the place of the Pope as the head of the Church, and looked to him for spiritual leadership. The failure of the papacy to offer such leadership, its insistence on temporal authority and its general worldliness contributed to a growing disillusionment with Orthodoxy, which led to the spread of **heresy**. The ecclesiastical institution surrounding the Papacy also became increasingly legalistic and bureaucratic in the era of the **Crusades**.

The Papacy largely created the crusading movement, promising remission of sins (**indulgences**) for those who fought to liberate and defend **Jerusalem** and the Eastern Church. However, in later times it exploited crusading as a weapon of papal supremacy, and called Crusades against its political enemies, notably **Frederick II** and then **Aragon**. In the course of the thirteenth century the papacy succeeded in casting off the influence of the **Holy Roman Empire**, at the cost of coming under the dominance of the **Capetian** dynasty of **France**. For most of the fourteenth century the papacy was based in **Avignon** and closely tied to the French court.

## Portugal

Portugal came into being as a separate kingdom under Alfonso Henriques, a patron and associate of the Templars, who encouraged the Order to establish itself there as part of the **Reconquista**. The Order of the Temple received its first grants early on, including towns and castles from rulers who hoped they would lend military assistance against the **Moors**. The earliest donation seems to have been the castle of Soure, given by the Countess Teresa, the mother of Alfonso Henriques. Alfonso's son Sancho continued to favour the Templars. The Order received many grants of land and castles on the frontier, as, with their help, the kingdom expanded southward. They also received ecclesiastical authority over the recovered land.

Local Templars participated in the capture of Lisbon from the Muslims, where Portuguese forces were assisted by northern European knights en-route to the **Second Crusade**. In 1160 the Templars built their fortress headquarters at **Tomar**, having also founded the town there. In 1190 the Templars withstood a siege at Tomar from the invading Moroccans, and successfully repulsed the Muslims from the region. The Templar Master of Portugal during this period was the formidable **Gualdim Pais**. One of the best surviving castles is **Almoural**. The Templars also operated a hospital for **pilgrims** in the north, granted by the local archbishop at Braga. The Templars in Portugal were never found guilty of heresy. Templar lands were passed to the **Knights of Christ**.

## Poverty

There is a strand within Christianity that regards poverty as something sacred, as though possessions and wealth would contaminate the spirit. Monks were bound to take a vow of poverty (as well as **celibacy** and **obedience**). St **Francis of Assisi** spoke of poverty as his bride. The Templars too were party to the cult of poverty. They renounced individual possessions themselves, and bound themselves to defending poor and vulnerable **pilgrims** as an act of **charitable** love. Like other Orders, though, the Templars became collectively very wealthy and this made individual poverty inconvenient for some.

## Preceptory

A Preceptory or Commandery was a foundation of the Knights Templar, ruled by a Preceptor. It might constitute a rural farm manor or an urban monastic establishment, sometimes called a house. Some Preceptories were fortified, and some were equipped to host guests and to look after **pilgrims**. A well-equipped provincial Preceptory might contain a number of buildings within its precincts. There would be a stone chapel, possibly a **round church**, not excessively decorated but perhaps containing **wall paintings** of patron saints and battle scenes to remind the brethren of their Order's purpose in the **Holy Land**. The chapel might also contain **Holy Relics**. There would be a burial ground adjoining. There would be halls (of stone or timber-framed) dormitories, and possibly a separate residence for the **Preceptor**. There might be a refectory, an armoury and training ground, and perhaps a defensive tower. There would be a kitchen, a brewery, a larder, a bake house, stables, a smithy and workshop, a kiln, several barns, an orchard and a vegetable garden. There would be fields of livestock – cattle and sheep, a sty for pigs, a dovecot for pigeons and a coop of hens. There might also be a prison cell for brethren who breached the Order's discipline.

## Prester John

Prester John was a legendary priest-king whom medieval European Christians imagined reigning over a Christian empire somewhere in the East, beyond the Islamic world. They thought he might be a descendant of the Biblical Magi, and there were various legends about his powers, his military prowess, and the fanciful wonders of his kingdom. He was said to wield an emerald sceptre. The myth of Prester John probably had its origin in the reality of the St Thomas Christians in India, and of the Nestorians among the **Mongols. Jacques de Vitry** had heard that Prester John's people were Nestorians. **Oliver of Paderborn** recorded rumours of a David, son of Prester John, whom the knights of the **Fifth Crusade** hoped would come to aid them against the **Muslims**, and to assist in the recover **Jerusalem**. In 1141 the **Seljuks** had suffered a defeat in the East (near Samarkand) by the Kara

Khitai, a Mongol people, some of whom were indeed Nestorian Christians. The chief of the Kara Khitai was named Yur-Khan. In muddled accounts that filtered through to the Crusaders, Yur-Khan could have become Johan. Oliver of Paderborn's Asiatic 'David' was reputed to be an instrument of divine vengeance, and was evidently an optimistic reading of reports of Genghis Khan. An alternative source for the Prester John myth may have been the Christian Empire of **Ethiopia**, beyond Islamic North Africa. The seafaring Portuguese **Knights of Christ** would later identify the Ethiopian ruler as Prester John.

## Priests

Priests were members of the ordained clergy with the authority to perform the sacraments of the **Mass**. The Templars were given their own priests in the Papal bull *Omne Datum Optimum*, issued in 1139 by **Innocent II**, which also placed the Order above Episcopal jurisdiction and bestowed other privileges. Even the Patriarch of Jerusalem lost his authority over the Templars with this bull, which was the making of the Order as a great political entity. Ordinary Templars, though they took religious vows, had no spiritual authority. They were religious but not priests. Of all the Templars, only the Priests could perform masses, baptise, hear confessions, offer absolution and preside at **burials**. They were also the members of the Order most likely to be well educated and literate and it is unsurprising that one of them, **Pierre de Bologna**, became the most effective defender and spokesman of the Order at their trials in **Paris**.

## Priory of Sion

The *Prieuré de Notre Dame de Mt Sion* or *Prieuré de Sion* (Priory of Sion) came to wider attention after the publication of *The Holy Blood and the Holy Grail*. The book portrays it as a clandestine society dating back to **Godfroi de Bouillon**, and preserving the secret that the bloodline of the deposed **Merovingian** dynasty survives in certain noble families – and that the Merovingians were themselves the descendants of **Mary Magdalene** and **Jesus Christ**. The Priory of Sion was actually invented by **Pierre Plantard** in the late 1950s. The Priory myth, and the related **Rennes le Château** 'mystery' (centring on the nineteenth-century Abbé **Bérengar Saunière** and his supposed sudden wealth) was concocted among Plantard and his associates Phillippe de Chérisy and **Gérard de Sède**. For his associates it was perhaps a confidence trick and a surrealist joke. For Plantard it was a vehicle to support his spurious claim of Merovingian descent.

## Provinces

The Templar order in the West was divided up into provinces called *Langues* (tongues) roughly corresponding to the areas in which different languages were spoken. These consisted of scattered estates through various kingdoms rather than being unified entities. Each province had its headquarters, where the provincial Master or **Grand Preceptor** of the region would preside and administer the dispersed region under his authority, and held authority over the Masters of scattered **Preceptories** and manors. The most important province was the **Kingdom of Jerusalem** (where the **Grand Master** and major officers resided). All the other provinces existed to sustain Jerusalem with a portion of the profits and produce of their various industries (mainly agricultural). Each house typically sent a cash donation (known as a responsion) of a third of its income to the Order in the East, channelled via the provincial headquarters. The Templar holdings in Iberia, however, were not expected to contribute so much to the East, as they were involved with opposing the **Moors**. The Templars' Rule in the 1160s listed the most important provinces as **Tripoli, Antioch, France, England, Poitiers, Aragon, Portugal**, Apulia and Hungary. Apulia seems to have included all of southern Italy and Sicily, while Hungary may have referred to Dalmatia and Eastern Europe. Later the list seems to have been revised, with regional Preceptors within France rising in importance. **Cyprus** also became a vital province.

## Provins

Provins was a mercantile town in the **Champagne** region, under the protection of the Counts of Champagne. Some of its medieval architecture, including mighty fortifications, survives to this day. **Henry I, Count of Champagne** built a chapel there where he installed a certain Holy Relic, the head of St Judas Cyriacus, which he had brought back from Jerusalem. Provins meanwhile also became an important Templar location, the Order having two **Preceptories** there by the end of the twelfth century, and numerous other properties in and around the town, including warehouses and rented properties, a tile factory, market stalls and vineyards.

## Punishment within the Order

Some Templar churches contained penitential cells in the walls, but it is unlikely people were deliberately left to die in these. There is some evidence that the Preceptor **Walter Bachelor** perished under sinister circumstances in the cell at **Temple Church** in London, while being punished for some transgression of the rule. Other crimes may have resulted in corporal punishment and humiliating penances, such as those ordained for **Adam de Wallaincourt**, who was made to eat on the floor with the dogs for a year. Demotion was another possible punishment. The most serious and shameful sentence was deemed to be expulsion from the Order, though those expelled might be expected to do penance at a **Cistercian** monastery. Templars judged their own, decisions were made at Chapter meetings, and the verdicts noted for use as precedents should similar cases arise. The **Catalan Rule** of the Templars contains such case studies. These include the case of Jacques de Ravane, who was imprisoned for raiding the Muslims without permission. Also that of one brother George the Mason, who deserted, was imprisoned on his recapture and perished there.

# Q

## *Qalawun (c. 1220–90)*

Qalawun (or Kalawun) al-Mansur was a **Mameluk** Sultan of **Egypt**. He rose to power in 1279, after a campaign against **Armenia**, and after leading a coup in Egypt. He continued **Baybars'** campaign against the crumbling **Kingdom of Jerusalem**, further diminishing **Frankish** power in the **Holy Land**. After a battle in 1280 Qalawun imposed his authority over the governor of **Damascus**, Sungur, and then united with Sungur to defeat **Mongol** forces near Homs. He initially made treaties with the Christian cities and the **Military Orders** (he seems to have reduced **Tyre** to a tributary state). In 1285, however, he besieged and captured the **Hospitaller** castle of Margat. In 1297 he invaded Lataika, the last port remaining to the Frankish principality of **Antioch**.

In 1289 he attacked **Tripoli**. A spy in the pay of the Templars, the Emir al-Fakhri, had told the Grand Master **Guillaume de Beaujeu** of the planned attack, and de Beaujeu had sent a warning, but it was not heeded. Thus Tripoli was unprepared for the onslaught, and was taken by storm. The Templar commander Peter de Moncada died during the defence. Afterwards Qalawun took the surviving population away as **slaves** and destroyed the city. Qalawun's last act was to organise the campaign against **Acre**, which would be completed by his son **al-Ashraf Khalil**.

# R

## *Ramon Lull (c. 1235–15)*

Ramon Lull was a Catalan writer, mystic, philosopher and **Crusade** strategist, born in Mallorca. He was known as the 'Illuminated Doctor'. He had been a tutor to **James II of Aragon**. He advocated the study of Arabic, in order to convert **Muslims** to Christianity through preaching. He also favoured the **merger** of the **Military Orders**. He taught in **Paris** and preached in Tunis, and his approach to theology was a synthesis of faith and reason. On the matter of the Templars he seems eventually to have been persuaded of their guilt of **heresy**. His own ideas however, (especially his attempt to reconcile faith and reason and his interest in astrology) were subsequently condemned by the **Catholic** Church. His name later came to be associated with alchemy.

## Ramon sa Guardia (born c. 1254)

Ramon sa Guardia was the last Templar Preceptor of **Mas Deu** in Rousillon. At the time of the suppression he held up in the castle of **Miravet** where he was ultimately besieged by **James II** of **Aragon**. Ramon protested the Order's innocence to the King, and also appealed to Blanche of Anjou, wife of James. Ramon hoped the Queen would intercede on behalf of the Templars. Ramon also reminded the King how the Templars had shed their blood for Aragon and been rewarded in the past, and that they had continued to serve the kingdom faithfully and courageously, not only fighting the **Muslims** but giving alms to the needy. It achieved little, for the King laid siege to Miravet, although he did not press the Templars aggressively. Ramon wrote sorrowfully to James that he pitied him and the King of **France**, and 'all **Catholics** in relation to the harm which arises from all this, more than ourselves which have to endure the evil'.

The siege was long and negotiations continued intermittently throughout. Ramon offered to surrender providing James undertook to protect the Templars so long as Pope **Clement V** remained under the power of King **Philip the Fair**. In the end he resolved to fight rather than be falsely condemned as a **heretic**. Ramon was eventually forced to abandon Miravet as its sixty or seventy defenders were starved into submission. Ramon finally surrendered in late November 1308 after nearly a year. He was subsequently extradited to Rousillon. When he came before a tribunal, he denied the charges, claimed the initiation ritual was wholly orthodox, and denied that any of the vile 'errors' in the **accusations** had ever existed in the Order.

## Raoul de Gizy (born c. 1261)

Raoul de Gizy was the Templar Preceptor of Lagny-le-Sec and Sommereaux near Beauvais, **France** (despite apparently being only a sergeant brother). He was one of the few Templars in **Paris** who initially cooperated with the accusers over the charges of **idolatry**. He described seeing the idolatrous **head** in seven different Chapter meetings, sometimes held by **Hugues de Pairaud**, and sometimes in the presence of **Gerard de Villiers**. According to him it was an object of terrible and **demonic** appearance, and when it appeared all the brethren prostrated themselves before it. He described the conventional reception at his **initiation ceremony** (where de Pairaud had presided), but then added the heretical practices, including being made to spit at a holy image in a book. Raoul later came before the Council of Sens (the trial organised by the ruthless Archbishop **Philip de Marigny**) and forsook the mantle of a Templar before being reconciled with the Church.

## Raoul de Presles (thirteenth–fourteenth century)

Raoul de Presles was a lawyer from the court of **Philip the Fair** and an influential figure. He testified as a hostile witness at the Templars' **trial in Paris** in

April 1310. He said that he had once been a friend of Gervais de Beauvais, preceptor of Laon. He claimed Gervais had often alluded to a deadly secret within the Order of the Temple, which he could never tell. He had also heard Gervais speak of the severity of the Order's prisons, where disobedient brethren were interred, even unto death.

## *Raymbaud de Caron* (1240–1308/09)

Raymbaud de Caron was Preceptor of **Outremer** (i.e. of **Cyprus**, by this stage). He accompanied **Jacques de Molay** to Europe when the **Grand Master** was summoned by **Clement V** in 1306. He was one of the high ranking Templars held and questioned at the castle of **Chinon** in August 1308. His testimony appears in the **Chinon Parchment**, a document recently rediscovered in the **Vatican Secret Archives**. He confessed to denouncing Christ at a reception that took place near Carpentras forty-three years previously, presided over by Preceptor Roncelin de Fos. After confessing before the cardinals, de Caron was declared absolved. Raymbaud disappeared mysteriously some time after giving this deposition. It seems likely he died in the castle.

## *Raymond de Bentho* (thirteenth–fourteenth century)

Raymond de Bentho was a knight who testified at the trial of the Templars on **Cyprus**. He had acted as a custodian of Templar prisoners after their arrest. He had been sent to guard them under house arrest at the fortress **Preceptory** at Khirokitia. He was at first suspicious of them, having heard of the evil **accusations** against them, and avoided their company. He then, however, witnessed the prisoners attending a **mass**, where the holy wafer elevated by the priest seemed twice normal size and particularly bright. He later asked the priest about it and was shown a supply of perfectly normal wafers, convincing him that the one he had seen at the mass constituted a miracle, and proved the Templars' innocence. This Raymond testified at the trial, also reporting that in the **Holy Land** he had seen them fighting against the Saracens as well or better than other Christians, and that he had often seen them revere the cross.[266]

## *Raymond of Poitiers/of Antioch* (1105–1149)

Raymond of Poitiers became the Prince of **Antioch** in 1136, on his marriage to **Constance of Antioch**. The following year he was reluctantly compelled to recognise the **Byzantine** Emperor **John II Comnenus** as his overlord, following a siege by Imperial forces. He later tried to rebel against Byzantine power, but was ultimately brought into line by the Emperor **Manuel I** and obliged to recognise a Greek **Patriarch**. Raymond's daughter Maria of Antioch was later married to Manuel. Raymond may have been responsible for some of the earliest donations of land and castles to the **Military Orders**. He seems to have had Templars and **Hospitallers** augmenting his army. During the **Second Crusade**, Raymond played host to **Louis VII** and **Eleanor of Aquitaine**, hoping to persuade Louis to remain in the area to assist him in a campaign against **Aleppo**. Louis however continued south to **Jerusalem**, thence to attack **Damascus** without success. Raymond was an uncle of Queen Eleanor, which did not prevent rumours circulating that he had an affair with her during her visit. Louis grew paranoid about their relationship. Raymond was later killed in battle against **Nur ed-Din** at **Inab**.

## Raymond II of Tripoli (1115–52)

Raymond II of **Tripoli** was the son of Pons of Tripoli and great grandson of **Raymond IV of Toulouse**. His wife Hodiera was a daughter of **Baldwin II** and sister of Queen **Melisende**. Raymond was involved in warfare against **Zenghi** of **Aleppo**, and was briefly a prisoner of the **Muslims**. He was also a patron of the Knights **Hospitaller**, granting them at least five castles in the county of Tripoli, including **Krak des Chevaliers** in 1144. In 1152 he was murdered by an **Assassin**, while riding back from escorting his estranged wife some way to **Jerusalem**. (He was the first Christian lord to fall victim to the sect, which had previously only targeted prominent Sunni **Muslims**.)

## Raymond III of Tripoli (1140–87)

Count Raymond III succeeded his father **Raymond II of Tripoli** at the age of twelve, and in these early times his mother Hodierna acted as regent of **Tripoli**. In 1164 Raymond joined with **Bohemond III, Prince of Antioch** to confront **Nur ed-Din's** encroaching forces at **Harenc**. The Christians were defeated and many were taken to **Aleppo** as prisoners. Raymond was only released in 1173 in return for a ransom. During his time in captivity he had learned Arabic, and observed **Arab** customs. He would remain one of the Latin barons most respected among the **Muslims**.

Raymond earned the enmity of an ambitious knight from the West called **Gerard de Ridefort**, who had taken service under Raymond, apparently on the understanding that he would be rewarded with the hand of a rich heiress, whom in the event Raymond gave to a Genoese merchant. Ridefort, enraged, departed from Raymond's court, and joined the Knights Templar.

On the death of **Amalric I**, Raymond sought to become regent of the **Kingdom of Jerusalem**, during the minority of **Baldwin IV**. As the King's closest male relative he had a claim. Conveniently the appointed Regent Miles of Plancy was soon murdered in **Acre**, allowing Raymond to govern. Raymond arranged **Sibylla of Jerusalem's** marriage to William 'Longsword' of Montferrat. After William's death, Raymond was instrumental in ensuring that William and Sibylla's son (later **Baldwin V**) was named as Baldwin IV's heir. In the event Raymond failed to prevent Sibylla's remarriage to **Guy de Lusignan** or Guy's eventual succession, especially as Guy has the support of the Knights Templar under their new Grand Master Gerard de Ridefort, who was still intensely hostile to Raymond. Soon after Guy's coronation Raymond withdrew to his northern territories. He made an independent truce with **Saladin**, distancing himself from the court in Jerusalem, which was doing nothing to stop the provocative raids on Muslim caravans by **Reynald de Chatillon** that would inevitably result in retaliation. Raymond allowed a Muslim army to cross his territory, prompting fears in Jerusalem that Raymond would ally with Saladin against the Kingdom. A Templar-led delegation was dispatched to negotiate with Raymond. Before it reached him it was annihilated by the Muslim force at **Cresson**. Only Gerard de Ridfort escaped. Still, according to **Ibn al-Athir**, the Count sided with Saladin, and was only shamed into realigning with the Christians when another delegation headed by the Patriarch arrived.

Raymond went to meet with the King and the court at **Acre**. During his absence, Saladin brought his army against Tiberias. Raymond's wife the countess Eschiva, holding out in the besieged Citadel, sent word of the situation. Despite this Raymond opposed the idea of launching out to relieve Tiberias. He did not believe Saladin capable of holding together his vast army, and deemed it prudent not to advance from the easier defended and well-watered position of Sephoria (to which the Franks had moved). He advised that if the army marched out across the desert attempting to relieve the city it would be an act of suicide. King Guy appeared to accept this argument, but was visited by Gerard de Ridefort. Gerard, supported by **Reynald de Chatillon**, persuaded Guy that Raymond was a traitor in league with Saladin, and that following Raymond's advice would make Guy appear weak. Predicting doom, Raymond accompanied the army across the arid wastes to the Battle of **Hattin**. He led two unsuccessful charges, but then fled, seeing that the situation was hopeless. It is possible the Muslims allowed him to go. He made away to Tripoli, but had lost the will to live, deeming himself to be forsaken by God, and died soon after.

## Raymond IV of Toulouse (Raymond I of Tripoli) (1052–1105)

Raymond IV de St Gilles, Count of Toulouse was the ruler of a large region of south-western France. He led the Provencal contingent during the **First Crusade**, having previously fought the **Moors** in **Iberia**. He refused to swear allegiance to **Alexius I Comnenus** in **Constantinople**, yet he of all the **Crusader** barons would have the most constructive relationship with the Emperor.

Raymond was accompanied on the First Crusade by his third wife Elvira, and by his eldest son Bertrand. Raymond fought at Nicæa and at **Dorylaeum**, and at **Antioch**. He left a garrison there, when he passed on towards **Jerusalem**, but this was ejected by the Norman **Bohemond of Taranto**, who intended to be sole ruler of Antioch. Raymond consequently looked for another potential fiefdom, and began to take land in Lebanon, which would later form the basis of Tripoli. Eventually the Crusaders, under Raymond, Tancred and **Godfroi de Bouillon**, arrived at **Jerusalem**. Raymond's forces secured the surrender of the **Tower of David**. The citadel's defenders were the only **Muslims** to be spared, and as a result Raymond has been judged the most honourable of the Crusaders. Subsequently he declined the crown. After assisting Godfroi in the south against the Egyptians (and sometimes quarrelling over the spoils), Raymond headed north and deprived Bohemond of Laodicia. He then went to Constantinople to ally with Alexius against the Norman's ambitions. He eventually returned to the vicinity of Tripoli and consolidated his power base there with the capture of Tortosa, with Greek help.

## *Raymond VI of Toulouse* (1156–1222)

Raymond VI de St Gilles became Count of Toulouse in 1194. He was **excommunicated** three times. He also had five wives in turn, the fourth being Joan Plantagenet, sister of **Richard the Lionheart**. He was a tolerant ruler who refused the demands of Pope **Innocent III**'s legate, Peter of Castelnau, that he clamp down on the heretical **Cathars**. The Church blamed Raymond for the murder of Castelnau, and used this as justification for launching the **Albigensian Crusade**. After the sieges of Béziers and **Carcassonne**, Raymond distanced himself from the 'Crusaders', and began to lead the opposition. He also travelled to **Rome** to attempt to clear himself of Castelnau's murder but his arguments were ignored, and he was officially deposed. **Simon de Montfort** took over Toulouse. In 1217, however, Raymond VI and his son Raymond VII returned to the city in secret and overthrew de Montfort's garrison. De Montfort was killed attempting to re-enter the city. The restored St Gilles Counts were widely recognised as the legitimate lords of Toulouse, by a nobility wary of the Church's claiming the right to depose other nobles.

## *Raynaud Bergeron* (born 1266)

Raynaud Bergeron was a Templar Serving Brother from Langres who testified during the **trials** in 1311. His story was quite unusual, for he was apparently a married Templar. In 1304, his local commander had invited him to join the Templars (perhaps as a way of settling financial debts). Raynaud had agreed to enter on condition that his wife could accompany him into the Order. During his initiation ceremony, however, he was horrified to learn from his receptor, Laurent de Beaune, of the requirement to take a vow of **chastity**. Raynaud had promptly got up and made to leave the building. The Templars had followed him, however, protesting that it was foolish to refuse the honour of admittance. They eventually persuaded him to return, saying that he and his wife could be sent to the same Preceptory. After this scene he, as he claimed, he was still required to vow chastity. Raynaud added that subsequently he had been taken to another chamber where the sordid things in the **accusations** against the order had taken place.

## Reconquista

The Iberian Reconquista has been called the story of **Outremer** in reverse, with Christian forces driving out **Muslim** invaders and settlers. The struggle was led by the Kings of **Portugal**, Castile and **Aragon**. Local **Military Orders** were founded to operate specifically in this theatre of warfare, which came to be seen by some as another front of the ongoing **Crusade**. The Knights Templar and **Hospitaller** were also extensively involved, and had significant land holdings and fortresses in the lands adjoining the frontier.

Spain had been invaded by **Muslim** forces, Arab, Syrian, Moroccan and Berber, in AD 711. These Muslims in Spain were collectively known as the **Moors**. Since 753, an exiled member of the **Umayyad** dynasty had arrived from Syria and set up a rival Caliphate to the **Abbasids**, based in Cordoba. Muslim raiders called razzias continued to prey on the northern kingdoms. Muslim Spain eventually fragmented into separate city-states (*taifas*), some of which paid tribute money to the Christian kingdoms in the north. The *taifas* were only united by the invasion of the Almohads from North Africa, who invaded in response to renewed Castilian aggression against the *taifas*. Subsequently, however, the Christian reconquest gathered momentum, sometimes with the assistance of **knights** from other corners of **Christendom**. In 1085, Alfonso VI of León-Castile captured Toledo, the ancient Visigothic capital, a major enhancement for his prestige, enabling him to style himself Emperor. Castile, where the Orders of **Calatrava** and **Santiago** flourished, gained the most land from the Reconquista, although both Portugal and Aragon, where the Templars were more prominent, also managed to expand southward. Fighters of the Reconquista adopted St James as their patron, who became *Santiago Matamoros* (the Moor killer). His shrine at Santiago de Compostella became a sacred site to rival any in the **Holy Land**, so the Reconquista, like the Crusade, had to it an element of **pilgrimage**. One of the greatest Christian victories of the reconquista was *las Navas de Tolosa*, (1212) where an alliance of royal armies and the Military Orders decimated a powerful invasion force under an Almohad Caliph, leading the way to a rapid push south against the Muslim lands.

Granada, the last Muslim entity of southern Spain, was conquered in 1492. Those Muslims who remained were subjected to forced conversion and the attentions of the **Inquisition**. From earlier times, however, there are depictions of Moors and Christians playing instruments together or games of chess, so clearly they were not always at each other's throats.

## Regnans in Coelis

*Regnans in Coelis* was a **papal bull** issued by **Clement V** after *Faciens Misiricordam*. In it the Pope lamented and bewailed the state of affairs in Christendom, and his grief concerning the discovery of the Templars' supposed crimes. He proposed the assembly of a Church council to rectify the situation. His would belatedly take place as the **Council of Vienne**.

## Reims

Reims (Or Rheims) is a city in Central **France**. Its towering cathedral, *Notre Dame de Reims*, was the traditional place of coronation for the Kings of France. The Templars maintained a Preceptory at Reims, founded in the 1160s. Their obituary roll survives from there, showing those donors for whom the Order said prayers on certain dates (ranging from **King Philip II Augustus** through members of the clergy and aristocracy to a humble baker).[267] At least nine Templars were burnt in Reims during the suppression.

## Renaud de Provins (born *c.* 1275)

Renaud de Provins was the Templar Preceptor of Orleans. He was one of the defence procurators at the Templars' mass trial in **Paris**, known as the Papal Commission, along with **Pierre de Bologna, Guillaume de Chambonnet** and **Bertrand de Sartiges**. Provins was also a **priest**. Ironically, he had considered joining the **Dominicans** before joining the Templars. Under **Inquisition** interrogation he had managed to avoid making a direct confession. Later, with Bologna, he made a submission protesting at the treatment his fellow Templars had received, kept in irons, poorly fed, and denied the sacraments, while those who died in prison had been refused decent Christian burial. Provins also argued compellingly that the initial charges of **heresy** and the **arrest** of the brethren had been irregular and unlawful. He said the defendants should be allowed funds to mount a proper legal defence. When the Archbishop of Sens **Philip de Marigny** began the burnings of the Templars under his own jurisdiction, the four procurators strongly protested. The Commission only acted when Provins himself was taken away to the Council of Sens. Provins was returned, along with Chambonnet and de Sartiges, but the Council of Sens soon degraded him from the Priesthood, so he was unable to serve as a procurator. Bologna, meanwhile, had vanished, and the defence of the Order had collapsed amid terror and farce.

## Rennes le Château

Rennes le Château is a small village below a castle in the French Pyrenees, in the area traditionally called the **Languedoc**. It has become associated with hidden **treasure**, secrets, **conspiracy theories** and the **Priory of Sion**. Rennes le Château contains an old church dedicated to St **Mary Magdalene**. The church was much remodelled by the priest Bérengar Saunière (1852–1917), who installed some unusual statuary and sculpture including a red demon being crushed under the font. The source of his apparently extensive funds and the meaning of some of the odd symbolism in his redecoration are questions at the heart of many of the theories regarding the Rennes le Château mystery. In 1891, Saunière is supposed to have found cryptic scrolls in this church, including a genealogy of **Dagobert II**. The Bishop of **Carcassonne** sent Sauniere to **Paris** for various meetings and to have the documents translated, possibly by Father Bieul of St Sulpice. He also met Emma Calve, famous soprano and occultist. Saunière returned south with copies of paintings including *Et in Arcadia Ego* by **Nicolas Poussin**, and subsequently exhibited the wealth leading to the later theory that he had received some sort of pay-off from the Church after discovering some potent secret. He also received visits from Jean-Stephane of Hapsburg and other grandees, and by 1900 had commenced lavish building projects like the Villa Bethania and the Magdala Tower, symbolic of **Holy Land** Locations. (Saunière derived some of his wealth, unscrupulously, by selling Church **masses**, for which he was sued in 1915.) If Saunière knew a secret it seems he left it to his servant/mistress Marie Denaud, but she took it to her grave. There is no direct evidence that the Templars were established at Rennes le Château, although there is some suggestion they had connections with the nearby castle of **le Bezu**.

## Revelation, Biblical Book of

The Revelation of St John the Divine (or the Apocalypse of John) is the last canonical book of the Christian Bible. It contains prophetic visions revealed to the author, who is sometimes identified with St John the Apostle, living on the Greek island of Patmos at the time. It tells of the apocalypse – the end of the world, preceded by the reign of the **Antichrist** (referred to as the 'Beast') – the Second Coming of **Christ**, the last battle at Armageddon and the Last Judgement. It incorporates some bizarre imagery and esoteric symbolism, which has been interpreted in many different ways. Theologians have looked to the book of Revelation seeking signs that they may be living in the last days. Apocalyptic (eschatological) speculation was very prevalent at the beginning of the Crusading era, and again at the time of the suppression of the Templars. The Holy Roman Emperor **Frederick II** was suspected by some of being the Antichrist.

## Reynald de Châtillon (1125–87)

Reynald de Châtillon was a knight from Champagne, who came to the **Kingdom of Jerusalem** and gained power by marrying successively two well-placed widows, making him master first of **Antioch** and then of **Kerak**. He was not a Templar but he was an ally of the Order. He fought alongside them and conducted raids with them. Reynald participated in **Baldwin III's** campaign with the Templars, which resulted in the capture of **Ascalon**. In 1153 he married **Constance of Antioch** (1127–63), the widow of **Raymond of Poitiers**. Becoming Lord of the region, Reynald allied with the Templars against the Cilician Armenians, before switching with them into an alliance with the Armenians against the **Byzantine Empire**. With the excuse that Manuel I Comnenus was delaying in paying what he had promised for the attack on Thoros II, and 'on advice of evil men by whom he was too greatly influenced', Reynald initiated a raid on **Cyprus**.[268] In 1156 he attacked the Byzantine island without **Baldwin III's** permission. Baldwin was almost as furious over all this as the Byzantine Emperor **Manuel I** was. Reynald had abused and terrorised the Latin **Patriarch** of Antioch in order to extract funds for the raid. He had chained the priest up at the top of a tower, smeared in honey and left him all day at the mercy of swarms of flies, until the Patriarch promised to release the money. On Cyprus, according to **William of Tyre**, de Châtillon's men, having overcome initial resistance, had rampaged and robbed at will. They had despoiled monasteries and 'shamefully abused nuns and tender maidens'.

Manual I subsequently brought his army to Antioch, where Reynald humbly submitted before him. Manuel, it seems, was placated by the show of penitence and pardoned Reynald. Soon after, Reynald, while raiding peasant villages, was captured and handed to the governor of **Aleppo**. Reynald was not released until 1176, after spending sixteen years in a dungeon. He soon married the twice-widowed Stephanie de Milly, lady of Kerak and daughter of the former **Grand Master** Templars **Philip de Milly of Nablus**. Reynald now controlled the castles of Kerak and Montreal, and dominated the Transjordan, as well as territory to the south extending to the Red Sea. He immediately began to terrorise his own subjects, as well as launching raids against Muslim caravans crossing between Arabia and Egypt. Meanwhile in 1177 Reynald joined with **Baldwin IV** and the Templars, and helped defeat **Saladin** at **Montguisard**.

Reynald was brave in battle, but many of these battles might not have been necessary but for the provocation he gave the Muslims. In 1181, Reynald broke the truce agreed by Baldwin and Saladin by launching a raid against another rich Muslim caravan. In 1185 he went on to launch piratical raids down the Red Sea, striking at the sacred heartland of Islam. Saladin developed a great hatred for Reynald and subsequently besieged him at Kerak. However he was compelled to withdraw by the arrival of Baldwin IV and his army. Reynald lived to foment discord another day. He became an ally of **Guy de Lusignan** and **Gerard de Ridefort**, undermining the more cautious influence of **Raymond III of Tripoli**. He also returned to raiding Muslim caravans. Saladin captured Reynald at **Hattin**. After the battle the Sultan had his principal captives brought to his tent. He confronted Reynald with his crimes and listed his acts of barbarism. Reynald is said to have responded: 'But this in truth is the custom of Kings, and I have only followed the beaten path.'[269] Saladin executed him, and then turned to Guy and said that one king does not kill another.

## *Reynald de Vichiers* (died 1256)

Reynald de Vichiers became the nineteenth **Grand Master** in 1250 after the death of **Guillaume de Sonnac** at **Mansourah** in **Egypt** during the **Seventh Crusade**. Previously he had been **Marshal** of the Temple, and had contributed to the preparation of the **Crusade**, arranging shipping for **Louis IX**'s armies. Reynald soon proved his worth as a redoubtable warrior with an independent streak. **Jean de Joinville**'s chronicle recalls how on the march south from **Damietta**, King Louis IX had ordered that none was to break formation in the face of enemy harassment. Then one of the Muslims gave a Knight Templar in the first rank so heavy a blow with his battle-axe that it felled him under the hooves of Reynald de Vichiers' horse. The marshal cried out: 'At them in the name of God for I cannot longer stand this!' He spurred his horse at the enemy, followed by his brethren, and, as the Templars' **horses** were fresh and the Turks' already weary, not a single enemy escaped.[270]

Reynald de Vichiers accompanied Louis IX to the **Acre**, following the defeat in Egypt. There, with Louis's backing, he was confirmed as the Grand Master. He acted as godfather to a son born to Louis and **Marguerite of Provence**, (born within **Pilgrims Castle**). Relations later deteriorated when Louis started to feel that the Templars had overstepped their authority, negotiating independently with Damascus. The King decided to make an example of the Order, compelling Reynald de Vichiers to exile from the Holy Land **Hugues de Jouy**, the new Marshal of the Order. Reynald de Vichiers also had to kneel before the King publicly and apologise.

## *Reynard the Fox*

Reynard (or Renart) the Fox is a cunning fox character who is the hero of various folk tales and literary satires from Medieval Europe, especially lampooning the puffed up and greedy Churchmen and aristocracy. In one version of 1289, *Renart le Nouvel* by the Fleming Jacquemart Giélée, the fox becomes **Pope**, and is met by a **Grand Master** of the Templars who pleads for aid for the **Holy Land** saying that if the Order does not increase in wealth they would have to abandon the land of Syria. It seems the plea had become so over-familiar as to become a joke, though it reflected the true situation well enough.

# Rhodes

Rhodes is a Greek island, one of the larger and more easterly of the Dodecanese. In medieval times it was part of the **Byzantine Empire**, with an Eastern Orthodox Christian population. It endured Muslim occupation from AD 672 but was restored to the Empire by **Alexius I Comnenus**. After 1308 it became the base of the Knights **Hospitaller**, (subsequently sometimes known as the Knights of Rhodes) who conquered the island turning it into their own Order-state and the fortress base for ongoing sea missions against the Muslims. They built great defences and a magnificent palace for their **Grand Master**. The island subsequently withstood determined sieges by **Ottoman Turkish** forces in 1444 and 1480, and was only taken with overwhelming force in 1522. The Hospitallers went on to establish themselves on **Malta**.

# Ribat

A Ribat was the **Islamic** equivalent of a fortified monastery, the occupants of which formed a society dedicated to religious discipline and *Jihad*. Some were associated with the *caravanserai* stationed along roads as shelters for trading caravans and pilgrims. They may have inspired the Christian **Military Orders**.[271]

# Ribston

Ribston was a Templar Preceptory in North Yorkshire, **England**. It was built on land in the valley of the River Nidd, donated by the Temple's patron Sir **Robert de Ros** (possibly the knight once buried under the effigy in **Temple Church, London**, with the de Ros arms on its shield). After the **suppression** of the Templars **Edward II** held on to Ribston until 1324, when Papal threats forced him to yield it to the **Hospitallers**. It later became a possession of the Goodricke family. The Templar chapel is all that remains of the Preceptory, joining on to the later stately home Ribston Hall. The other buildings were demolished in 1673 to make way for the house. The chapel contains some Victorian stained glass featuring Templar iconography. The last Preceptor of Ribston was **William de Grafton**. There is something of a mystery concerning his release from monastic vows, over twenty years after the suppression. This seems to indicate that there was still a **Master** and Brethren of the Temple to release him from those vows.

# Ricaut Bonomel (thirteenth century)

Ricaut Bonomel was a Knight Templar and a poet of melancholy verses written in about 1262, at the time of the **Mameluk** rampage through the **Kingdom of Jerusalem**:

> Anger and grief are so set in my heart
> That I all but kill myself at once;
> Or lay down the cross I took up
> In honour of Him who was put on the Cross;
> For neither cross nor law helps nor guides me
> Against the evil Turks, God curse them! ...

The poem goes on to lament the fall of **Caesarea** and **Arsuf**, and the fate of their defenders and the people. It was as though God were sleeping, allowing the Christians to face daily defeat:

> ... And Bafometz acts with all his power
> And spurs on Melicadefer.

Melicadifer seems to refer to the Sultan **Baybars**. Bafometz seems to be the **demon** (**Baphomet**). The name may be related to **Mohammed**. Bonomel also wrote bitterly how the **Pope** was very generous with indulgences against Italians, to **Charles of Anjou** and the French, but he 'pardons for money people who have taken our Cross'. Clearly the debasing of the Crusading ideal by the thirteenth-century Popes and the diverting of Crusades and money from Palestine in favour of the Papal wars in Italy was strongly resented among the Templars.

### Richard de Hastings (died *c.* 1164)
Richard de Hastings was the **Master of the Temple in England** from around 1155 to 1164. He was a loyal supporter of King **Henry II of England**. He served as one of the three Templar custodians of the castles of **Gisors** and Neafle, and offended the king of **France**, **Louis VII** by being quick to transfer the castles to Henry, the marriage of the royal children having been rushed through at Henry's behest. The castles formed part of the dowry of the French princess Marguerite. Louis expelled the three Templars for their partiality towards Henry II.

### Richard of Cornwall (1209–72)
Richard Plantagenet, Earl of Cornwall was the younger brother of **Henry III of England**. He married Isabel, the daughter of **William Marshal**, after the death of her first husband Gilbert de Clare. He took part in a **Crusade** between 1240 and 1242 and refortified **Ascalon**. He also signed a treaty with the Sultan As-Silah **Ayyub**, which reconstructed the **Kingdom of Jerusalem** at its greatest extent since before **Hattin**, and including the restoration of Galilee and the plains of **Jaffa**. **Jerusalem** was fully restored to Christian rule and emptied of **Muslims**. Richard was prevented from achieving more by the mistrust

of the local Barons, who were suspicious of him because he was the brother-in-law of **Frederick II**. However he is credited with some success, temporarily reconciling acrimonious factions including the Templars and **Hospitallers**.[272] Richard returned home and went on to take part in the Barons War against **Simon de Montfort, 6th Earl of Leicester**, and was captured after the battle of Lewis. He died at his castle of Berkhamsted.

## Richard the Lionheart (King Richard I of England) (1157–99)

King Richard I Plantagenet of **England** was one of the greatest generals of his age and the foremost leader of the **Third Crusade**. He won the epithet *Cœur de Lion*. He was the son of **Eleanor of Aquitaine** and **Henry II of England**. He was regarded as a hero in England, despite his neglecting the realm in favour of the **Holy Land** and the **Angevin** territories in what is now **France**. Richard was flame haired, tall, handsome and gallant, but lacking in tact. He was brought up at his mother's court in Aquitaine, rebelled against his father, and put down rebellions against his own authority in his domains (Aquitaine and Poitou), notably taking the strong castle of Taillebourg in 1172, which had been a rebel stronghold. He acceded to the English throne in July 1189, having been predeceased by two elder brothers, and having recently allied against his father with **Philip II Augustus**. His coronation was marred by outbreaks of mob violence against **Jews**, which Richard endeavoured to stop. Richard's immediate priority, meanwhile, was organizing the **Crusade**, which was to have been led by his estranged father. Richard had good relations with the Templars, who played a part in the preparation of the campaign and the collecting of funds. The King's relationships were not so cordial with his fellow Crusading leaders. His relationship with Philip II deteriorated, largely owing to Richard's snubbing of his fiancée, Alys of France, Philip's sister (on the grounds that she had become Henry II's mistress) and marrying Berengaria of Navarre instead.

After Richard's capture of **Cyprus** in 1191 he had sold the island to the Templars, although they were soon obliged to sell it back. The Templars had gone on to accompany Richard at the recovery of **Acre** and the victory over **Saladin** at **Arsuf**. When Richard heard that his brother Prince **John** had schemed against him and overthrown his regent William Longchamp, Richard was compelled to abandon the Crusade. It is said that he travelled incognito, disguised possibly as a Templar. Shipwrecked near Venice, he was later discovered on account of his ruby ring, which was not something a humble Templar would have worn. He was kept prisoner by the Duke of Austria and by the Duke's overlord the **Holy Roman Emperor, Henry VI**, who demanded an enormous ransom before agreeing to Richard's release. There is a story that Richard's place of imprisonment was discovered by a loyal minstrel called Blondel, who sought him travelling from castle to castle, singing a song composed by Richard, until the answering verse came down from a barred window. The ransom was eventually raised, and Richard returned to England in 1194. He forgave his brother's plotting, and not long afterwards embarked to fight Philip II in France (Philip and his allies having capitalised on Richard's absence by invaded the Angevin territories on the continent). He fought to recover his estates and built the great fortress, the Château-Gaillard. He died in April 1199 after receiving an arrow wound while laying siege to the town of Châlus in Limousin. He was nursed at the end by his mother and buried in Fontervaud Abbey near his father.

### Robert I, Count of Artois (1216–50)

Robert I, Count of Artois was the third son of Louis VIII and a younger brother of **Louis IX** of **France**. During the **Seventh Crusade** he led the vanguard of the army, moving south from **Damietta**. He led a reckless charge into **Mansourah**, goading the **Templars** and **William Longespee** into accompanying him. According to **Matthew Paris**, when the wary master of the Templars, **Guillaume de Sonnac** counselled caution, Robert of Artois directed at him the accusation that the **Military Orders** were traitors who had been holding up the Christian defeat of the **Saracens** for their own interests, because if the Crusades succeeded their supremacy would come to an end. The Templars, cut to the quick by these words, unfurled their banners and prepared to brave death in battle.[273] The advancing knights were trapped within the town and slaughtered. Robert defended himself in a house there for some time before being overwhelmed by the **Mameluk** enemy.

### Robert de Craon (c. 1100–c. 1147)

Robert de Craon became the second **Grand Master** of the Knights Templar in 1136. He was known as 'The Burgundian', despite being born in Anjou, and was a younger son of Renard de Craon. He had given up a fiancée in Aquitaine to join the newly formed Order in **Jerusalem**, serving under **Hugues de Payens**. He was also present at the **Council of Troyes**. He oversaw the continuing growth of the Order. Robert participated in some inconclusive campaigns against the forces of **Aleppo** in the **Holy Land**.

### Robert de Ros (c. 1177–1226/27)

Sir Robert de Ros of Furfan was probably the knight once buried under the effigy in **Temple Church, London,** with the de Ros arms on its shield. The effigy is unusual as it represents the knight with his mail hood down, exposing his wavy, shoulder-length hair. Robert de Ros was a patron of the Templars. He donated land in Yorkshire at **Ribston**, among other places. Robert, as a young knight, had been with King **Richard the Lionheart** in Normandy in 1197. He had been arrested for unknown offences and held in the Château of Bonville. His jailor Hugh de Spiney allowed him to escape, and apparently was hanged by the King for it. Robert was allowed to remain at large in exchange for a ransom. He returned to **England** during the reign of King **John** and received an inheritance including the Castle of Werke in Northumberland. Robert was married to Isabella, the sister of William I the Lion, King of **Scotland**. He escorted William to England when William swore fealty to King John. At some stage subsequently Robert became a monk and placed his lands in the custody of Philip d'Ulcote. Later he evidently returned to the world and served as Sheriff of Cumberland. Robert was also one of the signatories of the **Magna Carta** in 1215. He initially held favour with John during the ensuing Barons revolt. He was made governor of Carlisle, before switching sides. He later lent his support to the young **Henry III**, when Henry accepted the Magna Carta. He may have joined the Order on his deathbed.[274]

### *Robert de Sable* (died 1193)

A member of the **Third Crusade**, Robert de Sable became **Grand Master** of the Knights Templar in 1191. He had previously been a **vassal** of **Richard the Lionheart**. Robert oversaw the purchase of **Cyprus**.

### *Robert Hales* (died 1381)

Robert Hales was a **Hospitaller** Grand Prior of **England**, and also Royal Treasurer of England. He was responsible for a poll tax, which was one of the causes of the **Peasants' Revolt**. The peasants marched on London, burning the manor of **Cressing** on the way (which had passed to the Hospitallers). The rebels seized Hales in **London** and beheaded him.

### *Robert le Bougre* (died *c*. 1250)

Robert le Bougre, was a **Dominican** Friar, and probably a former **heretic**, to judge by his epithet. He was a notorious Inquisitor, commissioned by **Gregory IX** to extend the **Inquisition** into northern **France**, where the Institution had not previously taken hold due to an apparent absence of heretics. With general Episcopal support, Robert terrorised these previously peaceful regions, especially the provinces of Sens and **Reims**. He had a number of people **burnt** for heresy and sorcery. Others were imprisoned or made to shave their heads and wear crosses to mark them out.[275] Robert's career culminated in a mass burning of 180 supposed **Cathars** in Mont-Aimé in 1239, witnessed by a number of bishops and by **Theobald IV, Count of Champagne**. Robert was later deemed to have gone too far and to have persecuted innocents, and it seems he was removed from office and imprisoned. Later he secured pardon and ended his days as at **Clairvaux**.

## Robert the Bruce (1274–1329)

Robert the Bruce (Robert I) was a king of **Scotland**, most famous for his victory over the English at **Bannockburn**, securing Scotland's independence. As Earl of Carrick, Bruce, (like most Scottish nobles apart from **William Wallace**) had been unsure of his allegiance during the early wars with **England**. He had bided his time until the death of **Edward I**.

Bruce had a strong claim to the throne of Scotland, but had a rival in John 'the Red' Comyn. In 1306, the two men met in a church in Dumfries, where Bruce murdered Comyn. Pope **Clement V** soon **excommunicated** Bruce for this crime. Bruce meanwhile manoeuvred to be crowned King of Scotland at Scone. Bruce's rebellion got off to a bad start at the battle of Mithven (during which many of his supporters were captured). After that he adopted guerrilla tactics, resisting the English from the Western Isles. He gained more successes after the death of Edward I (who had in the meantime captured Robert's wife, sister and daughter and, it is said, kept them prisoner in cages at the top of castle towers).

There have been claims that Robert the Bruce, being an excommunicant, gave shelter to fugitive Templars after 1307, and did not suppress the Order in Scotland. This is not born out by some of the records: Robert, the younger son of Christaine of Esperton went to Robert the Bruce after 1312 and asked to have back the lands the Templars under **Brian de Jay** had seized from his mother. The rest of the estate seems to have been passed to the **Hospitallers**. Templar trials were only held south of the Firth of Forth, in English-controlled territory, and then only two or three Templars were heard. So Bruce may have looked favourably on refugee Templars.

By 1314 Bruce had taken control of most of Scotland above the Tay, and his title was even recognised by the Clergy, despite his excommunication. He achieved his greatest victory at Bannockburn, an engagement precipitated by his brother's capture of Stirling Castle. Later Bruce and his brother campaigned with limited success in **Ireland**. Bruce's excommunication was eventually lifted by **Pope John XXII**, and **Edward III** recognised Scottish independence a year before Robert's death. Bruce was regarded as a great hero in Scotland. He wished his heart to be buried in the **Holy Sepulchre** in **Jerusalem**, and a party of knights, including James de Douglas and **William Sinclair** undertook the pilgrimage to deliver it there. When Douglas, Sinclair and many others were killed near Cordoba in **Spain**, fighting against the **Moors**, the heart was brought back to Scotland, and buried instead in **Melrose Abbey**.

## Roger de Flor (1266–1306)

Roger de Flor (or Rutger von Blume) was a renegade Templar sea captain, who became a notorious pirate chief in the eastern Mediterranean. He was the son of the German falconer of **Frederick II**, and became a cabin boy on a Templar galley based at Brindisi. He eventually joined the Order as a **sergeant** brother, and came to command his own ship. At the siege of **Acre** in 1291 he showed his true colours by extorting great sums from rich matrons wishing to escape by sea from the city beset by **Mameluks**, aboard his ship the *Falcon*. For this dishonourable conduct he was expelled from the Order.[276]

He went to Italy and continued his freebooting career, commanding ships for **Charles of** Naples in his war with **Aragon** over Sicily. Eventually the king of Naples found himself unable to pay his Catalan mercenaries. Roger promised them rich pickings in the **Levant**, which was in a lawless state in the wake of the **Crusades**. Roger arrived in **Constantinople** with a fleet of thirty-two ships, and a small army of soldiers of fortune. They persuaded the Byzantine Emperor, Andronicus II, to take them on as mercenaries against the **Turks**, though it was as much a protection racket as a real service, as they themselves were a threat to **Byzantium**. Roger gained a Byzantine princess bride and the title of Grand Duke into the bargain. After some weeks spent brawling with the **Genoese**, he and his men eventually launched against the Turks, with some success. Roger later attacked Magnezia in **Greece** in an attempt to recover a treasure he had sent there. Afterwards he returned to Constantinople to intrigue against the ruler and to plunder the surrounding country to augment the pay his men were receiving from the Emperor. Eventually Roger was assassinated at the instigation of the new Emperor Michael IX Palaeologus. His band went on to attack the Greeks and to seize power in Athens, in 1311. They ruled it for the next seventy-seven years.

### *Roger de Moulins* (died 1187)

Roger de Moulins was elected **Grand Master** of the Knights **Hospitaller** in 1184. He accompanied his Templar counterpart, **Arnold of Tarroja**, and the Patriarch **Heraclius** on the tour of Europe during which Arnold died, the purpose of the tour being to appeal for aid for the **Holy Land**. Back in the East, Roger de Moulins opposed the faction of **Reynald de Chatillon** and **Guy de Lusignan** and was dismayed by the prospect of Guy becoming king. It is said that the royal regalia of Jerusalem was kept in a treasury that required two keys to open, the keys held by the Grand Masters of the **Military Orders**. Roger was compelled to produce his key but tossed it out of the window so that his counterpart **Gerard de Ridefort** had to go searching for it. Eventually it was found, the regalia were brought out, and the joint coronation of Guy and **Sibylla** went ahead. The following year Roger died, probably at the Battle of **Cresson**.

### *Roger de Mowbray* (*c.* 1116– *c.* 88)

Roger de Mowbray, Earl of Northumberland, was an accomplished knight and noble patron of the Knights Templar. At the age of 18 he was part of an English victory over the Scots at the Battle of the Standard. Roger was a supporter of King **Stephen** in his civil war against the Empress **Matilda**, and was captured alongside the King in battle near **Lincoln**. He was also a veteran of several **Crusading** expeditions. It was while serving in the **Holy Land** during the **Second Crusade** that he became an admirer of the **Military Orders**.

Roger's donations to the Templars in the 1160s and 70s included land in Yorkshire, notably **Penhill**, and **Balsall** in Warwickshire and other rents and lands in Lincolnshire. He also supported the **Order of St Lazarus**, and donated to them land in Leicestershire where they built their headquarters at Burton Lazarus. Roger was part of an unsuccessful revolt against **Henry II** with the backing of the Scots. He departed for the **Holy Land** on a pilgrimage, seeking absolution. He then came back West. Roger returned to the Holy Land when he was entering his seventies and participated in the Battle of **Hattin**. He survived to be ransomed (possibly by the Templars), but died soon after, and was buried in the East.

## Romanesque

Romanesque was the predominant style of **architecture** in the early medieval period. It was defined by round arches and by thick walls and columns. The term also applies to the stylised sculpture accompanying such buildings. During the early crusading period the style was giving way to the new style that would subsequently be known as **Gothic**. Many Templar buildings reflect this transition.

## Rome

Rome, known as the eternal city, was the traditional seat of the **Popes** through most of the Middle Ages, as in later times. It was the centre of the Papal state, dominating much of central Italy. It was regarded as a sacred city because it was believed that St **Paul of Tarsus** and **St Peter** had been **martyred** there. The city was the home of revered relics, too. These included the *Scala Sancta*, the steps from Pilate's palace in Judea, down which Christ had been led (removed to the Lateran), and the *Titulus Crucis*, the sign that was put over the **True Cross** (installed in the church of Santa Croce in Gerusalemme, on the site of the palace of St **Helena**). The Templars had established a Preceptory in Rome by 1138, standing on the Aventine Hill.

In medieval times the city of Rome was somewhat unstable, and lay under the shadow of numerous forbidding stone towers, built by rival aristocratic families as a means of physical and psychological warfare against one another. The important patrician clans included the Conti (the family of **Innocent III**), the Annibaldi, the Frangipani, the Colonna, and the Caetani. These families dominated Roman politics and the Roman Church. The Caetani Pope **Boniface VIII** would resort to calling a Crusade against the Colonna, who included two rebellious cardinals. The Papacy frequently had to seek refuge from Rome and in the early fourteenth century under **Clement V** abandoned it for **Avignon**. The Popes continued to assert their power in Rome by proxy, until **Gregory XI** restored the papacy to Rome in 1377.

## Rosicrucianism

The Rosicrucians (or the Fraternity of the Rosy Cross) were supposed to be an occult brotherhood. However, although there are modern groups based on Rosicrucian mythology and mysticism, there is some question whether there was really an order of enlightened initiates in the past. Between 1614 and 1616 three manifestos were published, purporting to be the work of the brotherhood, and telling of its founder, one Christian Rozenkreuz, a German pilgrim, supposedly living from 1378 to 1484 who was supposed to have been initiated into occult secrets by Eastern sages. The manifestos are filled with allegorical symbolism. Like a Grail Knight, Rozenkreuts arrives at a castle of wonders and assists the 'Chymical wedding' of the King and Queen. The badge of Rosicrucianism is a red cross with a rose at its centre. Rosicrucianism has been linked to **Gnosticism**, Alchemy and **Freemasonry**.

## Roslin, Battle of

The Battle of Roslin was a military engagement between English and Scottish forces in February 1303. As at the later **Bannockburn** the rebellious Scots were outnumbered but won a decisive victory. Also at stake was the hand of the beautiful Lady Margaret Ramsey of Dalhousie, whom the English commander Sir John de Segrave desired, though she was pledged to **Henry St Clair**. It was partly to prevent them marrying that Segrave invaded the St Clair estates of Roslin. Dalhousie Castle was meanwhile besieged by another part of the English army.

The Scots rallied and ambushed Segrave's camp by the river Esk on an early morning. They defeated him and then went to confront the other English forces that had been besieging Dalhousie. Again they triumphed, luring the English into an attack on their higher positions. They then managed to defeat a third English contingent, inspired, it is said, by the sight of a huge cloth saltire laid over the hillside, which seemed to burn in the evening light. It had been laid out by one Prior Abernethy, a Scottish **Cistercian** monk who, it is claimed, had previously been a Templar.

## Rosslyn Chapel

Rosslyn (Roslin) Chapel is a church in Midlothian, **Scotland**. **William St Clair**, Lord of Roslin and Prince of Orkney, began building it in 1446 as a collegiate chapel where retained priests would perform **masses** for the benefit of his soul. The chapel, dedicated to St Matthew, seems to be only one wing of an envisaged cruciform building. Unfinished transepts extend from the east wall. Oliver St Clair, William's son, hurriedly finished the building on a less ambitious scale. It has an unusual barrel vaulted roof and flying buttresses surround its exterior. Inside the surfaces are carved with many curious devises.

One of the pillars, more ornate than the rest, has come to be called the Apprentice Pillar, and it is at the centre of many **conspiracy theories**. The shaft of the Pillar has bands of ornately carved foliage twisting around it. At the base it has carvings of dragons (thought by some to refer to the serpent who gnaws at the tree of Yggdrasil in Viking mythology). At the top is a scene of **Abraham** about to sacrifice Isaac. The story attached to the pillar is that it was carved by a gifted apprentice while the master had gone to **Rome** to gain inspiration. The master retuned to find the work completed to a brilliant standard. In a fit of rage and jealousy he struck down the apprentice and killed him. Above the pillar, on an architrave, is carved a quote from a text found in some versions of the Bible: 'Wine is strong, a king is stronger, women are stronger still, but truth conquers all.' This relates to the **apocryphal** book of Esdras where three guards seek to win favour with King Darius by stating what is strongest. The third to speak, who named women and truth, was named as Zerubbabel, the man who would later rebuild the **Temple of Solomon**.

Rosslyn is close to **Ballentradoch**. It is unclear whether the chapel ever had anything to do with the historical Knights Templar. It was, after all, founded 136 years after the Order's demise. There is a **grave slab** in Rosslyn carved with the name 'William de St Cler'. Adjacent to the name is a floriated cross with a long stem and a stepped base, and on the other side is a sword. Below is a more modern inscription 'William de St. Clair Knight Templar'. The grave is indeed of a type used by the Templars, but there is nothing to say that the **William St Clair** in question (probably he of 1297–1330) was affiliated with the Order. The slab evidently predates the chapel. On the exterior of the building, near the lower frame of the window on the south-west corner, is a carving claimed by some to resemble the First Degree ritual of **Freemasonry**. There are two figures, one behind appearing to hold the end of a noose around the other's neck. Other carvings on the interior include musician angels, an upside-down angel bound in rope (Lucifer falling from heaven, perhaps), numerous '**Green Man**' heads, a horned **Moses** and a **knight** with a passenger on his horse. The chapel suffered somewhat during the Reformation and the Civil War (when parliamentarian troops used it as a stable), and for a time lay derelict. It was later restored as a place of worship of the Episcopalian Church. The building also serves as a venue for **Neo-Templar** gatherings.

## Rothley

Rothley was a Templar Preceptory in Leicestershire. The land was probably first donated to the Order by John de Harecourt in 1203. **Henry III** either confirmed or extended the grant on the manor in 1231. Today the Templar chapel survives. It dates from around 1240.

## Round Churches

Round churches were a distinctive type of Templar **Architecture**. It is said these were inspired by the Church of the **Holy Sepulchre** in **Jerusalem**. In **England** the Order constructed several such churches. The known Templar examples are: **Temple Church, London**, (which survives), Hereford (lost), **Garway, Bruer, Bristol** and **Dover** (all lost but with the foundations visible at their sites). There are other similar round churches still standing at **Cambridge, Northampton** and at Little Maplestead in Essex. There are ruined round chapels at Ludlow Castle and at Earl's Bu on the Orkneys. These were probably not built by the Templars, however. The Hospitallers also sometimes built round churches, including, reputedly, one at their headquarters in Clerkenwell, London (nothing of which survives). The round shape seems to have fallen from favour by the start of the thirteenth century, and the Templars themselves demolished some of their own round churches and replaced them with more conventional oblong structures.

There were many other round churches in Europe, including a number of Templar ones. One of the best surviving is at **Tomar** in Portugal. There was a magnificent round church at the **Paris Temple** but this vanished in the eighteenth or nineteenth century. There are also four round churches on the Island of Bornholm in the Baltic. Round churches are clearly more complicated to build than oblong ones. The arches around the central section, such as those at Temple Church, London, have to be constructed curving in two directions, which is quite a feat. Normally the round churches had an oblong chancel attached (so the churches were technically keyhole shaped as opposed to round). The oblong chancel was where **Mass** was performed and the Altar was placed. This poses the question what the circular part was for. A possible explanation might be some ritual with a central focus. **Chapter** meetings were probably also held here. Many Abbeys and cathedrals have round Chapter Houses.

## Royston Cave

Royston Cave is an underground chamber reached by a passage. It is found in the village of Royston, nine miles from **Baldock** in Hertfordshire, **England**. It lies below the crossroads of King's street (following the route of the ancient Roman Road of Ermine Street), and Melbourne Street (on the prehistoric Icknield Way). The chamber is man-made and conical in shape, and its chalky sides are covered in carvings. The cave and its carvings lay buried and forgotten for centuries and were only rediscovered in 1742. The passage's sealed entrance was discovered by workmen clearing space for a new bench, who put down a post, which struck the stone cover. The villagers cleared the chamber hoping to find treasure, but only found shards of pottery, a piece of brass, bones, and a seal bearing a fleur-de-lis.[278]

Some of the **symbolism** in the carvings provides reason to associate the cave with the Templars, as does its location in proximity to former Templar lands. The carvings are crude and obscured by later graffiti, but they clearly include many human and animal figures as well as mysterious symbols. The cave may have been a secret Templar chapel, or a place where Templars were imprisoned while being transferred (although given that the carvings are in raised relief the latter option sees unlikely). As in the dungeon carvings at **Lincoln** and **Chinon** there are many crosses and crucifixion scenes, and figures of saints. There is also the crowned figure of a man with raised arms, there are several great swords of the type used by the **Crusaders**, there is a prancing horse, and there is a bearded man with a cross on his chest brandishing a sword, identifiable as a Templar. There is a figure of **St Catherine of Alexandria** holding her wheel, and another of St Lawrence holding his gridiron. There is a St Christopher carrying **Christ** on his shoulder. There is also apparently a **St John the Baptist**. Other carvings show mysterious symbols, such as crosses with the upper arms connected by arch-shapes, and hearts within hands. There are also concentric circles. Other features in the cave include niches in the walls reminiscent of **piscinas**, supporting the view that the place may have had a ritual use. A shallow grave also indicates its function as a chapel. This, taken with the combination of military and mystical/religious iconography, makes it likely that this was indeed a Templar shrine.

## Rule of the Knights Templar

The 'Rule of the Poor Knighthood of the Temple' was the collection of rules and regulations drawn up to govern the Templars' way of life. In a sense it was also the Order's constitution. It was given to the Templars at the **Council of Troyes**, and was influenced by an outline of the mode of life that the Templars had already adopted, given to the Council by **Hugues de Payens**. It was also influenced by St **Bernard of Clairvaux**, who was eager to impose monastic discipline on this new knightly brotherhood. It was written down by the **Cistercian** notary **Jean Michael**.

The original Latin Rule originally ran to seventy-three clauses. Later the Rule was translated into French, and given additional articles relating to military issues, mostly overlooked in the Latin original. The opening passage encourages the Templars to live up to the ideals of **knighthood**, and also to follow the example of monks. As those who renounced their own wills, serving God with horses and arms, they should strive to hear Matins. God would be with them if they promised to 'despise the deceitful world in perpetual love of God, and scorned the temptations of the body'.[279] Nourished by God and religious instruction the Templars should have no need to fear going into battle if they 'henceforth wear the tonsure'. ('Tonsure' here is the translation of the original Latin for 'crown' and could refer to the Templars wearing a crown of **martyrdom**, rather than a monk's haircut.)

The rule stated that Brothers were not to be admitted lightly, but after a probation period, although **excommunicated** knights could be admitted for the salvation of their souls. New knights were to be of age and already trained in arms. Married men could be admitted (as **confraters**) so long as they willed their property to the Order and did not wear the white mantle. Brothers were to be **obedient** to the **Master** as though they were obeying **Christ** himself. No man was to make war or peace without the Master's say so. Brothers were to **confess** their faults to the Master and submit to his discipline. The Master of the community on the other hand was advised neither to be too harsh nor too lenient. His staff (**Baculus**) was to support the needy as well as to strike down the vices of the errant.

Templars were to renounce all personal property, neither could they expect privacy. Even personal letters were to be read aloud before the Master if required, and lockable bags were not allowed. Brothers were to sleep in their clothes in lit dormitories, which were to be illuminated through the night – presumably as a precaution against sin. Regarding crimes, things that would be considered as major offences included treachery, **heresy**, **sodomy**, disobedience, retreating from an enemy without permission, revealing the Order's **secrets** and killing Christians. The harshest punishment was said to be expulsion (which meant enlistment in a stricter monastic Order or imprisonment). Other punishments were to include scouring, humiliation and eating off the floor with the dogs.

The rule instructed Brothers to behave decently and humbly. It regulated their day, their **dress**, when and what they ate, and what prayers they said. Aged and sick brethren were to be cared for as it were Christ himself suffering. When a brother died, **Masses** were to be performed for his soul and **charity** given to the poor in his honour for forty days. The Templars were forbidden from attending jousts, from indulging in falconry and from hunting for pleasure – although the hunting of **lions** was permitted. Brothers were discouraged against speaking excessively. The rule said that to speak too much was not without sin, and also that life and death were in the power of the tongue. (Neither were Brothers allowed directly to ask for anything.) Meals were to be taken communally in the refectory in silence. The rule permitted the Templars to eat meat and drink wine in moderation. They had authority to collect tithes and to keep servants, so that they may devote their energies to striving to retain the Holy Land, and 'smiting the enemies of the Catholic faith without sin'.

The rule ordered the practice of admitting females to be done away with (implying it seems that **sisters** were already being admitted to the Order). It warned that it was dangerous even to look at a woman's face; the Devil used women's charms to lure men from the path to God. Brothers were to avoid staying under the same roof as a woman, and forbidden from kissing or embracing females, even their own mothers or sisters. They were, however, to honour female saints, including The **Blessed Virgin Mary**, **Mary Magdalene** and **Catherine**.

# S

## *Saint, Status of*
A saint is an individual recognised by the Church of being of exceptional holiness and worthy of reverence by the faithful. The process of officially recognizing a saint is termed canonisation. Saints are deemed to inhabit a high place in Heaven, to be able to intercede with God and (sometimes) to be associated with miracles on earth. **Catholic** writers recorded the deeds and wonders associated with saints in hagiographies such the Golden Legend.

There were two sainted Knights **Hospitallers**, but no Templar saints. This may be because the clergy were quite jealous of the Templars' privileges at the time so would not have accepted a Templar being made a saint. After the suppression the Templars' reputation was blackened, so not surprisingly no member of that Order was considered for canonisation thereafter. The Church tried to forget about the Templars. It seems to have played down their contribution to church history and the links that acknowledged saints had to them (saints like St **Bernard of Clairvaux** who had been an enthusiastic supporter of the Order).

Those Templars who died in battle were recognised as achieving **martyrdom**, but were not regarded as saintly. The best candidates for sainthood among the Templars may be those actually persecuted by the Church. Those who defended their innocence and orthodoxy in the face of the oppressors that would have them admit to being **heretics** and would force them to confess to **denial of Christ** when they never had. Men like **William de la More** and **Jacques de Molay** (who redeemed himself in his last hours), surely died as Christian martyrs. With one notable exception, however, the Church has not made a practice of recognizing its own victims as saints (that exception being Joan of Arc).

As for the Hospitaller saints, one was St Hugh of Genoa, a mystical Hospitaller who was devoted to ministering to the sick (probably after a Military career). Another was the serving brother Gerard Mercati, who later became a Franciscan hermit, but who still wore the white Hospitaller cross on his habit.

## St Clair Dynasty

The clan St Clair (later changed to Sinclair) was a family in **Scotland** holding the title Baron, later Earl, of Rosslyn (or Roslin). One of their Norman ancestors, William the Seemly, fought with William the Conqueror at Hastings, and gained estates in **England**. He later escorted the Saxon Princess St Margaret from exile in Hungary to marry Malcolm III of Scotland. Malcolm granted William land at Roslin, defending the approach to Edinburgh.

The Scottish St Clairs went on to fight in battles against the English and to serve as royal ambassadors. They also received the title *Guardians of the Holy Relics of Scotland*. It is unclear how closely these St Clairs were linked to the Templars. There is a myth that **Hugues de Payens** was once married to a Catherine de St Clair. Hugues did visit Scotland, and the earliest grant of land the Templars received in that realm was at **Balantradoch** near Roslin. They also shared a devotion to **St Catherine of Alexandria.**

At the trial of the two or three Templars arrested in Scotland, **Henry St Clair** (1297–1331) and either his son William or brother William gave unfavourable testimony, repeating the hearsay that if the Templars were holy they would not have lost Jerusalem. Henry and his sons both fought under Robert at **Bannockburn** and the sons went on to die in Spain fighting the Moors, while attempting with Sir James de Douglas to escort King Robert's heart to the **Holy Sepulchre.** Henry outlived his sons and was succeeded by his grandson, whose marriage brought the family the Earldoms of Caithness and Orkney. Under their son Henry, Orkney was elevated to a principality.

This Prince Henry was the one said to have voyaged to **America,** though that story is probably another myth. His son Henry St Clair, 2nd Prince of Orkney (who died in 1440) was captured along with King James I of Scotland when they were shipwrecked in England, and either paid a ransom or escaped. His son, **William St Clair,** 3rd and last St Clair Prince of Orkney, was the builder of **Rosslyn Chapel.** He died in 1484, most of his lands and titles going to his second son Oliver. The St Clairs also became hereditary Grand Masters of the Masons of Scotland, the progenitors of **Freemasonry.** Sir **Walter Scott** would record a legend that generations of St Clair knights were buried under Rosslyn Chapel in full armour.

The family remained Catholic long after the reformation. They were besieged at Roslin Castle by Parliamentary troops during what is inaccurately termed the 'English Civil War'. Sir William, the last male St Clair of the direct Rosslyn branch, died in 1778.[280]

## Sainte Eulalie de Cernon

Sainte Eulalie de Cernon was an important Templar Preceptory in southern **France**. It constituted a Templar stronghold and a fortified hilltop village, its walls guarding the inhabitants from local brigands. It was passed to the **Hospitallers**, who later remodelled the church and strengthened the walls.

## Sainte Felix de Carman

Sainte Felix de Carman is a town in southern **France**, situated near Castelnaudary. It is remarkable for being the scene of a **Cathar** council in 1167, attended by Cathar 'bishops' and presided over by Niquinta, the spiritual leader of the **Bogomils** who had come from the Balkans. Public debates and disputations were held with representatives of the orthodox **Catholic** clergy. Here, though, it was established that the Cathars' beliefs could not be reconciled with mainstream Christianity. Sainte Felix de Carman is notable also for being the birthplace of **Guillaume de Nogaret**. There is a story that his parents had been **burned** as **heretics** there, leading to conjecture that he may have nurtured a personal hatred for the Catholic Church.

## St Sabas, War of

The War of St Sabas was a civil war fought between Christian factions on the streets of **Acre**, at a time when the vestigial **Kingdom of Jerusalem** was under great peril from the **Mameluks**. The main rival factions were the **Venetian** and **Genoese** merchants. Conflict was sparked by a row over the monastery of St Sabas. The main period of hostility was 1256–8. The **Military Orders** and the local barons became partisan. The Templars and **Teutonic Knights** sided with the Venetians, while the **Hospitallers** sided with the Genoese. Eventually the Grand Masters, including **Thomas Bérard**, agreed to keep the peace, given a sense of urgency by the menacing advance of the **Mongols** into the region following the bloody conquest of **Baghdad**.

## Saladin (Salah ed-Din) (1137–93)

Salah ed-Din Yusuf ibn Ayyub, known in the West as Saladin, was a Kurdish warrior, champion of **Islam**, and the true founder of the **Ayyub** dynasty, which held power in both **Egypt** and Syria. He originated from Tikrit in modern Iraq, and was educated in **Damascus**. He accompanied his uncle, the general **Shirkuh**, in an army sent by **Nur ed-Din** to fight the Crusaders in Egypt. In 1169 Saladin succeeded Shirkuh as the effective ruler of Egypt. On the convenient death of the last **Fatimid** (Shi'ite) Caliph, he restored recognition in Egypt of the **Abbasid** (Sunni) Caliph of **Baghdad**. Once established as ruler of Egypt, Saladin made it clear that he no longer considered himself a subordinate of Nur ed-Din. On Nur ed-Din's death in 1174, Saladin took an army across Frankish territory into Syria, ultimately bringing all the Muslim territories in the region under his rule. He declared himself Sultan (undisputed after the death of the young son of Nur ed-Din in 1181). He fought campaigns to subjugate Damascus, **Aleppo** and Mosul, and establishing independence from the **Seljuks**. He then accelerated the *Jihad* against the Christian **Kingdom of Jerusalem**.

The Sultan was unexpectedly defeated in 1177 by **Baldwin IV** and the Templars at **Montguisard**. He reversed the verdict in 1179 winning a decisive victory over the Franks at **Jacobs Ford**, but failed to press home the victory. Later the activities of his mortal enemy **Reynald de Châtillon** gave Saladin cause to again invade the Frankish territory, first sending in a large scouting force that annihilated a small Templar detachment, which foolishly engaged it at **Cresson**. Saladin summoned the Muslim faithful to arms from Mosul to Syria and Egypt. He won his greatest victory at **Hattin** in July 1187, crowned in October by the conquest of **Jerusalem**, despite a spirited defence led by **Balian of Ibelin**. In 1188 Saladin's forces swept through the remainder of the Latin Kingdom, capturing nearly every major fortress and city except for **Tyre**.

Saladin became famous for his mercy when he spared the people of Jerusalem, albeit in exchange for ransom payments, and even granted amnesty to some of those who could not afford the ransom. However, many others were taken into **slavery**, and Saladin's mercy did not extend to the **Military Orders**. He vowed to cleanse the land of 'these two impure races'.[281] In the aftermath of Hattin, the day after his execution of Reynald, he had more than 100 Templar and **Hospitaller** prisoners beheaded by **Sufis** travelling with his army. Saladin spared only the **Grand Master**, **Gerard de Ridefort** (perhaps suspecting that if released Gerard, like **Guy de Lusignan**, would be more of a liability than an asset to the Christians). Saladin fought the armies of **Richard the Lionheart** during the **Third Crusade**, though the two leaders never met face to face. (Saladin sent his brother **al-Adil** to negotiate with the **Crusaders**.) The Crusaders retook **Acre**, and scattered Saladin's army at **Arsuf**. However Saladin prevented them from recapturing Jerusalem. Having survived many battles and attempts on his life by the **Assassins**, Saladin died a year after the end of the Crusade, in Damascus, where he was buried in a mausoleum near the Great Mosque. The Muslim unity he had forged disintegrated soon afterwards, but his descendants held positions of power in Egypt and the Middle East for several generations.

## San Bevignate

San Bevignate is a Templar church in Perugia, Umbria, Italy. It contains original medieval wall paintings, including riding knights carrying the **Beauseant** standard of the Order. A fresco there includes a group of monks in white habits confronting a **lion** outside their church. There is also an image of a **flagellant**. The Preceptory was established by 1250, and the church was completed by around 1262.

## Sandford

Sandford was a Templar manor or **Preceptory** in Oxfordshire. It was granted by Robert de Sandford in 1239, and absorbed the Order's older foundation at Crowley, two miles north. The 250-acre estate, developed by the **Hospitallers** after their takeover, included water mills, fisheries, orchards and dovecotes.

## San Gimignano

San Gimignano is a hilltop town in Tuscany, Italy, famous for its medieval towers and the **wall paintings** in its Collegiate Church. It also houses a medieval museum containing works of art and reliquaries (including the beautiful naturalistic **head** reliquary of St Fiona with gilded hair and shoulders). There is also a museum of **torture** equipment. There was a Templar Preceptory in the town, and a medieval hospital. On its Romanesque façade can be seem carvings including a Crusader-style cross and an **Agnus Dei**.

## Santiago, Order of

The Order of Santiago (also known as the Order of St James of Compostella) was a Spanish Military/Religious Order founded in the twelfth century. It had possessions in both Leon and Castile. It adopted a version of the Rule of St **Augustine** in 1171 and received Papal recognition four years later. The Order functioned both to protect **pilgrims** on the road to the shrine of Santiago de Compostella, and to fight the **Moors** in the **Reconquista**. It had affiliated Canons and Canonesses, concerned with religious observations and the care of pilgrims. There were two classes of knights, religious brethren living communally, and married knights (who had not vowed chastity) who might fight alongside them but who did not have votes in **chapter**. The Order's badge was an ornate red cross with a bladelike lower arm. The Order later suffered schisms. It was involved in maritime expeditions, as was the Order of **Knights of Christ**. After this it became customary that new knights had to have served six months at sea.

## Saphet, Castle

Saphet (or Safed) was a great Templar Castle in Galilee. The Templars obtained it in 1160. It fell to **Saladin** during his 1188 campaign, but was recovered in 1240 following a treaty with **Damascus**. The castle was rebuilt with the support of Benedict of Alignan, Bishop of Marseilles. The castle was again besieged in 1266, by **Baybars** and the **Mameluks**. The defenders mounted a valiant resistance, but were thwarted when the Egyptians started promising to spare any of the Templars' Syrian Christian mercenaries (**Turkopoles**) who abandoned the Castle. The Templars realised that no relief was coming, and that their local troops were drifting away. They therefore sent Leon Cazelier, a

Syrian **sergeant** brother, to negotiate the Castle's surrender. Cazelier returned and said the Sultan had offered safe passage through his lines to **Acre** for the garrison and the refugees sheltering in the castle. It was a lie, as the Templars should have guessed after the fate of **Arsuf** the previous year. Again the refugees, including many women and children, were dragged off to **slavery**. The Templars were given an ultimatum of Islam or death. The next day Baybars ringed the castle with their severed heads.

## Saracens

Saracens, meaning 'Easterners', was the term often used by the **Frankish** Christians to designate the **Muslims** of the Middle East, especially the **Arabs** and the **Egyptians**. Some Christians interpreted the word as meaning 'not of Sarah', because the Arabs were believed to descend from the Biblical Patriarch **Abraham** via his concubine Hagar rather than his wife Sarah.

## Sciarra Colonna (1217–1329)

Sciarra Colonna was a member of a powerful family in Italy, which included the cardinal Jacopo Colonna. Jacopo had been **excommunicated** by Pope **Boniface VIII** in 1297, contributing to a feud between the family and the Papacy. Sciarra plotted with the French and accompanied **Guillaume de Nogaret** in the attempt to arrest Boniface VIII at **Anagni** in 1303. Sciarra was reported to have struck the **Pope** and demanded his death, and though Boniface was rescued he died soon after.

## Scotland

The Templar presence in Scotland began some time after the visit of **Hugues de Payens**, the founder of the Order, in around 1127. The Order received its first grant of land there from King **David I**, who gave them **Balantradoch**, Lothian. Another holding was at **Maryculter**, Aberdeenshire and there must have been several others. The Templars were never officially suppressed in the area controlled by **Robert the Bruce**, and there has been speculation that some Templars found refuge in his realm. Such a small number of Templars (as few as two) were tried in Scotland (in the south under English auspices) that it seems likely many fled to the highlands. The two arrested Templars were both English – Walter Clifton Preceptor of Balantrodoch and Walter Middleton of Culter. They made no confessions before the bishops of St Andrews and the papal nuncio John de Solero, who tried them. Other witnesses were mostly hostile. The Abbot of Dunfermline and the Prior of Hollyrood had heard rumours of secretive rituals while servants from Balantrodoch also spoke of clandestine nocturnal gatherings. Templar estates in Scotland ultimately passed to the **Hospitallers**.

## Seal of the Templars

Most important people in medieval times, including the heads of religious orders, had a personal steal. This was a mould, usually round and resembling a coin, for leaving an impression in wax or lead, which was attached to official documents for purposes of validation and authentication. Seals usually incorporated heraldic devices and other meaningful **symbolism** relating to their owners. The Templars' official seal was kept in a safe at their headquarters in **Jerusalem**, which, it is said, could only be accessed by three keys – held by the **Grand Master** and two high officials.

The device of two riders on a single **horse** was the nearest thing to an exclusively Templar symbol, which appeared on various versions of the Order's official seal. The seal was changed with minor variations for every new Grand Master. The earliest known version of the two riders motif is that of the Grand Master **Bertrand de Blanquefort**, dating from about 1158. The emblem could refer to the dual function of the order – religious and military. It could also hint at the Templars' duty to support their needy brothers. Blanquefort's seal was encircled by Latin script reading '*Sigillum militum*', on the front, and '*Christi de Templo*' on the reverse (Seal of the soldiery of **Christ** and the Temple). A later version, the seal of Reginald de Vichiers, read '*Sigillum militum xpisti*'. The first letters of Chris's name are replaced with the Greek 'XP' (**Chi-Rho**). A domed building frequently appears on the reverse side of the Templars' official seal, with a cross at its apex. This appears to be the **Dome of the Rock** Mosque, converted into a church, although it is usually interpreted as being the **Holy Sepulchre**.

The **Masters** of Templar **Preceptories** came to issue their own seals, incorporating various symbols. The *Agnus Dei* was used by several **Masters of the Temple in England**, and also by the Master of Provence. Bearded **heads** also appear on the seals of two Templar Masters of Germany. **Hospitaller** seals also show similar heads, probably representing St **John the Baptist**. The seals of other Templar **Preceptors** have been found to include many other symbols, such as combinations of crosses and fleurs-de-lis in various configurations, castle towers, eagles, griffins, doves, horses and single mounted knights. A late seal of the Templar from England shows a **lion** stood below a crescent moon and a cross, between two six-pointed stars. One version of the seal carries an image of the **Abraxas** and the legend *Templi Secretum*.

## Second Crusade

The Second Crusade was preached by Pope **Eugenius III** in 1145, in response to the fall of **Edessa** to the **Muslims** under **Zenghi** of **Aleppo** the year before. The **Papal Bull** *Quantum Predecessores* called on the knights of Christendom to match the zeal and courage of the previous generation of **Crusaders**. The Pope also commissioned St **Bernard of Clairvaux** to preach the Crusade. It was the campaign wherein the Templars came of age as a **Military Order**, but was not a success. **Conrad III**, the German Emperor, and **Louis VII**, the King of France, both experienced difficulties passing through the **Byzantine Empire**, and came to suspect **Manuel I Comnenus** of deliberately hampering their progress. Below the walls of Constantinople the Germans actually fought against a Byzantine army, which included Turkish mercenaries. Conrad's army crossed to Anatolia but suffered a defeat at Turkish hands, and the King was compelled to retreat and to reconcile with Manuel.

The French also lost many men to enemy action during the Crossing of Anatolia. Louis's force during the second passage through the region would have faced annihilation at the hands of the **Turks** but for Templar organization and leadership. Their performance and their ability to look after their **horses** in the difficult conditions was praised by the chronicler Odo of Deuil, who was also a participant. He recorded that the Templars and their Grand Master set an honourable example to the others. The army established fraternity with the Order, agreeing to obey the officers assigned to them by the Templars and not to flee.[282] Odo suspected the Greeks of deliberately supplying inadequate guides and referred to them as much as enemies as the Turks.

Louis and his wife **Eleanor of Aquitaine** arrived in **Antioch**, but the King was reluctant to assist its ruler, **Raymond of Poitiers**, in any military action against Aleppo. Instead Louis (who seems to have been suspicious of Eleanor and Raymond's relationship) was keen to pass south to the **Holy Land** proper. In June 1148 a council of war was held in **Acre**, where Louis and Conrad met the leaders of the **Kingdom of Jerusalem**, including the young king-in-waiting, **Baldwin III**. The masters of the Military Orders were probably also present as military options were discussed. Some advocated an attack on **Ascalon**, but ultimately the controversial decision was made to attack **Damascus** (an entity which had hitherto been a good ally to the **Franks** against **Zenghi**). The siege of Damascus ended in fiasco and the Crusaders were forced to withdraw. The attack, a betrayal of faith, only drove **Unur** of Damascus into a reluctant alliance with **Nur ed-Din**.

The failure of the siege also exposed divisions between the Palestinian Frankish settlers, the western Crusaders and the Military Orders, and there were bitter recriminations. Some English and Dutch knights assisted in the capture of Lisbon in **Portugal** on the way to the **Holy Land**, but in the east none of the Crusade's objectives were achieved. The failure of the Damascus expedition caused something of a crisis of faith in many Christians. The **Grand Master** of the Templars, **Everard des Barres**, resigned in 1149 and retired into the **Cistercian Order**.

## Secret Doctrines and Secrecy

The Templars were said to be a secretive group. They held their chapter meetings *sub rosa*, perhaps understandably not wanting to reveal any of the

Order's internal problems to outside parties. Secrecy also surrounded their **initiation ritual**, which in the end proved the Order's undoing as it allowed its enemies to make all sorts of **accusations** about what went on.

There has been speculation about the existence of a secret **Rule** since the time of the **suppression**, but no authentic alternative Rule has ever been found.

## Selby Abbey

Selby Abbey was a **Benedictine** monastery in North Yorkshire, **England**. It was sponsored by the de Lacy family, who were also Templar patrons. The three-towered, cathedral-like church survives intact. Parts of the Church are of Norman date and **Romanesque** style. Selby's monastic community was joined by at least one penitent Templar after the **suppression**, that being **William de Grafton**, the former Preceptor of **Ribston**.

## Seljuk Turks

The Seljuk Turks were one of several **Turkic** tribes of nomadic raiders from the Central Asian Steppes. Known for their ferocity in battle and wearing their hair in long braids, they conquered Persia in the tenth century. The Caliphate of **Baghdad** in turn fell to them in 1055, and after this they adopted Sunni **Islam**. They enthroned their own Sultan to hold political power in a Great Seljuk Empire, but retained the **Abbasid** Caliph as a religious figurehead. When the **Holy Land** fell under their sway in 1065, they demonstrated less tolerance of Christian **pilgrims**. Motivated by a mixture of zeal for their new Muslim faith and by a love of plunder, the Seljuks continued the Islamic assault on the **Byzantine Empire**. In 1071 the Seljuk Sultan Alp Arslan defeated the Byzantine armies at Manzikert in Armenia, capturing the Emperor Romanus IV Diogenes, and facilitating the Turkish advance into Anatolia. They captured Nicæa (modern Iznik) in 1077, virtually on the doorstep of the imperial capital. The resultant threat to Constantinople prompted the Emperor **Alexius I Comnenus** to appeal to the West for military assistance, which resulted in the **First Crusade**. Internal divisions within the Seljuk Empire, meanwhile, especially the death of the Sultan Malik Shah, caused the empire's fragmentation, between rival emirates and atabegs (governorships), in Syria chiefly **Aleppo** and **Damascus**. The presence of the Shi'ite **Assassins** was also a destabilizing factor. The Seljuks were also occupied by Arab revolts, and yet it was Seljuk warlords like **Il-ghazi**, **Zenghi** and **Nur ed-Din** who would begin to rally the Muslims under the banner of *Jihad* against the Franks in Syria/Palestine. The coming of the **Mongols** would be a real disaster for the Seljuk Empire. The Turks of the Sultanate of Rum and the Danishmends broke away in Anatolia, meanwhile. Their descendants the **Ottomans** would complete the Conquest of Byzantium and also control much of the Seljuk Empire in the Middle East.

## Seneschal (Templar)

The Seneschal of the Knights Templar was a senior officer beneath the **Grand Master**. His duties and responsibilities seem to have included administration of lands, **horses**, food and provisions for the Order. Sometimes the Seneschal also acted as the Order's standard-bearer. On occasion a Seneschal was elected to succeed a Grand Master. Known Seneschals include:

| Seneschal | Mentioned in |
| --- | --- |
| Guillaume | 1130 |
| **André de Montbard** | 1148–54 |
| Guillaume de Guirehia | 1163 |
| Gautier | 1170 |
| Béranger | 1174–6 |
| Seiher de Mamedunc | 1174 |
| Godechaux de Turout | 1174 |
| **Walter de Mesnil** | 1174 |
| **Gérard de Ridefort** | 1183 |
| Hurson | 1187 |
| **Aimon de Ais** | 1190 |
| Reric de Cortina | 1191 (April to July) |
| Bryony Bonds | 1192 |

## Sénéxhaux

*Sénéxhaux* were agents of the French King, operating in the south of the country, as opposed to *baillis* in the north. They were the ones charged with the arrest of the Templars.

## Sens

Sens is a Cathedral town in **France**, in the **Burgundy** region. The Archbishop of Sens, by a quirk of administrative demarcation, had authority over an area including **Paris**. Therefore during the trial of the Templars the Archbishop **Philip de Marigny** was able to subvert the Papal Commission by calling Templars away from the general tribunal and to convict them as relapsed heretics on an individual basis. His tribunal, called the Council of Sens, seems actually to have taken place in another part of Paris.

## Sergeants

Sergeants (or Serving brothers) were the second class of Templars. They were those not born into noble families. They wore brown or black mantles instead of white, with the usual red cross. They formed an auxiliary, slightly lighter cavalry force in battle, and lived and ate separately from the **knight** brethren. Serving brothers were not necessarily warriors. They could be craftsmen such as stonemasons and carpenters, or agricultural employees.

## Seventh Crusade

The Seventh Crusade was called at the **Council of Lyons** of 1245, in response to the loss of **Jerusalem** to the **Khoresmians** and the defeat of the forces of the **Kingdom of Jerusalem** at **La Forbie** the year before. Continuing hostilities between the **Pope** and the Emperor **Frederick II** hampered the **Crusade**'s initial organization. **Louis IX**, the pious King of **France**, was keen to lead the Crusade. He was accompanied by his brothers **Charles of Anjou**, Alphonse, Count of Toulouse (who had married the daughter of Count Raymond VII and brought the **Languedoc** under **Capetian** control) and **Roger, Count of Artois**. The French included **Jean de Joinville**, who would later write an account of the campaign. The decline in the popularity of Crusading was evident by the smaller numbers involved (although the increased expense of warfare was also a factor in this). Louis mustered 2,800 knights and 8,000 foot soldiers – paid troops rather than zealous volunteers. An English contingent of about 200 knights was led by **William de Longespee**.

The Crusade got under way in 1248, and made **Cyprus** its first port of call. There the decision was made against the better judgement of some (including the Templars), to attack **Egypt** rather than the **Holy Land** proper, to gain its wealth and resources. The Crusade thus followed in the footsteps of the **Fifth Crusade**. After wintering in Cyprus, Louis captured **Damietta** early in 1249. The city fell after a successful amphibian operation. The Crusaders were detained there for many months, but eventually marched south, with their sights on Cairo. However the rashness of the Count of Artois cost the Crusaders their cavalry vanguard at the Battle of **Mansourah**. The leader of the Mameluks who defeated them after an ambush in the town was **Baybars**, who would go on to inflict more deadly damage on the Crusader State. Most of the Templar contingent, including the Grand Master **Guillaume de Sonnac**, were killed during or shortly after the engagement.

Conditions deteriorated for Louis as his camp came under sustained attack before Mansourah, and as hunger and sickness also took a toll on his remaining army. Louis, himself sick with dysentery, refused to abandon his men and was eventually captured. Meanwhile the ruthless Mameluks overthrew their former masters the **Ayyubid** Sultans at the same time. Louis was compelled to surrender Damietta and to provide a ransom, against Templar objections, to secure his liberty. (The Templars had to be pressurised by Jean de Joinville to break into their coffers.) Louis abandoned Egypt and went to **Acre**, with few forces left. He busied himself in that region for four more years, strengthening city defences and even trying to negotiate an alliance with the **Mongols**. He also punished the Templars for attempting (under **Reynald de Vichiers**) to negotiate their own treaty with the Syrian Muslims without his assent.

It was felt in **England** that William de Longespee had received rough treatment at the hands of the French Barons, that far from being a saintly hero, Louis had shown poor leadership, being unable to control his barons, and that Robert of Artois had caused William de Longespee's death. The Crusade therefore marked a deterioration of relations between the two countries. Meanwhile in France the burghers became resentful of the taxes they had to pay to contribute both to Louis's ransom and the cost of his activities in the Holy Land. It began to be argued that it was a better and holier thing to live quietly at home, and wiser not to journey far overseas to die expensively.

## Sheba, Queen of

Sheba (Saba) was probably a kingdom in southern Arabia, extending into **Ethiopia**. Its Queen, according to the Old Testament, visited King **Solomon**, having heard of his wisdom. A seduction occurred (she is regarded as the female partner in the 'Song of Solomon') and according to Ethiopian lore, a son was born, Menelik, who eventually returned to Jerusalem to remove the **Ark of the Covenant**.

## Shekinah

Shekinah is a **Jewish** concept relating to the dwelling place of God (the **Ark of the Covenant** or the **Temple of Solomon**). It also refers to the feminine aspect of the divinity. It is sometimes equated with the Holy Spirit.

## Shields

The shields the Templars carried underwent evolution between the twelfth and fourteenth centuries. Originally they would have carried the large, inverted teardrop-shaped shields of the type carried by the **Norman** knights depicted on the Bayeux Tapestry. Made of wood, they might have had a central metal boss with radiating bands to add strength. With improvements in armour, the shield shrank to the classic triangular shield of the thirteenth century. There are different versions of the design that the Templars carried on their shields. They do not appear to have carried family heraldry, at least after a certain time.

Some have it that the knights carried white shields with red crosses, echoing their garb. Other images show the shield as being half black and half white, echoing their **Beauseant** flag. **Matthew Paris**'s own illustration shows the shield as predominantly white, with a black upper part (chief). Wall paintings from **San Bevignate**, Perugia, however, show the design the other way around, with a small cross in the white upper section. Perhaps there was a regional variation, or it is possible that there were different designs for Templars of different ranks.

## Ships

The Templars maintained a number of ships for both military and merchant purposes. Some were based in **La Rochelle**, others in **Marseilles** and others in **Bristol**. They also had ships in the ports of the **Holy Land**. Some of these were used for transporting **pilgrims**. Much of the Templar fleet seems to have vanished at the time of the **suppression**. The **Military Orders** aspired to gaining a fleet so that as **Crusaders** they need not be reliant on the Italian **maritime republics**. Only the **Hospitallers** (reinvented as the Knights of **Rhodes**) really succeeded in this sphere however.

## Shirkuh (died 1169)

Shirkuh was the Kurdish general who commanded **Nur ed-Din**'s army during interventions in **Egypt**. He was forced to withdraw on several occassions by **Amalric I** and the Templars, but eventually established himself as Egypt's ruler, soon to be succeeded by his nephew **Saladin**.

## Sibylla of Jerusalem (1160–90)

Sibylla was the last Queen to reign in **Jerusalem** before its fall to **Saladin**. Her cunning streak was shown by her promise to annul her marriage to her unpopular husband, **Guy de Lusignan**, and to name a new consort on her accession. She did so, and, after being crowned by the patriarch **Heraclius**, named Guy as her chosen husband and King. Sibylla was the eldest daughter of King **Amalric I** of Jerusalem and **Agnes of Courtenay**. She was the elder sister of **Baldwin IV** and the half-sister of the young **Isabella of Jerusalem**. Her first marriage to the short-lived William de Montferrat had produced the short-lived heir **Baldwin V**. In 1180 Sibylla (at the behest of her mother) was remarried to Guy de Lusignan, an **Angevin** vassal. Baldwin IV approved the match, despite Guy's relatively lowly status, perhaps hoping that Guy, being a westerner, would be able to enlist western support for the **Kingdom of Jerusalem**.

Sibylla bore Guy two daughters, Alice and Maria. Guy's failure at **Hattin** made him generally unacceptable as king, in what little was left of the Kingdom. Guy was captured. Sibylla remained in Jerusalem and was present during the siege, where she cut off her hair as a sign of penitence. It didn't help. She subsequently went to **Tripoli**. When Guy was released by **Saladin**, but refused access to **Tyre** by **Conrad of Montferrat**, Sibylla went with Guy to commence the siege of **Acre**. After the death of Sibylla and their two infant daughters at the siege (during an epidemic), Guy's claim to the throne of the lost Jerusalem was widely rejected by the local barons.

## Sicard de Vaour of Narbonne

Sicard de Vaour, a canon of Narbonne, was one of the French **Inquisitors** who came to **England** in 1309 to investigate the Templars, and who sought to use **torture** against the defendants to secure **confessions** of guilt. The other was **Dieudonné** the Abbot of Lagny. **Edward II** was cautious about allowing the Inquisition to operate in England, but by the same token was reluctant to be seen to oppose the **Pope**. Templars were questioned in London, and then in **York** and **Lincoln**. When confessions were not forthcoming the inquisitors pressed for **Edward II's** permission to use torture, or to 'proceed according to ecclesiastical custom' as they put it. This they received, though with limitations.

## Sicilian Vespers

Sicilian Vespers is a name given to the revolt in Easter 1282 that dislodged **Charles of Anjou** as ruler of Sicily. An effect of this revolt was to weaken the grip of **Capetian/Angevin** power around the Mediterranean. It ultimately shifted the balance of power in the Crusader States, and facilitated the acknowledgement of the claim to the (nominal) kingship of Jerusalem by **Henry II of Cyprus**. The King of **Aragon** intervened on behalf of the Sicilian rebels, and as a consequence an anti-Aragonese Crusade was declared by the very pro-Capetian/Angevin Pope **Martin V**.

## Sidon

Sidon (in modern Lebanon) was an ancient Port city in the **Levant**, probably founded by the Phoenicians. One of its surviving monuments is a ruined **Crusader** castle facing the sea. The city fell to the Crusaders in 1110, after a combined operation with the forces of **Baldwin I** besieging it by land and a Norwegian fleet blockading it by sea (the Norwegian King Sigurd Magnusson having come East on an armed **pilgrimage**). Intimidated by the Crusaders' siege tower and receiving little or no maritime help from **Egypt**, the **Muslim** rulers of Sidon negotiated their surrender and were permitted to withdraw in safety. The city became part of the **Kingdom of Jerusalem**. It subsequently suffered at the hands of the **Mameluks** and of the **Mongols** (who sacked it in 1260). The fortress of Sidon was obtained by the Templars later in the same year. Sidon was also to be mentioned in the trial of the Templars when the strange story of the **Skull of Sidon** was repeated.

## Sigismund of Hungary (1368–1437)

Sigismund was King of Hungary and **Holy Roman Emperor** from 1410. He was a leader of what has been called the last **Crusade**. In Bulgaria in 1396, in alliance with **John of Nevers**, he confronted the **Ottoman Turks** at the battle of Nicopolis. The Christians were utterly defeated. Sigismund fled on a Venetian ship.

## Simon de Montfort, 5th Earl of Leicester (1160–1218)

Simon de Montfort was a French baron. He also had the English title Earl of Leicester, but was excluded from his English lands by King **John**. Simon participated in the **Fourth Crusade**, but became disenchanted when the **Crusade** was diverted towards Zara, and soon left the force. He then became a leader in the **Albigensian Crusade**, being present at the sack of Béziers and the capture of Carcassonne. He was the only one prepared to accept the title Viscount of **Carcassonne**, once Viscount Raymond-Roger Trencavel was deposed – to die in prison, probably under sinister circumstances.

Simon became Captain-General of the **Catholic** forces subduing the **Languedoc**. He developed a reputation for ruthlessness and cruelty as he continued the campaign, eventually establishing himself in Toulouse, and driving out Count **Raymond IV**. Simon's rule was harsh, and he was known throughout the **Languedoc** as Pharaoh, or as *the wolf*. In 1213, At Muret, he defeated and killed **King Pedro II of Aragon** who had attempted to intervene on Raymond IV's behalf.

In 1217 Simon was absent from Toulouse and the city rose up in support of the rightful count. Simon returned and attempted to recover the city, but during the battle was struck dead by a rock hurled from a catapult operated by women on the walls. He was buried in the cathedral of St Nazaire in Carcassonne.

## Simon de Montfort, 6th Earl of Leicester (1208–65)

Simon de Montfort, 6th Earl of Leicester was the younger son of the leader of the **Albigensian Crusade**. He settled in **England**, reclaiming family estates, and in 1238 married Eleanor, the sister of King **Henry III**. Later Simon quarrelled with the King, and in 1240 left the country on **Crusade** to escape the heat. He went to the **Holy Land**, but saw little action. On his return, Simon became Henry's governor of Gascony, but complaints over his harsh rule forced Henry to recall him. Meanwhile Simon became a focus of opposition to Henry III, especially among barons made jealous by the King's tendency to favour foreign courtiers (despite the fact that Simon himself was French). De Montfort led a rebellion in 1263. He captured the King, Prince Edward (**Edward I**) and Richard of Cornwall at the Battle of Lewes in May 1264. The following year Simon experimented with the establishment of a Parliamentary system of government, though real power remained in his own hands. The **Military Orders** were represented at this parliament, but their real loyalties remained with the monarchy, and the Templars probably permitted a raid on their treasury at the **New Temple, London** by Prince Edward, securing funds for the struggle against de Montfort. When Prince Edward escaped from Simon's custody, he rallied the Barons who had become wary of Simon's ambition and led them to victory over Simon at the Battle of Evesham. Simon was lured into a trap by Edward, who flew the banner of Simon's son. The Earl was killed in the battle.

## Sinan (died *c.* 1193)

Imam Rashid al-Din Sinan ibn Suleiman was the leader of the **Assassins** (Nizari Ismailis) in Syria, known as the **Old Man of the Mountains**. It was he who attempted to make a pact with **Amalric I**, which was thwarted by the Templars under **Odo de St Amand** when they killed the Nizari envoy. Sinn also sent Assassins against **Saladin**. It is said that they killed his guards and left a poisoned dagger on the sultan's pillow while he slept. Sinan was probably also the Assassin leader who ordered the murder of **Conrad of Montferrat.**

## Sisters of the Order

Nuns were affiliated with the Templars, despite the stipulations of the **Rule** discouraging the Brothers from having any contact with females. Sometimes, for example, the wives of **confrates** or **married brothers** also became associates of the Order, living on Templar land but not in the community as such. There was at least one convent of nuns under the authority of the Templars, at Muhlen in **Germany**. The female Templars (who can never have been numerous) did not take part in warfare (though female warriors were not unknown among **crusading** armies). They were probably involved with domestic or nursing work and with religion. Sometimes male Templar establishments employed female servants, for example in their dairies and laundries. Female donors sometimes retired to the Templars too. Azo, Archbishop of Canterbury, supported the request of Joanne de Chaldefielde to spend her final days at the Preceptory of Saddlescombe as a member of the Order. Joanne de Chaldefelde was one of a handful of recorded female Templars. Along with her husband Richard de Claldefielde, she took the vows of a Templar before Azo, it being established that she was too old to be a temptation to the brethren.

There seems to be no record of female Templars being interrogated or condemned during the **suppression**. There is a medieval document with a curious illustration showing some **tonsured** male Templars being burnt while King

Philip the Fair and his retinue look on. The interesting thing is that in this illustration, women in veils are being burned along with the brethren.[283] Sisters of the order, perhaps, though there is no record from the time of Templar nuns being incinerated with the male brethren. The word Templar can clearly be seen in the accompanying text, even so. This is from a copy of the Grand Chronicles of France produced a century after the destruction of the Templars, so its accuracy is open to question. A Templar heard at the **Paris** trials, **Ponsard de Gizy**, had alleged previously that the **Grand Master** swore in sisters as well as brothers to the order, making the sisters promise poverty, chastity and obedience, but once they had entered deflowered them (no attempt seems to have been made to locate any of these alleged sisters). Meanwhile in another incomplete record of Templar **Trials** examined by the German historian Heinrich Finke in the **Vatican Secret Archives**, five of the Templars interrogated refer to the presence of women at Templar rituals, perhaps **demons** in female form who had entered the sealed chamber by supernatural means. Two said they had copulated with these women. This last case perhaps reflects an attempt on the part of the **Inquisition** to link the Templars to **heretical, Devil-worshipping** sects who were routinely accused of attending orgies, something that would be a fixation, later, of the persecutors of **witchcraft**.

## Sixth Crusade

The Sixth Crusade embarked in 1228 under the leadership of the Emperor **Frederick II**. It began under a cloud when the Pope **Gregory IX** rashly **excommunicated** Frederick for delaying his departure due to illness, and when Frederick II embarked without waiting for the excommunication to be lifted. (The excommunication was actually more to do with the power struggle between the **Holy Roman Emperor** and the **Pope** that was under way in Italy.)

Frederick II arrived in the **Holy Land** and was initially greeted warmly. However his status as an excommunicant created difficulty, especially after two **Franciscans** arrived with Gregory's admonition that the Crusaders should acknowledge no allegiance to Frederick. Still there was a reluctance to allow the enterprise to disintegrate even after the papal attempt to sabotage it. The diplomatic **Hermann von Salza** was instrumental in keeping the army together, suggesting that members of the other **Military Orders** and those unhappy with obeying an excommunicant could take orders in the name of **Jesus Christ** rather than the Emperor. As Frederick marched on Jaffa in a show of force, even the Templars stayed with the army, albeit following behind.

After months of bargaining (with **Fakhr al-Din** as mediator) Frederick negotiated the restoration of **Jerusalem** to Christian hands from the **Ayyubid** Sultan **al-Kamil**, the ruler at that time of Egypt and most of Palestine. Al-Kamil had been having difficulties with his rebellious nephew an-Nasir, the (son of **al-Muazzam**) in **Damascus**, and was also concerned with the **Khoresmian** threat, so was keen to reach a settlement with the Crusaders. The treaty stipulated that all of Jerusalem would be restored to Christian hands apart from **Temple Mount**, which would remain Muslim. Galilee and **Bethlehem** would also be restored to Christian rule, and a truce would secure peace for ten years.

The Pope condemned the treaty. Frederick had roused the Roman Church's pique by succeeding in recovering Jerusalem without Papal control or the spilling of infidel blood. The Frankish barons and Military Orders were also resentful because the treaty had been ratified without their assent. Frederick provoked particular animosity from the Templars, but was supported by the **Teutonic Knights**, the Sicilian and English bishops and a host of German **pilgrims**. The Emperor entered Jerusalem on 17 March 1229 and the following day crowned himself in the **Holy Sepulchre**, ostensibly reigning on behalf of his infant son **Conrad IV**.[284] When he did so Jerusalem itself was placed under **interdict** by the Latin **Patriarch** Gerold, who remained at **Acre**. It must have seemed decidedly farcical, and hardly sent out a good message to ordinary Christians. All that mattered to them was that they could again visit the Holy Places, and in these basic terms the irregular Sixth Crusade was a great success. Frederick himself was equally interested in the Islamic sites. He toured the Jerusalem Mosques, with the qadi of Nablus as a guide, but did not remain more than a night or two in the city. A Muslim source had it that he feared the Templars, but the Order came onboard with his plans to begin the refortification of the citadel and other parts of the city, so it is difficult to judge the level of hostility between the Emperor and the Order at this stage.

It was alleged later that the Templars had been guilty of trying to arrange Frederick's murder, by writing to al-Kamil revealing when the Emperor would be vulnerable as he made a pilgrimage to the River Jordan. If so it suggests how mired in politics the Order had become. Frederick besieged the Templars at **Pilgrim's Castle**, but eventually had to return to his Italian lands, which were under attack from papal forces under **John of Brienne**. Frederick left Imperial representatives in the **Holy Land** and departed from a bitterly divided Acre, being pelted with offal by a hostile crowd on his way to his galley.

## Skull and Crossbones

The skull and crossed bones is a symbol with various meanings. It is a sign of danger, but is also a *memento mori* or reminder of human mortality. In that sense it can be a Christian symbol. The skull of Adam is sometimes depicted at the base of the crucifix, indicating that Adam's sin was the cause of death, while the sacrifice of **Christ** opened up the possibility of everlasting life. The skull and crossed bones became a popular symbol of death and pestilence, especially after the Black Death in 1348.

Centuries later it became a device used on **pirate** flags (the Jolly Roger). It was also a symbol used within **Freemasonry**, and as the badge of certain military regiments. The skull and crossed bones does not seem to have been a device commonly used by the Templars, even though the **accusations** mention that the idol they supposedly worshipped sometimes took the form of a skull. The symbol only appears on later gravestones, such at those that surround the ruined Templar church at Temple (**Balantradoch**). At the nearby **Rosslyn Chapel** there is a curious skull carved with foliage growing from its mouth, as though symbolizing life from death. At **Temple Church**, London, there are twelve carvings of **Green Man** heads above the portal to the **round church**, with four foliate shoots growing from the mouths in 'X' shapes. At first glance these could be mistaken for skulls and crossbones.

## Skull of Sidon

The Skull of **Sidon** features in a strange story, which was told to the Papal Commission during the **Trials** of the Templars in **Paris,** by witnesses responding to the notion of the Templars being associated with a magical severed **head**. The first version of the story was told by the Italian notary **Antonio Sicci de Vercelli**. He had heard at Sidon that a lord of the city secretly loved an **Armenian** lady. He never knew her in life, but after her death went to her tomb and violated the corpse. Afterwards he had heard a voice telling him to return when it was time for birth because he would find a head, his offspring. The lord had returned to the tomb and found a human head between the legs of the buried woman. The voice told him to guard the head because good things would come to him through it.

Hugues de Faure, a Templar from Lemoges, had not heard of any lord of Sidon being a Templar. However in **Cyprus** he had heard a similar story from the secular knight Jean de Tanis, bailli of Limassol. This time it was said that a noble had been in love with a damsel of the castle of Maraclea in **Tripoli**, but could not have her. When he heard that she had died he had her exhumed and had intercourse with her. Afterwards he cut off her head and was told by a voice that he should take care of the head, as whoever saw it would be vanquished. The protagonist kept the head in a chest, and used it against his enemies the Greeks. He later sailed to **Constantinople** to destroy them with the head, but a maid found the key to the chest, and opened it through curiosity, immediately sinking the ship. Another witness mentioned a legend of a head appearing on the sea amid a whirlwind at Satalia, bringing doom to any ship that sighted it.

This story seems to have medieval precedent unconnected to the Templars. **Walter Map** recorded a version where a poor shoemaker of Constantinople falls hopelessly in love with a noble young lady, and becomes a knight to make himself more worthy of her. Still he was scorned by the maiden's father, and so in a rage he went off to become a **pirate**. News later arrived that the object of his desire had died. He found her grave and performed the previously mentioned deed. As in Antonio Sicci de Vercelli's version the pirate heard the voice and returned to retrieve the head he had sired, which would be deadly to any enemy who beheld it. Eventually the pirate married a **Byzantine** princess. The princess was always curious about the mysterious chest the pirate always carried, and the key around his neck. Eventually, aboard ship, she took the key while he was sleeping and discovered the head in its chest. She challenged him with it, whereupon he was killed. Horrified, she had the head and its keeper cast into the sea, which became the accursed stretch of the gulf of Satalia. In some versions of the story, the dead lady is named as Yse. This hints that the story may be a muddled version of the myth of **Isis** and Osiris from **Egyptian** mythology, which seems to have been mixed up with the Greek myth of the **Gorgon Medusa**, whose severed head was used by Perseus to destroy his enemies, before it was finally cast in the sea. Elements from the story of Pandora and her box may also be traced.

## Slavery

Slavery was a little-known institution in Frankish Europe. Serfs may have been tied to the land, but the spectacle of human beings being bought and sold at the market place was rare. The slave trade was a part of everyday life in the Mediterranean and the Orient; however, despite its foreignness to the Franks they made no attempts to suppress the trade. Meanwhile victorious **Muslim** conquerors at times delighted in enslaving Christian captives, men for labour, women and sometimes children for harems. On occasion hundreds were taken at a time. Some sultans also kept slave soldiers. The **Mameluks** began life as slaves, many being captured in Georgia and converted to Islam at a young age. The Christian barons did not keep harems, but they did sometimes use the labour of slaves – possibly enslaved prisoners of war.

The **Military Orders** sometimes used slave labour in the construction of castles, and galleys were rowed by captive slaves, a particularly unpleasant fate. They also seem to have shipped slaves west to work their estates in Sicily and **Aragon**. (One of Pope **Gregory IX**'s complaints against **Frederick II** was that he had set free 100 Saracen slaves from the Templars and **Hospitallers** in Sicily and Apulia, and had not compensated the Orders.)[285] The African slave trade was already in existence at this time, the main slave takers being **Arabs**. Slaves were also sold through the port of Ayas in Cilicia.

## Sodomy

Sodomy referred to a sexual act deemed immoral or unnatural. It particularly applied to homosexual contact between men, which was condemned in the Old Testament and in the writings of St Paul (e.g. Romans 1:27). The name derived from the city of Sodom, which the Old Testament God saw fit to destroy for the sinfulness of its inhabitants, although the nature of their sinfulness is not actually specified. By the late thirteenth century there was a tendency to associate sodomy with **heresy**, and it was within the remit of the **Inquisition** to prosecute it. The accusation of being Sodomites was among the charges that the Templars most recoiled from and were most reluctant to confess, despite all the pressure placed on them. In fact sodomy was expressly outlawed within the Order. The fact that the **Rule** ordered Templars to sleep fully dressed in lightened dormitories may be taken as a measure to discourage it. The French Rule was even more specific in condemning it and brothers found to have engaged in the act were likely to face imprisonment and expulsion from the Order. In the confessions heard at **Chinon**, most of the senior Templars denied any knowledge of sodomy occurring within the Order. **Hugues de Pairaud**'s testimony becomes rather contradictory when in one line he confesses to instructing the brethren to engage in sodomy, and the next confirms **Raymbaud de Caron**'s account of three Templars who were found guilty of it being imprisoned. The Cardinals at Chinon evidently overlooked the discrepancy. The only Templar confessions relating to being told that sodomy was licit within the Order arose in France and Italy and were the result of the application of torture. Even then the defendants generally said that they never committed the act themselves.[286]

## Solar Temple

The Order of the Solar Temple was a modern apocalyptic cult, which ceased to be after the mass suicide/murder of most of its members in 1994 and 1995. The cult was founded in 1984 in Geneva by Luc Jouret, a charismatic Belgian homeopath, and Joseph di Mambro, a French jeweller. Di Mambro was a former member of a neo-**Rosicrucian** Order, the AMORC. The two gurus convinced their adherents that they were reincarnated Templars. They recruited many well-off members to the cult, which dressed in Templar-style regalia and conducted quasi-**masonic** rituals, with various grades of initiation. Holograms and other tricks were used during rituals to make it seem like spirits were present. The cult spread from Geneva into several other countries, including Canada, where the founders set up a commune in Quebec. Recruits were drawn in during Juret's lecture tours. Brainwashing must also have been involved, convincing members that the world was ending. Di Mambro began to preach that his daughter was a new solar Christ-child, who would lead the cult to a perfect new world, which existed in orbit of Sirius, and which they would reach on the other side of death. Jouret meanwhile, stockpiled firearms, while exploiting female members for sex. Soon after the murder in 1994 of a Canadian couple that had left the cult and the stabbing to death of their child, the other members in Switzerland performed mass suicide – or so it seemed. Some of the victims were drugged and killed by their comrades. The bodies were partly consumed in a fire. A second mass death occurred among other cult members in December 1995. Over seventy died in all.[287]

## *Solomon, King of Israel* (tenth–ninth century BC)

Solomon was the son of the Biblical King **David** of Israel and Bathsheba, the wife of Uriah the Hittite. As David's chosen heir, Solomon reigned in Jerusalem during what the Bible portrays as a golden age, and built the Temple (**Solomon's Temple**) where the **Ark of the Covenant** was installed. Solomon was reputedly gifted by God with great wisdom. Later legends (and the Koran) attributed Solomon with magical powers and control over animals and spirits. He was also linked to the Jewish **Cabbalah**. If Solomon's reign was a period of glory it was to be short-lived as his son's saw division and discord, with the ten northern tribes of Israel breaking away from the Kingdom of Judah. Solomon is supposed to have had many wives and concubines including the daughter of a Pharaoh of **Egypt**. He is also attributed as the author of the sensual 'Song of Songs', which may relate to his affair with the mysterious Queen of **Sheba** but which St **Bernard of Clairvaux** interpreted as an allegory of **Christ**'s spiritual relationship with the Church. King Solomon seems to have been sexually voracious, fond of luxury and in the end disobedient to God (in that he was steered away from monotheism by some of his wives). It is odd that the Templars incorporated his name into their full title (the Poor Knights of Christ and the Temple of Solomon) when they were pledged to chastity, poverty and obedience. He was an unlikely role model.

## *Solomon's Temple*

The Temple of Solomon was built on **Temple Mount** in **Jerusalem** in the tenth or ninth century BC, at the behest of King **Solomon**. Craftsmen and materials were sent by King Hiram of **Tyre**, so the building may have had some Phoenecian influences. It contained cherubim and a cauldron supported on the backs of bronze oxen, and enshrined the **Ark of the Covenant** in the Holy of Holies. The Glory of the Lord was said to manifest in the Temple in the form of a cloud. The forecourt of the building was a scene of large-scale animal sacrifice. Jerusalem fell to the Babylonian Empire in about 587 BC, and the Temple was destroyed. The Jews (or a large number of them) were taken away to exile in Babylon. They were permitted to return seventy years later by the Persians, who had conquered the Babylonians. The Jewish leader of this time was Zerubbabel, who rebuilt the temple to the same dimensions as before but without such rich ornament. This temple was remodelled and redecorated extensively by King Herod (a client king installed by **Rome**) in the first century, but was destroyed by the Romans to punish the Jews for rebelling against the Empire. Only the Western Wall of the sacred enclosure was allowed to remain. The buildings on the Temple platform were demolished. The site stood empty for hundreds of years until after the Arab conquest, when the **Dome of the Rock** was built. What the **Crusaders** knew as the Temple of Solomon (or sometimes as the Palace of Solomon) was actually the adjacent **Al Aqsa Mosque**. The Templars probably understood that the mosque where they were based was not the Biblical Temple.

## Spiritual Franciscans
The Spiritual Franciscans, or Fraticelli, were a purist splinter group from the Franciscan Order. They argued that religious persons should embrace apostolic poverty, and that priests should renounce all material possessions. This caused the Fraticelli to be condemned as **heretics** during the reign of Pope **John XXII**.

## Spying
The Templars used spies and scouts during the Crusades. They also employed informers, such as the emir al-Fahkri, who supplied **Guillaume de Beaujeu** with intelligence concerning **Mameluk** intentions. The Templars probably also used diplomatic missions as a cover for intelligence gathering. Their spy network may have operated within **Christendom** too, but failed to prevent their **suppression**. If the Order was successfully infiltrated by spies of **Philip the Fair** then it does not seem these were called to testify at the **trials**.

## Star of David (Star Symbols)
There is some evidence that the Templars used the six-pointed star (alternatively called the Star of **David** or the Seal of **Solomon**), now thought of mainly as a **Jewish** symbol. A six-pointed star may be discerned among the dungeon carvings in **Chinon** where Templars prisoners were incarcerated. Another may be seen in a mosaic floor at the early Templar Church in Shipley, West Sussex. Six-pointed stars can be traced in the plan at least two of the **round churches** the order built, with six columns supporting the central part (standing where the lines forming the star would intersect). One such building is **Temple Church, London**, and a building identical in plan once stood at the heart of the **Paris** Temple, the Templars' headquarters in Europe. A similar six-pointed design also appears repeatedly in the decora-

tions of **Montsaunes**. It resembles six petals within a circle, and is a symbol linked with the **Cistercians**.

## Stephen Harding (1165–34)

Stephen Harding was one of the founders of the **Cistercian Order**. He was an English monk of the dispossessed Saxon nobility, probably from Dorset, who became a loyal follower of the Abbot Robert of Molesme in **Burgundy**. He was of the party of twenty that in 1098 left Molesme to found Citeaux, which would become the Cistercian motherhouse. In 1109 Stephen became Abbot of Citeaux. He maintained the strict observance of the **Benedictine Rule**, and also instituted his own precepts, codified in the *Carta Caritatis* (charter of **charity**). Stephen was joined at Citeaux in 1112 by the zealous young Bernard de Fontaines Dijon, (who would become St **Bernard of Clairvaux**) and his thirty followers.

Stephen became a mentor to Bernard, who three years later moved on to establish his own monastery at **Clairvaux**. Meanwhile Stephen is said to have sought the help of learned **Jewish** rabbis in the translating of scripture. It has been suggested that this may have had some connection with the activities of **Hugues de Payens** and the early Templars at the site of **Solomon's Temple** in **Jerusalem**, and a possible quest for some lost **Holy Relic** or ancient **treasure**.[288] Stephen also attended the **Council of Troyes** where the Templars were officially incorporated.

## Stephen II, Count of Blois (1045–1102)

Count Stephen II of Blois was a leader of the **First Crusade**. He was infamous for abandoning the Crusade at the siege of **Antioch**, and for informing the Emperor **Alexius Comnenus** when he met him that the **Crusaders** had probably already been wiped out. Having earned the scorn of many back in Europe, (including his wife Adela, the daughter of William the Conqueror), he felt compelled to take part in the Crusade of 1101, to restore his honour and fulfil his original vow. He was killed in battle at Ramlah.

## Stephen of Blois (King Stephen of England) (1096–1154)

Stephen was the son of **Stephen II, Count of Blois**, and the younger brother of Count **Theobald of Champagne**. He married **Matilda, Countess of Boulogne**. In 1135 he seized the throne of **England** from the Empress **Matilda**, the daughter of **Henry I**. Some years of civil war ensued, a period called the Anarchy. Stephen was captured in battle against the Empress's champion the Earl of Gloucester at the battle of **Lincoln** in 1141. He was for a time imprisoned in Bristol, but was released when Gloucester himself was captured by Stephen's faction. Hostilities ended when Stephen recognised the Empress Matilda's son Henry (**Henry II**) as his heir, compensating his own surviving son, William of Blois with the titles Earl of Surrey and Count of Boulogne. Stephen was a generous patron of the early Templars, bestowing lands in England including the site of the **Old Temple** in London.

## *Stephen de Stapelbrugge* (thirteenth–fourteenth century)

Stephen de Stapelbrugge was an English Templar. During the **suppression** he went on the run but was caught in Salisbury in June 1311. He was interrogated at Newgate, **London**, in the presence of the Bishop of London, and became one of only a couple of English Templars to make any form of **confession**. He said there were two forms of **initiation ceremony** used by the Order, one orthodox, the other 'against the faith'. He claimed to have undergone the **heretical** reception (presided over by **Brian de Jay**) two years after his first initiation into the Order. His confession mentioned being compelled in the presence of brethren with drawn swords, to deny **Christ** and **Mary, the Blessed Virgin**, and to spit towards the cross. He admitted some of the other accusations and claimed to know that **Walter Bacheler**, the Preceptor of **Ireland**, had perished under **torture** at the hands of his fellow Templars at the **New Temple, London**. Stephen, having made these confessions, sought absolution. Later, with another Templar who had been persuaded to confess, **Thomas de Thoroldeby**, Stephen was called to publicly abjure the 'errors', and formally absolved in St Paul's Cathedral, in a ceremony presided over by the Archbishop of Canterbury.

## *Strood Manor*

Strood in Kent, **England**, has a surviving Templar manor house. The Preceptory stood near the River Medway, and on the road between **London** and **Dover**, and was probably in Templar hands some time before 1160, having been granted by **Henry II**. Little remains of the rest of the Preceptory, but the manor, which dates to 1240, has expansive **Gothic** vaults, reminiscent of **Crusader** architecture in the **Holy Land**.

## *Structure of the Order*

The Templars had a two-tier structure, with the **knight** brothers being superior to the **sergeant** or serving brothers. It was not as though a sergeant could easily be promoted to a knight, because knights considered themselves a breed apart. There was a case (mentioned in the **Catalan Rule**) where it was discovered that a long-serving knight was found not to have such noble-blooded parentage as he had led his brethren to believe. He was stripped of his white habit and made a sergeant (although he later became a **priest**). Even so there were examples of able sergeants holding important offices such as treasurer without being made knights, and there are also references to Sergeants running **Preceptories**. The exact hierarchy of the Templar Knights seems somewhat uncertain,[289] but the general rank structure was something like this:

**Grand Master**
**Visitor**
**Seneschal**
**Marshal**
**Grand Preceptor of Jerusalem**
Drapier
**Turkopolier**
**Grand Preceptor** (of other Langues or **Provinces**)
**Master/Preceptor** (of individual Preceptories)
**Knight** Brother
Squire

## Sufis

Sufis are followers of a tradition of mysticism within **Islam**. They were thought to be peaceful, poetic and spiritual ascetics. There were various esoteric Orders of Sufis, and their relationship to mainstream Islam was perhaps comparable to the relationship between the **Gnostic** sects and mainstream Christianity. For unclear reasons Saladin gave the task of beheading the captive Templars and **Hospitallers** to Sufis after the Battle of **Hattin**.

## Suger, Abbot of St Denis (1081–1151)

Abbot Suger was an influential French cleric, chronicler and statesman, who rose to prominence from relatively humble origins. He was close to Kings Louis VI and **Louis VII**, serving as regent for the latter during his absence on the **Seventh Crusade**. He is also remembered for his splendid rebuilding of his Abbey of St Denis near **Paris**, traditional burial place of the Kings of **France**.

## Suppression

The suppression of the Knights Templars was the process by which the powerful Order was brought down and finally abolished. It was a widespread operation, ruthlessly pursued. The main agencies of the suppression were the King of France **Philip the Fair**, the Pope **Clement V** (who was largely controlled by the King), the informer **Esquin de Floyran**, the Royal minister **Guillaume de Nogaret**, and the French **Inquisition**. Other monarchs including **Edward II** of **England, James II** of **Aragon** and **Henry II** of **Cyprus** also became involved in the destruction of the Order.

The suppression involved the **arrest** of the Templars, and their **trials** for **heresy**. A propaganda campaign was launched in France to turn popular opinion against the Order by publicizing the list of distasteful things of which the Templars were accused. Sermons and speeches were given denouncing the wickedness of the Order, and hysteria was whipped up. The authorities often employed terror tactics during the suppression, especially against the Templars in **France**. These included harsh imprisonment, fierce interrogation backed up by **torture** and ultimately execution by **burning**, which persuaded many Templars to confess to the **accusations** rather than suffer the fate of their comrades.

The suppression culminated with the formal abolition of the Order of the Temple at the **Council of Vienne** in 1312. The Templars who had escaped execution or who had not perished in prison were mostly pensioned off to scattered monasteries. Others may have joined other **Military Orders**, or became renegades. Most of the Templars' land was given to the Knights **Hospitaller**, though much money was demanded first by the secular powers.

## Sword Brethren

The Livonian Sword Brethren was a **Military Order** involved in the **Baltic Crusades**. It was founded in 1202 along Templar lines by the Bishop of Riga, Albrecht von Buxthoven. The brethren wore white mantles bearing a red *Croix Pattée* above a red sword, pointing downwards. They were formed to fight against the pagan Livonians, and played a part in the subjugation of northern Estonia, where they became based. The Order was decimated in 1236 at the Battle of Saule in Lithuania, against the Samogatian natives. The following year the remnants of the Order merged with the **Teutonic Knights**, although they retained their habit.

## Symbolism

The Knights Templar used a variety of symbols, many of which appeared on the **Seal of the Templars**. Their most common symbol, which appeared on their **dress**, was a red **cross** against white. (This was most commonly a Greek Cross or a *Croix Pattée*.) The **baculus** staff was the symbol of the authority of the **Grand Master**, while the banner **Beauseant** was the symbol of the Order's military prowess. The Templars also used on their seals such devices as the two riders, the **Agnus Dei**, a domed building, a bearded **head**, a **lion**, moons and stars, the **Chi-Rho**, and sometimes, unusually, the **Abraxas**.

The elongated cross with a stepped base (**Calvary Cross**) was often carved on Templar **grave slabs**, often alongside a **sword**. The cross also appeared in a Templar dungeon carving. In the castle of **Chinon** there is a **Star of David**. The circle was also an important symbol to the Templars, as may be seen from their preference for **round churches**. The Templars in addition used the devices of a cross or a flower of six petals (or a six-leafed pattern) within a circle (sometimes called a **Cistercian** Rose). These appear frequently on Templar monuments. The heart may have been another Templar symbol. It appears within a hand in the carvings at **Royston Cave**, and on one of the grave slabs at **Kilmory**.

# T

## *Tactics (Military)*

The Templars were primarily a mounted force. The knights fought as a heavy cavalry unit when a pitched battle was unavoidable. Their primary tactic was a thunderous charge, the squadron having wheeled into line, they would approach the enemy at increasing speed in close formation, intended to break through the enemy's ranks and scatter them. Such a charge would ideally follow a barrage of archery fire, and be followed by a charge of lighter cavalry, and then by an infantry charge, to deal with those knocked down or wounded by the horsemen. The Templars recruited **Turkopole** mercenaries to fill the role of mounted archers, useful for harrying enemy forces. The **Military Orders** were effective and disciplined in battle, as they cooperated and did not seek individual glory. The Templars' statutes laid out their operational procedures. Engaging in battle would begin with the marshal giving the command to form into orderly squadrons. Brothers were forbidden to break ranks or to charge without permission, unless to rescue a comrade once battle was joined. The Turkopoles and sergeants would also be deployed into formation behind the knights to fulfil their supporting role. All would follow the banner **Beauseant**. After singing the psalm (**Non Nobis**) they would couch their lances and initiate the united charge.

The Military Orders seldom had full strategic control over given battles though, as they normally only formed a component of a combined army under a secular commander. The Crusaders did not only rely on tactics to win battles. Faith in God and in relics such as the **Holy Spear** or the **True Cross** also played a part. The Templars were also involved in chevauchée raiding and in siege warfare, both offensive and defensive, which required a different set of tactics again.

## *Tancred de Hauteville* (1072–1112)

Tancred de Hauteville was a **Knight** of **Norman** extraction, who was prominent in the **First Crusade**. He was a nephew of **Bohemond of Taranto**, who was present at the capture of **Jerusalem**. He also captured **Bethlehem**. Afterwards he became the regent of **Antioch** and built the principality up into a powerful state.

## Taxation

The Templars were involved in the collection of the taxes that the Church levied to fund **Crusades**. Collecting for the 'Saladin Tithe' for the **Third Crusade** was entrusted to the local priests and a Templar and **Hospitaller**. The **New Temple, London** served as a depository of taxation money. In 1207 Innocent III wrote to the bishops of Ely and Norwich demanding payment of crusading tax arrears to the Temple, tax of a fortieth of Church incomes having been introduced in 1199 for the **Fourth Crusade**.[290]

## Tel-Danith

Tel-Danith was a battle between **Baldwin II** and **Il-ghazi** in August 1119. It gained a reprieve for **Antioch** as the **Muslims** were forced to withdraw. This was one of the first battles in which the **Crusaders** carried the **True Cross** into action. It boosted their morale and the success of the action contributed to their belief in its power to help them gain victories.

## Templarism

Templarism is a word coined for Templar revivalist groups and societies claiming to belong to the Templars' legacy. Templarism is sometimes defined as the belief that the Templars possessed and transmitted ancient wisdom.[291] The word is also used pejoratively for a genre of literature etc. devoted to the Templars, especially when promoting a romanticised view of the Templars as mystical initiates and the keepers of secrets. Templarism is often linked to **conspiracy theories**.

## Templar of Tyre (late thirteenth–early fourteenth century)

The 'Templar of Tyre' was the author of a history of the last days of the Latin presence in the **Holy Land**. His identity is not known. He was obviously closely associated with the **Grand Master William de Beaujeu**, probably serving some clerical role for him. 'The Templar of Tyre' had previously been a servant of Margaret of Antioch-Lusignan, sister of King Hugh III of **Cyprus**, who had married John of Montferrat in **Tyre**. The author described a peace treaty between the king of Cyprus and the Templars in 1285, and the second coronation of the king as titular King of Jerusalem in **Acre** later the same year, with attendant pageants including a strange cross-dressing joust. The 'Templar of Tyre' later became an advisor of William de Beaujeu, also serving as a messenger and possibly as an intelligence agent. He was present at the Grand Master's death during the final siege of Acre, and was presumably among the Templars who escaped by sea to **Sidon**. He was critical of **Theobald Gaudin**, blaming him for Sidon's subsequent loss. 'The Templar of Tyre' evacuated with the others to Cyprus, where he described the plight of the Frankish refugees from the Holy Land. He evidently distanced himself from the Order of the Temple after that, and was not arrested with the other brethren during the **suppression**.

## Temple Church, London

Temple Church, London is a **round church**, which previously occupied the heart of the Templars' headquarters in the city, the **New Temple**. The church is impressive in scale and precise in execution, as befits the church of such an important **Preceptory**. It is now surrounded by the elegant Inns of Court, off Fleet Street, where lawyers of the **Inner** and **Middle Temple** go about their profession.

The oldest part of the church is the rotunda, which was begun in the 1160s, and which was consecrated to the Blessed Mary in 1185 by **Heraclius**, the visiting **Patriarch** of **Jerusalem**. It shows a transitional style of architecture, with **Romanesque** windows but pointed **Gothic** arches supporting its central drum. A blind arcade surrounds the interior, with a series of carved **heads** in between the arches. Some of these are darkly comical, others grotesque, with grimacing expressions. Some show kings, others fools, others **demons**. Not all are original. The Romanesque doorway to the round nave has an elaborate Norman arch, with twelve 'Green Man' heads around the top of the door. Outside may be seen the plain stone coffins of the Templars. Inside are ten tomb covers, including nine effigy figures of **knights**. These are patrons and **confrates** of the Order, some of whom joined the Templars at the end of their lives. They include **Geoffrey de Mandeville**, **Robert de Ros**, **William Marshal, 1st Earl of Pembroke**, and William's son and grandson. These figures are not in their original locations. The round church opens into an oblong choir, rebuilt in the time of **Henry III**, who originally intended to be buried there. The choir contains another tomb, that of a bishop, in a recess near the altar. To one side of the three arches connecting the two parts of the church, a stairway leads up to a small chamber, said to be the penitential cell where expired the ill-fated **Walter Bacheler**. There was formerly a side chapel dedicated to St Anne, but this was later demolished. A stairway leading down from the side porch hints at the existence of an undercroft.

The church sustained damage during the Blitz when all its original furnishings were destroyed, and when the tomb figures were damaged. It was restored in a rather austere fashion. In late Templar times the decoration would have been rich, with sacred vessels on the altars in silver gilt and ivory, and with banners and probably paintings on the now bare walls. The building passed temporarily to the **Hospitallers**, but eventually became the chapel serving the legal societies of the **Inner Temple** and **Middle Temple**. It is a 'Royal Peculiar' independent of the diocese of London, with ministers appointed by the Crown. The priest serving the church (now part of the Church of England) has the grand title 'Master of the Temple'.

## Templecombe

Templecombe is a Templar village in Somerset, **England**. One Serlo FitzOdo granted the land to the Order in 1185. Four Templars were found to be in residence in the **Preceptory** at the time of the **suppression**. A painted image of a long-haired, bearded **head** on a board was found in Templecombe, buried within the ceiling of a medieval cottage's outhouse. The building was in West Court, off the High Street, and the discovery was made when wartime bombing damaged the outhouse. The head is painted on a large panel, and seems to be a devotional image. Evidently it had been deliberately hidden, probably by the Templars. It appears to be thirteenth century, stylistically, and has been carbon dated to 1280. The head is at the centre of a painted frame in the shape of a quatrefoil combined with a square. The head is now displayed in St Mary's Church, Templecombe. Some have interpreted it as an image of St **John the Baptist** or as **Jesus Christ**.

## Temple, Cornwall

The Templars possessed land in Cornwall including much of Bodmin Moor, of old known as Temple Moor, where they grazed sheep. The hamlet of Temple is at the centre of the moor. The Church at Temple was dedicated to St **Catherine of Alexandria**. The church passed to the **Hospitallers** and then became an independent church. By a quirk of administration it retained the Templars' freedom from Episcopal visitation. It had a bad reputation in the sixteenth century as a place where eloping couples married without official licence, and where suicides were buried on consecrated ground. The original church was eventually abandoned in the eighteenth century and most of it collapsed during a severe gale. An unfortunate local tramp, sheltering there from the storm was apparently crushed by the rubble. The small church was rebuilt in 1883 but retained one original Templar archway, and there is an outhouse, into the outer wall of which have been set various fragments from the earlier Templar building. As in several locations associated with the Templars, there are local myths telling of hidden tunnels and buried treasure around Temple.

## Temple Mount

Temple Mount is a rocky outcrop in the city of **Jerusalem**. It stands in the south-eastern corner of the old walled city. It was the site of the Jewish

Temples of Biblical antiquity. The **Temple of Solomon** was the earliest, though the oldest visible remains are from the time of Herod. Only the Western Wall was left standing by the Romans and this remains sacred to the **Jews**. The **Muslims** conquerors of Jerusalem built the **Al Aqsa** mosque and the **Dome of the Rock** atop Temple Mount. They called the mount the *Haram al Sharif*. They identified it as the 'most distant mosque' enigmatically referred to in the Koran but not named, from which occurred Mohammad's 'night flight' where he ascended to heaven on the back of a mythical beast in order to consult with Allah. The Al Aqsa mosque and the Dome of the Rock are the fourth and third most sacred sites in Islam. The Crusaders called them the Temple of Solomon and the Temple of the Lord, though they probably understood that the Original Temple of Solomon was long gone.

Temple Mount was captured by **Tancred** when the Crusaders stormed Jerusalem. The Dome of the Rock was converted into a church, where the **Canons of the Temple of the Lord** performed daily masses. According to **William of Tyre**, Baldwin II granted the Templars a temporary home in his palace (the former Al Aqsa Mosque) from which to maintain the safety of the pilgrim roads. The Canons of the Temple of the Lord also bequeathed the courtyard between the two buildings. If the donation was intended to be temporary, this was soon forgotten, as for more than seventy years the Knights Templar occupied Temple Mount. The royal court of Baldwin II abandoned the site for a new palace near the Citadel of David, leaving the Templars in complete control of the southern side of the mount. They continued to use the Al Aqsa mosque as their headquarters, adding auxiliary buildings to the eastern side of it and a cloister and hall on the west side, as well as a church that was never finished. Somewhere nearby they had a burial ground. Elsewhere in the area was a sculptors' workshop, producing carvings for the Templars' complex, and also the tombs of the Crusader kings.

Though the Dome of the Rock had been turned into a Church, privileged Muslim visitors were permitted to pray in the small shrine nearby. Christian pilgrims also had regular access to the Mount, entering through the Beautiful Gate, on the western side. A widespread **conspiracy** theory has it that the Templars were secretly busy carrying out excavations during their early years on the site. They are supposed to have found either a great treasure or a powerful secret that enabled them to blackmail the Church and secure their rise to wealth and power. However, given that pilgrims and priests continued to visit and use the site, it seems unlikely the Templars would have been able to keep such activities secret. Most of the Templars' additions were destroyed after **Saladin** captured Jerusalem. Temple Mount remained in Muslim hands after the recovery of Jerusalem by **Frederick II**, as per the emperor's negotiated deal with the Sultan **al-Kamil**. Afterwards the remaining Muslims left Jerusalem, but it is unclear whether the Templars ever returned to Temple Mount. Few seem to have been present in 1244 to defend Jerusalem when the **Khoresmian** onslaught came.

## Templi Secretum

There is a Templar seal bearing an **Abraxas** and wording referring to a secret of the Temple *(Templi Secretum)*. One possibility is that it was the sign of a secret Order within the Order. Clearly the majority of the Order remained loyal to the **Catholic** Church, and many shed their blood in defence of the medieval Catholic version of True Religion. There may, though, have been an inner core, the 'Templi Secretum', that was informed by **Cabbalistic** and **Gnostic** ideas. The original accusations proposed that only the senior knights were aware of the **heresy**, and at the time of the trials there were hints that there might have been a conspiratorial parallel hierarchy within the Templars, and that some sort of secret rule may have existed. As mentioned, the Abraxas seal seems to hint at this. Oddly, though, this seal, with its seeming occult allusions, is found on some rather prosaic and less than mystical documents. It appears on one from 1214, for example, that divides a certain forest between the Order of the Temple and the King of **France**.[292]

## Teutonic Knights

The Teutonic Knights were a Germanic **Military Order** inspired by the Templars and the **Hospitallers**. They were devoted to the **Virgin Mary** and were originally called the Hospitaller Order of St Mary of the Teutons. They were created during the **Third Crusade** at the Siege of **Acre**, where they operated a rudimentary hospital on the beachhead aiding the Crusade's German-speaking contingents. Their Rule was based on that of the Templars and they dressed similarly in white cloaks but with black crosses instead of red. Their original purpose was much like that of the Knights **Hospitaller**, but from the early 1200s they developed an almost exclusively military character. The Teutonic Knights had a sometimes acrimonious relationship with the older, francophone Military Orders. The Templars regarded the Teutons as upstarts and potential rivals. They prevented them from gaining too many possessions in the **Holy Land**. The castle of Montfort in Galilee was the Teutons' only major fortress in the region. They were also a significant presence in Acre.

The Teutonic Knights, under their *Hochmeister* (Grand Master) **Hermann von Salza** were among the most loyal supporters of the imperial faction of **Frederick II** during and after the **Sixth Crusade**, which again set them in opposition to the Templars. The Teutonic Order removed itself from the

Mediterranean area after the fall of Acre in 1291, and the end of the Crusader presence in the Holy Land. It had already found an alternative focus in north-eastern Europe where it had laid the foundations for its own *Ordensstaat* (Order State). The Knights had obtained Chelmo on the Vistula in 1226, and steadily expanded their territory subsequently at the expense of pagan tribes in Prussia, Lithuania and Latvia, as part of the **Baltic Crusade**. From the time of Pope **Alexander IV** they conducted what has been called a privatised, eternal Crusade.[293] In 1308 the Order seized Pomerania, and also took Gdansk from the Poles. In 1310 they relocated their headquarters from **Venice** to the Polish Castle of Marienberg (Malbork), the greatest of their brick-built, Gothic fortresses, which were termed *Ordensburgen*.[294] Marienberg became the seat of their *Hochmeister*, who took on the attributes of a prince in the region. The order had its enemies and critics within Christendom, but its sovereignty in its own territories made it largely impervious to outside interference. In 1305 a trial was commenced against members of the Livonian branch, who were accused, among other things, of corruption, of imprisoning the Archbishop of Riga, and of impeding missionary work. The Order shrugged off such interventions.

The Teutonic Knights briefly moved into Transylvania to combat the encroaching Cumans, but were expelled by the Hungarians for scheming to gain too much power and independence. Subsequently the Order waged sporadic war from Prussia against the Slavic armies of Poland and Muscovy. The Order under Ulrich von Jungingen was defeated by these at the Battle of Tannenberg (or Grundwald) in 1410, amid the Masurian lakes. They were defeated by Władysław II of Poland and Lithuania, a **Catholic**. The next *Hochmeister*, Herman von Plauen, was able to defend Marienberg when it came under siege. The Order survived into the Reformation and beyond in a reduced capacity. In 1525, the last *Hochmeister* of Prussia converted to Protestantism and became the first Duke of the Hohenzollern dynasty. The Order's black cross became a German military symbol.

## *Thaddeo of Naples* (late thirteenth century)

Thaddeo of Naples was an Italian resident in the Latin East, and an eyewitness to the fall of **Acre** in 1291. Possibly a cleric with links to the Templars, he wrote an account of the Christian disaster at Acre while at Messina at the end of that year. His vivid account was clearly intended to inspire a new generation of Crusaders to rise up to recover the lost kingdom. He mentioned details such as the desertion of the Italian contingent once the **Mameluks** started to pour into the city, the suicidal charge a group of priests made against the enemy armed only with the cross they carried, the trampling of children lost in the confusion by riderless horses, and the atrocities of the Muslims, including the raping of nuns and the desecration of churches.[295]

## Theobald II, Count of Champagne (1090–1151)

Count Theobald (or Thibaud) of Blois (a son of **Stephen of Blois** and brother of King **Stephen**) succeeded his uncle Count **Hugh of Champagne** in 1125, when Hugh joined the Knights Templar. Theobald was present at the **Council of Troyes**, and was one of the first to donate land to the Templars. In 1127 he donated property at Baronne-Fayel near Troyes, including a farm that still exists called *la Commanderie*. Theobald's tenure was marred by a breakdown of relations with **Louis VII**, and war waged between the king and the count between 1142 and 1144. The hostilities stemmed from Louis permitting the Count of Vermandois to repudiate his wife, who was Theobald's niece. During this time Champagne was invaded by royal forces and Vitry was brutally sacked. Theobald was married to Maria of Carinthia.

## Theboald IV, Count of Champagne/Theobald I of Navarre (1201–53)

Theobald IV was the posthumous son of Theobald III, Count of Champagne. During his minority his mother Blanche of Navarre acted as regent. The times were plagued by strife due to a rival claim to the succession of Champagne by Theobald's cousin Philippa, wife of Erard of Brienne, an ambitious baron, and by her sister Alice, Queen of Cyprus. Theobald, on attaining his majority, eventually paid these women to drop their claims. Theobald's relations were strained with the Kingdom of France and early in the reign of **Louis IX** he was associated with an unsuccessful revolt there. Rumours abounded that Theobald had poisoned Louis's father Louis VIII, and that he became the lover of Louis' mother **Blanche of Castile**, who ruled France until Louis IX's majority. During Blanche of Castile's regency Theobald would certainly become a powerful influence at court, provoking the resentment of other barons. Theobald later inherited the throne of Navarre, which alleviated his financial straits. The Count had experienced major difficulties, having inherited huge debts from his uncle **Henry II, Count of Champagne**, and had gone as far as attempting to repossess properties donated to the Templars by his predecessors.

Theobald was a notable romantic poet and also a Crusader, although his poems seldom concerned the **Crusades**. In 1238 the truce made between **Frederick II** and **al-Kamil** was due to expire. Theobald led an expedition to the **Holy Land**, sometimes known as the Barons' Crusade. This Crusade (not conventionally considered significant enough to be numbered with the other major expeditions) sought to capitalise on the death of the Sultan and the ensuing conflict between the various Muslim potentates. Theobald hesitated and poeticised on arrival in Acre and eventually decided to campaign around **Gaza** and **Ascalon** against the Egyptian garrisons. After initial success a major setback was encountered, when Henry, Count of Bar, against advice, launched a foray against the enemy, underestimating their strength and resulting in the annihilation of his contingent. (The Templars and **Hospitallers** received some criticism for failing to support Henry.) Theobald shifted policy later and attacked the territory of **Damascus**. The Crusaders experienced mixed fortunes, but persuaded the Damascene **Ayyubids** to conclude a truce restoring yet more land to Christian rule. This outcome also enabled the Templars to reoccupy a number of castles for a time. Theobald refused to accompany Louis IX on the **Seventh Crusade**, but encouraged some of his own vassals to take part, including **Jean de Joinville**.

### *Theobald Gaudin* (died *c.* 1293)

Theobald Gaudin was a Knight Templar who served in the Order for thirty years. He had held the ranks of **Turkopolier** and Preceptor of **Acre (Grand Preceptor)**. **Acre** had fallen under the massive onslaught of **al-Ashraf Khalil** and his **Mameluk** forces in May 1291. While still serving under **Guillaume de Beaujeu**, Theobald had attempted in vain to prevent a violent clash between **Pisan** and **Genoese** parties in Acre. Gaudin was elected the twenty-second (and penultimate) **Grand Master** of the battered remnants of the Order of the Temple, after the deaths of de Beaujeu and Peter de Sevrey in the battle. Theobald escaped from Acre by sea, three days before the final fall of the Templars' fortress, sailing to **Sidon** with the Order's **treasure**. In the month after the fall of Acre **Tyre** had surrendered and **Sidon** seemed hardly defensible. Gaudin withdrew to **Cyprus**, intending to return to Sidon with reinforcements. However the Templars seem to have been demoralised, and soon Sidon, Beirut and the fortresses of **Tortosa** and even **Pilgrim's Castle** were also abandoned. The mainland was entirely lost. Gaudin was succeeded on Cyprus by **Jacques de Molay**.

### *Theodora Comnena* (born 1145)

Theodora Comnena was a Byzantine princess, and a niece of the Emperor **Manuel I Comnenus**. She became the wife of King **Baldwin III** of **Jerusalem** in 1158. She was widowed in 1162. She later eloped with her kinsman **Andronicus Comnenus**, causing something of a scandal. The incestuous lovers went on the run, first to Damascus, and eventually established themselves in Anatolia.

### *Theresa of Portugal* (1080–1130)

Theresa Countess of **Portugal** was an illegitimate daughter of Alfonso VI of Castile. She was one of the Templars' earliest benefactors in Europe, donating the castle of Soure, on the Portuguese Muslim frontier, in 1228. Theresa's husband was Henry of **Burgundy**. Their son Alfonso Henriques became the first King of Portugal.

## Third Crusade

The Third Crusade was a response to the Battle of **Hattin** and the loss of **Jerusalem** to **Saladin** in 1187, and most of the Latin **Kingdom of Jerusalem** in the following year. The Crusade was proclaimed by Pope **Gregory VIII**. Many argued that the loss of Jerusalem had been a divine punishment for the sins of the Christians, and that a new show of military devotion was needed to recover it. Its first wave came from Germany and followed the Emperor **Frederick I Barbarossa** though Asia Minor. The Emperor was drowned while crossing a river, and after that his men lost spirit and began to drift homeward. Only a small contingent continued to the **Holy land**, under Duke Leopold of Austria. The bulk of the Crusade was to come from **England** and **France** (it was with the Anglo-French forces that the Templars and **Hospitallers** mainly operated, new brethren having been recruited from Europe to make up numbers after the slaughter of **Cressac** and **Hattin**).

Kings **Richard the Lionheart** of England and **Philip II Augustus** of France and their armies met in 1190 at **Vezelay**, where they planned their journey to the East. They marched south for **Marseilles**, and thence to Sicily, where they separated after quarrelling over Richard's marriage plans. Philip sailed directly to **Acre**, Richard met up with an English fleet which had sailed around the Iberian Peninsula, and then progressed to **Cyprus**. He encountered trouble from **Isaac Comnenus**, the renegade **Byzantine** prince who had set himself up as 'Emperor' of the island.

Richard's response, joined now by **Guy de Lusignan**, was to defeat Isaac and conquer the island. Richard then sailed to Acre in June 1191, where an epic siege was still under way, begun by Guy and reinforced by European **Crusaders**, who were simultaneously trying to capture the city while fending off attacks from Saladin's army.

Acre surrendered to the Crusaders on 12 July. Crusader unity was fragile, however, as arguments continued about the succession to the throne of the lost Jerusalem. In the end Philip and Leopold, having both fallen out with Richard, abandoned the Crusade, leaving Richard in sole command of the combined army that passed south along the coast, with the Templars and Hospitallers alternately defending the vanguard and rear. Saladin harried him all the way, attempting without success to coax the Crusaders into breaking their defensive formation.

On 7 September Saladin launched a major assault near **Arsuf**. The Crusaders counter-attacked, led by the **Military Orders**, and the **Muslim** forces were scattered. The Crusaders went on to recover **Jaffa**. After that they became bogged down in negotiations, factionalism and indecision. Later Saladin moved to reoccupy Jaffa with a strong army. Richard, who had returned to **Tyre**, hurried to Jaffa by sea and stormed ashore with a small company, fighting so gallantly against Saladin's thousands that the onlooking Sultan, it is said, felt such admiration that he sent the king fresh horses when his own was killed beneath him. Richard went on to recapture Jaffa, and to take Ascalon too, but his two attempts on Jerusalem proved abortive.

The Templars and Hospitallers seem to have had a hand in dissuading Richard from commencing a siege, supposedly believing that the forces they had were insufficient to hold onto the city even if they captured it. A year after Hattin Richard negotiated a treaty with Saladin's brother, and prepared to quit the Holy Land. According to the treaty, the safety of unarmed Christian pilgrims visiting Jerusalem was to be assured. The Christian Kingdom of Jerusalem was to survive, albeit as little more than a narrow strip of coast on the edge of a vast **Ayyubid** Empire.

### *Thomas Bérard* (died 1273)
Thomas Bérard became the twentieth **Grand Master** of the Templars in 1256. He sent word to Europe of the threat from the advancing **Mongols**, who had blazed their way across the Middle East. He reported their atrocities and predicted that unless help was given a horrible annihilation was inevitable. Bérard presided at the time when the **Mameluks** under **Baybars** were putting great pressure on the Crusader States, especially the principality of **Antioch**. While based in Acre, Bérard heard of the fall of Antioch, and that **Baghras** was under siege. Unable to send relief and knowing that the castle could not withstand the siege, Bérard sent a message ordering the beleaguered brethren there to surrender and withdraw to la Roch Guillaume. It was found that the garrison had already surrendered. Bérard did not have them permanently expelled, but held them to account, especially for failing to destroy everything before departing.

### *Thomas Cantilupe, St* (1218–82)
Thomas de Cantilupe was an English prelate statesman, who supported **Simon de Montfort 6th Earl of Leicester** during the Barons War. De Montfort made him Chancellor of England. Cantilupe eventually recovered favour after the death of de Montfort, and was appointed chancellor of Oxford University. He became a trusted advisor of **Edward I**, and subsequently was appointed Bishop of Hereford. He died in Italy in 1282 and his body was returned to **England**. He was canonised in the fourteenth century. Cantilupe's tomb in **Hereford** Cathedral is surrounded by fourteen carvings of **knights**, possibly Templars, in attitudes of mourning.

### *Thomas de Thoroldeby* (thirteenth–fourteenth century)
Thomas de Thoroldeby was an English Templar. At the time of the **suppression** he was held in **Lincoln**, where he received menaces from the Inquisitor **Dieudonné, Abbot of Lagny**. He escaped and went on the run. He apparently

remained in contact with the **Master** of **England (William de la More**, then in royal custody), and went on some sort of spying mission for him to the continent, or so he claimed. He was later apprehended and this time made confessions, and with **Stephen de Stapelbrugge** was absolved and reconciled with the church in a public ceremony in St Paul's Cathedral, **London**.

## Tomar

Tomar was the headquarters of the Knights Templar in central **Portugal**. Their fortress complex, the Convento di Cristo, contained a **round church**, which was extended by the Templars' successors, the **Knights of Christ**. The fortress was built in around 1160 by the **Master** of the Temple in Portugal, **Gualdim Pais**, who also fostered the development of the town. In 1190 the fortress repulsed a siege by the **Moors**, under the Sultan of Morocco. The fortress also protected the treasure of King Sancho I.

## Tonsures

It seems unclear whether Templars were required to be tonsured (the top of the head shaved in the monastic fashion alluding to the crown of thorns). The rule (in certain translations) makes brief mention of tonsures, and one well-known picture of the burning of de Molay and de Charney shows them with tonsures. Most of the time the Templars were shown with covered heads so it is hard to tell if this was the general custom. St **Bernard of Clairvaux** instructed the Templars to keep their hair short and tidy, but it is not certain they went so far as to wear monastic tonsures like their **Cistercian** counterparts. The Templars' **Rule** contains the line *none shall fear to go into battle if he henceforth wears the tonsure.*[296] The word 'coronam' in the Latin rule, translated by some as 'tonsure', could equally be translated as 'crown'. In the context in which it is found, this could refer to the crown of **martyrdom** that the Templars could win in battle.

## Tortosa (Syria)

Tortosa (modern Tartous) in Syria was a Port held by the **Crusaders**. It was within the county of **Tripoli**. The castle of Tortosa was passed to the Templars in 1152 by Bishop William of Tortosa, after an agreement with **Everard des Barres**, after an attack on the city by the forces of **Nur ed-Din** (followed by a brief and brutal occupation) had shown up its vulnerability. The Templars were seen as better able to rebuild and defend Tortosa and its people. The Franks evacuated Tortosa on 3 August 1291, soon after the fall of **Acre**. Just off Tortosa was the island of **Ruad**, which the Templars reoccupied in 1302.

## Torture

The use of torture during the inquiry process was permitted under Roman law, the basis of Ecclesiastical law. From 1253 the **Inquisition** had the Pope's official permission (given in the bull *Ad Extripanda*) to use torture against suspected **heretics** as a means to securing **confessions**. Torture and fear of torture went in tandem with intense sessions of questioning, and the Inquisition had various psychological methods of breaking their victims will and working on their emotions. Victims might be kept in chains, fed only on bread and water, prevented from sleeping over periods of weeks and months. That alone might be sufficient to produce the desired statement, but if not there were more horrific methods. The very sight of some of the instruments of torture might persuade the prisoner to confess. The favoured methods of torture were the rack and the strappado.

Roman law did not make many inroads in **England**, where common law was still in the main respected and where torture was not permitted during investigations. (It would not be regularly used in England until Tudor times). The Inquisition and its methods only operated briefly when two representatives arrived as guests of **Edward II** during the suppression of the Templars. In France the arrested Templars were subjected to torture almost immediately, and it must have been a bewildering and dreadful turn of events. The Royal officials evidently had as much of a hand in it as the friars of the Inquisition. The knight Gérard de Pasigo was one of the unfortunate Templars arrested in **France** in 1307. He was subjected to torture on the strappado by a royal *bailli* of Mâcon. This involved the victim's hands being tied behind their backs, the shackles attached to a rope, which ran over a high beam or pulley. They would be hoisted up on a windlass, and allowed to fall in a series of agonizing jolts, which among other things dislocated the shoulders. In Gérard de Pasigo's case the pain was increased by the weights his tormentors attached to his feet and other parts of his body.[297] Another method of torture was to secure the victim to a table with their feet smeared in fat and exposed to the flames of a brazier. Bernard de Vado, a Templar priest of Albi, suffered such torture until the blackened bones dropped from his feet.

## Tours

Tours cathedral was the place from which **Fulk V, Count of Anjou** embarked for the Holy Land. It was also the place where **Richard the Lionheart**, took the Cross after hearing of Jerusalem's fall. Tours was the capital of the former province of Touraine, which was part of the Angevin domain until taken by **Philip II** Augustus of France. **Philip the Fair** summoned a parliament in **Tours** in 1308, which was used to influence opinion against the Templars.

## Tower of David

The Tower of David is the citadel of **Jerusalem**, a strong fortress built into the city walls standing adjacent to Temple Mount. It was taken by **Raymond IV, Count of Toulouse** and his Provincial forces during the capture of Jerusalem in 1099 in the **First Crusade**. The citadel was built in ancient times, and was strengthened in turn by the Romans, the **Arabs** and the **Crusaders**. It was later rebuilt by the **Ottoman Turks**.

## Tower of London

The Tower of London is a castle. The oldest part, the central keep, known as the White Tower was built from 1078 by William the Conqueror, to stamp **Norman** authority on the city. The castle was extended by the **Angevin** Kings, especially **Henry III** and **Edward I**, for whom it was a Royal residence complete with exotic menagerie. The castle had a long history as a prison for traitors (or political prisoners as the case may be). **William de la More**, the Last **Master of the Temple in England**, died in a dungeon there in about 1213, as did **Imbert Blanke**. It seems a number of other Templars were incarcerated there in chains. Some may have been kept in the Martin Tower, where a Templar-style cross has been carved in the stone of the walls. Most were released after abjuring heresy during a ceremony at St Paul's Cathedral, while those too weak to make the journey abjured in the church on Tower Green. William de la More refused to abjure crimes he had not committed, and so died while awaiting papal judgement. Later, during the **Peasants' Revolt**, the Grand Prior of the **Hospitallers** would be murdered in the Tower, which was stormed by the rebels. The Tower's grim history as a prison really began in Tudor times. The Tower is also famed for its ravens, for its ghost stories, and as the home of the Crown Jewels.

## Treasure

The Templars have long been associated with treasure. Authors have speculated that the knights were on a secret quest for some treasure of both intrinsic and spiritual value. They have been linked to mythical treasures such as the **Holy Grail** and the **Ark of the Covenant**. Leaving aside such things, the Templars (despite their individual poverty) certainly possessed collectively great material wealth, only some of which was discovered during the persecution. It was believed at the time that they had hidden enormous quantities of treasure. In **England** it was still being searched for in the time of **Edward III**. In France it was believed that **Hugues de Pairaud** had hidden treasure, and he was questioned about it in prison years after the suppression of the Order, while there were stories of Templars making off with treasure on the eve of the **arrests**. The Templars on **Cyprus** were said to have hidden gold. It is known that the Templars rescued treasure from **Acre** before its fall to the **Mameluks**, and that they had certain **Holy Relics** of their own, as well as gold. The Templars did not just have their own treasure, but in their banking capacity also acted as treasurers, guarding the wealth of entire kingdoms as well as of prominent nobles such as **Hubert de Burgh**. That said, in their own right the Templars may not have been as wealthy as they have been perceived to be. They had extensive sources of revenue, but also expensive commitments. The building and maintaining of their castles cost them vast amounts.

## Trials

At least in terms of the numbers of accused, the trials of the Knights Templar were probably the biggest in history. They were also among the most widespread for they did not just take place in France but right across Christendom, from Scotland to Cyprus. The Trials in France fall into two distinct phases. The first, the Episcopal or Royal commission, was the initial set of hearings following the **arrests**. The second, the Papal Commission or Cardinals commission, followed the intervention of Pope **Clement V**. Clement intervened to suspend the original inquest, but the government of **Philip the Fair** soon pressured him into ordering the international arrest of the Templars. The Papal Commission, sitting in **Paris**, was to look into the guilt of the Order as a whole, the other trials to investigate the Templars as individuals. Generally speaking confessions were only heard when fear of torture or of being burned caused them to be made. In England, meanwhile, provincial trials were held in **York** and **Lincoln**, before the Templars were brought from these places and elsewhere to be tried in **London**.

## Tripoli

Tripoli (in northern Lebanon) is a port city south of Tortosa (Tartus, Syria). It was an important commercial and cultural centre in the Middle Ages. It was surrounded by the sea and could only be attacked by land along the eastern side, through a narrow passage. It was taken by the **Crusaders**, under Bertrand of Toulouse, the son of **Raymond IV of Toulouse**, in 1109, and became the main city of the Crusaders' county of Tripoli. Much later the **Grand Master** of the Templars **Guillaume de Beaujeu** learned from a paid informer in the **Mameluk** camp, the Emir al-Fakhri, that the Mameluks planned to attack Tripoli, and wrote to warn the city commune. Unfortunately the leaders of Tripoli neither trusted the Grand Master nor believed his warning, and consequently the Mameluks found Tripoli unprepared and took the city with relative ease. Internal factionalism and the rivalry of the **Genoese** and **Venetian** merchants had also weakened the city. Tripoli was captured by **Qalawun** in 1289. The Mameluks killed every Christian man in Tripoli including the Templar commander, Peter de Moncoda. The women and children were dragged off as **slaves**. The city was then largely destroyed.

## Troyes

Troyes was the capital of the county of **Champagne**, which was semi-independent until the reign of **Philip the Fair**, who united it to the **Capetian** domain in 1285. It was an important location in relation to the early Templars. Its ruler **Hugh Count of Champagne** had a palace and ancestral castle there. Hugh was one of the first backers of the Order of the Temple (as he was of the **Cistercian Order**). **Hugues de Payens** was from the region and the monastery of Clairvaux was close by. Troyes was the venue of the Church **Council of Troyes**, presided over by St **Bernard of Clairvaux**. The city was one of the venues of the **Champagne Fairs**. The Templars' **Preceptory** in Troyes was on the Rue du Temple, adjacent to the Rue de l'Epicerie. The Preceptory was destroyed in a fire in 1524.

## True Cross

The True Cross was the **Holy Relic** held most sacred by the **Crusaders**. They obtained it after the **First Crusade**, apparently after **Arnulf of Chocques** threatened force against the Eastern clergy in order to discover its location. It was a large fragment of a wooden cross, which had been discovered near the **Holy Sepulchre** by St **Helena**. This was believed to be the actual cross on which **Jesus Christ** was crucified. The Crusaders took to carrying it into desperate battles, attributing it with power to grant victory to God's faithful soldiers, much as the ancient Israelite warriors had with the **Ark of the Covenant**. The fragment was encased in a great, cross-shaped reliquary of gold, set with jewels. The Crusaders entrusted it to Syrian Christian guardians, and it was held in the Holy Sepulchre, brought out only in times of war. Its loss to Muslim forces at the Battle of **Hattin** caused great grief among the Christians, and was a worse blow to their morale than the capture of the King.

## Tunnels

The Templars dug out numerous tunnels and underground chambers, both in the **Holy Land** and in the West. A Templar tunnel exists in **Acre**, and another, perhaps in **Jerusalem**, leads towards the centre of **Temple Mount** from the south-eastern corner of the outcrop (**excavations**). This has been identified as a possible secret entrance for their fortified headquarters, or as an attempt on their part to dig into the centre of the mount in the search for ancient treasures. Alternatively it could be an ancient tunnel that they rediscovered. The archaeologists under Mier Ben-Dov, who in 1968 excavated the passage, could only progress so far before coming to the area under the authority of the Muslims, sacred ground deemed inviolable. Some Templar tunnels may have had a defensive purpose (e.g. sally ports under the walls of castles).

## Turkopoles

Turkopoles were oriental mercenaries employed by the **Crusaders**, mostly Syrian Christians. The Templars often employed Turkopoles as mounted archers and light cavalry and possibly also as foot solders. They were under a Templar officer called the *Turkopolier*.

## Turks

The Turkic peoples originated in Central Asia. They formed various tribal groupings. In the ninth and tenth centuries they conquered Persia and the Middle East, under the umbrella of the **Seljuk** Empire. They became masters of the **Arabs** in the region, from whom they mostly adopted **Islam.** (Previously they had adhered to a shamanic religion of nature worship.) In 1085 they captured **Baghdad**, establishing a Sultanate and reducing the Caliph to a figurehead. Now mostly Sunnis, the Turks also gained victories over the **Byzantine Empire**, including Manzikert in 1071. By the time of the **Crusades** the Seljuk Empire had fragmented somewhat. This disunity played some part in the Crusader's success. The Turkish Empire was farther destabilised by the activities of the **Assassins**.[299] The **Ottoman Turks** later conquered an extensive empire in the Near East and Eastern Europe, becoming masters of Greeks, Slavs and Armenians, as well as Arabs. Many Turkic peoples, including the **Khoresmians**, were pushed westward by the **Mongol** hordes, while others assimilated with them.

## Tyre

Tyre is an ancient port city in Lebanon. It was a centre of the Phoenician civilization. The ancient King Hiram of Tyre is said in the Bible to have assisted **Solomon** in building the Temple in **Jerusalem**. Tyre, situated between **Acre** and **Sidon**, was important to the Crusaders, who gained control of it in 1124. The Franks had intercepted a pigeon bringing a message to the defenders that reinforcements were on the way, and had substituted a forged note saying the opposite, and advising surrender.[300] Tyre became the seat of the archbishop **William of Tyre**, the statesman and chronicler. Tyre was one of the few cities to hold out against **Saladin**, and became the power base of **Conrad of Montferrat** during the Third **Crusade**. Tyre was one of the last Crusader strongholds in the East, being abandoned only after the fall of Acre in 1291.

# U

## Umayyad Dynasty
The Ummayads were the first dynasty of Sunni **Muslim** Caliphs. They reigned from **Damascus**. The **Abbasids** supplanted them but a branch of the dynasty took root in Spain.

## Unam Sanctum
*Unam Sanctum* (The One Holy) was a **Papal Bull** issued in November 1302 by **Boniface VII**. It proclaimed the doctrine that there can be no salvation or absolution outside of the **Catholic** Church. It also emphasised **Papal supremacy** and authority over temporal as well as spiritual matters. It was vital for salvation, the bull stated, that every human creature should be subject to the Roman Pontiff. The bull was shockingly direct in its claim to universal authority. King **Philip the Fair**, who was already feuding with Boniface over the right to tax the clergy, rejected the document as insolent, and commissioned a refutation of the Pope's assertions. The Pope **excommunicated** him.

## University of Paris
The University of **Paris** came into being in the twelfth century. Its masters and scholars became recognised arbiters in legal and theological matters. During the **suppression** of the Templars, **Philip the Fair** sought to legitimate his actions (in moving against an Order suspected of **heresy**) by gaining the support of the University theologians. In February 1308 he wrote to them, posing a list of questions on the matter, anticipating favourable answers. This was an attempt both to bypass the authority of **Clement V**, and to put pressure on him to reopen the suspended inquisitorial proceedings into the Templars. **Jacques de Molay** had been obliged to repeat his early confession to the University masters, and they were present at the end when he repudiated the **accusations against the Order**.

## Unur (died 1149)
The Emir Mu'in ad-Dur Unur was a Turkish commander of the forces of **Damascus**. He came to power in the city in 1140. He forged an alliance with the **Franks** against **Zenghi** of **Aleppo**, who had recently been besieging Damascus. Unur led a Damascene army with a large Frankish contingent to capture **Baniyas**, which was afterwards ceded to the Franks. Though the alliance had been productive, the Franks later broke it off and attacked Damascus during the **Second Crusade**, without success.

## Urban II (Pope) (1042–99)

Urban II (originally Odo of Lagery) was the **Pope** who called the **First Crusade**. He was a **Burgundian**, and became pope in 1088. At the Council of Piacenza in 1095 Urban received the emissaries of the **Byzantine** Emperor **Alexius I Comnenus**, who told of the threat from the **Turks** and appealed for military aid. Urban responded by preaching the **Crusade** at the **Council of Clermont** and at other locations, touring **France** amid great pomp and ceremony and delivering rousing sermons promising material and spiritual rewards to potential Crusaders, urging them to **take the Cross** and be redeemed from their sins.

## Urban III (Pope) (died 1187)

Urban III became **pope** in 1185. His reign was taken up with political disputes with **Frederick I Barbarossa**, the **Holy Roman Emperor**. He died in October 1187; it is said he died from sorrow on hearing of the Christian defeats in the **Holy Land**.

## Usama ibn Munqidh (1095–1188)

Usama ibn Murshid ibn Munqidh was a **Muslim** diplomat and merchant from Shaizar, who visited the **Kingdom of Jerusalem** and recorded his impressions. He had a low opinion of **Frankish** food, was astonished by their relatively lax and unjealous attitude to women, and ridiculed their medical practices.

Usama represented **Unur** the Governor of **Damascus** on a diplomatic mission to **Jerusalem** in 1138, where he discussed an alliance with the King (**Fulk V, Count of Anjou**) against Mosul. Usama had good words to say about the Templars, who permitted him to pray towards Mecca on **Temple Mount**, and defended him from a boorish Frank, a 'devil of a man', newly arrived from the West, who it seems mocked the Muslim's prayers. The Templars rebuked and jettisoned the interloper. This may have been politically motivated, but the episode belies the image of them as belligerent zealots. Generally Usama deemed the Franks to be 'animals possessing the virtue of courage and fighting but nothing else'.[301] He was one of the defenders of **Ascalon** when it was attacked and captured by the Franks, and perhaps crossed swords with his former friends the Templars during the fighting there.

# V

## Vasco da Gama (1469–1524)

Vasco da Gama was a great Portuguese sailor and explorer. He was commissioned by **Manuel I, King of Portugal** to sail to the East, seeking the legendary Christian empire of **Prester John**. Da Gama became the first European captain to sail around Africa to India. Da Gama reached Calicut in southern India in May 1498. His pioneering voyage opened the way for Portuguese trade and colonial expansion in the subcontinent. He was an associate of the **Knights of Christ**, the successors of the Templars in **Portugal**. One of the sons he left was **Christopher da Gama**, who died fighting **Muslims** in **Ethiopia**.

## Venerable Order of St John

The Most Venerable Order of the Hospital of St John of Jerusalem is a revival of the Knights **Hospitaller** in Britain. Its badge is a **Maltese cross** with lions and unicorns between its arms. It came into being in the early nineteenth century, and was later recognised as a Royal Order of **chivalry**. It is an ecumenical Christian association, and is distinct from the Catholic **Sovereign Military Order of Malta**. The Venerable Order possesses St John's Gate, the last surviving part of the headquarters of the Knights Hospitaller in Clerkenwell, **London**. The Order carries on the medical/charitable tradition of the Knights Hospitaller through its association with the St John Ambulance Brigade (created in 1887). The foundation of the English Order in the 1820s was encouraged by members of the French Langue of the Order of Malta, who had a quixotic plan to raise forces to recover Rhodes from the **Ottoman Turks**, who were then distracted by the Greek War of Independence. The plan came to nothing. However, the later support of Queen Victoria gave it a degree of legitimacy as a secular Order of Chivalry. The English Order supported the foundation of a hospital in east **Jerusalem**, specializing in ophthalmic surgery.

## Venice

Venice, amid its lagoon at the top of the Adriatic, was a powerful mercantile republic beginning an era of particular prosperity and imperial expansion at the time of the **Crusades**. The Venetians first gained a stake in the affairs of the **Holy Land** when they defeated an Egyptian fleet off **Ascalon** in 1123 and assisted the Crusaders to capture **Tyre** the following year. This became an important trading port for them. They gained trading concessions in other **Levantine** ports besides. Their disputes with the **Pisans** and **Genoese** in later days often sucked in local factions including the **Military Orders**. During the **War of St Sabas** the Templars sided with the Venetians and the Teutonic knights against the Genoese and the Hospitallers. The Venetians also continued to trade with the **Mameluks**. Venice's involvement caused the **Fourth Crusade** to divert and to attack the Christian cities of Zara and **Constantinople**. Venice was filled with looted **Byzantine** treasures, including the bronze horses that now adorn the façade of St Mark's basilica (a church built to hold the relics of St Mark, which an earlier generation of Venetian pirate-merchants had stolen from **Alexandria**).

The Templars' relationship with the Venetians was sometimes strained, and a serious dispute in the 1240s led to the Templars burning the Dalmatian town of Segna. By 1259, however, the relationship had improved and the Venetian government gave the Templars money to extend and improve their Preceptory in Venice. The Templars on the whole remained suspicious of the Venetians, whose first motive was profit.

## Vézelay

Vézelay is a city in **Burgundy, France**. It was important to **Crusading** history, being the point of departure for both the **Second Crusade** and the **Third Crusade** (when **Philip II Augustus** and **Richard the Lionheart** met to plan the recovery of the **Holy Land**). It was on the pilgrim road to Santiago de Compostella, and was a great centre of pilgrimage in its own right. Its grand **Romanesque** basilica (also a **Benedictine** abbey) laid claim to the bones of St **Mary Magdalene**. Its portals are surrounded by carvings incorporating scenes of the Last Judgement as well as the signs of the zodiac.

## Visitor

The Visitor of the Order was an important official of the Knights Templar. His duties involved inspecting Templar **Preceptories** in Western Europe to ensure proper practices were being observed and to make sure revenue was being collected for the Order's activities in the **Holy Land**.

## Vox in Excelso

*Vox in excelso* was a **Papal Bull** issued by **Clement V** at the **Council of Vienne** in 1312, ending the official existence of the Knights Templar. It explicitly stated: 'we abolish the aforesaid Order of the Temple and its constitution, habit and name, in an irrevocable and perpetually valid decree ... strictly forbidding anyone to presume to enter the said order in the future, or to receive or wear its habit, or to act as a Templar. Which if anyone acts against this, he will incur the sentence of excommunication *ipso facto.*'

## Vrána

Vrána is a Templar castle in Croatia, which survives in ruins. Templars from there resisted attack from **Mongol** invaders.

# W

## Waldensians

Waldensians (also called Vaudoise) were a sect of religious reformers in the Middle Ages, rashly condemned as **heretics** by the **Catholic** establishment at the **Fourth Lateran Council**. They were followers of one Peter Waldo, a former merchant of **Lyons** who became a popular preacher in the 1170s. They did not wildly diverge from Catholic doctrine initially, but disputed the exclusive authority of the ordained priesthood to preach and interpret the Gospels. They had certain ideas in common with both the **Cathars** and the **Spiritual Franciscans**. They became the subject of persecution at the hands of the **Inquisition** and were also accused of unholy worship. **Bernardo Gui**, in his manual for Inquisitors, accused them of engaging in orgiastic rites at which a diabolical **cat** appeared to receive their devotion. They in turn accused the **Pope** and Bishops of murder for promoting the **Crusades** and creating the Inquisition. They became strongly opposed to the church hierarchy, and believed themselves to be true heirs to the apostles. Though hunted, they survived in hiding, especially in remote parts of Switzerland and in **France** in secret. Later they found common cause with the Protestant Reformation.

## Wall paintings

Medieval **Catholic** churches were often richly decorated with wall paintings, usually depicting Biblical characters and episodes. Very little of the original decoration of Templar buildings has survived, and only exceptionally can original wall paintings be discovered. Good examples of chapels where Templar-era murals survive include (albeit in a degraded state) **Cressac** and **Montsaunes** in France and **San Bevignate** in Perugia, Italy. The paintings include **saints**, mounted **knights**, castles, animals, **crosses**, and strange, abstract, possibly astrological symbols.

## Walter Bacherler (died *c.* 1306)

Walter Bacheler (or Walter le Bachellor) was a former Templar Preceptor of **Ireland**. It seems he died imprisoned at the **New Temple, London**, having been found guilty of stealing Templar property. The circumstances of his death were inquired about during the **trials** of the Templars in **England**. A Templar called Ralph de Barton told the tribunal in **Holy Trinity Church, London** that Walter had died in fetters and had been refused burial in the Order's cemetery, because he had broken the Order's rule and was therefore considered **excommunicated**. Others said that Walter had died under natural circumstances, had been confessed before his death and was buried decently.[302] The penitential cell may have been the small chamber at the top of a stairway within **Temple Church London**.

## Walter de Mesnil (died *c.* early 1170s)

Walter (or Gautier) de Mesnil was a Templar in the **Kingdom of Jerusalem**. According to **William of Tyre**, he was the leader of the Templar ambush of the **Assassin** envoy, calculated to wreck the planned alliance between King **Amalric I** and the Syrian Assassins under Rashid ed-Din Sinan. He therefore has the unusual distinction of being an assassin of Assassins. William found the whole episode outrageous, and called Walter 'an evil, one-eyed man, *whose breath is in his nostrils*, a totally worthless man'.[303] Amalric demanded that Walter de Mesnil be handed over for punishment but the Grand Master **Odo de Saint-Amand** refused, asserting the Templars' independence of Royal authority. Odo declared his intention instead to send Walter to **Rome** for judgement by the **Pope**. Amalric, however, rode to **Sidon**, interrupting the Templar **Chapter** meeting. Walter was dragged away in chains and imprisoned in **Tyre**, though his ultimate fate is unknown. William of Tyre claimed that the whole kingdom was brought to the brink of ruin by the murder of the ambassador. It does not seem that Odo took responsibility for Walter's attack on the Assassin delegates, but it is unlikely that Walter acted independently, considering the emphasis the Templars always placed on obedience to their hierarchy.

## Walter IV of Brienne (1205–46)

Walter IV, Count of Brienne became Count of **Jaffa** and **Ascalon** in 1221, and married Princess Mary of **Cyprus**. Walter commanded the Christian contingent at the battle of **La Forbie**, which followed on from the loss of **Jerusalem** in 1244. The battle was a disaster for the **Kingdom of Jerusalem**. The Sultan **Ayyub** won a decisive victory, decimating the Templars and **Hospitallers** and capturing **Armand de Perigord**. Walter was captured and later murdered while in prison in Cairo.

## Walter Map (c. 1135–1210)

Walter Map was a chronicler, churchman and diplomat, probably from the west of **England**. He served as ambassador for **Henry II** at the French and Papal courts, before holding clerical posts in England, including Archdeacon of Oxford. Walter was obviously loyal to Henry, whom he praised as an affable, energetic and modest lawmaker. Walter wrote accounts of the diabolical rites that heretics were supposed to partake in. He described, for example, an orgiastic sect called Paterines, who worshipped a huge **cat** who descended to them on a rope, whom they would kiss on the feet and below the tail. Walter did not accuse the Templars of any **heresy**, but he did suspect them of loving violence too much. He reported their murder of the Assassin envoy, claiming that they did it because the Assassins were about to convert to Christianity, and the Templars feared the outbreak of peace through the disappearance of the Muslims' religion.[304]

## Walter of Hemingborough (thirteenth–fourteenth century)

Walter of Hemingborough was an English chronicler and the representative of **Edward II** at the **Council of Vienne**, where Pope **Clement V** caved into pressure from King **Philip the Fair** and abolished the Knights Templar. Walter recorded how the move was only supported by the French, and how fear of Philip was the main motivation for it. He called Philip the source of the whole scandal. He described how the Pope was sat between King Philip and his son the King of Navarre whilst he read out the bull *vox in excelso*, which ended the existence of the Order of the Temple. He also related how none were permitted to speak against the declaration on pain of **excommunication**.

## Walter Sans-Avoir (died 1096)

Walter (or Gautier) Sans-Avoir (the Penniless) was a **knight** who led one of the first bodies of **Crusaders** to set off during the **First Crusade**. He joined with **Peter the Hermit**. The contingent contained a large number of poorly armed **pilgrims**, many drawn from the poorer classes. Having crossed into Anatolia, they rashly engaged the Turks and faced near annihilation. Walter was killed. He may have served as example to the early Templars, who were also known as the Poor Knights.

## Walter Scott (1771–1832)

Sir Walter Scott was an author and poet from **Scotland**. He was the author of numerous historical novels. In two of these, namely *Ivanhoe* and *The Talisman* the medieval Knights Templar feature as villains. Paradoxically, Scott seems to have admired medieval **chivalry**, but disdained the **Crusades**, and his **Jewish** or **Saracen** characters were usually more favourably portrayed than his Templars. Scott also took an interest in **Rosslyn Chapel**, writing about its legends, and having copies of some of its carvings incorporated into his **Gothic**/baronial mansion at Abbotsford, which he built in the 1820s.

## Warwick Castle

Warwick Castle is a medieval fortress on the river Avon, and is one of the best-known castles in **England**. The oldest part is the mound or motte. Most of the present castle is fourteenth century. At the time of the Templars the Castle was held by the Beauchamp family. The Templars from Temple **Balsall** were imprisoned for a time in Warwick Castle. In a grim dungeon at the base of Caesar's Tower, many crosses, including **Calvary crosses**, can be seen, scratched into the stone walls. If the dungeon is contemporary with the Templars' suppression (which seems so, to judge from the architecture) then it is very likely that Templar prisoners left the crosses in its walls. The dungeon also held Royalist prisoners during the English Civil War.

## Weaponry

The Templars carried the same sort of weaponry as secular **knights** of the period, though it was to be without ostentatious ornament. For the most part the knights carried a straight, single-handed broadsword with a straight cross-guard and a round pommel (counter-weight), used either on foot or on horseback. The scabbard was made of leather-covered wood. **Shields** were also of wood. The sword, though prized, was their secondary weapon, however, as the knights' primary weapon was the lance, made of ash wood with an iron tip and carried couched (locked under the arm), and used in the mass cavalry charge. Each knight also had a knife or dagger (which, if he was captured, was technically the only ransom he was allowed to offer for his life). The dagger was designed for use in close quarter fighting, to stab through the eye slits of an enemy's helmet. Some knights also carried maces, battle-axes, war hammers, etc. There are also accounts of Templars using crossbows. Their Syrian mercenaries (**Turkopoles**) carried Saracen bows. These Turkopoles probably also had Arab style pattern-welded swords, designed for cutting rather than stabbing.

## Westerdale

Westerdale was the location of a Templar **Preceptory** in North Yorkshire, **England**. It was donated by one Guy de Bonaincurt, before 1203. **Grave slabs** have been found in the area with the trademark round-headed crosses with long stems and stepped bases carved on to them. These are now kept in Christ's Church, Westerdale. Another slab is carved with the outline of a bow and arrow and a dagger. There is a picturesque stone bridge nearby, believed to have been built by the Templars.[305] The last Preceptor of Westerdale was **William de la Fenne**.

## William de Grafton (thirteenth–fourteenth century)

William de Grafton was the last Templar Preceptor of **Ribston** in Yorkshire, **England**. He had been received into the Order in the **Master**'s rooms in the **New Temple, London**. After the **arrests** he was held and interrogated in **York**. He was probably taken with the others to face the **Inquisition** in **London**. Simon Brighton mentions an intriguing mystery concerning William's release from his religious vows, much later. After the suppression of the Templars in England, William, like most of the ex-brethren, was sent to serve out his penance in a monastery, in this case **Selby Abbey** back in Yorkshire. In 1331 he applied to be released from his monastic vows. Brighton cites Denis Gardner's translation of a contemporary document: 'The Master of the Temple, with the assent of the brethren absolves from his vow William de Grafton, one of the brethren of the Order and granted that having laid aside the habit of the Temple, he may be allowed to turn himself to the secular state which King **Edward II** and the Present King (i.e. **Edward III**) have confirmed.' The document seems to refer to a Grand Master or at least a Provincial Master. Could it mean the Master of the Hospitallers? The only man after the suppression to use the title 'Master of the Temple' officially was the priest serving Temple

Church, London, and it is doubtful he would be the one referred to here. The only alternative is that there was some not very secret Templar **continuity**.

## *William de la Fenne* (thirteenth–fourteenth century)

William de la Fenne was the last Preceptor of **Westerdale** (or possibly of Faxfleet) in Yorkshire. He was arrested at Westerdale, and was one of the Templars initially held in **York**, after the arrests, along with **William de Grafton**. William de la Fenne had been received as a Templar in Shipley, Sussex, in the dormitory. At the Templar trials in York it was alleged by the Sheriff of York **John de Eure** that William was in possession of a book with a loose page that contained **heretical** doctrines such as that **Christ** was not divine nor the son of a virgin, and that he was a false prophet crucified for his sins. William remembered lending the book to de Eure's wife but denied any knowledge of the alleged page with the heretical statements written on it. According to the Sheriff, however, when he confronted him, William had attributed the writings to a *Magnus Ribaldus* (great joker) and taken the book away.

## *William de la More* (died 1313)

William de la More was the last **Master of the Temple in England.** He succeeded **Brian de Jay.** He was imprisoned in the Tower of London, initially in quite comfortable conditions, which were made worse as the trials dragged on. During the Trials he defended the Order's innocence, and denied all of the **accusations**. On 29 April 1311 William read at out a statement at the Church of **All Hallows by the Tower, London**, where he had been brought from his place of confinement. He declared the Templars' belief in all that the Church taught. The Templars were devoted to **Christ** and **Mary the Blessed Virgin**. Their religion was founded on **obedience, poverty** and **chastity**, and the striving for the recovery of **Jerusalem**. He denied and contradicted all the **heretical** and wicked things that the Order was charged with. He said if they had erred through ignorance of a word, as unlettered men, then they stood ready to be punished and corrected, but prayed that they be treated as true children of the Church. Despite possibly being **tortured**, William subsequently refused to abjure crimes which he insisted he had never committed, rejecting therefore the face-saving solution devised by the English Church, (i.e. public abjurations and reconciliation ceremonies). William remained a prisoner in the Tower of London, awaiting papal judgement. His death was a result of harsh imprisonment in chains. He was dead by February 1313, never having compromised his principles.

## *William Le Maire* (died 1317)

William Le Maire, Bishop of Angers, was an attendee of the **Council of Vienne**. He submitted his opinion that the Order of the Temple should be abolished and its assets confiscated without further investigation because its reputation was now irredeemably sullied.

## William Longespee (1207–50)

William II Longespee (or Longsword), the dispossessed Earl of Salisbury, was an English noble who died at the debacle of **Mansourah** during the **Seventh Crusade**. He was a distinguished **Crusader** who had already made two pilgrimages to the **Holy Land**. He visited the **Pope** to gain support and contributed a contingent of 200 English **knights** to the mainly French army under **Louis IX** that attacked **Egypt**. **Matthew Paris** recorded Longespee's troubles with the jealous French barons who among other things conspired to deprive him of his private booty. His quarrels with Count **Robert, Count of Artois** drove him to quit the army for **Acre** for a while, though he later returned in time for the Battle of Mansourah.

William Longespee was killed along with Robert and most of the Templars. When news of Longespee's death got back to the English, they regarded him a **martyr** and as much a victim of the French as of the **Saracens**. Longespee's body was recovered and buried in Acre, and a commemorative effigy of him was also installed in Salisbury Cathedral.

## William Marshal, 1st Earl of Pembroke (1144?–1219)

William Marshal, 1st Earl of Pembroke, was a powerful English nobleman, and Lord Marshal of the Kingdom. Tall and doughty, he was a **knight** renowned both in tournament and on the battlefield. He was educated in the ways of knighthood in Normandy by his uncle William de Tancerville. He was knighted during wars between **Henry II** and **Louis VII**, and first earned distinction fighting to save Drincourt from the enemy (he earned much respect when it became clear that he fought to save the people rather than to take prisoners and make money from ransoms). William gained favour during the reign of Henry II, and presided at the knighting of the King's son Prince Henry (known as the Young King). William served in campaigns on the continent. He and the young Henry became estranged after William was accused of an affair with the Prince's wife, which obliged William to leave court circles and pursue a career as a knight errant. William and the young Henry were reconciled just before Henry's death. William pledged to deliver the ailing prince's cloak with its cross to the **Holy Sepulchre**, in symbolic fulfilment of the Prince's **Crusading** vow. William went to the **Holy Land** and remained between 1184 and 1186, probably taking part in action alongside the Templars and becoming an honorary associate of the Order.

William returned to the service of Henry II. In 1187 he intercepted the King's rebelling son **Richard the Lionheart**, and unhorsed him, but recoiled from killing Richard. Henry II rewarded William with the hand of the fair Isabel de Clare, the eighteen-year-old heiress of the Earldom of Pembroke. Soon afterwards Henry II died and William was reconciled with King Richard, before crossing to England to claim his bride. William remained in England during the **Third Crusade**, defending Richard's interests. He besieged Prince **John** at Windsor Castle, foiling John's attempted coup and facilitating Richard's return from captivity in Germany. At the death of King John, William became a protector of the infant **Henry III** and though in his mid-seventies led the loyalist forces against the French invaders and their allies, defeating them at the battle of **Lincoln**. On his deathbed, William was admitted into the Knights Templar, and he was buried at **Temple Church, London**, where his effigy may still be seen.

## *William V of Montferrat* (1115–91)

William V, Marquis of Montferrat was a Piedmontese noble and participant in the **Second Crusade**. He returned to the **Holy Land** in old age and was captured at the Battle of **Hattin**. The Muslims subsequently paraded William before the walls of Tyre in an attempt to persuade his son, **Conrad of Montferrat** to surrender the city. William shouted at his son to fight on and Conrad pointed an arrow at him saying he would rather slay his own father than surrender to **Saladin**. William was married to Judith, daughter of Leopold III of Austria.

## *William of Rubruck* (1200–56)

William of Rubruck was a **Franciscan** monk who went on a fact-finding mission to the **Mongols**. Close to **Louis IX**, he followed the **Seventh Crusade**, and was at **Acre** and **Tripoli** with the King, who aspired to convert the Mongols and ally with them against Islam. From 1253, Rubruck travelled to the Mongols via **Constantinople** and the Black Sea. He had no success converting the Mongol princes he encountered, but was sent on to the Mongol capital. He stayed at the court of Mongke Khan in Karakorum from 1254. He returned and found Louis in Tripoli in 1255.

He presented a report on his experiences and on the geography of the Mongol Empire. William dispelled the myth that the Mongols were likely converts. He claimed that the Mongols' Ruthenian subjects looked to the Germans, especially the **Teutonic Knights**, as potential liberators.[306]

## *William of Tyre* (c. 1130–85)

William, Archbishop of Tyre was a leading cleric and statesman in the Latin **Kingdom of Jerusalem**. He was also wrote a chronicle of the **Crusades**. He was born in **Jerusalem** but completed his extensive education in Italy and **France**. Returning to the Holy Land in 1165, he soon became a trusted courtier of **Amalric I**, who sent him to negotiate the alliance with **Manuel I Comnenus**, which would lead to their planning a combined invasion of **Egypt**. In the 1170s, William was appointed tutor to Amalric's only son Baldwin (**Baldwin IV**). Much to William's distress, he was the first tentatively to diagnose the prince's leprosy, when the prince cut himself while playing and felt no pain. Meanwhile William eventually rose to become Chancellor of the Kingdom and Archbishop of **Tyre** and remained influential through the reign of Baldwin IV. However, he lost out on becoming **Patriarch** of Jerusalem, a position that went to his rival **Heraclius**.

William called the Templars 'brave men and valiant nobles' when describing their being granted custody of **Gaza**.[307] But on other occasions his tone became very critical of the Order, perhaps as a result of their killing of the **Assassin** envoy, which had so angered Amalric, and which he clearly considered a scandal. William also took a dim view of the Templars' conduct at the capture of **Ascalon**, and recorded the only account of some Templars being hanged by Amalric for surrendering to the enemy a fortified cave beyond the Jordan. He gave a brief account of the Order's **foundation** by **Hugues de Payens** and **Godfroi de St Omer**, giving the year 1118 for this, but stated that after this worthy beginning, the Order had become arrogant. They were no longer obedient to the **Patriarch** of Jerusalem, and refused tithes and first fruit to the churches. He also criticised the conduct of the **Hospitallers**. In William's judgement, it was a 'great evil' that the Pope had freed them from the jurisdiction of the Patriarch and the bishops.[308] William attended the Third Lateran Council, where he probably repeated these complaints against the Orders. Despite making these criticisms, however, William evidently accepted that the Military Orders were indispensable in the defence of the Kingdom.

## *William Raven* (thirteenth–fourteenth century)

William Raven was one of the Templars in **England** at the time of the **suppression**. He was held in the **Tower of London** and questioned in **Holy Trinity Church, London**. He denied the **accusations against the Order**. Questioned about his **initiation ritual**, he said that he had been invested as a Templar by the **Master** of England, **William de la More**. This had taken place at **Templecombe**, in the presence of around 100 other people, including non-Templars. He described an orthodox reception including pledging **obedience** to the Master, service to God and **Mary, Blessed Virgin**, and never to harm a Christian.

## *William St Clair* (died 1330)

William St Clair was a Scottish noble of **Norman** extraction. He fought for **Scotland** at **Bannockburn** and was one of those who died with James de

Douglas in Spain, fighting the **Moors**, while attempting to take the head of **Robert the Bruce** for burial in the **Holy Land**. A small Templar-style **grave slab** in **Rosslyn Chapel** purports to be that of this William St Clair, and a modern inscription below claims him as a Knight Templar. (It could alternatively be the gravestone of William's uncle, another William St Clair who was the warlike bishop of Dunkeld, who took up arms and repelled an English raid in 1317.)

There is no evidence that either of these William St Clairs actually was a Templar. It seems possible the inscription is a forgery, and that the slab, which is indeed in a Templar style, was brought into the chapel from elsewhere in more recent times. At the trial of the two Templars arrested in Scotland, William and his brother both gave evidence against them. They said they had heard about secret Templar receptions, and that their father had blamed the Templars for losing the Holy Land.

## William St Clair (c. 1401–84)

William St Clair (or Sinclair) was the Earl of Caithness, Prince of Orkney and Lord of Roslin. He served for a time as Lord Chancellor of Scotland. Approaching his later years, he began to build the famous **Rosslyn Chapel** near Edinburgh. There is no evidence that he was a member of a secretly continuing Templar Order.

## William Sidney Smith (1764–1840)

Admiral Sir William Sidney Smith was a British naval officer. He served in the Royal Navy against the American revolutionaries, and then in the Swedish Navy against the Russians. He was made a knight of the Swedish Order of the Sword and later a Knight Commander of the Bath. He returned to the Royal Navy during the **French Revolutionary** wars, and after a series of daring actions was captured and imprisoned in the **Paris Temple**, charged with burning the French Fleet at Toulon. He escaped in 1798 with the help of French Royalists.

He went on to serve in the Navy in the Levant, as well as leading a diplomatic mission to the Sublime Porte, the court of the **Ottoman** Sultan in **Constantinople**. Smith then assisted Ottoman forces to defeat **Napoleon Bonaparte** at **Acre**. Smith went on to fight the French in Italy, and then returned to Turkey, where he met an Austrian ally, **Joseph von Hammer-Purgstall**.

After the Napoleonic wars he pursued a political career, campaigning against Barbary piracy and the **slave** trade. He later settled in **Paris**, and evidently became an associate of **Bernard-Raymond Fabré–Palaprat**, the founder of the revived Order of the Temple and producer of the **Larmenius Charter**. Perhaps Smith developed an interest in the historical Templars during his earlier captivity in their old fortress (by then demolished). In 1838 Smith, it seems, was elected Palaprat's successor as **Grand Master** of the neo-Templar Order.

## William Wallace (c. 1270–1305)

Sir William Wallace was the leader of Scottish resistance to English rule during the reign of the English King **Edward I**. He was a minor noble, probably of Welsh ancestry, but an ardent Scottish patriot. A fifteenth-century biographer, Blind Harry, had it that Wallace began by killing Sir William Heselrig, English Sheriff of Lanark, in revenge for his killing of a maiden named Marion Braidfute, whom Wallace had secretly married. At any rate, Wallace and his allies won several victories and led a determined guerrilla campaign, and he was one of the few Scottish leaders never to waver in his opposition to English hegemony.

William's greatest victory (allied with Andrew of Moray) was at Stirling Bridge in September 1297, where Scottish infantry with spears isolated the vanguard of the English cavalry and slaughtered them. Wallace was then knighted and proclaimed Guardian of **Scotland**. He led an invasion of England and attacked **York**. Wallace's first major defeat was at the Battle of **Falkirk** in April 1298, where he came up against Edward I himself, come from **Flanders**. Wallace nonetheless was able to slay the Templar Master **Brian de Jay**, who had contravened his Order's customary neutrality in wars between Christians to lead Welsh mercenaries. Wallace escaped from Falkirk. Afterwards he reputedly went to **France**, to try to win support from **Philip the Fair**. He returned to Scotland in 1303. In August 1305 he was captured. He was put on trial as a traitor in London and hanged, drawn and quartered by the vengeful Edward.

## Witchcraft

Witchcraft is conventionally defined as the practice of doing harm through magical powers. In the sixteenth and seventeenth century, witches were believed to have gained their power through a pact made with Satan who physically appeared to them. The prosecuting authorities regarded witches as members of a secret, subversive network, practising **Devil worship**. They accused witches of meeting at nocturnal Sabbaths to adore Satan, who might appear as a toad, a **cat** or a goat, and to abuse the cross and parody the mass before taking part in depraved rites. Infant sacrifice was also sometimes said to occur. The Devil might bestow on his disciples new powers and instruct them in future works of evil.

Though the **Inquisition** was occasionally involved in witch trials and produced the notorious *Malleus Maleficarum*, there were relatively few witch trials before the Reformation. **Germany** was the epicentre of the

Great Witch Hunt, which took place in both Protestant and Catholic areas. Most accused witches were women but they could also be men. Many of the accusers and witnesses at witch trials were also female. Accusations of witchcraft commonly arose out of disputes between neighbours. The cases spiralled into witch-hunts when authorities used **torture** on the accused to secure confessions not only of using magic but also of belonging to a coven, and then forced the accused to name others who attended the supposed unholy gatherings. The line of questioning used tended to produce confessions that supported the witch-hunters' expectations.

This preconceived model arose in part from propaganda used to demonise those denounced as **heretics**, including the **Waldensians** and **Cathars**. The accusations against the Templars and the suspicion surrounding the Order as a result of **Philip the Fair**'s campaign against them likewise informed attitudes about witchcraft. In 1531, Heinrich Cornelius Agrippa wrote *De Occulta Philosophia*. The work influenced later impressions of the Templars, mentioning them in the context of 'gnostic magicians' who could supposedly control demons, and saying 'similar things are known of the witches ... wandering into offenses of this sort'.

## Wolfram von Eschenbach (1170–1220)

Wolfram von Eschenbach was a German **knight** and poet. His most famous literary work was the epic poem *Parzival*, based on *Perceval, le Conte du Graal*, by **Chretien de Troyes**. The Grail romance follows the adventures of Parzival and other knights and also delves into the affairs of Parzeval's vainglorious father, which adds context to the son's quest for the **Holy Grail**, for self-knowledge and redemption. Wolfram claimed the work was based on a mysterious source, named Kyot of Provence, probably a reference to **Guiot of Provins**. In his work Wolfram included Templar-esque characters as guardians of the Grail. Wolfram's Grail is a mysterious stone, apparently fallen from Heaven, thus called the exiled stone (*Lapis Exillis*). This seems to be related to the Philosopher's Stone referred to by the Alchemists (*Lapis Exillir*).

## Women in the Crusades

Women accompanied many of the Crusades and on occasion took up arms. Anna Comnena, the chronicler and daughter of the Byzantine Emperor Alexius, refers disapprovingly to Frankish women, dressed in armour and using swords and lances like men. One such was Sigelgatia (a little before Anna), wife of the Norman baron Robert Guiscard, who herself led men into battle. Saracen chroniclers of the era of the **Third Crusade** also referred to capturing western women in armour. Frankish Palestinian women sometimes found themselves involved in the defence of cities besieged by the **Muslims**, whom they had every interest in resisting (as did any women in a city besieged by enemy soldiers in those times). Crusader leaders and fighters were frequently accompanied by their wives to the East, and many of these women became involved in events.

Kings who brought their wives included **Richard I** (who married **Berengaria of Navarre** on **Cyprus**), **Louis X** (whose wife **Marguerite of Provence** helped in the securing of his release from Egyptian custody), and **Edward I** (whose wife Queen Eleanor of Castile saved his life at **Acre** by sucking poison from a wound). **Eleanor of Aquitaine** accompanied her first husband **Louis VII** of France (having taken the cross in her own right). Many women also supported the Crusades from Europe by donating to the **Military Orders**, or by encouraging sons and husbands to take part (though on other occasions we hear of women locking up their menfolk to stop them leaving). Royal women such as Queens **Melisende of Jerusalem**, **Agnes of Courtenay** and **Sibylla** were also pivotal to the politics of the Crusader states.

## Wool Trade

Sheep farming was the mainstay of the Templars' agricultural and economic activities. Like the **Cistercians** they kept large flocks in **France**, and also in parts of **England**. It is therefore quite appropriate that one of the religious symbols they adopted was the **Agnus Dei** (Lamb of God). Wool production was a major source of income for the Templars, the profits being put towards their military activities. **Lincolnshire** in **England**, especially the **Preceptory** of Temple **Bruer**, was a major Templar centre of sheep farming and wool production.

# X

## Xpisti

'Xpisti' is a short form of the Latin word *Christi* (of Christ) but incorporating the Greek letters 'X' and 'P'. It appears on the face of some versions of the Templars' **seal** in the legend *Sigillum milium xpisti*.

# Y

## Yolande of Jerusalem (1212–28)

Yolande of **Jerusalem**, also known as Isabella, was the daughter of **John of Brienne**, and of Maria (1192–1212), the daughter of **Conrad of Montferrat** and **Isabella of Jerusalem**. In 1125, at the instigation of Pope **Honorius III**, Queen Yolande was betrothed to the widower **Frederick II**, as an incentive for him to recover **Jerusalem** on **Crusade**.[309] All this had been decided at a meeting in Ferentino, attended by the leaders of the Knights Templar and **Hospitallers**. It was rumoured that Frederick treated his wife badly, and certainly he soon brushed aside her father and asserted his own place as king. The unfortunate Yolande died giving birth to Frederick's son, **Conrad IV**, (much as her own mother had died after childbirth). Later Yolande's premature death was utilised by anti-Frederick propagandists who insinuated that he had killed her, but this was probably unfounded.

## York

York is a city in northern **England** that during medieval times was one of the largest and most prosperous in England. Its castle, the surviving part of which is known as **Clifford's Tower**, was one of the places where Templars were imprisoned and interrogated during the **suppression**. They were held in the custody of the Sheriff of York, **John de Eure**. Initially they were not kept in harsh conditions and were allowed to wander about the castle. Templars were brought to York for trial from Newcastle. They were also brought from various more local **Preceptories**. The Templars in York Castle were tried in April 1310. They pleaded innocent and denied the **accusations against the Order**. The prisoners were later transferred south to **London**.

# Z

## Zenghi (died 1146)

Imad ed-Din Zenghi was a **Seljuk** warlord, initially active in Mesopotamia. There was an unlikely rumour among the **Crusaders** that Zenghi was the son of Countess Ida of Austria, who had been lost during the Crusade of 1101. Zenghi rose to prominence putting down an **Arab** revolt against Seljuk rule by the **Abbasid** Caliph of **Baghdad**. Thereafter he became the governor (Atabeg) of Mosul and (after 1128) of **Aleppo**, where he founded the Zenghid dynasty. In 1137 Zenghi besieged Barin in the county of **Tripoli** and defeated the relief force under King **Fulk** of Jerusalem. Zenghi aspired to bring **Damascus** under his authority, but was repeatedly thwarted in this aim by its governor **Unur**, who soon allied with the **Franks** against the common threat. Returning north, Zenghi went on to capture **Edessa** at Christmas 1144, having outmanoeuvred Joscelin II de Courtenay. Previously Zenghi had taken the **Muslim** town of Baalbek and had its garrison crucified and their commander burned alive, despite a promise of safe passage. Zenghi claimed to be a zealous Muslim, despite such deeds. He had introduced *madrassas* into Syria and promoted *Jihad* against **Latin** Christians, turning the tide against the Franks. He showed clemency to the non-Frankish Christians of Edessa, however. Many Muslims welcomed his strong leadership, and he was seen to have restored justice. He was killed by a slave, supposedly while lying in a drunken stupor.

# *Zion*

Mount Zion/Sion is a hill overlooking **Jerusalem**, situated just to the south of the old city. The word Zion is sometimes used synecdochically to mean the Holy City itself, the **Holy Land**, or Israel. The neo-Romanesque Church of the Dormition was built there by German **Benedictines** in the early twentieth century, on the site of the death of the **Virgin Mary**. In medieval times the **Abbey of Notre Dame de Mt Sion** occupied the site, served by **Augustinian** canons. Nearby is the supposed site of the Last Supper. (It is possible the hill presently identified as Zion, where the Dormition monastery stands, is not the same location as the Biblical Zion. Zion itself is evidently not easily pinned down.)

Zionism is the doctrine that this region around Jerusalem is the Promised Land, destined for the Chosen People. In modern times Zionism was and is the attempt to build and sustain there a **Jewish** nation, the state of Israel. It may be argued that the **Crusades** represented Christian Zionism, and **Saladin**'s *Jihad* a type of **Islamic** Zionism. Zion has been the scene and cause of an ongoing human tragedy, in which the Templars played but a small part. The Crusades were one short chapter in this long story.

It appears as though that sacred soil will absorb more blood before history has run its course. There were compromises during the Crusades, though, that pointed to a possible better way. There were examples of respect and even friendship across the divide, such as the relationship between **Usama Ibn Munqudh** and the Templars, or that between **Frederick II** and **Al Kamil**. The settlement between the latter showed that a solution was possible, allowing coexistence in a Holy Land that allowed each side to keep what they valued most.[310]

# Notes

1 Barber, M., *The New Knighthood*, p. 8. Other forms included the *Knights of the Temple*, the *Order of the Temple*, the *Poor Knights*, the *Militia of Christ*, while one early Templar is called a *miles Sancti Stephani*, identifying him with the Church of St Stephen outside Jerusalem's Damascus Gate.
2 Maalouf, A., *The Crusades Through Arab Eyes*, p. 9.
3 Ralls, K., *The Templars and the Grail*, p. 40.
4 Barber, M., *The Trial of the Templars*, pp. 248–52.
5 Baha ad-Din in Gabrielli, F. (trans.), *Arab Historians of the Crusades*, pp. 223–4.
6 Tyerman, C., *God's War*, p. 819.
7 Barber, M., *The New Knighthood*, p. 177.
8 Barber, M., *The Trial of the Templars*, p. 149.
9 For the text of AD *Providam* see: http://www.templarhistory.com/providem.html
10 For the text of Nupter in Concilio see: http://www.templarhistory.com/nuper.html
11 Tyerman, C., *God's War*, p. 358.
12 Cited in Andrea, A.J., *Encyclopedia of the Crusades*, p. 5.
13 Maalouf, A., *The Crusades Through Arab Eyes*, p. 246.
14 'Annals of St Rudolph of Salzberg' in MGH. *Scriptores*, ix, p. 795 (sub anno 1260).
15 Jotischky, A., *Crusading and the Crusader States*, p. 162.
16 Billings, M., *The Crusades*, pp. 139–40.
17 For an introduction to the Albigensian Crusade see: Shea, S., *The Perfect Heresy*. See also: Jotischky, A., *Crusading and the Crusader States*, pp. 172–3.
18 For the Military Orders' response to the Albigensian Crusade see: Selwood, Dominic, *Knights of the Cloister: Templars and Hospitallers in Central-South Occitania, c. 1100– c. 1300*, pp. 1–50.
19 Read, P.P., *The Templars*, p. 142.
20 Philips, J., *The Fourth Crusade*, pp. 53–4.

21 Barber, M., *The New Knighthood*, p. 27.

22 Jotischky, A., *Crusading and the Crusader States*, p. 217.

23 Darbcock, E.A. and Krey, A.C. (trans. and ed.), *William, Archbishop of Tyre*, p. 312.

24 Read, P. P., *The Templars*, p. 148.

25 Barber, M., *The New Knighthood*, pp. 159, 266.

26 Knight, C. and Lomas, K., *The Hiram Key*, pp. 288–9.

27 Schafer, D., *A Preliminary Report on a Survey of the 'Westford Knight'*. This critique by a Harvard archaeologist found little substance to the carving, and dismissed the idea that it depicted a medieval European knight. Among other things, Schafer dismissed the supposed sword, and thought the 'blade' descending from the 'T' shape was actually the result of glacial scratchings, and that the 'T' shape of the hilt could have been made by two local boys in the nineteenth century.

28 Barber, M., *The New Knighthood*, p. 71.

29 Harris, J., *Byzantium and the Crusades*, pp. 124–5.

30 Helen Nicholson, http://www.cf.ac.uk/hisar/people/hn/MilitaryOrders/MILORDOCS7.htm

31 Menache, S., *Clement V*, pp. 15, 197.

32 Oldenbourg, Z., *The Crusades*, pp. 108–9.

33 Tyerman, C., *God's War*, p. 995.

34 *Ibid*, pp. 641–3.

35 Lord, E., *The Knights Templar in Britain*, p. 155.

36 Barber, M., *The Trial of the Templars*, pp. 204–10.

37 Barber, M., *The New Knighthood*, p. 394.

38 The 'Secret' archives have a website at: http://asv.vatican.va/en/arch/1_past.htm

39 Ralls, K., *The Templars and the Grail*, pp. 95–9.

40 Hancock, G., *The Sign and the Seal*, pp. 103–8.

41 Nicholson, H., *Knights Templar 1120–1312*, p. 63.

42 Jotischky, A., *Crusading and the Crusader States*, p. 172.

43 Oldenbourg, Z., *The Crusades*, p. 160.

44 Asbridge, T., *The First Crusade*, p. 322.

45 Menache, S., *Clement V*, pp. 206–7.

46 Tyerman, C., *God's War*, pp. 458–9.

47 *Interarium Peregrinorum et Gesta Regis Ricardi*, p. 246.

48 Folda, J., 'Art in the Latin East. 1095–1291' *The Oxford Illustrated History of the Crusades*, J.S.C. Riley Smith (ed.), p. 148.

49 Maalouf, A., *The Crusades Through Arab Eyes*, pp. 109–12.

50 Seward, D., *The Monks of War*, p. 49.

51 Shaw, M.R.A. (trans.), Joinville and *Villehardouin*, pp. 277–8.

52 Bartlett, W.B., *The Assassins*, pp. 173–9.

53 Riley-Smith, J., *What Were the Crusades?* pp. 6, 9, 27. A 'just war' required a just cause, legitimate princely authorisation, and right intentions. It was also to be a last resort.

54 Menache, S., *Clement V*, pp. 22–4.

55 Barber, M., *The Trial of the Templars*, p. 217.

56 Broadhurst, R.J.C., *A History of the Ayyubid Sultans of Egypt, translated from the Arabic of al-Marqizi*, p. 289.

57 Mackey, A., *Encyclopaedia of Freemasonry and its Kindred Sciences.* http://www.standrew518.co.uk/ENCYC/MacEncB1.htm

58 Burman, E., *The Templars, Knights of God*, p. 149.

59 Jotischky, A., *Crusading and the Crusader States*, p. 66.

60 Murray, A.V., *The Crusader Kingdom of Jerusalem, a Dynastic History*, pp. 120–204.

61 Philips, J., *The Fourth Crusade*, p. 50.

62 Tyerman, C., *God's War*, p. 371.

63 Ibn al-Athir in Gabrielli, F. (trans.), *Arab Historians of the Crusades*, pp. 139–40.

64 Barber, M., *The New Knighthood*, p. 67.

65 Barber, M., *The Trial of the Templars*, p. 62.

66 Tietze. H., 'The Psychology and Aesthetics of Forgery in Art', *Metropolitan Museum Studies*, pp. 1–2.

67 Maalouf, A., *The Crusades through Arab Eyes*, pp. 248–9.

68 Seward, D., *The Monks of War*, p. 81. Seward does not name the 'subject' of Baybars who is said to have made these comments.

69 Jotischky, A., *Crusading and the Crusader States*, p. 239.

70 Ibn abd az-Zahir in Gabrielli, F. (trans.), *Arab Historians of the Crusades*, pp. 308–12. Ibn abd az-Zahir was a Mameluk chancellor under the Sultans Baybars and Qalawun, and later their biographer.

71 Maalouf, A., *The Crusades through Arab Eyes*, p. 251.

72 Barber, M., *The New Knighthood*, p. 168.

73 Nicholson, H., private correspondence.

74 Menache, S., *Clement V*, p. 301.

75 Darbcock, E.A. and Krey, A.C. (trans. and ed.), *William, Archbishop of Tyre*, p. 227.

76 Frayling, C., *Strange Landscape*, p. 125.

77 William de St Thierry, *Life of St Bernard* (*c.* 1140). http://www.fordham.edu/halsall/source/1150bernard-2accs.html

78 Frayling, C., *Strange Landscape*, p. 125.

79 Barber, M., *The New Knighthood*, p. 12.

80 Dafoe, S. and Butler, A., *The Knights Templar Revealed*, p. 97.

81 Tyerman, C., *God's War*, p. 28.

82 Ralls, K., *The Templars and the Grail*, p. 69.

83 Jones, C., *The Cambridge Illustrated History of France*, p. 101.

84 Tyerman, C., *God's War*, p. 573.

85 Barber, M., *The New Knighthood*, p. 97.

86 Menache, S., *Clement V*, pp. 191–9.

87 Philips, J., *The Fourth Crusade*, p. 114.

88 Barber, M., *The Trial of the Templars*, p. 197. All things considered, Brian de Jay hardly seems to have embodied the finer qualities of his Order.

89 Lord, E., *The Knights Templar in Britain*, p. 186.

90 Barber, M., *The New Knighthood*, pp. 21, 212, 234.

91 Ibn al Athir, p. 278.

92 Barber, M., *The New Knighthood*, p. 185.

93 This claim appears in Sinclair, A., *The Sword and the Grail*, and in Laidler, K., *The Head of God*, pp. 239–41, but there is no evidence to support it.

If there is a small coffin, it must be a child's or a dwarf's because there is no other sensible explanation. Those buried in Templar graveyards were not only Templars, and the children of servants or patrons could have been given burial there.

94 Barber, M., *The Trial of the Templars*, p. 157.

95 Gibbon, E., *The Decline and Fall of the Roman Empire*, p. 1,005.

96 The correspondence between the Cabbala's 'tree of life' and the ceiling decorations of Montsaunes was first noted by Christian Tourenne, and mentioned in the discussion forums at http://www.templarhistory.com

97 Jotischky, A., *Crusading and the Crusader States*, p. 81.

98 Butler, A. and Dafoe, S., *The Knights Templar Revealed*, p. 183.

99 Barber, M., *The Trial of the Templars*, p. 163.

100 Nicolle, D., *Crusader Castles in the Holy Land 1097–1192*, p. 40.

101 Barber, M., *The New Knighthood*, pp. 246, 249. Forey, A, *The Templars in the Corona de Aragon* http://libro.uca.edu/forey/templar2.htm

102 O'Shea, S., *The Perfect Heresy*, p. 13.

103 Upton-Ward, J., (trans.), *Catalan Rule of the Temple*, p. 77.

104 Upton-Ward, J., (trans.), *Primitive Rule of the Templars*.

105 Lambert, M., *Medieval Heresy*, pp. 115–17.

106 Reynaldus (Chronicle extract) 'on the Accusations against the Albigensians'. *Internet Medieval Sourcebook*: http://www.fordham.edu/halsall/source/heresy1.html

107 Haskins, C.H., *Robert le Bougre and the Beginnings of the Inquisition in Northern France*, p. 365.

108 O'Shea, *The Perfect Heresy*, p. 35, explains the origin of the cat-worshipper theory. The link to the Arabic 'Kathir' is my own speculation.

109 Jotischky, A., *Crusading and the Crusader States*, p. 29. The *Filioque* controversy was over the origin of the Holy Spirit. The Eastern church preserved the original dogma that the Holy Spirit derived from God the Father, the Latins came to hold that it derived from the Father and the Son, and were too stubborn to back down from their position or to admit error.

110 O'Shea, *The Perfect Heresy*, p. 35.

111 Nicholson, H., trans. *Si je ne chant si souvent come jou faire soloye*, possibly the work of a Templar of Dourges. It begins:
'If I do not sing as often as I used to do,
It's because of the evil folk who are intent night and day
Watching to see if I make any sign or appearance of love
Towards you, worthy lady.'

112 Menache, S., *Clement V*, pp. 119–20.

113 Nicolle, D. *Crusader Castles in the Holy Land*, p. 41.

114 Ralls, K. *The Templars and the Grail*, pp. 56–7.

115 Tourenne, C. (Private conversation). This claim (concerning the Archbishop's giving the Templars warning about the King's plans) cannot be verified, though there are indeed inscriptions in the dungeons of Chinon.

116 Nicholson, H., *The Military Orders and their Relations with Women*, in Hunyadi, Z. and Laszolovsky, J. (ed.), *The Crusades and the Military Orders: Expanding the Frontiers of Medieval Latin Christianity*, p. 411.

117 Ralls, K. *The Templars and the Grail*, pp. 125–6.

118 Barber, M., *The Trial of the Templars*, p. 16.

119 Nicholson, H., *Knights Templar*, p. 93.

120 Roger of Hoveden, *Chronicle* http://www.fordham.edu/halsall/source/hoveden1187.html

121 Nicholson, H., *Knights Templar*, p. 133.

122 See Knight, C., and Lomas, R. *The Hiram Key*.

123 See von Hammer-Purgstall, J. *The Guilt of the Templars*

124 See Butler, A and Dafoe, S., *The Knights Templar Revealed*

125 See Cadet Gassaicourt, C., *The Tomb of James Molai*

126 See Baigent et al. *Holy Blood, Holy Grail*

127 See Hancock, G. *The Sign and the Seal*, and Ralls, K. *The Templars and the Grail*.

128 See Laidler, K., *The Head of God*.

129 See Picknett, L. and Price, C. *The Templar Revelation*.

130 See Lincoln, H, and Haagensen, E., *The Templars' Secret Island*.

131 See Baigent, M. and Leigh, R, *The Temple and the Lodge*, although the idea of the Templars becoming the Freemasons and being involved in anti-monarchistic conspiracies was around at least since Gassaicourt's *The Tomb of James Molai*.

132 Brighton, S., *In Search of the Knights Templar*, p. 16.

133 Ibn al-Athir, in Gabrielli, F. (trans.), *Arab Historians of the Crusades*, p. 117.

134 Nicholson, H., *The Knights Templar; a New History*, p. 35.

135 Gibbon, E., *The Decline and Fall of the Roman Empire*, p. 885.

136 Riley-Smith, J., *What were the Crusades?* p. 5.

137 Guibert de Nogent, *Gesta Dei per Francos*, p. 1.

138 Throop, P.A., 'Criticism of Papal Crusade Policy in Old French and Provençal', *Spectrum*, vol. 13, no. 4 (1938), p. 382.

139 Jotischky, A., *Crusading and the Crusader States*, p. 75.

140 Dostourian, A.E., *Matthew of Edessa*, p. 272.

141 Edbury, P.E., *The Military Orders in Cyprus*, in Hunyadi, Z. and Laszolovsky, J. (ed.), *The Crusades and the Military Orders: Expanding the Frontiers of Medieval Latin Christianity*, p. 407.

142 Newman, P., *A Short History of Cyprus*, p. 140.

143 Barber, M., *The Trial of the Templars*, p. 218.

144 Conrad Greenica, M. (trans.), Bernard of Clairvaux, *In Praise of the New Knighthood*. Cistercian Fathers Series: Number Nineteen B. (Introduction by Barber, M.)

145 Barber M., *The Trial of the Templars*, p. 201.

146 http://www.williamhenry.net/documents/TEMPLARGRAFITTIATDOMMElow.pdf

147 Ibn al-Athir in Gabrielli, F. (trans. and ed.), *Arab Historians of the Crusades*, p. 51.

148 Conspiracy theories making a link between the Templars and Ancient Egypt include those in: Knight, C. and Lomas, R., *The Hiram Key*; Laidler, K. *The Head of God*; Picknett, L. and Prince, C., *The Templar Revelation*.

149 Read, P.P., *The Templars*, p. 123.

150 Equestrian Order of the Holy Sepulchre (Lieutenancy of England and Wales) http://www.khs.org.uk/index.htm

151 Hancock, G., *The Sign and the Seal*, p. 503.

152 See for example: Knight, C. and Lomas, R., *The Hiram Key*, pp. 29, 267. The artefacts, which Knight and Lomas claim are Templar, are in the possession of one Robert Brydon, who is associated with Rosslyn Chapel. According to Stephen Dafoe, who contacted Mr Brydon subsequently, Brydon himself makes no such claims about the objects, which include spurs and a sword hilt. It seems Brydon's grandfather received them from a member of the Parker expedition, with whom he was in contact. A distorted version of Brydon's story has appeared in other books, including Knight and Lomas *The Second Messiah*; Ralls, K., *The Templars and the Grail*; Laidler, K., *The Head of God*.

153 Maalouf, A., *The Crusades Through Arab Eyes*, p. 226.

154 Oldenbourg, Z., *The Crusades*, pp. 248–9; Asbridge, T. and Edgington, S.B. (trans.) *Walter the Chancellor*, pp. 124–41.

155 For a detailed study of the Fifth Crusade see Powell, J.M., *Anatomy of a Crusade 1213–1221*.

156 Oliver of Paderborn, 'The Capture of Damietta' in Peters, E., *Christian Society and the Crusades*, p. 73.

157 Powell, J.M., *Anatomy of a Crusade 1213–1221*, p. 189.

158 Jones, T. and Eireia, A., *Crusades*, p. 177.

159 For a study of this Crusade see: Asbridge, T. *The First Crusade*; Primary accounts of the First Crusade include Fulcher of Chartres, Robert of Reims and Albert of Aachen.

160 William of Tyre in Barber, M., and Bate, K. (trans. and ed.), *The Templars: Selected Sources Translated and Annotated*, pp. 25–6.

161 Ralls, K., *The Templars and the Grail*, p. 30. Barber, M., *The New Knighthood*, p. 8.

162 Luttrell, A., *The Early Templars*. p. 195.

163 Philips, J., *The Fourth Crusade*, pp. 68–9.

164 Nicholson, H., *The Motivations of the Hospitallers and Templars in their involvement in the Fourth Crusade and its aftermath. Malta Study Centre Lecture 2003*, p. 2.

165 Philips, J., *The Fourth Crusade*, p. 130.

166 For a scholarly biography see: Abulafia, D., *Frederick II, A Medieval Emperor*.

167 Maalouf, A. *The Crusades Through Arab Eyes*, p. 229.

168 Cadet-Gassicourt, C.L., *The Tomb of James Molai*, p. 17.

169 Martin, Sean, *The Knights Templar*, p. 11, citing Baigent, Lincoln and Leigh, *The Holy Blood and the Holy Grail*, p. 51.

170 Housley, N. (ed. and trans.), *Documents of the Later Crusades, 1274–1580*, pp. 40–7.

171 Seward, Desmond, *The Monks of War*, p. 210.

172 Mayer, H.E., 'Studies in the History of Queen Melisende of Jerusalem', *Dumbarton Oaks Papers*, vol. 26, pp. 100–1.

173 Ibn Al-Athir in Gabrielli, F. (trans. and ed.), *Arab Historians of the Crusades*, pp. 42–3.

174 Darbcock, E.A. and Krey, A.C. (trans. and ed.), *William Archbishop of Tyre*, pp. 202–3.

175 Lord, E., *The Knights Templar in Britain*, p. 164.

176 Seward, Desmond, *The Monks of War*, p. 51.

177 Ibn al-Athir in Gabrieli, F. (trans.). *Arab Historians of the Crusades*, p. 118.

178 *Interarium Peregrinorum et Gesta Regis Ricardi*, p. 79.

179 Hancock, G., *The Sign and the Seal*, p. 161.

180 William de St Thierry. This chronicler mentions a William de St Omer, a former noble, living as a monk at Clairvaux in the 1140s. http://www.fordham.edu/halsall/source/1143clairvaux.html

181 Lord, E., *The Knights Templar in Britain*, p. 149. Citing Henderson's Annals of Lower Deeside (1892)

182 List of Knights Templar: http://en.wikipedia.org/wiki/List_of_Knights_Templar

183 'Auditia Tremendi' in Riley-Smith, L. and Riley-Smith, J. *The Crusades: Idea and Reality*, p. 64.

184 Haskins, C.H., *Robert le Bougre and the Beginnings of the Inquisition in Northern France*, pp. 632–3; O'Shea, S., *The Perfect Heresy*, pp. 193–7.

185 Housley, N., *The Italian Crusades*, pp. 21–18.

186 Barber, M., *The Trial of the Templars*, p. 145.

187 Menache, S., *Clement V*, p. 2 14.

188 Vaughn, Richard (trans. and ed.), *The Illustrated Chronicles of Matthew Paris*, p. 168.

189 Ibn al-Athir: in Gabrielli, F. (trans.), *Arab Historians of the Crusades*, p. 118.

190 Imad ad-Din in Gabrielli, F. (trans.), *Arab Historians of the Crusades*, p. 138.

191 Ibn al-Athir in Gabrielli, F. (trans.), *Arab Historians of the Crusades*, p. 124. *Itinerarium Peregrinorum et Gesta Regis Ricardi*, p. 34.

192 Oldenbourg, Z., *The Crusades*, p. 423.

193 *Itinerarium Peregrinorum et Gesta Regis Ricardi*, p. 34.

194 Brighton, S., *In Search of the Knights Templar*, p. 112.

195 For a discussion of Helena's role in early Christianity and her background see the early chapters of Thiede, C.P. and D'Ancona, M., *The Quest for the True Cross*.

196 Socrates Scholasticus, *Historia Ecclesiastica of Socrates Scholasticus*, chapter xvii. Socrates Scholasticus was a Byzantine historian of the fourth century.

197 Barber, M., *The New Knighthood*, p. 200.

198 Knight, C. and Lomas, R., *The Hiram Key*, p. 302.

199 Masson, G., *Frederick II of Hohenstaufen, a Life*, p. 142.

200 Kantowicz, E., *Frederick the Second 1194–1250*, p. 91.

210 Burkeman, O., *The Guardian*, 4 Jan 2005: http://www.guardian.co.uk/religion/Story/0,2763,1382899,00.html

202 See Murray, M., *The Witch Cult in Western Europe*. (1921)

203 See Cohn, N., *Europe's Inner Demons*.

204 Barber, M., *The Trial of the Templars*, p. 183. It is possible that perhaps the Templars made up such tales under torture in order to deflect their inquisitors from pursuing the embarrassing allegation of sodomy.

205 Ralls, K., *The Templars and the Grail*, p. 138.

206 Martin, S., *The Knights Templar*, p. 22.

207 Knight, C. and Lomas, R., *The Hiram Key*, pp. 283–305.

208 Tyerman, C., *God's War*, p. 253.

209 Demurgue, A., *Les Templiers, Une Chevalerie Chretienne au Moyen Age*.

210 Asbridge, T. and Edgington, S., *Walter the Chancellor's 'The Antiochene Wars'*, pp. 129–31.

211 Riley-Smith, J., *What were the Crusades?* p. 10.

212 Throop, P.A., *Criticism of Papal Crusade Policy in Old French and Provençal*, p. 389.

213 O'Shea, S., *The Perfect Heresy*, p. 159.

214 Lambert, M., *Medieval Heresy*, p. 197.

215 Tyerman, C., *God's War*, p. 602. Tyerman rather plays down the brutality of the medieval Inquisition, stating that death sentences were only passed in a small minority of cases. What he seems to miss is the point that regular mass killings are not necessary to maintain a climate of fear.

216 Nicholson, H., 'Serving King and Crusade: The Military Orders in Royal Service in Ireland, 1220–1400' in Bull, M. and Housley, N. (eds), *The Experience of Crusading*, pp. 235–6.

217 Asbridge, T., *The First Crusade*, p. 309.

218 Cadet-Gassaicourt, C.L., *The Tomb of James Molai*, p. 8.

219 William of Tyre in Barber, M. and Bate, K. (ed. and trans.), *The Templars: Selected Sources Translated and Annotated*, pp. 78–9.

220 Lev, Yacacov, 'Prisoners of War during the Fatimid-Ayyubid wars with the Crusades' in Gervais, M. and Powell, J.M. (eds), *Tolerance and Intolerance: Social Conflict in the Age of the Crusades*, p. 14.

221 *Interarium Peregrinorum et Gesta Regis Ricardi*, pp. 5–6.

222 Rau, I., (trans.) *A letter of Jacques de Vitry*. http://www.leeds.ac.uk/history/weblearning/MedievalHistoryTextCentre/James%20of%20Vitry.doc

223 Bartlett, R., *The Making of Europe* , p. 25.

224 For a study of Joinville's relationship with the Crusading movement see: Smith, C., *Crusading in the Age of Joinville*.

225 William of Tyre, *Historia*, Book Fourteen, p. 93.

226 Barber, M., *The New Knighthood*, p. 77, citing the Byzantine historian John Kinnamos.

227 Nicolle, D., *Crusader Castles in the Holy Land 1097–1192*, p. 20.

228 Jones, T. and Ereira, A., *Crusades*, p. 185.

229 Riley-Smith, J., in the *Daily Telegraph* (London) was quoted as decrying *Kingdom of Heaven* as 'rubbish, ridiculous, and complete fiction', as well as 'dangerous to Arab relations'. This was apparently on the basis of having read an inaccurate synopsis of the film, and before production had finished. His complaint that the film portrays the somewhat outdated colonial concept of the Crusaders is valid, however.

230 Jotischky, A., *Crusading and the Crusader States*, p. 231.

231 Tourenne, C., 'The Templars in the Eastern Pyrenees: The Legend of a Treasure', in *Templar History Magazine*, Issue 13, Dafoe, S. (ed.), p. 23.

232 Seward, D., *The Monks of War*, p. 104.

233 Lord, E., *The Knights Templar in Britain*, p. 79. The Jews of Lincoln were persecuted after rumour spread in 1255 that they had tortured and murdered a Christian boy later known as Little St Hugh of Lincoln. A Jew named Koppin and eighteen others supposedly confessed and were executed. This rumour made it easier for Edward I to rob and expel the Jews of England *c.* 1290.

234 O'Shea, S., *The Perfect Heresy*, p. 169.

235 Barber, M., *The New Knighthood*, pp. 1, 200.

236 Mackey, A.C., *Encyclopaedia of Freemasonry and its Kindred Sciences* http://www.standrew518.co.uk/ENCYC/MacEncM1.htm

237 Prawer, J. *The World of the Crusaders*, p. 117.

238 Vaughan, R. (trans.), *The Illustrated Chronicles of Matthew Paris*, pp. 166–9.

239 Shaw, M.R.B., *Joinville and Villehardouin*, p. 219.

240 Joinville, p. 329.

241 Vaughan, R. (trans.), *The Illustrated Chronicles of Matthew Paris*

242 Mayer, H.E., 'Studies in the History of Queen Melisende of Jerusalem', *Dumbarton Oaks Papers*, vol. 26, pp. 100–1.

243 Tabrham, C., *Melrose Abbey, Official Guide*, Historic Scotland, p. 28.

244 John of Plano Carpini, 'History of the Mongols', p. 65.

245 Ralls, K., *The Templars and the Grail*, pp. 147–8. Haagensen, E., and Lincoln, H., *The Templars' Secret Island*, pp. 98–9.

246 Cronin, V., *Napoleon* (Harper Collins, 1971), p. 147.

247 William of Tyre in Barber, M. and Bate, K. (ed. and trans.), *The Templars: Selected Sources*, p. 26.

248 Burman, E., *The Templars, Knights of God*, p. 45.

249 Lord, E., *The Knights Templar in Britain*, p. 194. These numbers seem hardly adequate to run the estates that the Order is known to have possessed in these lands.

250 Tourenne, C., in *Templar History Magazine*, issue No. 11, Dafoe, S. (ed.), p. 45.

251 William of Tyre in Barber, M. and Bate, K. (ed. and trans.), *The Templars: Selected Sources Translated and Annotated*, p. 81.

252 Peters, E. (ed.), *Christian Society and the Crusades, 1198–1229*, p. 101.

253 Mees, B.T., 'Hitler and the Austrian Order of New Templars', *Templar History Magazine*, issue No. 14, Dafoe. S. (ed.), p. 37.

254 Luttrell, A., *The Early Templars*, p. 199.

255 Lacroix, P. *Military and Religious Life in the Middle Ages and at the Period of the Renaissance*, p. 187.

256 See Robinson, J.J., *Born in Blood*.

257 Brighton, S., *In Search of the Knights Templar*, pp. 184–7.

258 Seward, D., *The Monks of War*, p. 73. Seward claims the two de Montaigu Grand Masters were brothers. Others question this assertion.

259 Ralls, K., *The Templars and the Grail*, p. 40.

260 This latter argument was advanced, for example in: Cohn, N., *Europes Inner Demons*, and in: Partner, P., *The Murdered Magicians*.

261 Mayer, H.E., *Studies in the History of Queen Melisende of Jerusalem*, p. 119.

262 Littrell, A., 'The Hospitallers in twelfth-century Constantinople', in Bull, M. and Housley, N. (eds), *The Experience of Crusading*, p. 227.

263 Atiya, A.S., *The Crusades in the Late Middle Ages*, pp. 49–51.

264 Gilmour-Bryson, A., *Sodomy and the Knights Templar*, p. 116.

265 Oliver of Paderborn, 'The Capture of Damietta' in Edwards, P., *Christian Society and the Crusades*, pp. 57–8.

266 Barber, M., *The Trial of the Templars*, p. 219.

267 Barber, M., *The New Knighthood*, p. 257.

268 Darbcock, E.A. and Krey, A.C. (trans. and ed.), *William, Archbishop of Tyre*, p. 254.

269 Oldenbourg, Z., *The Crusades*, p. 416.

270 Joinville and Villehardouin, *Chronicles of the Crusades*, p. 211.

271 Forey, A., *The Military Orders*, pp. 7–8.

272 Burman, E., *The Templars, Knights of God*, p. 149.

273 Vaughn, R., *Chronicles of Matthew Paris*, p. 167.

274 Ross family http://www.tudorplace.com.ar/ROS.htm

275 Haskins, C.H., *Robert le Bougre and the Beginnings of the Inquisition in Northern France*, p. 364.

276 Read, P.P., *The Templars*, p. 250.

277 Laidler, K., *The Head of God*, pp. 368–75.

278 Brighton, S., *In Search of the Knights Templar*, p. 98.

279 Upton Ward, J. (trans.), *The Primitive Rule of the Temple*. (Clause 9) http://www.ordotempli.org/ancient_templar_rule_of_order.htm (This anti-worldly instruction reflects a Manichean/Augustinian view, but is also found in scripture, e.g. the First Epistle of John 2:15)

280 Earl of Rosslyn, *Rosslyn Chapel*, p. 48.

281 Imad ad-Din in Gabrielli, F. (trans.), *Arab Historians of the Crusades*. p. 138.

282 Berry. V.G. (ed. and trans.) Odo of Deuil, *De Profectione Ludovici VII in Orientem*, p. 125.

283 *Les Grandes Chroniques de France, c.* 1410–20. British Library. See http://ibs001.colo.firstnet.net.uk/britishlibrary/controller/subjectidsearch?id=8856andandidx=1andstartid=6761

284 Jones, T. and Ereira, A., *Crusades*, p. 181; Masson, G. *Frederick II of Hohenstaufen, a Life*, p. 142.

285 Barber, M., *The New Knighthood*, p. 240.

286 Gilmour-Bryson, A., *Sodomy and the Knights Templar*, pp. 153, 173.

287 Dafoe, S., 'The Tragedy of the Solar Temple Cult', *Templar History Magazine*. Vol. 2.

288 Read, P.P., *The Templars*, p. 305, citing the speculation of Michel Lamy (dismissively).

289 Burman, E., *The Templars: Knights of God*, p. 43. Burman gives the hierarchy as follows: Master, Seneschal, Marshal, Commander of the Kingdom of Jerusalem, Commander of the City of Jerusalem, Commander of Tripoli and Antioch, Drapier, Commander of Houses, Commander of Knights, Knight brothers and Sergeants of the Convent, Turkopolier, Under Marshal (a sergeant) Standard Bearer (a sergeant) Sergeant Brothers Commanders of Houses, rural brothers, sick attendant brothers and servant brothers.

290 Siberry, E., *Criticism of Crusading*, p. 127

291 For an exploration of this theme see: Partner, P. *The Murdered Magicians.*

292 Rimy, M., Les *Templiers, ces grands seigneurs aux blancs manteaux.*

293 Tyerman, C., *The Invention of the Crusades*, p. 41.

294 Barber, M., *The New Knighthood*, p. 310.

295 Atiya, A.S., *The Crusades in the Late Middle Ages*, p. 31.

296 Upton-Ward, J. (trans.), *Primitive Rule of the Templars* (paragraph 9)

297 Barber M., *The Trial of the Templars*, p. 56.

298 Butler, A. and Dafoe, S., *The Knights Templar Revealed*, pp. 124, 163–7, 221–4.

299 See the first chapter of Bartlett, W.B., *The Assassins*.

300 Edgington, S.B., *The Doves of War*, p. 170.

301 Usama Ibn Munqudh, excerpts at http://www.fordham.edu/halsall/ source/usamah2.html

302 Lord, E., *The Knights Templar in Britain*, p. 140.

303 William of Tyre in Barber, M., and Bate, K. (ed. and trans.), *The Templars: Selected Sources Translated and Annotated*, p. 6.

304 Walter Map in Barber, M. and Bate, K. (ed. and trans.), *The Templars: Selected Sources*, p. 77. Perhaps Walter was being ironic, as it is hard to believe anyone was naïve enough to think that Islam would melt away, even if the Assassins (who weren't Orthodox Muslims anyway) had con- verted to Christianity.

305 Brighton, S., *In Search of the Knights Templar*, p. 194.

306 Saad, R., *William of Rubruck's Account of the Mongols*, p. 30.

307 Darbcock, E.A. and Krey, A.C. (trans. and ed.), *William, Archbishop of Tyre*, p. 202.

308 Edbury, P.W. and Rowe, J.G., *William of Tyre: Historian of the Latin East*, p. 124.

309 Abulafia, D., *Frederick II*, p. 150.

310 Echoing sentiments expressed in Abulafia, D., 'The Frederick al-Kamil compromise of 1229'. Letter to the *Daily Star*, 13/8/2003.

# Bibliography

## Primary Sources

Anonymous
Nicholson, Helen (trans.), *Chronicle of the Third Crusade: A Translation of the Intinearium Peregrinorum et Gesta Regis Ricardi*, Aldershot, Ashgate, 1997

Bernard of Clairvaux
Greenia, C. (trans.), Werblowsky, R.J.Z. (intro.), 'In Praise of the New Knighthood' in *Works of St Bernard of Clairvaux*, vol. VII, treatises, 3

Fulcher of Chartres
Peters, Edward (ed.), *The First Crusade: The Chronicle of Fulcher of Chartres and Other Source Materials*, 2nd edn, University of Pennsylvania Press, 1998

Guibert of Nogent
Levine, Robert (trans.), *The Deeds of God through the Franks: Guibert de Nogent's Gesta Dei per Francos*, Boydell Press, 1997

Ibn al-Athir
Richards, D.S. (trans.) *The Chronicle of Ibn al-Athir, Part 1. The Years 491– 541/1097–1146: The Coming of the Franks*, Aldershot, Ashgate, 2006

Ibn al-Marqizi
Broadhurst, R.J.C. (trans.), *A History of the Ayyubid Sultans of Egypt, translated from the Arabic of al-Marqizi*, Boston, Twayne, 1912

Jean de Joinville
Shaw, Margaret R.B. (trans.), *Joinville and Villehardouin, Chronicles of the Crusades*, London, Penguin Classics, 1963

John of Plano Carpini
Dawson, Christopher (ed.), *The Mission to Asia/The Mongol Mission*, London, 1980

Matthew of Edessa and Gregory the Priest
Dostourian, Ara Edmond (trans.) and Maksoudian, Kilkos H. (foreword), *Armenia and the Crusades: Tenth to Twelfth Century*, University Press of Armenia, London, 1993

Matthew Paris
Vaughn, Richard (trans. and ed.), *The Illustrated Chronicles of Matthew Paris: Observations on Thirteenth-Century Life* (Matthew Paris's *Chronica Majora* 1247–50), Stroud, Sutton, 1993

Odo of Deuil
Virginia Ginerick Berry (ed. and trans.), *De Profectione Ludovici VII in Orientem*. New York, Columbia University Press, 1948

Oliver of Paderborn
Peters, Edward (ed.), *Christian Society and the Crusades, 1198–1229, Sources in translation including the Capture of Damietta by Oliver of Paderborn*, University of Pennsylvania Press, 1971

The Templars' Rule
Upton-Ward, Judi (trans.), *The Rule of the Templars: The French Text of the Rule of the Order of Knights Templar*, Woodbridge, Boydell Press, 1992

Upton-Ward, Judi (trans.) *The Catalan Rule of the Templars*, Woodbridge, Boydell Press, 2003

Usama ibn-Munqidh
Hitti, Philip (trans.), *An Arab-Syrian Gentleman and Warrior in the Period of the Crusades*, Beirut, Khayats, 1929
Walter Bower:
Watt, D.E.R. (ed. and trans.), *A History Book for Scots: Selections from the Schotichronicon*, University of St Andrews, 1998

Walter the Chancellor
Asbridge, Thomas and Edgington, Susan (trans.), *Walter the Chancellor's 'The Antiochene Wars'* Crusader Texts in Translation 4, Aldershot, Ashgate, 1999

William of Rubruck
Saad, Rana and Rockhill, William W. (trans. and ed.), *William of Rubruck's Account of the Mongols*. Maryland, 2005

William of Tyre
Atweiler Darbcock, Emily and Krey, A.C., *William, Archbishop of Tyre: A History of Deeds Done Beyond the Sea*, Vol. 2, New York, Columbia University Press, 1943 Also excerpts in Barber and Bate (see below)

## Various

Barber, Malcolm, and Bate, Keith (ed. and trans.), *The Templars: Selected Sources Translated and Annotated*, Manchester, Medieval Sources, 2002

Gabrielli, Francesco (ed. and trans.) Costello, E.J. (trans. from Italian), *Arab Historians of the Crusades*, London, Routledge and Kegan Paul, 1969

Housley, Norman (ed. and trans.), *Documents of the Later Crusades, 1274–1580*, Macmillan, London, 1966

Riley-Smith, Louise and Riley-Smith, Jonathan (eds. and trans.) *The Crusades: Idea and Reality*, Edward Arnold, London, 1981

## Secondary Sources

Addison, Charles G., *The History of the Knights Templars, the Temple Church and the Temple*, London, 1842

Anderson, William, *Green Man*, London, Harper Collins, 1990

Andrea, Alfred J., *Encyclopedia of the Crusades*, Greenwood Press, Westport, 2003

Asbridge, Thomas, *The First Crusade: A New History*, London, Free Press, 2004

Atiya, Aziz Suryal, *The Crusades in the Late Middle Ages*, London, 1938

Baigent, Michael, Leigh, Richard, and Lincoln, Henry, *The Holy Blood and the Holy Grail*, London, Corgi, 1982

Baigent, Michael and Leigh, Richard, *The Temple and the Lodge*, London, Jonathan Cape, 1989

Barber, Malcolm, *The New Knighthood: A History of the Order of the Temple*, Cambridge, CUP, 1993

Barber, Malcolm, *The Trial of the Templars*, Cambridge, CUP, 1978

Barber, Malcolm, 'The Social Context of the Templars', Transactions of the Royal Historical Society, 1984, pp. 27–46

Bartlett, Robert, *The Making of Europe: Conquest, Colonization and Cultural Change, 950–1350*, London, Penguin, 1993

Bartlett, W.B., *The Assassins: the Story of Medieval Islam's Secret Sect*, Stroud, Sutton, 2002

Benvenisti, Meron, *The Crusaders in the Holy Land*, New York, Macmillan, 1972

Billings, Malcolm, *The Cross and the Crescent*, London, BBC Books, 1981

Billings, Malcolm, *The Crusades*, Stroud, Tempus, 2000

Brighton, Simon, *In Search of the Knights Templar: A Guide to the Sites in Britain*, Weidenfeld and Nicholson, 2006

Bull, Marcus and Housley, Norman (eds.), *The Experience of Crusading: Western Approaches*, Cambridge, CUP, 2003

Burman, Edward, *The Assassins: Holy Killers of Islam*, London, Harper Collins, 1998

Burman, Edward, *Supremely Abominable Crimes: The Trial of the Knights Templar*, Allison and Busby, 1994

Burman, Edward, *The Templars, Knights of God: The Rise and Fall of the Knights Templars*, UK, Crucible, 1986

Butler, Alan and Dafoe, Stephen, *The Knights Templar Revealed*. London, Magpie Books, 2006

Cadet-Gassicourt, C.L., *The Tomb of James Molai, or The Secret of the Conspirators* (Trans. by a gentleman of Boston) Boston, Benjamin Edes, 1797

Cohn, Norman, *Europe's Inner Demons*, Sussex, SUP, 1975

Currer-Briggs, Noel, *The Shroud and the Grail*, London, Weidenfeld and Nicholson, 1979

Dafoe, Stephen, *Unholy Worship: The Myth of the Baphomet Templar/Freemason Connection*, Templar Books, 1998

Demurgue, Alan, *The Last Templar: The Tragedy of Jacques de Molay*, London, Profile, 2005

Edbury, Peter W. and Rowe, John Gordon, *William of Tyre: Historian of the Latin East*, Cambridge, CUP, 1988

Edgington, Susan B., 'The Doves of War: The Part Played by Carrier Pigeons in the Crusades', Balard, Michel (ed.), *Autour de la Première Croisade: Actes du Colloque de la Society for the Study of the Crusades in the Latin East* (Clermont-Ferrand, 22–25 juin 1995), *(Paris, 1996), pp. 167–175*

Folda, Jaroslav, 'The Figural Arts in Crusader Syria and Palestine, 1187–1291', *Dumbarton Oaks Papers*, 2004

Frayling, Christopher, *Strange Landscape: A Journey Through the Middle Ages*, London, BBC, 1995

Forey, Alan, *The Military Orders: From the Twelfth to the Early Fourteenth Centuries*, Basingstoke, Macmillan, 1992

George, Leonard, *The Encyclopaedia of Heresies and Heretics* London, Robson, 1995

Gervais, M. and Powell, J.M. (eds.), *Tolerance and Intolerance: Social Conflict in the Age of the Crusades*, New York, Syracuse University Press, 2001

Gibbon, Edward, *The Rise and Fall of the Roman Empire*, Ware, Wordsworth Editions, 1998 (original 1788)

Gies, Frances and Gies, Joseph, *Daily Life in Medieval Times*, Rochester, Grange Books, 2005

Gilmour-Bryson, Anne, 'Sodomy and the Knights Templar', *Journal of the History of Sexuality*, 1996, p. 151–83

Godwin, Malcolm, *The Holy Grail, its Origins, Secrets and Meaning Revealed*, London, Bloomsbury, 1994

Haagensen, Erling and Lincoln, Henry, *The Templars' Secret Island*, Moreton-in-Marsh, Windrush, 2000

Hancock, Graham, *The Sign and the Seal: A Quest for the Ark of the Covenant*, London, Mandarin, 1992

Harris, J., *Byzantium and the Crusades*, Hambledon, Contunuum, 2006

Haskins, Charles H., 'Robert le Bougre and the Beginnings of the Inquisition in Northern France', *American Historical Review*, vol. 7, no. 4

Holmes, George (ed.), *The Oxford Illustrated History of Medieval Europe*, Oxford, OUP, 1988

Howarth, Stephen, *The Knights Templar*, London, William Collins and Sons, 1982

Housley, Norman, *The Italian Crusades: The Papal-Angevin Alliance and the Crusades against Christian Lay Powers, 1254–1345*, Oxford, OUP, 1984

Hunyadi, Zsolt and Laszolovsky, Josef (eds), *The Crusades and the Military Orders: Expanding the Frontiers of Medieval Latin Christianity*, Budapest, Central European University, 2001

Jones, Terry and Eireia, Alan, *Crusades*, London, Penguin/BBC, 1996

Jotischky, Andrew, *Crusading and the Crusader States*, Harlow, Longman, 2004

Kantowicz, Ernst, *Frederick the Second 1194–1250*, New York, Frederick Ungar Publishing, 1931

Kedar, Benjamin, 'Gerard of Nazareth a Neglected Twelfth-Century Writer in the Latin East: A Contribution to the Intellectual and Monastic History of the Crusader States.' *Dumbarton Oaks Papers*, 1983, pp. 55–77

Knight, Christopher, and Lomas, Robert, *The Hiram Key*, London, Century, 1996

Lacroix, P., *Military and Religious Life in the Middle Ages and at the Period of the Renaissance*, London, Bickers and Sons, pre-1877

Laidler, Keith, *The Head of God: The Lost Treasure of the Templars*, London, Orion, 1999

Lambert, Malcolm, *Medieval Heresy: Popular Movements from the Gregorian Reform to the Reformation* (3rd edn), Oxford, Blackwell, 2002

Lea, Henry Charles, *A History of the Inquisition in the Middle Ages*, vol. III, New York, 1888

Lord, Evelyn, *The Knights Templar in Britain*, Harlow, Longman, 2002

Luttrel, Anthony 'The Early Templars' Balard, Michel (ed.), *Autour de la Première Croisade: Actes du Colloque de la* Society for the Study of the Crusades in the Latin East *(Clermont-Ferrand, 22–25 juin 1995)*. (Paris, 1996), pp. 193–202

McGlynn, Sean, *Blood Cries Afar: The Forgotten Invasion of England 1216*, Stroud, Spellmount, 2013

Markale, Jean, *The Templar Treasure at Gisors*, Inner Traditions, 2003

Martin, Sean, *The Knights Templar: The History and Myths of the Legendary Military Order*, Harpenden, Pocket Essentials, 2004

Masson, Georgina, *Frederick II of Hohenstaufen, a Life*, London, Secker and Warburg, 1957

Maxwell-Stuart, P.G., *Chronicles of the Popes*, London, Thames and Hudson, 1997

Mayer, H.E., 'Studies in the History of Queen Melisende of Jerusalem', *Dumbarton Oaks Papers*, vol. 26, 1972

Menache, Sophia, *Clement V*, Cambridge, CUP, 1998

Murray, A.V., *The Crusader Kingdom of Jerusalem, a Dynastic History Prosopographica et Genealogica*, Oxford, 2000

Napier, Gordon, *The Rise and Fall of the Knights Templar: The Order of the Temple, 1118–1314, A True History of Faith, Glory, Betrayal and Tragedy*, Stroud, Spellmount, 2003

Nicolle, David, *Crusader Castles of the Holy Land*, Oxford, Osprey, 2004

Nicholson, Helen, *The Knights Templar: A New History*, Stroud, Sutton, 2001

Nicholson, Helen, *Knights Templar 1120–1312*, Botley, Osprey, 2003

Nicholson, Helen, *Templars, Hospitallers and Teutonic Knights: Images of the Military Orders*, Leicester, LUP, 1993

Oldenbourg, Zoé, *The Crusades*, London, Weidenfeld and Nicholson, 1966

O'Shea, Stephen, *The Perfect Heresy, the Life and Death of the Cathars*, London, Profile Books, 2000

Partner, Peter, *The Murdered Magicians*, Oxford, OUP, 1981

Picknett, Lynn, and Price, Clive, *The Templar Revelation: Secret Guardians of the True Identity of Christ*, London, Bantam Press, 1997

Ralls, Karen, *The Templars and the Grail*, Wheaton, IL, Quest Books, 2003

Reston, James Jr, *Warriors of God: Richard the Lionheart and Saladin in the Third Crusade*, Faber and Faber, 2002

Riley-Smith, Jonathan (ed.), *The Oxford Illustrated History of the Crusades*, Oxford, OUP, 1995

Riley-Smith, Jonathan, *What Were the Crusades?* (3rd edn), San Francisco, Ignatius Press, 2002

Riley-Smith, Jonathan, 'The Templars and the Castle of Tortosa in Syria: An Unknown Document Concerning the Acquisition of the Fortress', *English Historical Review*, April 1969, pp. 278–88

Robson, John J., *Born in Blood: The Lost Secrets of Freemasonry*, London, Evans, 1990

Sanello, Frank, *The Knights Templars: God's Warriors, the Devil's Bankers*, Taylor Trade Publishing, 2003

Sconfield, Hugh, *The Essene Odyssey*, London, Element Books, 1984

Selwood, Dominic, *Knights of the Cloister: Templars and Hospitallers in Central-South Occitania, c. 1100– c. 1300*, London, Boydell, 1999

Seward, Desmond, *The Monks of War: The Military Religious Orders*, London, Penguin, 1992

Siberry, Elizabeth, *Criticism of Crusading*, Oxford, Clarenden Press, 1985

Sinclair, Andrew, *The Sword and the Grail*, London, Century, 1995

Smith, Caroline, *Crusading in the Age of Joinville*, Aldershot, Ashgate, 2006

Thiede, Carsten Peter and D'Ancona, Matthew, *The Quest for the True Cross*, London, Wiedenfeld and Nicholson, 2000

Throop, Palmer A., 'Criticism of Papal Crusade Policy in Old French and Provençal', *Speclum*, vol. 13, no. 4. October 1938

Tietze, Hans, 'The Psychology and Aesthetics of Forgery in Art', *Metropolitan Museum Studies*, 1934

Turner, Ralph V. and Heiser, Richard R., *The Reign of Richard the Lionheart: Ruler of the Angevin Empire 1189–1199*, Longman, 2000

Tyerman, Christopher, *God's War: A New History of the Crusades*, London, Penguin, 2006

Tyerman, Christopher, *The Invention of the Crusades*, London, Macmillan, 1998

Waley, David, *Late Medieval Europe*, London, Longmans, 1964

Wilkinson, J. (ed.), *Jerusalem Pilgrimage, 1099–1185*, London, 1988

Vessay, Norman, *The Medieval Solder*, London, Arthur Baker, 1971

*Useful Websites:*
Catholic Encyclopaedia (entry on Templars)
http://www.catholicity.com/encyclopedia/t/templars,knights.html

Chinon Parchment
http://www.inrebus.com/chinon.html

Great Orders of Chivalry (discusses self-styled Templar Orders)
http://www.chivalricorders.org/orders/templars/templars.htm

La Régle du Temple as a Military Manual (Templar tactics and military organization) http://www.deremilitari.org/RESOURCES/ARTICLES/bennett1.htm

OSMTH. (modern Templars, Portuguese faction)
http://www.theknightstemplar.org/

Rule of the Temple: Upton Ward, Judi (trans.) Temple.
http://www.ordotempli.org/ancient_templar_rule_of_order.htm

Templar History (includes articles on Templar history, myths and mysteries, and discussion forums)
http://www.templarhistory.com/index.html

Temple Church, London (official site)
http://www.templechurch.com/

The Truth about Da Vinci (looks at the historical claims in the *Da Vinci Code*)
http://www.thetruthaboutdavinci.com/

William Marshall, the Flower of Chivalry (devoted to the famed knight)
http://bladezone.com/marshal/

If you enjoyed this book, you may also be interested in …

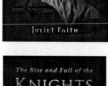

## Glastonbury, the Templars and the Sovran Cloth

JULIET FAITH

This book illustrates links between Glastonbury and Cornwall and examines old tales of an object of great importance - known as 'the Sovran cloth' - secretly hidden at both places. Richly illustrated, this book is sure to appeal to everyone interested in the Knights Templar and their Somerset history.

9780752470252

## The Rise & Fall of the Knights Templar

GORDON NAPIER

The Knights Templar, a mysterious fraternity of warrior monks, pledged their swords to defend pilgrims to the Holy Land from the bandits and marauders of the roads. This title unravels the many mysteries that surround the Knights Templar and their sudden fall from grace.

9780752453828

## The Knights Templar and Scotland

ROBERT FERGUSON

Templar and Scottish history is intertwined. From the foundation of the Order in the early twelfth century right up to the present day, this title examines the part the Templars played, in Bannockburn and beyond, and compares the Scottish Templars to their brethren in other parts of the world.

9780752493381

Visit our website and discover thousands of other History Press books.

**www.thehistorypress.co.uk**

Lightning Source UK Ltd.
Milton Keynes UK
UKOW05f2336130314

228095UK00008B/47/P